T0234673

Lecture Notes in Computer Science   14463

The series Lecture Notes in Computer Science (LNCS), including its subseries Lecture Notes in Artificial Intelligence (LNAI) and Lecture Notes in Bioinformatics (LNBI), has established itself as a medium for the publication of new developments in computer science and information technology research, teaching, and education.

LNCS enjoys close cooperation with the computer science R & D community, the series counts many renowned academics among its volume editors and paper authors, and collaborates with prestigious societies. Its mission is to serve this international community by providing an invaluable service, mainly focused on the publication of conference and workshop proceedings and postproceedings. LNCS commenced publication in 1973.

Wei Jia · Wenxiong Kang · Zaiyu Pan ·
Xianye Ben · Zhengfu Bian · Shiqi Yu ·
Zhaofeng He · Jun Wang
Editors

Biometric Recognition

17th Chinese Conference, CCBR 2023
Xuzhou, China, December 1–3, 2023
Proceedings

Springer

Editors
Wei Jia
Hefei University of Technology
Hefei, China

Zaiyu Pan
China University of Mining and Technology
Xuzhou, China

Zhengfu Bian
China University of Mining and Technology
Xuzhou, China

Zhaofeng He
Chinese Academy of Sciences
Beijing, China

Wenxiong Kang
South China University of Technology
Guangzhou, China

Xianye Ben
Shandong University
Jinan, China

Shiqi Yu ⓘ
Southern University of Science
and Technology
Shenzhen, China

Jun Wang
China University of Mining and Technology
Xuzhou, China

ISSN 0302-9743   ISSN 1611-3349 (electronic)
Lecture Notes in Computer Science
ISBN 978-981-99-8564-7   ISBN 978-981-99-8565-4 (eBook)
https://doi.org/10.1007/978-981-99-8565-4

This Springer imprint is published by the registered company Springer Nature Singapore Pte Ltd.
The registered company address is: 152 Beach Road, #21-01/04 Gateway East, Singapore 189721, Singapore

Paper in this product is recyclable.

Preface

Biometric technology, which enables automatic person recognition based on physiological or behavioral traits such as face, fingerprint, iris, gait, and signature, finds extensive applications in modern society. In recent years, biometric recognition systems have been widely deployed globally, spanning law enforcement, government, and consumer sectors. Developing diverse and reliable approaches for trustworthy biometric applications has become imperative. In China, the proliferation of the Internet and smartphones among its vast population, coupled with substantial government investments in security and privacy protection, has led to the rapid growth of the biometric market. Consequently, biometric research in the country has garnered increasing attention. Researchers have been actively addressing various scientific challenges in biometrics, exploring diverse biometric techniques, and making significant contributions to the field. The Chinese Conference on Biometric Recognition (CCBR), an annual event held in China, serves as a pivotal platform for biometric researchers. It provides an excellent opportunity to exchange knowledge, share progress, and discuss ideas related to the development and applications of biometric theory, technology, and systems.

CCBR 2023 took place in Xuzhou from December 1–3, marking the 17th edition in a series of successful conferences held in prominent cities like Beijing, Hangzhou, Xi'an, Guangzhou, Jinan, Shenyang, Tianjin, Chengdu, Shenzhen, Urumqi, Zhuzhou, and Shanghai since 2000. The conference received 79 submissions, each meticulously reviewed by a minimum of three experts from the Program Committee. Following a rigorous evaluation process, 41 papers were chosen for presentation (51.9% acceptance rate). These papers comprise this volume of the CCBR 2023 conference proceedings, which covers a wide range of topics: Fingerprint, Palmprint and Vein Recognition; Face Detection, Recognition and Tracking; Affective Computing and Human-Computer Interface; Gait, Iris and Other Biometrics; Trustworthiness, Privacy and Personal Data Security; Medical and Other Applications.

We would like to thank all the authors, reviewers, invited speakers, volunteers, and organizing committee members, without whom CCBR 2023 would not have been successful. We also wish to acknowledge the support of the China Society of Image and Graphics, the Chinese Association for Artificial Intelligence, Institute of Automation of Chinese Academy of Sciences, Springer, and China University of Mining and Technology for sponsoring this conference.

December 2023

Zhengfu Bian
Shiqi Yu
Zhaofeng He
Jun Wang
Wei Jia
Wenxiong Kang
Zaiyu Pan
Xianye Ben

Organization

Academic Advisory Committee

Tieniu Tan	Institute of Automation, Chinese Academy of Sciences, China
Anil K. Jain	Michigan State University, USA
Qiang Yang	WeBank, China
Jie Zhou	Tsinghua University, China
David Zhang	Chinese University of Hong Kong (Shenzhen), China

Industry Advisory Committee

Zhifei Wang	Information Center of Ministry of Human Resources and Social Security, China
Hongchuan Hou	First Research Institute of the Ministry of Public Security, China
Cong Liu	Iflytek Co., Ltd, China

General Chairs

Zhengfu Bian	China University of Mining and Technology, China
Shiqi Yu	Southern University of Science and Technology, China
Zhaofeng He	Beijing University of Posts and Telecommunications, China
Jun Wang	China University of Mining and Technology, China

Program Committee Chairs

Wei Jia	Hefei University of Technology, China
Wenxiong Kang	South China University of Technology, China
Zaiyu Pan	China University of Mining and Technology, China
Xianye Ben	Shandong University, China

Organizing Committee Chairs

Yi Jin	Beijing Jiaotong University, China
Ying Fu	Beijing Institute of Technology, China
Qi Li	Institute of Automation, Chinese Academy of Sciences, China
Shihai Chen	China University of Mining and Technology, China
Jie Gui	Southeast University, China

Publicity Chairs

Lei Zhu	Shangdong Normal University, China
Kuerban Wubli	Xinjiang University, China

Forum Chairs

Xiangbo Shu	Nanjing University of Science and Technology, China
Shunli Zhang	Beijing Jiaotong University, China
Hao Liu	Ningxia University, China
Xiushen Wei	Nanjing University of Science and Technology, China
Dexing Zhong	Xi'an Jiaotong University, China
Lunke Fei	Guangdong University of Technology, China
Zhe Jin	Anhui University, China
Peipei Li	Beijing University of Posts and Telecommunications, China
Cong Wang	Northwestern Polytechnical University, China
Xu Jia	Liaoning University of Technology, China

Publication Chairs

Qijun Zha	Sichuan University, China
Dan Zeng	Southern University of Science and Technology, China

Competition Chair

Caiyong Wang	Beijing University of Civil Engineering and Architecture, China

Contents

Fingerprint, Palmprint and Vein Recognition

Face Detection, Recognition and Tracking

Affective Computing and Human-Computer Interface

Gait, Iris and Other Biometrics

Trustyworth, Privacy and Persondal Data Security

Medical and Other Applications

Fingerprint, Palmprint and Vein Recognition

Unsupervised Fingerprint Dense Registration

Yuwei Jia, Zhe Cui$^{(\boxtimes)}$, and Fei Su

Beijing Key Laboratory of Network System and Network Culture,
Beijing University of Posts and Telecommunications, Beijing, China
`cuizhe@bupt.edu.cn`

Abstract. Fingerprint registration is still a challenging task due to the large variation of fingerprint quality. Meanwhile, existing supervised fingerprint registration methods need sufficient amount of labeled fingerprint pairs which are difficult to obtain. In addition, the training data itself may not include enough variety of fingerprints thus limit such methods' performance. In this work, we propose an unsupervised end-to-end framework for fingerprint registration which doesn't require labeled fingerprint data. The proposed network is based on spatial transformer networks, and can be applied flexibly to achieve a better results by being used recursively. Experiment results show that our method gets the state-of-the-art matching scores while preserving the good ridge structure of fingerprints, and achieves competitive matching accuracy through score fusion when compared with supervised methods.

Keywords: Fingerprint Registration · Unsupervised Learning ·
Spatial Transformer Network · Recursive Registration

1 Introduction

Fingerprint is one of the most widely used biometric trait today. Despite the widespread deployment of fingerprint recognition algorithms, large variation of fingerprint images still leads to a significant decrease in the performance of fingerprint matching algorithms [21]. In recent years, several supervised fingerprint registration algorithms have been proposed to improve fingerprint matching performance [1–5]. These methods have made significant contributions by estimating elastic skin deformations to align fingerprints before matching. However, there are still remained issues of insufficient registration accuracy due to the lack of high quality fingerprint data. Cui et al. [2] proposes a phase-based fingerprint registration algorithm that achieves high matching scores but its speed and accuracy are limited. Deep learning-based methods [3, 4] exhibit faster speed, but the registration results and matching scores are not satisfactory enough due to the lack of training data with large variation. The method proposed in [4] achieves state-of-the-art performance in fingerprint registration, but this method still faces the challenge of annotating the dataset, making it difficult to obtain a large and diverse training set that includes an adequate variety of skin deformation types.

Unsupervised learning is an important approach to address the challenge of annotating data and has been widely applied in tasks such as optical flow estimation [8,9,16] and medical image registration [10,22] which are similar to fingerprint registration task. Although such methods based on unsupervised learning don't outperform supervised methods on benchmarks, they are still commonly concerned due to the availability of a much larger amount of data without manual labeling that can be utilized for unsupervised learning. As a result, there are still many ongoing research efforts focused on unsupervised registration. However, these methods often do not consider the issue of impostor matches. Directly applying these methods can result in high matching scores even in the presence of impostor matches. Moreover, due to the lack of consideration for false matches, these methods have a weak regularization strength on the predicted deformation field, leading to the distortion of the ridge structure in input fingerprints. Although Yu et al. [6] has applied unsupervised learning methods to fingerprint registration, it has not considered its influence on fingerprint matching, making it difficult to apply this method in practical fingerprint recognition scenarios.

In this paper, we propose a fingerprint registration method which is based on unsupervised learning and addresses the challenges of balancing speed, matching scores and matching accuracy that have troubled previous fingerprint dense registration methods. Our method uses Spatial Transformer Network (STN) to perform fixed-interval sampling on the input fingerprint and searches for corresponding points of these sampled points in the target fingerprint. These point pairs are then interpolated as parameters of a thin-plate spline (TPS) model to obtain a dense deformation field. The obtained dense deformation field is used to warp the input fingerprint to align it with the reference fingerprint. Furthermore, we can recursively apply the proposed network to the input fingerprint pairs as a refinement process to achieve higher matching scores. The main steps of this method are as follows: (1) The minutiae features of fingerprint pairs are extracted. (2) Minutiae-based initial registration is performed. (3) Network refine registration is conducted after the initial registration. The methods used in the first two steps are the same as those used in previous dense registration methods [4].

The rest of this paper is organized as follows: Sect. 2 presents a literature review of related work on fingerprint registration tasks. Section 3 describes the details of the proposed method. Section 4 reports the experiment results of the method. Section 5 concludes our findings.

2   Related Work

2.1   Fingerprints Dense Registration

Si et al. [1] introduce the problem of fingerprint dense registration and propose a correlation-based method to solve this problem, which significantly increases matching accuracy and greatly benefited fingerprint matching tasks. Subsequently, Cui et al. [2] make full use of the phase characteristics of fingerprints, further increasing matching accuracy. However, it has slow registration speeds, often taking about 2 s, which can affect user experience in everyday applications. Deep learning methods [3,4] are further utilized to address the target of increasing matching accuracy. These methods have faster registration speeds, but result in lower matching scores. Additionally, existing deep learning-based methods require the annotation of deformation fields for a pair of fingerprints in order to perform training. However, obtaining accurate deformation fields is highly challenging. These methods often synthesize fingerprint pairs by applying existing deformation fields to a single fingerprint and using the synthesized pairs as training data. This approach limits the variety of fingerprints, which is the reason for lower matching scores.

2.2 STN for Fingerprint Registration

The Spatial Transformer Networks (STN) [7] has proposed a framework for unsupervised image registration, which is used to unwrap input images. Dabouei et al. [11] and Grosz et al. [12] apply STN to the unwrapping of contactless fingerprints, achieving good results. However, these works only take a single fingerprint as input and focus on perspective distortion correction for contactless fingerprints. He et al. [17,20] apply STN in fingerprint matching, but it's only for partial fingerprint. Schuch et al. [16] use STN to predict the angular difference between fingerprint pairs for registration, but applying rotation transformation alone cannot achieve accurate registration results and only serves as an initial alignment, which is less effective than methods based on key points. Tang et al. [19] use STN to predict the affine transformation between fingerprint pairs for registration, also only serving as the initial alignment process. Yu et al. [6] are the first to apply STN in fingerprint registration. However, this method only takes genuine matching into consideration and is not fit for fingerprint matching problem. Additionally, the method they proposed obtain a sparse deformation field, which is then converted into a dense deformation field through bi-cubic interpolation which does not simulate the deformations of the fingerprint skin.

2.3 Unsupervised Image Registration

Methods for unsupervised image registration are designed based on STN, such as unsupervised approaches in optical flow estimation [8,9,16] and in medical image registration [10,22]. These methods make every effort to find the correspondences between two images, but they rarely consider the scenario where the content in the input image pairs belongs to different instances or categories. Therefore, these methods cannot be directly applied in fingerprint dense registration. In fingerprint dense registration, if we attempt to align both genuine and impostor pairs as accurately as possible, the improvement in the matching score for impostor pairs is often greater than that for genuine pairs's. This results in lower matching accuracy and ultimately fails to provide positive assistance to the entire fingerprint recognition system. The main reason for the decrease in matching accuracy is that the smoothing approach used by these methods, often by minimizing deformation field gradients, is not suitable for fingerprint dense registration. Our method integrates TPS into an end-to-end training process, resulting in a sufficiently smooth deformation field, thus improves matching accuracy. Additionally, our method can be applied recursively to input images, ensuring high matching scores.

3   Proposed Method

Three main steps of our method are: (1) Extracting the minutiae features of fingerprint pairs. (2) Minutiae-based initial registration. (3) Network refine registration. Step (1) and (2) are same as Cui et al. [4]. Minutiae features are extracted by Verifinger SDK. Then, we compute the similarity between these minutiaes and use spectral clustering to match them. With these matched minutiaes, we employ TPS interpolation to obtain the initial registration deformation field, aligning the input fingerprint to the reference fingerprint. Finally, we apply network refine registration to the input fingerprint as follows.

3.1   Network Structure

The structure of the proposed unsupervised registration network is shown in Fig. 1. In our network, two 256×256 images, I_i and I_r, are first inputted. They then pass through a siamese network to extract features, resulting in F_i and F_r. The dimensions of F_i and F_t are $256 \times 256 \times 32$. Afterwards, the extracted features F_i, F_t, and the element-wise Hadamard product of F_i and F_t are fused by concatenating them along the channel axis. This results in the fused feature F which has the size of $256 \times 256 \times 96$. F is then fed into the LocalisationNet, which outputs the corresponding points P_r of the input fingerprint to the fixed points P_i of the reference fingerprint. Using these corresponding points, Thin Plate Spline (TPS) interpolation is performed to obtain a dense deformation field, F_d. This dense deformation field is then applied to I_i to generate I_w. The intersection of I_w, I_r, and the mask M generated from I_w and I_r is used to calculate the loss.

In this network, the FeatureNet is used to extract image features and its structure is similar to [4]. It consists of 4 convolutional blocks, each comprising a 7×7 convolutional layer, a batch normalization layer, and a ReLU activation function. The first convolutional block has an input with 1 channel and output with 32 channels, while the remaining three blocks have inputs and outputs with 32 channels. The feature extraction layer is optional, as similar results can be achieved by directly feeding the images into the LocalisationNet without including the feature extraction layer.

LocalisationNet performs convolution and pooling operations on FeatureNet or the input image itself to obtain sparse key points. There are two commonly used structures for LocalisationNet, one with a sampling interval that is a multiple of 2, and the other with a sampling interval that is a multiple of 5. High matching accuracy can be achieved when the sampling interval is 16 or 20.

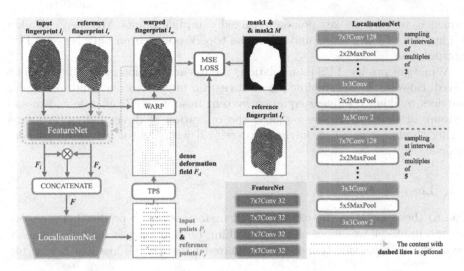

Fig. 1. Architecture of the proposed unsupervised fingerprint dense registration network. Overall process is presented on a light purple background. FeatureNet is presented on a light green background. LocalisationNet is presented on a light yellow background. Elements in dashed lines or dashed arrows are optional. (Color figure online)

Since our prediction results are sparse, when using the warped fingerprint as the input to the network, even though the sampling positions are the same, the corresponding regions of the fingerprint are different. Therefore, we can use the warped fingerprint as the input fingerprint and continue to feed it into the network for recursive training or testing. Moreover, the number of recursive iterations can be different for training and testing. This provides our network with great flexibility.

3.2   TPS Module

Unlike Yu et al. [6], which uses bicubic interpolation to interpolate sparse deformation fields into dense deformation fields, we adopted TPS [13] transformation that better simulates human skin deformations. To incorporate TPS into end-to-end training of the network, we made improvements to TPS, including key point selection and solving linear equations using pseudo-inverse during TPS computation.

Our network is a fully convolutional network that can be applied to images of any size, but when the image size becomes too large, TPS interpolation requires a significant amount of GPU memory which is proportional to the product of the length and width of the image. Therefore, we have implemented point selection to mitigate this issue. The key points output by the LocalisationNet are the corresponding points on the input fingerprint for fixed sampling points on the reference fingerprint. We calculate the L2 distance for each corresponding point pair and sort them in descending order to obtain an ordered sequence. Using this sequence, we sort the key points and fixed sampling points. We then calculate the number of pixels in M and select the top N points from both sets for TPS interpolation.

While performing TPS interpolation, the linear equation system needs to be solved. However, fixed sampling points at regular intervals often result in singular matrices, making the linear equation system unsolvable. To enable end-to-end training of the network, we replaced the operation of direct matrix inversion during the linear equation solving process [13] with the calculation of pseudo-inverse.

3.3   Loss Function

Due to the smooth nature of the TPS transformation we predict between two images, unlike [4] we do not need a smoothing term in our loss function. Instead, we utilize a simple variation of Mean Squared Error (MSE) loss like E_D in [14],

$$E_D(I_r, I_w, M) = M * \rho(1 - I_r, 1 - I_w) \tag{1}$$

where I_r is the target fingerprint, I_w is the warped fingerprint. M is the mask generated by I_r and I_w. We get two mask form I_t and I_w using the closing operation in morphology and obtain the intersection of these two masks as M. $\rho(x) = (x^2 + \epsilon^2)^\gamma$ is an empirical function with $\gamma = 0.4$ and $\epsilon = 10^{-7}$.

4   Experiments

4.1   Implementation Details

The experiments are conducted on Intel(R) Xeon(R) CPU E5-2620 v4 and two NVIDIA GeForce1080Ti with 11G memory. The training and evaluating of network are based on the Pytorch 1.10.2. We use Adam [15] optimizer with parameters: learning rate = 0.0001, $\beta_1 = 0.9$, $\beta_2 = 0.999$. We train 25 epochs with batch size 16. We mainly used the training data from [4] as our training set, but only utilized 20,918 pairs of latent fingerprints as training data. The data augmentation methods were the same as [4].

4.2   Experiments Result

We performed testing on FVC2004 DB1_A. Following [3], we also employed score fusion to increase matching accuracy. For score fusion, we used a Multi-Layer Perceptron (MLP) with one input layer, one output layer, and two hidden layers, where the activation function was set as ReLU. We randomly sampled 5,500 pairs of genuine and impostor fingerprint matches from the training set of unsupervised registration. The sampling intervals were set at 16, 20, and 32, and the recursive iteration numbers were 1, 2, and 2 for the three networks, respectively. By testing these combinations, we obtained three sets of matching scores. These

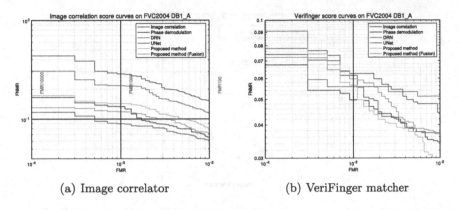

(a) Image correlator   (b) VeriFinger matcher

Fig. 2. DET curves of image correlator and VeriFinger matcher on FVC2004 DB1_A

Table 1. Matching accuray of different dense registration algorithms for processing fingerprints in FVC2004 DB1_A. In each cell, the FNMR on the left represents the result calculated by the image correlator, and on the right represents the result calculated by the Verifinger matcher.

Method	EER	FNMR@FMR=0	FNMR@FMR=10^{-2}
Image Correlation [1]	0.073, 0.036	0.436, 0.074	0.151, 0.044
Phase Demodulation [2]	**0.041**, 0.030	0.166, **0.068**	0.065, 0.034
DRN [3]	0.058, 0.040	0.306, 0.091	0.114, 0.051
UNet Registration [4]	0.045, 0.033	**0.117**, 0.078	**0.061**, 0.037
Ours	0.045, **0.020**	0.173, 0.078	0.078, **0.029**
Ours (Fusion)	0.042, 0.028	0.131, 0.072	0.071, 0.037

scores, along with the corresponding labels indicating whether they were genuine matches, were utilized as training data to train the MLP. Score fusion was applied to enhance the matching accuracy to a certain extent."

With sampling every 20 points, our method achieves comparable matching accuracy to [2] without score fusion, and significantly outperforms [3], which employs supervised deep learning. When score fusion is applied, our method surpasses [2] in terms of matching accuracy. The DET curves on FVC2004 DB1_A by VeriFinger matcher and image correlator are shown in Fig. 2. The matching accuracy on FVC2004 DB1_A by VeriFinger matcher and image correlator are shown in Table 1.

Although there is a gap between our method and the state-of-the-art in terms of matching accuracy, we can achieve the highest matching score while preserving the fingerprint ridge structure, as shown in Fig. 3. The average matching scores of methods [1–4] on 2800 genuine pairs in FVC2004 DB1_A are 0.7662, 0.8473, 0.7979 and 0.7778, while our method achieves the highest score of 0.8597. This result is obtained by recursively applying our method with sampling every 16

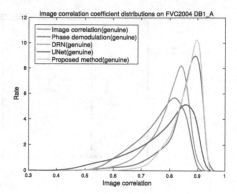

Fig. 3. Genuine image pairs correlation distributions on FVC2004 DB1_A.

points for five recursions. As shown in Fig. 4, when sampled every 10 points and recursively iterated 10 times, even the samples that perform unsatisfactory in [1,2,4] can be surpassed by our proposed method in terms of VeriFinger score and correlation coefficient.

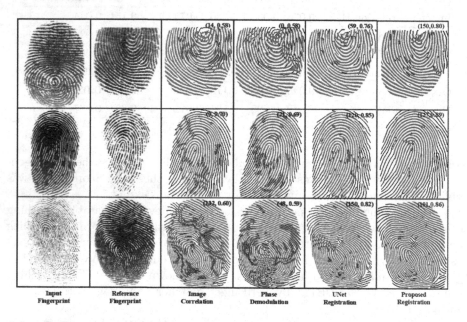

Fig. 4. Registration examples of different dense registration methods for genuine matching fingerprints. The numbers in the brackets are matching scores by VeriFinger matcher and image correlator.

4.3 Efficiency

When tested on FVC2004 DB1_A ,using two Nvidia 1080Ti GPUs, the time required for dense registration is 0.08 s, and the fastest average time without FeatureNet is 0.04 s. Both are much faster than the 0.15 s reported in [4]. Table 2 shows average time Costs of different dense registration algorithms for processing a pair of fingerprints in FVC2004 DB1_A.

Table 2. Average time costs (in seconds) of different dense registration algorithms for processing a pair of fingerprints in FVC2004 DB1_A.

Method	Image Correlation [1]	Phase Demodulation [2]	UNet Registration [4]	The Proposed Method
Time/s	3	1.99	0.53	0.46

5 Conclusion

This paper presents an unsupervised framework for fingerprint dense registration. Our method is the first to apply TPS in end-to-end training of fingerprint registration networks, which overcomes the challenge of annotating ground truth data in learning-based fingerprint registration tasks. Our method enables the use of trained networks to achieve the highest registration scores by adjusting the recursion iterations. It can also to approach state-of-the-art matching accuracy by combining multiple network scores. However, our method still faces issues such as difficult parameter adjustment, insufficient matching on certain datasets. In future work, we aim to enhance the matching accuracy by exploring more advanced initial registration methods.

Acknowledgments. This work was supported by the National Natural Science Foundation of China 62206026.

References

1. Si, X., Feng, J., Yuan, B., Zhou, J.: Dense registration of fingerprints. Pattern Recognit. **63**, 87–101 (2017)
2. Cui, Z., Feng, J., Li, S., Lu, J., Zhou, J.: 2-D phase demodulation for deformable fingerprint registration. IEEE Trans. Inf. Forensics Secur. **13**(12), 3153–3165 (2018)
3. Cui, Z., Feng, J., Zhou, J.: Dense fingerprint registration via displacement regression network. In: 2019 International Conference on Biometrics (ICB), pp. 1–8. IEEE (2019)
4. Cui, Z., Feng, J., Zhou, J.: Dense registration and mosaicking of fingerprints by training an end-to-end network. IEEE Trans. Inf. Forensics Secur. **99**, 1 (2020)
5. Lan, S., Guo, Z., You, J.: A non-rigid registration method with application to distorted fingerprint matching. Pattern Recognit. **95**, 48–57 (2019)

6. Yu, Y., Wang, H., Zhang, Y., Chen, P.: A STN-based self-supervised network for dense fingerprint registration. In: Feng, J., Zhang, J., Liu, M., Fang, Y. (eds.) CCBR 2021. LNCS, vol. 12878, pp. 277–286. Springer, Cham (2021). https://doi.org/10.1007/978-3-030-86608-2_31

7. Jaderberg, M., Simonyan, K., Zisserman, A., et al.: Spatial transformer networks. Adv. Neural Inf. Process. Syst. 2017–2025 (2015)

8. Yu, J.J., Harley, A.W., Derpanis, K.G.: Back to basics: unsupervised learning of optical flow via brightness constancy and motion smoothness. In: Hua, G., Jégou, H. (eds.) ECCV 2016. LNCS, vol. 9915, pp. 3–10. Springer, Cham (2016). https://doi.org/10.1007/978-3-319-49409-8_1

9. Ren, Z., Yan, J., Ni, B., Liu, B., Yang, X., Zha, H.: Unsupervised deep learning for optical flow estimation. In: Proceedings of the AAAI Conference on Artificial Intelligence, vol. 31, no. 1 (2017)

10. Balakrishnan, G., Zhao, A., Sabuncu, M.R., Guttag, J., Dalca, A.V.: Voxelmorph: a learning framework for deformable medical image registration. IEEE Trans. Med. Imaging **38**(8), 1788–1800 (2019)

11. Dabouei, A., Soleymani, S., Dawson, J., Nasrabadi, N.M.: Deep contactless fingerprint unwarping. In: 2019 International Conference on Biometrics (ICB), pp. 1–8. IEEE (2019)

12. Grosz, S. A., Engelsma, J. J., Liu, E., Jain, A. K.: C2CL: contact to contactless fingerprint matching. IEEE Trans. Inf. Forensics Secur. **17**, 196–210 (2021)

13. Bookstein, F.L.: Principal warps: thin-plate splines and the decomposition of deformations. IEEE Trans. Pattern Anal. Mach. Intell. **11**(6), 570 (1989)

14. Meister, S., Hur, J., Roth, S.: Unflow: unsupervised learning of optical flow with a bidirectional census loss. In: Proceedings of the AAAI Conference on Artificial Intelligence, vol. 32, no. 1 (2018)

15. Kingma, D.P., Ba, J.: Adam: a method for stochastic optimization. In: International Conference on Learning Representations (ICLR), vol. 5 (2015)

16. Schuch, P., May, J.M., Busch, C.: Unsupervised learning of fingerprint rotations. In: 2018 International Conference of the Biometrics Special Interest Group (BIOSIG), pp. 1–6 (2018)

17. He, Z., Liu, E., Xiang, Z.: Partial fingerprint verification via spatial transformer networks. In: 2020 IEEE International Joint Conference on Biometrics (IJCB), pp. 1–10 (2020)

18. Wang, C., Pedrycz, W., Li, Z., Zhou, M., Zhao, J.: Residual-sparse fuzzy C-Means clustering incorporating morphological reconstruction and wavelet frame. IEEE Trans. Fuzzy Syst. **29**(12), 3910–3924 (2021)

19. Tang, S., Han, C., Li, M., Guo, T.: An end-to-end algorithm based on spatial transformer for fingerprint matching. In: 2022 7th International Conference on Computer and Communication Systems (ICCCS), pp. 320–325 (2022)

20. He, Z., Zhang, J., Pang, L., Liu, E.: PFVNet: a partial fingerprint verification network learned from large fingerprint matching. IEEE Trans. Inf. Forensics Secur. **17**, 3706–3719 (2022)

21. Maltoni, D., Maio, D., Jain, A.K., Prabhakar, S., Feng J.: Handbook of Fingerprint Recognition. Springer, Switzerland (2022). https://doi.org/10.1007/978-3-030-83624-5

22. Balakrishnan, G., Zhao, A., Sabuncu, M.R., Guttag, J., Dalca, A.V.: An unsupervised learning model for deformable medical image registration. In: Proceedings of the IEEE Conference on Computer Vision and Pattern Recognition, pp. 9252–9260 (2018)

Research on Accurate ROI Localization Algorithm for Omnidirectional Palm Vein Recognition Based on Improved SSD Model

Xu Chen and Yang Genke[✉]

Shanghai Jiao Tong University, No. 800 Dongchuan Road, Minhang District, Shanghai 200240, China

{c-xu21,gkyang}@sjtu.edu.cn

Abstract. Palm vein recognition technology offers advantages in terms of security and privacy. However, traditional methods rely on predefined rules about hand shape and positioning, affecting user experience. This paper focuses on the research of ROI extraction algorithm for palm vein recognition, utilizing an improved SSD [1] network to achieve multiple tasks such as palm classification, ROI localization, and gesture correction. It enhances the localization accuracy under various scenarios, including complex backgrounds and special hand shapes. The proposed approach in this paper enables non-contact palm recognition technology, implementing 360-degree omnidirectional recognition, thereby improving convenience and feasibility in its usage.

Keywords: Non-contact Palm vein recognition · multi-task fusion object detection network · ROI extraction · complex scenarios

1 Introduction

In recent years, biometric technology and security products have received widespread attention and expectations [3]. Biometric features based on surface characteristics such as fingerprints and faces are easily obtained and forged, posing security risks. As an internal biometric feature, palm vein recognition technology has the characteristics of accuracy, stability, and real-time processing. Palm vein recognition technology uses near-infrared imaging to capture the vein pattern information of a user's palm, ensuring the privacy and accuracy of the information data, and meeting the requirements for high-security level applications.

ROI (Region of Interest) [3] extraction is an important step in palm vein recognition technology, used to locate the region of the palm image that contains valid information. A multi-task fusion object detection network can simultaneously handle multiple related tasks in object detection process, such as bounding box regression, classification, and key-point detection. This can be applied to the research of ROI extraction algorithms in palm vein recognition, improving the overall efficiency and accuracy of the palm vein recognition system.

W. Jia et al. (Eds.): CCBR 2023, LNCS 14463, pp. 13–23, 2023.
https://doi.org/10.1007/978-981-99-8565-4_2

This article introduces the software and hardware design scheme of a non-contact palm vein recognition system, focusing on the design ideas and implementation process of the palm ROI extraction algorithm. Based on the collection of data samples in complex scenarios and special gestures, precision testing experiments are conducted on ROI extraction, and the new algorithm is applied to the palm vein recognition system. The experimental results indicate that the new algorithm supports recognition in a plane of 360 degrees. Under the same conditions in other aspects, the palm vein recognition system based on the new algorithm improves the false acceptance rate and the true rejection rate.

The remaining part of this article is organized as follows: Sect. 2 provides an overview of palm vein recognition and ROI extraction related works. Section 3 describes the proposed method of ROI extraction based on the improved SSD model. Section 4 presents the experimental results and performance evaluation. Finally, Sect. 5 summarizes this article and discusses future research directions for palm vein recognition technology.

2 Related Works

2.1 Traditional ROI Extraction Method

Palm vein recognition technology uses infrared cameras to capture images of palm veins, including the background and palm area. Traditional methods for ROI extraction involve edge detection algorithms to obtain the hand contour, followed by locating specific points such as the base of fingers, fingertips, and midpoint of the wrist to determine the ROI [4] (Fig. 1).

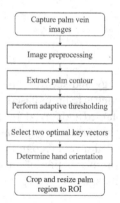

Fig. 1. Flowchart for ROI extraction method.

The algorithm processing steps are as follows: 1) Cropping and scaling. 2) Segmentation: The hand region is separated from background. 3) Finding key vectors: Key vectors or reference points, such as the wrist or center point, are used to locate the ROI. 4) Selecting two optimal key vectors: One is selected between little finger and ring finger, another is between index finger and middle finger. 5) Locating the palm ROI: The position relationship between the two key vectors is determined to indicate the hand's orientation. 6) Extracting the palm ROI: Before cropping the ROI, the palm image is rotated in the 2D plane based on the rotation angle θ calculated from the two optimal key vectors. To address the limitation when the hand rotates in 3D space, a four-point perspective transformation function is used to obtain the palm ROI.

These methods are known for their efficiency and clear logic. However, they heavily rely on clear hand contours and accurate point positions, resulting in limited effectiveness in scenarios with complex backgrounds and hand poses. Detection performance for palm targets in such cases is generally suboptimal.

2.2 SSD Model for Multi-task Object Detection

Single Shot MultiBox Detector(SSD) [1] is a popular object detection model that efficiently performs object detection and localization in images. It was introduced by Liu et al. in 2016 and is known for its high accuracy, real-time performance, and simplicity. SSD utilizes a series of convolutional layers to predict a set of default bounding boxes at different scales and aspect ratios in the image. These default bounding boxes, also known as anchor boxes or prior boxes, serve as templates for capturing objects of various sizes and shapes.

The base network of SSD is typically a pre-trained convolutional neural network (CNN), such as VGG16 or ResNet [2]. SSD incorporates feature maps from multiple layers of the base network to capture objects at different scales. Lower-level feature maps contain high-resolution details necessary for detecting small objects, while higher-level feature maps capture more semantic information useful for detecting larger objects. For each predictor layer, a predefined set of default anchors at different scales and aspect ratios is associated. The SSD model predicts the offsets and class probabilities for each default box, adjusting them to match the ground-truth objects during training. The model uses a combination of classification loss (e.g., softmax loss) and localization loss (e.g., $smooth_{L1}$ loss) to optimize the network parameters.

While the SSD model performs well in rectangular object detection, it may have limitations in locating distorted and irregular shapes. Since SSD uses predefined default anchors that are typically rectangular, it may not accurately locate non-rectangular objects. When objects have significant shape variations or complex contours, SSD may struggle to capture the precise location of the object.

This paper proposes a novel approach to address these limitations and improve the accuracy of ROI extraction. The approach leverages advanced techniques based on an improved SSD multitask object detection network to robustly extract hand regions from palm vein images captured by infrared cameras, even in challenging scenarios with complex backgrounds and gestures. Experimental results demonstrate that our proposed approach performs better in terms of effectiveness and robustness compared to traditional methods.

3 System Design

Develop an integrated palm vein recognition system that combines data acquisition and identification, including hardware devices, embedded drivers, and upper computer software. The system utilizes a wide dynamic range infrared lens and a fast exposure sensor design to ensure clear and stable image acquisition in various complex environments.

3.1 Acquisition Equipment

Develop a high-precision and highly reliable palm vein recognition device with an image resolution of no less than 1 million pixels. The hardware adopts a reflective imaging structure, including core components such as an infrared filter, light source driver, and main control circuit. The infrared filter allows only specific wavelengths of near-infrared light to pass through, filtering out ambient light and enhancing imaging contrast. The light source driver is responsible for controlling the brightness of the near-infrared light source. The main control circuit manages the control of light intensity and processes the image acquisition and transmission processes.

The diagram below illustrates palm vein acquisition module (Fig. 2).

Fig. 2. Prototype diagram of acquisition device.

3.2 Software System

The algorithm design process mainly includes the following steps: image acquisition, denoising, ROI extraction, rotation correction, feature extraction, feature encoding, and feature matching. Firstly, adjusting the exposure parameters for image capture. Secondly, perform denoising on the images to reduce the influence of optical and electronic noise. Thirdly, extract the ROI to obtain relevant information and remove background interference. Next is rotation correction to eliminate the impact of rotation on recognition results. Then, perform normalization to eliminate the influence of image brightness on recognition results. The final steps involve feature extraction, feature encoding, compressing the features to improve matching efficiency; and feature matching, calculating similarity for matching purposes (Fig. 3).

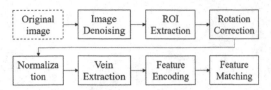

Fig. 3. Algorithm flow.

Design an interactive software based on the QT framework. The software will have the following functionalities: image acquisition, registration and recognition. The software can display the acquired palm vein images in real-time. Additionally, the software will display information such as recognition time and scores (Fig. 4).

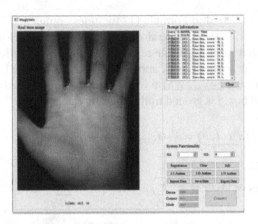

Fig. 4. Software presentation diagram.

3.3   Improved SSD Model Algorithm

Based in the analysis above, a multiple-task fusion object detection network can be developed. This network combines classification and bounding box regression tasks to detect the presence of palms in complex scenes and accurately localize them. By simultaneously addressing these tasks, the network can achieve improved performance in challenging scenarios and provide more accurate hand region detection results (Fig. 5).

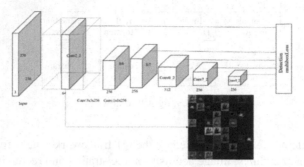

Fig. 5. Improved SSD model structure. The input image size is $256 \times 256 \times 3$. View the results of a specific convolutional layer conv2_2. ·

The loss function referred to Formula (1) includes confidence loss $L_{conf}(x, c)$ and localization loss $L_{loc}(x, l, g)$. In general cases, the localization loss is composed of four parameters (x, y, w, h). Coordinate regression predicts the difference between the predicted box p and the anchor box d, approaching the difference between the ground truth box g and the anchor box d. Where N is positive sample based on the anchor box, i represents predicted box, j is ground truth box, k is category [2].

$$L(x, c, l, g) = \frac{1}{N}(L_{conf}(x, c) + \alpha L_{loc}(x, l, g)) \tag{1}$$

$$L_{conf}(x, c) = -\sum_{i \in Pos}^{N} x_{ij}^{p} log(\hat{c}_i^p) - \sum_{i \in Neg} log(\hat{c}_i^0) \tag{2}$$

$$L_{loc}(x, l, g) = \sum_{i \in Pos}^{N} \sum_{m \in \{cx, cy, w, h\}} x_{ij}^k \text{smooth}_{L1}\left(l_i^m - \hat{g}_j^m\right) \tag{3}$$

where $\hat{c}_i^p = \frac{\exp(c_i^p)}{\sum_p \exp(c_i^p)}, \hat{g}_j^{cx} = (g_j^{cx} - d_i^{cx})/d_i^w, \hat{g}_j^{cy} = (g_j^{cy} - d_i^{cy})/d_i^h, \hat{g}_j^w = \log(\frac{g_j^w}{d_j^w}),$

$\hat{g}_j^h = \log\left(\frac{g_j^h}{d_j^h}\right), \text{smooth}_{L1}(x) = \begin{cases} 0.5x^2 & if |x| < 1 \\ |x| - 0.5 & otherwise \end{cases}$

As SSD has limitations in terms of position prediction parameters (x, y, w, h), it can only accommodate horizontal boxes. For cases involving rotated positions, the position boxes may contain unnecessary background regions, and the labeled (x, y, w, h) lacks practical meaning.

To address this problem, implement a method for locating arbitrary quadrilateral boxes. Represent anchor box d_0 using point coordinates $(x_{01}, y_{01}, x_{02}, y_{02}, x_{03}, y_{03}, x_{04}, y_{04})$ and dimensions (w_0, h_0), where $d_{0m} = (x_{0m}, y_{0m})$ represents the coordinates of a vertex of the quadrilateral box, and $m = \{1, 2, 3, 4\}$. For the ground truth, since it could be a polygon, using an enclosing rectangle G_b and four point coordinates G_q to represent it. The purpose of the enclosing rectangle is to determine the order of the four point coordinates, and obtain (x_0, y_0, w_0, h_0) as a result (Fig. 6).

Fig. 6. Anchor illustration diagram

$$L_{loc}(l, g) = \sum_{i \in Pos}^{N} \sum_{m \in \{1,2,3,4\}} \text{smooth}_{L1}\left(l_i^m - g^m\right) \tag{4}$$

$$g^m = \frac{Gq^m - d_i^{0m}}{w_i^0} \tag{5}$$

$$l^m = \frac{p^m - d_i^{0m}}{h_i^0} \tag{6}$$

The predicted box $p = (x_1, y_1, x_2, y_2, x_3, y_3, x_4, y_4)$ can be represented as below:

$$x_m = x_{0m} + w_0 \times \Delta x_m$$
$$y_m = y_{0m} + h_0 \times \Delta y_m \tag{7}$$

For m = {1, 2, 3, 4}, where x_m, y_m represent the coordinates of the predicted box p at each corner, x_{0m}, y_{0m} represent the coordinates of the anchor box d_0 at each corner, w_0 and h_0 represent the width and height of the anchor box d_0, Δx_m, Δy_m represent the offsets for each corner of the box.

In order to add key-point detection for subsequent tasks in object detection and classification, we have added three additional points: G_{q5}, G_{q6}, and G_{q7}. The reference point is chosen as the center point of the anchor box (x_0, y_0). Therefore, the index m can take values from 1 to 7, where $d_{05} = d_{06} = d_{07} = (x_0, y_0)$.

4   Experimental Results

4.1   Database Construction

Based on self-developed hardware device, the obtained data can be divided to seven types. The examples of each type are shown as follows (Fig. 7):

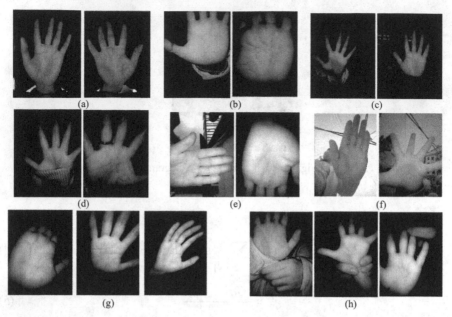

Fig. 7. Types of collected samples. (a) Single-colored background, appropriate size, clear palm. (b) Partial hand, complete palm, clear image. (c) Large movable range, clear image. (d) Obstruction or accessories. (e) Different angles. (f) Complex background: including but not limited to environmental brightness, external objects, self-interference, etc. (g) Different postures: fingers clenched, bent; palm tilted, deformed, etc. (h) Multiple hands coexist.

Data annotation software enables automatic data labeling, supporting for different resolutions, real-time saving, and undoing modifications. With this software the annotation time for training sample set is about 10 images in 1 min (Fig. 8).

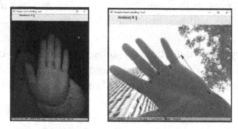

Fig. 8. Annotation software illustration. After marking mark1, mark2, and mark3, pressing the key 'a' will automatically generate rectangular bounding boxes.

4.2 Experimental Analysis

In this section, we conducted a series of tests to evaluate the performance of our proposed method for localizing arbitrary quadrilateral boxes. Firstly, we implemented ROI extraction based on traditional algorithms as a control experiment (Fig. 9).

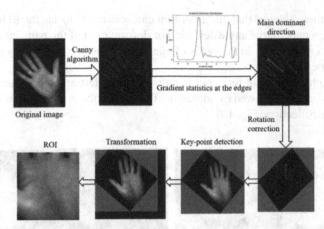

Fig. 9. Experimental Process and results.

Then, we conducted experiments based on the new algorithm model. We compared the predicted boxes with the ground truth boxes using evaluation metric Intersection over Union (IoU). The IoU measures the overlap between these two boxes. A total of 2600 images were used as training samples.

By establishing two different test sets, we can verify the impact of deviation angles on the test results. For the dataset test1 consists of hand rotations ranging from −90° degrees to 90°, as well as dataset 2 consists of hand rotations ranging from −45° to 45°. Each dataset underwent two types of testing, with different confidence threshold and localization error.

In the first experiment, the confidence threshold was set to 0.98, indicating that only output bounding boxes with a prediction score higher than this threshold were considered for further processing. This helped ensure high-confidence predictions and reduce the chances of false positives. The localization error of the system was measured to be 0.21, indicating the average distance between the predicted bounding box and the ground truth bounding box. A lower localization error signified better accuracy in localizing the ROI. While in the second experiment, the confidence threshold was set to 0.79 and the localization error to be 0.40 (Table 1).

Table 1. Experiment results of recognition rate

Dataset	Left hand detection	Right hand detection	Average rate
Test1-1	0.752143	0.881077	0.817939
Test1-2	0.787997	0.9454	0.868321
Test2-1	0.834174	0.941092	0.887729
Test2-2	0.871665	0.976293	0.924073

The experiment showed that this algorithm can accurately locate the ROI and extract key points. Even under large angle deviation or deformation of the palm, accurate localization was still achievable. In the case of fingers being close together, key points of the fingertips can be detected.

Despite slightly different recognition rates between left and right hands, it is suggested that this can be improved by addressing the imbalance in the training data through additional data collection (Fig. 10).

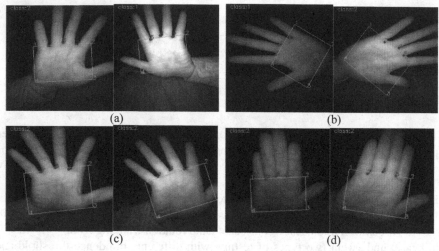

Fig. 10. Recognition output. Class 1 means left hand, and class 2 means right hand. ROI area displayed with green anchors, three key points G_{q5}, G_{q6}, G_{q7} were also identified and marked. (a) Output graphs of appropriate palm. (b) Output graphs of palm in different angles. (c) Output graphs of palm with large angle deviation or deformation. (d) Output graphs of key point detection in the case of fingers being close together.

5   Conclusion

Palm vein recognition technology will have greater development prospects and application scenarios. Through experimental analysis, the new algorithm demonstrates improved accuracy in ROI extraction and localization of palm vein images. It can adapt to complex scenarios and hand gestures, playing a crucial role in enhancing the accuracy, speed, and user experience of palm vein recognition system. Meanwhile, this algorithm shows promise in achieving precise arbitrary quadrilateral object detection and key point detection, offering potential applications in areas such as contactless palm print system and multimodal biometric system. In the future, we will move towards the comprehensive scenario of 'palm vein recognition+', constructing a multidimensional information data application platform.

References

1. Liu, W., et al.: SSD: single shot multibox detector. In: Leibe, B., Matas, J., Sebe, N., Welling, M. (eds.) ECCV 2016. LNCS, vol. 9905, pp. 21–37. Springer, Cham (2016). https://doi.org/10.1007/978-3-319-46448-0_2
2. Liao, M., Shi, B., Bai, X.: Textboxes++: a single-shot oriented scene text detector. IEEE Trans. Image Process. **27**(8), 3676–3690 (2018)
3. Sun, Z., et al.: Overview of biometrics research. J. Image Graph. **26**, 1254–1329 (2021). 生物特征识别学科发展报告.中国图象图形学报 **26**, 1254–1329 (2021)
4. Lin, C.L., Fan, K.C.: Biometric verification using thermal images of palm-dorsa vein patterns. IEEE Trans. Circuits Syst. Video Technol. **14**(2), 199–213 (2004)
5. Kang, W., Wu, Q.: Contactless palm vein recognition using a mutual foreground-based local binary pattern. IEEE Trans. Inf. Forensics Secur. **9**(11), 1974–1985 (2014)
6. Zhou, Y., Kumar, A.: Human identification using palm-vein images. IEEE Trans. Inf. Forensics Secur. **6**, 1259–1274 (2011)
7. Qin, H., El-Yacoubi, M.A., Li, Y., Liu, C.: Multi-scale and multi-direction GAN for CNN-based single palm-vein identification. IEEE Trans. Inf. Forensics Secur. **16**, 2652–2666 (2021)

U-PISRNet: A Unet-Shape Palmprint Image Super-Resolution Network

Yao Wang[1], Lunke Fei[1(✉)], Tingting Chai[2], Shuping Zhao[1], Peipei Kang[1], and Wei Jia[3]

[1] School of Computer Science and Technology,
Guangdong University of Technology, Guangzhou, China
flksxm@126.com
[2] School of Computer Science and Technology,
Harbin Institute of Technology, Shenzhen, China
[3] School of Computer and Information, Hefei University of Technology, Hefei, China

Abstract. Palmprint has gained significant attention in recent years due to its reliability and uniqueness for biometric recognition. However, most existing palmprint recognition methods focus only feature representation and matching under an assumption that palmprint images are high-quality, while practical palmprint images are usually captured by various cameras under diverse backgrounds, heavily reducing the quality of palmprint images. To address this, in this paper, we propose a Unet-shape palmprint image super-resolution network (U-PISRNet) by learning and recovering multi-scale palmprint-specific characteristics of palmprint images. First, we project the palmprint images into the high-dimensional shallow representation. Then, we employ the transformer-based Unet-shape Encoder-Decoder architecture with skip-connections to simultaneously learn multi-scale local and global semantic features of palmprint images. Lastly, we reconstruct the super-resolution palmprint images with clear palmprint-specific texture and edge characteristics via two convolutional layers with embedding a PixelShuffle. Experimental results on three public palmprint databases clearly show the effectiveness of the proposed palmprint image super-resolution network.

Keywords: Super-resolution · palmprint images · swin transformer · Unet

1 Introduction

For biometric recognition, palmprint has served as one of the most promising biometric traits due to its rich unique characteristics, non-invasiveness, user-friendliness and hygienic contactless acquisition manner [1]. Over the past decades, there have been a number of methods proposed for palmprint recognition, such as the sub-space-based, local direction encoding-based, and deep learning-based methods. It is noted that most existing palmprint recognition methods focus only on feature representation and matching under an assumption that the palmprint images are high-quality. However, in real-world scenarios,

© The Author(s), under exclusive license to Springer Nature Singapore Pte Ltd. 2023
W. Jia et al. (Eds.): CCBR 2023, LNCS 14463, pp. 24–33, 2023.
https://doi.org/10.1007/978-981-99-8565-4_3

palmprint images are usually captured by various cameras with differing resolutions under diverse backgrounds and lighting conditions, which heavily affect the quality of palmprint images. For this reason, how to improve the quality of palmprint images plays a critical role for reliable palmprint recognition.

Image super-resolution (SR) has shown great potential in enhancing the perceptual quality of images by reconstructing high-resolution (HR) images from their low-resolution (LR) counterparts. In the literature, there have been a variety of methods proposed for image SR, such as interpolation-based, reconstruction-based, and learning-based methods. Due to the remarkable success of deep learning in image processing and computer vision tasks, numerous deep learning-based SR methods have been introduced in recent years. For instance, Zhang et al. [2] proposed a channel attention-based RCAN to selectively enhance informative features for improving SR images. Chen et al. [3] presented a pure transformer-based network by employing self-attention mechanisms to capture long-range dependencies and spatial information for various image restoration tasks, including super-resolution, denoising, and deraining. While these SR methods have achieved encouraging performance, they usually cannot be directly used for palmprint image SR due to the intrinsic characteristics of palmprints, such as palmar ridge patterns and palmar flexion creases. To address this, this paper specially focuses on the study of SR for palmprint images.

In this paper, we propose a Unet-shape palmprint image super-resolution network (U-PISRNet) for palmprint image SR. Figure 1 shows the basic framework of the proposed U-PISRNet, which consists of shallow feature extraction, encoder, FRM, decoder, and image reconstruction sub-networks. First, the shallow feature extraction sub-network converts the original palmprint images into its high-dimensional shallow representation via a single convolutional layer. Then, the encoder sub-network utilizes three groups of global local feature extraction modules (GLEMs) and down-sampling blocks to learn multi-scale pixel-level and structure-level features of palmprint images. Third, we introduce a bank of Feature Refinement Modules (FRM) to further refine the multi-scale palmprint features by adaptively enhancing informative features. After that, we employ the decoder sub-network to gradually recover the high-resolution feature maps of palmprint images. Finally, based on both the shallow and high-level palmprint feature maps, we reconstruct the super-resolution palmprint image via two convolutional layers with embedding a PixelShuffle layer. Experimental results on three widely used palmprint databases clearly show the effectiveness of the proposed method.

The remaining sections of this paper are organized as follows: Sect. 2 provides a brief review of related topics. Section 3 presents the proposed U-PISRNet. Section 4 discusses the experimental results. Finally, Sect. 5 concludes this paper.

2   Related Work

Unet mainly consists of an encoder and a decoder with skip connections, allowing the flow of information from the encoder to the decoder. This enables the Unet can simultaneously learn both the global and local features. For this reason,

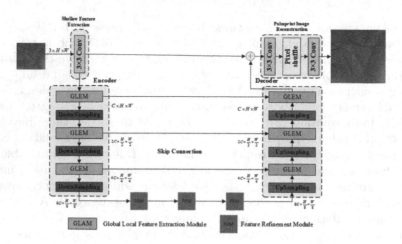

Fig. 1. The main framework of the proposed U-PISRNet.

Unet has been widely used for various computer vision tasks, such as objection detection and semantic segmentation, and achieved remarkable performance. Recently, Unet has also been successfully applied for image super-resolution due to its ability to capture fine-grained details and recover high-resolution minute characteristics. For example, Lu et al. [4] proposed a modified Unet that removes all batch normalization layers, one convolution layer, and introduces a mixed gradient error for image super-resolution. Min et al. [5] propose a dual decoder Unet (D2UNet) to explore both the detail and edge information of the data for seismic image SR. In this paper, we propose a new Unet-shape palmprint image super-resolution network by exploring the multi-scale palmprint-specific features.

3   The Proposed U-PISRNet

As shown in Fig. 1, the proposed U-PISRNet consists of the shallow feature extraction, encoder, FRM, decoder, and image reconstruction sub-networks. In the following, we elaborate each component of the U-PISRNet.

3.1   Shallow Feature Extraction

Let $I_{LR} \in \mathbb{R}^{3 \times H \times W}$ denotes the input low-resolution (LR) palmprint images, the shallow feature extraction sub-network employs a 3×3 convolution layer to extract the low-level feature representation of palmprint images as follows.

$$F_l = f_{in}(I_{LR}),\tag{1}$$

where $f_{in}(\cdot)$ represents the function of the 3×3 convolutional layer. $F_l \in \mathbb{R}^{C \times H \times W}$ is the extracted low-level feature map, where C, H and W are the numbers of the channel, height and width of F_l, respectively.

3.2   Encoder

Having obtained the shallow palmprint representation, we design an encoder sub-network to further exploit the intrinsic high-level semantic features of the low-resolution palmprint images. The encoder sub-network (see Fig. 1) consists of three global local feature extraction modules, each of which is followed with a down-sampling block. Figure 2(a) shows the main idea of the GLEM, which consists of N layers of swin-transformer for building the global feature long-range dependencies, and two 3 × 3 convolution layers for extracting local features.

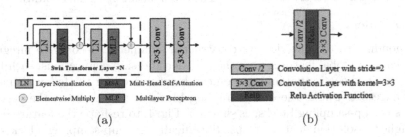

(a)   (b)

Fig. 2. (a) The basic architecture of the global local feature extraction module (GLEM), and (b) the basic idea of the down-sampling block.

To obtain fine grained high-level palmprint features, we employ the down-sampling block to produce different scales of high-dimensional features. Figure 2(b) depicts the basic architecture of the down-sampling block, which consists of a 3 × 3 convolution layer with the *stride* = 2, a Relu activation function, and a 3 × 3 convolution layer with the *stride* = 1. The down-sampling block can be functioned as follows.

$$G_d \in \mathbb{R}^{2C \times \frac{H}{2} \times \frac{W}{2}} = \varphi(f_\downarrow(G_{out})), \tag{2}$$

where $f_\downarrow(\cdot)$ is the down-sampling function with the scaling factor of 2, and $\varphi(\cdot)$ represents the Relu activation function. G_{out} is the palmprint feature map generated by GLEM. The feature map generated by the entire encoder is $G_e \in \mathbb{R}^{8C \times \frac{H}{8} \times \frac{W}{8}}$.

3.3   Feature Refinement Module (FRM)

To continuously refine and enhance the important encoded features of the palmprint, we embed three feature refinement modules (FRMs) between the encoder and decoder. Figure 3 shows the basic structure of the FRM, which consists of two symmetrical channel attention modules, convolution layers, and also two swin-transformer layers. The channel attention selectively amplifies informative channels while suppressing less relevant ones, allowing us to focus most on discriminative texture and edge features of palmprints. Simultaneously, the swin-transformer layer captures long-range dependencies within the feature maps, facilitating the integration of contextual information. By doing this, FRM can refine the representation of the palmprint feature maps.

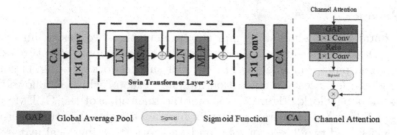

Fig. 3. The basic architecture of the feature refinement module (FRM).

3.4 Decoder

Corresponding to the encoder, we construct a symmetric decoder to integrate both local and global features from the encoder and skip connections, such that the fine-grained contextual information can be preserved for the following palm-print image SR. Unlike the down-sampling blocks in the encoder, the decoder employs the up-sampling blocks, as shown in Fig. 4, to reshape the feature maps into higher resolution feature maps. Specifically, the up-sampling block consists of a 2×2 deconvolution layer with $stride = 2$, a Relu activation function, and a 3×3 convolution layer with $stride = 1$. First, the deconvolution layer decreases the channel dimension by $2\times$ and increases the spatial dimension by $2\times$ to the original dimension. Then, the ReLU activation function introduces the non-linearity into the network to capture the complex patterns and relationships in the palmprint features. After that, the convolution layer with $stride = 1$ is employed to further refine the fusion palmprint features.

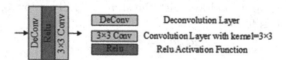

Fig. 4. The basic architecture of the up-sampling block.

The skip connections are used to fuse the multi-scale features from the encoder with the up-sampled features from the decoder. In addition, the shallow features extracted from the GLEM in encoder and the deep features extracted from the up-sampling blocks are concatenated to reduce the loss of spatial information caused by down-sampling.

3.5 Palmprint Image Reconstruction

Having obtained the fine-gained aggregation of multi-scale feature map (e.g., G_{last}), the palmprint image reconstruction sub-network reconstructs the super-resolution palmprint image via two 3×3 convolution layers with inserting a pixel shuffle layer, as follows.

$$I_{SR} = f_{out}(G_{last}) + I_{LR}, \tag{3}$$

where $I_{SR} \in \mathbb{R}^{3 \times H \times W}$ is the reconstructed super-resolution palmprint image, and $f_{out}(\cdot)$ denotes the convolution layers in the reconstruction sub-network.

4 Experiments

In this section, we conduct comparative experiments to evaluate our proposed network. For the proposed U-PISRNet, we set the scale of up-sampling block and down-sampling block to 2. Additionally, we used a channel number of 60 for the shallow feature extraction sub-network. We selected ReLU as the activation function and optimized our model using the Adam optimizer, with and. The initial learning rate was set to 2×10^{-4}, and we reduced it by half every 200 epochs. We implemented our model on the PyTorch framework and trained it with one NVIDIA 3060Ti GPU.

4.1 Databases

The PolyU Multispectral Palmprint Database [6]: The PolyU Multispectral Palmprint Database consists of 24,000 palmprint images captured from 250 volunteers using four different spectral bands: blue, green, red, and near-infrared (NIR). Each volunteer provided 12 palmprint images under each spectral band, resulting in four separate datasets with 6,000 images each.

The TJI Palmprint Database [7]: The TJI Palmprint Database contains 12,000 palmprint images collected from 300 individuals, and 20 palmprint images were acquired for each palm of an individual.

The XJTU-UP Database [8]: The XJTU-UP Database contains 20,000 palmprint images obtained from 100 subjects by using five different mobile phones, including the iPhone 6S, HUAWEI Mate8, LG G4, Samsung Galaxy Note5, and MI8, in two different environmental conditions. As a result, the XJTU-UP actually contains ten sub-datasets, and each dataset consists of 2,000 palmprint images from 200 different palms.

Figure 5 shows some typical palmprint images selected from the PolyU, TJI and XJTU-UP databases. In the experiments, we train our proposed U-PISRNet using 12000 training images from the PolyU database (including PolyU-Red and PolyU-NIR). For fairness, we randomly selected five images per each palm from the PolyU-Green, PolyU-Red, TONGJI, XJTU-UP, respectively, to form four test sample set.

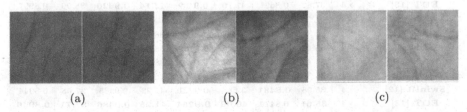

(a)   (b)   (c)

Fig. 5. Some representative palmprint ROI images selected from the (a) PolyU, (b) TJI, and (c) XJTU-UP databases.

4.2 Palmprint Image SR

To better evaluate the proposed U-PISRNet, we calculate the peak signal-to-noise ratio (PSNR) and structural similarity (SSIM) of the U-PISRNet on palmprint image SR, and compare it with the state-of-the-art methods, including RCAN [2], SAN [9], HAN [10], NLSA [11], SwinIR [12], and EDT [13]. Table 1 tabulates the SR results of different methods for palmprint image SR with scaling factors of 2, 3, and 4 SR task. It can be seen that our proposed method outperforms the CNN-based methods, such as RCAN, SAN, and HAN. This is because our proposed method employs the transformer mechanism to capture long-range dependency, while the CNN-based methods usually focus only on the local regions, such that more texture and edge features can be captured by our proposed method for image super-resolution. Furthermore, the proposed U-PISRNet also achieves higher PSNR and SSIM than the transformer-based methods such as SwinIR and EDT for different SR scale factors. The possible reason is that U-PISRNet leverages a fusion of the swin-transformer and Unet architectures, such that multi-scale and global feature maps can be simultaneously learned. In contrast, the existing transformer-based methods usually adopt a stacked chain architecture, making it hard to propagate and exploit lower-level features, and resulting to a high information loss.

Table 1. The average PSNR and SSIM obtained by different methods for palmprint image super-resolution with the scale factors of 2, 3 and 4 on the PolyU-Green, PolyU-Red, TJI and XJTU-UP, respectively.

Method	Scale	PolyU-Green		PolyU-Red		TJI		XJTU-UP	
		PSNR	SSIM	PSNR	SSIM	PSNR	SSIM	PSNR	SSIM
RCAN [2]	×2	39.31	0.9180	41.89	0.9450	46.37	0.9812	40.07	0.9501
SAN [9]	×2	39.34	0.9186	42.07	0.9452	46.51	0.9820	40.16	0.9567
HAN [10]	×2	39.32	0.9181	42.14	0.9461	46.54	0.9823	40.06	0.9548
NLSA [11]	×2	39.59	0.9217	42.17	0.9469	46.52	0.9821	40.16	0.9573
SwinIR [12]	×2	39.72	0.9230	42.24	0.9475	46.76	0.9826	40.25	0.9611
EDT [13]	×2	**39.75**	**0.9232**	**42.27**	**0.9479**	**46.77**	**0.9827**	**40.28**	**0.9614**
U-PISRNet(Ours)	×2	39.77	0.9234	42.30	0.9481	46.78	0.9828	40.31	0.9619
RCAN [2]	×3	37.17	0.8496	40.81	0.9256	41.75	0.956	37.51	0.8837
SAN [9]	×3	37.14	0.8487	40.79	0.9243	41.41	0.9525	37.87	0.8897
HAN [10]	×3	37.17	0.8497	40.82	0.9258	41.76	0.9561	37.53	0.8838
NLSA [11]	×3	37.28	0.8502	40.94	0.9262	41.78	0.9562	37.65	0.8843
SwinIR [12]	×3	**37.84**	**0.8692**	**41.71**	**0.9403**	41.66	0.9539	**38.11**	**0.9007**
EDT [13]	×3	37.82	0.8691	41.70	0.9402	**42.14**	**0.9620**	38.09	0.8997
U-PISRNet(Ours)	×3	37.94	0.8712	42.05	0.9419	42.61	0.9668	39.25	0.9428
RCAN [2]	×4	35.36	0.8472	38.97	0.912	38.76	0.9352	37.32	0.8923
SAN [9]	×4	35.42	0.8475	39.15	0.9129	38.83	0.9355	37.38	0.8929
HAN [10]	×4	35.42	0.8475	39.27	0.9135	38.91	0.9359	37.39	0.8929
NLSA [11]	×4	35.31	0.8465	39.28	0.9134	39.11	0.9378	37.42	0.8931
SwinIR [12]	×4	35.58	**0.8481**	39.83	0.9221	41.23	0.9485	37.68	0.8944
EDT [13]	×4	**35.61**	0.8479	**40.09**	**0.9251**	**41.25**	**0.9486**	**37.71**	**0.8946**
U-PISRNet(Ours)	×4	35.97	0.8485	40.16	0.9261	41.27	0.9489	37.83	0.9209

4.3 Ablation Analysis

Our proposed U-PISRNet employs the swin-transformer layer for exploiting the global relationship of palmprint features, the U-shape architecture for utilizing the multi-scale palmprint features and the skip connection for multi-scale feature fusion. In the following, we conduct a series of ablation experiments to evaluate the effectiveness of these modules.

Effect of the Skip Connections: The skip connections in our U-PISRNet are strategically incorporated at the 1, 1/2, and 1/4 resolution scales. To investigate the impact of skip connections in U-PISRNet, we varied the number of skip connections to 0, 1, 2, and 3, respectively, and correspondingly calculated the PSNR and SSIM for image SR, as summarized in Table 2. We see that our U-PISRNet improves the reconstruction performance with an increasing number of skip connection. Hence, in this study, we empirically set the number of the skip connections to 3 to better enhance the robustness of the proposed method.

Table 2. The PSNR and SSIM of the proposed network with varying number of the skip connection

Skip Connection	PolyU-Green		PolyU-Red		TONGJI		XJTU-UP	
	PSNR	SSIM	PSNR	SSIM	PSNR	SSIM	PSNR	SSIM
0	39.55	0.9218	42.03	0.9461	46.57	0.9805	40.06	0.9594
1	39.61	0.9225	42.15	0.947	46.65	0.9818	40.12	0.9598
2	39.64	0.9227	42.19	0.9472	46.69	0.9821	40.17	0.9601
3	**39.77**	**0.9234**	**42.30**	**0.9481**	**46.78**	**0.9828**	**40.31**	**0.9616**

Effect of the FRM: To test the FRM, we gradually increased the FRM number of the proposed network in the range of , and perform palmprint image SR, as tabulated in Table 3. It shows that the proposed U-PISRNet with no FRM (i.e., U-PISRNet-V0) achieves the lowest PSNR and SSIM, demonstrating the importance of embedding FRM into our U-PISRNet. Moreover, it is observed that our proposed network achieves the best image SR performance when the number of FRM is set to 3. To this end, we empirically embed three FRMs into our proposed U-PISRNet.

Effect of the GLEM: GLEM combines both CNN and transformer to simultaneously learn the local features and global structural information. To verify the effectiveness of the GLEM, we formed three variants of the proposed network: (1) the U-PISRNet with embedding no GLEM (referred to as w/o GLEM), (2) the U-PISRNet with embedding only the convolution layers in GLEM (referred to as GLEM w/o swin), and (3) the U-PISRNet with embedding only the swin-transformer layers in GLEM (referred to as GLEM w/o CNN). Table 4 tables the palmprint image SR results by using different U-PISRNet variants. It can be seen

Table 3. The PSNR and SSIM of the proposed network with varying number of the FRM.

Methods	PolyU-Green		PolyU-Red		TONGJI		XJTU-UP	
	PSNR	SSIM	PSNR	SSIM	PSNR	SSIM	PSNR	SSIM
U-PISRNet-V0	39.52	0.9217	42.01	0.9459	46.55	0.9803	40.02	0.959
U-PISRNet-V1	39.67	0.9229	42.21	0.9475	46.71	0.9823	40.22	0.9602
U-PISRNet-V3	**39.77**	**0.9234**	**42.30**	**0.9481**	**46.78**	**0.9828**	**40.31**	**0.9616**
U-PISRNet-V5	39.51	0.9216	42.15	0.9467	46.52	0.9809	40.13	0.9604

that the proposed U-PISRNet with embedding the complete GLEM consistently outperforms the other three variants, demonstrating the promising effectiveness of the GLEM. This is because the convolution layers of the GLEM can effectively exploit the local palmprint characteristics, and meanwhile the swin-transformer layers of the GLEM can capture the global palmprint structural information, such that more complementary local and global information can be extracted for the final super-resolved image reconstruction.

Table 4. The PSNR and SSIM of the proposed network with three variants of GLEM

Methods	PolyU-Green		PolyU-Red		TONGJI		XJTU-UP	
	PSNR	SSIM	PSNR	SSIM	PSNR	SSIM	PSNR	SSIM
w/o GLEM	37.49	0.9012	40.07	0.9162	44.66	0.9509	38.09	0.9298
GLEM w/o swin	39.67	0.9227	42.22	0.9473	46.71	0.9822	40.23	0.9605
GLEM w/o CNN	39.74	0.9232	42.27	0.9478	46.76	0.9826	40.27	0.9612
GLEM	**39.77**	**0.9234**	**42.30**	**0.9481**	**46.78**	**0.9828**	**40.31**	**0.9616**

5   Conclusion

In this paper, we propose a Unet-shape palmprint image super-resolution network for palmprint image SR. The proposed method first maps a palmprint image into the high-dimensional pixel-level representation and then simultaneously learns the multi-scale local and global palmprint-specific features via encoder and decoder sub-networks. To clearly recover the intrinsic local patterns of palmprint images, we further design GLEM and FRM to specially capture the local palmprint details and global palmprint structural information. Experimental results on three benchmark databases have demonstrated the promising effectiveness of the proposed U-PISRNet for palmprint image super-resolution. For future work, it seems to be an interesting direction to extend our proposed network to other hand-based biometric SR tasks such as palm-vein and finger-vein image SR.

Acknowledgments. This work was supported in part by the National Natural Science Foundation of China under Grants 62176066 and 62106052, in part by the Natural Science Foundation of Guangdong Province under Grant 2023A1515012717, and in part by the Natural Science Foundation of Shandong Province under Grant ZR2023QF030.

References

1. Fei, L., Wong, W.K., Zhao, S., Wen, J., Zhu, J., Xu, Y.: Learning spectrum-invariance representation for cross-spectral palmprint recognition. IEEE Trans. Syst. Man Cybern. Syst. (2023)
2. Zhang, Y., Li, K., Li, K., Wang, L., Zhong, B., Fu, Y.: Image super-resolution using very deep residual channel attention networks. In: Proceedings of the European Conference on Computer Vision (ECCV), pp. 286–301 (2018)
3. Chen, H., et al.: Pre-trained image processing transformer. In: Proceedings of the IEEE/CVF Conference on Computer Vision and Pattern Recognition, pp. 12299–12310 (2021)
4. Lu, Z., Chen, Y.: Single image super-resolution based on a modified U-Net with mixed gradient loss. Signal Image Video Process. 1–9 (2022)
5. Min, F., Wang, L., Pan, S., Song, G.: D2UNet: dual decoder U-Net for seismic image super-resolution reconstruction. IEEE Trans. Geosci. Remote Sens. **61**, 1–13 (2023)
6. Zhang, D., Guo, Z., Lu, G., Zhang, L., Zuo, W.: An online system of multispectral palmprint verification. IEEE Trans. Instrum. Meas. **59**(2), 480–490 (2009)
7. Zhang, L., Li, L., Yang, A., Shen, Y., Yang, M.: Towards contactless palmprint recognition: a novel device, a new benchmark, and a collaborative representation based identification approach. Pattern Recognit. **69**, 199–212 (2017)
8. Shao, H., Zhong, D., Du, X.: Deep distillation hashing for unconstrained palmprint recognition. IEEE Trans. Instrum. Meas. **70**, 1–13 (2021)
9. Dai, T., Cai, J., Zhang, Y., Xia, S.T., Zhang, L.: Second-order attention network for single image super-resolution. In: Proceedings of the IEEE/CVF Conference on Computer Vision and Pattern Recognition, pp. 11065–11074 (2019)
10. Niu, B., et al.: Single image super-resolution via a holistic attention network. In: Vedaldi, A., Bischof, H., Brox, T., Frahm, J.-M. (eds.) ECCV 2020. LNCS, vol. 12357, pp. 191–207. Springer, Cham (2020). https://doi.org/10.1007/978-3-030-58610-2_12
11. Mei, Y., Fan, Y., Zhou, Y.: Image super-resolution with non-local sparse attention. In: Proceedings of the IEEE/CVF Conference on Computer Vision and Pattern Recognition, pp. 3517–3526 (2021)
12. Liang, J., Cao, J., Sun, G., Zhang, K., Van Gool, L., Timofte, R.: SwinIR: image restoration using swin transformer. In: Proceedings of the IEEE/CVF International Conference on Computer Vision, pp. 1833–1844 (2021)
13. Li, W., Lu, X., Lu, J., Zhang, X., Jia, J.: On efficient transformer and image pre-training for low-level vision. arXiv preprint arXiv:2112.10175 (2021). **3**(7), 8

Region of Interest Extraction for Closed Palm with Complex Background

Kaijun Zhou$^{(\boxtimes)}$, Xiaoyong Sun, Xiancheng Zhou, and Qi Zeng

School of Intelligent Engineering and Intelligent Manufacturing, Hunan University of
Technology and Business, No. 569, Yuelu Avenue, Changsha 410000, China
zkj@hutb.edu.cn

Abstract. The tilt of the closed palm can make it impossible to accurately locate
the region of interest (ROI) in contactless palmprint recognition systems. In order
to accurately extract the closed palm ROI in the tilted stance, firstly, this paper
combines the skeleton point detection and perspective transformation techniques
for the correction of tilted images, and then adopts DeepLabv3+ network to eliminate complex backgrounds and combines Gaussian skin colour model to improve
segmentation accuracy. Convex packet detection is used to obtain the hand depression points, and combined with horizontal edge detection to filter out the final
valley points. Experiments on the open-source dataset 11k Hands and the homemade dataset HUTB_Hands prove that the extraction success rate of the proposed
method reaches more than 95%, which is superior to other methods under the
same conditions.

Keywords: Contactless palmprint recognition · Tilt correction · Image
segmentation · Closed palm · Region of interest extraction

1 Introduction

Biometric identification has been an established research field, aiming to use biometric
features to identify individuals for access control. Among them, palm prints have received
much attention due to their unique advantages such as rich features, high stability and
not easy to wear out.

A typical palmprint recognition system generally consists of four modules: image
acquisition, region of interest (ROI) extraction, feature extraction, feature matching and
recognition. With the advancement of technology and health care needs, image acquisition technology gradually develops towards non-contact, which inevitably leads to the
problem of palm tilting, which in turn leads to deformation, distortion, and inaccurate
positioning of ROIs in the palmprint image. Extracting palm ROIs is one of the key steps
in palmprint recognition, which is the basis for subsequent feature matching. Most of
the existing methods require a lot of time and human resources, and are easily affected
by skin colour and light with poor segmentation accuracy.

W. Jia et al. (Eds.): CCBR 2023, LNCS 14463, pp. 34–45, 2023.
https://doi.org/10.1007/978-981-99-8565-4_4

1.1   Current Status of Research on Palm Tilt Correction Methods

Skew correction of palm images is a hotspot and difficult problem within the field of non-contact palmprint recognition. Currently, the mainstream correction methods are depth information method and pose transformation method.

Depth information-based palm correction mainly uses 3D scanning equipment or binocular stereo camera to obtain the depth coordinate information of the palm surface, and then calculates the palm plane before correction. Zheng et al. [1] proposed a hand recognition method based on features invariant to the projective transformation of the map area, and achieved good results in a small sample database. Smith [2] et al. used a 3D system for non-contact mode acquisition, and used high-resolution photometric stereo to compensate for the resolution gap, so as to effectively obtain the palm texture features. Palm correction by changing the hand posture is mainly done by changing the tilt posture. Mikolajczyk et al. [3] applied 3D vision to the field of palmprint recognition, which can correct for a small range of palm tilts. Cong Gao et al. [4], on the other hand, proposed a new tilt correction method that focuses on correcting the tilt of labelled images with salient features.

1.2   State of the Art in Closed Palm Region of Interest Extraction Research

Among the existing works, there are few studies on extracting regions of interest using closed palms. The most common methods are edge detection, template matching, and methods that combine techniques such as deep learning and computer vision.

In 2015, Ito et al. [6] proposed an edge detection-based method for extracting palm ROIs by constructing palm contours by subtracting the main lines of finger edges for binarised palm images. Shao et al. [7] determined the location of ROIs directly by marking the points in unconstrained palmprint recognition. With the development of techniques such as deep learning and computer vision, convolutional neural networks have been used to handle palmprint ROI extraction. Bao et al. [8] used the CASIA palmprint database to determine the location of finger valleys using a shallow network consisting of four convolutional layers and two fully connected layers, and the extraction results were comparable to Zhang [5].

In summary, although the extraction of a closed palm region of interest can be achieved using mainstream methods, it is necessary to obtain a finer palm contour. Most of the existing methods are unable to achieve the balance between the accuracy of the region of interest extraction and the tilt correction of the palm in a non-contact environment.

1.3 Related Work

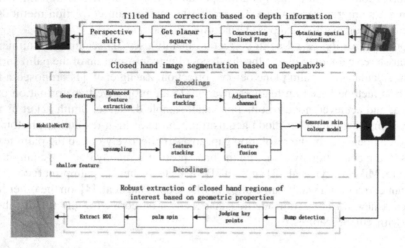

Fig. 1. Algorithmic framework diagram.

In this paper, a closed palm ROI extraction method is proposed to address the problems of difficulty and lack of accuracy in the extraction of the closed palm region of interest under tilted posture (Fig. 1), based on the existing research at home and abroad. The palm is corrected to face the camera for the error caused by the palm in the tilted posture. For the closed palm region of interest extraction, the segmentation accuracy is improved by using DeepLabv3+ in combination with the Gaussian skin colour model. Then, the connection between the palm marker points is constructed to accurately extract the closed palm region of interest.

2 Tilt Correction of Palm Image Based on Depth Information

The method of palm image tilt correction based on depth information consists of three steps. First, the skeleton point detection technique is used to obtain the depth information of the marked points of the palm. Then the super-definite equations are constructed and solved to obtain the plane coefficients to construct the outer rectangle of the palm. Finally, the palm is corrected by perspective transformation.

2.1 Palm Plane Construction

To construct a 3D plane of the palm, a 3D plane needs to be fitted by obtaining the depth coordinate information of the skeleton points of the palm. As in Fig. 2, the marked points 0, 5, 9, 13 and 17 are used as the coordinate points of the palms P1, P2, P3, P4 and P5 and substituted into the plane equation $Z = aX + bY + c$, i.e.

$$\begin{bmatrix} x_1 & y_1 & 1 \\ x_2 & y_2 & 1 \\ x_3 & y_3 & 1 \\ x_4 & y_4 & 1 \\ x_5 & y_5 & 1 \end{bmatrix} \cdot \begin{bmatrix} a \\ b \\ c \end{bmatrix} = \begin{bmatrix} z_1 \\ z_2 \\ z_3 \\ z_4 \\ z_5 \end{bmatrix}. \tag{1}$$

where x_1, y_1, z_1 are the position coordinates of the pixels in the spatial domain and a, b, c are the plane equation coefficients. The fitted plane coefficients $X(a, b, c)$ are obtained by solving the equation.

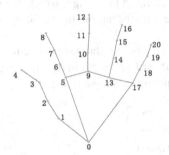

Fig. 2. Palm Skeleton Point Information.

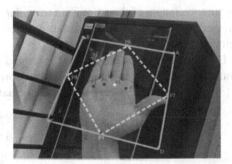

Fig. 3. Tilt-corrected feature point infographic.

2.2 Rectangular Construction Outside the Palm of the Hand

Constructing a hand outer rectangle by the obtained plane coefficients such that the rectangle encompasses the entire palm. After that, P3 is used as a reference point to make the symmetry point P6 of P1 and obtain the coordinates of P6.

$$P6(x, y, z) = 2 * P3(x, y, z) - P1(x, y, z). \tag{2}$$

where (x, y, z) is the three-dimensional coordinate information of the point. In order to derive the coordinates of the four key points of the rectangle, assuming the three-dimensional coordinates of P7. P7 should satisfy the following three conditions:

① The distance from P7 to P3 should be equal to the distance from P6 to P3;
② The vector formed by P7 and P3 should be perpendicular to the vector formed by P6 and P3;
③ P7 should lie in the fitting plane.

Let the coordinates of P3 be (x_3, y_3, z_3) and P6 be (x_6, y_6, z_6), then the system of equations is derived

$$\begin{cases} (x_7 - x_3)^2 + (y_7 - y_3)^2 + (z_7 - z_3)^2 - (x_6 - x_3)^2 - (y_6 - y_3)^2 - (z_6 - z_3)^2 = 0 \\ (x_6 - x_3) * (x_7 - x_3) + (y_6 - y_3) * (y_7 - y_3) + (z_6 - z_3) * (z_7 - z_3) = 0 \\ a * x_7 + b * y_7 - z_7 + c = 0 \end{cases}. \tag{3}$$

where a, b and c are the coefficients of plane equation. Solve the system of equations to obtain the coordinates of P7, and then use P3 as the reference point to make the symmetry point P8 of P7.

Repeat the above steps, assuming that the point **A** is obtained, the symmetry can be obtained by the symmetry of the points **B**, **C** and **D** respectively. The outer rectangle of the palm is then obtained, as shown in Fig. 3.

2.3 Palm Image Perspective Transformation

The outer rectangle of the palm is an irregular quadrilateral in the image, which can be corrected to a rectangle on the image by a perspective transformation, thus making the palm corrected.

The obtained points **A**, **B**, **C** and **D** are fed as parameters into the perspective transformation function so that the four points form a standard rectangle under the image coordinate system. The perspective transformation equation is shown in Eq. (4).

$$\begin{bmatrix} x' & y' & w' \end{bmatrix} = \begin{bmatrix} u & v & w \end{bmatrix} \begin{bmatrix} a_{11} & a_{12} & a_{13} \\ a_{21} & a_{22} & a_{23} \\ a_{31} & a_{32} & a_{33} \end{bmatrix}. \tag{4}$$

where u, v, w are the original image coordinates, corresponding to get the transformed image chi-square coordinates as x', y', w', and $a11$–$a33$ is the transformation matrix. The transformed image coordinates x and y can be obtained according to the chi-square coordinates.

$$x = \frac{x'}{w'} = \frac{a_{11}u + a_{21}v + a_{31}}{a_{13}u + a_{23}v + a_{33}}. \tag{5}$$

$$y = \frac{y'}{w'} = \frac{a_{12}u + a_{22}v + a_{32}}{a_{13}u + a_{23}v + a_{33}}. \tag{6}$$

Correctly deriving the coordinates of the four points in the 3D plane and including the whole hand in the rectangular area are the keys to good or bad calibration. If the coordinate information is inaccurate, the subsequent series of equation coefficients will be inaccurate, resulting in a false calibration effect. If the whole hand is not captured, the hand part will be distorted in the calibration, and the calibration effect will be unsatisfactory.

3 Research on the Extraction of ROI for Closed Hand in Complex Backgrounds

In palmprint recognition process, interference from complex backgrounds can make it difficult to extract and recognise palmprint features. There are many types of complex backgrounds, including skin folds and sweat, shadows and lighting variations in palm images, background texture interference and background colour diversity interference factors. The method proposed in this chapter mainly focuses on the above factors of lighting variations, background colour diversity and background texture interference in the complex background. Combined with the actual palmprint acquisition process, it is proposed to use semantic segmentation to minimise the interference of the complex background and improve the extraction accuracy of the palm contour.

3.1 Segmentation of the Palm Area on a Complex Background

The palm region segmentation algorithm is mainly divided into 4 steps. At first, the palm image with complex background is coarsely segmented using DeepLabv3+ semantic neural network to remove most of the complex background region. Then the mask is inflated so that the size covers the palm region. After that, the Gaussian skin colour model is used to obtain the fine palm contour. Finally, the palm contour is smoothed using the median filter.

Taking semantic segmentation to a new level, the DeepLabv3+ network can accurately match every pixel point in an image to the correct object class. It uses null convolution to increase the perceptual field of the convolution kernel and improve the perceptual range. It reduces parameter computation and improves model training and inference speed by using depth-separable convolution. It uses multi-scale prediction and pyramid technique for accurate segmentation of images of different scales and sizes, and improves the accuracy of segmentation boundaries (Fig. 4).

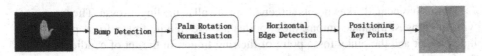

Fig. 4. Framework diagram of the region of interest extraction algorithm for the closed hand.

3.2 Closed Hand Region of Interest Extraction

Convex package detection is performed on the obtained binarised closed palm image to obtain the group of depression points between the fingers. The coordinates of each depression point are determined according to the positional relationship between the centre of mass point and the depression point. Using the relationship between the coordinate points two-by-two, two lines *L1* and *L2* passing through the middle finger of the index finger and the little finger seam of the ring finger are obtained. Finally, the end point information of the horizontal edge of the palm is extracted by horizontal edge detection. And **L1** and **L2** are used as reference lines to screen out the final finger valley points. The specific palm key points are shown in Fig. 5.

Critical Point Screening. The distance from each candidate point to the centre of mass and the distance from each candidate point to the connecting lines L1 and L2 are calculated. Candidate points that are not in the three finger fossae are first removed with the constraints shown in Eqs. (7) and (8). Where **P** is the coordinate of the candidate point, **i** is the subscript of the coordinate point in the candidate point set, **C** is the centre of mass point, **L1** and **L2** are the derived finger seam lines.

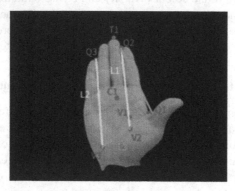

Fig. 5. Information map of feature points extracted from the region of interest.

$$dist(P_i(x, y, z), C_1(x, y, z)) \leq 1/2 \times dist(L_1, L_2), \forall i \in Z^+. \tag{7}$$

$$dist(P_i(x, y, z), L_1) \leq 1/2 \times dist(L_1, L_2), \ or$$
$$dist(P_i(x, y, z), L_2) \leq 1/2 \times dist(L_1, L_2), \forall i \in Z^+. \tag{8}$$

At this moment, the key points screened out are all at the finger fossa. The two points with the longest distance among these points are the middle finger fossa point of the index finger and the pinky fossa point of the ring finger. In the set of candidate points, the formula for calculating the maximum value of the two-by-two distance is shown in (9).

$$VP = arg \max_{i,j} \{ dist(CP_i(x, y, z), CP_j(x, y, z)) \}, \forall i \in Z^+. \tag{9}$$

where **P** refers to the key point, and **i, j** are the subscripts of the key point set.

Convex packet detection is used to get the concave points and image processing is performed using the connection between the marked points on the palm to finally obtain the palm valley points and extract the region of interest of the palm.

4   Experiments

The experimental configuration and training parameters are shown in Table 1 below.

Table 1. Experimental parameters.

Configuration	Parameter	Configuration	Parameter
GPU	2060Ti	Programming Language	Python
Batch_size	16	learn rate	7e−3
Optimiser	Sgd	Momentum	0.9
Weight Decay	1e−4	Loss	Cross Entropy Loss + Dice Loss

4.1 Palm Tilt Correction Experiment

4.1.1 Datasets

In this section of the experiment, the homemade dataset HUTB_Hands was used. Both left and right hands of 50 subjects were collected as the initial database by using the OAK-D binocular stereo camera. 20 images (10 for each left and right hand) were collected for each subject. During the acquisition process, the hand was in a naturally closed posture (i.e., the four fingers were naturally together and the thumb was open). The appropriate distance from the camera was maintained as much as possible, and the tilt angle and rotational direction of the palm were slowly changed. In the database, we ensure that the palm can be captured at tilt angles of 0°, 10°, 20°, and 30°. Finally, we detect the palm skeleton marker points through Google's open-source MediaPipe, to ensure to obtain the depth information of the marker points at multiple angles of the palm.

4.1.2 Tilt Correction Experiment Results

The calibration results for the HUTB_Hands dataset are shown in Table 2. From the experimental results, it can be seen that the palm tilt correction method proposed in this paper can accurately correct the tilted palm back when the depth information of the palm mark points is correctly captured.

Table 2. Tilt Correction Results.

Number of Skewed Pictures	Number of successful calibrations	Success rate
1000	1000	100%

The results of visualization the tilted palm correction are shown in Fig. 6.

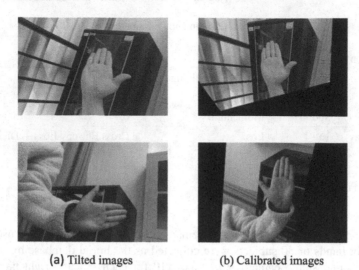

(a) Tilted images   (b) Calibrated images

Fig. 6. Palm tilt correction effect.

4.1.3 Performance Analysis of Tilt Correction Methods

In the palm correction method, this paper uses palm images with different tilt angles for experiments and uses cosine similarity, hash similarity, and histogram distance similarity to check the robustness of the algorithm. The results are shown in Table 3.

Table 3. Comparative analysis of similarity of calibration results.

Tilt angle	Cos similarity/(%)	Hash similarity/(%)	histogram distance similarity/(%)
10°	95.23	94.54	95.87
20°	90.58	89.65	91.65
30°	87.69	86.23	86.36

As can be seen from the table, the similarities are all above 85%, and the similarity decreases as the tilt angle increases, which indicates that the method proposed in this paper is more accurate and robust.

4.2 Closed Hand Region of Interest Extraction Experiment

4.2.1 Datasets

The corrected HUTB_Hands dataset was expanded to 3,000 sheets with panning, rotation and colour enhancement to ensure the diversity of the dataset.

4.2.2 Performance Analysis of Closed Hand Region of Interest Extraction Methods

The selection of key points is crucial in the palm ROI extraction process. In this paper, the correct key points are determined manually. The extraction is considered successful if the selected key point region is detected to be within 20 pixel points of the correct region.The ROI extraction success rate is the percentage of the number of images from which palm ROIs have been successfully extracted to the total number of images in the dataset. In this paper, among the total of 3000 database palm images, we compare the proposed method with the traditional method proposed by Michael [9], the method proposed by Ito [6], the palm ROI extraction using MediaPipe [11] skeleton points, and the neural network [10] method using manually defined key point locations. The results are shown in Table 4.

Table 4. ROI extraction success rate.

Method	Successes/total	Rate
Michael [9]	37/3000	1.2%
Ito [6]	2683/3000	89.43%
Neural Network [10]	2762/3000	92.07%
MediaPipe [11]	2843/3000	94.77%
Ours	2867/3000	95.47%

As can be seen from the table, the method proposed in this paper achieves more than 95% success rate in ROI extraction, which is better than other methods.

In addition, in order to prove the effectiveness of the method proposed in this paper, 314 high-quality closed palm images were extracted from the 11k Hands [12] public palmprint image database for testing, as shown in Table 5.

From the table, it can be seen that the success rate of the proposed method reaches 98.4%, which is higher than other palmprint region of interest extraction methods, proving the stability and effectiveness of the method in this paper.

Table 5. Public database ROI extraction success rate.

Method	Successes/total	Rate
Michael [9]	4/314	1.3%
Ito [6]	252/314	80.25%
Neural Network [10]	301/314	95.86%
MediaPipe [11]	305/314	97.13%
Ours	309/314	98.4%

In order to test the robustness and universality of the proposed method, this paper verifies the accuracy of ROI recognition in HUTB_Hands and 11k Hands datasets using the algorithms of AlexNet, ResNet, VGG16 and CompCode, respectively. The results are shown in Table 6 and Table 7.

Table 6. ROI recognition accuracy for HUTB_Hands dataset.

Method	AlexNet	ResNet34	VGG16	CompCode
Ito [6]	87.68%	93.53%	85.35%	95.68%
Neural Network [10]	92.56%	95.61%	89.28%	93.89%
MediaPipe [11]	90.58%	96.88%	91.54%	98.13%
Ours	95.85%	96.38%	93.61%	96.48%

Table 7. ROI recognition accuracy for 11k Hands dataset.

Method	AlexNet	ResNet34	VGG16	CompCode
Ito [6]	87.61%	90.43%	87.36%	90.56%
Neural Network [10]	89.23%	93.23%	85.59%	93.89%
MediaPipe [11]	92.33%	94.46%	90.18%	91.49%
Ours	90.56%	96.11%	89.46%	92.48%

From the recognition results, it can be seen that the method proposed in this paper performs stably in each recognition algorithm, and the results are basically optimal. This proves that the algorithm has strong robustness.

5 Conclusion

In this paper, a region of interest extraction method for closed palm under tilted state is proposed to address the problems of tilted and closed palm posture. The proposed framework firstly corrects the tilted posture by palm depth information, and then combines DeepLabv3+ neural network with Gaussian skin colour model to achieve fine segmentation and obtain a complete palm image. Finally, convex packet detection and horizontal edge detection are used to filter the key points to extract the palm ROI. Experiments on the homemade dataset HUTB_Hands as well as the open-source dataset 11k Hands have demonstrated that the extraction rate of the proposed method in this paper reaches more than 95% in both cases.

Although the method proposed in this paper can stably and successfully correct palm images with tilted poses during palm tilt correction, and can stably and efficiently extract palm ROI regions during subsequent closed palm regions of interest extraction, this method is only applicable to the study of region of interest extraction methods for specific closed palm cases, and is only applicable to complete palms rendered across the entire image, which has relatively weak applicability. In the future research, we will work on improving and enhancing the robustness and universality of the algorithm.

Acknowledgements. This research received partial support from the National Natural Science Foundation of China (61976088) and Research Foundation of Education Bureau of Hunan Province, China (22A0440). The authors would like to extend their sincere gratitude to York University, Assiut University and scholars for their generous provision of the palmprint dataset and other publicly available information.

References

1. Zheng, G., Wang, C.J., Boult, T.E.: Application of projective invariants in hand geometry biometrics. IEEE Trans. Inf. Forensics Secur.Secur. **2**(4), 758–768 (2007)
2. Smith, L.N., Langhof, M.P., Hansen, M.F., et al.: Contactless robust 3D palm-print identification using photometric stereo. In: Applications of Digital Image Processing XLIV, vol. 11842, pp. 612–630. SPIE (2021)
3. Mikolajczyk, K., Schmid, C.: An affine invariant interest point detector. In: Heyden, A., Sparr, G., Nielsen, M., Johansen, P. (eds.) Computer Vision — ECCV 2002. ECCV 2002. LNCS, vol. 2350, pp. 128–142. Springer, Berlin, Heidelberg (2002). https://doi.org/10.1007/3-540-47969-4_9
4. Gao, C.: Research on tilt correction method for labelled images with salient features. Internet Things Technol. **12**(08), 105–108 (2022). (in Chinese)
5. Zhang, D., Kong, W.K., You, J., et al.: Online palmprint identification. IEEE Trans. Pattern Anal. Mach. Intell.Intell. **25**(9), 1041–1050 (2003)
6. Ito, K., Sato, T., Aoyama, S., et al.: Palm region extraction for contactless palmprint recognition. In: 2015 International Conference on Biometrics (ICB), pp. 334–340. IEEE (2015)
7. Shao, H., Zhong, D., Du, X.: Efficient deep palmprint recognition via distilled hashing coding. In: Proceedings of the IEEE/CVF Conference on Computer Vision and Pattern Recognition Workshops (2019)
8. Bao, X., Guo, Z.: Extracting region of interest for palmprint by convolutional neural networks. In: 2016 Sixth International Conference on Image Processing Theory, Tools and Applications (IPTA), pp. 1–6. IEEE (2016)
9. Michael, G.K.O., Connie, T., Teoh, A.B.J.: Touch-less palm print biometrics: novel design and implementation. Image Vis. Comput.Comput. **26**(12), 1551–1560 (2008)
10. Matkowski, W.M., Chai, T., Kong, A.W.K.: Palmprint recognition in uncontrolled and uncooperative environment. IEEE Trans. Inf. Forensics Secur.Secur. **15**, 1601–1615 (2019)
11. Kocakulak, M., Acir, N.: Dynamic ROI extraction for palmprints using mediapipe hands. In: 2022 30th Signal Processing and Communications Applications Conference (SIU), pp. 1–4. IEEE (2022)
12. Afifi, M.: 11K Hands: gender recognition and biometric identification using a large dataset of hand images. Multimed. Tools Appl. **78**, 20835–20854 (2019)

A Comparative Study on Canonical Correlation Analysis-Based Multi-feature Fusion for Palmprint Recognition

Yihang Wu[1,2] and Junlin Hu[1(✉)]

[1] School of Software, Beihang University, Beijing, China
hujunlin@buaa.edu.cn
[2] School of Computing, National University of Singapore, Singapore, Singapore

Abstract. Contactless palmprint recognition provides high-accuracy and friendly experience for users without directly contacting the recognition device. Currently, many existing methods have shown relatively satisfying performance, but there are still several problems such as the limited patterns extracted by single feature extraction approach and the huge gap between hand-crafted feature-based approaches and deep learning feature-based approaches. To this end, in this paper, we make use of multiple palmprint features and exploit the benefits of hand-crafted features and deep features in a unified framework using Canonical Correlation Analysis (CCA) method, and present a comparative study on CCA-based multi-feature fusion for palmprint recognition. In the experiments, the best feature fusion scheme achieves 100% accuracy on Tongji palmprint dataset and shows good generalization ability on IITD and CASIA palmprint datasets. Extensive comparative experiments of different approaches on three palmprint datasets demonstrate the effectiveness of CCA-based multi-feature fusion method and the prospects of applying feature fusion techniques in palmprint recognition.

Keywords: Palmprint recognition · multi-feature fusion · Canonical Correlation Analysis · deep feature

1 Introduction

Faced with massive demand for accurate and reliable identity verification techniques, biometrics are now playing indispensable roles in various fields. Among existing biometric technologies, palmprint recognition has received increasing attention. Palmprint has rich texture details such as main lines, wrinkles, ridges, and valleys [1]. In addition to having a larger feature area, palmprint recognition has the advantages of high privacy, resistance to wear, and less susceptible to emotions, age, and plastic surgery. Furthermore, it offers low-cost and user-friendly acquisition process, thus having extensive application potential.

In the field of contactless palmprint recognition, most of methods mainly utilize the single feature and obtain some considerable results. To exploit the multiple features for further improving the recognition accuracy, various feature fusion

W. Jia et al. (Eds.): CCBR 2023, LNCS 14463, pp. 46–54, 2023.
https://doi.org/10.1007/978-981-99-8565-4_5

methods are introduced, and a widely-used feature fusion approach is based on simple linear concatenation of different features, which has shown satisfactory results in some cases. However, the linear concatenation-based method is not an ideal choice when dealing with features with complex dimensions. In feature-level fusion stage, a simple serial concatenation strategy is likely to bring a significant amount of noise and redundancy to the fused features, adversely affecting the discriminative power. Among existing feature fusion methods, canonical correlation analysis (CCA) [2] is well-known method for fusing multiple features in machine learning and pattern recognition.

In this paper, we select CCA as our feature fusion method for exploiting multiple features, making use of the benefits of hand-crafted features and deep features, and analyzing how different features contribute to final performance in contactless palmprint recognition task. We specially make a comparative study on multiple sets of CCA fusion schemes using ResNet [3], PCA [4], LDA [5], and CompCode [6] as individual features. Extensive experiments on Tongji [7], CAISA [8] and IITD [9] palmprint datasets are conducted to evaluate the effectiveness and robustness of CCA-based feature fusion method.

2 Related Work

Recent years has witnessed the emergence of many effective palmprint recognition algorithms, which can be generally classified into two categories: classic hand-crafted-based methods and deep learning-based methods.

Handcrafted-based methods often extract lines, textures, and directional information in palmprint using manually designed filters, dimensionality reduction techniques, and feature descriptors. Huang et al. [10] propose an enhanced limited Radon transform to extract main line features. The pixel-to-area ratio comparison is employed in the feature matching period. Gayathri et al. [11] utilize the high-order Zernike moments to extract palmprint features and KNN algorithm is used for palmprint classification. Li et al. [12] optimize the Hilditch algorithm to extract main line features and employ edge detection techniques to remove noise such as branches and short lines. Then the broken lines are connected to obtain a single-pixel palmprint main line image. Jia et al. [13] propose histogram of oriented lines (HOL) based on histogram of oriented gradient, using filters and an improved limited Radon transform to extract line orientation responses of palmprint pixels. These methods are able to achieve relatively accurate recognition results.

Deep learning-based methods can learn more complex feature structures, thus performing stronger generalization abilities. However, most networks are proposed and optimized for other tasks such as face recognition and image classification. When such methods are applied to palmprint recognition, some possible improvements can be made. Zhong et al. [14] utilize ResNet-20 to extract palmprint features and propose the centralized large margin cosine loss function to maximize inter-class differences while minimizing intra-class differences. Liu et al. [15] design a fully convolutional network with a soft-link triplet loss function for contactless palmprint recognition. Jia et al. [16] develop the EEPNet specifically for palmprint recognition by compressing the layers and enlarging the convolutional kernels of MobileNet-V3 and five strategies are also introduced to improve accuracy. All these models achieve favorable results on multiple datasets, demonstrating the powerful capabilities of deep learning-based methods in palmprint recognition tasks.

All the above methods have proposed and optimized palmprint recognition system from different perspectives, showing relatively satisfying performance, but there are still problems such as limited pattern extracted by single recognition approach and huge gap between traditional approaches and deep learning approaches. In this case, feature fusion may be one of the potential solutions for a more accurate and robust palmprint recognition system.

The core idea of feature-level fusion is to fuse multiple feature vectors through operations such as dimensionality reduction and concatenation. In the scenario of contactless palmprint recognition, Jaswal et al. [17] fuse scale-invariant feature transform (SIFT) features and statistical features based on texture-encoded co-occurrence matrices. Bidirectional two-dimensional principal component analysis is used to represent feature space, following with SVM for classification. Li et al. [12] concatenate features of local binary patterns and two-dimensional local preserving projection with Euclidean distance used for matching. These feature fusion methods achieve the improved performance compared to their corresponding single-feature approaches, demonstrating the effectiveness of feature fusion for contactless palmprint recognition.

3   CCA-Based Multi-feature Fusion

Canonical Correlation Analysis (CCA) aims to find an optimal projection that maximizes the correlation between multi-sets of features.

Taking two feature sets as an example, $X = [x_1, x_2, ..., x_n] \in \mathbb{R}^{p \times n}$ and $Y = [y_1, y_2, ..., y_n] \in \mathbb{R}^{q \times n}$, assuming that both sets have n samples and dimensions p and q, respectively, the goal of CCA is to find a series of linear transformations $W_X = [\alpha_1, \alpha_2, ..., \alpha_r] \in \mathbb{R}^{p \times r}$ and $W_Y = [\beta_1, \beta_2, ..., \beta_r] \in \mathbb{R}^{q \times r}$ to transform X and Y to $W_X^T X \in \mathbb{R}^{r \times n}$ and $W_Y^T Y \in \mathbb{R}^{r \times n}$ with the maximum correlation.

Specifically, the first step is to calculate the covariance matrices of X and Y:

$$S = \begin{pmatrix} Var(X) & Cov(X,Y) \\ Cov(Y,X) & Var(Y) \end{pmatrix} = \begin{pmatrix} S_{XX} & S_{XY} \\ S_{YX} & S_{YY} \end{pmatrix}, \tag{1}$$

where $S_{XX} = Var(X)$ denotes the variance of X, and $S_{XY} = Cov(X,Y)$ means the covariance of X and Y. Furthermore, the variance and covariance of the transformed $\alpha^T X$ and $\beta^T Y$ after the linear transformations $\alpha \in \mathbb{R}^p$ and $\beta \in \mathbb{R}^q$ can be computed:

$$Var(\alpha^T X) = \alpha^T Var(X)\alpha = \alpha^T S_{XX}\alpha,$$
$$Var(\beta^T Y) = \beta^T Var(Y)\beta = \beta^T S_{YY}\beta, \tag{2}$$
$$Cov(\alpha^T X, \beta^T Y) = \alpha^T Cov(X,Y)\beta = \alpha^T S_{XY}\beta.$$

Based on the above expressions, the objective of CCA can be denoted as:

$$\max \quad J(\alpha, \beta) = \frac{\alpha^T S_{XY} \beta}{\sqrt{(\alpha^T S_{XX} \alpha) \cdot (\beta^T S_{YY} \beta)}} \tag{3}$$

which can be further expressed in a constrained form as follows:

$$\max \quad \alpha^T S_{XY} \beta,$$
$$\text{s.t.} \quad \alpha^T S_{XX} \alpha = 1, \quad \beta^T S_{YY} \beta = 1. \tag{4}$$

It is possible for α (or β) to be singular, which can be addressed by regularizing the singular α (or β). Subsequently, α and β can be solved using eigenvalue decomposition [2] or singular value decomposition (SVD) [18].

When dealing with multi-feature CCA problems, generalized CCA (gCCA) [19] can be employed in a similar way. For instance, when incorporating a new feature set $Z \in \mathbb{R}^{o \times n}$ to be projected with X and Y using CCA, the covariance matrices between Z and X, as well as Z and Y, can be calculated separately according to Eq. (1). Let's denote the desired weight matrix corresponding to the Z as $W_Z = [\gamma_1, \gamma_2, ..., \gamma_r] \in \mathbb{R}^{o \times r}$, and the objective of gCCA can be defined as follows:

$$\max \quad J(\alpha, \beta, \gamma) = \frac{\alpha^T S_{XY} \beta}{\sqrt{(\alpha^T S_{XX} \alpha) \cdot (\beta^T S_{YY} \beta)}} + \frac{\beta^T S_{YZ} \gamma}{\sqrt{(\beta^T S_{YY} \beta) \cdot (\gamma^T S_{ZZ} \gamma)}}$$
$$+ \frac{\alpha^T S_{XZ} \gamma}{\sqrt{(\alpha^T S_{XX} \alpha) \cdot (\gamma^T S_{ZZ} \gamma)}}. \tag{5}$$

Then, similar methods can be employed to solve for W_X, W_Y and W_Z. Once the weight matrices, also known as the projection matrices, are obtained, the original multiple feature sets X, Y and Z can be projected onto the shared feature space as $[W_X^T X; W_Y^T Y; W_Z^T Z] \in \mathbb{R}^{3r \times n}$, yielding a set of features with the maximum mutual correlation.

4 Experiments

In this section, we conduct a series of comparative experiments to thoroughly evaluate the performance of CCA-based multi-feature fusion for contactless palmprint recognition. Specifically, we select four types of features, i.e., ResNet-34 [3] as deep feature, PCA [4] and LDA [5] as subspace features, and Comp-Code [6] as hand-crafted feature. The dimensions of these features are listed in Table 1.

Table 1. Dimensions of different features

Features	ResNet-34	PCA	LDA	CompCode
Dimensions	256	120	80	1024

4.1   Datasets

We conduct experiments on the Tongji, CASIA, and IITD palmprint datasets.

Tongji [7] is a large-scale contactless palmprint dataset built by Tongji University, containing a total of 12,000 images from 600 different palms. During the acquisition process, 300 subjects provide 10 palmprint images on each of their left and right hands in two intervals. These collection samples include 192 males and 108 females among which 235 are in the age group of 20–30 years old and the rest are in the age group of 30–50 years old.

CASIA [8] is a contactless palmprint database established by the Institute of Automation, Chinese Academy of Sciences, containing a total of 5502 palmprint images on 620 different palms. The whole acquisition process is based on its self-developed contactless palmprint acquisition device, and the image format obtained is 648 × 480 JPEG grey-scale images.

IITD [9] is a contactless palm print database established by the Indian Institute of Technology, containing a total of 2603 palm print images of 460 different palms. A total of 230 subjects, all aged 12 to 57 years, participate in the acquisition of this database. During this process, the subjects provide seven palmprint images of each of their left and right hands in different poses, all in a bitmap format of 800 × 600.

4.2   Experimental Results and Analysis

During the training phase of the ResNet-34, we divide Tongji dataset into a training set of 9,600 palmprint images and a test set of 2,400 palmprint images. The network is trained on the training set for 420 epochs until it converges. Then we conduct within-dataset experiments on Tongji and cross-dataset experiments on CASIA and IITD using the pre-trained ResNet-34. We evaluate multiple fusion methods, including linear concatenation fusion and CCA-based multifeature fusion. The main experimental results are summarized in Table 2. We can observe that among the various fusion methods, CCA-based approach achieves a stable performance on all three datasets, and performs better than single feature-based and linear concatenation fusion-based methods.

Comparison with Single Feature. The results shown in Table 2 indicate that three classic single feature-based methods exhibit the limited recognition performance, and deep learning-based features shows better accuracy than handcrafted features and subspace features. In addition, most CCA-based fusion methods achieve a significant improvement in both accuracy and robustness compared to single-features on all three datasets.

Table 2. Accuracy (%) of different methods on Tongji, CASIA and IITD datasets.

Methods	Features	Tongji	CASIA	IITD
Single Feature	ResNet	98.4	91.1	94.1
	PCA	55.0	91.1	94.1
	LDA	83.3	88.2	88.2
	CompCode	71.5	86.8	92.0
Linear Concatenation Fusion	ResNet+PCA	89.7	86.9	87.7
	ResNet+PCA+LDA	96.1	88.4	82.1
	ResNet+PCA+CompCode	67.4	84.9	91.7
	ResNet+LDA+CompCode	78.6	89.5	92.0
	ResNet+PCA+LDA+CompCode	78.6	89.6	92.0
CCA-based Multi-Feature Fusion	ResNet+PCA	99.8	91.5	93.8
	CompCode+PCA	97.6	87.7	88.6
	ResNet+CompCode	95.5	84.7	82.0
	ResNet+LDA	97.3	91.0	90.4
	CompCode+LDA	86.3	84.7	86.4
	PCA+LDA+CompCode	82.3	91.1	89.4
	ResNet+PCA+LDA	99.9	92.6	**94.4**
	ResNet+PCA+CompCode	89.9	92.8	92.7
	ResNet+LDA+CompCode	**100**	**94.4**	93.7
	ResNet+PCA+LDA+CompCode	94.1	93.8	93.0

Comparison with Linear Concatenation Fusion. We also evaluate three settings using linear concatenation fusion. The results indicate that all the three linear concatenation fusion methods exhibit unstable performance, especially the fusion setting with four features shows a significant drop in performance on Tongji dataset. Furthermore, it can be seen that when traditional features are directly concatenated with deep learning feature, the accuracy improves compared to single traditional features, but it still shows a poor performance compared to deep learning feature alone. The reason for this phenomena may be that linear concatenation leads to high dimension with a large amount of noise and redundancy from different feature spaces, which can easily result in over-fitting or under-fitting. Therefore, concatenation fusion is not an ideal solution.

Comparison of CCA-Based Multi-feature Fusion. We conduct multiple sets of two-feature, three-feature, and four-feature CCA fusion experiments. To evaluate the influences of feature normalization on the experimental results, we compare four feature normalization methods, i.e., no normalization (None), mean normalization (MeanStd), min-max normalization (MinMax) and unit-length normalization (UnitLength), as shown in Fig. 1. It can be observed that among the these feature normalization methods, unit-length normalization gets relatively better results. Using unit-length normalization, most methods perform more stably on the three datasets.

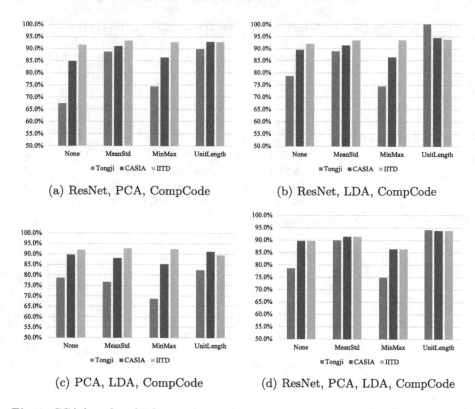

(a) ResNet, PCA, CompCode   (b) ResNet, LDA, CompCode

(c) PCA, LDA, CompCode   (d) ResNet, PCA, LDA, CompCode

Fig. 1. CCA-based multi-feature fusion with different feature normalization methods.

As shown in Table 2, most of the CCA-based fusion methods exhibit superior recognition accuracy and generalization capabilities compared to individual features, particularly ResNet+PCA and ResNet+LDA+CompCode. These two methods not only achieve highly recognition results on the Tongji dataset but also show the improved generalization on the CASIA and IITD datasets. Compared to two-feature CCA fusion, three/four-feature CCA fusion generally shows the improved generalization capabilities on the CASIA and IITD datasets. This implies that CCA fusion enhances the model's ability to generalize to unseen data. We also observe that ResNet+CompCode, ResNet+LDA+CompCode, and PCA+LDA+CompCode show a significant decrease in accuracy on the Tongji dataset. Therefore, we may conclude that the performance of CCA-based multi-feature fusion depends on the combination of different features, and the selection of appropriate features for CCA fusion becomes a crucial issue in practical application scenarios.

Comparison with Other Methods. We also compare CCA-based multi-feature fusion palmprint recognition methods with other representative methods including deep learning -based methods and descriptor-based methods on the

Tongji dataset. The results are summarized in the Table 3. It can be observed that the CCA-based feature fusion methods still outperform these compared methods, showcasing their superior performance.

Table 3. Comparison with other methods on Tongji dataset.

Type	Methods	Accuracy (%)
CCA-based Multi-feature Fusion	ResNet+PCA	99.80
	ResNet+PCA+LDA	99.90
	ResNet+LDA+CompCode	100
Deep Learning-based	C-LMCL [14]	99.97
	VGG-16 [20]	98.93
	PalmNet [21]	99.80
Descriptor-based	LLDP [22]	99.71
	CR_CompCode [7]	98.78
	HOL [13]	99.64

5   Conclusions

In this paper, we provide a comparative study on CCA-based multi-feature fusion method for contactless palmprint recognition. The CCA-based fusion method exploits multiple features and makes use of the benefits of hand-crafted features and deep features for improving the performance of palmprint recognition. In experiments, deep feature, subspace features, and hand-crafted feature are extracted by ResNet, PCA, LDA, and CompCode, respectively, and different settings of feature fusion methods are designed. Extensive experimental comparisons on Tongji, CASIA, and IITD palmprint datasets show the effectiveness and robustness of CCA-based multi-feature fusion method.

Acknowledgments. This work was supported by the National Natural Science Foundation of China under Grant 62006013.

References

1. Zhang, D., Zuo, W., Yue, F.: A comparative study of palmprint recognition algorithms. ACM Comput. Surv. **44**(1), 1–37 (2012)
2. Guo, C., Wu, D.: Canonical correlation analysis (CCA) based multi-view learning: an overview. arXiv preprint arXiv:1907.01693 (2019)
3. He, K., Zhang, X., Ren, S., Sun, J.: Deep residual learning for image recognition. In: IEEE Conference on Computer Vision and Pattern Recognition, pp. 770–778 (2016)

4. Lu, G., Zhang, D., Wang, K.: Palmprint recognition using eigenpalms features. Pattern Recogn. Lett. **24**(9–10), 1463–1467 (2003)
5. Wu, X.Q., Wang, K.Q., Zhang, D.: Palmprint recognition using fisher's linear discriminant. In: International Conference on Machine Learning and Cybernetics, pp. 3150–3154 (2003)
6. Kong, A.K., Zhang, D.: Competitive coding scheme for palmprint verification. In: International Conference on Pattern Recognition, pp. 520–523 (2004)
7. Zhang, L., Li, L., Yang, A., Shen, Y., Yang, M.: Towards contactless palmprint recognition: a novel device, a new benchmark, and a collaborative representation based identification approach. Pattern Recogn. **69**, 199–212 (2017)
8. Sun, Z., Tan, T., Wang, Y., Li, S.Z.: Ordinal palmprint represention for personal identification. In: IEEE Conference on Computer Vision and Pattern Recognition, vol. 1, pp. 279–284 (2005)
9. Fei, L., Xu, Y., Tang, W., Zhang, D.: Double-orientation code and nonlinear matching scheme for palmprint recognition. Pattern Recogn. **49**, 89–101 (2016)
10. Huang, D.S., Jia, W., Zhang, D.: Palmprint verification based on principal lines. Pattern Recogn. **41**(4), 1316–1328 (2008)
11. Gayathri, R., Ramamoorthy, P.: Automatic palmprint identification based on high order Zernike moment. Am. J. Appl. Sci. **9**(5), 759 (2012)
12. Li, C., Liu, F., Zhang, Y.: A principal palm-line extraction method for palmprint images based on diversity and contrast. In: International Congress on Image and Signal Processing, pp. 1772–1777 (2010)
13. Jia, W., Hu, R.X., Lei, Y.K., Zhao, Y., Gui, J.: Histogram of oriented lines for palmprint recognition. IEEE Trans. Syst. Man, Cybern. Syst. **44**(3), 385–395 (2013)
14. Zhong, D., Zhu, J.: Centralized large margin cosine loss for open-set deep palmprint recognition. IEEE Trans. Circ. Syst. Video Technol. **30**(6), 1559–1568 (2019)
15. Liu, Y., Kumar, A.: Contactless palmprint identification using deeply learned residual features. IEEE Trans. Biometrics, Behav. Identity Sci. **2**(2), 172–181 (2020)
16. Jia, W., Ren, Q., Zhao, Y., Li, S., Min, H., Chen, Y.: EEPNet: an efficient and effective convolutional neural network for palmprint recognition. Pattern Recogn. Lett. **159**, 140–149 (2022)
17. Jaswal, G., Kaul, A., Nath, R.: Multiple feature fusion for unconstrained palm print authentication. Comput. Electr. Eng. **72**, 53–78 (2018)
18. Andrew, G., Arora, R., Bilmes, J., Livescu, K.: Deep canonical correlation analysis. In: International Conference on Machine Learning, pp. 1247–1255 (2013)
19. Shen, C., Sun, M., Tang, M., Priebe, C.E.: Generalized canonical correlation analysis for classification. J. Multivar. Anal. **130**, 310–322 (2014)
20. Tarawneh, A.S., Chetverikov, D., Hassanat, A.B.: Pilot comparative study of different deep features for palmprint identification in low-quality images. arXiv preprint arXiv:1804.04602 (2018)
21. Genovese, A., Piuri, V., Plataniotis, K.N., Scotti, F.: PalmNet: Gabor-PCA convolutional networks for touchless palmprint recognition. IEEE Trans. Inf. Forensics Secur. **14**(12), 3160–3174 (2019)
22. Luo, Y.T., et al.: Local line directional pattern for palmprint recognition. Pattern Recogn. **50**, 26–44 (2016)

Finger Vein Recognition Based on Unsupervised Spiking Neural Network

Li Yang[1]($\boxtimes$), Xiang Xu[2], and Qiong Yao[2]

[1] School of Computer Science and Engineering, University of Electronic Science and Technology of China, Chengdu 610000, China
2631839168@qq.com
[2] University of Electronic Science and Technology of China, Zhongshan Institute, Zhongshan 528402, China

Abstract. At present, although the deep learning models represented by convolutional neural networks and Transformers have achieved promising recognition accuracies in finger vein (FV) recognition, there still remain some unresolved issues, including high model complexity and memory cost, as well as insufficient training samples. To address these issues, we propose an unsupervised spiking neural network for finger vein recognition (hereinafter dubbed 'FV-SNN'), which utilizes Difference of Gaussian filter to encode the original image signal into a kind of spiking signal as input to the network, then, the FV-SNN model is trained in an unsupervised manner and the learned spiking features are fed to a LinearSVM classifier for final recognition. The experiments are performed on two benchmark FV datasets, and experimental results show that our proposed FV-SNN not only achieves competitive recognition accuracies, but also exhibits lower model complexity and faster training speed.

Keywords: Finger vein recognition · Unsupervised spiking neural network · Difference of Gaussian filter

1 Introduction

With the increasing security requirements of personal identity authentication, the traditional identity authentication technologies based on identity tags or identity information will no longer meet the current needs. Relatively speaking, biometric traits (e.g., fingerprint, facial, speech, gait, iris, and vein) have more stable security by using physical characteristics of individual. Among, finger vein (FV) traits have more friendly and safe properties than the other biometric traits, due to the fact that finger veins are distributed under the epidermis of the fingers, which can only be captured in vivo, and are hard to forge and steal. Besides, the acquisition devices of FV can be designed to be smaller and non-contact, which are more convenient and hygienic for users.

X. Xu–This work was supported by National Natural Science Foundation of China under Grant 62271130 and 62002053.

The imaging principle of FV images is mainly because the hemoglobin in vein blood can absorb near-infrared light to form shadows. However, due to the variances of finger position, uneven light and noise, high quality imaging has always been a luxury. In order to compensate for the impact of low-quality FV images, some image enhancement techniques are used as preprocessing means, and then feature extraction is carried out on the enhanced FV images.

Recently, deep convolutional neural networks (DCNNs) have achieved great success in FV recognition tasks due to their ability to hierarchically learn high-level semantic features. Among, some popular large-scale models, such as ResNet and AlexNet, etc., have been introduced for end-to-end FV recognition. Considering that generally vein texture and structure features are used for discrimination, model lightweight is preferable. In [1], a dual-channel and lightweight deep learning network was developed. In [2], a lightweight convolutional neural network combined with convolutional block attention module (CBAM) was designed for FV recognition. In [3], a lightweight network, consisting of a stem block and a stage block, was constructed for FV recognition.

As noted earlier, although the aforementioned network models have shown good feature representation ability, they still face many problems of complex model structures and excessive memory overhead. To address these issues and seek more economical network model, we propose a novel FV recognition framework based on an unsupervised spiking neural network (dubbed 'FV-SNN'). The backbone of the proposed FV-SNN contains two layers of spiking convolutional block. First, Difference of Gaussian (DoG) filter is utilized to encode the original image signal into a kind of spiking signal as input to the network, then, the FV-SNN model is trained and the learned spiking features are fed to a LinearSVC classifier to obtain the final recognition results. Compared with some popular deep learning based FV recognition networks, our proposed FV-SNN not only achieves competitive recognition accuracies, but also exhibits lower model complexity and faster training speed.

2 Proposed FV-SNN Model

2.1 Framework of the FV-SNN Model

The schematic diagram of the basic flow of FV-SNN for FV recognition is shown in Fig. 1. First, in the preprocessing step, the original image and corresponding skeleton image are superimposed on top of each other, so as to highlight the vein skeleton information. Then, the preprocessed image is further enhanced by using the DoG filter, and is encoded into a discrete spike signal. Such spike signal contains time steps corresponding to the delay encoding of image pixel intensity, which will be used as input of the subsequent unsupervised spiking neural network (SNN). Here, the designed SNN just provided two layers of spiking neurons for feature learning, and the learning rule is based on the unsupervised spike timing dependent plasticity (STDP). After finishing the training of SNN, the output feature vectors of training samples are fed to the LinearSVC of svm in the sklearn library for classifier training, and specify the penalty function

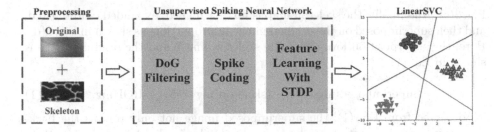

Fig. 1. Schematic diagram of the basic flow of FV-SNN for FV recognition.

as C = 2.4. And finally, in the test step, the test image samples are processed through the whole flow, and the outputs of the LinearSVC classifier are used to determine their categories.

2.2 Preprocessing Strategy

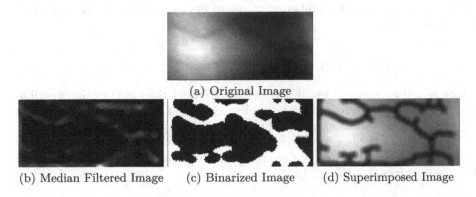

(a) Original Image

(b) Median Filtered Image   (c) Binarized Image   (d) Superimposed Image

Fig. 2. Example of original image and corresponding preprocessed images.

In order to highlight the vein structure and relieve the background interference to the FV image, we carry out a series of preprocessing operations. First, histogram equalization and mean filtering are sequentially executed to enhance the contrast and remove Gaussian noise. Then, Laplacian edge detection and median filtering are performed afterward, here, the Laplacian operator is a second-order differential operator that can sharpen the image to highlight the effect of finger veins, and median filter can remove isolated noise in the background. Figure 2(a) and (b) show an example of the original image and the preprocessed image after median filtering. Subsequently, histogram equalization and morphological operations are performed again to discard small connected regions and holes in the image, and connect broken lines and edges simultaneously. After, the current image is further binarized and refined to obtain the skeleton map, as shown in

Fig. 2(c). And finally, the skeleton map is further refined, expanded, and blurred, and then superimposed on the original image in proportion, as shown in Fig. 2(d). Here, the superposition formula of the skeleton image and the original image is shown in Eq. (1).

$$SuperimposedImg = (1 - (skeletonImg/255)) \times ROIImg. \tag{1}$$

As observed from Eq. (1), the superimposed image not only retains the background information, but also reduces the pixel value in the skeleton image, thus, the skeleton map is enhanced and it is more conducive to the subsequent edges extraction of FV images.

2.3   DoG Filtering and Spike Coding

According to the rules of SNN, the input data should be spike signals with time information. At the same time, considering that STDP needs to learn the correlations between input spikes, we adopt DoG filter to help STDP for encoding spike signals and constructing meaningful correlations. DoG filter can simulate ganglion cell receptive field of the retinal in the visual pathway, which consists of two Gaussian filters with different standard deviations, the specific formula is shown in Eq. (2).

$$D(x, y, \delta_1, \delta_2) = \frac{1}{\sqrt{2\pi}\delta_1}e^{-\frac{x^2+y^2}{2\delta_1^2}} - \frac{1}{\sqrt{2\pi}\delta_2}e^{-\frac{x^2+y^2}{2\delta_2^2}}, \tag{2}$$

where δ_1 and δ_2 represent two different standard deviations of Gaussian distribution, x and y are position coordinates of pixels, and $D(x, y, \delta_1, \delta_2)$ is the output of DoG filtering, which represents the contrast information of the image.

When the DoG filter is performed on the input FV image, it can efficiently extract edges from the image. Concretely, the extracted FV edge features can be obtained by using Eq. (3).

$$F(x, y) = I(x, y) \oplus \hat{D}(x, y, \delta_1, \delta_2), \tag{3}$$

where $F(x, y)$ is the extracted FV edge features, $\oplus$ is convolution operator, and $\hat{D}$ is the normalization of D, as calculated by using Eq. (4).

$$\hat{D}(x, y, \delta_1, \delta_2) = \frac{D(x, y, \delta_1, \delta_2) - D(x, y, \delta_1, \delta_2)_{mean}}{D(x, y, \delta_1, \delta_2)_{max}}. \tag{4}$$

As noted that in our FV-SNN model, we employ two DoG filters with the same kernel size of 7, one DoG filter has two standard deviations of 1 and 2, which is used to simulate on-center ganglion cells for providing excitatory input, while the second DoG filter has two standard deviations of 2 and 1, which is used to simulate off-center ganglion cells for providing inhibitory input. For visual intuition, the preprocessed input image sample as well as two DoG filtered feature maps are shown in Fig. 3.

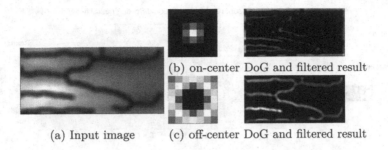

(a) Input image

(b) on-center DoG and filtered result

(c) off-center DoG and filtered result

Fig. 3. Preprocessed input image as well as two DoG filtered feature maps.

After obtaining the DoG filtered image, we need to encode the pixel intensity of the image into discrete spike signals. Here, in order to inject time information into the representation of the spike signals, we use the intensity delay, which means, the time step to occupy the first dimension of the image tensor is introduced, and considering that the larger the pixel intensity, the stronger the external visual stimulus, we divide all image pixels into a batch of specified time-steps. Supposing an input is represented by F number of feature maps, each constitutes a network of $H \times W$ neurons. Let T_{max} be the maximum time-step, $T_{f,r,c}$ represents the spike time of the neuron which located at the position (r, c) in the feature map f, in which $0 \leq f < F$, $0 \leq r < H$, $0 \leq c < W$, and $T_{f,r,c} \in \{0, 1, \ldots, T_{max} - 1\} \bigcup \{\infty\}$. Symbol ∞ indicates no spike. Therefore, the input image is converted from $2 \times H \times W$ to a four-dimensional binary spike-wave tensor $S[t, f, r, c]$ with a size of $T_{max} \times 2 \times H \times W$, in which, $S[t, f, r, c]$ is calculated by Eq. (5).

$$S[t, f, r, c] = \begin{cases} 0, & t < T_{f,r,c}, \\ 1, & \text{otherwise.} \end{cases} \tag{5}$$

These spikes retention (cumulative structure) may repeat the spikes to increase memory usage in future time steps, but can process all time-steps simultaneously and produce the corresponding outputs with very fast speed [4].

2.4 Structure of Unsupervised SNN

Drawing on the design concept of traditional CNN networks, our SNN model provides a two-layer spiking convolutional block, and each block contains a spiking convolutional layer and a pooling layer. The structure of the presented unsupervised SNN is shown in Fig. 4, in which T denotes the time step, $C1$ represents the number of feature maps in the first spiking convolutional layer, and $C2$ represents the number of feature maps in the second spiking convolutional layer. First, the preprocessed image is input into an image encoding layer of the SNN, then, the encoded spike signal is processed by two sets of continuous spiking convolutional layer and pooling layer, so as to obtain the final output spiking feature representation.

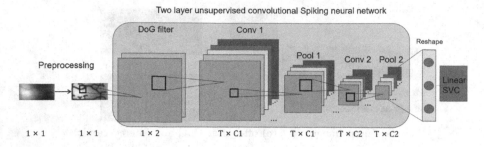

Fig. 4. Structure of the presented unsupervised spiking convolutional neural network.

In each spiking convolutional layer, the neuron is the non-leaky integrate and fire model with at most one spike per stimulus. Each convolutional layer obtains the potentials tensor by convolving the discrete spike-wave tensor, and only when the neurons reach a given threshold, it will fire the spike again, thus continuing to generate the spike-wave tensor transmission to the next layer. In addition, each convolutional layer is updated by the STDP learning rule, as well as the winners-take-all (WTA) and lateral inhibition mechanism. The STDP learning rule follows the definition in [4] and its specific formula is as follows:

$$\Delta W_{i,j} = \begin{cases} A^+ \times (W_{i,j} - \text{LB}) \times (\text{UB} - W_{i,j}) & \text{if } T_j \leq T_i, \\ A^- \times (W_{i,j} - \text{LB}) \times (\text{UB} - W_{i,j}) & \text{if } T_j < T_i. \end{cases} \tag{6}$$

where, $\Delta W_{i,j}$ is the amount of weight change of the synapse that connecting the postsynaptic neuron i and presynaptic neuron j, A^+ and A^- are the learning rate and $A^+ > 0$, $A^- < 0$. $(W_{i,j} - \text{LB}) \times (\text{UB} - W_{i,j})$ is a stabilizer that slows down the weight changes when the synaptic weight $W_{i,j}$ approaches the lower limit LB or the upper limit UB. Here, the synaptic weight change does not consider the exact time difference between two spikes, but only the order of the spikes.

Before performing the STDP learning rule, the neuronal synapses first use the WTA mechanism, which means, the winner first chooses according to the earliest spike time and then according to the maximum potential. The winning neuron inhibits other neurons in the feature map, but just be updated and copies the updated weights into those neurons, such strategy ensures that a feature map only learns specific features. In addition, the lateral inhibition mechanism is used to inhibit the neuron distribution of other feature maps at the winner position, thus also increases the chance of learning different features from different feature maps.

3   Experimental Results and Discussion

3.1   Datasets

The FV datasets used in our experiments include MMCBNU_6000 [5] and FV-USM [6], which both provide the original and ROI images. Figure 5 shows the original images, ROI images and preprocessed images of two datasets.

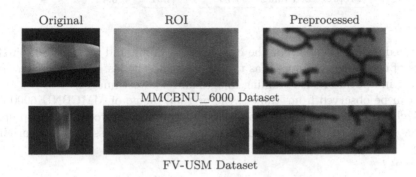

Original   ROI   Preprocessed

MMCBNU_6000 Dataset

FV-USM Dataset

Fig. 5. Original, ROI, and preprocessed images of two FV datasets.

3.2   Experiments on MMCBNU_6000

For the MMCBNU_6000 dataset, the image coding layer adopts two DoG filters with kernel size of 7, the first DoG filter has standard deviations of 1 and 2, and the second filter has standard deviations of 2 and 1. In the image intensity delay encoding, 15 time steps are used. Following the structure in Fig. 4, the first convolutional layer consists of 16 feature maps with a convolution window size of 5×5 and firing threshold of 10. The second convolutional layer consists of 24 feature maps with a convolution window size of 2×2 and firing threshold of 2. Two pooling layers have a pooling window with size of 2×2, and a step size of 2 and a padding of 1. The learning rate of all convolutional layers is set to $A^+ = 0.004$, $A^- = -0.003$, to speed up convergence, the first convolutional layer introduces an adjustment mechanism of the learning rate, when A^+ is less than 0.15, the learning rate A^+ is multiplied by 2 per training session of 500 images until $A^+ = 0.15$, where the ratio of A^- and A^+ is always the same as the original. The first convolutional layer trains 2 epochs, and the second convolutional layer trains 5 epochs.

Table 1 shows the results of recognition accuracy, model training and classification time, and EERs corresponding to the original image, ROI image and preprocessed input images respectively that performed on the MMCBNU_6000 dataset. The original image was adjusted to a size of 96×128 by using a bilinear interpolation algorithm. ROI images are provided by the dataset itself and directly utilized in the experiments. Preprocessed input images are derived from

Table 1. Results of recognition accuracy, model training and classification time, and EERs of the proposed FV-SNN on the original image, ROI image, preprocessed input image of the MMCBNU_6000 dataset.

Input	Accuracy(%)	Time(s)	EER(%)
Original Image	97.50	858	1.25
ROI Image	98.83	547	0.83
Preprocessed Image	99.16	491	0.42

the procedure in Sect. 2.2. For the division of training and test sets, the first 9 images of each finger were used as training set and the last 1 image as test set, resulting in a total of 5400 training images and 600 test images.

It can be observed from Table 1, the original image of MMCBNU_6000 can effectively improve the recognition accuracy after ROI interception and preprocessing. Besides, the training and classification time is less than the original image.

3.3   Experiments on FV-USM

For the FV-USM dataset, the network structure is similar to that has been used for MMCBNU_6000 dataset, but the firing threshold of the first convolutional layer is set to 4, thus, the output of the second convolutional layer is changed to 20 feature maps, and the firing threshold of the second convolutional layer is set to 1.

Table 2. Results of recognition accuracy, model training and classification time, and EERs of the proposed FV-SNN on the original image, ROI image, preprocessed input image of the FV-USM dataset.

Input	Accuracy(%)	Time(s)	EER(%)
Original Image	98.67	858	0.66
ROI Image	96.13	321	1.93
Preprocessed Image	98.78	567	0.61

In the experiment, the bilinear interpolation algorithm was used to adjust the original image to 128×96, and the ROI image of the second stage was adjusted to 150×50, so that the ROI image of both stages could be trained and tested together. 5 images of each finger class in each stage were selected as training samples, with one remaining image as test sample, resulting in a total of 4920 training images and 984 test images. Table 2 shows the results of recognition accuracy, model training and classification time, and EERs corresponding to the original image, ROI image and preprocessed input images respectively that performed on the FV-USM dataset. It can be seen obviously, the preprocessed input images of the FV-USM dataset can effectively improve the recognition accuracy, and the training and classification takes less time than the original images.

3.4   Comparison with Some FV Recognition Networks

In order to further evaluate the performance of the proposed FV-SNN model, we compared it with two popular CNN-style models from the perspective of classification results and computational overhead, including pre-trained ResNet-152 and AlexNet, both have been well trained on ImageNet dataset. Considering that above models both have very deep and complicated network structures, we also introduced a purely supervised convolutional network with similar structures to the FV-SNN, which is dubbed 'Simple CNN', concretely, the first convolutional layer of Simple CNN outputs 16 feature maps with convolution kernel size of 5×5, and the output of the second convolutional layer is 32 feature maps with convolution kernel size of 2×2. In each convolutional layer, ReLU activation is used, and the last decision layer is a fully connected layer and a Softmax layer with cross-entropy loss. It should be noted that the final decision layer performed a 50% dropout. At the same time, in order to evaluate the effect of DoG filtering, we also carried out experiments on Simple DCNN to determine whether to use DoG filtering. Meanwhile, [2] has also been compared, in the reproduction, the original parameter settings were maintained, but the dataset partitioning method proposed in this article was adopted.

Table 3 and Table 4 show the comparison results of recognition accuracy, model training and classification time, EER, and parameters quantity of the compared models on MMCBNU_6000 and FV-USM datasets, respectively. The results are obtained by using preprocessed input images. To accommodate the AlexNet model, the preprocessed image in the MMCBNU_6000 dataset was expanded to 120×256, and the preprocessed image in the FV-USM dataset was set to 300×100. Overall, the number of parameters of the proposed FV-SNN is far smaller than that of the CNN-style networks, but it still achieved competitive accuracy and consumed relatively less time.

Table 3. Comparison results of recognition accuracy, model training and classification time, EER, and parameters quantity of the compared models on MMCBNU_6000 dataset.

Models	Accuracy(%)	Time(s)	EER(%)	Parameters
ResNet-152	99.33	2094	0.17	116,544,432
AlexNet	99.16	370	0.21	60,730,355
Simple CNN	93.07	1435	1.83	15,964,092
Simple CNN + DoG	94.93	1654	1.21	15,964,492
CNN+CBAM [2]	99.30	655	0.17	1,261,848
FV-SNN	99.16	491	0.42	2336

Table 4. Comparison results of recognition accuracy, model training and classification time, EER, and parameters quantity of the compared models on FV-USM dataset.

Models	Accuracy(%)	Time(s)	EER(%)	Parameters
ResNet-152	99.28	1290	0.34	116,323,140
AlexNet	99.16	360	0.21	60,287,879
Simple CNN	77.56	1483	7.03	14,703,988
Simple CNN + DoG	87.91	1536	4.73	14,704,388
CNN+CBAM [2]	99.48	662	0.18	958,380
FV-SNN	98.78	567	0.61	2080

4   Conclusion

In this paper, we have proposed a two-layer unsupervised spiking convolutional neural network for FV recognition, which namely FV-SNN. By introducing DoG filtering and a series of preprocessing operations, we can obtain a kind of discrete spiking signal coding that adaptively represents the correlation of pixels in the image. Considering the huge number of parameters and high model complexity of the popular deep CNNs, the proposed FV-SNN achieves the competitive recognition accuracies as well as far smaller parameters than those of deep CNNs. In addition, our FV-SNN can be trained in an unsupervised manner, thus, the requirement for a large number of labeled samples has also been greatly eased. In the future, we will focus on the supervised spiking convolutional neural networks to extract more discriminative vein features. In addition, we will also pay attention to the combination with reward mechanisms, so as to avoid the use of additional external classifiers.

References

1. Fang, Y., Wu, Q., Kang, W.: A novel finger vein verification system based on two-stream convolutional network learning. Neurocomputing **290**, 100–107 (2018)
2. Zhang, Z., Wang, M.: Convolutional neural network with convolutional block attention module for finger vein recognition. arXiv e-prints (2022)
3. Shen, J., et al.: Finger vein recognition algorithm based on lightweight deep convolutional neural network. IEEE Trans. Instrum. Meas. **71**, 1–13 (2022)
4. Mozafari, M., Ganjtabesh, M., Nowzari-Dalini, A., Masquelier, T.: SpykeTorch: efficient simulation of convolutional spiking neural networks with at most one spike per neuron. Front. Neurosci. **13**, 625 (2019)
5. Lu, Y., Xie, S., Yoon, S., Yang, J., Park, D.: Robust finger vein ROI localization based on flexible segmentation. Sensors **13**, 14339–14366 (2013)
6. Asaari, M.S.M., Suandi, S.A., Rosdi, B.A.: Fusion of band limited phase only correlation and width centroid contour distance for finger based biometrics. Expert Syst. Appl. **41**, 3367–3382 (2014)

Feature-Fused Deep Convolutional Neural Network for Dorsal Hand Vein Recognition

Gaokai Liu[1], Yinfei Zheng[2]([✉]), and Zeyi Luo[2]

[1] Intelligent Sensing Laboratory, Huzhou Institute of Zhejiang University, Huzhou, China
[2] College of Biomedical Engineering and Instrument Science, Zhejiang University, Hangzhou, China
zyfnjupt@zju.edu.cn

Abstract. Dorsal hand vein recognition has attracted more and more attention from researchers due to its advantages of high recognition accuracy and good anti-attack performance. However, in practical applications, it is inevitably affected by certain external environments and bring out performance reduction, such as the droplet problem, which is rarely solved in current research works nevertheless. Facing this challenge, this paper proposes a feature-fused dorsal hand vein recognition model. Firstly, both dorsal hand vein matching and classification tasks are constructed via typical methods. Then, we introduce another classification task to learn the droplet and non-droplet features. Finally, the output feature vector of the droplet classification task is merged into other two tasks, meanwhile all the tasks are jointly optimized for the core purpose of promoting the performance of the dorsal hand vein matching task. The experimental result on our self-built dataset shows that the poposed model reaches 99.43% recognition accuracy and 0.563% EER, which achieves significant performance improvement in EER metric compared with the typical model.

Keywords: Dorsal hand vein recognition · Feature-fused · Droplet problem · Convolutional neural network

1 Introduction

As a kind of vein recognition, dorsal hand vein recognition has the characteristics of live detection, difficult to forge, and stronger anti-counterfeiting features compared with other biometric technologies such as fingerprint, face, iris. In addition, with respect to finger hand and palm hand veins, dorsal hand vein recognition take the advantages that it is usually thicker and therefore more robust to the surrounding environment such as temperature, pollution and physical damage.

From the perspective of its development, dorsal hand vein recognition can be divided into traditional methods and deep learning methods, among which the typical traditional methods can be listed as, SIFT [1], PCA [2], Sparse Representation [3], Graph Matching [4], and avelet decomposition [5] et al.

These methods above can recognize dorsal hand vein quickly. However, the disadvantage is that these features are usually designed manually and are not a universal

W. Jia et al. (Eds.): CCBR 2023, LNCS 14463, pp. 65–72, 2023.
https://doi.org/10.1007/978-981-99-8565-4_7

method. Moreover, these features are usually low-level or intermediate features, and it is difficult to extract high-level semantic features of dorsal hand vein.

Deep learning model can be as the effective solution scheme to the above problems. Compared with traditional methods, as a data-driven model, deep learning-based models are no need to design specific manual features for different datasets. Moreover, considering the design of nonlinearity and depth, the high-level semantic features that are closer to the essence of things can be extracted. Therefore, higher recognition accuracy can aiso be obtained usually. Xiaoxia Li [6] et al. introduces deep learning into the field of dorsal hand vein recognition for the first time, compares the performance of several classical models, and confirms the necessity of fine tuning. H Wan [7] et al. extract the region of interest (ROI) of dorsal hand vein images and the contrast limited adaptive histogram equalization (CLAHE), meanwhile gaussian smoothing filter algorithm is used to preprocess the images, then the deep learning model is used to extract the features, finally the recognition is carried out based on logistic regression. Gaojie Gu [8] et al. proposes a transfer learning method to integrate local binary pattern (LBP) features into the ResNet-50 framework to alleviate the loss of local information. Zhenghua Shu [9] et al. design a recognition system for dorsal hand vein based on deep residual network and attention mechanism (DRNAM) to extract cross-channel and spatial information features. Jiaquan Shen [10] et al. put forward a triplet loss based finger vein recognition method, which can improve the recognition accuracy and not need to re-train the new categories of follow-up data.

Although the above deep learning-based models usually have good recognition performance, there is extremely scarce the relevant research work for the scenario with liquid droplets as far as we know. Through our experiments, it is found that the presence of liquid droplets has a great influence on the performance of models. To solve this problem, a feature-fused dorsal hand vein recognition model is proposed in this paper. Specifically, by means of introducing the extra droplet classification task, the shared features in backbone network can be allowed to extract the higher differentiation features. Meanwhile the matching ability of models can be further improved owing to fusing droplet classification features.

2   Datasets and Models

2.1   Datasets

The images used in this paper are acquired by a self-designed dorsal hand vein acquisition device as shown in Fig. 1(left). The device adopts a near-infrared light source with a wavelength of 850 nm.

The datasets is assessed from 33 people with the age span of 18–50 years old. Each person is captured with images of both left and right hands, and therefore the dataset contains 66 categories. The training set and test set includes 414 and 383 images respectively, and the verification set is splited 20% from the training set. To improve algorithm robustness and alleviate overfitting, image enhancement operations such as scaling, flipping, size and color distortion are adopted. A example of vein images is shown in Fig. 1(middle,right). The image in middle includes droplets,while the image in right not.

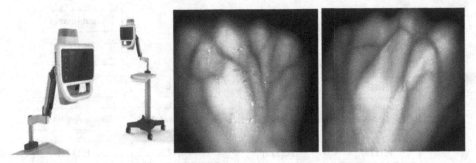

Fig. 1. Experimental equipment (left) and vein images (middle, right)

2.2 Models

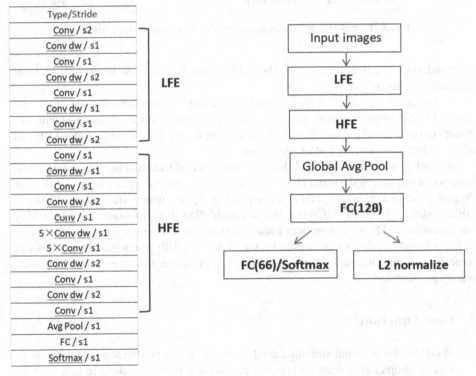

Fig. 2. Mobilenet (left) and the typical model (right, referenced by [12])

In order to take into account the application on embedded devices in the subsequent work, the basic framework here adopts the lightweight model Mobilenet [11] as shown in Fig. 2(left), and the structure is shown in the Fig. 2(left). It can be seen that the model uses conv and conv dw(depthwise) for image feature extraction many times. Besides, the following classification process is completed by 7×7 average pooling, full connection

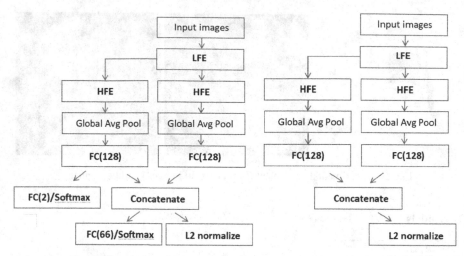

Fig. 3. Proposed (training stage, left) and Proposed (test stage, right)

layer and softmax activation function. Here LFE and HFE means low-level and high-level feature extraction respectively.

Figure 2(right) shows the typical model structure which adopts the idea from the paper [12]. Likewise, we introduce the dorsal hand vein classification task to facilitates better convergence of the matching task. Moreover, the typical model includes LFE and HFE modules the same as that of Mobilenet.

According to the problem that the existence of droplets limits model performance, meanwhile inspired by the paper [13], a parallel branch for droplet classification (whether droplet exists or not) is designed as shown in Fig. 3(left), which also utilizes LFE and HFE modules The main difference lies in considering that this branch is as a binary classification problem, the number of neurons from the last fully connected layer is set to 2. Furthermore, the output feature vector of the first fully connected layer with 128 dimensions is concatenated into the typical model for the purpose of promote the feature learning of droplets.

3   Loss Function

Based on the above model structure, the loss function can be divided into three parts, namely, the droplet classification loss, the dorsal hand vein classification loss, and the dorsal hand vein matching loss, which can be expressed by the formula as follows.

$$L = L1 + L2 + L3. \tag{1}$$

$$L1 = -\sum_k t_k \log y_k. \tag{2}$$

$$L2 = -\sum_k p_t \log q_t. \tag{3}$$

$$L3=\max(d(\text{anchor, positive})-d(\text{anchor, negative})+\text{margin},0) . \tag{4}$$

Here $L1$, $L2$ and $L3$ indicate the loss of droplet classification task, dorsal hand vein classification task and matching task, respectively. t and p are the true values, while y and q are the predicted values. It can be seen that the two classification branches both adopt cross-entropy function, and the difference lies in that the number of categories for different problems is different. The droplet classification problem is served as a binary classification problem, so the category number $k = 2$, while the dorsal hand vein classification problem is used to classify different dorsal hand veins, which reflects a multi-classification problem with a category number $t = 66$.

For the triplet matching loss of the main task of the dorsal hand vein matching, the optimization process is completed by constructing triples and calculating the similarity distance of the feature vectors between the same class and different classes, and the core idea lies in making the similarity distance between the same class smaller and smaller while the similarity distance of different classes is optimized larger and larger. Where anchor, positive, and negative indicates the feature vector of reference image, the feature vector with the same category as reference image, and the feature vector with the different category as reference image respectively. In addition, $d(\cdot)$ indicates euclidean distance and margin is a constant with the value of 0.2.

4 Training and Prediction

The model structure during training is shown in Fig. 3(left), and the optimal weight can be obtained through the joint optimization of the different tasks above. As a contrast, Fig. 3(right) shows the model structure during prediction. It can be clearly seen that only the dorsal hand vein matching task participates in the prediction process based on the weight previously trained. So the other two tasks can both be regarded as auxiliary tasks to promote the optimization of the main task of the dorsa hand vein matching, and finally improve the performance of the model.

5 Metrics

For matching tasks, the evaluation indexes commonly used are Accuracy, FAR (false acceptance rate), TAR(true acceptance rate), and equal error rate (EER). Considering that FAR and TAR are trade-off relation as the matching threshold changes. So for the convenience of comparison, EER can represent the comprehensive performance between FAR and TAR. Then,

$$\text{Accuracy}=(TP+TN)/(TP+TN+FP+FN). \tag{5}$$

$$\text{EER}=\text{FRR}=\text{FAR} \tag{6}$$

$$\text{FAR}=FP/(FP+TN). \tag{7}$$

$$FRR=FN/(TP+FN). \tag{8}$$

$$TAR=1-FRR. \tag{9}$$

Here FRR signifies false positive rate, and TP, FP, TN,FN are the number of true positive matching cases, false positive matching cases, true negative matching cases and false negative matching cases, respectively.

Under different matching thresholds, relevant FAR and TAR can be obtained, thus a TAR-FAR curve can be constructed to visually observe the change trend of them. From Eq. (6), (7), (8), (9), we can see that EER can be acquired by the horizontal coordinate of intersection point between TAR-FAR curve and straight line $y = -x+1$.

6 Experiments

The comparison experiments are conducted between the proposed model and the typical model. Here the model hyperparameters are set as that, epochs with the value 100 are equally divided into two phases, where the learning rates are initialized as 1e–3 and 1e–4 respectively. ADAM optimizer is used to optimize the loss function, and dropout is adopted after the global average pooling layer with a rate of 0.4.

From Table 1 we can clearly see that after fusing the output vector of the droplet classification branch, the accuracy of the model is not significantly improved, but the EER value is greatly reduced. The effectiveness above can be mainly explained from two perspectives. On the one hand, the introduce of droplet classification branches promotes the learning involved droplet information on shared features in the backbone network, which refers to LFE module. On the one hand, the fusion feature can further learn the feature representation of the samples containing droplets from the droplet classification branch. Finally, the reason for the lack of significant improvement in accuracy can be explained by the fact that although the improved model can promote the matching performance via the above two aspects, however, the small number of such samples containing droplets lead to the little impact on accuracy. We can also get a more intuitive visual experience to compared EER through Fig. 4.

Table 1. Comparison experiments(Here bold indicates better).

Methods/metrics	Accuracy	EER
Typical model	99.38%	0.679%
Proposed	**99.43%**	**0.563%**

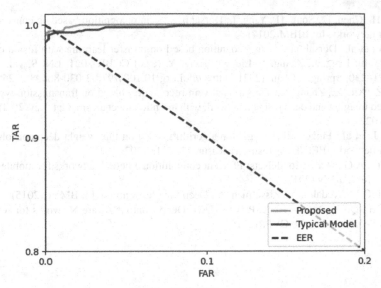

Fig. 4. TAR-FAR curves

7 Conclusion

This paper put forward a hand vein recognition model for droplet problems. Specifically, a droplet classification task is introduced and jointly optimized. Under the circumstances, the shared features add extra droplet information, meanwhile the droplet features are integrated into the original tasks. Accordingly, the sample features containing droplets can be well learned through the above two ways. The experimental results have verified the effectiveness of the improved model, and in the future, we plan to further study better feature fusion modes.

References

1. Wang, Y., Wang, D., Liu T.: Local SIFT analysis for hand vein pattern verification. In: Proceedings of the International Conference on Optical Instruments and Technology: Optoelectronic Information Security, vol. 7512, pp. 30–37(2009)
2. Khan, M.H.M., Subramanian, R., Khan, N.M.: Low dimensional representation of dorsal hand vein features using principle component analysis (PCA). World Acad. Sci. Eng. Technol. **49**, 1001–1007 (2009)
3. Joardar, S., Chatterjee, A., Rakshit, A.: A real-time palm dorsa subcutaneous vein pattern recognition system using collaborative representation-based classification. IEEE Trans. Instrum. Meas.Instrum. Meas. **64**(4), 959–966 (2015)
4. Lajevardi, S.M., Arakala, A., Davis, S., Horadam, K.J.: Hand vein authentication using biometric graph matching. IET Biometrics **3**(4), 302–313 (2014)
5. Wang, Y., Liu, T., Jiang, J.: A multi-resolution wavelet algorithm for hand vein pattern recognition. Chin. Optics Lett. **6**(9), 657–660 (2008)
6. Li, X., Huang, D., Wang, Y.: Comparative study of deep learning methods on dorsal hand vein recognition. In: CCBR(2016)

7. Wan, H., Chen, L., Song, H., Yang, J.: Dorsal hand vein recognition based on convolutional neural networks. In: BIBM(2017)

8. Gu, G., et al.: Dorsal hand vein recognition based on transfer learning with fusion of LBP feature. In: Feng, J., Zhang, J., Liu, M., Fang, Y. (eds.) CCBR 2021. LNCS, vol. 12878, pp. 221–230. Springer, Cham (2021). https://doi.org/10.1007/978-3-030-86608-2_25

9. Shu, Z., Xie, Z., Zhang, C.: Dorsal hand vein recognition based on transmission-type near infrared imaging and deep residual network with attention mechanism. Opt. Rev. **29**(4), 335–342 (2022)

10. Shen, J., et al.: Finger vein recognition algorithm based on lightweight deep convolutional neural network. IEEE Trans Instrum Measur. **71**, 1–13 (2021)

11. Howard, A.G., et al.: MobileNets: Efficient convolutional neural networks for mobile vision applications. arXiv (2017)

12. Parkhi, O.M., Vedaldi, A., Zisserman, A.: Deep face recognition. In: BMVC(2015)

13. Chen, H., Qi, X., Yu, L., Heng, P. A.: DCAN: Deep Contour-Aware Networks for Accurate Gland Segmentation. In: CVPR(2016)

3D Fingerprint Reconstruction and Registration Based on Binocular Structured Light

Jingjing Wang[1,2], Yuping Ye[1,2], Wei Cao[1,2], Juan Zhao[1,2], and Zhan Song[1,2(✉)]

[1] Shenzhen Institute of Advanced Technology, Chinese Academy of Sciences, Shenzhen 518055, China
jj.wang3@siat.ac.cn
[2] University of Chinese Academy of Sciences, Beijing 100049, China

Abstract. Fingerprint recognition is assuming an increasingly pivotal role in our modern information society. Its applications span across civil domains such as door locks and mobile phone security, to more critical realms like public security and legal identification. However, traditional contact-based fingerprint recognition methods bear the drawbacks of compromising the fingerprint's intrinsic 3D structure and being susceptible to contamination. In contrast, prevailing non-contact 3D fingerprint collection methods encounter challenges related to limited coverage area and the complexity of capturing an absolute height 3D representation. In light of these issues, we present a novel approach: a 3D fingerprint reconstruction and registration technique rooted in high-precision binocular structured light. This innovative method promises to deliver comprehensive and remarkably precise 3D fingerprint representations, addressing the limitations of current methodologies.

Keywords: 3D fingerprint · binocular structured light · 3D fingerprint reconstruction · 3D fingerprint registration

1 Introduction

Biometric identification is assuming an increasingly pivotal role in the modern information-driven society. Among the various biometric traits, fingerprints stand out due to their uniqueness, ease of collection, and resilience against damage. Conventional fingerprint recognition primarily relies on contact-based fingerprints. However, this approach often compromises the spatial attributes of one-dimensional fingerprints. Additionally, the collection process is susceptible to factors like contamination and slippage. Consequently, scientists have turned their attention towards non-contact 3D fingerprint techniques.

The current methodologies for 3D fingerprint reconstruction encompass techniques grounded in stereo vision, structured light, photometry, as well as optical coherence tomography (OCT) and ultrasound. Of these, stereo vision approaches typically employ two or more cameras. However, these solutions tend to be cost-prohibitive and can encounter difficulties in addressing feature point matching, making them ill-suited for objects rich in feature points, like fingerprints. Photometry-based methods offer accurate high-frequency reconstruction, albeit they cannot ascertain the absolute height of the 3D fingerprint. While OCT-based strategies can reconstruct both epidermal and subdermal fingerprint layers, the exorbitant cost of OCT sensors and their limited capacity for large-scale 3D fingerprint imaging pose challenges. Ultrasound-based 3D fingerprint imaging captures subsurface details but isn't entirely non-contact and is relatively compact. In comparison, the structured light approach employs multiple cameras and a projector to yield highly accurate 3D fingerprint reconstructions; however, the area of fingerprint capture is restricted.

Hence, we propose a novel method for 3D fingerprint reconstruction utilizing a binocular structured light system. This system empowers two synchronized cameras to capture fingerprint images of a single finger, generating dual 3D point clouds. Subsequent software processing accomplishes registration and alignment on the fingerprint plane, leading to precise registration parameters. As a result, a meticulous alignment and fusion of the two fingerprint point clouds are achieved.

2   Related Work

The existing 3D fingerprint imaging methods can be mainly divided into the following categories: (1) 3D fingerprint imaging based on photometry; (2) 3D fingerprint imaging based on structured light; (3) 3D fingerprint imaging based on stereo vision; (4) 3D fingerprint reconstruction based on ultrasound; (5) 3D fingerprint imaging based on OCT fingerprint imaging. Among them, 3D fingerprint imaging based on photometry, structured light and stereo vision principles can only image from the finger surface, while 3D fingerprint imaging based on ultrasound and OCT can realize finger surface and internal and fingerprint imaging.

Methods based on stereo vision usually require more than two cameras to capture objects simultaneously and then match them based on disparity or feature correspondence. Parziale et al. [12] developed a contactless volume-equivalent fingerprint capture device, The Surround Imager^{TM}, using five cameras and an array of 16 green LEDs. They first estimate the finger volume based on the shape from silhouette method and unfold the 3D fingerprint to a 2D plane, which can minimize the distortion of the fingerprint during the unfolding process and establish the correspondence between image pixels. Then, based on the corresponding relationship between the images, 3D fingerprint reconstruction is realized by using stereo vision and photogrammetry algorithms. This method can accurately reconstruct the shape of the fingerprint, but it is difficult to accurately reproduce high-frequency information. Liu et al. [10,11] used SIFT, ridge features, and details to establish the relationship between 3D fingerprints and 2D contactless fingerprint images based on the principle of stereo vision. They used three cameras to reconstruct 3D fingerprints and used this method to build a database of 3D fingerprint stitched images of 541 fingers. 3D fingerprint reconstruction based on the principle of stereo vision often suffers from the problems of bulky equipment and difficult matching of feature points.

Photometric-based methods usually need to use multiple LEDs or other light sources to create different lighting conditions and collect images, and then process the collected images to calculate the surface normal of the object to recover the shape information of the object. Xie et al. [16] proposed a real-time 3D fingerprint acquisition method based on photometric stereo, using a camera and some white LED lights, which can capture high-quality fingerprints. Kumar et al. [8] used photometric stereo to restore the surface normal, using 7 symmetrically distributed LEDs and a low-cost camera to reconstruct 3D fingerprints by collecting 7 images, but this method is prone to distortion due to finger movement. Lin et al. [9] built a photometric system using a camera and six colored LEDs, which can achieve 3D fingerprint reconstruction with an average MSE = 0.1202 accuracy in 0.5 s with two shots. In addition, they built a database containing 5520 color 2D fingerprints and 2760 3D fingerprints. The advantage of the photometry-based method is that it can reconstruct the high-frequency information in the fingerprint more accurately, which is beneficial for the recovery of the ridge-valley features. However, the three-dimensional information obtained by this method is the height of the normal integral of the fingerprint, not the absolute height.

The structured light-based method usually requires the use of multiple cameras and projectors to project the pattern onto the object, and then to capture the deformed pattern and recover the depth information of the object according to the deformation of the pattern. Wang et al. [15] used phase measurement profilometry to reconstruct 3D fingerprints with ridge details based on the principle of structured light. They also created a set of 430 2D fingerprint images and corresponding 430 3D fingerprint unfolded images from 12 subjects. Yalla et al. [17] proposed a method of sub-window technology based on the principle of structured light, which can achieve high-quality 3D fingerprint acquisition. The advantage of this method is that high-quality and high-resolution PPI 3D fingerprints can be obtained. Huang et al. [6] proposed a novel 3D fingerprint imaging system based on fringe projection technology, which uses a color CCD camera and a DLP projector, combined with a four-step phase shift and an optimal three-stripe selection algorithm, can obtain 3D fingerprint features and corresponding color texture information. Chatterjee et al. [3] used a single structured light system consisting of LED lights, sinusoidal gratings, and a CCD camera to reconstruct 3D fingerprints using the Fourier transform analysis method (FTM). The advantage of this method is the single-frame imaging, which can avoid noise and influence caused by finger shaking. The advantage of structured light-based 3D fingerprint imaging is that it can achieve high-precision imaging, but there are certain equipment requirements. High-speed, high-resolution cameras and projectors are often the basis for powerful structured light systems.

OCT-based 3D fingerprint reconstruction is typically based on the principle of interferometry. An OCT scanner is used to collect interference patterns, and information at different depths is obtained by measuring the time of flight of different light beams. Considering the shortcomings of slow speed and unnecessary data generation when using OCT for frontal imaging, Auksorius et al. [2] used full-field optical coherence tomography to perform fingerprint imaging from inside the finger, proving that full-field optical coherence tomography (FF-OCT) scanning can be used to generate images of sweat pores and internal fingerprints. Auksorius et al. [1] collected fingerprints using a full-field optical tomography system consisting of a silicon camera and a near-infrared light source, which can image fingerprints and sweat glands inside the human body. Ding et al. [5] proposed an improved U-Net method (BCL-U Net) for OCT volumetric data segmentation and fingerprint reconstruction, achieving the first simultaneous automatic extraction of surface fingerprints, internal fingerprints, and sweat glands. Ding et al. [4] proposed an end-to-end convolutional neural network-based fingerprint reconstruction method that can extract both internal and surface fingerprints from noisy OCT. The disadvantage of this method is that the finger is placed on the glass during the capture process, so it is not a complete non-contact fingerprint capture. The advantage of OCT-based fingerprint imaging is that it is fast and can reconstruct the internal fingerprint, but such systems are often expensive and do not take advantage of large-scale deployment.

Ultrasonic 3D fingerprint reconstruction usually requires the use of professional ultrasonic transmitting and receiving equipment, and the processing of received signals requires certain professional knowledge and experience of the operator. Saijo et al. [13] developed an ultrasonic microscope system with a center frequency of 100 MHz, which can realize ultrasonic impedance imaging and three-dimensional ultrasonic imaging of living fingerprints, and realize the observation of sweat glands on the surface of fingerprints and glands on the back of fingerprints. Jiang et al. [7] were the first to demonstrate the ability of MEMS ultrasonic fingerprint sensors to image epidermal and subsurface layers of fingerprints. Zhao et al. [18] proposed a prototype resonance-based multi-transducer ultrasonic imaging system that could reconstruct fingerprints from the deep skin layer by poropore location and epidermal structure. The advantage of using ultrasound technology to reconstruct 3D fingerprints is that high-resolution 3D fingerprints can be obtained, but it is difficult to extract features for fingerprint identification.

3   Proposed Method

Note that the coordinates of a point M in three-dimensional space in the world coordinate system, camera coordinate system, and projector coordinate system are M_W, M_C, M_P. After being projected by the projector and photographed by the camera, the coordinates of the point in the camera pixel coordinate system and the projector pixel coordinate system are m_c and m_p, respectively. By calibrating the camera and projector, respectively, the internal and external parameters of the camera and projector can be obtained A_C, A_P, E_C, E_P, where E_C, E_P are external parameters of the camera and projector relative to the same world coordinate system. Then the coordinate m_c of point M in the camera pixel coordinate system and its coordinate M_C in the camera coordinate system have the following relationship as Eq. (1) shows, where I_3 is the 3 × 3 unit matrix:

$$\begin{bmatrix} m_c \\ 1 \end{bmatrix} \cong A_C \begin{bmatrix} & 0 \\ I_3 & 0 \\ & 0 \end{bmatrix} \begin{bmatrix} M_C \\ 1 \end{bmatrix} \tag{1}$$

Similarly, the coordinates m_p of point M in the projector coordinate system and its coordinates M_P in the projector coordinate system have the following relationship as Eq. (2) shows, where I_3 is the 3 × 3 unit matrix:

$$\begin{bmatrix} m_P \\ 1 \end{bmatrix} \cong A_P \begin{bmatrix} & 0 \\ I_3 & 0 \\ & 0 \end{bmatrix} \begin{bmatrix} M_P \\ 1 \end{bmatrix} \tag{2}$$

In addition, there is the following relationship between the coordinate M_C of point M in the camera coordinate system and its coordinate M_W in the world coordinate system. Among them, R_C and T_C are the rotation matrix and translation vector from the world coordinate system to the camera coordinate system, respectively as Eq. (3) shows,

$$\begin{bmatrix} M_C \\ 1 \end{bmatrix} = E_C \begin{bmatrix} M_W \\ 1 \end{bmatrix} = \begin{bmatrix} R_C & T_C \\ 0 & 1 \end{bmatrix} \begin{bmatrix} M_W \\ 1 \end{bmatrix} \tag{3}$$

Similarly, there is the following relationship between the coordinate M_P of point M in the projector coordinate system and its coordinate M_W in the world coordinate system, where R_C and T_C are the rotation matrix and the translation vector from the world coordinate system to the camera coordinate system, respectively as Eq. (4) shows,

$$\begin{bmatrix} M_p \\ 1 \end{bmatrix} = E_p \begin{bmatrix} M_W \\ 1 \end{bmatrix} = \begin{bmatrix} R_p & T_p \\ 0 & 1 \end{bmatrix} \begin{bmatrix} M_W \\ 1 \end{bmatrix} \tag{4}$$

Suppose the transformation relation between the camera coordinate system and the projector coordinate system is represented by $E = \begin{bmatrix} R & T \\ 0 & 1 \end{bmatrix}$, then the point M in the camera coordinate system is The coordinates M_C and its coordinates M_P in the projector coordinate system have the following relationship as Eq. (5) shows, where R and T are from the projector coordinate system to the phase.

$$\begin{bmatrix} M_C \\ 1 \end{bmatrix} \cong \begin{bmatrix} R & T \\ 0 & 1 \end{bmatrix} \begin{bmatrix} M_p \\ 1 \end{bmatrix} \tag{5}$$

After the camera calibration, you can get E_C, E_P, and substitute Eq. (3) and Eq. (4) to get E. Then, according to the corresponding relationship between M_C and M_P And triangulation principle can get the depth of point M.

The algorithm we use in the coarse registration stage is the N-point SVD decomposition algorithm, and the fine registration stage uses the ICP algorithm. The basic principle of the ICP algorithm is to find the nearest neighbor points in the source point cloud and the target point cloud according to certain constraints, and then calculate the optimal registration parameters to minimize the error function. The error function is shown in Eq. (6),

$$\min_{R_2,T_2} E = \frac{1}{n} \sum_{i=1}^{n} ||q_i - (R_2 q_i + T_2)||^2 \tag{6}$$

Among them, P and Q are the source point cloud and the target point cloud, respectively, n is the number of nearest neighbor point pairs, p_i is a point in the target point cloud p, q_i is the nearest point corresponding to p_i in the source point cloud Q, (p_i, q_i) is the nearest neighbor point, R_2 is the rotation matrix, and T_2 is the translation vector.

Figure 1 shows the structure of the binocular structured light system. The system consists of two cameras, a projector, and a computer. There are two-way trigger and control lines between the left camera and the projector, and two-way trigger and control lines between the projector and the right camera. There is a one-way trigger line between the two cameras, and a two-way control and data transmission line between the computer and the two cameras. When the device is working, the left camera triggers the projector to project, and the projector sends shooting signals to the left and right cameras. After that, the 19 deformed patterns projected by the projector on the surface of the finger can be captured by the left and right cameras, and the image data is also stored in the computer.

Figure 2 shows the complete process of 3D fingerprint reconstruction and registration using a binocular structured light system. First, 19 binary fringes are generated by software, then they are burned into a projector, and the binary fringes are continuously projected on the finger surface, the binary fringes are deformed by the height modulation of the finger surface. At this time, the left and right cameras record at the same time, and two sets of deformed fringe images are obtained, each with 19 pieces, corresponding to the deformed fringe images recorded by the left and right cameras. Then, according to the calibration parameters of the system, we using a stripe edge-based structured light method [14] processes the two sets of images separately, and two sets of fingerprint point clouds can be obtained.

After obtaining two sets of fingerprint point clouds, we use our registration method based on standard parts to obtain the calibration parameters for the height plane where the system fingerprints are located, and then perform high-precision registration on the two fingerprint point clouds. The fingerprint registration method based on standard parts can be described as follows. First, the average finger thickness d is calculated. Then, use a facet plate with tiny features as a master and place the master at a height d from the reference plane. Then, select at least three rough registration points on the standard part, and use the N-point SVD decomposition algorithm and rough matching points to perform rough matching to obtain rough registration parameters. Then, on this

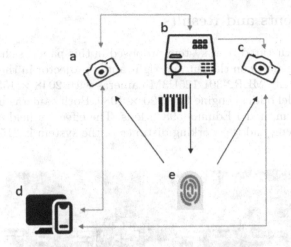

Fig. 1. System structure diagram (a) left-camera (b) projector (c) right-camera (d) computer (e) fingerprint

basis, use the ICP algorithm to fine register the standard parts to obtain the final registration parameters. The advantage of this method is that high-precision registration parameters can be obtained near the finger surface, that is, near the fingerprint imaging surface, which is conducive to high-precision registration of fingerprints and avoids noise due to insufficient registration precision.

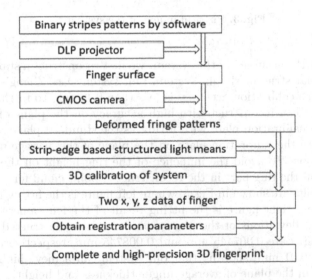

Fig. 2. Flow chart of obtaining 3D fingerprint

4   Experiments and Results

The binocular structured light system proposed in this paper is shown in Fig. 3. It includes two cameras on the left and right and a projector in the center. Both cameras are Daheng MER2-301-125U3M cameras with 2048 × 1536 resolution. Anhua 4710 model optical engine for 1920 × 1080. Both cameras have the same focal length 35 mm model Edmund59872 lens. The effective field of view of the system is 5cmx4cm, and the working distance of the system is 215 mm.

Fig. 3. Physical image of the system

To measure the accuracy of the system, we first reconstruct a standard plane using a binocular structured light system. Our system uses Zhang's calibration method, and the calibration accuracy is less than 0.1 mm. To further illustrate that the system can reconstruct with high accuracy on the plane of the fingerprint, we use a calibration plate with a ring as the standard plane, as shown in Fig. 4, and place the calibration plate on the plane of the average finger height for reconstruction. To avoid the influence of the ring height on the calibration plate, we cut off the ring part in the reconstructed point cloud for plane fitting. The fitting results are shown in Fig. 5, where left figure is the fitting result of the right camera and right figure is the fitting result of the left camera. The plane fitting standard deviations of the plane point clouds reconstructed by the left and right cameras are 0.007445 mm and 0.008745 mm, respectively, which are both less than 0.01 mm, showing that our system can achieve highly accurate reconstruction in the plane of average finger thickness and height.

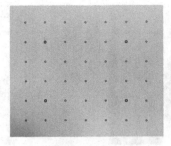

Fig. 4. Calibration plate for plane fitting

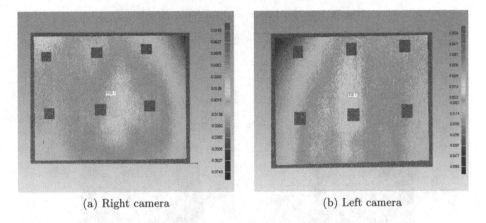

(a) Right camera   (b) Left camera

Fig. 5. Plane Fitting Accuracy of the System

The standard part used in the registration process is a small flat sheet with fine small characters, as shown in Fig. 6. Considering that the area occupied by the fingerprint is slightly smaller than the standard part, and we prefer to use the part with fine small characters for registration, we cut off the smooth and flat part on the right side of the point cloud of the standard part. We select eight symmetrical points in the small patch and one point in the center as the rough matching points (as shown in right figure of Fig. 6), and use the N-point SVD algorithm for rough matching, and then use the ICP algorithm for fine matching, and obtain The registration error of the standard parts is about 0.009 mm. Then we use the binocular structured light system to reconstruct the fingerprint. The reconstruction result of the right camera is shown in Fig. 9, and the reconstruction result of the left camera is shown in Fig. 7. It can be seen from the encapsulated meshes of the two point clouds that the ridge-valley information of the fingerprint has been effectively reconstructed. Using the registration parameters obtained from the standard parts, the two fingerprints are registered. The registration results are shown in Fig. 8. It can be seen that the reconstruction results contain not only the ridge and valley information, but also the combined fingerprints. The larger area contains more ridge-valley and detail features, which is conducive to improving the accuracy of fingerprint recognition.

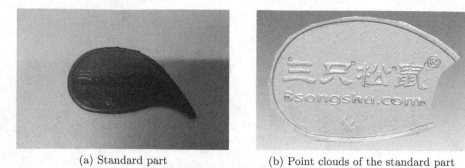

(a) Standard part   (b) Point clouds of the standard part

Fig. 6. Standard part and its point cloud

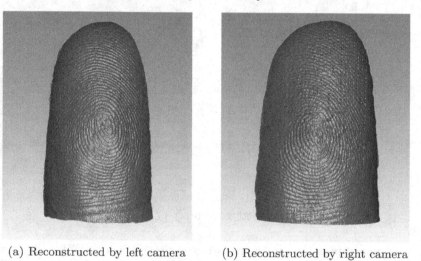

(a) Reconstructed by left camera   (b) Reconstructed by right camera

Fig. 7. Fingerprint mesh

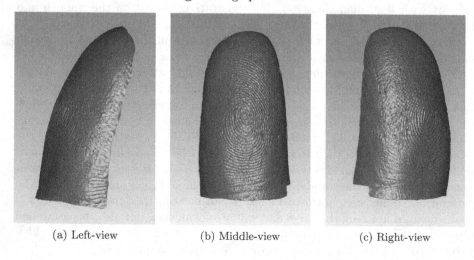

(a) Left-view   (b) Middle-view   (c) Right-view

Fig. 8. The merged fingerprint mesh

5   Conclusion

In general, by building a binocular structured light system and using a high-precision structured light reconstruction algorithm, we collected two 3D fingerprint point clouds, and completed the high-precision fingerprint point cloud matching based on standard parts to enable registration parameters. Our work provides fingerprint point clouds with more effective areas, which is conducive to improving the accuracy of fingerprint recognition. In the future, we will further map and expand the merged fingerprint grids to obtain extended fingerprints compatible with 2D fingerprints.

References

1. Auksorius, E., Boccara, A.C.: Fast subsurface fingerprint imaging with full-field optical coherence tomography system equipped with a silicon camera. J. Biomed. Opt. **22**(09), 1 (2017). ISSN: 1083–3668, https://www.spiedigitallibrary. org/journals/journal-of-biomedical-optics/volume-22/issue-09/096002/Fast-subsurface-fingerprint-imaging-with-fullfield-optical-coherence-tomography/10. 1117/1.JBO.22.9.096002.full, https://doi.org/10.1117/1.JBO.22.9.096002
2. Auksorius, E., Boccara, A.C.: Fingerprint imaging from the inside of a finger with full-field optical coherence tomography. Biomed. Opt. Express **6**(11), 4465 (2015). ISSN: 2156–7085, 2156–7085, https://opg.optica.org/abstract.cfm?URI=boe-6-11-4465, https://doi.org/10.1364/BOE.6.004465
3. Chatterjee, A., et al.: Anti-spoof touchless 3D fingerprint recognition system using single shot fringe projection and biospeckle analysis. Opt. Lasers Eng. (2017). https://doi.org/10.1016/j.optlaseng.2017.03.007
4. Ding, B., et al.: End-to-End surface and internal fingerprint reconstruction from optical coherence tomography based on contour regression. IEEE Trans. Inf. Forensics Secur. **18** (2023)
5. Ding, B., et al.: Surface and internal fingerprint reconstruction from optical coherence tomography through convolutional neural network. IEEE Trans. Inform. Forensic Secur. **16**, 685–700 (2021). ISSN: 1556–6013, 1556–6021, https://ieeexplore.ieee.org/document/9167283/, https://doi.org/10.1109/TIFS.2020.3016829
6. Huang, S., et al.: 3D fingerprint imaging system based on full-field fringe projection profilometry. Opt. Lasers Eng. **52**, 123–130 (2014). ISSN: 01438166, https://linkinghub.elsevier.com/retrieve/pii/S0143816613002091, https://doi.org/10.1016/j.optlaseng.2013.07.001
7. Jiang, X., et al.: Monolithic ultrasound fingerprint sensor. Microsyst. Nanoeng. **3**(1), 17059 (2017). ISSN: 2055–7434, https://www.nature.com/articles/micronano201759, https://doi.org/10.1038/micronano.2017.59
8. Kumar, A., Kwong, C.: Towards contactless, low-cost and accurate 3D fingerprint identification. IEEE Trans. Pattern Anal. Mach. Intell. **37**(3) (2015)
9. Lin, C., Kumar, A.: Tetrahedron based fast 3D fingerprint identification using colored LEDs illumination. IEEE Trans. Pattern Anal. Mach. Intell. **40**(12), 3022–3033 (2018). ISSN: 0162–8828, 2160–9292, 1939–3539, https://ieeexplore.ieee.org/document/8100983/, https://doi.org/10.1109/TPAMI.2017.2771292

10. Liu, F., Zhang, D.: 3D fingerprint reconstruction system using feature correspondences and prior estimated finger model. Pattern Recognit. **47**(1), 178–193 (2014). ISSN: 00313203, https://linkinghub.elsevier.com/retrieve/pii/S0031320313002616, https://doi.org/10.1016/j.patcog.2013.06.009
11. Liu, F., et al.: Touchless multiview fingerprint acquisition and mosaicking. IEEE Trans. Instrum. Meas. **62**(9), 2492–2502 (2013). ISSN: 0018–9456, 1557–9662, http://ieeexplore.ieee.org/document/6562785/, https://doi.org/10.1109/TIM.2013.2258248
12. Parziale, G., Diaz-Santana, E., Hauke, R.: The surround imager^{TM}: a multicamera touchless device to acquire 3D rolled-equivalent fingerprints
13. Saijo, Y., et al.: High frequency ultrasound imaging of surface and subsurface structures of fingerprints. In: 2008 30th Annual International Conference of the IEEE Engineering in Medicine and Biology Society, pp. 2173–2176. IEEE, Vancouver, BC, August 2008. ISBN: 978-1-4244-1814-5, https://ieeexplore.ieee.org/document/4649625/, https://doi.org/10.1109/IEMBS.2008.4649625
14. Song, Z., Chung, R., Zhang, X.T.: An accurate and robust strip-edge- based structured light means for shiny surface micromeasurement in 3-D. IEEE Trans. Ind. Electron. **60**(3), 1023–1032 (2013). ISSN: 0278–0046, 1557–9948, http://ieeexplore.ieee.org/document/6157617/, https://doi.org/10.1109/TIE.2012.2188875
15. Wang, Y., Hassebrook, L.G., Lau, D.L.: Data acquisition and processing of 3-D fingerprints. IEEE Trans. Inf. Forensics Secur.–JCI 1.90 Q1 5.4 (2010)
16. Xie, W., Song, Z., Chung, R.: Real-time three-dimensional fingerprint acquisition via a new photometric stereo means. Opt. Eng. **52**(10), 103103 (2013). ISSN: 0091–3286, http://opticalengineering.spiedigitallibrary.org/article.aspx?doi=10.1117/1.OE.52.10.103103, https://doi.org/10.1117/1.OE.52.10.103103
17. Yalla, V., et al.: High-quality 3D fingerprint acquisition using a novel subwindowbased structured light illumination approach. In: Proceedings of SPIE (2010). https://doi.org/10.1117/12.855513
18. Zhao, C., et al.: Ultrasonic guided wave inversion based on deep learning restoration for fingerprint recognition. IEEE Trans. Ultrason. Ferroelectr. Freq. Control **69**(10), 2965–2974 (2022). ISSN: 0885–3010, 1525–8955, https://ieeexplore.ieee.org/document/9856608/, https://doi.org/10.1109/TUFFC.2022.3198503

Cross-Sensor Fingerprint Recognition Based on Style Transfer Network and Score Fusion

Chuan Cheng, Jiachen Yu, Linkai Niu, Zhicheng Cao, and Heng Zhao[✉]

School of Life Science and Technology, Xidian University, Xi'an 710071, China
hengzhao@mail.xidian.edu.cn

Abstract. With the emergence of various types of fingerprint sensors, the fingerprint images collected by different sensors are distinct from each other due to systemic deformation and the different imaging style. Most of the existing fingerprint recognition methods fail to consider the problem of cross-sensor fingerprint verification. This paper proposes a cross-sensor fingerprint recognition system based on style transfer and score fusion. The method uses a CycleGAN to unify the styles of fingerprint images from different sensors and combines ResNeSt-50 with a spatial transformation network (STN) to extract fixed-length texture features with two properties of domain alignment and spatial alignment. The texture features are used to calculate the Texture Comparison Score, which is fused with Minutiae Comparison Score to produce the final similarity score. Experiments are carried out on the MOLF database and the self-collected database by the Xidian University and show that the proposed method has achieved excellent results.

Keywords: Fingerprint Recognition · Cross-Sensor · Style Transfer · Score Fusion

1 Introduction

At present, a large number of fingerprint recognition algorithms have been proposed. When the same sensor is used for registration and verification, the existing fingerprint recognition methods are considered effective. With the update of sensor technology and the development of the Internet, the situation of authentication using different sensors is becoming more and more diversified. Fingerprints for registration and verification are captured by sensors with different acquisition technologies and interaction types. Most of the existing methods do not consider the problems caused by the systemic deformation and the different imaging principles of different sensors for registration and verification. In the last few years, deep learning have shown very high potential in many research areas as well as in the field of fingerprint-based biometrics [1, 2]. For fingerprint recognition methods based on deep learning, due to the gap of datasets, when a model trained on a unique dataset is directly applied to another dataset, the performance may become poor [3], leading to defects in the practical application of most existing methods based on deep learning.

© The Author(s), under exclusive license to Springer Nature Singapore Pte Ltd. 2023
W. Jia et al. (Eds.): CCBR 2023, LNCS 14463, pp. 85–95, 2023.
https://doi.org/10.1007/978-981-99-8565-4_9

Improving the recognition accuracy between fingerprint images of the same person from different sensors has become one of the key issues. The differences in image style and the texture deformation are the main cause of performance degradation. In this paper, a new cross-sensor fingerprint recognition method is proposed. This method adopts the strategy of fusion of image texture and minutiae features. Firstly, the CycleGAN is used to unify the style of images from the different sensors, and then a deep network with spatial transformation network (STN) is designed for fixed-length feature extraction. Then the comparison score is calculated, and finally it is fused with the comparison score based on the minutiae to obtain the final recognition result.

2   Related Work

Research results in recent years have shown that the study of the influence of different fingerprint sensors on automatic fingerprint comparison is of great significance [4]. Ross et al. [5] proved that when two different sensors are used to capture fingerprints, the performance of the system drops sharply. Subsequently, Ross et al. [6] proposed a non-linear calibration method, using the TPS model to register a pair of fingerprints captured by different sensors and model the deformation of the fingerprints. Alshehri et al. [7] proposed a method of fusing comparison scores based on direction, gradient and Gabor-Hog descriptor by weighted summation rules to solve the problem of cross-sensor fingerprint comparison. These methods focus on using feature descriptors, as well as the fusion of fingerprint scaling and nonlinear deformation correction. Tan et al. [8] used two branches of minutiae attention network with reciprocal distance loss to recover the features correspondence for contactless and contact-based fingerprint images from the same fingers. Grosz et al. [9] proposed an end-to-end automatic fingerprint recognition system that extracted minutiae texture features for comparison. Their methods were implemented in PolyU Contactless 2D to Contact-based 2D Images Database and UWA Benchmark 3D Fingerprint Database. Shao et al. [10] proposed a Joint Pixel and Feature Alignment (JPFA) framework, which used a two-stage alignment method on the source and target datasets to obtain adaptive features for palmprint recognition across datasets. The performance of their method was not stable on different source and target databases. Alrashidi et al. [11] proposed the Siamese network with the features extracted by the Gabor-HoG descriptor, which was trained by adversarial learning. It can be seen that researchers have made a lot of efforts, but the performance of the current solution is unsatisfactory. This problem has important practical application value and deserves further in-depth research.

In the process of fingerprint identification, the fingerprint minutiae are one of the widely adopted fingerprint features. Besides, local structure features of minutiae, end-to-end local texture features and fingerprint features based on the fusion of minutiae and texture have also been extensively studied. Especially with the application of deep learning in the field of fingerprint recognition, the fusion of texture and minutiae features has received more and more attention. One of the most representative feature descriptors that combines fingerprint minutiae and local structures is the Minutia Cylinder-Code (MCC) descriptor [12]. Jin et al. [13] used the kernel principal component analysis and thermal kernel function to construct the projection matrix of the fingerprint comparison score of the training data set, and then used dynamic quantization technology to assign binary bits to each feature element to obtain fingerprint fixed-length feature vector. Li et al. [14] presented a kernel learning-based real-valued fingerprint feature and converted it into compact and cancellable binary code via one permutation hashing. This scheme enables accurate and efficient comparison as well as high security. Engelsma [15] designed a double-branch feature extraction framework based on the Inception network, in which one branch represented texture information, the other represented fingerprint minutiae information, and 512-dimensional fixed-length features of fingerprints were extracted after stitching. This framework achieved the effect close to the traditional method, but its structure was more complicated and required higher computing resources. Since fingerprint fixed-length feature representation on deep learning network has the huge advantages of no need to manually design feature extraction operators and convenient subsequent integration with template protection algorithms, this paper mainly focuses on the fixed-length texture feature extraction based on deep learning and the fusion with minutiae features to improve the efficiency of cross-sensor fingerprint recognition.

3 Proposed Method

We propose a cross-sensor fingerprint recognition framework from the perspective of style transfer and correction of systematic deformation, including image preprocessing, feature extraction and comparison strategy. Image preprocessing mainly includes style transfer and fast enhancement. After that, the spatially aligned fixed-length texture feature is extracted by deep network with STN to calculate the texture comparison score. At the same time, Verifinger is used to calculate the minutiae comparison score for the pre-processed fingerprint image, and the final comparison score is obtained by fusing

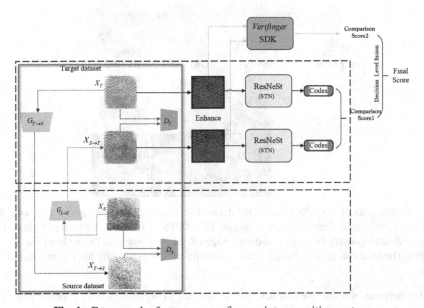

Fig. 1. Framework of cross-sensor fingerprint recognition system.

the texture Comparison score and the minutiae comparison score. The framework of cross-sensor fingerprint recognition is shown in Fig. 1.

3.1 Style Transfer Based on CycleGAN

Cross-sensor fingerprint recognition is mainly aimed at fingerprint images from different sensors. Different imaging conditions will produce different image styles, which will seriously affect the recognition performance. Domain adaptation is an effective scheme to solve the problem of image style differences. The core of domain adaptation is to extract domain alignment features in different data sets and bring the knowledge learned in one field into another different but related field to complete the target task [10]. Inspired by this idea, a pixel-level alignment framework based on style transfer is proposed in order to unify the style. It should be noted that the synthesized images generated after style transfer must meet the following two conditions: 1) the synthesized target image should be as similar to the target image as possible in style in order to reduce the gap, 2) the synthesized target images need to maintain the identity information in the source database, that is, synthesized images generated from the same category still belong to the same category. For meeting the above requirements, CycleGAN [16] is used to generate synthesized images from the source images. In Fig. 1, the solid red wire box is the pixel-level alignment part, implemented with CycleGAN. Where X_T represents target image, X_S represents source image, $X_{S \to T}$ represents pseudo target image, $X_{T \to S}$ represents pseudo source image, $G_{T \to S}$ represents source domain image generator, $G_{S \to T}$ represents target domain image generator, D_T and D_S represent discriminators of target domain and source domain respectively.

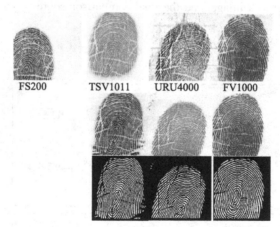

Fig. 2. Fingerprints of the self-collected database. The first row is the images of the same fingerprint generated by different sensors, including FS200, TSV1011, URU4000 and FV1000. The second row is to convert the corresponding image of the first row into the style of the FS200 database. The third row is to do image enhancement on the corresponding fingerprint images.

The purpose of using the fast texture enhancement algorithm is to improve the definition of the ridge structure in the recoverable area of the fingerprint image and remove the unrecoverable area. According to the estimated local ridge direction and frequency, the ridge and valley structures in the fingerprint images are adaptively sharpened. The directional Gabor filter is used to enhance the fingerprint image [17]. The enhanced fingerprint image on the self-collected database is shown in Fig. 2. It can be seen that the image style of the image processed by CycleGAN is indeed closer to the image style of the target domain. Fingerprint images that are less missing in the source domain are filled in and slightly conglutinated lines become clearer. The sharpness of the ridge after the fast fingerprint enhancement algorithm is higher, which is convenient for subsequent extraction of distinctive depth texture features.

3.2 Fingerprint Fixed-Length Feature Extraction Based ResNeSt with STN

In the end-to-end fingerprint fixed-length feature extraction, the ResNeSt [18] network is used as the backbone. It can adaptively adjust the size of the receptive field to obtain information of different receptive fields, effectively improving the feature extraction ability of the network. We use the ResNeSt-50 to extract 1024-dimensional fixed-length feature of fingerprint. The network model parameters of ResNeSt-50 are shown in Table 1. Here we set the relevant parameters cardinal $k = 1$, and split to $r = 2$.

Table 1. The detailed model structure parameters of the ResNeSt-50 network we used (SA stands for Split-Attention block)

Layer name	Output size	ResNeSt-50($2 \times 64d$)
Conv1	112×112	7×7, 64, stride 2
		3×3 max pool, stride 2
Conv2_x	56×56	$\begin{bmatrix} 1 \times 1, 128 \\ SA[r = 2, k = 1], 128 \\ 1 \times 1, 256 \end{bmatrix} \times 3$
Conv3_x	28×28	$\begin{bmatrix} 1 \times 1, 256 \\ SA[r = 2, k = 1], 256 \\ 1 \times 1, 512 \end{bmatrix} \times 4$
Conv4_x	14×14	$\begin{bmatrix} 1 \times 1, 512 \\ SA[r = 2, k = 1], 512 \\ 1 \times 1, 1024 \end{bmatrix} \times 6$
Conv5_x	7×7	$\begin{bmatrix} 1 \times 1, 1024 \\ SA[r = 2, k = 1], 1024 \\ 1 \times 1, 2048 \end{bmatrix} \times 3$
	1×1	global average pool, softmax

Although convolutional neural networks define powerful classification models, they are still limited by the lack of computational and parameter efficiency in terms of spatial invariance to input data. It is necessary to extract fingerprint discriminative features with spatial deformation alignment ability. A learnable module, Spatial Transformer Network (STN), is introduced to allow the network to explicitly exploit the spatial information of the images, perform spatial transformations based on the feature maps themselves without the additional training supervision or modifying the optimization process and learn invariance to translations, scaling, rotations and more common distortions. The fixed-length feature extraction network framework with spatial alignment properties is shown in Fig. 3. Experiments have shown that just correcting the rotation angle is sufficient for fingerprint recognition [19] and only one value θ is returned to the localization network. The fingerprint images before and after the transformation by the visualization space transformation module are shown in Fig. 4.

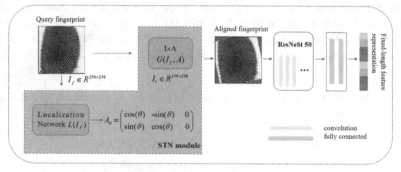

Fig. 3. A fixed-length feature extraction network framework with spatial alignment properties

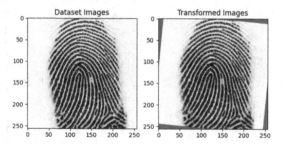

Fig. 4. Example of fingerprint images before and after the spatial transformation module

In the entire training process, the loss function CurricularFace [20] based on adaptive curriculum learning appears be used to adaptively adjust the easy and difficult samples in different training stages. At each stage, according to the difficulty of different samples, different importance is assigned. This can make the intra-class distance larger and inter-class distance smaller, so as to enhance the fingerprint recognition capabilities.

3.3 Comparison by Decision-Level Fusion

The minutiae are the most commonly used feature of fingerprint images. Therefore, we consider adding fingerprint minutiae information at the decision-making level. We use Verifinger to extract fingerprint minutiae features, and obtain minutiae Comparison scores. Then fingerprint texture Comparison score and minutiae Comparison score are fused according to the formula $s = \omega_t s_t + \omega_m s_m$ to obtain the final similarity score for calculating EER. In that, ω_t, ω_m are the weights of fingerprint texture features and minutiae features respectively. Here we set $\omega_t = 0.7$, $\omega_m = 0.3$. The parameter is obtained from experimental experience.

4 Experimental Results and Comparison

4.1 Experimental Setup

Databases. The public databases in the experiment are the MOLF DB1 and MOLF DB2 fingerprint databases [21, 22], published by the Image Analysis and Biometrics Lab of the Indian Institute of Technology (IIT). The self-collection cross-sensor fingerprint database was established by Xidian University, including the corresponding fingerprint templates obtained by four kinds of collection instruments: FS200, TSV1011, URU4000 and FV1000. The collection plan for four databases is to require each of 20 volunteers to collect fingerprints from the left ring finger to the right ring finger in turn, and collect 20 images for each finger. Each database has collected 160 types of different fingerprint templates.

Image Cropping. Since the sizes of the images collected by each collection instrument are not the same, we select the smallest image size as a fixed size for the MOLF DB1 and MOLF DB2, and crop all fingerprint images into a square ROI at this fixed size. Here the fixed size is set to 256×256.

Synthesized Target Databases Generation. Data with better imaging quality was selected as the target database of CycleGAN, and the images collected by other sensors are used to generate corresponding synthesized target database with a style similar to the target database. In this paper, MOLF DB1 and FS200 data are used as the target database of the public database and the self-collecting database respectively.

Training and Testing Dataset Setup. In the fixed-length feature extraction experiment, for the public database, MOLF DB1 and enhanced images are used as training data, and MOLF DB2 and enhanced images are used as testing data. For self-acquisition libraries, FS200 and enhanced images are used as training data, and the remaining libraries and enhanced images are used as testing data.

Comparison Protocol. The cross-sensor comparison experiments are carried out on the FVC protocols.

4.2   Experimental Results

Experiment 1. In this experiment, the cross-sensor fingerprint comparison EERs on texture feature, on minutiae feature and on the fusion of both are shown in the Table 2. In the table, "Tr" means the original images have been transferred by CycleGAN. "Enh" means images are regulated by Fast Texture Enhancement. Molf-1 means MOLF DB1. Molf-2 means MOLF DB2. As can be seen from the Table 2, when texture features are used for comparison, CycleGAN style transfer has a positive effect on the comparison results on all databases. At the same time, on the basis of style transfer, the performance is further improved by using the texture enhancement algorithm. After the texture comparison score based on fixed-length feature and the one based on minutiae are fused, the cross-sensor fingerprint recognition performance is greatly improved. And the recognition results reflect that texture fixed-length features and fingerprint minutiae can complement each other effectively. The performance on MOLF data is worse than the others because the fingerprint images in MOLF DB2 have different degrees of defects.

Table 2. Experimental results with the fusion of minutiae and texture features (EER (%)).

Databases		Texture			Minutiae		Fusion
Target	Source	Original	Tr	Tr + Enh	Original	Tr + Enh	Tr + Enh
FS200	TSV1011	14.00	9.18	7.12	0.626	0.54	**0.38**
	URU4000	14.61	11.05	6.45	0.638	0.55	**0.36**
	FV1000	13.97	10.21	7.62	0.649	0.58	**0.47**
MOLF-1	MOLF-2	37.51	21.12	19.66	5.06	4.98	**4.87**

Experiment 2. On the basis of Experiment 1, the STN module was embedded in the fixed-length feature extraction network. The experimental results are shown in Table 3. Because the Verifinger SDK for Minutiae extraction does not require fingerprint orientation correction, the "Minutiae" section does not increase the results of "STN". The results of "Tr + Enh + STN" under "Fusion" in Table 3 express that "Texture Feature" are obtained by "Tr + Enh + STN" and "Minutiae" scores are obtained by "Tr + Enh". The addition of the STN module has improved most of the recognition results of the self-collected databases to a certain extent. Only when using texture features for MOLF database comparison, the index becomes worse, and the reason is that the fingerprint of the MOLF dataset after cropped in the early stage has almost filled the image and has no fingertip information, causing the spatial transformation to be counterproductive.

Table 3. Comparison of fingerprint identification of embedded STN modules (EER (%))

Databases		Texture		Fusion
Target	Source	Tr + STN	Tr + Enh + STN	Tr + Enh + STN
FS200	TSV1011	8.35	6.56	**0.30**
	URU4000	10.62	5.65	**0.29**
	FV1000	8.54	7.41	**0.36**
MOLF-1	MOLF-2	23.30	21.28	**4.70**

4.3 Comparison of Results

Table 4. The results of comparing the previous methods on MOLF databases.

Data (MOLF DB1- DB2)	Method	EER (%)
200 classes	Alshehri [7]	2.08
	proposed method	**0.82**
1000 classes	Alrashidi [11]	10.23
	proposed method	**4.70**

The comparison results with the existing methods on the public cross-sensor finger-print database are shown in Table 4. MOLF DB1 is target database and MOLF DB2 is source database. In the case of selecting 200 classes of fingerprints in the database, the EER of our proposed method is 0.82%, better than the method of Alshehri et al. [7]. When all the fingerprint categories in the public databases are used, the EER rises to 4.70% due to the poor quality of fingerprint images in some categories. However, compared with the method of Alrashidi et al. [11], the superiority of our method is obvious.

5 Conclusion

A new cross-sensor fingerprint recognition method based on style transfer and score fusion is proposed in this paper. The method achieves style transfer on cross-sensor fingerprint images through CycleGAN network, uses ResNeSt-50 with STN to extract fixed-length fingerprint texture feature representations, performs domain alignment and deformation alignment on fingerprints, and obtains the final cross-sensor comparison by decision-level fusion of Texture comparison Scores and Minutiae comparison Scores. Experiments on two public fingerprint databases and four self-collected fingerprint databases all achieves lower EER. Although the fingerprints differ in scale and reso-lution, the main structure is invariant among fingerprints captured by different sensors, which includes ridge patterns, ridge orientations, and minutiae. In view of this, future studies should develop fingerprint enhancement algorithms for cross-sensor compari-son that can enhance ridge patterns and minutiae and suppress inconsistencies such as micro-texture patterns. In addition, cross-sensor comparison requires the development of new feature extraction techniques that are robust against variations of orientations, scale, and resolution.

Acknowledgements. This work was partly supported by the National Natural Science Foundation of China under Grants 61876139 and Instrumental Analysis Center of Xidian University.

References

1. Militello, C., Rundo, L., Vitabile, S., Conti, V.: Fingerprint classification based on deep learning approaches: experimental findings and comparisons," symmetry, **13**(5), 750 (2021)
2. Zeng, F., Hu, S., Xiao, K.: Research on partial fingerprint recognition algorithm based on deep learning. Neural Comput. Appl. **31**(9), 4789–4798 (2019)
3. Pan, S.J., Yang, Q.: A survey on transfer learning. IEEE Trans. Knowl. Data Eng. **22**(10), 1345–1359 (2010)
4. Lugini, L., Marasco, E., Cukic, B., Gashi, I.: Interoperability in fingerprint recognition: a large-scale empirical study. In: 2013 43rd Annual IEEE/IFIP Conference on Dependable Systems and Networks Workshop (DSN-W), pp. 1–6 (2013)
5. Ross, A., Jain, A.: Biometric sensor interoperability: a case study in fingerprints. In: Maltoni, D., Jain, A.K. (eds.) BioAW 2004. LNCS, vol. 3087, pp. 134–145. Springer, Heidelberg (2004). https://doi.org/10.1007/978-3-540-25976-3_13
6. Ross, A., Nadgir, R.: A thin-plate spline calibration model for fingerprint sensor interoperability. IEEE Trans. Knowl. Data Eng. **20**(8), 1097–1110 (2008)
7. Alshehri, H., Hussain, M., Aboalsamh, H.A., Zuair, M.A.A.: Cross-sensor fingerprint matching method based on orientation, gradient, and Gabor-HoG descriptors with score level fusion. IEEE Access **6**, 28951–28968 (2018)
8. Tan, H., Kumar, A.: Minutiae attention network with reciprocal distance loss for contactless to contact-based fingerprint identification. IEEE Trans. Inf. Forensics Secur. **16**, 3299–3311 (2021)
9. Grosz, S.A., Engelsma, J.J., Liu, E., Jain, A.K.: C2CL: contact to contactless fingerprint matching. IEEE Trans. Inf. Forensics Secur. **17**, 196–210 (2022)
10. Shao, H., Zhong, D.: Towards cross-dataset Palmprint recognition via joint pixel and feature alignment. IEEE Trans. Image Process. **30**, 3764–3777 (2021)
11. Alrashidi, A., Alotaibi, A., Hussain, M., AlShehri, H., AboAlSamh, H.A., Bebis, G.: Cross-sensor fingerprint matching using Siamese network and adversarial learning. Sensors **21**(11), 3657 (2021)
12. Cappelli, R., Ferrara, M., Maltoni, D.: Minutia cylinder-code: a new representation and matching technique for fingerprint recognition. IEEE Trans. Pattern Anal. Mach. Intell. **32**(12), 2128–2141 (2010)
13. Jin, Z., Lim, M.H., Teoh, A.B.J., Goi, B.M., Tay, Y.H.: Generating fixed-length representation from minutiae using kernel methods for fingerprint authentication. IEEE Trans. Syst. Man Cybern. Syst. **46**(10), 1415–1428 (2016)
14. Li, Y., Zhao, H., Cao, Z., Liu, E., Pang, L.: Compact and cancelable fingerprint binary codes generation via one permutation hashing. IEEE Signal Process. Lett. **28**, 738–742 (2021)
15. Engelsma, J.J., Cao, K., Jain, A.K.: Learning a fixed-length fingerprint representation. IEEE Trans. Pattern Anal. Mach. Intell. **43**(6), 1981–1997 (2021)
16. Zhu, J.Y., Park, T., Isola, P., Efros, A.A.: Unpaired image-to-image translation using cycle-consistent adversarial networks. In: 2017 IEEE International Conference on Computer Vision (ICCV), pp. 2242-2251 (2017)

17. Lin, H., Yifei, W., Jain, A.: Fingerprint image enhancement: algorithm and performance evaluation. IEEE Trans. Pattern Anal. Mach. Intell. **20**(8), 777–789 (1998)
18. Zhang, H., et al.: ResNeSt: split-attention networks. In: 2022 IEEE/CVF Conference on Computer Vision and Pattern Recognition Workshops (CVPRW), pp. 2735-2745 (2022)
19. Takahashi, A., Koda, Y., Ito, K., Aoki, T.: Fingerprint feature extraction by combining texture, minutiae, and frequency spectrum using multi-task CNN. In: 2020 IEEE International Joint Conference on Biometrics (IJCB), pp. 1-8 (2020)
20. Huang, Y., et al.: CurricularFace: adaptive curriculum learning loss for deep face recognition. In: 2020 IEEE/CVF Conference on Computer Vision and Pattern Recognition (CVPR), pp. 5900-5909 (2020)
21. Sankaran, A., Vatsa, M., Singh, R.: Latent fingerprint matching: a survey. IEEE Access **2**, 982–1004 (2014)
22. Sankaran, A., Vatsa, M., Singh, R.: Multisensor optical and latent fingerprint database. IEEE Access **3**, 653–665 (2015)

Sparse Coding of Deep Residual Descriptors for Vein Recognition

Zhengwen Shen, Xinfang Qin, Zaiyu Pan, and Jun Wang(✉)

School of Information and Control Engineering, China University of Mining and Technology, Xuzhou, Jiangsu 221116, China
jrobot@126.com

Abstract. Vein recognition has been drawing more attention recently because it is highly secure and reliable for practical biometric applications. However, the underlying issues such as uneven illumination, low contrast, and sparse patterns with high inter-class similarities make the traditional vein recognition systems based on hand-engineered features unreliable. To address the difficulty of direct training or fine-tuning a CNN with existing small-scale vein databases, a new knowledge transfer approach is formulated by using pre-trained CNN models together with a training dataset as a robust descriptor generation machine. A very discriminative model, sparse coding of residual descriptors (SCRD), is proposed by a hierarchical design of dictionary learning, coding, and classifier training procedures with the generated deep residual descriptors. Rigorous experiments are conducted with a high-quality hand-dorsa vein database, and superior recognition results compared with state-of-the-art models fully demonstrate the effectiveness of the proposed models. An additional experiment with the PolyU multispectral palmprint database is designed to illustrate the generalization ability.

Keywords: CNN · deep residual descriptors · sparse coding · vein recognition

1 Introduction

Vein pattern, an intrinsic biometric pattern imaged under near-infrared (NIR) light, has emerged as a promising alternative for person identification. Compared with extrinsic biometric features such as face, fingerprint, palm-print, and iris, vein patterns including finger-vein, dorsa-vein, and palm-vein are highly secure, private, and convenient. These properties are the basic requirements for practical applications and are attracting more attention [1–3]. Despite the advantages of adopting vein patterns for person identification, there still exist some inherent issues (e.g., unavoidable environmental illuminations [4–6], ambient temperature effects [2,6], uncontrollable user behaviours [4,5] and NIR device degradation [7–9]) which make the design of robust and accurate vein recognition systems a challenging task. To alleviate the inherent influence of these issues,

W. Jia et al. (Eds.): CCBR 2023, LNCS 14463, pp. 96–105, 2023.
https://doi.org/10.1007/978-981-99-8565-4_10

researchers [10,11] have proposed different algorithms targeted at a specific step of the traditional vein recognition framework such as designing restoration methods to recover the details and proposing better feature extraction methods and more robust matching strategies.

More recently, hand-engineered feature representation has been significantly outperformed by CNN in almost all domains of image understanding including object detection [12], categorization [13], and segmentation [14]. To find out an improved solution for utilizing powerful CNN for discriminating vein patterns, the idea of transferring the semantic knowledge encoded by both a pre-trained CNN and the training dataset (e.g., ImageNet) as the representation of vein patterns is proposed in this paper as the basis for constructing robust vein recognition systems. Trained on large-scale datasets with a pre-defined architecture, CNN has been shown to achieve much better results on different image understanding tasks [12–14] than those using traditional hand-engineered features. Driven by the success of CNN, it is sensible to embrace deep learning for vein recognition tasks. As shown in Fig. 1, the proposed descriptors are free from the burstiness problem that exists in traditional SIFT features, where some of the detected keypoints are repeated, thus degrading the discriminative ability of the descriptors.

2 Sparse Dictionary Learning with Deep Residual Descriptors

Based on the selected robust and discriminative deep residual descriptors, the bag of feature (BoF) model is analyzed and deployed for final feature generation and classification. Considering that the final descriptors for each sample should be sparse and by setting the threshold relatively high for generating the feature selection matrix in Stage II as shown in Fig. 1, an overcomplete dictionary and soft membership indicators [15] are desired for obtaining good results.

2.1 Deep Residual Descriptors

In the proposed model, CNN together with its training dataset is defined as a descriptor generation machine, and the output of the defined machine is a discriminative feature descriptor pool as shown in Fig. 2.

When feeding a vein image into the pre-trained CNN of the machine as shown in Fig. 1, the value of the softmax layer output, which indicates the relative similarity of input to a certain class in the training data is obtained. Subsequently, by setting a suitable threshold, the feature selection (FS) matrix can be calculated as given in Eq. (1):

$$FS_{\text{top-}K} = [F_1, F_2, \ldots, F_{1000}]; F_i = \{1, \ i \leqslant \ k; 0, \ other\} \tag{1}$$

With the matrix, the deep residual descriptors may be obtained by element-wise matrix multiplication between FS and the original descriptor pool, as described in Eq. (2):

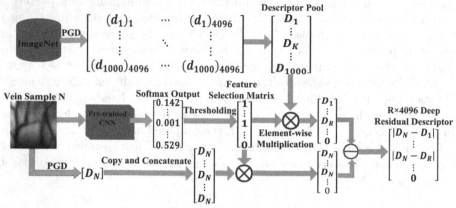

(a) Procedure of Generating Descriptors (PGD) from a pre-trained CNN for category K containing M samples

(b) Procedure of generating a descriptor pool and deep residual descriptor for a given vein sample

Fig. 1. Overview of the proposed deep residual descriptor generation system.

$$\mathbf{D} = (FS_{\text{top-}K})^T [D_1, D_2, \ldots, D_{1000}] \qquad (2)$$

where D_i is $(\sum_{j=1}^{M} d_i^j)/M$ with d_i^j being a 1×4096-D feature vector from the previous 4096-D fully-connected layer and M is the total number of samples in each training category. With such feature vectors describing one vein image, high-level feature encoding methods with sparse dictionary learning algorithms are realized for linear SVM training. Note that PCA is adopted to reduce the dimension of the descriptors from 4096 to 1000.

2.2   Learning Discriminative Representation with SCRD

Considering the difference between the residual descriptors and the traditional SIFT descriptors, suitable dictionary generation methods by modification to the selected basis are analyzed.

Let $\mathbf{X}$ be a set of deep residual descriptors lying in a D-dimensional feature space, i.e., $\mathbf{X} = [X_1, \ldots, X_N]^T \in \mathbb{R}^{N \times D}$. The most widely used codebook optimization model, the vector quantization (VQ) algorithm [16], is adopted by applying K-means to solve the following objective function (3):

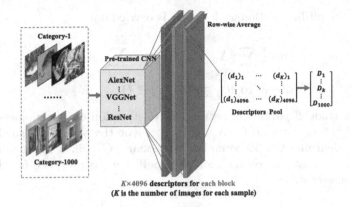

Fig. 2. Deep descriptor pool of the defined machine.

$$\min_{C} \sum_{n=1}^{N} \min_{k=1,\ldots,K} \|X_n - C_k\|_2^2 \tag{3}$$

where $C = [C_1, \ldots, C_K]^T$ is the codebook to be optimized, and $\| \cdot \|_2^2$ represents the ℓ_2-norm of the reconstruction residual matrix. The encoding problem can be solved by updating C_k with $A_k C$, and $A = [A_1, \ldots, A_K]^T$ represents the reconstruction coefficients. The overall optimization problem for solving the codebook and coefficients simultaneously can be realized by re-formulating the objective function (3) as:

$$\min_{C, A_k} \sum_{n=1}^{N} \|X_n - A_k C\|_2^2 \tag{4}$$

$$\text{subject to } Card(A_k) = 1, \|A_k\|_1 = 1, A_k \succeq 0, \forall k$$

where $Card(A_k = 1)$ requires that only one element of A_k is nonzero, and $A_k \succeq 0$ restricts that all elements of A_k are nonnegative. $\|A_k\|_1$ is the ℓ_1-norm operation, which defines the summation of the absolute value of each element in A_k. Based on these constraints, it can be concluded that the hard assignment [16] with $Card(A_k) = 1$ in VQ will undoubtedly result in a coarse reconstruction with large residual errors, thus degrading the discriminability of the coefficient representation. When adopting VQ based dictionary generation and coding methods for the residual descriptors, the performance will be worsened if N in $\mathbf{X}$ is small, which is the prerequisite to ensure that the generated residual descriptors are separable without intersection. To fully utilize the discriminability of the proposed deep residual descriptors, different constraints are added to the dictionary training and representation learning problems, resulting in functions (5)–(6), with which the off-line dictionary learning is carried out:

$$\min_{C,A_k} \frac{1}{2}\sum_{n=1}^{N}\|X_n - A_kC\|_2^2 + \alpha\sum_{n=1}^{N}\|A_k\|_1 \tag{5}$$

$$\text{subject to } \|C_j\|_2^2 \leq 1 \quad \forall j \in \{1,\ldots,K\}$$

where α is a tradeoff parameter between reconstruction error and sparsity constraint, and the ℓ_2-norm on C_j is used to prevent the arbitrarily small values of A_k. After learning the overcomplete dictionary C [16], a similar model by adding another constraint on the obtained coefficients is proposed for obtaining the final representation:

$$\min_{A_k} \frac{1}{2}\|X_n - A_kC\|_2^2 + \beta_1\|A_k\|_1 + \frac{\beta_2}{2}\|A_k\|_2^2 \tag{6}$$

By optimizing function (6) under the ℓ_1 and ℓ_2 sparse coding scheme [16], a discriminative and stable representation with the learned dictionary is obtained for later classifier training and vein recognition.

To solve the recognition problem with multiple classes, the one-against-all strategy is adopted to train multiple binary linear SVMs. Given the training dataset $\{(F_i,y_i)\}_{i=1}^{L}$, $y_i \in \mathbf{Y} = \{1,\ldots,L\}$, the classifier aims at learning L linear and binary functions $\{w_c^T F | c \in \mathbf{Y}\}$, and the label for a certain input F can be predicted by Eq. (7):

$$y = \min_{c\in\mathbf{Y}} w_c^T F \tag{7}$$

The parameters w_c of the kernel can be obtained by solving the following unconstrained convex function $J(w_c)$ with w_c as a variable:

$$\min_{w_c}\{J(w_c) = \|w_c\|_2^2 + C\sum_{i=1}^{L}\mathrm{L}(w_c, y_i^c, F_i)\} \tag{8}$$

where y_i^c equals 1 if the class label y_i is 1, otherwise y_i equals -1, and $\mathrm{L}(\cdot)$ is an improved hinge loss function defined as:

$$\mathrm{L}(w_c, y_i^c, F_i) = [\max(0, w_c^T F y_i^c - 1)]^2 \tag{9}$$

3   Experiments and Discussion

3.1   Database and Baseline Model Setup

Dataset Setup. Experiments for baseline model setup and performance comparison were conducted with the hand-dorsa vein database from CUMT-Dataset [11], which was obtained from 98 females and 102 males with ages varying from 19 to 62. Similar to other work [11], the region of interest (ROI) for each image in this database was extracted and normalized to a size of 224×224 pixels. When carrying out experiments, half of the examples are randomly selected as training data, and the remaining images are utilized for testing.

As the key parameter to obtain the residual descriptor, the size for the dimension of the feature selection matrix in Fig. 1 was determined by 5-fold cross-validation from $\{1, \ldots, 50\}$ with the training set. After obtaining the dimension R, PCA was adopted for transforming the $R \times 4096$ descriptors to $R \times 1000$ descriptors for better dictionary generation. For SCRD, the codebook size was fixed as 512.

Baseline Model Setup. With the availability of the numbers of pre-trained CNN models (e.g., VGG-16 [17], GoogLeNet [18], and ResNet-128 [19]) for descriptor pool generation, an experiment on finding out the most appropriate one for SCRD was designed, and three models including VGG-16 [17], GoogLeNet [18], and ResNet-128 [19]) pre-trained with ImageNet were involved. As shown in Table 1, the overall recognition rate using VGG was better than the others for the SCRD model by a large margin, and the VGG based models were used as the baseline for comparative experiments. Furthermore, the experimental results also reveal that the VGG based network structure is more capable of discriminating the sparse vein structures.

Table 1. Recognition rate (%) of SCRD with different pre-trained models.

	VGG	GoogLeNet	ResNet
SCRD	**98.83 ± 1.02**	91.25 ± 0.65	90.41 ± 0.78

3.2   Comparison with State-of-the-Arts

After obtaining the baseline formulations of SCRD, rigorous comparison experiments are designed to demonstrate the superiority of the proposed model over the current state-of-the-arts. After finding out the best parameter setup by cross-validation with the training dataset, the genuine matching and imposter matching on the testing set are conducted with the trained SCRD for obtaining the FAR and FRR respectively, with which we obtain the EER as shown in Table 2 and Fig. 3.

To demonstrate the superiority of the proposed encoding and recognition method over other types of CNN-based models on the hand-dorsa vein dataset, four different kinds of formulations on utilizing CNN for vein recognition tasks. The experimental results of these models with the hand-dorsa vein database are listed in Table 2. It also indicates that modifying the methods of feature extraction (e.g., generating the deep residual descriptors) and feature encoding methods simultaneously may result in state-of-the-art performance. In addition, the proposed generic approach of adopting CNN together with the training dataset for deep descriptor generation may also be applicable to other image classification tasks.

Table 2. EER (%) with different pre-trained models, the benchmark performance of the first four groups are the highlighted ones. Group 1 represents Direct Training (DT) from scratch; Group 2 represents Fine-Tuning (FT); Group 3 represents Off-line Feature Extractor (OFEx); Group 4 represents Off-line Feature Encoding (OFEn). A: FingerveinNet; B: AlexNet; C: VGG; D: FV; E: VLAD.

Group	DT		FT		OFEx		OFEn		Proposed
Methods	A	B	B	C	B	C	D	E	SCRD
Accuracy (%)	2.089	2.711	3.104	3.641	4.215	2.835	1.028	1.031	0.016

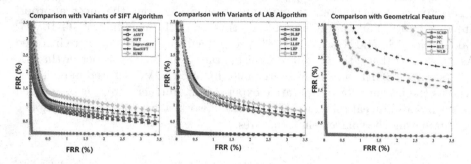

Fig. 3. Comparison of ROC curves between the proposed models and representative hand-engineered methods including (left) SIFT-based models, (middle) LBP-based models, and (right) Geometrical feature-based models.

Comparison with Hand-Engineered Feature Based Models: The specific EER results of different models are shown in Fig. 3. Judging from the EER result of identification with the hand-dorsal vein database, it can be concluded that the proposed deep residual descriptor encoding models perform better than the local invariant feature (LIF) models with an EER of 0.016whereas the best of LIF is 0.820 of LBPs is 0.058 recognition results fully demonstrate the ability of the proposed model in discriminating the sparse vein patterns with high inter-class similarity.

Comparison with Geometrical Feature-Based Models: As can be seen from the samples, different topological patterns between images make it possible to use vein patterns for authentication. In this section, four representative methods including the maximum curvature (MC) from [20], the wide line detector (WLD) [5], the principal curvature (PC) [21] and the repeated line tracking (RLT) method from [22] are selected for performance comparison. The specific EER results of different models are shown in Fig. 3.

As shown in Fig. 3, similar to the results from models based on hand-crafted features, large performance improvements using the proposed model over the other representative methods are shown as ranging from 1.841% to 3.005% on the hand-dorsa vein dataset. Besides, by comparing the results in Fig. 3, the performance gap between the best hand-crafted feature (DLBP) and the best geometrical feature (MEC) indicates the limitation of geometrical features, which can only work well on some specific patterns [23] and are sensitive to different variations. However, benefited from the proposed discriminative knowledge transfer mechanism and the hierarchical descriptor encoding methods (e.g., the sparse coding in this paper), the proposed model performs well across different biometrical patterns, as evidenced by the superior results with the palmprint datasets described in the following section.

3.3 Generalization Ability Evaluation

Table 3. Summary of EERs derived from recently published palm vein recognition models using PolyU Multispectral Palmprint database.

Method	Performance (EER %)
NPVM [24]	0.557
OPI [25]	0.012
NMRT; Hessian [26]	0.004; 0.430
CCGF [27]	0.102
CPOF [28]	0.140
QSHVR [11]	0.079
Proposed	0.021

In addition to the comparative experiments with hand-dorsa veins, the PolyU Multispectral Palmprint Database was employed in this section to evaluate the generalization ability of the proposed deep residual descriptor generation and encoding algorithms, and only the NIR images of the PolyU database were used for matching since the focus of the experiment is palm-vein identification. Similar to the experiments setup in the previous sections, the NIR part of the whole dataset is split into training and testing components randomly, with each of them containing the same number of samples. The best parameter configuration for SCRD is obtained by 5-fold cross-validation on the training dataset. After finishing the training of palm-vein matching models, the genuine and imposter matching are conducted on the testing set for obtaining the EER as reported in Table 3 and Fig. 3, the proposed framework, utilizing deep residual descriptors for pattern encoding and sparse coding for classification, is robust and general for vein pattern based person identification.

4   Conclusion

The main contribution of this paper is a completely new knowledge transfer concept of defining a pre-trained CNN together with its training dataset as a robust descriptor pool, from which representation knowledge is transferred to enrich the domain-specific image representation and to increase the final classification results. With the deep residual descriptor generation mechanism, discriminative representations for describing the sparse vein patterns with high inter-class similarity were obtained by the proposed SCRD model, which incorporated the sparse dictionary learning scheme for improving the semantic properties of the representation. VGG was adopted as the basis for generating the baseline model, and rigorous comparative experiments with both CNN-based models and other state-of-the-art algorithms demonstrate the representation and generalization ability of the proposed model. Furthermore, research on utilizing the proposed model for other domain-specific image recognition tasks is ongoing.

Acknowledgments. This work was partially supported by the Scientific Innovation 2030 Major Project for New Generation of AI under Grant 2020AAA0107300. The Fundamental Research Funds for the Central Universities under Grant 2023Q N1077.

References

1. Amira Yahi, S.D.: Multimodal biometric recognition systems using deep learning based on the finger vein and finger knuckle print fusion. IET Image Process. **14**(15), 3859–3868 (2020)
2. Pan, Z., Wang, J., Wang, G., Zhu, J.: Multi-scale deep representation aggregation for vein recognition. IEEE Trans. Inf. Forensics Secur. **16**, 1–15 (2020)
3. Pan, Z., Wang, J., Shen, Z., Han, S.: Disentangled representation and enhancement network for vein recognition. IEEE Trans. Circ. Syst. Video Technol. **33**, 4164–4176 (2023)
4. Maeda, Y., Hasegawa, T.: Analysis of finger vein variety in patients with various diseases using vein authentication technology. J. Biophotonics **12**(4), e201800354 (2019)
5. Huang, B., Dai, Y., Li, R., Tang, D., Li, W.: Finger-vein authentication based on wide line detector and pattern normalization. In: 20th International Conference on Pattern Recognition (ICPR), pp. 1269–1272. Istanbul (2010)
6. Pan, Z., Wang, J., Shen, Z., Chen, X., Li, M.: Multi-layer convolutional features concatenation with semantic feature selector for vein recognition. IEEE Access **7**, 90608–90619 (2019)
7. Cheong, W., Prahl, S., Welch, A.: A review of the optical properties of biological tissues. IEEE J. Quantum Electron. **26**(12), 2166–2185 (1990)
8. Lee, E., Park, K.: Image restoration of skin scattering and optical blurring for finger vein recognition. Opt. Lasers Eng. **49**(7), 816–828 (2011)
9. Yang, Y., Shi, Y.: Towards finger-vein image restoration and enhancement for finger-vein recognition. Inf. Sci. **268**, 33–52 (2014)
10. Wang, J., Wang, G., Li, M., Yu, W., Tian, H.: An improved hand vein image acquisition method based on the proposed image quality evaluation system. Comput. Model. New Technol. **18**(11), 1204–1208 (2014)
11. Wang, J., Wang, G.: Quality-specific hand vein recognition system. IEEE Trans. Inf. Forensics Secur. **12**(11), 2599–2610 (2017)
12. Mulyono, D., Jinn, H.: Rich feature hierarchies for accurate object detection and semantic segmentation. In: IEEE Conference on Computer Vision and Pattern Recognition (CVPR), pp. 580–587. Columbus, USA (2014)

13. Yang, W., Luo, W., Kang, W., Huang, Z., Wu, Q.: Fvras-net: an embedded finger-vein recognition and antispoofing system using a unified CNN. IEEE Trans. Instrum. Meas. **69**(11), 8690–8701 (2020)
14. Hariharan, B., Arbeláez, P., Girshick, R., Malik, J.: Simultaneous detection and segmentation. In: Fleet, D., Pajdla, T., Schiele, B., Tuytelaars, T. (eds.) ECCV 2014. LNCS, vol. 8695, pp. 297–312. Springer, Cham (2014). https://doi.org/10.1007/978-3-319-10584-0_20
15. Yang, J., Yu, K., Gong, Y., Huang, T.: Linear spatial pyramid matching using sparse coding for image classification. In: IEEE Conference on Computer Vision and Pattern Recognition (CVPR), pp. 1794–1801. Miami, USA (2009)
16. Koniusz, P., Yan, F., Gosselin, P., Mikolajczyk, K.: Higher-order occurrence pooling on mid-and low-level features: visual concept detection. IEEE Trans. Pattern Anal. Mach. Intell. **39**(2), 313–326 (2017)
17. Simonyan, K., Zisserman, A.: Very deep convolutional networks for large-scale image recognition, arXiv preprint arXiv:1409.1556 (2014)
18. Mulyono, D., Jinn, H.: Going deeper with convolutions. In: IEEE Conference on Computer Vision and Pattern Recognition (CVPR), pp. 1–9. Boston, USA (2015)
19. He, K., Zhang, X., Ren, S., Sun, J.: Deep residual learning for image recognition. In: IEEE Conference on Computer Vision and Pattern Recognition (CVPR), pp. 770–778. Las Vegas, USA (2016)
20. Miura, N., Nagasaka, A., Miyatake, T.: Extraction of finger-vein patterns using maximum curvature points in image profiles. IEICE Trans. Inf. Syst. **90**(8), 1185–1194 (2007)
21. Choi, J., Song, W., Kim, T., Lee, S., Kim, H.: Finger vein extraction using gradient normalization and principal curvature. In: SPIE Electronic Imaging, pp. 827–834. California, USA (2009)
22. Miura, N., Nagasaka, A., Miyatake, T.: Feature extraction of finger-vein patterns based on repeated line tracking and its application to personal identification. Mach. Vis. Appl. **15**(4), 194–203 (2004)
23. Wang, J., Wang, G.: SIFT based vein recognition models: analysis and improvement. Comput. Math. Methods Med. **50**(5), 1–14 (2017)
24. Chen, H., Lu, G., Wang, R.: A new palm vein matching method based on ICP algorithm. In: 2nd International Conference on Interaction Sciences: Information Technology, Culture and Human, pp. 1207–12118. Seoul, Korea (2009)
25. Zhang, D., Kong, W., You, J., Wong, M.: Online palmprint identification. IEEE Trans. Pattern Anal. Mach. Intell. **25**(9), 1041–1050 (2003)
26. Zhou, Y., Kumar, A.: Human identification using palm-vein images. IEEE Trans. Inf. Forensics Secur. **6**(4), 1259–1274 (2011)
27. Sun, J., Abdulla, W.: Palm vein recognition by combining curvelet transform and Gabor filter. In: 2nd International Conference on Interaction Sciences: Information Technology, Culture and Human, pp. 314–321. Jinan, China (2013)
28. Zhou, Y., Liu, Y., Feng, Q., Yang, F., Huang, J., Nie, Y.: Palm-vein classification based on principal orientation features. PLoS ONE **9**(11), e112429 (2014)

MultiBioGM: A Hand Multimodal Biometric Model Combining Texture Prior Knowledge to Enhance Generalization Ability

Zexing Zhang[1], Huimin Lu[1(✉)], Pengcheng Sang[1], and Jinghang Wang[2]

[1] School of Computer Science and Engineering, Changchun University of Technology, Changchun 130102, China
luhuimin@ccut.edu.cn
[2] School of Information Science and Technology, Northeast Normal University, Changchun 130024, China
wangjh@nenu.edu.cn

Abstract. Authentication through hand texture features is one of the crucial directions in biometric identification, and some recognition methods based on traditional machine learning or deep learning have been proposed. However, the generalization ability of these methods is not satisfying due to the different entities, backgrounds, and sensors. In this paper, based on the three modalities of fingerprint, fingervein, and palmprint, the texture prior knowledge extractor (PKE) is innovatively designed as a unified paradigm for texture extraction, aiming to improve the model generalization ability through prior knowledge. The feature vectors of texture images are obtained for matching by a knowledge embedding extractor (KEG) based on the Siamese Network. The credibility algorithm is proposed for multimodal decision-level feature fusion. Cascading PKE and KEG is our proposed multimodal biometric generalization model MultiBioGM. Experimental results on three multimodal datasets demonstrate the effectiveness of our model for biometrics, which achieves 0.098%, 0.024%, and 0.117% EERs on unobserved data.

Keywords: Biometric · Multimodal fusion · Generalization · Prior knowledge

1 Introduction

Domain $\mathcal{D}$ can be defined as a hypothetical feature space $\mathcal{X}$ and a marginal probability distribution $p(\mathbf{X})$, where the sampling space $\mathbf{X} = \{x_1, ..., x_N\} \in \mathcal{X}$. Biometric recognition has made great progress with the rise of machine learning, but most are based on the assumption that the sample data are independent and identically distributed. If the $p(\mathbf{X})$ of the test data domain differs from the training domain, e.g., different environmental backgrounds and different sensors used for sampling, the performance of the model will be degraded [1], which often needs to be solved by retraining or fine-tuning the model. For traditional methods, different data domains require different parameters to be set to extract features for recognition, and method procedures also need to be improved if necessary. Alternatively, overfitting is due to the pursuit of high recognition accuracy in the training set to the extent that it performs poorly on new samples that the model has not observed in an individual. Convex optimization and regularization is a good solution in this case.

To address the above issues, we propose MultiBioGM, a hand multimodal biometric generalization model that can be used across datasets, which enhances the generalization performance through human prior knowledge and solves the open-set problem through deep metric learning. Excellent recognition results can be achieved without retraining or parameter tuning on unobserved data. To the best of our knowledge, MultiBioGM is the first hand multimodal recognition model that combines fingerprints, fingerveins, and palmprints.

From the human prior knowledge, it is known that the hand texture features of different individuals are unique. Therefore, we utilize the U-Net network with an attention mechanism to learn stable texture intermediate domains $\mathcal{D}_M$ as the prior knowledge and change it to a multichannel stacked input structure to accomplish the multimodal texture extraction task through a single model. In order to balance the three modal of supervised training, we propose the probabilistic balancing algorithm. For the pixel sample imbalance problem, the original cross-entropy loss is replaced by focal loss, and the γ factor is modified to a smoothed γ factor. We named the improved prior knowledge extractor Balanced Stacked Network (BSNet). Feature vectors of the prior knowledge are obtained through the Siamese Network to be matched using the proposed multimodal decision-level feature fusion credibility algorithm. We provide the related code at https://github.com/ZacheryZhang/MultiBioGM. The multimodal dataset is combined using multiple publicly available unimodal datasets that do not intersect, and the specific dataset information is shown in Table 1.

Table 1. Information about the combined multimodal datasets

Multimodal	Fingerprint	Fingervein	Palmprint	Categories	Samples
Union DB1	FVC2000-DB1 [2]	FV-USM [3]	IITD [4]	80	400
Union DB2	NUPT-FPV [5]	SCUT FVD [6]	MPD [7]	100	500
Union DB3	NIST SD-10 [8]	MMCBNU [9]	TCPD [10]	550	5500

The rest of the paper is organized as follows. In Sect. 2, we discuss the related work and the feasibility of our model. Section 3 describes the proposed model MultiBioGM in detail, and Sect. 4 shows our experiments on three different multimodal datasets and analyzes the results. Finally, Sect. 5 summarizes the present work and provides recommendations for future research.

2   Related Work

One of the reasons for the rise of deep learning is the automation of the feature extraction process, the convolutional neural network (CNN) is the most popular deep learning model in computer vision, Radzi et al. [11] successfully introduced CNN into biometrics earlier. However, the performance of neural networks in unconstrained environments is challenged and often requires more training data and a more refined network structure to improve performance [12]. Domain transfer is another approach to address the performance degradation of neural networks under unconstrained conditions. Shao Huikai et al. [13] proposed using an autoencoder as a domain transfer method to accomplish cross-domain recognition of palmprints. Nevertheless, such methods must train new knowledge transfer models for different data domain samples.

Bimodal fingerprint and palmprint [14], fingervein and palmprint [15], and fingerprint and fingervein [16] recognition methods have been proposed and achieved recognition accuracies of 98.82%, 94.12%, and 99.70%, respectively. Multimodal biometrics can outperform the traditional single-modal methods, but most do not consider the generalization performance of the models. The probability distributions are often different for heterogeneous datasets, and traditional deep learning methods need to learn as many different distributions as possible [11]. However, the differences are often due to redundant image information. It is feasible to use human prior knowledge to select features and thus ignore redundant information, e.g., Rijun Liao et al. [17] proposed a gait recognition method based on pose estimation, which reduces the influence of the view background and clothing by extracting spatiotemporal features of the pose by human design in order to improve the robustness of the system.

In the multimodal fusion problem, the model-independent approach is the basic idea of traditional multimodal fusion [18], which can be divided into feature fusion, decision fusion, and hybrid methods, and the credibility algorithm proposed in this paper is a decision fusion method.

3   Proposed Method

MultiBioGM accomplishes multimodal recognition tasks with a secondary structure, including a texture prior knowledge extractor PKE and a knowledge embedding generator KEG (see Fig. 1). PKE processes the different modality original images to obtain the prior knowledge images as the input of KEG. The embedding vectors obtained by KEG and those stored in the template repository are fed into the credibility algorithm to obtain matching results.

3.1   Prior Knowledge Extractor (PKE)

BSNet is proposed to simultaneously accomplish the task of image semantic segmentation of fingerprint, fingervein, and palmprint by superimposing the channels based on U-Net. For the goal of better unrelated information elimination, we use the attention mechanism to learn the $\mathcal{D}_M$ representation.

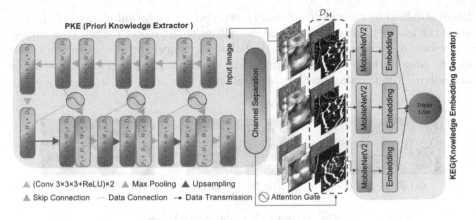

Fig. 1. The structure of MultiBioGM

$\mathcal{D}_M$ is obtained by eliminating the feature dimensions with low or redundant recognition contributions from the original sample space to obtain the dimensionality reduction subspace. Compared with the disordered distribution and large class spacing of the original data (Fig. 2b), the dimensionality reduction results in a uniform distribution of the data falling into the hypersphere (Fig. 2a), which enables the data to be mapped into a uniform feature space. Unlike linear transformation dimensionality reduction such as PCA, this method intuitively enhances the dimensionality reduction interpretability. The unobserved data can be more uniformly distributed in $\mathbf{X}$, improving the recognition model' generalization performance. The image segmentation soft labels are obtained by extracting the texture grayscale images of fingerprints, fingerveins, and palmprints using traditional methods, where the grayscale images' values are viewed as the probabilities of being a texture. However, since the probabilities in the soft

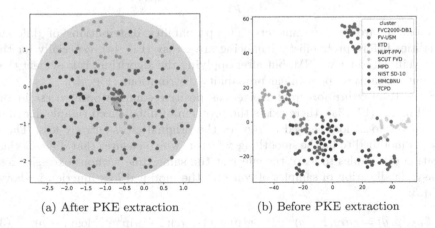

(a) After PKE extraction   (b) Before PKE extraction

Fig. 2. Different datasets after t-SNE visualization

labels obtained by different traditional methods tend to be unbalanced (Fig. 3), it leads the model to segment only the modalities with greater overall gray values. Therefore, our proposed probabilistic balancing algorithm processes the labels in real time during training, clarifying the pixel points' predicted probabilities and solving the training underfitting problem.

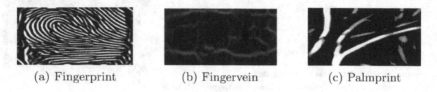

(a) Fingerprint   (b) Fingervein   (c) Palmprint

Fig. 3. Probability imbalance labels

The probabilistic balancing algorithm first selects the top λ gray values in the corresponding channels of the three modes to compute the mean triple $(\bar{p}_0, \bar{p}_1, \bar{p}_2)$ and selects the maximum mean among them, $\bar{p} = max\,(\bar{p}_k)$, where $k = 0, 1, 2$, and the channels corresponding to $\bar{p}$ are maximally probabilistically complemented through Eq. 1.

$$M = M\left(1 + \frac{1 - \bar{p}}{\bar{p}}\right) \tag{1}$$

where M is the channel image, after the maximum probability complementation then recalculate the highest μ gray values of the mean triple $(\bar{p}_0{}', \bar{p}_1{}', \bar{p}_2{}')$, and the probabilities of the different channels are then separately balanced with weighting through Eq. 2.

$$M_k = M_k \frac{\max\left(\bar{p}_k{}'\right)}{\bar{p}_k{}'}, k = 0, 1, 2. \tag{2}$$

λ and μ are hyperparameters. The probability distributions of different modalities before probabilistic balancing are messy (Fig. 4a), especially for the finger vein dataset FV-USM, but after applying the algorithm, it is evident that different modalities obey similar probability distributions (Fig. 4b).

Since the texture foreground pixels as positive samples occupy less in the overall image (Fig. 3a), there exists the problem of unbalanced sample distribution, so the focal loss is used to replace the original cross-entropy loss. The γ factor is modified to be the smoothing γ factor, which ensures that difficult classification of samples to learn the effect at the same time without excessive loss of easy classification of samples of concern, the modified loss function is shown in Eq. 3.

$$\mathcal{L}_{bfc}(p, y) = -\alpha y(1 - p)^{\log(\gamma)} \log(p) - (1 - \alpha)(1 - y)p^{\log(\gamma)} \log(1 - p) \tag{3}$$

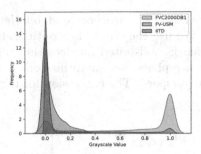 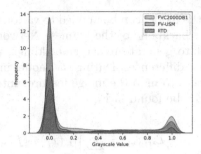

(a) Before the probabilistic balance (b) After the probabilistic balance

Fig. 4. Kernel density estimation (KDE) image presentation in Union DB1 dataset

p is the predicted probability, and y is the true labeling probability. In addition, adjusting α can make the positive examples learn better.

3.2 Knowledge Embedding Generator (KEG)

Algorithm 1. Credibility algorithm

Input: The group of trimodal images to be matched (x, y, z), i-th match in the template database (x_i, y_i, z_i).

Output: Result of matching success or failure.

1: $result \leftarrow$ success
2: $credibility \leftarrow 0$
3: $step \leftarrow 1$
4: $dists \leftarrow \left\| \hat{f}(x, y, z) - \hat{f}(x_i, y_i, z_i) \right\|_2$
5: **for** $dist$ in $dists$ **do**
6:   **if** $dist <= threshold$ **then**
7:     $credibility \leftarrow credibility + step$
8:   **end if**
9: **end for**
10: **if** $credibility = step$ **then**
11:   **if** $\left\| \hat{f}(y) - \hat{f}(y_i) \right\|_2 > threshold$ **then**
12:     $result \leftarrow$ failure
13:   **end if**
14: **else if** $credibility = 0$ **then**
15:   $result \leftarrow$ failure
16: **end if**
17: **return** $result$

In the KEG section, we use MobileNetV2, a widely used computer vision model known for its ability to extract image features. This model uses a deeply separable convolution technique that helps to create a lightweight network. To ensure that the model can be applied to various scenarios, we incorporate MobileNetV2 as the backbone of the Siamese Network. We use the triplet loss optimization target to generate image embeddings, which is well-suited for detecting slight texture differences. During the model inference phase, we only utilize one of the branches to map the image features into hyperspace. The expression for triplet loss can be found in Eq. 4.

$$\mathcal{L}_{\text{triplet}} = \sum_{i}^{N} \left[|f(x_i^a) - f(x_i^p)|^2 - |f(x_i^a) - f(x_i^n)|^2 + \delta \right] \tag{4}$$

The input is triple (x_i^a, x_i^p, x_i^n), which are the anchor sample, the positive sample, negative sample, and i stands for being the i-th input. x_i^p are samples from the same individual as the anchor example, x_i^n are samples from different individuals. $f(x)$ represents the image embedding generated by the backbone network, and δ is a positive real constant that serves to prevent model training from taking shortcuts by placing the embeddings of x_i^n closer to x_i^p resulting in a lower loss.

Let $\hat{f}$ be the trained KEG and $\hat{f}(x)$ be the embedding vector of the input image x. In order to realize accurate multimodal recognition, we propose the credibility algorithm for decision-level feature fusion, which is described in Algorithm 1.

4   Experiments

4.1   Implementation Details

In our experiments, the biometric images were uniformly resampled to 256×512 size, and the images were all feature enhanced using the CLAHE algorithm. We trained the BSNet using only 80% of the data from Union DB1, in addition, only 60% of the fingervein data from Union DB1 was selected for training the Siamese Network, and the rest of the data was used for testing. The hyperparameters of the BSNet in the PKE were set to $\alpha = 0.25, \lambda = 5, \mu = 20, \gamma = 10$, batch size was four and trained for 250 epochs, and the learning rate was set to 0.0002. The KEG's Siamese Network width multiplier is set to 1, and 10 epochs are fine-tuned on the model based on ImageNet. All experiments were performed on eight Nvidia Tesla v100 GPUs.

4.2   Evaluation and Analysis

The performance of MultiBioGM on unimodal datasets was first tested (see Fig. 5). On the left side are the ROC curves of the model on different datasets, which shows that the model still has a notable capability on unimodal, and on the right are the samples of the original images. The examples of the prior knowledge images extracted by PKE, which are fingerprint, fingervein, and palmprint from top to bottom, show that it is clear the irrelevant information has been effectively

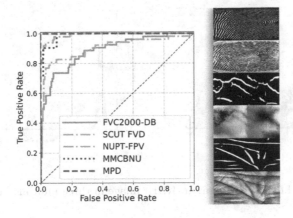

Fig. 5. Single modal testing

removed, and the texture information used for recognition has been accurately preserved.

To demonstrate the effectiveness of MultiBioGM, the performance of no prior knowledge and plain U-Net based on the same KEG and multimodal decision benchmarks were tested, as shown in Table 2.

Table 2. Biometric performance testing

	Union DB1			Union DB2			Union DB3		
	EER(%)	F1(%)	AUC(%)	EER(%)	F1(%)	AUC(%)	EER(%)	F1(%)	AUC(%)
KEG	7.21	80.528	77.460	13.68	75.371	71.550	26.13	63.705	67.132
U-Net+KEG	4.368	83.965	81.463	6.769	73.465	79.104	11.928	80.747	74.013
MultiBioGM	0.098	97.655	99.487	0.024	95.817	98.680	0.117	94.864	95.054

A horizontal comparison reveals that the recognition methods without prior knowledge, especially on the large-scale dataset Union DB3, all have declined in the generalization performance of the model, and the model does not have a good performance improvement against different data distributions. By removing the irrelevant background, plain U-Net performs well on the datasets involved in training, with a slight performance improvement on the other datasets. Vertically, if prior texture knowledge is not well learned, i.e., features are missing, the model's recognition performance is even worse than that of a model with no prior knowledge, but with our proposed PKE, the model will learn accurate texture knowledge and obey a uniform data distribution (Fig. 6). Combined with our proposed MultiBioGM framework and plausibility algorithm, the EER was reduced by 13.656% and 26.013% on heterogeneous datasets.

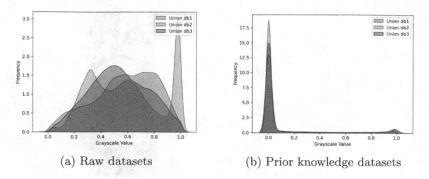

(a) Raw datasets　　　　　　　　(b) Prior knowledge datasets

Fig. 6. Kernel density estimation (KDE) image in three multimodal datasets

5　Conclusion

This work introduces human prior knowledge into a multimodal biometric model based on hand features and achieves good generalization performance. U-Net is improved to achieve good prior knowledge learning, and a credibility algorithm is proposed to achieve multimodal decision fusion. The prior texture knowledge learning is the decisive factor for the subsequent recognition effect, so the better and lighter PKE texture extraction structure is a promising improvement direction in the future, and the generative model can also complement the feature information inference to improve the model performance.

Acknowledgments. This research was supported by the 2023 Jilin Provincial Development and Reform Commission Industrial Technology Research and Development Project (No. 2023C042-6) and the 2023 Jilin Provincial Department of Education Science and Technology Research Planning Key Project (No. JJKH20230763KJ).

References

1. Anand, V., Kanhangad, V.: PoreNet: CNN-based pore descriptor for high-resolution fingerprint recognition. IEEE Sens. J. **20**(16), 9305–9313 (2020)
2. Maio, D., Maltoni, D., Cappelli, R., Wayman, J.L., Jain, A.K.: FVC 2000: fingerprint verification competition. IEEE Trans. Pattern Anal. Mach. Intell. **24**(3), 402–412 (2002)
3. Asaari, M.S.M., Suandi, S.A., Rosdi, B.A.: Fusion of band limited phase only correlation and width centroid contour distance for finger based biometrics. Expert Syst. Appl. **41**(7), 3367–3382 (2014)
4. Kumar, A.: Incorporating cohort information for reliable palmprint authentication. In: 2008 Sixth Indian Conference on Computer Vision, Graphics & Image Processing, pp. 583–590. IEEE (2008)
5. Ren, H., Sun, L., Guo, J., Han, C.: A dataset and benchmark for multimodal biometric recognition based on fingerprint and finger vein. IEEE Trans. Inf. Forensics Secur. **17**, 2030–2043 (2022)

6. Qiu, X., Kang, W., Tian, S., Jia, W., Huang, Z.: Finger vein presentation attack detection using total variation decomposition. IEEE Trans. Inf. Forensics Secur. **13**(2), 465–477 (2017)
7. Zhang, Y., Zhang, L., Zhang, R., Li, S., Li, J., Huang, F.: Towards palmprint verification on smartphones. arXiv preprint arXiv:2003.13266 (2020)
8. Watson, C.I.: NIST special database 10. NIST supplemental fingerprint card data (SFCD)(for special database 9-8-bit gray scale images) (2008)
9. Lu, Y., Xie, S.J., Yoon, S., Wang, Z., Park, D.S.: An available database for the research of finger vein recognition. In: 2013 6th International Congress on Image and Signal Processing (CISP), vol. 1, pp. 410–415. IEEE (2013)
10. Zhang, L., Li, L., Yang, A., Shen, Y., Yang, M.: Towards contactless palmprint recognition: a novel device, a new benchmark, and a collaborative representation based identification approach. Pattern Recogn. **69**, 199–212 (2017)
11. Radzi, S.A., Hani, M.K., Bakhteri, R.: Finger-vein biometric identification using convolutional neural network. Turk. J. Electr. Eng. Comput. Sci. **24**(3), 1863–1878 (2016)
12. Bazrafkan, S., Thavalengal, S., Corcoran, P.: An end to end deep neural network for iris segmentation in unconstrained scenarios. Neural Netw. **106**, 79–95 (2018)
13. Shao, H., Zhong, D., Du, X.: Cross-domain palmprint recognition based on transfer convolutional autoencoder. In: 2019 IEEE International Conference on Image Processing (ICIP), pp. 1153–1157. IEEE (2019)
14. Gayathri, R., Ramamoorthy, P.: A fingerprint and palmprint recognition approach based on multiple feature extraction. Eur. J. Sci. Res. **76**(4), 514–526 (2012)
15. Al-Mahafzah, H., AbuKhalil, T., Alksasbeh, M., Alqaralleh, B.: Multi-modal palmprint and hand-vein biometric recognition at sensor level fusion. Int. J. Electr. Comput. Eng. **13**(2), 2088–8708 (2023)
16. Nguyen, D.T., Park, Y.H., Lee, H.C., Shin, K.Y., Kang, B.J., Park, K.R.: Combining touched fingerprint and finger-vein of a finger, and its usability evaluation. Adv. Sci. Lett. **5**(1), 85–95 (2012)
17. Zhang, D., Kong, W.K., You, J., Wong, M.: Online palmprint identification. IEEE Trans. Pattern Anal. Mach. Intell. **25**(9), 1041–1050 (2003)
18. Baltrušaitis, T., Ahuja, C., Morency, L.P.: Multimodal machine learning: a survey and taxonomy. IEEE Trans. Pattern Anal. Mach. Intell. **41**(2), 423–443 (2018)

Face Detection, Recognition and Tracking

RRFAE-Net: Robust RGB-D Facial Age Estimation Network

Wenwen He[1], Lunke Fei[1(✉)], Shuping Zhao[1], Wei Zhang[1], Shaohua Teng[1], and Imad Rida[2]

[1] School of Computer Science and Technology, Guangdong University of Technology, Guangzhou, China
flksxm@126.com
[2] Centre de Recherches de Royallieu, Université de Technologie de Compiègne, 20529-60205 Compiègne, France

Abstract. Learning age estimation from face images has attracted much attention due to its favorable of various practical applications such as age-invariant identity-related representation. However, most existing facial age estimation methods usually extract age features from the RGB images, making them sensitive to the gender, race, pose and illumination changes. In this paper, we propose an end-to-end multi-feature integrated network for robust RGB-D facial age estimation, which consists of a 2D triple-type characteristic learning net and a 3D depth features leaning net. The triple-type characteristic learning net aims to extensively exploit multiple aging-related information including the gender, race features as well as the preliminary age features from RGB images, while the depth-feature learning net learns the pose and illumination-invariant age-related features from depth images. By incorporating these multi-dimensional feature nets, our proposed integrated network can extract the robust and complementary age features between RGB and depth modalities. Extensive experimental results on the widely used databases clearly demonstrate the effectiveness of our proposed method.

Keywords: Age estimation · RGB-D images · Multimodal · Multi-feature fusion

1 Introduction

Age estimation attempts to predict the real age value of a subject from one's face images, which has drawn wide research attentions in recent years due to its broad practical applications such as age-invariant identity-related representation, demographics analysis and human-computer interface [1]. Over the past decades, there have been a number of methods proposed for facial age estimation, which can be roughly classified into two categories: single-feature-based and multi-feature-based methods. The single-feature-based methods mainly extract the age features from an RGB image for age estimation. For example, Akbari et

al. [2] proposed an optimal transport-based learning framework for chronological age estimation from a face image. Giovanna et al. [3] designed a fully automated system to perform face detection and subsequent age estimation based on
RGB image. However, the face age of facial images is the typical demographic
attribute, which is usually affected by several factors such as gender and race in
age estimation [4,5].

To improve the accuracy of age estimation, many recent studies have focused
on multi-feature learning [6,7]. For example, Kong et al. [8] proposed a deep
multi-stream ordinal facial age estimation network by learning multiple global
and contextual feature through a spatial attention mechanism. Deng et al. [6]
proposed a two-stream convolutional neural network to simultaneously learn the
age and gender features for age estimation. More state-of-the-arts can be found in
the recent facial age estimation survey [9]. However, these multi-feature methods
are usually sensitive to variations in pose and illuminations. It is well recognized
that depth image is robust to variations in illuminations pose and can provide
the complementary depth information of the facial features, and recent studies
also show that multi-features learned from RGB-D images can achieve significant
performance improvement on various vision task [10]. Motivated by this, in this
paper, we utilize both RGB and depth images for aging feature learning and age
estimation.

In this paper, we propose a joint multi-feature learning network for robust
facial age estimation based on RGB-D face images. Specifically, we simultaneously learn multiple features including the preliminary age features, race features
and gender features from RGB images, and learn the depth features from the corresponding depth images. Then, inspired by the fact that attention mechanism
can focus most on specific feature learning, we concatenate these feature maps
based on a channel attention module to learn the robust aging features. Finally,
we use a regression-rank age estimator to predict the final age number, which
can better utilize the order and continuity of age labels. Experimental results on
the widely used database show that our proposed network successfully learns the
robust age features from RGB-D face images and achieves promising estimation
performance.

The main contributions can be summarized as follows:

- We propose a joint 2D and 3D feature learning network for robust facial age
  estimation based on RGB-D images. By integrating the complementary 2D
  and 3D features, our proposed method can learn more discriminative age
  features, and show promising robustness to variations in gender, race, pose
  and illuminations.
- Unlike traditional multi-feature fusion, we use a channel attention module to
  fuse the preliminary age, gender, race and depth feature map for adaptive
  feature refinement and further learn robust age feature from the refined joint
  features.
- We conduct extensive experiments on the baseline databases and the experimental results clearly show that our proposed method achieves higher age
  estimation accuracies than other state-of-the-arts.

The remainder of this paper is organized as follows. Section 2 reviews the related work. Section 3 shows the details of our proposed method. Section 4 presents the experimental results. Section 5 draws the conclusion of this paper.

2 Related Work

In this section, we briefly review two related topics, including the feature learning of RGB-D images and the facial age estimation.

2.1 Feature Learning of RGB-D Images

RGB images have been widely used for feature learning and representation in pattern recognition and computer vision tasks. However, they only contain the 2D information of the objects, which usually show large intra-class variances due to pose and illumination changes. To address this, RGB-D images, which contains not only 2D RGB descriptions but also the depth-based information, has been successfully used for feature learning. In recent year, there have been a number of feature learning methods based on RGB-D images for pattern recognition. For example, Grati et al. [11] designed a RGB-D learned local representation for face recognition based on facial patch description and matching. Uppal et al. [10] proposed a two-level attention-based fusion learning for RGB-D face recognition, which uses LSTM recurrent learning to fuse the feature maps of two modalities. In this work, we jointly learn multi-type and multi-dimensional features from RGB-D images for facial age estimation.

2.2 Facial Age Estimation

The facial age estimation aims to estimate the age number of a face, which can be treated as the typical multiple classification problem. For example, Zheng et al. [12] proposed a PCANet for age estimation, which treating each age as an independent category. However, age is a continuous and ordered value. Therefore, to make use of the continuity or order of age label, there has been various regression-based and ranking-based methods proposed for age estimation in recent years. For example, Xie et al. [13] used a expected value on the softmax probabilities to calculate the regression age. Chen et al. [14] proposed a ranking-CNN model by converting age estimation problem into multiple binary classification tasks. Inspired by existing studies, in this paper, we simultaneously utilize regression and ranking age prediction schemes to convert the age features into the final age number.

3 Proposed Method

In this section, we first present the overall framework of the proposed method. Then, we show how to perform the multi-feature learning and fusion of RGB-D images for age estimation.

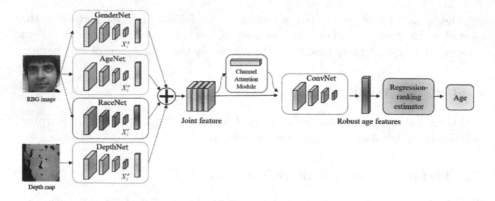

Fig. 1. An overview of the proposed method. We first use four subnetworks to learn the gender, preliminary age, race and depth features from the RGB-D images. Then, we fuse these features based on the channel attention module and learn robust age feature from the refined joint feature. Finally, we input the robust age feature into the regression-ranking estimator to predict the final age.

3.1 The Framework of Proposed Network

Human aging estimation has several affected factors such as identity, gender, race, and extrinsic factors. In addition, RGB-based age estimation methods are sensitive to pose and illumination changes [10,15]. To overcome these, we aim to learn multiple features from RGB-D images and fuse them to form the more robust features for age estimation. Figure 1 shows the basic idea of the proposed method, which mainly consists of multi-feature learning and fusion. For multi-feature learning, we utilize three subnetworks to learn gender, race and preliminary age features from RGB images, respectively. Then, we utilize one subnetwork to learn depth features from the corresponding depth images. For multi-feature fusion, we first use a channel attention module to connect the multiple types of feature maps. Then, we utilize a ConvNet to further learn the robust age features. Finally, we fed the robust age features into the regression-ranking estimator [14] to predict the final age. In the following, we present the detailed procedures of the multi-feature learning and fusion of our proposed method.

3.2 Multi-feature Learning

To learn more discriminative and robust features, we employ four subnetworks to learn the preliminary age feature, gender feature, race feature and depth feature from RGB-D images. As shown in Fig. 1, each subnetwork consists of 4 convolution blocks and 1 fully connected layer. Each convolution block includes a convolutional layer, a nonlinear activation, a batch normalization, and a pooling layer. For the GenderNet, the output of fully connected layer is a two-bits vector such as [1, 0] for male and [0, 1] for female. For the RaceNet, the output of fully connected layer is a three-bits vector such as [1, 0, 0] for Asian, [0,1,0] for African and [0, 0, 1] for European. For the AgeNet and DepthNet, the output of fully connected layer is a one hundred-bits vector, which represents the preliminary age such as [1, 0, ..., 0] for 1 year old and [0, 0, ..., 1] for 100 years old. Inspired by the fact that the feature map of the last convolution layer contains more discriminative features, we select the feature maps from the last convolution blocks of each subnetwork to represent the gender features, the race features, the preliminary age features and the complementary depth features. After that, we fuse these features based on channel attention mechanism for robust age estimation.

3.3   Multi-feature Fusion

Having learned multiple features from RGB-D images, we further fuse the gender features, race features, the preliminary age features and the complementary depth feature maps based on the channel attention module. Thus, the learning network can focus most on those feature maps with more contribution. Specifically, we first denote X_i^g, X_i^a, X_i^r and $X_i^d \in R^{c \times w \times h}$ as the gender, age, race and depth feature maps, respectively, and the joint feature map=$[X_i^g, X_i^a, X_i^r, X_i^d] \in R^{4c \times w \times h}$ is formed by channel connection. Then, the joint feature map is reshaped to $4C$ vectors by max-pooling and fed into channel attention module, which is composed of multi-layer perceptron with one hidden layer. The output of the attention module is $\theta_{am} \in R^{4C \times 1}$, which is normalized to $[0, 1]$ with the sigmoid function. Third, the refined joint feature maps are calculated as:

$$F' = F \times \theta_{am}, \tag{1}$$

where F is the joint feature map and F' indicates the refined the joint feature map. After that, we feed the refined joint features F' into the traditional ConvNet to further learn the robust age feature. Finally, we input the robust age features into the regression-ranking estimator to predict the final age.

4   Experiments

In this section, we conducted age estimation experiments on the IIIT-D (RGB-D) dataset [15,16] to evaluate the performance of our proposed method. Our method was implemented within the PyTorch framework and the parameters of the proposed networks were all initialized with the Xavier initialization. In addition, the Adam was used as the optimizer. The learning rate and batch size were empirically set to 0.001 and 16, respectively. The RLRP algorithm was used to automatically adjust the learning rate. All experiments were performed on the same machine with a GTX 2060s graphics card (including 2176 CUDA cores), a i5-9600KF CPU, and a 32 GB RAM.

4.1   Datasets and Preprocessing

The IIIT-D dataset contains 4,605 RGB-D images of 106 subjects. Due to its limited samples, to enlarge the sample set, we first flip each image to obtain two mirror-symmetric samples and then rotate them by $\pm 5°$ and $\pm 10°$. Moreover, we add Gaussian white noise with variance of 0.001, 0.005, 0.01, 0.015 and 0.02 on the original and the synthetic samples, such that each RGB-D image is finally extended to 40 samples. Figure 2 shows the typical samples selected from the IIIT-D dataset. In addition, we used MORPH2 (RGB) [17], FG-NET (RGB) [18], and LAP (RGB) [19] datasets to pre-train the GenderNet, AgeNet and RaceNet.

Fig. 2. Some typical RGB and the corresponding depth images selected from the IIIT-D dataset.

4.2   Comparisons with the State-of-the-Art

To evaluate the performance of our proposed method on age estimation, we compare the proposed method with four representative age estimation methods, including the MFCL [20], FRUK [15], DCCFL [21], and TAFL [10]. Following the standard age estimation proposal [22], we first train our method based on training samples. Then, we predict the age number of the testing samples to calculate the Mean Absolute Error (MAE) [23]. Table 1 tabulates the age estimation results of different methods on the IIIT-D databases.

Table 1. The MAEs of different age estimation methods on the IIIT-D databases.

Method	Modality	Fusion	MAEs
MFCL [20]	RGB	–	4.92
FRUK [15]	RGB-D	Score-based	4.34
DCCFL [21]	RGB-D	Feature-based	3.89
TAFL [10]	RGB-D	Attention-based	3.74
Ours	**RGB-D**	**Attention-based**	**3.56**

From Table 1, we can see that our proposed method consistently outperforms the compared RGB-D-based methods by achieving lower MAEs. This is because our proposed method can extensively exploit the age-related features, such as the gender, race, age and depth features. Moreover, our proposed network concatenates the multiple age-related feature maps based on a channel attention module, such that more adaptive aging features can be refined. In addition, we utilize a regression-ranking age estimator to predict the final age, such that our proposed method can make a better trade-off between the continuity and order of the age label. It is also noted that the RGB-D-based methods perform better performance than the RGB-based methods for age estimation. The possible reason is that RGB and depth images contains two modalities of information (face texture and 3D shape information), which provide more complementary robust age-related features, such that a better age estimation performance can be obtained.

4.3 Ablation Analysis

It is seen that the proposed network comprises of four components: the GenderNet, RaceNet, AgeNet and DepthNet. To better evaluate the effectiveness of each component, in this section, we conduct ablation experiments to analyze the performance of them. Specifically, we remove each component from the proposed network and use the remainder to perform age feature extraction and calculation, including the proposed networks (a) without embedding GenderNet (joint feature without X_i^g), (b) without embedding RaceNet (joint feature without X_i^r), (c) without embedding AgeNet (joint feature without X_i^a) and (d) without embedding DepthNet (joint feature without X_i^d). Figure 3(a) shows the MAEs of the comparative experiments based on different components of the proposed network on the IIIT-D dataset. We can see that the performance of the proposed method is obviously reduced when any component is removed from the network, demonstrating the effectiveness of the each component of the proposed network.

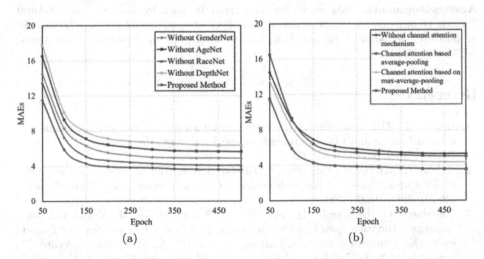

Fig. 3. The MAEs of the proposed method with (a) removing various components, and (b) various fusion mechanism on the IIIT-D dataset.

In addition, our proposed network uses the channel attention mechanism based on max-pooling to fuse multiple features for age estimation. To validate the effectiveness of our fusion method, we compare our fusion mechanism with three cases: including the proposed networks (a) without using channel attention mechanism, (b) with using channel attention mechanism based on average-pooling, (c) with using channel attention mechanism based on both max and average-pooling. Figure 3(b) depicts the experimental results of the proposed network with various fusion mechanism. It is observed that case (a) without using channel attention mechanism has the worst performance. This demonstrates that the channel attention mechanism can better extract the age-specific features. Compared with case (c) and our proposed method, case (b) with channel attention mechanism based on average-pooling achieves an obvious lower MAE. This is probably due to the fact that depth data is noisy. The case (b) based on the average-pooling possibly extracts more noise features than the max-pooling and max-average-pooling-based features.

5   Conclusion

In this paper, we propose a multi-modal learning framework for RGB-D age estimation. We first simultaneously learn multiple age-related features including the preliminary age features, race features and gender features from RGB images, and further learn the depth features from the corresponding depth images. Then we present a channel attention module based on max-pooling to effectively fuse the multiple features, such that more robust age-specific features can be obtained. Finally, we input the robust age features into regression-ranking estimator to predict the final age. Extensive experimental results on the widely used databases clearly demonstrate the effectiveness of our proposed method.

Acknowledgments. This work was supported in part by the National Natural Science Foundation of China under Grants 62176066, 62106052 and 61972102, and in part by the Natural Science Foundation of Guangdong Province under Grant 2023A1515012717.

References

1. Huang, Z., Zhang, J., Shan, H.: When age-invariant face recognition meets face age synthesis: a multi-task learning framework and a new benchmark. IEEE Trans. Pattern Anal. Mach. Intell. (2022)
2. Akbari, A., Awais, M., Fatemifar, S., Khalid, S.S., Kittler, J.: A novel ground metric for optimal transport-based chronological age estimation. IEEE Trans. Cybern. **52**(10), 9986–9999 (2021)
3. Castellano, G., De Carolis, B., Marvulli, N., Sciancalepore, M., Vessio, G.: Real-time age estimation from facial images using YOLO and EfficientNet. In: Tsapatsoulis, N., Panayides, A., Theocharides, T., Lanitis, A., Pattichis, C., Vento, M. (eds.) CAIP 2021. LNCS, vol. 13053, pp. 275–284. Springer, Cham (2021). https://doi.org/10.1007/978-3-030-89131-2_25

4. Huang, Z., Chen, S., Zhang, J., Shan, H.: PFA-GAN: progressive face aging with generative adversarial network. IEEE Trans. Inf. Forensics Secur. **16**, 2031–2045 (2020)
5. Deng, Y., et al.: Joint multi-feature learning for facial age estimation. In: Wallraven, C., Liu, Q., Nagahara, H. (eds.) ACPR 2021. LNCS, vol. 13188, pp. 513–524. Springer, Cham (2021). https://doi.org/10.1007/978-3-031-02375-0_38
6. Deng, Y., Fei, L., Teng, S., Zhang, W., Liu, D., Hou, Y.: Towards efficient age estimation by embedding potential gender features. In: ICASSP 2021–2021 IEEE International Conference on Acoustics, Speech and Signal Processing (ICASSP), pp. 2850–2854. IEEE (2021)
7. Deng, Y., Teng, S., Fei, L., Zhang, W., Rida, I.: A multifeature learning and fusion network for facial age estimation. Sensors **21**(13), 4597 (2021)
8. Kong, C., Wang, H., Luo, Q., Mao, R., Chen, G.: Deep multi-input multi-stream ordinal model for age estimation: based on spatial attention learning. Futur. Gener. Comput. Syst. **140**, 173–184 (2023)
9. Agbo-Ajala, O., Viriri, S.: Deep learning approach for facial age classification: a survey of the state-of-the-art. Artif. Intell. Rev. **54**, 179–213 (2021)
10. Uppal, H., Sepas-Moghaddam, A., Greenspan, M., Etemad, A.: Two-level attention-based fusion learning for RGB-D face recognition. In: 2020 25th International Conference on Pattern Recognition (ICPR), pp. 10120–10127. IEEE (2021)
11. Grati, N., Ben-Hamadou, A., Hammami, M.: Learning local representations for scalable RGB-D face recognition. Exp. Syst. Appl. **150**, 113319 (2020)
12. Zheng, D.P., Du, J.X., Fan, W.T., Wang, J., Zhai, C.M.: Deep learning with PCANet for human age estimation. In: Huang, D.-S., Jo, K.-H. (eds.) ICIC 2016. LNCS, vol. 9772, pp. 300–310. Springer, Cham (2016). https://doi.org/10.1007/978-3-319-42294-7_26
13. Xie, J.C., Pun, C.M.: Deep and ordinal ensemble learning for human age estimation from facial images. IEEE Trans. Inf. Forensics Secur. **15**, 2361–2374 (2020)
14. Chen, S., Zhang, C., Dong, M., Le, J., Rao, M.: Using ranking-CNN for age estimation. In: Proceedings of the IEEE Conference on Computer Vision and Pattern Recognition, pp. 5183–5192 (2017)
15. Goswami, G., Vatsa, M., Singh, R.: RGB-D face recognition with texture and attribute features. IEEE Trans. Inf. Forensics Secur. **9**(10), 1629–1640 (2014)
16. Goswami, G., Bharadwaj, S., Vatsa, M., Singh, R.: On RGB-D face recognition using Kinect. In: 2013 IEEE Sixth International Conference on Biometrics: Theory, Applications and Systems (BTAS), pp. 1–6. IEEE (2013)
17. Ricanek, K., Tesafaye, T.: Morph: a longitudinal image database of normal adult age-progression. In: 7th International Conference on Automatic Face and Gesture Recognition (FGR06), pp. 341–345. IEEE (2006)
18. Hsu, G.S.J., Wu, H.Y., Yap, M.H.: A comprehensive study on loss functions for cross-factor face recognition. In: Proceedings of the IEEE/CVF Conference on Computer Vision and Pattern Recognition Workshops, pp. 826–827 (2020)
19. Escalera, S., et al.: Chalearn looking at people 2015: apparent age and cultural event recognition datasets and results. In: Proceedings of the IEEE International Conference on Computer Vision Workshops, 1–9 (2015)
20. Xia, M., Zhang, X., Weng, L., Xu, Y., et al.: Multi-stage feature constraints learning for age estimation. IEEE Trans. Inf. Forensics Secur. **15**, 2417–2428 (2020)
21. Zhang, H., Han, H., Cui, J., Shan, S., Chen, X.: RGB-D face recognition via deep complementary and common feature learning. In: 2018 13th IEEE International Conference on Automatic Face & Gesture Recognition (FG 2018), pp. 8–15. IEEE (2018)

22. Rothe, R., Timofte, R., Van Gool, L.: Deep expectation of real and apparent age from a single image without facial landmarks. Int. J. Comput. Vision **126**(2–4), 144–157 (2018)
23. Tan, Z., Wan, J., Lei, Z., Zhi, R., Guo, G., Li, S.Z.: Efficient group-n encoding and decoding for facial age estimation. IEEE Trans. Pattern Anal. Mach. Intell. **40**(11), 2610–2623 (2017)

Human Identification Using Tooth Based on PointNet++

Xinyi Liu[1], Li Yuan[1(✉)], Chunyu Jiang[2], JiannanYu[3], and Yanfeng Li[3]

[1] School of Automation and Electrical Engineering, University of Science and Technology Beijing, Beijing 100083, China
lyuan@ustb.edu.cn
[2] Sino-German College Applied Sciences, Tongji University, Shanghai 201804, People's Republic of China
[3] The Fourth Medical Center, Chinese PLA General Hospital, Beijing 100037, China

Abstract. Human identification using tooth plays a crucial role in disaster victim identification. Traditional tooth recognition methods like iterative closest point (ICP) require laborious pairwise registration, so in this paper we focus on deep learning methods for human identification using tooth. We propose a complete workflow for tooth segmentation and recognition based on PointNet++ using the 3D intraoral scanning (IOS) model. Our method consists of two main components: an improved PointNet++ based tooth segmentation approach and a tooth recognition method that combines curvature feature extraction with improved PointNet++ using the segmented tooth part. To evaluate the identification method, we collect 240 IOS models, in which 208 models are used for training, and 32 models acquired for the second time are used for testing. The experimental results achieve a recognition accuracy of 96.88% on the test set, which demonstrates the potential of using the IOS model and deep learning methods for fully-automatedly human identification using tooth.

Keywords: 3D intraoral scan · human identification using tooth · tooth segmentation

1 Introduction

Human identification is one of the important issues in modern society. Technologies such as fingerprint recognition and facial recognition have been applied in various aspects of life, such as unlocking mobile devices and access control systems. However, in large-scale disasters, some commonly used biometric features for identity recognition, such as face, fingerprints and iris, can easily damaged, making it difficult to identify the victims. Human identification using tooth (hereinafter referred to as tooth recognition) is a reliable method of identification after large-scale disasters because tooth, being one of the hardest tissues in the human body, are better preserved. Currently, DNA comparison technology is the most widely used and effective individual identification technique in forensic science. However, the investigation of mixed traces still poses a challenge in forensic DNA analysis [1]. In addition, in cases such as identical twins and bone marrow transplants, DNA is unable to accurately identify individuals [2]. In these situations, tooth recognition remains a valuable complementary method.

Common dental imaging techniques include panoramic dental radiographs (PDR), cone-beam computed tomography (CBCT) and intraoral scanning (IOS). PDR employs X-rays to generate 2D images of the oral cavity, providing information about the teeth and their internal structures. CBCT provides high-resolution 3D images that can capture fine details of the teeth and oral structures. However, CBCT requires expensive equipment and specialized technical support, making it challenging to perform CBCT scans on victims after large-scale disasters. IOS (see Fig. 1) is a non-radiation-based method that is considered safer for patients. It enables fast acquisition of 3D images of the oral structures, making it convenient for capturing and comparing data of victims. Therefore, we choose IOS data for identity recognition research.

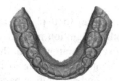

Fig. 1. An IOS model

Deep learning methods are employed for tooth segmentation and recognition in this study because they can automatically learn useful features without the need for manual feature engineering and exhibit better robustness in handling issues such as noise, deformation, and scale variations in dental models. Compared to traditional iterative closest point (ICP) [3, 4] methods that require laborious pairwise registration, deep learning methods are more suitable for large-scale dental sample identification tasks.

Since 3D intraoral scanning captures complete information of the teeth and gingiva, we first perform tooth segmentation on the IOS models, then utilize the segmented tooth regions for identity recognition. PointNet [5] is a classic method for deep learning on point clouds and can be used for segmentation and recognition of IOS models. However, the PointNet series utilizes max pooling to obtain global features for recognition, which ignores other features besides the maximum feature. In this paper, an improved model is proposed based on PointNet++ [6], where the input of the model is augmented with curvature information to enhance the important features such as tooth fissures that are crucial for recognition and the network structure replaces max pooling with a weighted feature aggregation mechanism (WFA) to better perform feature aggregation. The proposed method has two different networks for segmentation and recognition, enabling automatic segmentation of the tooth region in IOS models and identity recognition.

The main contributions of this paper are as follows:

1. A complete workflow for segmenting the tooth region in IOS models and performing identity recognition.
2. Using deep learning recognition networks to perform tooth recognition instead of superimposition to fill the gap in this field of research.

3. The introduction of curvature extraction and weighted feature aggregation to overcome the limitations of the PointNet++ model.

By employing the proposed method for segmenting IOS models and performing recognition, the identity recognition accuracy achieves 96.88% on 32 tooth models.

2　Related Works

Tooth recognition is commonly used to determine the identities of victims in large-scale disasters such as tsunamis and earthquakes. Traditional methods of tooth recognition rely on manual comparison of dental records. However, relying on manual identification is slow and inefficient. Since 2004, several studies [7, 8] have developed different methods for encoding teeth and dental arches in PDRs for personal identification. These methods utilize traditional computer vision techniques to manually design feature extraction and feature matching methods for individual identification. However, they lack generalizability and work well in small-sample environments but struggle to perform on larger datasets.

Given the advancements of deep learning in the field of face recognition, some studies have applied deep learning algorithms to tooth identification from 2D images. This approach avoids the need for manual feature design in traditional methods and enhances generalizability. Fan et al. proposed DentNet [9] using convolutional neural networks to extract features from PDRs for identity verification, achieving an accuracy of 85.16% on a test set of 173 individuals. Lai et al. proposed LCANet [10], which further improved the accuracy of deep learning-based tooth recognition algorithms. However, these methods primarily rely on 2D images for recognition, and compared to 3D images, they contain less information.

Currently, human identification using 3D tooth models involves performing 3D superimposition of pre-mortem and post-mortem models and quantitatively analyzing the degree of overlap for tooth recognition. The superimposition procedure requires point cloud registration, for example Cheng et al. [11] used correspondence-based six-degree-of-freedom (6-DoF) pose estimation for 3D point cloud registration. Gibelli et al. conducted 3D-3D superimposition of tooth morphology on a small sample size, specifically the maxillary first and second molars on both sides, demonstrating its potential applicability in tooth identification [12–14]. Reesu and Abduo employed the iterative closest point (ICP) algorithm for 3D model registration in both dental arch and tooth-level digital models and tooth recognition [3, 4]. Qnma et al. performed 3D superimposition of the entire dental arch and introduced mutual information to address noise and outliers in the traditional ICP algorithm for registration [15]. These methods have achieved good accuracy, but the comparison time exponentially increases when each tooth model needs to be superimposed and compared with all models in the database, making them unsuitable for large-scale sample identification. Deep learning has demonstrated high-level performance in medical image processing, such as disease diagnosis [16]. However, there is little research on 3D tooth recognition using deep learning models, and our research is dedicated to filling this gap.

3   A Complete Workflow for Tooth Segmentation and Recognition Based on PointNet++

Our approach consists of two parts: 1) A tooth segmentation method based on improved PointNet++. 2) A tooth recognition method that combines curvature feature extraction and an improved PointNet++. The tooth recognition process using this method is illustrated in Fig. 2. First, the tooth segmentation network is used to segment the tooth part of the IOS model. Then a set of segmented tooth parts with identity labels are used to train the tooth recognition network. Finally, a set of tooth parts with corresponding labels are used to test the identification result.

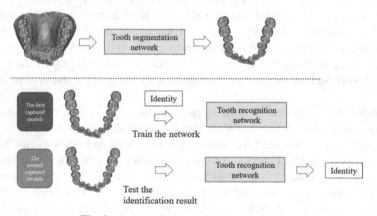

Fig. 2. System diagram of tooth recognition

3.1   Unit Network Structure and Set Abstraction Layer

Both tooth segmentation and recognition model need to extract features from the point cloud of IOS model. In the feature extraction section, both networks use the same unit structure. This unit structure consists of a multi-layer perceptron (MLP) followed by feature aggregation using the weighted feature aggregation (WFA) method, as shown in Fig. 3. With this unit structure, feature extraction can be performed on a set of points.

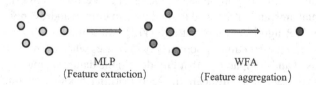

Fig. 3.   Unit network structure

This unit is performed in a local region of points with a center point. Let p_i denote the coordinate of the center point of the region, and let $P^i_{local} = \{p_{i1}, p_{i2}, \ldots p_{ik}\}$ represent the coordinates of k points in the whole local region. Each point p_{ij} is calculated by MLP to get a feature vector f_{ij}:

$$f_{ij} = \mathrm{MLP}(p_{ij}). \tag{1}$$

Then, WFA is performed to aggregate multiple features extracted by MLP into a single feature. It is accomplished by using a sub-network to learn weights and then applying these learned weights to perform weighted summation of the features. To perform feature aggregation for all features $\{f_{i1}, f_{i2}, \ldots f_{ik}\}$ within the region, the following formula is used to learn the weights:

$$\alpha_{ij} = \mathrm{MLP}((p_{ij} - p_i) \oplus (f_{ij} - f_i^{mean})), \tag{2}$$

here, $p_{ij} - p_i$ represents the subtraction of the coordinates of the neighborhood points from the corresponding center point coordinates, and f_i^{mean} is the mean of all features $\{f_{i1}, f_{i2}, \ldots f_{ik}\}$ within the region. The aggregated feature f_i is obtained by weighting the feature vectors f_{ij} with the weight vector α_{ij}, and can be expressed as:

$$f_i = \sum_{j=1}^{k} \alpha_{ij} \odot f_{ij}, \tag{3}$$

where $\odot$ denotes the Hadamard product.

The module used for feature extraction in both segmentation and recognition network is referred to as the set abstraction (SA) layer as shown in Fig. 4. The SA layer is composed of the aforementioned unit structure. It starts by down-sampling the point cloud using farthest point sampling (FPS) [6] to obtain a set of central points. These central points are then used as centers to divide the space into spherical regions. Within each spherical region, the unit structure mentioned earlier is applied to extract features. Each SA layer has adjustable parameters, including the number of sampled points, denoted as N_i, and the spherical radius, denoted as r. The SA layer enables the network to capture multi-scale feature information by processing different regions of the point cloud with varying N_i and r.

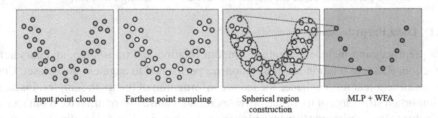

| Input point cloud | Farthest point sampling | Spherical region construction | MLP + WFA |

Fig. 4. Structure of the SA Layer

3.2 Tooth Segmentation Model

The proposed network architecture for tooth segmentation in this paper is shown in Fig. 5. The input of the network is the point cloud data of the tooth model, represented as an

Nx9 matrix. Here, N represents the number of points, and each point is represented by a 9-dimensional vector, including the 3D coordinates of the original position, 3D normal vectors, and 3D zero-centered coordinates.

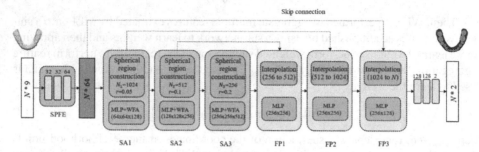

Fig. 5. Network structure of the tooth segmentation model

To better extract detailed information from the tooth model, there is a three-layer MLP serving as a single-point preliminary feature extraction (SPFE) module before the SA layers. More specific details of SPEF can be seen in our pervious study [17]. Following the SPFE are three SA layers that extract features at different scales. The number of sampled points in each layer is 1024/512/256, and the spherical radius is 0.05/0.1/0.2, respectively. After the SA layers, feature propagation (FP) [6, 17] layers which consist of interpolation, skip connection, and MLP are used for gradually restoring the original number of points in the point cloud. Finally, a three-layer MLP outputs the class labels (tooth or other) for each point.

3.3   Tooth Recognition Model

After tooth segmentation, the segmented tooth regions are used for human identification. The tooth recognition method involves preprocessing the segmented tooth regions, training the identification network on the preprocessed samples to learn identity information and testing the performance of the trained model on the testing samples.

3.3.1   Data Preprocessing

Data preprocessing includes sampling, random rotation and translation, and curvature extraction. Random rotation and translation are performed to augment the dataset. Curvature extraction aims to enhance the feature information of the tooth samples. Fissures are important structures of tooth and provide crucial feature information for tooth recognition due to their resistance to wear and change. As shown in Fig. 6, significant curvature variations are observed in the fissure regions (yellow and red), distinguishing it from other parts of tooth. Therefore, we extract curvature from the segmented tooth models to strengthen these important features.

After data preprocessing, the point cloud models can be represented as an Nx7 matrix, where the first three dimensions represent the coordinates of the point cloud, the fourth dimension represents curvature, and the last three dimensions represent the normal vector of each point.

Fig. 6. Visualization of curvature extraction of an IOS model (Color figure online)

3.3.2 Network Architecture for Tooth Recognition

The network architecture of the tooth recognition model consists of a feature extraction part and fully connected layers as shown in Fig. 7. In the feature extraction part, the input point cloud is processed to generate a global feature that is used for identification. The fully connected layers serve as the classification component of the model, taking the global feature as input and producing the output identity labels.

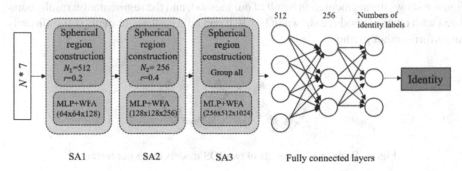

Fig. 7. Network structure of the tooth recognition model

The feature extraction part consists of three SA layers. The numbers of sampled points for the first two SA layers are 512 and 256, respectively, and the corresponding sphere radius values are 0.2 and 0.4. In the last SA layer, all the feature vectors obtained from the previous layer are aggregated to generate a global feature. The global feature is then passed through three fully connected layers which are responsible for learning the relationships and patterns within the global feature. Finally, the output of the last fully connected layer is the predicted class label that corresponds to the tooth model being identified.

4 Experimental Results

4.1 Datasets

For tooth segmentation, we have collected 202 IOS models from 101 volunteers (one upper tooth model and one lower tooth model for a volunteer), in which 160 for training and 52 for testing. Each model is sampled to 32,768 points.

For tooth recognition, we have collected 240 IOS models from 104 volunteers. For the first time, 208 models were collected from 104 people for training, and for the second time, 32 models were re-collected from 16 out of these 104 people for testing. Both training and testing models are sampled to 10,000 points.

4.2 Implementation Details

The two networks are implemented using PyTorch, with a GPU version of Tesla V100 and Windows operating system. Both networks use the Adam optimizer, NLL loss function and an initial learning rate of 0.001. Both networks use a learning rate reduced by a factor of 0.7 every 20 epochs and are trained for a total of 100 epochs. For the tooth segmentation network, the batch size is set to 4 during training. For the tooth recognition network, the batch size was set to 8 during training.

4.3 Tooth Segmentation Performance

Figure 8 shows the segmentation result of our method, and the segmentation results compared with other method are shown in Fig. 9. It can be seen that our method significantly outperforms other method.

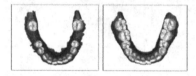

Fig. 8. Segmentation results of two IOS models using our method

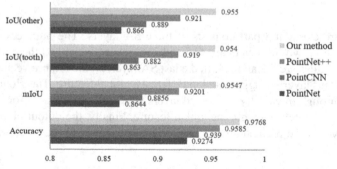

Fig. 9. Experimental results of tooth segmentation compared with PointNet, PointNet++ and PointCNN

4.4 Tooth Recognition Performance

Our recognition method tested on 32 tooth models achieves an accuracy of 96.88%, correctly identifies 31 models of the total 32 models. Table. 1 shows the recognition results of our method compared with PointNet and PointNet++. Figure 10 shows the training accuracy curve of our method and PointNet++ during training. By introducing curvature extraction and WFA, our method significantly improves recognition rate and has faster training speed as well.

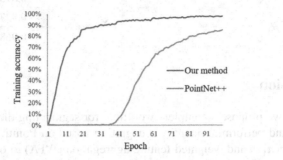

Fig. 10. Training accuracy curve of our method and PointNet++

Table 1. Experimental results of tooth recognition compared with PointNet and PointNet++

Model	Recognition rate
PointNet	0.7500
PointNet + +	0.8125
Our method	0.9688

4.5 Ablation Study

For tooth recognition, we conduct ablation study on curvature extraction and WFA. Table. 2 shows the experimental results of our method with neither curvature extraction nor WFA (Model 1), only with curvature extraction (Model 2), only with WFA (Model 3), and with both mechanisms (Model 4), respectively. Model 1 and Model 2 used max pooling instead of the WFA. Because WFA can better utilize the internal information of spherical neighbors and avoid information loss caused by max pooling, the recognition rate has been greatly improved. Curvature extraction used for data preprocessing further improves recognition rate by enhancing key information at the fissures.

Table 2. Ablation study for tooth recognition

Model	Curvature extraction	WFA	Recognition rate
1			0.8125
2	✓		0.8750
3		✓	0.9375
4	✓	✓	0.9688

5 Conclusion

In this paper, we propose a complete workflow for segmenting the tooth region in 3D IOS models and performing identity recognition based on PointNet++. We introduce curvature extraction and weighted feature aggregation (WFA) to overcome the limitations of the PointNet++ model. Tooth segmentation is performed to isolate the tooth region from the rest of the dental structure. This step allows for focused analysis and reduces the computational complexity of subsequent stages. Tooth identification stage first compute curvature to enhance the information of fissures, then feature extraction is carried out using MLP and aggregate by WFA to better use the information of each feature, finally fully connected layers outputs the recognition results. By leveraging deep learning techniques and curvature patterns, the proposed identification method reaches an accuracy of 96.88% on 32 testing dataset. The method has the potential to be applied in various scenarios, including forensic investigations, disaster victim identification, and dental records management. In our future research, as tooth arrangement may vary due to orthodontic treatments or destruction of the disasters. Therefore, our next research direction involves investigating tooth recognition using single tooth or developing recognition methods that are independent of tooth arrangement.

References

1. Anslinger, K., Bayer, B.: Whose blood is it? Application of DEPArray technology for the identification of individuals who contributed blood to a mixed stain. Legal Med. **133**(2), 419–426 (2019)
2. Lyu, T., Tian, X.: The necessity and possibility of dental identification in China. Forensic Med. **4**, 321 (2019)
3. Reesu, G.V., Woodsend, B., Scheila, M., et al.: Automated Identification from Dental Data (AutoIDD): A New Development in Digital Forensics. Forensic Sci. Int. **309**, 110218 (2020)
4. Abduo, J., Bennamoun, M.: Three-dimensional image registration as a tool for forensic odontology: a preliminary investigation. Am. J. Forensic Med. Pathol. **34**(3), 260–266 (2013)
5. Qi, C.R., Su, H., Mo, K., et al.: PointNet: deep learning on point sets for 3D classification and segmentation. In: IEEE Conference on Computer Vision and Pattern Recognition (CVPR), pp. 77–85. IEEE Press (2017)
6. Qi, C.R., Yi, L., Su, H., Guibas, L.J.: PointNet++: deep hierarchical feature learning on point sets in a metric space. In: Guyon, I., Von Luxburg, U., Bengio, S., et al., (Eds.) Advances in Neural Information Processing Systems, vol. 30, pp. 5099–5108. Curran Associates, Red Hook (2017)

7. Lee, S.S., Choi, J.H., et al.: The diversity of dental patterns in the orthopanthomography and its significance in human identification. Forensic Sci. (Wiley-Blackwell) **49**(4), 784–786 (2004)
8. Franco, A., Orestes, S.G.F., de Fátima Coimbra, E., et al.: Comparing dental identifier charting in cone beam computed tomography scans and panoramic radiographs using INTERPOL coding for human identification. Forensic Sci. Int., 1872–6283 (2020)
9. Fan, F., Ke, W.C., Wu, W., et al.: Automatic human identification from panoramic dental radiographs using the convolutional neural network. Forensic Sci. Int. **314**, 110416 (2020)
10. Lai, Y.C., Fan, F., Wu, Q.S., et al.: LCANet: learnable connected attention network for human identification using dental images. IEEE Trans. Med. Imaging **40**(3), 905–915 (2021)
11. Cheng, Y., Huang, Z., Quan, S., et al.: Sampling locally, hypothesis globally: accurate 3D point cloud registration with a RANSAC variant. Vis. Intell. **1**, 20 (2023)
12. Gibelli, D., De Angelis, D., Riboli, F., Dolci, C., Cattaneo, C., Sforza, C.: Quantification of odontological differences of the upper first and second molar by 3D–3D superimposition: a novel method to assess anatomical matches. Forensic Sci. **15**(4), 570–573 (2019)
13. Franco, A., Willems, G., Souza, P.H.C., Coucke, W., Thevissen, P.: Uniqueness of the anterior dentition three-dimensionally assessed for forensic bitemark analysis. Forensic Leg. Med. **46**, 58–65 (2017)
14. Chong, G., Forgie, A.: A pilot study to analyze the uniqueness of anterior teeth using a novel three-dimensional approach. Forensic Identif. **67**, 381–398 (2017)
15. Qnma, B., Llja, B., Yan, L.C., et al.: Three-dimensional superimposition of digital models for individual identification. Forensic Sci. Int. **318**, 110597 (2020)
16. Yang, Y., Cui, Z., Xu, J., et al.: Continual learning with Bayesian model based on a fixed pre-trained feature extractor. Vis. Intell. **1**, 5 (2023)
17. Yuan, L., Liu, X., Yu, J., Li, Y.: A full-set tooth segmentation model based on improved PointNet++. Vis. Intell. **1**, 21 (2023)

Intra-variance Guided Metric Learning
for Face Forgery Detection

Zhentao Chen and Junlin Hu[✉]

School of Software, Beihang University, Beijing, China
{chenzt,hujunlin}@buaa.edu.cn

Abstract. Since facial manipulation technology has raised serious concerns, facial forgery detection has also attracted increasing attention. Although recent work has made good achievements, the detection of unseen fake faces is still a big challenge. In this paper, we tackle facial forgery detection problem from the perspective of distance metric learning, and design a new Intra-Variance guided Metric Learning (IVML) method to drive classification and adopt Vision Transformer (ViT) as the backbone, which aims to improve the generalization ability of face forgery detection methods. Specifically, considering that there is a large gap between different real faces, our proposed IVML method increases the distance between real and fake faces while maintaining a certain distance within real faces. We choose ViT as the backbone as our experiments prove that ViT has better generalization ability in face forgery detection. A large number of experiments demonstrate the effectiveness and superiority of our IVML method in cross-dataset evaluation.

Keywords: face forgery detection · metric learning · dynamic margin · vit

1 Introduction

Recent years, face forgery generation methods have made some considerable progress. Advances in deep learning, generative adversarial networks [1] and the variational autoencoders [2], in particular, have made it very easy to generate high-quality forged faces. Using this technology, attackers can easily create fake news, smear celebrities, or compromise identity verification, leading to serious political, social, and security consequences. Therefore, in order to reduce the malicious abuse of face forgery, the development of effective detection methods is the best solution.

In earlier face forgery detection researches [3–6], face forgery detection is generally treated as a binary image classification task. Specifically, these methods typically use convolutional neural networks (CNNs) for image classification. Using the existing CNN backbone and directly taking a face image as input, it then classifies this face image as true or false. These methods can learn the data distribution of the training set to achieve considerable performance in in-domain

© The Author(s), under exclusive license to Springer Nature Singapore Pte Ltd. 2023
W. Jia et al. (Eds.): CCBR 2023, LNCS 14463, pp. 140–149, 2023.
https://doi.org/10.1007/978-981-99-8565-4_14

test. However, these simple classification guidelines tend to find specific detection points within the data set and have poor generalization, indicating that deep networks lack an understanding of forgery [7]. Since then, the mainstream of face forgery detection research has gradually shifted to a more reasonable search for falsified information, such as noise characteristics [8,9], local textures [10,11], and frequency information [6,12] to more specifically identify fake information in fake faces. Although the above methods achieve good results, they are easily limited to the seen forgery methods and difficult to detect unknown forgery schemes. However, in the practical application process, there will always be new forgery means and all kinds of noise disturbance, so the scheme without enough generalization ability is easy to appear low accuracy.

To solve the problems mentioned above, we put forward two main considerations to enhance the learning representation of face forgery detection. First of all, for feature extraction network, Vision Transformer can be considered. Since ViT series models divide images into multiple patches, it is easier and more likely to explore the relationship between patches, and face forgery detection needs to find out the differences between some patches and other patches. Secondly, in order to ensure that we can learn the difference between real faces and fake faces, it is necessary to use appropriate metric learning methods, so that the learned representation is able to capture the essential difference between real faces and fake faces, so as to guide the classification process through the difference of projected features.

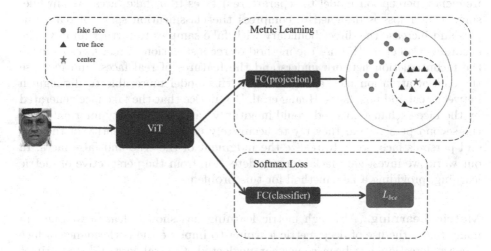

Fig. 1. The pipeline of our IVML method. A face image is inputted into the Vision Transformer, and the extracted features are passed into the classifier and projector composed of full connected layers (FC) respectively. L_{bce} is the binary cross entropy loss. The entire framework is trained under the joint optimization of metric learning loss and softmax loss.

In this paper, we study facial forgery detection problem from the perspective of distance metric learning, and propose an intra-variance guided metric learning (IVML) approach to drive classification and adopt ViT as the backbone. The proposed IVML approach increases the inter-class difference between true and false faces while ensuring that there are large differences of real faces. The pipeline of our IVML method is shown in Fig. 1. Extensive experiments prove the effectiveness of our proposed method, especially in cross-dataset evaluation.

2   Related Work

Face Forgery Detection. In order to improve the performance of face forgery detection [3,6,7], many efforts have been made. Earlier work, such as [4,13], utilizes state-of-the-art image classification backbones such as Xception [14] to extract features from the cropped facial images, and then classifies them directly through the fully connected network. However, such classification methods alone tend to overfit training data and fail to explore the nuances between real and fake face images. Therefore, many methods of distinguishing between true and false based on fake face patterns have been proposed. Zhao et al. [11] propose a multi-attention network architecture to capture local discrimination features from multiple face attention regions. Zhou et al. [9] introduce a two-stream deep network to detect fake faces by focusing on visual appearance and local noise, respectively. Li et al. [12] consider the details of frequency and propose a frequency perception model to separate real faces from fake faces. Meanwhile, single-center loss is designed to compress the classification space of real samples and increase the direct boundary with fake samples to further improve the accuracy. Cao et al. [15] use the method of reconstruction of real faces to make the reconstruction network understand the features of real faces, and increase the spatial attention mechanism to make the model more able to distinguish between real and fake faces. Huang et al. [16] notice that the fake face generated by the face exchange method would inevitably carry the identity information of the second person, and they try to accurately capture the identity of the second person's face, so as to realize the judgment of the true and false faces. In our work, we investigate facial forgery detection from the perspective of metric learning, providing a new method for this problem.

Metric Learning. Although metric learning has shown clear advantages in many tasks, the use of deep metric learning to improve the performance of face forgery detection has been somewhat neglected. Central loss [17] and triplet loss [18] are among the most commonly used methods in metric learning and center loss is highly relevant to our work. The purpose of center loss is to learn the characteristics of each class and push the characteristics of the same class closer to its own center. But an obvious disadvantage of central loss is that it only focuses on the proximity of the distance within the class, and does not consider whether the distance between the classes is large enough. Triplet loss drives the features of data samples with the same label closer to each other than features of data samples with different identities, while taking into account the reduction of intra-class distance and the expansion of inter-class distance. However, triplet losses can lead to problems with mining and huge data expansion. Kumar et al. [19] adopt a triplet loss supervision network to detect face forgery. But the triplet loss does not perform well on the pre-trained trunk. The single-center loss (SCL) proposed by Li et al. [12] takes into account the diversity of forgery situations, so only the center point of the real face is set, which makes the real face more concentrated while the fake face is further away from the center of the real face. However, SCL does not take into account that real faces are also very different from each other, and it may be too strict for real faces. Our proposed IVML method considers the intra-variance of real face images when distinguishing real faces from fake ones.

3 Proposed Method

3.1 Intra-variance Guided Metric Learning

Softmax loss is usually used in the supervised training of deep networks for face forgery detection. However, the features learned by softmax loss are inherently less discriminative, as softmax loss only focuses on finding a decision boundary to distinguish between different classes. Clearly, deep metric learning is a solution to the limitations of softmax loss, which generally compresses the intra-class distance between true and false faces in projected space. The feature distribution of fake faces varies according to the manipulation method. This is because generating models, manipulated regions, and some special operations bring unique falsified information. The characteristic difference of samples produced by different operation methods makes it hard to get all the fake faces together in one center. Therefore, forcing the forged faces together in the projected space often leads to the poor accuracy. In addition, there is a very large gap between real faces, and blindly reducing the intra-class distance of real faces may easily lead to overfitting, so that the unseen real faces will be mixed with fake faces.

To address the above issues, we propose an intra-variance guided metric learning (IVML) method, which not only enlarges the inter-class distance of fake and real faces as much as possible, but also ensures that the intra-class distance of real faces is large enough. As shown in Fig. 1, we take the real face farthest from the real face center $\mathbf{x}_c^r$ as the boundary of the real face, and expect the distance of the fake face and real face center $\mathbf{x}_c^r$ to be greater than the distance of the farthest real face and the real face center $\mathbf{x}_c^r$. This design can increase the inter-class distance between real and fake faces, and ensure a relatively loose intra-class distance between real faces. In order to facilitate optimization, our method utilizes the average distance between fake faces and $\mathbf{x}_c^r$ in a batch and increases the closest distance between real faces and $\mathbf{x}_c^r$. In addition, it is also necessary to consider properly reducing the intra-class distance of real faces, and optimizing the distance between real faces and $\mathbf{x}_c^r$. Then, the intra-variance loss function of our IVML method is formulated as follows:

$$L_{iv} = -\log \frac{\exp\left(d(\mathbf{x}^r_{max}, \mathbf{x}^r_c) + d(\mathbf{x}^r_{min}, \mathbf{x}^r_c)\right)}{\exp\left(d(\mathbf{x}^r_{max}, \mathbf{x}^r_c) + d(\mathbf{x}^r_{min}, \mathbf{x}^r_c)\right) + \frac{1}{N}\sum_{n=1}^{N}\exp\left(d(\mathbf{x}^f_n, \mathbf{x}^r_c)\right)}, \quad (1)$$

where $\mathbf{x}^r_{max}$ represents the real face farthest from $\mathbf{x}^r_c$, and $\mathbf{x}^r_{min}$ denotes the real face closest to $\mathbf{x}^r_c$. The batch size is $2N$, in which N real samples and N fake samples are taken, and $\mathbf{x}^f_n$ is the n-th fake face in each batch. $d(\mathbf{x}, \mathbf{y})$ represents the Euclidean distance or cosine distance between vectors $\mathbf{x}$ and $\mathbf{y}$, i.e.,

$$d_E(\mathbf{x}, \mathbf{y}) = -||\mathbf{x} - \mathbf{y}||_2, \quad (2)$$

$$d_{cos}(\mathbf{x}, \mathbf{y}) = \frac{\mathbf{x}\mathbf{y}^T}{||\mathbf{x}||_2||\mathbf{y}||_2}. \quad (3)$$

Therefore, by integrating the softmax loss and the intra-variance loss, the total loss function of our IVML method is given as

$$L_{total} = L_{bce} + \lambda L_{iv} \quad (4)$$

in which L_{bce} is binary cross entropy loss, i.e., binary softmax loss, and λ is a hyper-parameter that controls the trade-off between intra-variance loss and binary softmax loss.

3.2   Vision Transformers

In our experiment, we use the ViT backbone proposed by Alexey et al [20]. It splits the input image into 16×16 pixel blocks, and all the patches are first flattened and then inserted into the insert block by linear projection. Before entering the encoder, the vector obtained from the above processing is also connected with the positional embedding. In addition, this set of vectors includes an additional "category" tag. After the above operations are completed, the resulting combined vectors are then input into a Transformer encoder [21]. It consists of multiple layers of multi-headed self-attention (MSA) and MLP blocks. A LayerNorm is required before input into each block, and after block processing, a residual connection module is required. Finally, the feature outputted by the conversion encoder is used to represent the feature of the image.

VIT-S [22] is a model with a smaller number of parameters in the ViT, and it has only six heads in the MSA, unlike the basic version, which has 12 heads. The number of parameters for ViT-S is 22M, and the number of parameters for Xception [4] is also 22M. In our experiments, we employ VIT-S and Xception as backbones. Compared with CNN, Vision Transformer requires more training content. As suggested by Alexey et al. [20], a straightforward solution is using some larger data sets. ImageNet-21k [23] contains approximately 14 million images, grouped into 21K classes. The pre-trained model of ViT-S on ImageNet-21k is public, so we directly use this public pre-trained model in the experiments.

4   Experiments

4.1   Experimental Setup

Dataset. We evaluate our proposed IVML method on two challenging datasets, FaceForensics++ (FF++) [4] and Celeb-DF [24]. FF++ is the most widely used forgery dataset, including 720 videos for training, 140 videos for verification and 140 videos for test. It contains four manipulation methods, including identity swapping methods (DeepFakes[1], FaceSwap[2]) and expression swapping methods (Face2Face [25], and NeuralTexture [26]), which is suitable for evaluating the generalization of the model. Depending on the degree of compression, the FF++ dataset comes in three versions: c0 for raw data, c23 for lightly compressed version data (high quality), and c40 for heavily compressed version data (low quality). The high quality version (c23) is selected for our experiments. Celeb-DF [24] is generated by face swapping for 59 pairs of subjects, which contains 590 real videos and 5,639 high-quality fake videos.

Evaluation Metric. We employ the common metric, Area Under the Receiver Operating Characteristic Curve (AUC), to evaluate our method.

Implementation Detail. Our IVML approach is implemented by the PyTorch deep learning framework [27], with the batch size of 256 on an NVIDIA GTX 3090 GPU. All face images are cropped and normalized to 224×224. In order to ensure that the forged information will not be changed and improve the robustness of the model, we only use random horizontal flipping for data enhancement. Our method is optimized by the AdamW, the learning rate is 3e-5, and λ in Eq. (4) is set to 1. All experiments are trained on FF++(c23) dataset. Experiments on FF++ dataset belong to the intra-test results and on Celeb-DF dataset represent the cross-dataset test.

4.2   Quantitative Results

Comparison of Different Backbones. This subsection compares the results of ViT as backbone with the results of CNN as backbone, where ViT chooses ViT-S and CNN chooses Xception. The test process is that images are extracted by backbone and inputted into a one-layer full connected network to directly give classification results. The results are shown in Table 1. We can see that ViT-S is much higher than Xception both on the intra-testing and on cross-dataset tests, especially on cross-dataset tests. The results proves the correctness of choosing ViT-S as the backbone of face forgery detection method.

---

[1] https://github.com/deepfakes/faceswap.
[2] https://github.com/MarekKowalski/FaceSwap.

Table 1. The AUC (%) comparison between CNN-based methods (Xception) and ViT-based methods (ViT-S).

Backbone	FF++	Celeb-DF
Xception [4]	95.73	65.27
ViT-S [22]	**98.37**	**76.34**

Comparison of Our IVML with Different Backbones. To prove the effectiveness of our proposed IVML method, we take Xception and ViT-S as backbones respectively. The results are shown in Table 2. These experimental results remarkably show that our IVML method is effective for face forgery detection.

Table 2. The AUC (%) comparison of our IVML method with different backbones.

Method	Backbone	FF++	Celeb-DF
Xception [4]	Xception	95.73	65.27
IVML	Xception	**96.51**	**72.73**
ViT-S [22]	ViT-S	98.37	76.34
IVML	ViT-S	**99.33**	**78.86**

Comparison of Our IVML with Euclidean Distance and Cosine Distance. In our IVML method, the calculation of distance is a very important part. This subsection evaluate the performance of our IVML using Euclidean distance and cosine distance, as shown in Table 3. It can be seen from this table that the results of our IVML method with Euclidean distance and cosine distance are similar on two datasets.

Table 3. The AUC (%) comparison of our IVML method with Euclidean distance and cosine distance on two datasets.

Method	Distance	FF++	Celeb-DF
IVML	Euclidean	**99.33**	78.86
IVML	Cosine	99.21	**79.00**

Comparison with State-of-the-Art Methods. To verify the performance of our IVML method for face forgery detection, we compare our method with the classic and recent state-of-the-art methods on FF++ and Celeb-DF datasets. From the Table 4, we find that our IVML method is competitive to these state-of-the-art methods on FF++ and Celeb-DF datasets.

Table 4. The AUC (%) comparison with state-of-the-art methods.

Method	FF++	Celeb-DF
Xception [4]	95.73	65.27
EN-b4 [28]	99.22	68.52
Face X-ray [6]	87.40	74.20
MLDG [29]	98.99	74.56
MAT(EN-b4) [11]	99.27	76.65
GFF [30]	98.36	75.31
Local-relation [10]	**99.46**	78.26
IVML	99.33	**78.86**

5   Conclusion

In this paper, we propose a metric learning method called intra-variance guided metric learning (IVML) for face forgery detection. Specifically, our proposed IVML method compresses the distance within real samples via the softmax loss, enlarges the distance between the real and fake samples, and maintains a large distance within the real samples via the intra-variance loss. Our experiments also show that the generalization of Vision Transformer in face forgery detection is much stronger than that of Xception. Extensive experiments on two datasets have verified the effectiveness of our IVML method. In the future, we will explore more deep metric learning methods, give full play to the role of metric learning, and further improve the generalization ability of face forgery detection methods.

Acknowledgments. This work was supported by the National Natural Science Foundation of China under Grant 62006013.

References

1. Goodfellow, I.J., et al.: Generative adversarial networks. Commun. ACM **63**, 139–144 (2020)
2. Kingma, D.P., Welling, M.: Auto-encoding variational Bayes. In: International Conference on Learning Representations (2014)
3. Afchar, D., Nozick, V., Yamagishi, J., Echizen, I.: MesoNet: a compact facial video forgery detection network. In: IEEE International Workshop on Information Forensics and Security, pp. 1–7 (2018)
4. Rössler, A., Cozzolino, D., Verdoliva, L., Riess, C., Thies, J., Nießner, M.: Faceforensics++: learning to detect manipulated facial images. In: International Conference on Computer Vision, pp. 1–11 (2019)
5. Dang, H., Liu, F., Stehouwer, J., Liu, X., Jain, A.K.: On the detection of digital face manipulation. In: IEEE Conference on Computer Vision and Pattern Recognition, pp. 5780–5789 (2020)
6. Li, L., et al.: Face x-ray for more general face forgery detection. In: IEEE Conference on Computer Vision and Pattern Recognition, pp. 5000–5009 (2020)

7. Wang, C., Deng, W.: Representative forgery mining for fake face detection. In: IEEE Conference on Computer Vision and Pattern Recognition, pp. 14923–14932 (2021)
8. Gu, Q., Chen, S., Yao, T., Chen, Y., Ding, S., Yi, R.: Exploiting fine-grained face forgery clues via progressive enhancement learning. In: AAAI Conference on Artificial Intelligence, pp. 735–743 (2022)
9. Zhou, P., Han, X., Morariu, V.I., Davis, L.S.: Two-stream neural networks for tampered face detection. In: IEEE Conference on Computer Vision and Pattern Recognition Workshops, pp. 1831–1839 (2017)
10. Chen, S., Yao, T., Chen, Y., Ding, S., Li, J., Ji, R.: Local relation learning for face forgery detection. In: AAAI Conference on Artificial Intelligence, pp. 1081–1088 (2021)
11. Zhao, H., Zhou, W., Chen, D., Wei, T., Zhang, W., Yu, N.: Multi-attentional deepfake detection. In: IEEE Conference on Computer Vision and Pattern Recognition, pp. 2185–2194 (2021)
12. Li, J., Xie, H., Li, J., Wang, Z., Zhang, Y.: Frequency-aware discriminative feature learning supervised by single-center loss for face forgery detection. In: IEEE Conference on Computer Vision and Pattern Recognition, pp. 6458–6467 (2021)
13. Nguyen, H.H., Yamagishi, J., Echizen, I.: Capsule-forensics: Using capsule networks to detect forged images and videos. In: International Conference on Acoustics, Speech and Signal Processing, pp. 2307–2311 (2019)
14. Chollet, F.: Xception: deep learning with depthwise separable convolutions. In: IEEE Conference on Computer Vision and Pattern Recognition, pp. 1800–1807 (2017)
15. Cao, J., Ma, C., Yao, T., Chen, S., Ding, S., Yang, X.: End-to-end reconstruction-classification learning for face forgery detection. In: IEEE/CVF Conference on Computer Vision and Pattern Recognition, pp. 4103–4112 (2022)
16. Huang, B., et al.: Implicit identity driven deepfake face swapping detection. In: IEEE/CVF Conference on Computer Vision and Pattern Recognition, pp. 4490–4499 (2023)
17. Wen, Y., Zhang, K., Li, Z., Qiao, Y.: A discriminative feature learning approach for deep face recognition. In: European Conference on Computer Vision, pp. 499–515 (2016)
18. Schroff, F., Kalenichenko, D., Philbin, J.: FaceNet: a unified embedding for face recognition and clustering. In: IEEE Conference on Computer Vision and Pattern Recognition, pp. 815–823 (2015)
19. Kumar, A., Bhavsar, A., Verma, R.: Detecting deepfakes with metric learning. In: International Workshop on Biometrics and Forensics, pp. 1–6 (2020)
20. Dosovitskiy, A., et al.: An image is worth 16x16 words: transformers for image recognition at scale. In: International Conference on Learning Representations (2021)
21. Vaswani, A., et al.: Attention is all you need. In: Advances in Neural Information Processing Systems, pp. 5998–6008 (2017)
22. Steiner, A., Kolesnikov, A., Zhai, X., Wightman, R., Uszkoreit, J., Beyer, L.: How to train your vit? data, augmentation, and regularization in vision transformers. Trans. Mach. Learn. Res. 2022 (2022)
23. Deng, J., Dong, W., Socher, R., Li, L.J., Li, K., Fei-Fei, L.: Imagenet: a large-scale hierarchical image database. In: IEEE Conference on Computer Vision and Pattern Recognition, pp. 248–255 (2009)

24. Li, Y., Yang, X., Sun, P., Qi, H., Lyu, S.: Celeb-DF: a large-scale challenging dataset for deepfake forensics. In: IEEE/CVF Conference on Computer Vision and Pattern Recognition, pp. 3204–3213 (2020)
25. Thies, J., Zollhöfer, M., Stamminger, M., Theobalt, C., Nießner, M.: Face2face: real-time face capture and reenactment of RGB videos. Commun. ACM **62**(1), 96–104 (2019)
26. Thies, J., Zollhöfer, M., Nießner, M.: Deferred neural rendering: image synthesis using neural textures. ACM Trans. Graph. **38**(4) 66:1–66:12 (2019)
27. Paszke, A., et al.: Automatic differentiation in pytorch. In: Advances in Neural Information Processing Systems Workshop (2017)
28. Tan, M., Le, Q.V.: Efficientnet: rethinking model scaling for convolutional neural networks. In: International Conference on Machine Learning, pp. 6105–6114 (2019)
29. Li, D., Yang, Y., Song, Y., Hospedales, T.M.: Learning to generalize: meta-learning for domain generalization. In: AAAI Conference on Artificial Intelligence, pp. 3490–3497 (2018)
30. Luo, Y., Zhang, Y., Yan, J., Liu, W.: Generalizing face forgery detection with high-frequency features. In: IEEE Conference on Computer Vision and Pattern Recognition, pp. 16317–16326 (2021)

Text-Based Face Retrieval: Methods and Challenges

Yuchuan Deng, Qijun Zhao$^{(\boxtimes)}$, Zhanpeng Hu, and Zixiang Xu

College of Computer Science, Sichuan University, Chengdu, China
qjzhao@scu.edu.cn

Abstract. Previous researches on face retrieval have concentrated on using image-based queries. In this paper, we focus on the task of retrieving faces from a database based on queries given as texts, which holds significant potential for practical applications in public security and multimedia. Our approach employs a vision-language pre-training model as the backbone, effectively incorporating contrastive learning, image-text matching learning, and masked language modeling tasks. Furthermore, it employs a coarse-to-fine retrieval strategy to enhance the accuracy of text-based face retrieval. We present CelebA-Text-Identity dataset, comprising of 202,599 facial images of 10,178 unique identities, each paired with an accompanying textual description. The experimental results we obtained on CelebA-Text-Identity demonstrate the inherent challenges of text-based face retrieval. We expect that our proposed benchmark will encourage the advancement of biometric retrieval techniques and expand the range of applications for text-image retrieval technology.

Keywords: Text-based Face Retrieval · Visual-Language Pre-trainning

1 Introduction

Face retrieval aims to sort the gallery face images according to their similarity to the query [1]. Its practical applications in law enforcement, security, and marketing have made it increasingly significant, particularly in aiding the work of law enforcement agencies during criminal investigations. Typically, the query is given as an image. Yet, face images might be not always available, or the image quality is too low to be usable due to various factors such as large head poses or non-uniform illumination. Using texts is another way to define the query for face image retrieval. Text-based face image retrieval allows users to describe a face in natural language without relying on photographic material, which enhances accessibility and convenience. Additionally, facial descriptions can naturally provide hierarchical, from coarse to fine, information about a person's appearance. Law enforcement agencies could leverage such information to identify suspects based on eyewitness accounts. Figure 1 schematically shows the process of text-based face image retrieval.

Text-based image retrieval techniques have achieved promising results in identifying pedestrians [2–4]. However, there are differences between the way

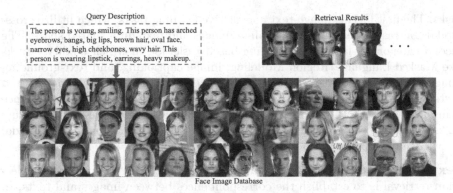

Query Description

The person is young, smiling. This person has arched eyebrows, bangs, big lips, brown hair, oval face, narrow eyes, high cheekbones, wavy hair. This person is wearing lipstick, earrings, heavy makeup.

Retrieval Results

Face Image Database

Fig. 1. An Example of Text-based Face Retrieval. Given natural language description of a face, our face retrieval system searches through a large-scale face database then retrieve the most relevant face samples.

describing faces and pedestrians. The facial description often emphasizes local facial features, while the description of pedestrians prioritizes overall behavior and clothing. When observing a face, people usually form a general perception first and focus on local features then. Furthermore, the absence of data poses another hurdle in text-based facial recognition tasks. The sensitive nature of privacy concerns hinders the acquisition of a substantial amount of data, rendering it both arduous and costly to obtain.

In response to these problems, drawing inspiration from [5], we present CelebA-Text-Identity dataset, along with a vision-language pre-training based baseline method and a coarse-to-fine retrieval strategy. We evaluate the proposed method through experiments on CelebA-Text-Identity. The main contributions of this study can be summarized as follows:

1. We propose a simple but effective approach as a baseline to establish a benchmark for text-based face retrieval, inspired by existing vision-language pre-training models and text-based pedestrian retrieval methods.
2. We present a coarse-to-fine retrieval strategy to mimic the coarse-to-fine way of human beings to identify faces.
3. We propose the CelebA-Text-Identity dataset, comprising a total of 30,000 facial images stemmed from 6,217 distinct identities, with each image being accompanied by a corresponding textual description. We conduct experiments on CelebA-Text-Identity dataset, establish a benchmark for text-based face retrieval.

2   Related Work

Vision-Language Pre-training. Vision-Language pre-training (VLP) models can be broadly classified into two categories based on their pre-training tasks. The first [6,7] is image-text contrastive learning tasks, which utilize cross-modal contrastive learning loss to align images and texts in a shared space. The second category is language modeling-based tasks [8], in which auxiliary tasks like Masked Language/Region Modeling, image captioning, and text-grounding image generation are used to establish correspondences between images and texts. Subsequent research [9,10] has confirmed the considerable performance gains achieved by VLP models for cross-modal tasks and fine-grained visual tasks. Our proposed approach utilizes the CLIP model, with ample cross-modal knowledge to improve the performance of the text-based face retrieval task.

Text-Based Pedestrian Retrieval. The main challenge of text-based pedestrian retrieval is to establish the correspondences between images and texts. In the initial stages of research, various cross-modal matching losses [11,12] were introduced to align image-text features within a joint embedding space. Recently, several research works [2-4] have explored knowledge from the CLIP model. These studies have effectively directed the focus of the model towards intricate details and inter-modal correlations, thereby narrowing down the semantic gaps between text and image domains. In this work, we aim to improve the performance of text-based face retrieval, by exploring effective fine-grained information and diverse optimization objectives.

3   Proposed Method

To transfer the ample cross-modal knowledge of VLP to text-based face retrieval task, our method builds upon the CLIP [6]. Given the unique characteristics of faces, we modify the optimization objectives and propose a coarse-to-fine retrieval strategy to better retrieve faces according to the text queries.

3.1   Model Architecture

As illustrated in Fig. 2, our method consists of an image encoder, a text encoder, and a cross-modal encoder. Following Moco [13], we maintain paired momentum encoders for unimodal encoders of the online model by exponential moving average (EMA) strategy to help guide the online model to learn superior representations. The EMA algorithm is formulated as follows: $\hat{\theta} = m\hat{\theta} + (1 - m)\theta$, where $\hat{\theta}$ and θ denote the parameters of the momentum and online encoders, respectively. The momentum coefficient $m \in [0, 1]$ controls the contribution of previous parameter values to the current value.

Image Encoder. To avoid distortion to intra-modal information [9], we utilize the approach described in CFine [4]. Specifically, we use a CLIP pre-trained ViT model with the projector removed as our image encoder. Given an input image I, we split the input into N_I non-overlapping patches embedded with positional information. A learnable class token $[CLS]$ is prepended to the image patches as an image-level global representations. Then, the $N_I + 1$ patches are passed into the transformer layers of image encoder, yielding a set of image embeddings $\{v_{cls}, v_1, ..., v_{N_I}\} \in \mathbb{R}^{(N_I+1) \times d}$.

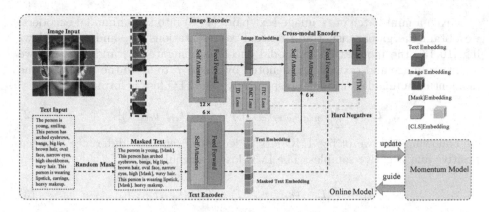

Fig. 2. The architecture of the vision-language pre-training based model we proposed. It comprises an image encoder, a text encoder and a cross-modal encoder. In order to improve learning with noisy data, we use the momentum model as additional supervision during training. Modules connected by dashed lines will be removed during inference stage.

Text Encoder. We utilize BERT [14] as text encoder. The input text T is first tokenized as $N_T + 1$ tokens, within a $[CLS]$ token to indicate position. The resulting token sequence is then passed through the first 6 layers of BERT resulting text embeddings $\{t_{cls}, t_1, ..., t_{N_T}\} \in \mathbb{R}^{(N_T+1) \times d}$.

Cross-Modal Encoder. Following [10], the cross-modal encoder is initialized using the last 6 layers of the BERT. The image and text embeddings are fed into cross-modal encoder, and fused by the cross attention mechanism to capture their semantic relationship. And the joint representation can be denoted by $\{f_{cls}, f_1, ..., f_{N_T}\}$, where f_{cls} denotes the joint representation of I and T, and $f_i(i = 1, ..., N_T)$ can be regarded as the joint representation of the image I and the i-th token in the text T.

3.2   Optimization Objectives

We integrate contrastive learning (CL), image-text matching learning (ITM), and masked language modeling (MLM) tasks, which serve to enforce the alignment constraints to discern subtle distinctions between faces.

Contrastive Learning. To make the subsequent cross-modal fusion easier, we introduce CL task on the representations from the unimodal encoders, which is divided into image-text contrastive (ITC) learning and intra-modal contrastive (IMC) learning tasks. InfoNCE loss [15] is a widely-used CL loss, denoted as:

$$\mathcal{L}_{nce}(u, v, Q) = -\frac{1}{2}\mathbb{E}_{(u,v)} \log \frac{exp(sim(u, v)/\tau)}{\sum_{v_i \in Q} exp(sim(u, v_i)/\tau)} \tag{1}$$

where the $sim(u, v) = \frac{u^T v}{\|u\|\|v\|}$ denotes the cosine similarity, Q denotes a maintained queue, and τ is a learnable temperature parameter.

Given a mini-batch of N image-text pairs (I, T) into the unimodal encoders, we obtain the global visual and textual representations v_{cls} and t_{cls}. Following [10,13], the momentum unimodal encoders generate $\hat{v}_{cls}$ and $\hat{t}_{cls}$, and we maintain image and text queues denoted by $\hat{I}$ and $\hat{T}$ to store the output of the momentum unimodal encoders, respectively. The ITC loss is formulated as:

$$\mathcal{L}_{itc} = \frac{1}{2}[\mathcal{L}_{nce}(v_{cls}, \hat{t}_{cls}, \hat{T}) + \mathcal{L}_{nce}(t_{cls}, \hat{v}_{cls}, \hat{I})] \tag{2}$$

Following [16], we utilize IMC loss to learn the semantic difference between positive and negative samples. The IMC loss is formulated as:

$$\mathcal{L}_{imc} = \frac{1}{2}[\mathcal{L}_{nce}(v_{cls}, \hat{v}_{cls}, \hat{I}) + \mathcal{L}_{nce}(t_{cls}, \hat{t}_{cls}, \hat{T})] \tag{3}$$

And the overall loss for Contrastive Learning is:

$$\mathcal{L}_{cl} = \mathcal{L}_{itc} + \mathcal{L}_{imc} \tag{4}$$

Image-Text Matching. In order to fuse vision and language representations, we adopt ITM which is widely used in previous VLP studies. However, previous ITM methods [10] ignore the sensitivity to sparsity and mismatch between different modalities. To overcome these limitations, we use similarity distribution matching (SDM) [3] loss, which is better at capturing the relationship between various modes, and can better handle modal mismatch and sparsity. We use f_{cls} as the joint representation of the input image-text pair and fed into a fully-connected layer to predict the matching probability $\phi(I, T)$. We assume that matched image-text pair (I, T) is positive (with label 1) and construct negative examples (with label 0) through batch-sampling [10]. The SDM loss can be denoted as:

$$\mathcal{L}_{sdm} = \mathbb{E}_{(I,T)} KL(\phi(I, T) \| y^{(I,T)}) \tag{5}$$

where $KL(\|)$ is KL divergence and $y^{(I,T)}$ is the true matching probability.

We refer to ALBEF [10], utilize the contrastive similarity between image and text from Eq. 2, and then select the top 128 images with the highest similarities to send them to the cross-modal encoder.

Masked Language Modeling. We employ MLM from BERT [14] to predict masked textual tokens. Following BERT, the replacements consist of 10% randomly selected tokens, 10% unchanged tokens, and 80% [MASK] placeholders. Given a image-text pair with masked text (I, T^{msk}), MLM loss is defined as the cross-entropy $\mathcal{H}$ between ϕ^{mlm} and y^{mlm}:

$$\mathcal{L}_{mlm} = \mathbb{E}_{p(I,T^{msk})} \mathcal{H}(y^{mlm}, \phi^{mlm}(I, T^{msk})), \tag{6}$$

where y^{mlm} is a one-hot vector denoting the ground truth of the masked token and $\phi^{mlm}(I, T^{msk})$ is the predicted probability for the masked token based on the information of the contextual text T^{msk} and the paired image I.

Joint Learning. Additionally, we incorporate ID loss [17] to reinforce the feature representations of identical identities. And the overall optimization objective is defined as:

$$\mathcal{L} = \mathcal{L}_{cl} + \mathcal{L}_{sdm} + \mathcal{L}_{mlm} + \mathcal{L}_{id}. \tag{7}$$

3.3   Retrieval Strategy

We propose a coarse-to-fine retrieval strategy for face retrieval tasks, where each query is represented by a set (T_g, T_l) of global, local features. T_g cover the over-all appearance of the face, such as facial contour, facial shape, eye position, and mouth shape, to describe the overall structure and appearance of the face. T_l focus on the remaining local areas or details of the face, such as the eyes, nose, mouth, and eyebrows. We use T_g before T_l for retrieval. For each round of retrieval, we sort the resulting similarity and select the top $p\%$ samples as candidates for the next round of retrieval.

4   Experiments

4.1   Experimental Settings

Dataset. Due to the lack of available face datasets with natural language descriptions, we propose the CelebA-Text-Identity dataset for text-based face retrieval based on the public CelebA face dataset [18]. The CelebA-Text-Identity dataset comprises of 205,599 facial images of 6,217 unique identities, each accompanied by a corresponding textual description. Following the example of Multi-Modal-CelebA-HQ [5], the facial descriptions in CelebA-Text-Identity are generated by utilizing all the facial attributes linked with the CelebA dataset. Textual descriptions are produced using a context-free grammar (CFG) based on the provided attributes. To better align with common describing practices, the generated description first provides overall impression, before focusing on facial details and features. Figure 3 displays some examples from the CelebA-Text-Identity dataset.

Fig. 3. Selected image-text pairs from CelebA-Text-Identity. Face images are selected from CelebA and normalized to 256×256, with each image being accompanied by a corresponding textual description. Our textual descriptions covers all the attributes contained in this person.

Evaluation Protocol. The dataset is classified into three distinct subsets: the training subset, validation subset, and testing subset. The training subset comprises 162,779 images featuring 8,190 unique identities; the validation subset includes 19,867 images containing 985 identities; and the testing subset consists of 19,962 images featuring 1,001 identities. There are no overlapping identities between the training, validation, and testing subsets. Additionally, the simple-testing subset contains 2,825 images with 605 unique identities, while the hard-testing subset encompasses all 19,962 images with 1,001 unique identities. To create the simple-testing subset, we selected front posed facial images while excluding those with poor illumination and excessive blurriness.

Evaluation Metrics. We have chosen to utilize the Rank-k metrics (k = 1, 5, 10) as our primary evaluation criteria, which are widely employed in text-based pedestrians retrieval research. The Rank-k measures the likelihood of locating at least one corresponding image of a person within the top-k list of candidates when a textual description is provided as a query. Moreover, for a comprehensive evaluation, we have also incorporated the mean Average Precision (mAP) and mean Inverse Negative Penalty (mINP) [19] as additional retrieval standards. The mAP metric assesses the model's ability to accurately detect objects across all classes, while the mINP metric places greater emphasis on detecting rare objects. A higher Rank-k, mAP, and mINP values indicates better performance.

Implement Details. We use a 12-layer visual transformer CLIP-ViT-B/16 as the pre-trained image encoder. The text encoder is initialized using the first 6 layers of the BERT [14], and the cross-modal encoder is initialized using the last 6 layers of the BERT. During the training process, the input image is initially resized to 224×224 and augmented through random horizontal flipping, random cropping with padding, random erasing, and normalization. The maximum length of the token sequence N_T is set to 80, while the representation dimension d is set to 768. We use Adam optimize for 50 epochs with a learning rate initialized to 1×10^{-5} and cosine learning rate decay. At the beginning, we spend 5 warm-up epochs linearly increasing the learning rate from 1×10^{-6} to 1×10^{-5}. For random-initialized modules, we set the initial learning rate to 5×10^{-5}. During the retrieval process, we set p to 30. The models are implemented on PyTorch and are trained on a NVIDIA RTX 4090 24G GPU.

4.2   Results

At present, there is no specifically designed method to address the challenge of text-based face retrieval. We use methods based on state-of-the-art text-based pedestrian retrieval for comparisons, and use the default parameters to train on the CelebA-Text-Identity.

Table 1 contains the performance comparisons in terms of Rank-1/5/10 accuracies, map, and mINP, including the CLIP models fine-tuned with the InfoNCE [15] loss. Our proposed method surpasses the current state-of-the-art network IRRA [3] on both Simple and Hard testing, demonstrating the effectiveness of our proposed method in text-based face retrieval. Specifically, we gains a significant Rank-1 improvement of 3.45% and 1.57% on Simple and Hard testing, respectively. Additionally, it can be seen that the CLIP-ViT-B/16 image encoder yields better results. Thus, in this paper's ablation study, we set the image encoder as CLIP-ViT-B/16.

Table 1. Performance comparisons with state-of-the-art methods on CelebA-Text-Identity dataset.

Methods	Simple-testing					Hard-testing				
	Rank-1	Rank-5	Rank-10	mAP	mINP	Rank-1	Rank-5	Rank-10	mAP	mINP
CMPM/C [12]	36.03	65.44	74.26	18.58	5.52	20.23	43.44	55.99	6.82	0.63
ViTAA [20]	38.47	69.31	80.21	19.92	6.18	21.19	44.75	56.81	7.29	0.76
Han *et al.* [2]	41.95	72.71	83.76	22.32	7.70	21.57	45.41	57.97	7.39	0.82
IRRA [3]	43.79	75.62	84.60	22.65	7.63	22.67	45.98	58.43	7.50	0.84
Baseline (CLIP-RN50)	38.24	69.23	80.99	20.70	6.71	21.89	44.65	57.32	7.48	0.73
Baseline (CLIP-ViT-B/32)	39.93	69.91	81.27	20.80	6.59	21.21	45.84	57.21	7.31	0.76
Baseline (CLIP-ViT-B/16)	41.31	71.86	83.16	21.63	7.49	21.72	46.06	57.18	7.44	0.80
Ours	**47.24**	**75.72**	**87.32**	**24.10**	**8.43**	**24.24**	**46.73**	**60.02**	**7.92**	**0.91**

4.3 Ablation Study

Effectiveness of Optimization Objectives. Since there is no public baseline for text-based face retrieval task, we adopt the CLIP-ViT-B/16 model with InfoNCE [15] loss as the baseline to facilitate the ablation study. The Rank-1, Rank-5, Rank-10 accuracies (%) for are reported in Table 2. The experimental results obtained by comparing models No.0 to No.1 demonstrate the efficacy of CL loss in discerning semantic nuances between similar text and images. To demonstrate the effectiveness of SDM loss, we compare it with the commonly used Image-text matching (ITM) loss [13] (No.2 to No.3), the SDM loss promotes the Rank-1 accuracy of the ITM loss by 1.16% and 0.74%, respectively. These results demonstrate that SDM loss well capturing the relationship between the two modalities. Additionally, the outcomes garnered from comparing No.1 to No.4 and No.6 to No.8 underscore the effectiveness of ID loss. Similarly, the results of contrasting No.0 to No.5 and No.7 to No.9 provide compelling proof for the efficiency of MLM loss.

Table 2. Ablation study on CelebA-Text-Identity without retrieval strategy.

No.	Methods	Components				Simple-testing			Hard-testing		
		$\mathcal{L}_{cl}$	$\mathcal{L}_{sdm}$	$\mathcal{L}_{id}$	$\mathcal{L}_{mlm}$	Rank-1	Rank-5	Rank-10	Rank-1	Rank-5	Rank-10
0	Baseline					41.31	71.86	83.16	21.72	46.06	57.18
1	$+\mathcal{L}_{cl}$	✓				42.54	72.68	83.42	21.96	45.77	58.27
2	$+\mathcal{L}_{sdm}$		✓			42.35	72.30	82.44	22.61	46.40	59.02
3	$+\mathcal{L}_{itm}$ [10]					41.19	71.92	83.67	21.87	45.58	57.39
4	$+\mathcal{L}_{id}$			✓		39.50	69.98	81.45	20.82	43.44	55.99
5	$+\mathcal{L}_{mlm}$				✓	42.05	72.63	83.50	21.47	45.41	57.61
6	$+\mathcal{L}_{cl}+\mathcal{L}_{sdm}$	✓	✓			43.79	74.62	83.49	22.28	46.23	56.84
7	$+\mathcal{L}_{cl}+\mathcal{L}_{id}$	✓		✓		43.27	73.01	84.77	22.20	46.01	57.74
8	$+\mathcal{L}_{cl}+\mathcal{L}_{sdm}+\mathcal{L}_{id}$	✓	✓	✓		44.09	73.29	84.15	23.45	46.43	58.43
9	$+\mathcal{L}_{cl}+\mathcal{L}_{id}+\mathcal{L}_{mlm}$	✓		✓	✓	44.54	73.76	84.68	23.39	46.18	58.25
10	Ours	✓	✓	✓	✓	45.82	74.35	85.32	24.06	46.62	58.15

Effectiveness of Retrieval Strategy. To investigate the impact of retrieval strategy, we attempted distinct approaches: (1) Exclusively relying on local feature-based retrieval, (2) Utilizing all features concurrently, (3) Using local features before global features, and (4) Using global features before local features. The outcomes in Table 3, (1) suggest that relying on facial features can roughly portray an individual's identity. Implementing a sequential retrieval strategy yields significant results on simple-testing when comparing (2), (3), and (4). Using global features before local features is the best choice and using local features before global features is the worst. It suggest that using local features before global features may result in the information of global features being covered by local features. However, sequential retrieval lacks efficacy when applied to hard-testing. To our analysis, this is due to the visibility of facial features in simple-testing is better, making it easier to extract crucial information about their identity through sequential retrieval.

Table 3. Performance comparisons with differnt retrieval strategies on CelebA-Text-Identity dataset.

Strategies	Simple-testing			Hard-testing		
	Rank-1	Rank-5	Rank-10	Rank-1	Rank-5	Rank-10
(1)	41.26	71.49	80.74	20.05	43.29	53.80
(2)	45.82	74.35	85.32	24.06	46.62	58.15
(3)	44.76	74.31	84.17	23.93	46.54	58.22
(4) (**ours**)	47.24	75.72	87.32	24.24	46.73	60.02

5   Conclusion

In this paper, we study the problem of retrieving faces through texts. To our best knowledge, this is the first study to explore this topic. We introduce the CelebA-Text-Identity dataset, and employed a CLIP-based model as a baseline to establish a benchmark for text-based face retrieval. We integrate contrastive learning (CL), image-text matching learning (ITM), and masked language modeling (MLM) tasks, and propose a coarse-to-fine retrieval strategy to learn the fine-grained information of faces and texts. The experimental results prove the superiority and effectiveness of our proposed method. Although our study primarily focuses on text-based face retrieval, we believe that the techniques proposed herein can be extended to other biometric recognition problems.

References

1. Jang, Y.K., Cho, N.I.: Similarity guided deep face image retrieval. arXiv preprint arXiv:2107.05025 (2021)
2. Han, X., He, S., Zhang, L., Xiang, T.: Text-based person search with limited data. arXiv preprint arXiv:2110.10807 (2021)
3. Jiang, D., Ye, M.: Cross-modal implicit relation reasoning and aligning for text-to-image person retrieval. In: IEEE International Conference on Computer Vision and Pattern Recognition (CVPR) (2023)

4. Yan, S., Dong, N., Zhang, L., Tang, J.: Clip-driven fine-grained text-image person re-identification. arXiv preprint arXiv:2210.10276 (2022)
5. Xia, W., Yang, Y., Xue, J.H., Wu, B.: TediGAN: text-guided diverse face image generation and manipulation. In: IEEE Conference on Computer Vision and Pattern Recognition (CVPR) (2021)
6. Radford, A., et al.: Learning transferable visual models from natural language supervision. In: International Conference on Machine Learning, pp. 8748–8763. PMLR (2021)
7. Li, J., Li, D., Xiong, C., Hoi, S.: BLIP: bootstrapping language-image pre-training for unified vision-language understanding and generation. In: International Conference on Machine Learning, pp. 12888–12900. PMLR (2022)
8. Chen, Y.-C., et al.: UNITER: UNiversal Image-TExt Representation Learning. In: Vedaldi, A., Bischof, H., Brox, T., Frahm, J.-M. (eds.) ECCV 2020. LNCS, vol. 12375, pp. 104–120. Springer, Cham (2020). https://doi.org/10.1007/978-3-030-58577-8_7
9. Bai, J., et al.: LaT: latent translation with cycle-consistency for video-text retrieval. arXiv preprint arXiv:2207.04858 (2022)
10. Li, J., Selvaraju, R., Gotmare, A., Joty, S., Xiong, C., Hoi, S.C.H.: Align before fuse: vision and language representation learning with momentum distillation. In: Advances in Neural Information Processing Systems, vol. 34, pp. 9694–9705 (2021)
11. Li, S., Xiao, T., Li, H., Zhou, B., Yue, D., Wang, X.: Person search with natural language description. In: Proceedings of the IEEE Conference on Computer Vision and Pattern Recognition, pp. 1970–1979 (2017)
12. Zhang, Y., Lu, H.: Deep cross-modal projection learning for image-text matching. In: Ferrari, V., Hebert, M., Sminchisescu, C., Weiss, Y. (eds.) ECCV 2018. LNCS, vol. 11205, pp. 707–723. Springer, Cham (2018). https://doi.org/10.1007/978-3-030-01246-5_42
13. He, K., Fan, H., Wu, Y., Xie, S., Girshick, R.: Momentum contrast for unsupervised visual representation learning. In: Proceedings of the IEEE/CVF Conference on Computer Vision and Pattern Recognition, pp. 9729–9738 (2020)
14. Devlin, J., Chang, M.-W., Lee, K., Toutanova, K.: BERT: pre-training of deep bidirectional transformers for language understanding. In: Proceedings of NAACL-HLT, pp. 4171–4186 (2019)
15. van den Oord, A., Li, Y., Vinyals, O.: Representation learning with contrastive predictive coding. arXiv preprint arXiv:1807.03748 (2018)
16. Gao, T., Yao, X., Chen, D.: SimCSE: simple contrastive learning of sentence embeddings. arXiv preprint arXiv:2104.08821 (2021)
17. Zheng, Z., Zheng, L., Garrett, M., Yang, Y., Xu, M., Shen, Y.D.: Dual-path convolutional image-text embeddings with instance loss. ACM Trans. Multimedia Comput. Commun. Appl. (TOMM) 16(2), 1–23 (2020)
18. Liu, Z., Luo, P., Wang, X., Tang, X.: Deep learning face attributes in the wild. In: Proceedings of International Conference on Computer Vision (ICCV) (2015)
19. Ye, M., Shen, J., Lin, G., Xiang, T., Shao, L., Hoi, S.C.: Deep learning for person re-identification: a survey and outlook. IEEE Trans. Pattern Anal. Mach. Intell. 44(6), 2872–2893 (2021)
20. Wang, Z., Fang, Z., Wang, J., Yang, Y.: *ViTAA*: visual-textual attributes alignment in person search by natural language. In: Vedaldi, A., Bischof, H., Brox, T., Frahm, J.-M. (eds.) ECCV 2020. LNCS, vol. 12357, pp. 402–420. Springer, Cham (2020). https://doi.org/10.1007/978-3-030-58610-2_24

Facial Adversarial Sample Augmentation for Robust Low-Quality 3D Face Recognition

Fengxun Sun, Cuican Yu, and Huibin Li$^{(\boxtimes)}$

School of Mathematics and Statistics, Xi'an Jiaotong University, Xi'an 710049, China
`huibinli@mail.xjtu.edu.cn`

Abstract. Compared with traditional 3D face recognition tasks using high precision 3D face scans, 3D face recognition based on low-quality data captured by consumer depth cameras is more practicable for real-world applications. However, it is also more challenging to deal with the variations of facial expressions, poses, occlusions, data noises, scanning distance, and so on. In this paper, we propose a novel robust low-quality 3D face recognition method based on Facial Adversarial Sample Augmentation, namely FASA-3DFR. It consists of two modules, namely facial adversarial sample generation, and facial adversarial sample training. For the first module, to enlarge the diversity of facial adversarial samples and boost the robustness of 3DFR, we propose to utilize the Kullback-Leibler divergence to maximize the distribution distance between the original and adversarial facial samples. For the second module, a distribution alignment loss is designed to make the distribution of facial adversarial samples gradually close to the one of the original facial samples, and the common and valuable information from both distributions can be effectively extracted. Extensive experiments conducted on the CAS-AIR-3D Face database show the effectiveness of the proposed method.

Keywords: Robust low-quality 3D face recognition · Facial adversarial sample augmentation

1 Introduction

Over the past two decades, 3D face recognition (3DFR) solutions have demonstrated impressive accuracy [1] when evaluated on high-precision 3D face databases, such as Bosphorus and FRGC, etc. Despite these achievements, the practical implementation of 3DFR still faces many challenges due to the limitations of acquiring high-precision data. Sensors used for high-precision data collection are bulky, expensive, and time-consuming. In contrast, the increasing popularity of consumer depth cameras, such as Microsoft Kinect and RealSense, has made it feasible to capture 3D facial data more efficiently and cost-effectively. However, the low resolution, noises and facial variations always lead to the data acquired by these sensors with a low quality. Consequently, improving the accuracy and robustness of low-quality 3DFR becomes a significant and pressing challenge.

© The Author(s), under exclusive license to Springer Nature Singapore Pte Ltd. 2023
W. Jia et al. (Eds.): CCBR 2023, LNCS 14463, pp. 160–169, 2023.
https://doi.org/10.1007/978-981-99-8565-4_16

To address this issue, we introduce a facial adversarial sample augmentation method from the viewpoint of general adversarial data augmentation [2]. Generally, adversarial data augmentation can introduce a rich diversity of facial samples into the training set, thereby enhancing the robustness of the deep 3DFR network [3]. Recently, some studies have utilized adversarial data to enhance 3DFR [4]. However, adversarial data augmentation is susceptible to the problem of robust over-fitting, resulting in reduced accuracy on the original clean facial samples [5]. We attribute this issue to the distribution mismatch between facial adversarial samples and the original facial samples, which hinders the network's ability to effectively extract shared features from both distributions, as depicted in Fig. 1. To mitigate this challenge, we propose to decouple and maximize the distance between the distribution of facial adversarial samples and the one of their corresponding original samples during the facial adversarial sample generation module. Then during the facial adversarial sample training module, we minimize the discrepancy between the distribution of facial adversarial samples and the one of their corresponding original samples to extract their common information and improve the recognition accuracy. This approach guides the model to better represent the data. Experimental results on the CAS-AIR-3D Face dataset demonstrate the effectiveness of our proposed method.

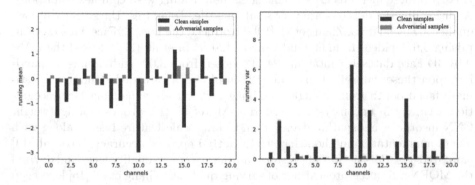

Fig. 1. The channel-wise Batch Normalization statistics on randomly sampled 20 channels in Arcface18's first layer for the clean and adversarial facial samples. It appears that the clean and adversarial facial samples exhibit distinct feature statistics, suggesting that they are sampled from different underlying distributions.

2   Related Work

2.1   Adversarial Data Augmentation

Adversarial data augmentation generates adversarial samples as additional training data by introducing small perturbations to the original inputs, which can cause the model to make incorrect predictions. The objective of adversarial data augmentation is to simulate real-world adversarial scenarios and enhance the network's robustness. However, existing studies have shown that the presence of adversarial samples may adversely affect the accuracy of objective classification on original clean images. Madry et al. [6] demonstrated the effectiveness of reliable adversarial training in defending against adversarial attacks by deep neural networks. Sinha et al. [7] proposed an efficient approach to ensure distributional robustness through adversarial training. Kannan et al. [8] focused on matching the logits obtained from clean images and their corresponding adversarial counterparts, which guides the model to improve its internal representations of the data. Recently, Xie et al. [9] argued that adversarial and clean samples are drawn from distinct distributions, and they proposed to use Auxiliary Batch Normalization (AuxBN) during adversarial training to improve the classification accuracy over the original clean images. In this paper, we not only adopt the AuxBN strategy to decouple the distribution of clean samples and adversarial samples but also introduce a distribution decoupling loss for generating diverse adversarial samples. This strategy can effectively separate the two distributions, and enable more accurate updates of the distribution parameters.

2.2 Low-Quality 3D Face Recognition

Early research on low-quality 3DFR relied on manually crafted facial descriptors. However, these methods faced challenges when dealing with complex conditions. Additionally, the datasets are very small in scale. To address the scarcity of low-quality 3D facial data, Zhang et al. [10] introduced the Lock3DFace dataset, comprising 5,671 videos from 509 individuals. Later, Li et al. [11] released the CAS-AIR-3D Face dataset, containing 24,713 videos from 3,093 individuals. Expanding upon these datasets, Cui et al. [12] employed a cascaded structure to estimate facial depth from a single face image, effectively enhancing face recognition accuracy in unconstrained scenarios. Mu et al. [13] proposed a lightweight CNN incorporating spatial attention and multi-scale feature fusion, along with a data augmentation method that significantly improved accuracy. Lin et al. [14] employed a pix2pix network to restore the quality of low-quality faces and devised the MQFNet to integrate features of varying qualities. Zhang et al. [15] leveraged Continuous Normalizing Flow to transform the facial-specific distribution into a flexible distribution for low-quality 3DFR. Jiang et al. [16] introduced Point-Face which directly processes 3D facial point cloud data. Zhao et al. [17] designed the LMFNet to better preserve low-level and high-level features extracted by the network. In comparison with these low-quality 3D face recognition methods, this paper focuses on the utilization of adversarial samples to augment data quantity and diversity. Moreover, to address the balance between the accuracy of the original clean samples and the robustness of facial variations, we proposed a distribution alignment approach to enhance the 3DFR accuracy.

3 Proposed Method

Figure 2 shows the framework of our method. In the facial adversarial sample generation module, we use the original clean facial depth map x_{cln} as input to the network F_θ which can be ArcFace18, LightCNN, etc. And we optimize the perturbation ϵ through maxing decoupling object loss L_{dis}. Through iterations, we generate the facial adversarial sample x_{adv}. Note that the original clean sample x_{cln} and adversarial sample x_{adv} pass through different Batch Normalization branches in the network. In the module of facial adversarial sample training, we train the deep network F_θ to perform the 3DFR task using both the original clean and adversarial facial samples. We calculate the adversarial loss L_{adv} on the adversarial samples, the classification loss L_{cln} on the clean samples, and the distribution matching loss L_{dis} over both of them. These three loss functions are employed for the training of the 3DFR network.

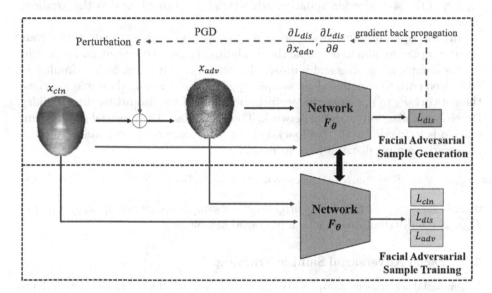

Fig. 2. The framework of the proposed robust low-quality 3D face recognition method based on Facial Adversarial Sample Augmentation, namely FASA-3DFR.

3.1 Facial Adversarial Sample Generation

For the task of 3DFR with deep network F_θ, the objective function can be formulated as:

$$\min_\theta \mathbb{E}_{(x,y)\sim D}[\mathcal{L}(x,y;\theta)] \tag{1}$$

where $(x,y) \sim D$ represents the data distribution, $\mathcal{L}$ represents the classification loss like cross-entropy loss, θ corresponds to the network parameters, and x represents the training sample along with the true label y.

We can generate a facial adversarial sample for the given facial depth map x by introducing a perturbation. This perturbation is designed to make the model give an incorrect prediction for the adversarial sample. The vanilla facial adversarial sample generation is maximizing the following optimization problem:

$$\max_{\epsilon \in \Delta} \mathbb{E}_{(x,y)\sim D}[\mathcal{L}(x + \epsilon, y; \theta)] \tag{2}$$

where ϵ is an adversarial perturbation, Δ is the space of perturbation. Through randomly initializing a perturbation ϵ, adversarial samples x_{adv} can be denoted as $x_{adv} = x_{cln} + \epsilon$. And x_{adv} can be iteratively generated by the Projected Gradient Descent (PGD) algorithm [6] as follows.

$$x_{adv}^{t+1} = x_{adv}^{t} + \eta \cdot \text{sign}\left(\nabla_x \mathcal{L}(x_{adv}^{t} + \epsilon, y; \theta)\right) \tag{3}$$

where x_{adv}^{t+1} and x_{adv}^{t} are adversarial examples with $t + 1$ and t iterations, $x_{adv}^{0} = x_{cln}$, η is the step size for updating adversarial perturbation. ∇ is the gradient operator.

In this paper, different from the above general approach for generating adversarial samples, we aim to decouple the two kinds of sample distribution for enriching the sample diversities and improve the network robustness. So we simultaneously feed both the original clean sample x_{cln} and the adversarial sample x_{adv} into the network F_θ to optimize the perturbation ϵ. And we also utilize an Auxiliary Batch Normalization [9] in the network. The goal of facial adversarial sample generation is to maximize the Kullback-Leibler divergence of the original clean and adversarial sample distributions, as below.

$$\max_{\epsilon \in \Delta} \mathbb{E}_{(x_{cln}\sim D_{cln}, x_{adv}\sim D_{adv})} \mathcal{D}_{\mathcal{KL}}\left(F_\theta(x_{adv})||F_\theta(x_{cln})\right) \tag{4}$$

where $(x_{cln}, y_{cln}) \sim D_{cln}$ is the original clean sample distribution, $(x_{adv}, y_{adv}) \sim D_{adv}$ is the distribution of facial adversarial sample.

3.2   Facial Adversarial Sample Training

When facial adversarial samples are generated, how to effectively use these adversarial samples becomes a key issue. In this paper, we introduced a sample distribution alignment loss to improve the accuracy of low-quality 3DFR. That is, we feed both the original clean and adversarial samples into the same network, but with different BN layers [9]. The main BN layer is used for the clean samples, while the auxiliary BN layer is used for the facial adversarial samples. And then the deep model is trained with the following sample distribution alignment loss.

The sample distribution alignment loss function is composed of three key components. First, the distribution alignment term plays a crucial role in aligning the distributions of clean and adversarial samples. It encourages the network to extract features that are shared between these two sample domains, promoting a smoother decision boundary, shown in Eq. 5. This term minimizes the discrepancy between the predictions of x_{cln} and x_{adv}, effectively reducing the impact of distribution mismatch and driving the decision boundary away from the samples.

$$\mathcal{L}_{dis} = \mathbb{E}_{(x_{cln}\sim D_{cln}, x_{adv}\sim D_{adv})} \mathcal{D}_{\mathcal{KL}}\left(F_\theta(x_{adv})||F_\theta(x_{cln})\right) \tag{5}$$

Second, the empirical risk term L_{cln} ensures that the network effectively extracts relevant features from the clean sample distribution. This term promotes the accurate classification of the clean facial samples and prevents over-fitting. The formula for L_{cln} is shown below.

$$\mathcal{L}_{cln} = \mathbb{E}_{(x_{cln}, y_{cln}) \sim D_{cln}} [- \sum_{i=1}^{c} y_{cln,i} \log (F_\theta(x_{cln,i}))] \tag{6}$$

Third, in order to enhance the network's robustness, we also introduce a common adversarial sample classification loss L_{adv} shown in Eq. 7. This loss encourages the model to learn more resilient representations and improves its ability to withstand the adversarial perturbations.

$$\mathcal{L}_{adv} = \mathbb{E}_{(x_{adv}, y_{adv}) \sim D_{adv}} [- \sum_{i=1}^{c} y_{adv,i} \log (F_\theta(x_{adv,i}))] \tag{7}$$

Overall, the final objective function for low-quality 3DFR can be formulated as follows:

$$\mathcal{L}_{total} = \mathcal{L}_{cln} + \alpha \mathcal{L}_{dis} + \beta \mathcal{L}_{adv} \tag{8}$$

where α and β are hyper-parameters, both of which are 0.1 in our experiments.

Algorithm 1 describes the proposed method in detail.

Algorithm 1. Pseudo code of the proposed FASA-3DFR method

Input: A training database of face depth map, a Network F with parameters θ, hyper-parameters α, β, adversarial step size η , and attack step T

Output: An optimized network F_θ for 3DFR

    for A mini-batch of face depth map sampled from the database **do**

        Initialize the adversarial perturbation $\epsilon \leftarrow 0$.

        for t = 1, 2, . . ., T **do**

            x_{cln} and x_{adv} go through the corresponding network structure respectively

            Generate a mini-batch of adversarial samples using Eq. 4

        end for

        Update the model F_θ with the combined loss of L_{cln}, L_{dis}, and L_{adv} using Eq. 8

    end for

    return

---

4 Experiments

4.1 Databases

CAS-AIR-3D Face Database [11]. CAS-AIR-3D Face is a low-quality 3D face database captured by Intel RealSense SR305. It consists of a total of 3093 individuals and 24713 videos with a video resolution set to 640 × 480. It records 8 videos for each individual, including 2 distance variations, 2 expression variations, 1 neutral, and 1 occlusion variation. To the best of our knowledge, CAS-AIR-3D Face is the largest low-quality 3D face database in terms of the number of individuals and sample variations. Figure 3 shows some samples of the database.

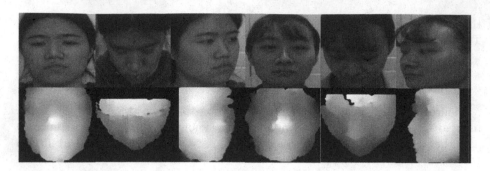

Fig. 3. Examples of CAS-AIR-3D Face dataset. The first row is the preprocessed facial RGB images, and the second is their corresponding facial depth maps.

4.2   Implementation Details

Preprocessing. We perform preprocessing on low-quality 3D face scans following [11]. Firstly, we employ the RetinaFace [18] to detect the facial region, and use the PFLD method [19] to detect facial landmarks. These are used for cropping the face depth maps. Next, we recover the 3D point clouds from the depth maps and utilize the Point Cloud Spherical Cropping Method (SCM) [13] to remove the background noise in the depth maps. Then, we apply a statistical filter to remove outliers of the point cloud and project the 3D point cloud face back to the depth map. Finally, we normalize the depth value to [0,255].

Implementation. We randomly flip the given facial depth maps to increase the amount of data. The SGD optimizer is chosen with a learning rate of 0.01, which decreases by 10% every 5 epochs. Weight decay and momentum are set to 0.0005 and 0.9, respectively. The batch size is 128, the step size η and attack step T in adversarial training are set to 4/255 and 2.

4.3   Experimental Results

For a fair comparison, we follow the close-set protocol and data process pipeline presented in [12]. We randomly sample 800 individuals as the testing set, and the other 2293 individuals as the training set. In the testing set, we select one frontal depth map with neutral expression at 0.5m as the gallery set, and the rest depth maps are used as the probe set. The probe set is divided into six test subsets (PS, PS+GL, PS+EP, DT+PS, DT+PS+GL, DT+PS+EP). The comparison results are shown in Table 1.

As shown in Table 1, our proposed FASA-3DFR method combined with different network models has effect improvements. The network combined with Arcface18 obtains the highest average accuracy of 85.36% and achieves the state-of-the-art performance on all subsets except DT+PS+EP. Specifically, on the experiments with Arcface18 as the backbone, the gains were 0.95%, 2.26%, 1.00%, 1.08%, and 1.86% for the five subsets of PS, PS+GL, PS+EP, DT+PS, and

Table 1. Comparison on the CAS-AIR-3D Face Dataset. Avg: average, PS: pose, GL: glasses, EP: expression, DT: distance

Backbone	Input	Output	Top-1 Identification Accuracy (%)						
			PS	PS+GL	PS+EP	DT+PS	DT+PS+GL	DT+PS+EP	AVG
LightCNN [20]	(128,128,1)	256	91.91	84.00	83.77	67.66	55.75	58.67	73.08
FaceNet [21]	(160,160,3)	512	92.82	85.35	87.70	70.93	58.74	64.28	76.69
MobileNet [22]	(112,112,3)	512	96.39	91.62	93.14	78.57	68.20	72.61	83.47
ArcFace18 [23]	(128,128,1)	512	96.58	91.97	93.55	79.93	69.60	**75.06**	84.58
Ours+LightCNN	(128,128,1)	256	94.84	88.89	89.26	73.52	62.90	66.05	78.89
Ours+ArcFace18	(128,128,1)	512	**97.53**	**94.23**	**94.55**	**81.01**	**71.46**	74.62	**85.36**

DT+PS+GL, respectively. And we also conducted experiments on LightCNN (without BatchNorm in the network structure). The results show that the average accuracy is even improved by 5.81%, and there is a significant improvement on all subsets, proving the effectiveness of our method. In conclusion, our proposed method is effective for low-quality 3D face recognition, and can better solve the problem of accuracy degradation on the original clean facial samples caused by the facial adversarial samples.

In Fig. 4, we further visualize the learned distributions of the original clean samples and the generated facial adversarial samples. Compared to Fig. 1, it is evident that the disparity between the distributions of the two sample types has noticeably reduced. This indicates that the distribution of clean samples and the one of facial adversarial samples can be well-aligned to each other, converging into a unified distribution space.

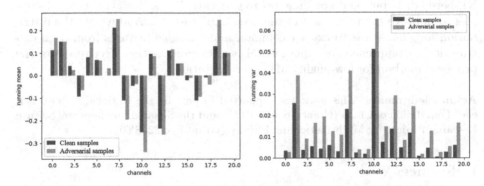

Fig. 4. Channel-wise Batch Normalization statistics on randomly sampled 20 channels in Arcface18's first layer for the clean and adversarial facial samples. It shows that the discrepancy between the clean and adversarial sample distribution diminishes, progressively converging toward a unified distribution space.

Ablation Study. To further demonstrate the effectiveness of the method, we conducted ablation experiments under the CAS-AIR-3D Face setting. We verify the impact of different loss items in our method by using the backbone network Arcface18. In particular, we trained four networks: (1) using the original clean sample classification loss only; (2) using both clean sample classification loss and the adversarial sample classification loss; (3) using both clean sample classification loss and the distribution alignment loss; (4) using clean sample classification loss, adversarial sample classification loss, and distribution alignment loss. Table 2 summarizes the recognition accuracy of all these models.

As can be seen from Table 2, all components improve the network to different degrees compared to the baseline network except the DT+PS+EP subset, indicating that these modules can effectively improve the feature extraction capability of the backbone network and reduce the loss of features for low-quality 3DFR.

Table 2. Ablation study on the CAS-AIR-3D Face dataset.

$\mathcal{L}_{cln}$	$\mathcal{L}_{adv}$	$\mathcal{L}_{dis}$	Top-1 Identification Accuracy (%)						
			PS	PS+GL	PS+EP	DT+PS	DT+PS+GL	DT+PS+EP	AVG
✓			96.58	91.97	93.55	79.93	69.60	**75.06**	84.58
✓	✓		97.43	93.96	94.34	80.47	70.57	74.04	84.96
✓		✓	97.43	94.06	94.48	80.77	71.06	74.29	85.14
✓	✓	✓	**97.53**	**94.23**	**94.55**	**81.01**	**71.46**	74.62	**85.36**

5   Conclusion

In this paper, we introduce a novel robust low-quality 3DFR method based on the Facial Adversarial Sample Augmentation strategy. In particular, we use the KL-based distribution decoupling loss to generate diverse facial adversarial samples to improve the robustness of the deep 3DFR model. And we use the distribution alignment loss to extract common and valuable features from both distributions. Comprehensive experimental results validate the effectiveness of the proposed method for low-quality 3D face recognition.

Acknowledgments. This work was supported in part by the National Natural Science Foundation of China (Grant No. 61976173) and the Shaanxi Fundamental Science Research Project for Mathematics and Physics (Grant No. 22JSY011).

References

1. Zhou, S., Xiao, S.: 3D face recognition: a survey. HCIS **8**(1), 1–27 (2018)
2. Rebuffi, S.-A., et al.: Data augmentation can improve robustness. In: Advances in Neural Information Processing Systems, vol. 34, pp. 29935–29948 (2021)
3. Schlett, T., Rathgeb, C., Busch, C.: Deep learning-based single image face depth data enhancement. Comput. Vis. Image Underst. **210**, 103247 (2021)
4. Yu, C., et al.: Meta-learning-based adversarial training for deep 3D face recognition on point clouds. Pattern Recogn. **134**, 109065 (2023)
5. Tang, S., et al.: RobustART: benchmarking robustness on architecture design and training techniques. arXiv preprint arXiv:2109.05211 (2021)

6. Madry, A., Makelov, A., Schmidt, L., Tsipras, D., Vladu, A.: Towards deep learning models resistant to adversarial attacks. In: Proceedings of ICLR (2018)
7. Sinha, A., Namkoong, H., Volpi, R., Duchi, J.: Certifying some distributional robustness with principled adversarial training. In: Proceedings of ICLR (2018)
8. Kang, D., Sun, Y., et al.: Transfer of adversarial robustness between perturbation types. arXiv preprint arXiv:1905.01034 (2019)
9. Xie, C., Tan, M., Gong, B., Wang, J., Yuille, A.L., Le, Q.V.: Adversarial examples improve image recognition. In: Proceedings of the IEEE/CVF Conference on Computer Vision and Pattern Recognition, pp. 819–828 (2020)
10. Zhang, J., Huang, D., Wang, Y., Sun, J.: Lock3DFace: a large-scale database of low-cost kinect 3D faces. In: International Conference on Biometrics, pp. 1–8 (2016)
11. Li, Q., Dong, X., Wang, W., Shan, C.: CAS-AIR-3D Face: a low-quality, multi-modal and multi-pose 3D face database. In: IEEE International Joint Conference on Biometrics, pp. 1–8 (2021)
12. Cui, J., Zhang, H., et al.: Improving 2D face recognition via discriminative face depth estimation. In: International Conference on Biometrics, pp. 140–147 (2018)
13. Mu, G., Huang, D., et al.: Led3D: a lightweight and efficient deep approach to recognizing low-quality 3D faces. In: Proceedings of the IEEE/CVF Conference on Computer Vision and Pattern Recognition, pp. 5773–5782 (2019)
14. Lin, S., Jiang, C., Liu, F., Shen, L.: High quality facial data synthesis and fusion for 3D low-quality face recognition. In: IEEE International Joint Conference on Biometrics, pp. 1–8 (2021)
15. Zhang, Z., Yu, C., Xu, S., Li, H.: Learning flexibly distributional representation for low-quality 3D face recognition. In: Proceedings of the AAAI Conference on Artificial Intelligence, pp. 3465–3473 (2021)
16. Jiang, C., Lin, S., Chen, W., Liu, F., Shen, L.: PointFace: point set based feature learning for 3D face recognition. In: IEEE International Joint Conference on Biometrics, pp. 1–8 (2021)
17. Zhao, P., Ming, Y., Meng, X., Yu, H.: LMFNet: a lightweight multiscale fusion network with hierarchical structure for low-quality 3-D face recognition. IEEE Trans. Hum.-Mach. Syst. 53(1), 239–52 (2022)
18. Deng, J., Guo, J., Ververas, E., Kotsia, I., Zafeiriou, S.: RetinaFace: single-shot multi-level face localisation in the wild. In: Proceedings of the IEEE/CVF Conference on Computer Vision and Pattern Recognition, pp. 5203–5212 (2020)
19. Guo, X., et al.: PFLD: a practical facial landmark detector. arXiv preprint arXiv:1902.10859 (2019)
20. Wu, X., He, R., et al.: A light CNN for deep face representation with noisy labels. IEEE Trans. Inf. Forensics Secur. 13(11), 2884–2896 (2018)
21. Taigman, Y., Yang, M., Ranzato, M.A., Wolf, L.: DeepFace: closing the gap to human-level performance in face verification. In: Proceedings of the IEEE Conference on Computer Vision and Pattern Recognition, pp. 1701–1708 (2014)
22. Howard, A.G., et al.: MobileNets: efficient convolutional neural networks for mobile vision applications. arXiv preprint arXiv:1704.04861 (2017)
23. Deng, J., Guo, J., et al.: ArcFace: additive angular margin loss for deep face recognition. In: Proceedings of the IEEE/CVF Conference on Computer Vision and Pattern Recognition, pp. 4690–4699 (2019)

Affective Prior Topology Graph Guided Facial Expression Recognition

Ruotong Wang[1,3] and Xiao Sun[2,3(✉)]

[1] AHU-IAI AI Joint Laboratory, Anhui University, Hefei, China
[2] School of Computer Science and Information Engineering, Hefei University
of Technology, Hefei, China
sunx@hfut.edu.cn
[3] Institute of Artificial Intelligence, Hefei Comprehensive National Science Center,
Hefei, China

Abstract. Facial expression recognition (FER) aims to comprehend human emotional states by analyzing facial features. However, previous studies have predominantly concentrated on emotion classification or sentiment levels, disregarding the crucial dependencies between these factors that are vital for perceiving human emotions. To address this problem, we propose a novel affective priori topology graph network (AptGATs). AptGATs explicitly captures the topological relationship between the two labels and predicts both emotional categories and sentiment estimation for robust multi-task learning of FER. Specifically, we first constructed an Affective Priori Topology Graph (AptG) to elucidate the topological relationships between affective labels. It employs different affective labels as nodes and establishes edges from the level of cognitive psychology. We then introduced a graph attention network based on AptG that models the relationships within the affective labels. Moreover, we propose a parallel superposition mechanism to obtain a richer information representation. Experiments on the wild datasets AffectNet and Aff-Wild2 validate the effectiveness of our method. The results of public benchmark tests show that our model outperforms the current state-of-the-art methods.

Keywords: Facial Expression Recognition · Multi-Task Learning · Graph Attention Networks

1 Introduction

Facial expression recognition has been a long-standing focus in the field of computer vision. Nowadays, the automatic analysis system for recognizing facial expressions has been extensively applied in various industries such as online education, special medical services, intelligent transportation, and virtual reality [1].

Nevertheless, it still faces serious challenges that restrict its application in realistic scenarios, such as large intra-class differences, small inter-class differences, subjectivity, and ambiguity of discrete categories [2]. Consequently, researchers have introduced VA models [3] that can broadly characterize emotions to compensate for the lack of intricate details. Muse [4] introduced a challenge tournament to evaluate uncontrolled dimensions. Toisoul et al. [5] has developed an end-to-end federated estimation framework with integrated face alignment. However, these works tend to solely focus on mining information from individual labels, disregarding the inherent dependencies across different label spaces. In fact, these relationships encompass crucial semantic information. Therefore, we propose a dependency-guided Multitask learning framework that captures intricate details while preserving intuitive information.

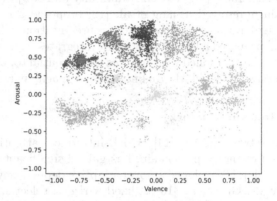

Fig. 1. Representation of the spatial relationship distribution of emotion on AffectNet.

In addition, we observed the presence of topological relationships in the multi-label data. Wang et al. [6] leverages label co-occurrence counts to guide the information transfer in Graph Convolutional Network. Lee et al. [7] employed structured knowledge graphs to model the relationships between labels. To effectively utilize this dependency, we propose a novel topology-based graph attention network for modeling real relations. We visualize the data distribution of valence arousal and discrete expression in Fig. 1. The contributions of this work can be summarized as follows:

- We design a versatile topological graph (AptG) to explore real-world emotion expressions. AptG has the capability to hierarchically aggregate label dependencies, aiding Graph Attention Network in guiding emotion representations. Our AptG can be easily extended to various emotion recognition scenarios.
- We introduce a parallel superposition mechanism designed to achieve multi-scale interaction between visual and topological information. This mechanism enhances the acquisition of more comprehensive representations.
- Experimental results on several challenging datasets show the effectiveness of our proposed model.

2   Related Works

2.1   Facial Expression Recognition

With the development of convolutional neural networks, deep learning methods began to be widely used in FER with remarkable results [1]. Farzaneh [8] introduced a deep centre of attention loss method to estimate feature attention weights to enhance discrimination. Jang et al. [9] present a novel single shot face-related task analysis method. Xue et al. [10,11] proposed a Transformer-based module for correcting attention and pooling noise. Although the aforementioned methods have made considerable progress, the ambiguity and subjectivity of discrete expressions remain unresolved. Huang et al. [12] proposed a multi-task framework for learning age-invariant identity-related representations while synthesizing faces. He et al. [13] proposed a loss function that integrates expression and action units. Nonetheless, the mentioned work ignores the potential topological relationships between affective labels, which still limits their capacity in realistic scenarios.

2.2   Graph Attention Networks

Graph Attention Network (GAT) [14], which introduces attention mechanisms specifically tailored to the graph domain, has gained significant traction among researchers. Wu et al. [15] developed a novel adaptive dependency matrix to capture temporal trends. Guo et al. [16] utilized a region selection mechanism to extract target structure and part-level information. Liu et al. [17] introduced a multi-scale aggregation scheme to capture robust motion patterns in skeleton-based action recognition. For FER, Kumar [18] leveraged the relationship between landmark and optical flow patches to aid micro-expression classification. Panagiotis et al. [19] employed random relations to support the recognition task. In contrast, we propose a topological relationship graph that cross-fertilizes with cognitive psychology theory, capturing the potential associations of affective labels.

3   Method

To link affective informations with image representations, we propose the affective priori topological graph-guided framework (AptGATs) that jointly learns sentiment estimation and expression classification, as shown in Fig. 2. We design AptG for the hierarchical aggregation of label topology information, and we have also introduce AptGAT to further learn label dependencies. Furthermore, we propose the parallel superposition mechanism that integrates label dependencies and image representations, leading to enhanced feature representations.

3.1   Affective Priori Topology Graph (AptG)

Affective Priori Topological Relationships. The topological relationship between affective labels include priori topological relationships and affective topological relationships. They focus on intra-space and inter-space relationships of

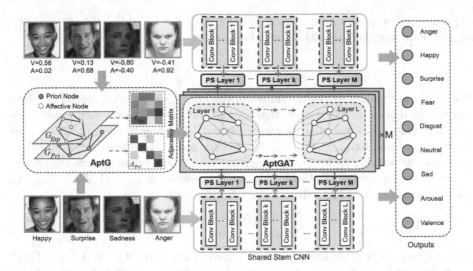

Fig. 2. Overview of our proposed model. The shared stem CNN extracts features from a batch of labelled face images. AptGAT models the label information derived from AptG. Lastly, PS incorporates the affective label information generated by AptGAT with the image features at M different stages, which are subsequently fed into the classifier. The final output of the model is a combined prediction of the inputs.

labels, respectively. We perform hierarchical aggregation of topological features to enhance the adequacy and robustness of the final features. By incorporating scales commonly employed in cognitive psychology [20], we standardize the affective topological relations as

$$A_R = \begin{bmatrix} -0.51 & -0.40 & -0.64 & 0.40 & -0.40 & 0.20 & 1.00 \\ 0.59 & 0.20 & 0.60 & 0.20 & -0.20 & 0.45 & 1.00 \end{bmatrix}, \tag{1}$$

where each row represents the value of the transformation of the seven axis of the basic emotion space to the axis of the VA (Valence-Arousal) sentiment space.

Topology Graph Construction. To make efficient use of label information, we propose a versatile method for constructing an affective priori topological graph. The affective priori topological graph $G_{Apt} = (V, E_{Apt}, A_{Apt})$ establishes the topological relationships among the various labeled nodes, where V represents the set of labels $V = \{V_1, V_2, ..., V_N\}$, N is the number of vertices. E refers to the set of edges. $A \in \mathbb{R}^{N \times N}$ is a weight matrix, where each element (i, j) denotes the weight assigned to the edges connecting nodes V_i and V_j. Specifically, our topology graph comprises two components: affective topology graph $G_{exp} = (V, E_{exp}, A_{exp})$, and priori topology graph $G_{pri} = (V, E_{pri}, A_{pri})$.

As we all know, most extraneous noise will make samples from different classes look more similar. To suppress extraneous noise and minimize computational expenses, we propose a mask matrix $Mask \in \mathbb{R}^{N \times N}$ to enable self-loops and disregard node associations within the label space:

$$Mask_{ij} = \begin{cases} 1, & \text{if } i = j \\ 0, & \text{if } i \neq j \end{cases}. \tag{2}$$

We utilize the matrix $Mask$ to transform the conventional prior matrix [19] into our modified prior matrix $A_{pri} = Mask \odot A_{emo}$, where $\odot$ is the element-wise product. Therefore, A_{pri} will allocate greater attention to highly relevant nodes. Furthermore, although $G_{pri} = (V, E_{pri}, A_{pri})$ yields more robust features while reducing computational complexity, this aggregation within spaces ignores the dependencies between spaces. To tackle this issue, we devise $G_{exp} = (V, E_{exp}, A_{exp})$ to enable the network to learn the topology between labels:

$$[A_{exp}]_{ij} = \begin{cases} |a_{ij}|, & \text{if}(i \in \text{Cat} \wedge j \in \text{Dim})\|(j \in \text{Cat} \wedge i \in \text{Dim}) \\ 0, & \text{else} \end{cases}, \tag{3}$$

where a_{ij} represents the value of column j in row i of matrix A_R. "Cat" and "Dim" are indexed sets representing the classification and dimension labels, respectively. Additionally, we employ absolute values to disregard the polarity of the values. This approach allows us to emphasize the magnitude of the data and prevent the learning of noisy information. Meanwhile, since A_{exp} and A_{pri} are non-negative, the aggregation of the two may produce extreme maxima.

$$[A_{Apt}]_{ij} = \begin{cases} \left|[A_{exp}]_{ij}\right| + \left|[A_{pri}]_{ij}\right|, \text{if } \left|[A_{exp}]_{ij}\right| + \left|[A_{pri}]_{ij}\right| < \tau \\ 1, & \text{if } \left|[A_{exp}]_{ij}\right| + \left|[A_{pri}]_{ij}\right| \geq \tau \end{cases} \tag{4}$$

denotes the final correlation matrix obtained through summation calculations. In our experiments, we empirically set a threshold $\tau = 1$ to suppress outliers.

3.2 AptG Guided GAT (AptGAT)

To fully leverage the constructed topological graph G_{Apt}, a graph guided graph attention module (AptGAT) was designed to implement the modelling of affective label dependencies. Specifically, the update process for the kth level nodes is:

$$H_w^{(k+1)} = AptGAT(A_{Apt} H_w^{(k)} W^k), \tag{5}$$

where $H_w^{(k)} = \{\vec{h}_1, \vec{h}_2, ..., \vec{h}_N\}$, $\vec{h}_i \in \mathbb{R}^F$ represents the node representations in the kth layer, $W \in \mathbb{R}^{F \times F}$ is a learnable matrix. Specifically, we compute linear combinations of features corresponding to the normalized attention coefficients e_{ij} like [14], which are attributed to the neighboring nodes. Thus, we produce the output of each node:

$$\vec{h_i}^{(k+1)} = LeakyReLU \left(\sum_{j \in N_i} \frac{\exp(e_{ij})}{\sum_{k \in N_i} \exp(e_{ik})} W \vec{h_j}^{(k)} \right), \tag{6}$$

where N_i is some neighborhood of node i in G_{Apt}. Our initial label embedding h_0 is obtained from a 300-dimensional GloVe embedding trained on the Wikipedia [21].

3.3   Parallel Stacking of AptGAT and CNN

We propose a parallel stacking (PS) interaction mechanism. This mechanism can drive multi-scale interactions between visual information extracted from stem CNN and topological information derived from AptGAT:

$$y^{(k)} = Conv_{1 \times 1}(x^{(k)} \otimes \sigma(H^{(k)^{T}})) + x^{(k)}, \qquad (7)$$

where $(\cdot)^{T}$, $\otimes$, and $+$ denote matrix transpose, multiplication, and sum operations respectively. $x^{(k)}$ and $H^{(k)}$ are the image feature and label dependencies at the kth AptGAT layer. Unlike solely overlaying label information in the final identification stage, the inclusion of multiple residual operations allows for the maximization of both geometric and semantic information utilization.

4   Experiments

4.1   Datasets

We trained and evaluated our model using the publicly available FER datasets AffectNet [22] and Aff-Wild2 [23]. AffectNet is currently the largest publicly available dataset in real-world conditions. It comprises over 1 million facial images obtained from the Internet. Aff-Wild2 is the pioneering dataset encompassing annotations for the three behavioral tasks of Expression, AUs, and VA, comprising 564 videos with approximately 2.8 million frames. Following our methodology, we train and evaluate our model exclusively on a subset of the database containing frames annotated with classification and VA labels.

4.2   Comparison with the State of the Art

Table 1 and Table 2 report the performance comparison of our method against the state-of-the-art methods on Aff-Wild2 and AffectNet datasets. Our model outperforms these recent state-of-the-art methods with 66.91% and 49.69%. [11] utilized a significantly larger number of parameters (65M) to achieve a comparable effect to ours (8M). We achieve comparable performance to [5] in VA metrics despite their tailored loss function and large-scale feature extraction network.

Table 1. Performance comparison on Aff-Wild2.

Methods	Acc.(%)	CCC-A	CCC-V
Baseline (DenseNet121)	46.77	0.44	0.41
EmoGCN [19]	48.92	0.51	0.46
AptGATs (Ours)	**49.69**	**0.51**	**0.48**

Table 2. Performance comparison of our method against the state-of-the-art methods on AffectNet. * indicates Transformer-based models.

Methods	Acc.(%)	Valence				Arousal			
		CCC	PCC	RMSE$^\downarrow$	SAGR	CCC	PCC	RMSE$^\downarrow$	SAGR
AffectNet [22]	58	0.60	0.66	0.37	0.74	0.34	0.54	0.41	0.65
Face-SSD [9]	–	0.57	0.58	0.44	0.73	0.47	0.50	0.39	0.71
VGG-FACE [24]	60	0.62	0.66	0.37	0.78	0.54	0.55	0.39	0.75
ResNet-18	–	0.66	0.66	0.39	0.78	0.60	0.60	0.34	0.77
EmoFAN [5]	62	0.73	0.73	0.33	**0.81**	0.65	0.65	**0.30**	**0.81**
DACL [8]	65.20	–	–	–	–	–	–	–	–
EmotionGCN [19]	66.46	0.77	–	–	–	0.65	–	–	–
TransFER* [10]	66.23	–	–	–	–	–	–	–	–
MViT* [25]	64.57	–	–	–	–	–	–	–	–
APViT* [11]	**66.91**	–	–	–	–	–	–	–	–
Baseline(DenseNet121)	64.06	0.75	0.73	0.33	0.80	0.65	0.65	0.33	0.79
AptGATs(Ours)	**66.91**	**0.78**	**0.78**	**0.32**	**0.81**	**0.69**	**0.69**	0.31	**0.81**

4.3 Ablation Studies

Evaluation of Different Graph. Experimental results shown in Table 3 show that G_{pri} performs worse than G_{exp} and G_{Apt}, which is caused by the lack of relationships between label spaces and by the over-smoothing effect resulting from the presence of numerous low-quality noise edges. The fusion of priori information provides an accuracy gain of 0.2% to our affective topographical information.

Table 3. Performance comparisons of different graphs on AffectNet. All variants have the same framework. Indicators with $^\downarrow$ are expected to have a smaller value.

Methods	Acc.(%)	Valence				Arousal			
		CCC	PCC	RMSE$^\downarrow$	SAGR	CCC	PCC	RMSE$^\downarrow$	SAGR
AptGATs(G_{pri})	65.31	0.77	0.77	0.33	0.81	0.68	0.68	0.32	0.79
AptGATs(G_{exp})	66.71	**0.78**	**0.79**	**0.32**	**0.82**	**0.69**	**0.69**	0.32	**0.81**
AptGATs(G_{Apt})	**66.91**	**0.78**	0.78	**0.32**	**0.82**	**0.69**	**0.69**	0.31	**0.81**

Evaluation on AptGAT Module. To showcase the effectiveness of the module, we incorporated a single AptGAT into four different stem CNNs. Table 4 illustrates the observed improvements in all case, with accuracy boosts ranging from 0.87% to 1.67%. This improvement can be attributed to the module's ability to capture the dependencies between affective labels, thus providing a robust and contributing representation. Moreover, the versatility of our gain module extends to any emotional data as it is decoupled from the dataset itself.

Table 4. Evaluation of different backbones on AffectNet. The result is denoted by the tuple (a, b), where 'a' represents the baseline and 'b' represents adding the AptGAT.

BackBone	Acc.(%)	Δ(%)	CCC-A	CCC-V
Resnet50	(64.92, 65.79)	+0.87	(0.66, 0.67)	(0.77, 0.77)
IR50	(63.94, 65.61)	+1.67	(0.65, 0.62)	(0.76, 0.76)
DenseNet121	(64.06, 65.04)	+0.98	(0.65, 0.66)	(0.75, 0.76)
MobileNetv2	(64.48, 65.34)	+0.98	(0.64, 0.68)	(0.75, 0.76)

4.4 Hyper-parameters Analysis

Impact of the Number of AptGAT. The results depicted in Fig. 3 demonstrate superior performance in all scenarios compared to the case without Apt-GAT. The performance starts to drop off when exceeds 5. This is due to the problem of vanishing gradients caused by the overstacking of GAT layers.

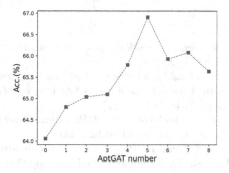

Fig. 3. The evaluation of number(M) of AptGAT on AffectNet.

Table 5. Evaluation(%) on AffectNet using different values for α and ρ.

α	ρ			
	0.1	0.2	0.3	0.4
0.2	66.29	**66.91**	65.99	65.79
0.3	66.02	65.79	66.82	65.37
0.4	66.17	65.82	66.68	65.10
0.5	65.99	66.77	66.47	66.05

Impact of α and ρ in GAT α is the hyperparameter of the activation function in GAT, ρ represents the drop rate. Table 5 demonstrates that optimal results were achieved when all values were set to 0.2. A small value of ρ is not conducive to gathering information during node updates. Conversely, a large value of ρ can result in over-smoothing.

5 Conclusion

We present a novel topological graph-guided network for facial expression recognition that addresses the issue of small inter-class differences and ambiguity of discrete categories. Specifically, our approach incorporates an affective priori topological graph-guided module to establish connections between and within diverse emotion spaces. Moreover, we introduce a parallel fusion mechanism to enhance the richness of representations. Our method outperforms existing approaches, highlighting the potential of discrete models in achieving generalized sentiment representation. For future research, we suggest exploring the utilization of multi-label modeling relationships to assist relabeling methods in addressing label uncertainty, which is a common challenge across various datasets.

References

1. Li, S., Deng, W.: Deep facial expression recognition: a survey. IEEE Trans. Affect. Comput. **13**(3), 1195–1215 (2022)
2. Kim, D., Song, B.C.: Contrastive adversarial learning for person independent facial emotion recognition. In: Proceedings of the AAAI Conference on Artificial Intelligence, vol. 35, no. 7, pp. 5948–5956 (2021)
3. Russell, J.A.: A circumplex model of affect. J. Pers. Soc. Psychol. **39**(6), 1161 (1980)
4. Christ, L., et al.: The muse 2022 multimodal sentiment analysis challenge: humor, emotional reactions, and stress. In: Proceedings of the 3rd International on Multimodal Sentiment Analysis Workshop and Challenge, pp. 5–14 (2022)
5. Toisoul, A., Kossaifi, J., Bulat, A., Tzimiropoulos, G., Pantic, M.: Estimation of continuous valence and arousal levels from faces in naturalistic conditions. Nat. Mach. Intell. **3**(1), 42–50 (2021)
6. Wang, Y., et al.: Multi-label classification with label graph superimposing. In: Proceedings of the AAAI Conference on Artificial Intelligence, vol. 34, no. 0), pp. 12265–12272 (2020)
7. Lee, C.W., Fang, W., Yeh, C.K., Wang, Y.C.F.: Multi-label zero-shot learning with structured knowledge graphs. In: 2018 IEEE Conference on Computer Vision and Pattern Recognition, CVPR 2018, Salt Lake City, UT, USA, 18–22, June 2018, pp. 1576–1585 (2018)
8. Farzaneh, A.H., Qi, X.: Facial expression recognition in the wild via deep attentive center loss. In: IEEE Winter Conference on Applications of Computer Vision, WACV 2021, Waikoloa, HI, USA, 3–8 January 2021, pp. 2402–2411 (2021)
9. Jang, Y., Gunes, H., Patras, I.: Registration-free face-SSD: single shot analysis of smiles, facial attributes, and affect in the wild. Comput. Vis. Image Underst. **182**, 17–29 (2019)
10. Xue, F., Wang, Q., Guo, G.: Transfer: learning relation-aware facial expression representations with transformers. In: 2021 IEEE/CVF International Conference on Computer Vision, ICCV 2021, Montreal, QC, Canada, 10–17 October 2021, pp. 3581–3590 (2021)

11. Xue, F., Wang, Q., Tan, Z., Ma, Z., Guo, G.: Vision transformer with attentive pooling for robust facial expression recognition. CoRR abs/2212.05463 (2022)
12. Huang, Z., Zhang, J., Shan, H.: When age-invariant face recognition meets face age synthesis: a multi-task learning framework. In: IEEE Conference on Computer Vision and Pattern Recognition, CVPR 2021, virtual, 19–25 June 2021, pp. 7282–7291 (2021)
13. He, J., Yu, X., Sun, B., Yu, L.: Facial expression and action unit recognition augmented by their dependencies on graph convolutional networks. J. Multimodal User Interfaces 15(4), 429–440 (2021)
14. Veličković, P., Cucurull, G., Casanova, A., Romero, A., Lio, P., Bengio, Y.: Graph attention networks. CoRR abs/1710.10903 (2017)
15. Wu, Z., Pan, S., Long, G., Jiang, J., Zhang, C.: Graph waveNet for deep spatial-temporal graph modeling. In: Proceedings of the Twenty-Eighth International Joint Conference on Artificial Intelligence, IJCAI 2019, Macao, China, 10–16 August 2019, pp. 1907–1913 (2019)
16. Guo, D., Shao, Y., Cui, Y., Wang, Z., Zhang, L., Shen, C.: Graph attention tracking. In: IEEE Conference on Computer Vision and Pattern Recognition, CVPR 2021, virtual, 19–25 June 2021, 9543–9552 (2021)
17. Liu, Z., Zhang, H., Chen, Z., Wang, Z., Ouyang, W.: Disentangling and unifying graph convolutions for skeleton-based action recognition. In: 2020 IEEE/CVF Conference on Computer Vision and Pattern Recognition, CVPR 2020, Seattle, WA, USA, 13–19 June 2020, pp. 140–149 (2020)
18. Kumar, A.J.R., Bhanu, B.: Micro-expression classification based on landmark relations with graph attention convolutional network. In: Proceedings of the IEEE/CVF Conference on Computer Vision and Pattern Recognition (CVPR) Workshops, pp. 1511–1520 (2021)
19. Panagiotis, A., Filntisis, P.P., Maragos, P.: Exploiting emotional dependencies with graph convolutional networks for facial expression recognition. In: 16th IEEE International Conference on Automatic Face and Gesture Recognition, FG 2021, Jodhpur, India, 15–18 December 2021, pp. 1–8 (2021)
20. Gebhard, P.: ALMA: a layered model of affect. In: 4th International Joint Conference on Autonomous Agents and Multiagent Systems (AAMAS 2005), 25–29 July 2005, Utrecht, The Netherlands, pp. 29–36 (2005)
21. Pennington, J., Socher, R., Manning, C.D.: Glove: global vectors for word representation. In: Proceedings of the 2014 Conference on Empirical Methods in Natural Language Processing, EMNLP 2014, 25–29 October 2014, Doha, Qatar, A meeting of SIGDAT, a Special Interest Group of the ACL, pp. 1532–1543 (2014)
22. Mollahosseini, A., Hasani, B., Mahoor, M.H.: AffectNet: a database for facial expression, valence, and arousal computing in the wild. IEEE Trans. Affect. Comput. 10(1), 18–31 (2019)
23. Kollias, D., Zafeiriou, S.: Aff-wild2: extending the Aff-wild database for affect recognition. CoRR abs/1811.07770 (2018)
24. Kollias, D., Cheng, S., Ververas, E., Kotsia, I., Zafeiriou, S.: Deep neural network augmentation: generating faces for affect analysis. Int. J. Comput. Vis. 128(5), 1455–1484 (2020)
25. Li, H., Sui, M., Zhao, F., Zha, Z., Wu, F.: MViT: mask vision transformer for facial expression recognition in the wild. CoRR abs/2106.04520 (2021)

Detect Any Deepfakes: Segment Anything Meets Face Forgery Detection and Localization

Yingxin Lai[1], Zhiming Luo[1], and Zitong Yu[2]([✉])

[1] Department of Artificial Intelligence, Xiamen University, Xiamen, China
[2] School of Computing and Information Technology, Great Bay University, Dongguan, China
zitong.yu@ieee.org

Abstract. The rapid advancements in computer vision have stimulated remarkable progress in face forgery techniques, capturing the dedicated attention of researchers committed to detecting forgeries and precisely localizing manipulated areas. Nonetheless, with limited fine-grained pixel-wise supervision labels, deepfake detection models perform unsatisfactorily on precise forgery detection and localization. To address this challenge, we introduce the well-trained vision segmentation foundation model, i.e., Segment Anything Model (SAM) in face forgery detection and localization. Based on SAM, we propose the Detect Any Deepfakes (DADF) framework with the Multiscale Adapter, which can capture short- and long-range forgery contexts for efficient fine-tuning. Moreover, to better identify forged traces and augment the model's sensitivity towards forgery regions, Reconstruction Guided Attention (RGA) module is proposed. The proposed framework seamlessly integrates end-to-end forgery localization and detection optimization. Extensive experiments on three benchmark datasets demonstrate the superiority of our approach for both forgery detection and localization. The codes are available at Link.

Keywords: Deepfake · SAM · Adapter · Reconstruction learning

1 Introduction

Amongst the diverse human biometric traits, the face is endowed with relatively abundant information and holds significant prominence in identity authentication and recognition. Nonetheless, with the rapid progress of computer vision technology, an array of face-changing techniques has emerged. Therefore, both industry and academia are in urgent need of robust detection methods to mitigate the potential misuse of face forgery technology.

Supplementary Information The online version contains supplementary material available at https://doi.org/10.1007/978-981-99-8565-4_18.

Currently, the majority of forgery detection methods treat the task as a binary classification problem [1–3] and utilize convolutional neural networks (CNNs) for feature extraction and classification. Although continuous advancements in forged face detection technology in recent years, accurate localization of forged regions remains a challenge, particularly for models that solely provide classification results. The precise identification of forged regions holds the utmost importance for uncovering the intentions and interpretability of the perpetrators. It allows individuals to discern fake images based on the forged regions and observe the discrepancies between forged and genuine images.

Due to the limited fine-grained pixel-wise forgery labels, some forgery localization methods [4–6] trained from scratch usually suffer overfitting. Recently, Meta introduces the pioneering foundational segmentation model, i.e., Segment Anything Model (SAM) [7,8], demonstrating robust zero-shot segmentation capabilities. Subsequently, researchers have explored diverse approaches such as Low-Rank Adaptation (LoRA) [9] to fine-tune SAM on downstream tasks including medical image segmentation and anomaly detection. However, these methods usually yield unsatisfactory positioning outcomes in face forgery localization due to their weak forgery local and global context modeling capacities.

This study focuses on: **1)** investigating how SAM and its variants perform in the deepfake detection and localization task; **2)** designing accurate and robust pixel-level forgery localization methods across various datasets. For the former one, due to the limited multiscale and subtle forgery context representation capacity, SAM [7] without or with fine-tuning [9,10] cannot achieve satisfactory forgery detection and localization results, which can be alleviated via the proposed SAM based Multiscale Adapter. On the other hand, we find that SAM and its variants are sensitive by the forgery boundary and domain shifts, which can be mitigated by the proposed Reconstruction Guided Attention module.

Our main contributions are summarized as follows: (1) We are the first to explore the availability of SAM and its fine-tuning strategies in the deepfake detection area. Based on SAM, a novel and efficient Detect Any Deepfakes (DADF) framework is proposed. (2) We propose the Multiscale Adapter in SAM, which can capture short- and long-range forgery contexts for efficient fine-tuning. (3) We propose the Reconstruction Guided Attention (RGA) module to enhance forged traces and augment the model's sensitivity towards forgery regions.

2 Related Work

Binary Classification Based Face Forgery Detection. Face forgery detection is predominantly treated as a binary (real/fake) classification task. Plenty of deep learning based methods are developed for detecting face forgery. Dang et al. [11] incorporated an attention mechanism to emphasize the forgery area, leading to improved accuracy in forgery classification. Alternatively, Nguyen et al. [12] proposed a capsule network designed specifically for identifying counterfeit images or videos. However, the above-mentioned methods only provide the result of forgery on the scale of the whole image, thus ignoring the identification of the forged region, which lack sufficient interpretability.

Joint Face Fogery Detection and Localization. Face forgery localization precisely identifies manipulated regions of a face at the pixel level. A hybrid CNN-LSTM model [13] was proposed for learning the distinctive boundary variations between manipulated and non-manipulated regions. Nguyen et al. [14] proposed to utilize multi-task learning to detect and locate manipulated regions in both images and videos. However, there are still no works investigating vision segmentation foundation models for joint face forgery detection and localization.

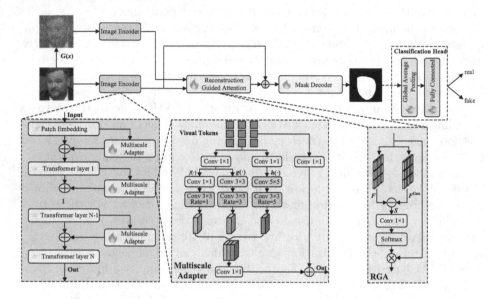

Fig. 1. Framework of the proposed Detect Any Deepfakes (DADF).

3   Methodology

As illustrated in Fig. 1, the proposed SAM-based [7] architecture involves an image encoder with the Multiscale Adapters for feature extraction, a Reconstruction Guided Attention (RGA) module for forged feature refinement and a mask decoder for forgery mask prediction. Based on the predicted mask, a classification head consisting of global average pooling and fully connected layers is cascaded for real/fake classification. In consideration of the limited data scale in the face forgery detection task, we freeze the main parameters (i.e., Transformer layers) of the SAM encoder and insert learnable specific modules to mine task-aware forgery clues. Specifically, we incorporate a concise and efficient Multiscale Adapter module along each transformer layer to capture forgery clues with diverse receptive fields using a multi-scale fashion.

First, we tokenize the input image x into visual tokens $x_p = P(x)$ via the Patch Embedding layer (denoted as $P(\cdot)$). During this process, defaulted patch size 14×14 is used. Then N fixed Transformer layers $L_i, i \in \{1, ..., N\}$ with learnable Multiscale Adapter $R(\cdot)$ are used for extracting short- and long-range contextual features Z_{tran}, which is then mapped to task-aware forgery features F via a dimension-matched learnable linear Task Head $T(\cdot)$. The feature encoding procedure can be formulated as

$$Z_{\text{tran}} = L_n(...L_2(R(L_1(R(x_p)))), \quad F = T(Z_{\text{tran}}). \tag{1}$$

As for the Multiscale Adapter (see the middle red block in Fig. 1 and Fig in Supplementary Materials, the output features x' of each Transformer layer are passed by a 1×1 convolution, and then split into three branches $f(\cdot)$, $g(\cdot)$, and $h(\cdot)$. Each branch uses different convolution kernel sizes and dilated rates for complementary forgery context mining. Therefore, the multiscale short- and long-range features $Sout_1$ can be formulated as:

$$
\begin{aligned}
Sout' &= \text{Concat}(f(\text{Conv}_{1\times1}(x')), g(\text{Conv}_{1\times1}(x')), h(\text{Conv}'_{1\times1}(x'))), \\
Sout_1 &= \text{Conv}''_{1\times1}(Sout'),
\end{aligned} \tag{2}
$$

where $f(\cdot)$, $g(\cdot)$ and $h(\cdot)$ denote a convolution with kernel size 1×1 cascaded with a convolution with kernel size 3×3 and dilated rates 1, a convolution with kernel size 3×3 cascaded with a convolution with kernel size 3×3 and dilated rates 3, and a convolution with kernel size 5×5 cascaded with a convolution with kernel size 3×3 and dilated rates 5, respectively. $Sout'$ is the result of merging features of the three branches, which is then re-projected to the original channel size via a 1×1 convolution to obtain $Sout_1$.

Finally, the resultant multi-scale features $Sout_1$ are added together to the original features x' passed over a 1×1 convolution operation $\text{Conv}'''_{1\times1}$, ensuring the preservation of the original information. The final multiscale contextual features $Sout$ can be formulated as:

$$Sout = Sout_1 + \text{Conv}'''_{1\times1}(x'). \tag{3}$$

3.1 Reconstruction Guided Attention

In order to enhance the sensitivity to deep forged regions and explore the common and compact feature patterns of real faces, we propose a reconstruction learning method, namely Reconstruction Guided Attention (RGA). In the training process, we simulate the forged faces by introducing white noise $G(\cdot)$ on the real faces. Based on the noisy inputs, the model gradually performs feature reconstruction to obtain the reconstructed features F^{Gau}.

$$x^{\text{Gau}} = G(x), \quad F^{\text{Gau}} = \Phi(x^{\text{Gau}}), \tag{4}$$

where Φ denotes the whole image encoder. After the feature reconstruction process performed by the image encoder, we compute the absolute difference S between the original features and the reconstructed features. In this calculation, the function $|.|$ represents the absolute value function.

$$S = |F^{\text{Gau}} - F|. \tag{5}$$

Subsequently, an enhancer $\varphi(\cdot)$ with 1×1 convolution is employed to high-light and enhance regions that might contain forgeries, which is cascaded with the Softmax function layer $\alpha(\cdot)$ to generate the forgery-aware attention map. Finally, we perform element-wise multiplication based refinement operation $\otimes$ between the obtained attention weights and the original features to obtain the final features F_{final}, which are then sent for the mask decoder. The procedure can be formulated as:

$$F_{\text{final}} = [\alpha(\varphi(S)) \otimes \varphi(F)] + F. \tag{6}$$

After obtaining the features F from the real faces and the reconstructed features F^{Gau} from the anomalies/forgeries simulation, we calculate the reconstruction loss $\mathcal{L}_{\text{rec}}$ for each batch M with $L1$ norm. Notably, the reconstruction loss L_{rec} is exclusively trained on real samples. Ablation studies on calculating $\mathcal{L}_{\text{rec}}$ for fake faces and all (real+fake) faces can be found in Table 5.

$$\mathcal{L}_{\text{rec}} = \frac{1}{M} \sum_{i \in M} \left\| F_i^{\text{Gau}} - F_i \right\|_1. \tag{7}$$

In the training stage, the RGA module leverages the abnormal simulated faces as one of the inputs and gradually recovers the intrinsic features of the real faces. Through this reconstruction process, SAM models can better understand the common and compact feature patterns of real faces, and even pay more attention to unknown forged regions in the inference stage.

3.2 Loss Function

The overall loss function $\mathcal{L}_{\text{overall}}$ of DADF consists of three components: segmentation loss $\mathcal{L}_{\text{seg}}$, classification loss $\mathcal{L}_{\text{cls}}$, and feature reconstruction loss $\mathcal{L}_{\text{rec}}$. The segmentation loss $\mathcal{L}_{\text{seg}}$ represents the semantic loss, while the binary cross-entropy loss $\mathcal{L}_{\text{cls}}$ measures the binary real/fake classification error. The feature reconstruction los $\mathcal{L}_{\text{rec}}$ captures the reconstruction error.

$$\mathcal{L}_{\text{overall}} = \mathcal{L}_{\text{seg}} + \lambda_1 \mathcal{L}_{\text{rec}} + \lambda_2 \mathcal{L}_{\text{cls}}, \tag{8}$$

where the hyperparameters λ_1 and λ_2 are used to balance the different components of the loss, which are set to 0.1 according to empirical observations.

4 Experiments

4.1 Datasets and Experimental Setup

Datasets. FaceForensics++ (FF++) [15] utilizes four different algorithms. The video data also provide versions with different compression ratios: original quality (quantization = 0), high quality (HQ, quantization = 23) and low quality (LQ, quantization = 40). **DF-TIMI** [16] dataset contained 16 pairs of similar people, each of whom lived 10 videos. **DFD** [15] was created specifically for

DeepFake technology. These videos were procured from the YouTube platform, consisting of 363 authentic videos and 3068 fabricated videos, which have been further categorized as high-quality (HQ) and low-quality (LQ). **FMLD** [4] comprises 40,000 synthetic faces generated using StyleGAN and PGGAN models.

Implementation Details. We use the SAM-based [7] ViT-H model as the backbone with a null input prompt setting. We train models with a batch size of 4 and adopt the AdamW optimizer with a learning rate (lr) 0.05. We train models with maximum 50 epochs while lr halves every 20 epochs. As for the RGA module, white noise is employed as a noise source, which is incorporated into the data using a normal distribution with a zero mean and a variance of $1e - 6$.

Evaluation Metrics. Two commonly used metrics, namely Binary Classification Accuracy (PBCA) and Inverse Intersection Non-Containment (IINC) [11] are employed for forgery localization. For fair comparisons, we follow the same evaluation protocols as [4] for face forgery localization. In terms of evaluating the performance of face forgery detection, Accuracy (ACC) is adopted.

4.2   Intra-dataset Testing

Results of Face Forgery Localization. Table 1 presents the results of the forgery localization on FF++ (HQ) [15] and FMLD [4]. The proposed DADF outperform the classical face forgery localization model [4] by 0.87% and 0.2% PBCA on FF++ (HQ) and FMLD, respectively. We can also find from the results of SAM [7] that direct finetuning SAM cannot achieve acceptable face forgery localization performance due to its heavy model parameters and limited task-aware data. Despite slight improvement via parameter-efficient fine-tuning strategies, SAM with LoRA or Prompt still has performance gaps with the previous localization method [4]. Thanks to the rich forgery contexts from the Multiscale Adapter and the strong forgery attention ability of RGA module, the proposed DADF improves baseline SAM [7] by 3.67%/−1.04% and 1.97%/−0.76% PBCA/IINC on FF++ (HQ) and FMLD, respectively.

Results of Face Forgery Detection. Table 2 presents the detection accuracy (ACC) of our model on various forgery techniques, namely Deepfake (DF), Face2Face (FF), FaceSwap (FS), and NeuralTextures (NT), using the challenging FF++ (LQ) [15]. It is clear that the proposed DADF performs significant improvements in classification accuracy compared to previous methods among different forgery techniques. This highlights the effectiveness of our Multiscale Adapter and RGA module in enhancing the detection capabilities, compared with the original SAM [7] and its variants (SAM+LoRA [9] and SAM+Prompt [10]). Specifically, the proposed DADF improves more than 3% ACC compared with the second-best method on Face2Face detection.

Table 1. Results of the forgery localization on FF++ (HQ) [15] and FMLD [4].

| Dataset | FF++ (HQ) | | FMLD | |
Methods	PBCA(%)↑	IINC(%)↓	PBCA(%)↑	IINC(%)↓
Multitask [14]	94.88	4.46	98.59	3.52
DFFD Reg [11]	94.85	4.57	98.72	3.31
DFFD Mam [11]	91.45	13.09	96.86	23.93
Locate [4]	95.77	3.62	99.06	**2.53**
SAM [7]	92.97	4.25	97.29	3.40
SAM+LoRA [9]	93.12	4.78	98.06	3.51
SAM+Prompt [10]	94.60	3.48	98.01	2.82
DADF (Ours)	**96.64**	**3.21**	**99.26**	2.64

Table 2. The forgery detection performance (ACC(%)) on FF++ (LQ) [15].

Methods	DF	FF	FS	NT	Average
Steg. Features [17]	67.00	48.00	49.00	56.00	55.00
Cozzolino [18]	75.00	56.00	51.00	62.00	61.00
Bayar & Stamm [19]	87.00	82.00	74.00	74.00	79.25
Rahmouni [20]	80.00	62.00	59.00	59.00	65.00
MesoNet [21]	90.00	83.00	83.00	75.00	82.75
SPSL [22]	93.48	86.02	92.26	**92.26**	91.00
Xception [22]	97.16	91.02	96.71	82.88	91.94
Locate [4]	97.25	94.46	97.13	84.63	93.36
SAM [7]	89.32	84.56	91.19	80.01	86.27
SAM+LoRA [9]	90.12	85.41	91.28	80.15	86.74
SAM+Prompt [10]	97.34	95.84	97.44	84.72	93.83
DADF (Ours)	**99.02**	**98.92**	**98.23**	87.61	**95.94**

4.3   Cross-Dataset Testing

In order to assess the generalization ability of our method on unseen domains and unknown deepfakes, we conducted cross-dataset experiments by training and testing on different datasets. Specifically, we train models on FF++ (LQ), and then test them on DFD (LQ), DF-TIMIT (HQ), and DF-TIMIT (LQ). The results shown in Table 3 demonstrate that the proposed DADF outperforms other methods in terms of average performance among the three testing settings.

4.4   Ablation Study

To validate the effectiveness of the Multiscale Adapter and Reconstruction Guided Attention module, ablation experiments are conducted on FF++ (HQ).

Table 3. Results of cross-dataset face forgery detection.

Dataset	DFD (LQ)		DF-TIMIT (HQ)		DF-TIMIT (LQ)		Average	
Method	AUC(%)↑	EER(%)↓	AUC(%)↑	EER(%)↓	AUC(%)↑	EER(%)↓	AUC(%)↑	EER(%)↓
MesoNet [20]	52.25	48.65	33.61	60.16	45.08	53.04	34.64	53.95
MesoIncep4 [20]	**63.27**	40.37	16.12	76.18	27.47	66.77	35.62	61.10
ResNet50 [23]	60.61	42.23	41.95	55.97	47.27	52.33	49.94	50.17
Face X-ray [24]	62.89	39.58	42.52	55.07	50.05	**49.11**	51.81	47.92
DFFD [11]	60.60	42.32	32.91	61.16	39.32	57.06	44.27	53.51
Multi-task [14]	58.61	44.49	16.53	77.86	15.59	78.50	30.24	66.95
F3Net [25]	58.89	39.87	29.12	58.33	45.67	52.72	44.56	50.30
Xception [22]	59.73	43.12	33.82	62.83	40.79	57.44	44.78	54.46
SAM [7]	50.61	49.13	43.19	57.94	45.71	54.39	46.50	53.82
SAM+LoRA [9]	53.71	48.29	43.64	56.67	47.64	53.02	48.33	52.66
SAM+Prompt [10]	57.25	45.28	44.32	55.07	48.17	52.54	49.91	50.96
DADF (Ours)	63.21	**39.52**	**46.37**	**53.20**	**50.62**	49.74	**53.40**	**47.48**

Efficacy of the Multiscale Adapter. It can be seen from the first two rows of Table 4 that compared with baseline SAM-only fine-tuning, SAM with Multiscale Adapter improves 3.34%/−0.85% PBLA/IINC for forgery localization and 8.21% ACC for forgery detection on the FF++ (HQ).

Table 4. Ablation studies on the FF++ (HQ) [15] dataset.

Baseline (SAM)	Multiscale Adapter	RGA	Localization		Detection
			PBLA(%)↑	IINC(%)↓	ACC(%)↑
✓			92.97	4.25	86.27
✓	✓		96.31	3.40	94.48
✓		✓✓	95.61	3.96	92.64
✓	✓	✓	**96.64**	**3.21**	**95.94**

Efficacy of the RGA. As shown in the last two rows of Table 4, equipping with RGA module can improve the baseline SAM by 2.64%/−0.29% PBLA/IINC for forgery localization and 6.37% ACC for forgery detection on the FF++ (HQ). Similarly, based on the SAM with Multiscale Adapter, the RGA module can further benefit the forgery localization by 0.33% PBLA and detection by 1.46% ACC. As for the loss function $\mathcal{L}_{rec}$ calculation for RGA, it can be seen from Table 5 that the performance drops sharply when $\mathcal{L}_{rec}$ calculated for fake faces and all (real+fake) faces, which might result from the redundant features of real faces and less attention on anomalies.

4.5 Visualization and Discussion

We visualize some representative forgery samples with their mask labels and predictions in Fig. 2. It is evident that the forgery localization quality from the

Table 5. Ablation studies of $\mathcal{L}_{rec}$ calculation on FF++ (HQ) [15] dataset.

Data	Localization		Detection
	PBLA(%)↑	IINC(%)↓	ACC(%)↑
Real & Fake	92.15	3.62	91.42
Fake	93.34	3.56	92.16
Real	**96.64**	**3.21**	**95.94**

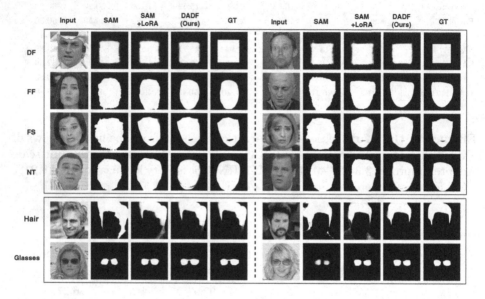

Fig. 2. Visualization of face forgery localization results of various methods.

proposed DADF outperforms SAM and its LoRA fine-tuning in accurately localizing and closely resembling the ground truth, particularly in fine-grained details such as edge, boundary, and face-head contexts. Besides, the proposed Multiscale Adapter is a parameter-efficient fine-tuning strategy alternative to tune the entire Transformer layers. Remarkably, by adjusting only 18.64% parameters of the SAM, substantial benefits on face forgery detection and localization are achieved, including reduced training costs and improved practical performance.

5   Conclusion

In this paper, we introduce a Segment Anything Model based face forgery detection and localization framework, namely Detect Any Deepfakes (DADF). Specifically, we propose the Multiscale Adapter and Reconstruction Guided Attention (RGA) to efficiently fine-tune SAM with rich contextual forgery clues and enhance the robustness of forgery localization. Extensive experimental results validate the effectiveness of the proposed DADF across different qualities of face images and even under cross-domain scenarios.

Acknowledgement. This work was supported by the National Natural Science Foundation of China (No. 62276221, No. 62306061), the Natural Science Foundation of Fujian Province of China (No. 2022J01002), the Science and Technology Plan Project of Xiamen (No. 3502Z20221025).

References

1. Lukáš, J., Fridrich, J., Goljan, M.: Detecting digital image forgeries using sensor pattern noise. In: Security, Steganography, and Watermarking of Multimedia Contents VIII. SPIE (2006)
2. Swaminathan, A., Wu, M., Liu, K.R.: Digital image forensics via intrinsic fingerprints. IEEE TIFS **3**, 101–117 (2008)
3. Chierchia, G., Parrilli, S., Poggi, G., Verdoliva, L., Sansone, C.: PRNU-based detection of small-size image forgeries. In: IEEE DSP (2011)
4. Kong, C., Chen, B., Li, H., Wang, S., Rocha, A., Kwong, S.: Detect and locate: exposing face manipulation by semantic-and noise-level telltales. IEEE TIFS **17**, 1741–1756 (2022)
5. Huang, Y., Juefei-Xu, F., Guo, Q., Liu, Y., Pu, G.: FakeLocator: robust localization of GAN-based face manipulations. IEEE TIFS **17**, 2657–2672 (2022)
6. Guo, X., Liu, X., Ren, Z., Grosz, S., Masi, I., Liu, X.: Hierarchical fine-grained image forgery detection and localization. In: IEEE CVPR (2023)
7. Kirillov, A., et al.: Segment anything. arXiv preprint arXiv:2304.02643 (2023)
8. Zhang, C., et al.: A comprehensive survey on segment anything model for vision and beyond. arXiv preprint arXiv:2305.08196 (2023)
9. Zhou, X., Yang, C., Zhao, H., Yu, W.: Low-rank modeling and its applications in image analysis. ACM Comput. Surv. (CSUR) **47**, 1–33 (2014)
10. Qiu, Z., Hu, Y., Li, H., Liu, J.: Learnable ophthalmology SAM. arXiv preprint arXiv:2304.13425 (2023)
11. Dang, H., Liu, F., Stehouwer, J., Liu, X., Jain, A.K.: On the detection of digital face manipulation. In: IEEE CVPR (2020)
12. Nguyen, H.H., Yamagishi, J., Echizen, I.: Capsule-forensics: using capsule networks to detect forged images and videos. In: IEEE ICASSP (2019)
13. Bappy, J.H., Roy-Chowdhury, A.K., Bunk, J., Nataraj, L., Manjunath, B.: Exploiting spatial structure for localizing manipulated image regions. In: IEEE ICCV (2017)
14. Nguyen, H.H., Fang, F., Yamagishi, J., Echizen, I.: Multi-task learning for detecting and segmenting manipulated facial images and videos. In: IEEE BTAS (2019)
15. Rössler, A., Cozzolino, D., Verdoliva, L., Riess, C., Thies, J., Nießner, M.: FaceForensics: a large-scale video dataset for forgery detection in human faces. arXiv preprint arXiv:1803.09179 (2018)
16. Korshunov, P., Marcel, S.: DeepFakes: a new threat to face recognition? Assessment and detection. arXiv preprint arXiv:1812.08685 (2018)
17. Fridrich, J., Kodovsky, J.: Rich models for steganalysis of digital images. IEEE TIFS **7**, 868–882 (2012)
18. Cao, J., Ma, C., Yao, T., Chen, S., Ding, S., Yang, X.: End-to-end reconstruction-classification learning for face forgery detection. In: CVPR (2022)

19. Bayar, B., Stamm, M.C.: A deep learning approach to universal image manipulation detection using a new convolutional layer. In: ACM Workshop on Information Hiding and Multimedia Security (2016)
20. Afchar, D., Nozick, V., Yamagishi, J., Echizen, I.: MesoNet: a compact facial video forgery detection network. In: IEEE WIFS (2018)
21. Liu, X., et al.: P-tuning v2: prompt tuning can be comparable to fine-tuning universally across scales and tasks. arXiv preprint arXiv:2110.07602 (2021)
22. Chollet, F.: Xception: deep learning with depthwise separable convolutions. In: IEEE CVPR (2017)
23. He, K., Zhang, X., Ren, S., Sun, J.: Deep residual learning for image recognition. In: IEEE CVPR (2016)
24. Li, L., et al.: Face X-ray for more general face forgery detection. In: IEEE CVPR (2020)
25. Qian, Y., Yin, G., Sheng, L., Chen, Z., Shao, J.: Thinking in frequency: face forgery detection by mining frequency-aware clues. In: Vedaldi, A., Bischof, H., Brox, T., Frahm, J.-M. (eds.) ECCV 2020. LNCS, vol. 12357, pp. 86–103. Springer, Cham (2020). https://doi.org/10.1007/978-3-030-58610-2_6

Dynamic Face Expression Generation with Efficient Neural Radiation Field

Te Yang[1,2], Xiangyu Zhu[1,2(✉)], and Zhen Lei[1,2,3]

[1] State Key Laboratory of Multimodal Artificial Intelligence Systems,
CASIA, Beijing, China
yangte2021@ia.ac.cn
[2] School of Artificial Intelligence, University of Chinese Academy of Sciences
(UCAS), Beijing, China
{xiangyu.zhu,zlei}@nlpr.ia.ac.cn
[3] The Centre for Artificial Intelligence and Robotics, Hong Kong Institute of Science
and Innovation, Chinese Academy of Sciences, Pak Shek Kok, Hong Kong

Abstract. Lacking of sufficient generalization ability on novel perspectives and expressions, drivable face NeRF, is still a challenging problem. In this paper, we concentrate on two aspects of the drivable face NeRF, the representation power of the driving signal and the efficiency of NeRF rendering. Firstly, we look into the utilization of world-space keypoints as the driving signal of the dynamic face. We realize this by a keypoint lifting strategy based on front keypoints to obtain stable and robust world-space keypoints, which are used to drive the deformation field and the Neural Radiance Field in the canonical space simultaneously. Second, the world-space keypoints are utilized to guide the NeRF to efficiently sample points near the face surface, and the coarse level in the original NeRF can be skipped, which significantly accelerates the rendering speed. We have verified the effectiveness and superiority of our method through good experiments.

Keywords: Neural radiance field · Novel expression synthesis · Novel view synthesis · Dynamic NeRF

1 Introduction

Generating realistic and controllable portraits, is a highly important and challenging problem in the field of computer vision. There are a wide range of applications, such as remote conferencing, virtual anchors, film production, and more. In the foreseeable future, the metaverse will increasingly occupy people's lives. Generating high-quality avatars for each individual is an indispensable step in building the metaverse.

© The Author(s), under exclusive license to Springer Nature Singapore Pte Ltd. 2023
W. Jia et al. (Eds.): CCBR 2023, LNCS 14463, pp. 191–201, 2023.
https://doi.org/10.1007/978-981-99-8565-4_19

In recent years, neural rendering has garnered widespread attention. It utilizes neural networks to implicitly represent three-dimensional scenes, thereby exhibiting excellent 3D consistency. Also, it requires only sparse images as input and can render remarkably high-quality images from any viewpoint. However, the initial framework of NeRF suffers from the limitation of static scenes and low rendering speed, which limits its applications.

In this paper, we apply neural rendering techniques to the tasks of novel viewpoint synthesis and facial expression driving for human faces and realize a drivable dynamic face NeRF, which can perform any expressions according to the driving signals as illustrated in Fig. 1. Our approach takes as input multiview images of faces with different expressions and outputs facial images with specified expressions from any arbitrary viewpoint. This method can be employed to create realistic facial avatars for users. To the best of our knowledge, our model is the first to simultaneously satisfy the criteria of utilizing stereo data, modeling dense expressions, and being uncomplicated in its preprocessing requirements.

In the course of conducting this research, we predominantly face two challenges: Firstly, devising an effective approach to make the model movable, which encompasses determining the optimal model architecture and selecting the suitable driving signal. The second issue we consider is how to optimize the model's training and testing speed as much as possible. To tackle the first challenge, we employ a strategy that fuses conditional NeRF and deformation field to establish a dynamic NeRF model. We develop a keypoint lifting strategy that yields precise world-space keypoints as driving signal. In response to the second challenge, we utilize keypoints in the world-coordinate system to guide NeRF sampling. We bypass the coarse level of NeRF and focus solely on sampling points which are in close proximity to facial keypoints. This substantially enhances rendering efficiency and diminishes the overall model size. The main contributions of this paper are summarized as follows:

(1) We proposed a new drivable dynamic face NeRF that is capable of synthesizing high-fidelity photos from any viewpoints of human faces, which can perform realistic expressions according to driving signals.
(2) We introduce the world-space keypoints into the framework, which not only improves the fidelity of the driven faces, however, also helps accelerate the model.
(3) The experiments show that our method outperforms previous methods and achieves faster speed.

Fig. 1. First column: the world-space keypoints that are utilized as the driving signals. Other columns: the corresponding rendered images from different perspectives.

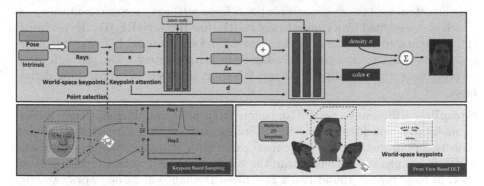

Fig. 2. Overview of our drivable face NeRF pipeline. Leveraging multi-view images and camera poses, 2D keypoints are extracted for each viewpoint using a face tracker. Employing Front view-based Direct Linear Transformation (DLT), 3D keypoints are acquired, enhancing sampling probability near the face during ray sampling. The sample points, world space keypoints' driving signals, and latent code are fed into a deformation network, transitioning them into the canonical space, where color and voxel density of sample points are computed. Through the rendering equation, the color of rays is determined. (Color figure online)

2   Related Work

Neural Rendering. The Neural Radiance Field [10] has received widespread attention since its inception. It directly models the color and occupancy of the scene as an implicit field, which is represented by a neural network. Then, novel views of the scene can be obtained by applying the rendering equation to the implicit field. Since then, numerous studies have made significant contributions to NeRF in static scenes from various perspectives, including extending NeRF to scenes in the wild [8] and at a large scale [12,16], integrating NeRF with computational imaging [7,9], and others. For a comprehensive account of the progress, interested readers may refer to [13].

Dynamic Neural Radiance Field. A straightforward idea to make NeRF models drivable is to make NeRF be conditioned on driving signals like time [2] or expressions [1,3,17]. NeRFACE [1] performs 3D facial reconstruction from monocular videos. However, it approximates images of different head poses under the same viewpoint as if they originate from distinct perspectives., resulting in jittering in the torso region during head pose changes. In our work, we utilize genuine stereo data, thereby eliminating such issues. Works such as MofaNeRF [17] and HeadNeRF [3] explore the construction of parametric facial models using conditional neural radiance fields. However, their methods only suitable for discrete expressions, which are insufficient for creating facial avatars. In our work, we utilize Meta's MultiFace dataset, which encompasses a rich variety of facial expressions. As a result, our model can generate realistic facial images with continuous expressions. Another related technique of dynamic NeRF is to integrate a deformation field to warp a sample point from picture space to canonical space which is represented by a conventional NeRF, like HyperNeRF [11]. HyperNeRF [11] is dedicated to addressing the issue of deformation fields being unable to capture topological changes. The adaptively learned latent codes, though uninterpretable, excel at interpolation but fall short in effectively controlling digital faces.

Sampling Efficiency. NeRF [10] suffers from poor sampling efficiency. NSVF [4] maintains explicit sparse voxels to concentrate sampling in regions containing objects. In our method, we don't need extra data structures like sparse voxels. MVP [5] samples exclusively within the volume anchored to facial meshes. However, in most cases, ground truth face mesh is unknown. In our work, we only use keypoints lifted from 2d keypoints by face tracker to guide sampling, which also effectively improves sampling efficiency.

3 Proposed Approach

The overall framework of our drivable face NeRF is shown in Fig. 2. In this section, we first introduce the architecture of drivable face NeRF, where a keypoint attention module is employed to capture the relations between world-space keypoints and the relations are sent to MLPs to model pose and expression variations. Then, we introduce how to get the world-space keypoints from the multi-view images. Finally, we elaborate a keypoints-based sampling strategy that only samples the points near the face surface to boost sampling efficiency.

3.1 Dynamic Face NeRF

The dynamic face NeRF is composed of three parts, world-space keypoints attention model, deformation field and canonical radiance field.

World-Space Keypoints Attention. Given world-space keypoints $a \in \mathbb{R}^{k \times 3}$ which are human face keypoints in world coordinate, k denotes the number of world-space keypoints, we use a self-attention module [14] to capture the relationship between different world-space keypoints. World-space keypoints are linear embedded to $Q, K \in \mathbb{R}^{k \times 10}, V \in \mathbb{R}^{k \times 3}$ by $W_q, W_k \in \mathbb{R}^{3 \times 10}, W_v \in \mathbb{R}^{3 \times 3}$, where

$$Q = aW_q, K = aW_k, V = aW_v. \tag{1}$$

Then

$$att = softmax(\frac{QK^T}{\sqrt{d}})V + k. \tag{2}$$

Deformation Field. Conventional NeRF model has trouble in modeling large head and torso movement. Therefore, we employ a deformation field to capture the significant movement, transforming sampling points from the photo space to the canonical space. A deformation field is defined as $D : (x, att) \rightarrow \Delta x$, where x is the sampling point which has been positional encoded. By $x \rightarrow x + \Delta x$, we transform it to canonical space.

Canonical Radiance Field. Although deformation field can represent humans' movement, small changes over different frames such as micro-expressions, are out of the ability of a single deformation field. So we concatenate world-space keypoints attention into the input of the canonical radiance field, promoting our model to more accurate expressions. Our canonical model is defined as

$$F : (x, \mathbf{d}, att) \rightarrow \sigma, c, \tag{3}$$

where x is the three dimensional coordinate of sampling points and $\mathbf{d}$ is the corresponding view direction, both are positional embedded. We use the following rendering equation to turn the result volume density and color into RGB values of rays.

$$RGB = \int_{z_{near}}^{z_{far}} \sigma(\mathbf{r}(t))c(\mathbf{r}(t), \mathbf{d})T(t)dt, \tag{4}$$

where

$$T(t) = exp(-\int_{z_{near}}^{t} \sigma(\mathbf{r}(s))ds. \tag{5}$$

We use image reconstruction loss to train our model.

3.2   Driving NeRF by World-Space Keypoints

Let I denote a set of cameras. Given a set of 2d points $\{p_i | i \in I\}$ that are projections from different views of a 3D point, solving a set of over-determined equations defined by projection relations through SVD can recover the coordinate of the 3D point, which is also called direct linear transformation (DLT).

In practice, the 2D detection models cannot perform well in every view. In most of the cases, keypoints from the front view are more accurate and stable than that from the side views, as we can see in Fig. 4. Therefore, we propose front view based DLT to find the potentially best world-space 3D points matching the 2d positions.

Consider a 3D point, denote the homogeneous coordinate of its front view projection as $p_0 = (x_0, y_0, 1)$, its depth from front view as d and its 3D position in world coordinate as q_w, and denote intrinsic and extrinsic parameters of the front view camera as K_0, T_0, we know

$$q_w = T_0^{-1} K_0^{-1} \begin{bmatrix} dp_0 \\ 1 \end{bmatrix}. \tag{6}$$

Given another view i and the corresponding projection matrix from world space to the photo space as P_i, we have $p_i \times P_i q_w = 0$. Denote $[L|R] = P_i T_0^{-1} K_0^{-1}$, where $L \in \mathbb{R}^{3\times3}$, $R \in \mathbb{R}^{3\times1}$, we have $(p_i \times Lp_0)d + (p_i \times R) = 0$, which finally gives us an equation of type

$$\begin{bmatrix} f_1^i \\ f_2^i \end{bmatrix} d + \begin{bmatrix} g_1^i \\ g_2^i \end{bmatrix} = 0. \tag{7}$$

Considering equations corresponding to all $\{i \in I | i \neq 0\}$, let $F = [f_1^1, f_2^1, \ldots, f_1^i, f_2^i, \ldots]^T$, $G = [g_1^1, g_2^1, \ldots, g_1^i, g_2^i, \ldots]^T$, the solution can be written as

$$d = \frac{F \cdot -G}{F \cdot F}. \tag{8}$$

3.3   Keypoint-Based Efficient Sampling

In the original NeRF [10], a two-stage model is proposed to capture the detail of the scene: a coarse-level model that samples random points along the ray and models the rough geometry, and a fine-level model in which points along a ray are more likely to be selected if they have higher volume density in coarse level model.

In our method, we find that with world-space keypoints, we only need to sample the points which have the shortest distance to the set of world-space keypoints. It helps us get rid of the coarse level model, leading to higher speed and lower GPU memory cost. Specifically, we first sample N points uniformly for each ray and calculate keypoints distance. We define the distance between a sample point p and the keypoint set S as

$$d_p = \frac{1}{3} \min_{i,j,k \in S, i \neq j \neq k} (\|i - p\|_2 + \|j - p\|_2 + \|k - p\|_2), \tag{9}$$

where i, j, k traverse the set of keypoints S. If the minor distance along the ray r, $d_{min} = \min_{p \in r} d_p$ is smaller than a threshold, we randomly sample half points between the two points with the smallest distance among the N points and half points randomly. Otherwise, we randomly sample all points.

3.4 Training

Loss Function. The drivable face NeRF is trained using the loss function: $L = L_{recon} + \lambda L_{latent}$. The first term is the reconstruction loss, which measures the L2 distance between the predicted color and the ground truth color The second term is a regularization term of latent code as in [1], which penalizes large values of latent code.

4 Experimental Results

Dataset. We use the publicly available dataset Multiface [15], a dataset for research on high quality digital humans released by Meta Reality Labs Research, to verify the effectiveness of our model. Five types of data are given: Multiview photos, unwrapped textures, meshes, audio and metadata which mainly provide intrinsic and extrinsic data of cameras. Since the whole dataset takes over 100T hardware memory, we take the data from id 00264381 to conduct the following experiments.

Data Pre-processing. We resize all images to 333×512 to maintain a proper i/o speed. Then we use the opensource package mediapipe [6] to detect 2d facial keypoints. The world-space keypoints are then generated as described in Sect. 3.2.

Implementation Details. The deformation network and canonical network share a structure that contains 6 hidden layers and a skip connection from the input layer to the 4-th hidden layer. We use Adam optimizer to train our model and set the initial learning rate to $5e^{-4}$. An exponential learning rate decay strategy with a 0.1 decay factor and 250000 decay steps is adopted. The model is trained with 400000 iterations to get convergence. In each iteration, we sample 128 random rays. The algorithm is implemented on pytorch 1.10.2, and is run on Ubuntu 18.04.4 system. We use 8 Nvidia 3090Ti GPUs to train our model, with a batch size of 32.

4.1 Comparison with SOTA

We compare our results with the state-of-the-art method NerFACE [1]. We report two metrics PSNR and LPSIS, which are widely used in evaluating NeRF-type models.

Fig. 3. First line: Qualitative results of novel expression synthesis. Second line: Qualitative results of novel view synthesis. From left to right: Original image, NerFACE, ours w/o kpts sampling, and ours.

Novel View Synthesis. In this experiment, we take all images with different expressions and divide the images into training and testing datasets according to different cameras. We have two settings, 37 views for training and three views for testing, 27 views for training and 13 views for testing. The results are shown in first row of Fig. 3 and Table 1. One can see that using 3D keypoint can effectively improve the model's performance and our method outperforms the NerFACE.

Table 1. Results for novel view synthesis

	37 Train views		27 Train views	
	PSNR	LPSIS	PSNR	LPSIS
NerFACE [1]	26.851	0.084	25.683	0.141
ours(w/o kpts sampling)	27.012	**0.081**	25.873	**0.136**
ours	**27.621**	0.088	**25.98**	0.145

Novel Expressions Synthesis. In this experiment, we take 40 expressions for training and 2 expressions for testing. Example results are shown in Fig. 3. It can be seen that the proposed method has achieved better rendering results than NerFACE. We list novel expressions synthesis results in Table 2. To demonstrate the experimental results comprehensively, we divided the 40 test angles into five groups according to their yaw. We can see that using world-space keypoints or not has a substantial impact on the model's generalization ability, which shows that the relationship between world-space keypoints and the whole scene can be captured more easily than 2d keypoints.

Table 2. Result for novel expressions synthesis

	group1		group2		group3		group4		group5		average	
	PSNR	LPSIS	PSNR	LPSIS	PSNR	LPSIS	PSNR	LPSIS	PSNR	LPSIS	PSNR	LPSIS
NerFACE [1]	30.08	**0.108**	29.537	**0.098**	28.601	**0.106**	28.502	**0.116**	29.418	0.117	28.724	**0.111**
ours (w/o kpts sampling)	**30.806**	0.116	**30.316**	0.108	29.048	0.112	29.138	0.126	**30.462**	0.124	29.406	0.119
ours	29.973	0.123	30.252	0.117	**30.182**	0.108	**29.474**	0.121	30.143	**0.114**	**29.906**	0.116

4.2 Ablation Study

We conduct two ablation studies to show the effectiveness of our method.

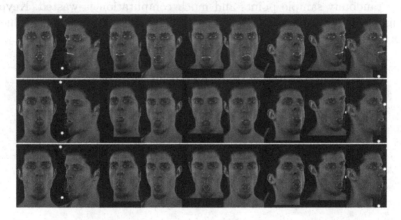

Fig. 4. Comparison of face tracker, reprojection of DLT-obtained results and ours result (from top to bottom). The red box highlights the areas where our results significantly outperform the others. (Color figure online)

Front View vs DLT. We compare Front view based direct linear transformation with direct linear transformation as in Fig. 4. Since the ground truth of world-space keypoints is unknown, we can only assess the performance of our method by projecting world-space keypoints to different perspectives. Images from various perspectives are selected to comprehensively demonstrate our experimental results. From Fig. 4, qualities of tracking results of different viewpoints are not equal and those from front views are often better because landmark detection model is expected to perform poorly in large poses. When the face tracker has a larger error in a certain perspective, results of DLT will shift in the wrong direction, which can be reflected in the reprojection results. This is because DLT assigns equal weights to all viewpoints. In our method, we assign infinite weight to the front view, which has smaller errors, in order to produce more stable results than DLT. Even though the face tracker may produce significant errors in some perspectives, Front view based DLT is barely affected and can still obtain high-quality world-space keypoints.

Table 3. Comparison of inference time and model size

	inference time	model size
ours(w/o kpts sampling)	7.26 s	2.25M
ours	**5.23 s**	**1.41M**

Keypoint Based Sampling Rendering. As we can see in Table 3, compared with the two stage method, keypoint based sampling reduces inference time and have a smaller model size. On the other hand, we compare our model with one stage model and one stage NerFACE as in Table 4. One stage methods can only randomly sample points and much computation is wasted. Keypoint sampling enable the model to sample more points near the face, thus achieving high performance.

Table 4. Ablation study of keypoint based sampling

	37views	27views	novel expression
NerFACE [1]	24.894	25.696	28.386
one stage	24.844	26.044	28.766
ours	**25.98**	**27.621**	**29.772**

5 Conclusion

In this paper, we have presented a novel method for dynamic face modeling. We first acquire high quality world-space keypoints from multi-view photos. Utilizing world-space keypoints, we achieve better performance compared to the previous method. Moreover, we propose keypoints based sampling to reduce inference time and model size.

Acknowledgement. This work was supported in part by Chinese National Natural Science Foundation Projects 62176256, 62276254, 62206280, 62106264, Beijing Natural Science Foundation under no. L221013, the Youth Innovation Promotion Association CAS (Y2021131) and the InnoHK program.

References

1. Gafni, G., Thies, J., Zollhöfer, M., Nießner, M.: Dynamic neural radiance fields for monocular 4D facial avatar reconstruction. In: Proceedings of the IEEE/CVF Conference on Computer Vision and Pattern Recognition (2021)
2. Gao, C., Saraf, A., Kopf, J., Huang, J.B.: Dynamic view synthesis from dynamic monocular video. In: Proceedings of the IEEE/CVF International Conference on Computer Vision (2021)

3. Hong, Y., Peng, B., Xiao, H., Liu, L., Zhang, J.: HeadNeRF: a real-time nerf-based parametric head model (2022)
4. Liu, L., Gu, J., Zaw Lin, K., Chua, T.S., Theobalt, C.: Neural sparse voxel fields. In: Advances in Neural Information Processing Systems (2020)
5. Lombardi, S., Simon, T., Schwartz, G., Zollhoefer, M., Sheikh, Y., Saragih, J.: Mixture of volumetric primitives for efficient neural rendering. ACM Trans. Graph. (ToG) **40**(4), 1–13 (2021)
6. Lugaresi, C., et al.: MediaPipe: a framework for building perception pipelines. arXiv preprint arXiv:1906.08172 (2019)
7. Ma, L., et al.: Deblur-NeRF: neural radiance fields from blurry images. In: Proceedings of the IEEE/CVF Conference on Computer Vision and Pattern Recognition (2022)
8. Martin-Brualla, R., Radwan, N., Sajjadi, M.S., Barron, J.T., Dosovitskiy, A., Duckworth, D.: NeRF in the wild: neural radiance fields for unconstrained photo collections. In: Proceedings of the IEEE/CVF Conference on Computer Vision and Pattern Recognition (2021)
9. Mildenhall, B., Hedman, P., Martin-Brualla, R., Srinivasan, P.P., Barron, J.T.: NeRF in the dark: high dynamic range view synthesis from noisy raw images. In: Proceedings of the IEEE/CVF Conference on Computer Vision and Pattern Recognition (2022)
10. Mildenhall, B., Srinivasan, P.P., Tancik, M., Barron, J.T., Ramamoorthi, R., Ng, R.: NeRF: representing scenes as neural radiance fields for view synthesis. In: Vedaldi, A., Bischof, H., Brox, T., Frahm, J.-M. (eds.) ECCV 2020. LNCS, vol. 12346, pp. 405–421. Springer, Cham (2020). https://doi.org/10.1007/978-3-030-58452-8_24
11. Park, K., et al.: HyperNeRF: a higher-dimensional representation for topologically varying neural radiance fields. ACM Trans. Graph. (TOG) **40**(6), 1–12 (2021)
12. Tancik, M., et al.: Block-NeRF: scalable large scene neural view synthesis. In: Proceedings of the IEEE/CVF Conference on Computer Vision and Pattern Recognition (2022)
13. Tewari, A., et al.: Advances in neural rendering. In: Computer Graphics Forum, vol. 41, pp. 703–735 (2022)
14. Vaswani, A., et al.: Attention is all you need. In: Advances in Neural Information Processing Systems (2017)
15. Wuu, C., et al.: MultiFace: a dataset for neural face rendering. arXiv preprint arXiv:2207.11243 (2022)
16. Xiangli, Y., et al.: BungeeNeRF: progressive neural radiance field for extreme multi-scale scene rendering. In: Avidan, S., Brostow, G., Cissé, M., Farinella, G.M., Hassner, T. (eds.) ECCV 2022. LNCS, vol. 13692, pp. 106–122. Springer, Cham (2022). https://doi.org/10.1007/978-3-031-19824-3_7
17. Zhuang, Y., Zhu, H., Sun, X., Cao, X.: MoFaNeRF: morphable facial neural radiance field. In: Avidan, S., Brostow, G., Cissé, M., Farinella, G.M., Hassner, T. (eds.) ECCV 2022. LNCS, vol. 13663, pp. 268–285. Springer, Cham (2022). https://doi.org/10.1007/978-3-031-20062-5_16

Adversarial Face Example Generation in AMBTC Compressed Domain

Rui Lou[1], Lu Leng[1(✉)], Hanrui Wang[2], and Zhe Jin[3]

[1] School of Software, Nanchang Hangkong University, Nanchang 330063, Jiangxi, People's Republic of China
leng@nchu.edu.cn
[2] School of Information Technology, Monash University Malaysia, 47500 Subang Jaya, Selangor, Malaysia
[3] Anhui Provincial Key Laboratory of Secure Artificial Intelligence, School of Artificial Intelligence, Anhui University, Hefei 230093, China

Abstract. In recent years, adversarial examples have played a significant role in protecting image privacy and improving the robustness of deep learning models. Most adversarial example generations are conducted in uncompressed domain; however, most images are compressed in storage and network transmission, and the compression definitely degrades the adversarial effectiveness. Absolute moment block truncation coding (AMBTC) is popular for image compression. This paper aims to study the adversarial face example generation for AMBTC format. The method is proposed and optimized in compressed trio-data domain (CTD), the adversarial face example generation is optimized directly on the trio data of each block rather than on each pix. Since CTD method optimizes the trio data, it reduces the computational overhead. The experiments on LFW face database confirm that CTD method has satisfactory anti-compression ability for AMBTC format, and simultaneously has satisfactory image quality.

Keywords: Adversarial face example · AMBTC · Anti-compression

1 Introduction

In recent years, deep learning models have been widely used in many fields. However, various studies have shown that these models are highly susceptible to adversarial attacks, resulting in security concerns. Therefore, adversarial examples are crucial for evaluating the robustness of deep learning models. Meanwhile, adversarial examples can lead to some positive and beneficial effects. For example, a large number of face images are shared on some social networks (such as Facebook and Instagram). Adversarial examples can successfully fool face detection models, and protect the privacy of face photo.

Most adversarial examples are generated in uncompressed domain. In practice, in order to save transmission bandwidth or storage space, the original images are generally compressed to remove redundancy. However, the adversarial examples are highly sensitive to image compression. The distortion introduced by the image compression greatly reduces adversarial effectiveness [1, 2]. Moreover, attackers can only intercept the lossy compressed data of images rather than the original images. And some channels do not support transmitting uncompressed adversarial images. Therefore, the adversarial example generation in compressed domain is more practical than that in uncompressed domain.

The generated adversarial examples should still maintain certain adversarial effectiveness after compression. However, due to the distortions caused by compression, the adversarial optimization process must be designed specifically for various compression formats, because the procedures of different compression formats are completely different.

Absolute moment block truncation coding (AMBTC) is a popular image compression format due to its fast encoding speed and low computational cost [3, 4]. However, as a lossy compression format, it also introduces distortions that reduce the adversarial effectiveness. Currently, no research has been done to generate adversarial examples for AMBTC format. Since face is one of the most widely used biometric modality, this paper proposes the adversarial face example generation method for AMBTC. The main contributions of this work are summarized as follows.

(1) In compressed trio-data domain (CTD), the adversarial face example generation is optimized directly on the trio data of the blocks.
(2) The proposed CTD method has both anti-compression ability for AMBTC format in untargeted and targeted attack modes, and and simultaneously has satisfactory image quality.
(3) Since CTD method optimizes the trio data instead of each pix, it reduces the computational overhead and can strongly suppress the adversarial effectiveness loss due to compression.

2 Related Works

The early adversarial examples are generated in uncompressed domain. Szegedy et al. [5] used the Limited Memory Broyden-Fletcher-Goldfarb-Shanno algorithm (L-BFGS) to solve the least perturbation equation that misclassifies the outputs. Goodfellow et al. believed that the success of adversarial attacks stemmed from the linear structure of the network models, and proposed a Fast Gradient Sign Method (FGSM) [6]. Kurakin et al. proposed a basic iterative approach (BIM) [7] to generate adversarial examples that were closer to normal examples. As a extension of FGSM, BIM sometimes is also called iteration FGSM (I-FGSM). Madry et al. proposed the projected gradient descent (PGD) algorithm [8] based on BIM.

In traditional adversarial examples generations, the adversarial effectiveness definitely degrades in compressed domain, such as JPEG, AMBTC and other compression formats. This is because the adversarial perturbations are greatly weakened and destroyed by compression. To solve this problem, a special design is required according to the principles and characteristics of the compression formats. To resist JPEG compression, Shin et al. [9] leveraged the differentiable operations to approximate the non-differentiable rounding process. Wang et al. [10] designed a compression approximation model (ComModel) based on coding and decoding. The model learned the transforms from the original-compressed pairs of images to approximate JPEG compression format.

Some adversarial example generation methods in compressed domain are conducted in frequency domain. Shi et al. [11] used the gradients in the frequency domain to guide rounding to produce the quantization discrete cosine transform (DCT) coefficients of the adversarial image. Sharma et al. [12] added the perturbation to low frequencies to avoid the adversarial effectiveness loss due to JPEG compression. Duan et al. [13] removed the image details (high-frequency coefficients) to generate adversarial examples. Zhou et al. [14] employed a low-pass filter to impose adversarial perturbations on the low frequency bands. Zhang et al. [15] no longer restricted adversarial perturbations, but regularized the source model to use more low-frequency features through adversarial training.

Although AMBTC is a popular image compression format, the anti-compression adversarial examples for AMBTC are absent. The compression/decompression procedures of JPEG and AMBTC are completely different, so the existing works for JPEG format are unsuitable for AMBTC. In this paper, a CTD method is designed for adversarial face example generation in AMBTC domain.

3 Methodology

3.1 Absolute Moment Block Truncation Coding

AMBTC [16] is a lossy compression format. First, an original image is divided into several non-overlapping blocks of size $m \times m$. For each block P, the average value $\bar{p}$ is:

$$\bar{p} = \frac{\sum_{j=1}^{m \times m} p_j}{m \times m} \qquad (1)$$

where p_j is the j-th pixel in P. The bitmap in each block is M, which is divided into two groups, M^0 and M^1, where $M = M^0 \cup M^1$ and $M^0 \cap M^1 = \varnothing$, $M^0 = \{0_0, 0_1, ..., 0_q\}$ and $M^1 = \{1_0, 1_1, ..., 1_{(m \times m - q)}\}$. q and $m \times m - q$ represent the pixel numbers of "0" and "1", respectively. The lowlight and highlight values, namely the mean pixel values in M^0 and M^1, are:

$$L = \left\lfloor \frac{1}{q} \sum_{p_j < \bar{p}} p_j \right\rfloor \qquad (2)$$

$$H = \left\lfloor \frac{1}{m \times m - q} \sum_{p_j \geq \bar{p}} p_j \right\rfloor \qquad (3)$$

In decompression, the pixels in M^0 are replaced by L; while the pixels in M^1 are replaced by H.

For color images, the Red, Green, and Blue components are separated into R, G, and B channels. AMBTC is conducted on each channel separately.

Figure 1 shows an example of AMBTC compression and decompression. For ease of explanation, the pixel values are normalized to the range of [0,1].

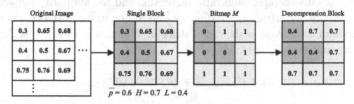

Fig. 1. AMBTC compression and decompression.

3.2 Method in Uncompressed Domain

The output of a classifier is $C(x) \in \Delta^K$, where x is an example, Δ is the probability simplex, K is the number of classes. An untargeted adversarial example x' satisfies:

$$\arg \max_k C(x')k \neq y \tag{4}$$

where y is the true label of x, k refers to the predicted class, and $\|x'-x\|$ should be small for some distance metric $\|\cdot\|$.

x' can be found by solving $\arg \max_{x'} l(C(x'), 1_y)$ s.t. $\|x'-x\|<d$, where $l(\cdot,\cdot)$ is the loss function, and $1_y \in R^K$ is a one-hot coding vector and the y-th element is set to 1.

For FGSM [8]:

$$x' + x + \epsilon \cdot \text{sign}(\nabla_{x'}[l(C(x'), 1y)]_{x'=x}) \tag{5}$$

where ϵ represents the total perturbation amplitude.

3.3 Threat Model

In uncompressed domain, the adversarial images are generated on the original image, and are transmitted to the model through the network. However, in order to save transmission bandwidth or storage space, the original images are generally compressed to remove redundancy in practice. The situation is shown in Fig. 2.

The detailed process is specified as follows. Firstly, the adversarial example x' is compressed to $t_{x'}$ by AMBTC:

$$t_{x'} = trio\_Blocks(x\prime, m) = \{\{H_1, L_1, M_1\}, \cdots, \{H_i, L_i, M_i\}, \cdots \{H_n, L_n, M_n\}\} \tag{6}$$

Each block has a piece of trio data. An image is divided into n blocks. H_i, L_i, and M_i refer to the highlight value, lowlight value and bitmap of the i-th block, respectively.

m is the side length of the block. $t_{x'}$ must be decompressed to obtain the decompressed image x_1:

$$x_1 = I(t_{x'}) \tag{7}$$

If m increases, the compression ratio increases, and the similarity between x' and x_1 decreases. Many perturbations are directly erased due to the AMBTC compression, so the adversarial effectiveness degrades sharply. When m is larger, this degradation becomes more remarkable, and leads to:

$$\arg\max_k C(x')_k \neq \arg\max_k C(x_1)_k \tag{8}$$

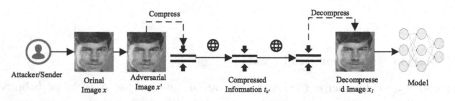

Fig. 2. Traditional attack through the network for compression.

As shown in Fig. 3, an attacker intercepts the compressed information t and generates the adversarial compressed information t'. t' replaces t and is transmitted to the model over the network.

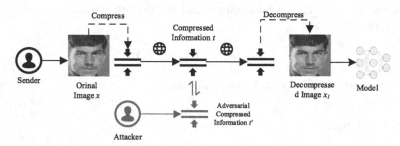

Fig. 3. Attack in compressed domain through the network for compressed format.

3.4 Method in Compressed Trio-Data Domain

CTD method directly optimizes the trio data, avoiding the perturbation loss caused by compression. Only the trio data need to be optimized, so the compression process is not included in each iteration process, and the computational overhead is reduced.

The whole process is shown in Fig. 4. The decompressed image I is put into the model to calculate the loss with the Target Label y'. Then the gradients of the trio data are obtained, and gradient descent optimization is performed to decrease the loss. The optimized intermediate trio data is t'.

Given the trio data of an original image, a step gradient is calculated by Eq. (9).

$$G = \nabla_{(H_i, L_i)} l\big(C(I(trio\_Blocks(x, m))), y'\big) \tag{9}$$

where $l(\cdot, \cdot)$ represents the loss function. For classification tasks, it computes the cross-entropy of the predicted label and actual output. For feature extraction tasks, it computes the similarity between features.

The i-the block has the trio data $\{H_i, L_i, M_i\}$. The bitmap M_i contains only 0 and 1, the direct optimization causes the highlight mean value and lowlight mean value at a pixel to be converted to each other, which definitely seriously reduces the image quality. Thus only the highlight mean value H_i and the lowlight mean information L_i are optimized.

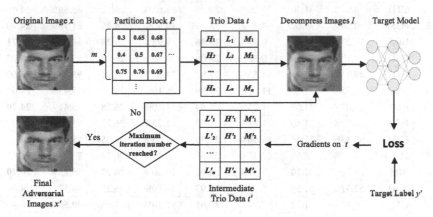

Fig. 4. CTD method for generating adversarial images in AMBTC format.

4 Experiments and Discussions

4.1 Dataset and Implementation Details

The experiments are carried out on the facial recognition system (FRS). IResnet50 [17] is used as the backbone and ArcFace [18] is used as supervisory head during training. FRS is trained on CASIA-WebFace. It is tested on LFW and the accuracy reaches 97.3%.

Both untargeted attacks and targeted attacks are tested. For untargeted attacks, 3000 face images are selected from LFW. If FRS identifies the images x and adversarial x' as two different identities, the attack is successful. For targeted attacks, 3000 pairs of face images with different identities are selected, and one image of each pair is attacked. If FRS identifies the adversarial image x' and the other face image in the pair as the same identity, the attack is successful. m is set to 4, 8, 12, 16 for compression.

FGSM, BIM, and PGD are conducted for comparisons. In PGD and CTD, infinite norms limit the disturbance amplitude.

4.2 Comparisons

Untargeted Attack. Table 1 shows the SR and PSNR in untargeted attacks. SR is attack success rate, and PSNR measures the similarity between the final decompressed adversarial examples and its original image. The larger the two, the better the attack effect and image quality. ϵ limits the disturbance amplitude.

Table 1. Anti-compression testing of adversarial examples for AMBTC in untargeted attacks

		$m = 4$		$m = 8$		$m = 12$		$m = 16$	
		SR	PSNR	SR	PSNR	SR	PSNR	SR	PSNR
$\epsilon = 2$	FGSM	0.27%	32.00	1.13%	28.07	12.13%	26.28	56.83%	24.70
	BIM	0.90%	32.10	0.60%	**28.08**	8.73%	**26.29**	53.30%	**24.71**
	PGD	0.60%	**32.12**	0.43%	28.08	8.33%	26.29	52.63%	24.71
	CTD	**6.07%**	31.96	**21.20%**	27.98	**51.63%**	26.22	**85.80%**	24.65
$\epsilon = 3$	FGSM	0.50%	31.67	4.37%	28.01	18.90%	26.26	61.73%	24.70
	BIM	11.23%	**31.99**	0.87%	**28.06**	9.93%	**26.28**	54.07%	**24.71**
	PGD	3.40%	31.99	0.50%	28.06	9.30%	26.28	53.70%	24.70
	CTD	**49.93%**	31.73	**61.63%**	27.87	**77.83%**	26.14	**95.20%**	24.60
$\epsilon = 4$	FGSM	1.57%	31.17	11.77%	27.89	28.10%	26.21	67.43%	24.68
	BIM	49.03%	**31.85**	1.73%	**28.04**	11.10%	**26.28**	55.47%	**24.70**
	PGD	24.50%	31.80	1.23%	28.03	11.23%	26.27	55.70%	24.70
	CTD	**90.33%**	31.48	**88.60%**	27.75	**91.93%**	26.05	**98.43%**	24.53
$\epsilon = 5$	FGSM	4.77%	30.56	22.47%	27.69	40.50%	26.13	73.27%	24.65
	BIM	84.20%	**31.70**	4.30%	**28.02**	12.80%	**26.27**	56.83%	**24.70**
	PGD	62.37%	31.56	5.07%	27.97	14.10%	26.25	58.57%	24.69
	CTD	**99.17%**	31.22	**97.90%**	27.61	**97.10%**	25.95	**99.50%**	24.46

The scatters corresponding to SR and PSNR are plotted in Fig. 5, in which the image quality and SR are simultaneously considered. ϵ values are from 1 to 10. The closer to the upper righter corner the curve is, the better attack performance is. At $m = 4$, BIM sometimes achieves similar performance to CTD. This is because the loss caused by compression is very small if m is small. When m increases, CTD outperforms other methods more remarkably.

Targeted Attack. Table 2 shows the SR and PSNR in targeted attacks. The comparison results are similar to those of untargeted attack. CTD has both satisfactory anti-compression ability and image quality.

The scatters corresponding to SR and PSNR are plotted in Fig. 6. With the increase of m, the image quality gradually decreases. The increase of SR is accompanied by the decrease of image quality for each method. But CTD has a highest SR at the same PSNR.

Figure 7 shows that the adversarial images at different m values for untargeted and targeted attack. *"None"* is the compressed image without attacks of the original image.

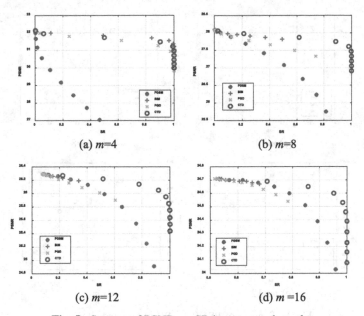

(a) $m=4$　　　　　　　　(b) $m=8$

(c) $m=12$　　　　　　　　(d) $m=16$

Fig. 5. Scatters of PSNR vs. SR in untargeted attacks.

Table 2. Anti-compression testing of adversarial examples for AMBTC in targeted attacks

		$m=4$		$m=8$		$m=12$		$m=16$	
		SR	PSNR	SR	PSNR	SR	PSNR	SR	PSNR
$\epsilon=1$	FGSM	23.83%	32.23	5.20%	28.12	2.20%	**26.32**	0.83%	**24.75**
	BIM	28.00%	32.24	4.27%	**28.13**	1.87%	26.32	0.80%	24.75
	PGD	16.83%	**32.25**	3.07%	28.13	1.63%	26.32	0.77%	24.75
	CTD	**54.73%**	32.19	**24.63%**	28.10	**12.30%**	26.29	**3.77%**	24.73
$\epsilon=2$	FGSM	62.17%	32.06	15.37%	28.10	4.33%	26.31	1.27%	**24.74**
	BIM	75.50%	32.17	8.83%	**28.12**	2.50%	**26.31**	0.87%	24.74
	PGD	56.47%	**32.18**	6.57%	28.12	2.13%	26.31	0.83%	24.74
	CTD	**96.30%**	32.02	**71.87%**	28.02	**41.17%**	26.24	**14.40%**	24.69
$\epsilon=3$	FGSM	82.93%	31.72	33.93%	28.04	9.47%	26.28	1.93%	**24.74**
	BIM	95.30%	**32.07**	14.63%	**28.10**	3.23%	**26.31**	0.97%	24.74
	PGD	87.30%	32.06	11.90%	28.10	3.03%	26.31	0.90%	24.74
	CTD	**99.80%**	31.80	**94.23%**	27.92	**71.47%**	26.17	**30.83%**	24.64
$\epsilon=4$	FGSM	91.47%	31.23	53.03%	27.92	17.60%	26.23	3.00%	24.72
	BIM	99.27%	**31.96**	21.77%	**28.09**	4.10%	**26.30**	1.00%	**24.74**
	PGD	97.47%	31.87	21.17%	28.06	4.47%	26.29	1.17%	24.74
	CTD	**100%**	31.58	**98.90%**	27.80	**88.57%**	26.08	**48.37%**	24.58

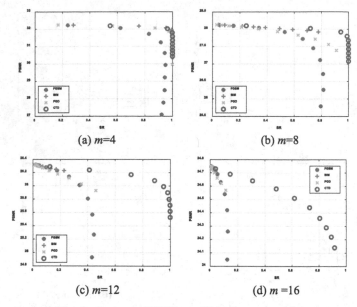

Fig. 6. Scatters of PSNR vs. SR in targeted attacks.

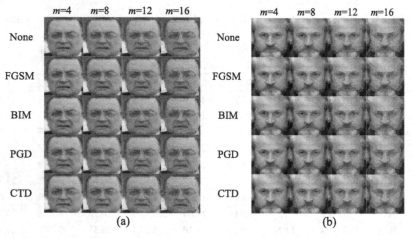

Fig. 7. Compressed adversarial images with $\epsilon = 4$. (a) untargeted attack; (b) targeted attack.

5   Conclusions

This paper proposes CTD method for generating AMBTC-resistant adversarial examples. It focuses on optimizing directly on trio data. CTD method has both satisfactory compression resistance and image quality. The compression process is not included in each iteration process, so the computational overhead is reduced. The experiments on LFW database show that the adversarial face examples confirm the advantages of CTD method. In future works, we will try to extend our method to other compression formats.

Acknowledgments. This research was supported by the National Natural Science Foundation of China (61866028) and (62376003), the Technology Innovation Guidance Program Project (Special Project of Technology Cooperation, Science and Technology Department of Jiangxi Province) (20212BDH81003).

References

1. Guo, C., Rana, M., Cisse, M., Van, D.M.L.: Countering adversarial images using input transformations. arXiv preprint arXiv:1711.00117 (2017)
2. Jia, X., Wei, X., Cao X., Foroosh H.: ComDefend: an efficient image compression model to defend adversarial examples. In: Proceedings of the IEEE/CVF Conference on Computer Vision and Pattern Recognition (CVPR), pp. 6084–6092 (2019)
3. Kim, C., Shin, D., Yang, C., Leng, L.: Data hiding method for color AMBTC compressed images using color difference. Appl. Sci. **11**, 3418 (2021)
4. Kim, C., Shin, D., Yang, C.N., Leng L.: Hybrid data hiding based on AMBTC using enhanced hamming code. Appl. Sci. **10**, 5336 (2020)
5. Szegedy, C., et al.: Intriguing properties of neural networks. arXiv preprint arXiv:1312.6199 (2014)
6. Goodfellow, I., Shlens, J., Szegedy, C.: Explaining and harnessing adversarial examples. arXiv preprint arXiv:1412.6572 (2014)
7. Kurakin, A., Goodfellow, I., Bengio, S.: Adversarial machine learning at scale. arXiv preprint arXiv:1611.01236 (2016)
8. Madry, A., Makelov, A., Schmidt, L., Tsipras, D., Vladu, A.: Towards deep learning models resistant to adversarial attacks. arXiv preprint arXiv:1706.06083 (2017)
9. Shin, R., Song, D.: Jpeg-resistant adversarial images. In: NIPS 2017 Workshop on Machine Learning and Computer Security, pp. 1–8 (2017)
10. Wang, Z., et al.: Towards compression-resistant privacy-preserving photo sharing on social networks. In: Proceedings of the 21th International Symposium on Theory, Algorithmic Foundations, and Protocol Design for Mobile Networks and Mobile Computing, pp. 81–90 (2020)
11. Shi, M., Li, S., Yin, Z., Zhang, X., Qian, Z.: On generating JPEG adversarial images. In: 2021 IEEE International Conference on Multimedia and Expo (ICME), pp. 1–6. IEEE (2021)
12. Sharma, Y., Ding, G., Brubaker, M.: On the effectiveness of low frequency perturbations. arXiv preprint arXiv:1903.00073 (2019)
13. Duan, R., Chen, Y., Niu, D., Yang, Y., Qin, A.K., He, Y.: AdvDrop: adversarial attack to DNNs by dropping information. In: Proceedings of the IEEE/CVF International Conference on Computer Vision (CVPR), pp. 7506–7515 (2021)
14. Zhou, W., et al.: Transferable adversarial perturbations. In: Proceedings of the European Conference on Computer Vision (ECCV), pp. 452–467 (2018)
15. Zhang, J., Yi, Q., Sang J., Sang, J.: JPEG compression-resistant low-mid adversarial perturbation against unauthorized face recognition system. arXiv preprint arXiv:2206.09410 (2022)
16. Lema, M., Mitchell, O.: Absolute moment block truncation coding and its application to color images. IEEE Trans. Commun. **32**, 1148–1157 (1984)
17. Deng, J., Guo, J., Xue, N., Zafeiriou, S.: ArcFace: additive angular margin loss for deep face recognition. In: Proceedings of the IEEE Conference on Computer Vision and Pattern Recognition (CVPR), pp. 4690–4699 (2019)
18. Duta, I.C., Liu, L., Zhu, F.: Improved residual networks for image and video recognition. In 2020 25th International Conference on Pattern Recognition (ICPR), pp. 9415–9422. IEEE (2021)

Single Sample Face Recognition Based on Identity-Attribute Disentanglement and Adversarial Feature Augmentation

Liang Yao, Fan Liu$^{(\boxtimes)}$, Zhiquan Ou, Fei Wang, and Delong Chen

College of Computer and Information, Hohai University, Nanjing 211100, China
{liangyao,fanliu,zhiquanou,fei_wang,chendelong}@hhu.edu.cn

Abstract. To address the issue of facial variation interference, this paper proposes a novel approach for single sample face recognition. Inspired by human visual perception, we introduce an attribute disentanglement module to separate identity features from attribute features using canonical correlation analysis. Due to the lack of attribute labels in the single sample set, we utilize the attribute features of the generic set to construct the SOM attribute space. Then, we fine-tune the network by reducing the distance between the attribute features of single sample and the attribute space. Finally, we use feature adversarial augmentation module to generate more intra-class features and train more robust classifier. Experimental results on AR, LFW and FERET datasets show significant improvements in accuracy and generalization performance compared to other methods.

Keywords: Single-sample Face Recognition · Attribute Disentanglement · Adversarial Feature Generation

1 Introduction

Face recognition is a widely used biometric recognition method due to its non-invasive nature, high accuracy, and convenient data acquisition. However, in real-world applications, face recognition systems often face the challenge of having access to only one sample per identity, which significantly limits their performance. Under such single-sample per person (SSPP) [13] constraint, facial attributes like expression, mustache, hair style, and eyeglasses are strongly coupled with facial identity, posing a significant challenge for learning accurate face representation.

F. Liu—This work was partially supported by National Nature Science Foundation of China(62372155), Joint Fund of Ministry of Education for Equipment Pre-research(8091B022123), Research Fund from Science and Technology on Underwater Vehicle Technology Laboratory(2021JCJQ-SYSJJ-LB06905), Key Laboratory of Information System Requirements, No: LHZZ 2021-M04, Water Science and Technology Project of Jiangsu Province under grant No.2021063, Qinglan Project of Jiangsu Province.

This challenge leads to the need for performing *identity-attribute disentanglement* during the face representation learning process. In this paper, we aim to make face features more robust to attribute variations, allowing identity information to be captured more precisely. Specifically, based on Canonical Correlation Analysis (CCA), we set up an additional attribute classifier and designed a novel loss function, which aims to lower the correlation coefficients of attribute information and identity information to encourage the separation of these two components.

However, this method only works well on datasets with human labeling of facial attributes, which we utilized as a generic set for representation pretraining. When it comes to single sample sets for downstream recognition, attribute annotations are usually inaccessible. This problem poses a significant challenge for learning identity-attribute disentanglement on single sample sets. To solve this issue, this paper constructs a Self Organizing Map (SOM) [14]-based attribute space using the attribute feature set obtained from the disentanglement result of the generic dataset. Then, we fine-tune the network by reducing the distance between the attribute features of single sample and the attribute space.

Additionally, to further enhance the learning of disentanglement on single sample sets, we propose using adversarial feature augmentation to generate virtual face features. We set up a Generative Adversarial Network (GAN) [15] to learn the probabilistic distribution of facial attribute and identity features, then sample a large number of virtual features to enlarge the training set. With sufficient training instances, learning a decent identity-attribute disentanglement becomes easier.

We evaluated our method on the AR [16], LFW [8], and FERET [17] datasets, achieving high face recognition accuracies of 95.2%, 98.34%, and 99.30%, respectively. This represents an absolute improvement of +0.53%, +0.43%, and +5.40% compared to previous methods. Rigorous ablation experiments prove that both identity-attribute disentanglement and adversarial feature augmentation make noticeable contributions to the overall model performance.

2   Related Work

Existing deep single-sample face recognition methods can be divided into two categories: virtual sample methods and generic learning methods [9–11]. When training deep models directly using a single-sample training set, limited training samples often lead to model over fitting. Therefore, the direct solution is to generate multiple virtual samples or features based on a single training sample to expand the training set, thereby transforming the single-sample problem into a general face recognition problem. Generic learning methods introduce an additional generic sample set with rich intra-class variation information to learn variation information as prior knowledge for the network, improving the accuracy of single-sample face recognition problems.

The key to virtual sample methods is to increase intra-class variation within the samples. Because the newly generated virtual samples are highly correlated with the original single-sample dataset, their contribution to classification improvement is limited. In recent years, various deep learning-based virtual sample methods have been proposed to better simulate the real intra-class distribution of facial images. Some methods employ novel network architectures and generation processes, using GANs to create virtual samples. For example, Zakharov et al. [1] represent intra-class variations using extracted facial landmarks and employ meta-learning strategies to generate high-quality virtual samples during adversarial training. Tran et al. [2] introduced a Disentangled Representation learning-Generative Adversarial Network (DR-GAN) to separate pose features from the features, enabling pose-controllable face generation.

Some researchers argue that generating virtual images also requires input feature extractors, when remapped to the feature space, may lead to identity information loss. Therefore, several methods based on virtual features have been proposed. For instance, Yin et al. [3] assume that intra-class variations of feature vectors follow a Gaussian distribution, allowing the sampling of different virtual features for individual samples from the corresponding distribution. Min et al. [4] learn intra-class variation information from a general sample set through feature clustering.

The aforementioned methods often treat the features extracted from individual samples as the centers of their respective classes, without considering the inherent variation information carried by each individual training sample. Consequently, feature correction methods have also gained widespread attention. In recent years, Pang et al. introduced the Variation Disentangling Generative Adversarial Network (VD-GAN) [5] and the Disentangling Prototype plus Variation model (DisP+V) [6], which generate image centers and feature centers of the training images separately.

3   Method

3.1   Design of Network Structure

To address the issue of attribute interference in single-sample training data, this paper introduces a method based on attribute disentanglement and adversarial generation. It employs a attribute disentanglement network to separate identity information and attribute information within deep facial features and introduces a attribute disentanglement loss to measure the degree of information separation. Simultaneously, a generative adversarial network is constructed to generate features based on the disentangled identity features, enhancing the robustness of the classification network to intra-class variations in facial images. The network architecture is illustrated in Fig. 1.

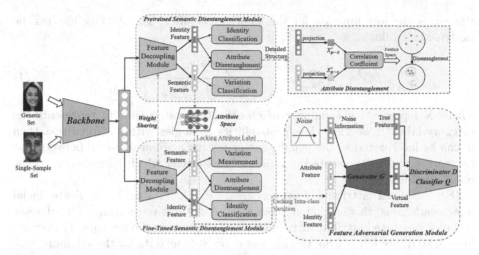

Fig. 1. Framework of our Method. **Step 1**: Train the backbone network and attribute disentanglement module by using the CelebA dataset as a generic set. **Step 2**: Use the attribute features disentangled from the generic set to construct the SOM attribute space, and align single sample attribute features with the attribute space. **Step 3**: Generate feature to increase intra-class variations.

3.2   Pretrained Attribute Disentanglement

The pre-trained attribute disentanglement module consists of four components: feature separation, identity feature classification, attribute disentanglement, and attribute classification. It separates the original features into identity and attribute features. The identity features are used for facial identity recognition, while the attribute features contain information related to facial variations in the image. A attribute disentanglement loss is then used to minimize the correlation between these features by utilizing the correlation coefficient. This loss term enhances facial identity recognition and reduces the impact of facial changes.

Deep Feature Extraction and Disentanglement. We employ FaceNet as the deep feature extraction network to map facial images to a deep feature space, represented as $x = \text{FaceNet}(I_m)$, where $x \in i^{1\times512}$ represents the image features, and I_m represents the original image. Based on the principles of the 'P+V' model at the feature level, image features x simultaneously contain identity-related features and attribute features related to variations. So we used a feature disentanglement module to separate identity features $x_d \in \mathbb{R}^{1\times512}$ and attribute features $x_s \in \mathbb{R}^{1\times512}$, as shown in Fig. 1.

Identity and Attribute Classifiers. After obtaining the identity features of the facial image, denoted as $x_d \in \mathbb{R}^{1\times512}$, the aim is to map the identity information into the feature category space using a deep neural network. To achieve this, we use the Arcface loss, which increases the angular margin between classes, as the loss function for the identity classifier. The Arcface loss can be expressed as follows:

$$L_{id} = -\frac{1}{N}\sum_{i=1}^{N}\log\frac{e^{s\cos(\theta_{y_i}+m)}}{e^{s\cos(\theta_{y_i}+m)}+\sum_{j\neq y_i}e^{s\cos\theta_j}} \tag{1}$$

where N represents the number of classification categories, y_i represents the category label. If we view class probabilities as angles within a full circle, then m can be interpreted as the penalty factor for the angular distance between two categories, and s represents the radius of this circle, which corresponds to the regularized feature.

For acquired attribute features $x_s \in \mathbb{R}^{1\times512}$, due to intricate facial image variations, this section employs CelebA dataset pretraining. This dataset includes annotated attribute attributes, used to pretrain the network. 17 discriminative attribute labels from this dataset serve as label data for the attribute classifier. To counter noise, noise label classification is introduced during attribute classification, assuming noise in every facial image. This leads to 18 attribute labels. Given each image's noise label, the data's noise part lacks facial information; this label is set to 1 in one-hot encoding. The final loss for the attribute classifier can be expressed as:

$$L_a = -\frac{1}{N}\sum_{i=1}^{N}y_i\log\left(f\left(x_s\right)\right) = -\frac{1}{N}\sum_{i=1}^{N}\frac{e^{s\cos(\theta_{y_i})}}{e^{s\cos(\theta_{y_i})}+\sum_{j\neq y_i}e^{s\cos(\theta_j)}} \tag{2}$$

where N represents the number of attribute categories, set to 18.

Attribute Disentanglement Loss. After separating identity features x_d and attribute features x_s, their correlation acts as regularization to aid feature disentanglement. Batches of facial images are employed to compute correlations, mitigating feature randomness. Therefore, batch identity features are represented as $X_{p-d} = [x_{d1}, x_{d2}, ..., x_{dn}]$, and batch attribute features are represented as $X_{p-s} = [x_{s1}, x_{s2}, ..., x_{sn}]$, where n represents the number of features. For ease of calculation, batch identity and attribute features are mapped to one-dimensional vectors:

$$X'_{p-d} = W_d^T X_{p-d}, \quad X'_{p-s} = W_s^T X_{p-s} \tag{3}$$

where, W_d^T and $W_s^T \in \mathbb{R}^{L\times1}$ represent mapping matrices that map X_{p-d} and X_{p-s} to X'_{p-d} and $X'_{p-s} \in \mathbb{R}^{1\times n}$, respectively. At this point, vectors X_{p-d}' and $X'_{p-s} \in \mathbb{R}^{1\times n}$ represent identity and attribute features within this batch. The calculation of the correlation coefficient between these two is as follows:

$$\rho\left(X'_{p-d}, X'_{p-s}\right) = \frac{\mathrm{cov}\left(X'_{p-d}, X'_{p-s}\right)}{\sqrt{D\left(X'_{p-d}\right)}\sqrt{D\left(X'_{p-s}\right)}} \tag{4}$$

Since the covariance between two independent random variables is zero, ρ can be used as a loss term for measuring correlation to reduce the correlation between identity and attribute features. For ease of calculation, ρ^2 is used as the correlation loss and can be expressed as:

$$L_c = \rho^2 \left(W_d^T X_{p-d}, W_s^T X_{p-s} \right) \tag{5}$$

Finally, the sum of the identity category loss, attribute category loss, and identity-attribute correlation loss mentioned above is computed as the ultimate network loss:

$$L_{loss} = \alpha L_{id} + \beta L_a + \gamma L_c \tag{6}$$

where α, β, and γ represent the respective coefficients for the loss terms.

3.3   Fine-Tuned Attribute Disentanglement

Transitioning to single-sample tasks, lacking attribute labels hampers proper attribute classifier usage. To address this, the CelebA dataset serves as a generic set for creating a attribute space with its features. Then, we calculate the distance between the attribute features and the feature spaces. Recognizing human visual systems' advantage in complex information processing, we used a Self-Organizing Map (SOM) network to construct the attribute space, shown in Fig. 1. Assuming the set of attribute features separated from the generic set is $X_s^c = [x_s^{c1}, x_s^{c2}, ..., x_s^{cM}]$, where M represents the number of attribute features in the generic set, X_s^c is used as input to construct the SOM network S_c as the attribute space.

For a single-sample image feature x^t, identity features $x_d^t = F_{split}(x^t)$, and attribute features $x_s^t = x^t - F_{split}(x^t)$ are computed using F_{split} network. Identity features x_d^t are trained with the identity classifier in Sect. 3.2. For attribute features x_s^t, Mean Square Error (MSE) loss measures the distance to attribute space, facilitating attribute feature training. The attribute loss can be expressed as:

$$L_{mse} = \frac{1}{m} \sum_{i=1}^{m} \left(x_s^{ti} - n_c^i \right) \tag{7}$$

where, m is feature dimension, x_s^{ti} is the i-th dimension of attribute feature x_s^t, and n_c^i is the i-th dimension of winning neuron for x_s^t in attribute space.

3.4   Feature Adversarial Generation

In single sample face recognition, limited training samples and diverse test samples cause disentanglement networks to deviate from true category centers. Misclassification is common due to small intra-class distances and sample variations. To address this, we propose using obtained identity features as category centers and generating virtual features. This improves classification margin and mitigates center deviations.

Unlike traditional GANs, infoGAN uses real features and noise for interpretable attribute generation. The mutual information constraint between generated features and input information ensures the interpretability of the generation process. It includes a feature generator (G), discriminator (D), and category classifier (Q) for authenticating features and categories.

Using the attribute space S_c constructed in Sect. 3.3, the identity feature x_d is used as input, and the obtained winning neurons are used as attribute feature x_s. The generated attribute feature x_s, disentangled identity feature x_d, and noise information are sampled and input into the Generative Adversarial Network, represented as follows:

$$\hat{x} = G\left(f\left(x_d\right)\right) = G\left(x_d + x_s + W_c c\right) \tag{8}$$

where $\hat{x}$ is the generated image feature, W_c are noise weights, and $c \in \mathbb{R}^{1 \times 512}$ is Gaussian noise, simulating diverse facial image variations.

The use of randomly generated Gaussian noise can generate numerous intra-class variation images, denoted as $\hat{X} = [\hat{x}^0, \hat{x}^2, \ldots, \hat{x}^C]$, where C represents the number of virtual features generated for the same class, set to 100.

Here, feature classifier Q measures the correlation between undisentangled real feature x and virtually generated feature $\hat{x}$. Both maintain identical identity labels before and after generations. The identity classifier ensures consistent labeling, preserving identity information during feature generation. This method prioritizes identity preservation, boosting classification efficiency over pre- and post-generation mutual information calculations.

The final feature generation network loss can be expressed as:

$$\begin{aligned} \text{Loss} = E_{x \sim p_z(z)} \left[\log\left(1 - D\left(G\left(x_d + x_s + W_c c\right)\right)\right)\right] \\ + E_{x \sim p_{\text{data}}(x)}[\log D(x)] - \lambda[\text{soft max}(x) + \text{softmax}(\hat{x})] \end{aligned} \tag{9}$$

4   Experimental Results

To validate our method's efficacy in single-sample face recognition, we conducted experiments, comparing them with state-of-the-art techniques. The AR [16], LFW [8], and FERET [17] datasets were employed, with FaceNet extracting 512-dimensional deep facial features. The disentanglement network pre-training utilized the CelebA dataset [7] to enhance identity and attribute features separation. In training, a attribute classifier used 17 selective variation labels, and images were resized to 160×160. As in prior works [12], we adopted Accuracy (acc) as our metric.

4.1   Results on AR Dataset

In this section, we conducted experiments using 100 classes from the AR dataset. 80 classes were used for training and testing in single-sample, while the remaining 20 classes were used as a generic set. The first image of each class was used as the training sample. We compared our proposed method with commonly

Table 1. AR Dataset Comparison Experiment

Method	Acc	Method	Acc
AGL	59.95	SSAE	85.21
BlockFLD	62.92	SSLD	94.67
ESRC	71.88	SSPP-DAN	93.33
SVDL	72.56	KWV	94.31
RHDA	90.65	VD-GAN	79.70
SGL	87.30	FaceNet	86.30
FDDL	95.00	**ours**	**95.20**

used algorithms for single-sample face recognition, including traditional and deep learning methods. The results are shown in Table 1.

According to the experimental results, our proposed method achieved a minimum 5% improvement compared to traditional methods like AGL, RHDA, and SVDL. Additionally, our proposed method achieved a 0.53% improvement over other deep learning methods like SSLD and KWV. These results highlight the robustness of our proposed method in handling facial variations such as expressions, lighting, and occlusions.

4.2 Results on LFW Dataset

Compared to AR, LFW contains a greater amount of unconstrained variation information, including over 13,000 facial images from more than 5,000 categories. We used 158 classes from LFW for training and testing in single-sample recognition, and 1522 classes for the generic set. Results are in Table 2.

Table 2. LFW Dataset Comparison Experiment

Method	Acc	Method	Acc
AGL	31.90	SSPP-DAN	97.91
BlockFLD	18.10	Center-Fea	90.60
ESRC	33.60	CJR-RACF	95.50
SVDL	33.50	DisP+V	96.70
VQ	42.92	UP	94.80
RHDA	32.90	FaceNet	93.80
SSLD	92.70	**ours**	**98.34**

Our proposed method achieved a high classification accuracy of 98.34% even with complex and unconstrained facial variations. Compared to other deep learning methods, our proposed method showed a minimum of 0.43% improvement in accuracy. In comparison to the DisP+V method of generating virtual features, our proposed method still achieves a 1.64% improvement.

4.3   Results on FERET Dataset

In this section, we used the FERET-b dataset, where 200 classes were used for experimental validation, with each class containing 7 intra-class samples. The experimental results are shown in Table 3.

Table 3. FERET Dataset Comparison Experiment

Method	Acc	Method	Acc
SRC	53.44	SSPP-DAN	93.30
ESRC	58.90	KCFT	93.17
CPL	93.67	FaceNet	91.40
TDL	89.33	**ours**	**99.30**

Our proposed method outperformed traditional methods like SRC, ESRC, CPL, and deep learning methods like SSPP-DAN and KCFT by at least 5.4%. These results highlight the effectiveness of our method in achieving high classification accuracy, even in the presence of common facial variations such as lighting and pose changes.

4.4   Ablation Study

To validate the effectiveness of our method, this section conducted ablation experiments on two modules to compare the accuracy on different datasets. The experimental results are shown in Table 4.

Table 4. Ablation on Attribute Disentanglement and Feature Augmentation Module

Attribute Disentanglement	Feature Augmentation	Acc		
		AR	LFW	FERET
		86.3	93.8	91.4
✓		92.2	96.8	98.3
✓	✓	**95.2**	**98.3**	**99.3**

Experimental results reveal the substantial enhancements from the proposed attribute disentanglement and feature augmentation modules compared to relying solely on FaceNet-extracted features. The disentanglement and augmentation modules achieved 5.9% and 3% improvements on the AR dataset, respectively. The disentanglement module alone achieves 92.2% accuracy in AR's natural images. Despite LFW dataset variations, the augmentation module outperforms the disentanglement module, adding 1.5% accuracy.

Ablation experiments confirm the disentanglement module's effectiveness in mitigating attribute variations' impact on accuracy, while the featrue augmentation module enhances accuracy against common and complex scenarios.

5   Conclusion

This study addresses the challenge of balancing visual and attribute information in single-sample face recognition. We propose an approach using attribute
disentanglement and adversarial augmentation. Our method employs a feature
disentanglement network to separate identity from attribute features. Utilizing
identity features as category centers, a generative adversarial network creates
virtual features, enhancing classification accuracy. Experimental results on AR,
LFW, and FERET datasets show our method maintains strong classification performance under complex facial variations, effectively distinguishing intra-class
and inter-class differences.

References

1. Zakharov, E., Shysheya, A., Burkov, E., Lempitsky, V.: Few-shot adversarial learning of realistic neural talking head models. In: Proceedings of the IEEE/CVF
   International Conference on Computer Vision, pp. 9459–9468 (2019)
2. Tran, L., Yin, X., Liu, X.: Representation learning by rotating your faces. IEEE
   Trans. Pattern Anal. Mach. Intell. **41**(12), 3007–3021 (2018)
3. Yin, X., Yu, X., Sohn, K., Liu, X., Chandraker, M.: Feature transfer learning for
   face recognition with under-represented data. In: Proceedings of the IEEE/CVF
   Conference on Computer Vision and Pattern Recognition, pp. 5704–5713 (2019)
4. Min, R., Xu, S., Cui, Z.: Single-sample face recognition based on feature expansion.
   IEEE Access **7**, 45219–45229 (2019)
5. Pang, M., Wang, B., Cheung, Y., Chen, Y., Wen, B.: VD-GAN: a unified framework
   for joint prototype and representation learning from contaminated single sample
   per person. IEEE Trans. Inf. Forensics Secur. **16**, 2246–2259 (2021)
6. Pang, M., Wang, B., Ye, M., Chen, Y., Wen, B.: Disentangling prototype and
   variation for single sample face recognition. In: 2021 IEEE International Conference
   on Multimedia and Expo (ICME), pp. 1–6. IEEE (2021)
7. Liu, Z., Luo, P., Wang, X., Tang, X.: Deep learning face attributes in the wild.
   In: Proceedings of the IEEE International Conference on Computer Vision, pp.
   3730–3738 (2015)
8. Huang, G.B., Mattar, M., Berg, T., Learned-Miller, E.: Labeled faces in the wild:
   a database for studying face recognition in unconstrained environments. Month
   (2008)
9. Duan, Q., Zhang, L.: Look more into occlusion: Realistic face frontalization and
   recognition with BoostGAN. IEEE Trans. Neural Netw. Learn. Syst. **31**(1), 214–
   228 (2020)
10. Zhou, J., Chen, J., Liang, C., Chen, J.: One-shot face recognition with feature
    rectification via adversarial learning. In: Ro, Y.M., et al. (eds.) MMM 2020. LNCS,
    vol. 11961, pp. 290–302. Springer, Cham (2020). https://doi.org/10.1007/978-3-
    030-37731-1_24
11. Pang, M., Cheung, Y.M., Wang, B., Lou, J.: Synergistic generic learning for face
    recognition from a contaminated single sample per person. IEEE Trans. Inf. Foren-
    sics Secur. **15**(1), 195–209 (2020)
12. Wang, X., Zhang, B., Yang, M., Ke, K., Zheng, W.: Robust joint representation
    with triple local feature for face recognition with single sample per person. Knowl.
    Based Syst. **181**, 104790 (2019)

13. Liu, F., Chen, D., Wang, F., Li, Z., Xu, F.: Deep learning based single sample face recognition: a survey. Artif. Intell. Rev. Int. Sci. Eng. J. **56**, 2723–2748 (2023)
14. Kohonen, T.: The self-organizing map. IEEE Proc. ICNN **1**(1–3), 1–6 (1990)
15. Choe, J., Park, S., Kim, K., Park, J.H., Kim, D., Shim, H.: Face generation for low-shot learning using generative adversarial networks. In: IEEE International Conference on Computer Vision Workshop, pp. 1940–1948 (2017)
16. Martinez, A., Benavente, R.: The AR face database: CVC technical report, 24 (1998)
17. Phillips, P.J., Wechsler, H., Huang, J., Rauss, P.J.: The FERET database and evaluation procedure for face-recognition algorithms. Image Vis. Comput. **16**(5), 295–306 (1998)

Affective Computing
and Human-Computer Interface

Dynamic Graph-Guided Transferable Regression for Cross-Domain Speech Emotion Recognition

Shenjie Jiang[1], Peng Song[1(⊠)], Run Wang[1], Shaokai Li[1,2,3],
and Wenming Zheng[4]

[1] School of Computer and Control Engineering, Yantai University,
Yantai 264005, China
pengsong@ytu.edu.cn
[2] The State Key Laboratory of Tibetan Intelligent Information Processing
and Application, Xining 810008, China
[3] Tibetan Information Processing and Machine Translation Key Laboratory
of Qinghai Province, Xining 810008, China
[4] Key Laboratory of Child Development and Learning Science of Ministry
of Education, Southeast University, Nanjing 210096, China

Abstract. To deal with the problem of cross-domain speech emotion recognition (SER), in this paper, we propose a novel dynamic graph-guided transferable regression (DGTR) method. Specifically, a retargeted discriminant linear regression in the source domain is utilized to make the projection matrix discriminative. Meanwhile, an adaptive maximum entropy graph is designed for similarity measurement for different domains. Experiments on four popular datasets show that our method can achieve better performance compared with several related state-of-the-art methods.

Keywords: regression · transfer learning · speech emotion recognition

1 Introduction

Speech emotion recognition (SER) can automatically identify human emotions from speech signals. It has demonstrated impressive performance in a variety of practical applications, e.g., forensic trials, intelligent interaction, in-car board systems [1]. The objective of SER is to train a classifier with labeled speech samples and identify the unlabeled samples into emotion categories, including happiness, surprise, disgust, sadness, anger, and fear. In practice, the training samples might significantly differ from the testing samples due to altered recording conditions, different languages, or different reception equipment, which would lead to different distributions of training and test data and poor recognition performance [2].

To tackle the above problem, transfer learning is an efficient technique, which can facilitate the knowledge transfer from the source domain to the target

W. Jia et al. (Eds.): CCBR 2023, LNCS 14463, pp. 225–234, 2023.
https://doi.org/10.1007/978-981-99-8565-4_22

domain. Over the past two decades, numerous transfer learning methods have been proposed [3]. For example, in [4], Pan et al. propose a transfer component analysis (TCA) approach for domain adaptation. In [5,6], Long et al. present a joint distribution adaptation (JDA) algorithm and a transfer joint matching (TJM) algorithm, which can efficiently mitigate the distance across domains. In [7], Wang et al. present a novel balanced distribution adaptation (BDA) algorithm to deal with the cross-domain recognition problem. In [8], Zhang et al. put forward a joint transfer subspace learning and regression (JTSLR) method for hyperspectral image classification. In [9], Li et al. propose a transferable linear regression method to improve the performance of cross-domain SER.

The aforementioned methods can achieve appealing performance, but they neglect the relevance of category spaces between source and target domains and do not efficiently utilize label information of the source domain. Moreover, the similarity metrics are usually fixed, which cannot well describe the similarities across domains. To this end, motivated by linear regression and transfer learning, we propose a novel cross-domain SER method, named dynamic graph-guided transferable regression (DGTR). It utilizes the source labels to guide the procedures of transfer, and designs a dynamic graph to effectively minimize the distribution gap across two domains.

2 Proposed Method

2.1 Problem Formulation

The Discriminant Regression. As a classic method commonly used in classification tasks, linear regression is used to measure the correlation between samples and labels, which can be formulated as follows:

$$\min_{W} \|Y - W^T X\|_F^2 \tag{1}$$

where $X \in \mathbb{R}^{d \times n}$ is the feature matrix, n and d denote the numbers of samples and features, respectively, $W \in \mathbb{R}^{d \times c}$ is the projection matrix, and $Y \in \mathbb{R}^{c \times n}$ is the label matrix. To alleviate the inherent tension between the model flexibility and overfitting [10], Eq. (1) can be rewritten as

$$\min_{W} \|T - W^T X\|_F^2$$
$$\text{s.t. } \forall \{i, j, j \neq l_i\}, T_{l_i, i} - T_{j,i} \geq 1 \tag{2}$$

where l_i represents the class number of the i-th sample and $l_i = k$ if the i-th sample belongs to the k-th class. $T \in \mathbb{R}^{c \times n_s}$ is the retargeted label matrix to be trained. If x_i belongs to the j-th class, $T_{j,i}$ is 1. Otherwise, it is 0.

To make the model be more tolerant to noises, we impose an $\ell_{2,1}$-norm on the projection matrix W. Then we can obtain

$$\min_{W} \|T - W^T X\|_F^2 + \|W\|_{2,1}$$
$$\text{s.t. } \forall \{i, j, j \neq l_i\}, T_{l_i, i} - T_{j,i} \geq 1 \tag{3}$$

where $\|W\|_{2,1}$ is defined as $\sum_{i=1}^{d} \sqrt{\sum_{j=1}^{c} W_{ij}^2}$.

The Dynamic Graph Regularization. During the projection from high-dimensional space to low-dimensional subspace, the inherent local geometric structure of data may be destroyed. To address this issue, we introduce a graph Laplacian, which is expressed as

$$L_s = \frac{D_s - (S^T + S)}{2} \tag{4}$$

where L_s is the Laplacian matrix, D_s is a diagonal matrix, whose elements are represented as $\sum_j \frac{s_{ij} + s_{ji}}{2}$. S is the similarity matrix and its optimal form is a block diagonal structure. According to [11], by imposing a rank constraint, the similarity matrix S can exhibit the desired block diagonal structure, while the corresponding graph will possess c connected components. The rank constraint is mathematically expressed as follows:

$$rank(L_s) = n - c \tag{5}$$

To reduce the computational complexity, according to [12], Eq. (5) can be rewritten as

$$\min_{S} \sum_{i=1}^{c} \sigma_i(L_s) = 0 \tag{6}$$

$$\text{s.t. } s_i^T 1 = 1, 0 \leqslant s_i \leqslant 1$$

where $\sigma_i(L_s)$ is the i-th smallest eigenvalue of L_s and $\sigma_i(L_s) \geqslant 0$. According to Ky Fan's theorem [13], we have

$$\sum_{i=1}^{c} \sigma_i(L_s) = \min_{W^T W = I} Tr(W^T X L_s X^T W) \tag{7}$$

where $W^T X$ represents a low-dimensional feature matrix. The orthogonal constraint $W^T W = I$ is imposed to prevent trivial solutions.

We introduce an adaptive learning strategy into the process of transfer learning, which can learn an adaptive manifold structure by adaptively updating the similarity matrix [14]. As discussed in information entropy theory, the information entropy reflects the average uncertainty of all possible positions where the information from the information sources is transmitted. It can be expressed as

$$\gamma = \sum_{i=1}^{k} p_i log \frac{1}{p_i} \tag{8}$$

Here, k represents the number of information sources, and p_i represents the probability of the i-th information source for a sample. A smaller γ indicates an unstable state. We aim to continuously update the similarity matrix S until it reaches a stable state. Thus, we maximize the following information entropy of S:

$$\max_{\sum_{j=1}^{n} s_{ij}=1, s_{ij}>0} \sum_{i=1}^{n} \sum_{j=1}^{n} (-s_{ij} log s_{ij}) \tag{9}$$

where s_{ij} is the (i,j)-th entry of S. We embed S into the graph constraint of the low-dimensional feature matrix $W^T X$, resulting in a dynamic maximum entropy graph constrained model. Then we can obtain

$$\min_{F,S} Tr(W^T X L_s X^T W) + \sum_{i=1}^{n} \sum_{j=1}^{n} (s_{ij} log s_{ij})$$

$$\text{s.t. } W^T W = I, \sum_{j=1}^{n} s_{ij} = 1, s_{ij} > 0 \tag{10}$$

Objective Function. By combining Eq. (3) and Eq. (10), the objective function of DGTR is formulated as follows:

$$\min_{W,T,S} \|T - W^T X_s\|_F^2 + 2\alpha (Tr(W^T X L_s X^T W) + \beta \sum_{i=1}^{n} \sum_{j=1}^{n} (s_{ij} \log s_{ij})) + \gamma \|W\|_{2,1}$$

$$\text{s.t. } \forall \{i,j, j \neq l_i\}, T_{l_i,i} - T_{j,i} \geq 1, W^T W = I, \sum_{j=1}^{n} s_{ij} = 1, s_{ij} > 0 \tag{11}$$

where α, β, and γ are the trade-off parameters.

2.2 Optimization

Since Eq. (11) has an $\ell_{2,1}$-norm, which is tricky to optimize. Thus, we first transform Eq. (11) into the following form:

$$\mathcal{L} = \|T - W^T X_s\|_F^2 + 2\alpha (Tr(W^T X L_s X^T W) + \beta \sum_{i=1}^{n} \sum_{j=1}^{n} (s_{ij} \log s_{ij}))$$

$$+ \gamma Tr(W^T G W) + Tr(\phi(W^T W - I)) \tag{12}$$

where ϕ is a Lagrange constraint. $G \in \mathbb{R}^{d \times d}$ is a diagonal matrix and its i-th element is

$$G_{ii} = \frac{1}{2\|w^i\|_2 + \varepsilon} \tag{13}$$

where w^i represents the i-th row of W and ε represents a constraint with small values. Equation (12) can be solved by updating one variable while fixing the others. The steps are given as follows:

(1) **Fix S, W and update T:** The sub-problem of updating T can be written as follows:

$$\min_{\forall \{i,j, j \neq l_i\}, T_{l_i,i} - T_{j,i} \geq 1} \|T - W^T X_s\|_F^2 \tag{14}$$

Here we define $V = W^T X_s$, so Eq. (14) can be rewritten as

$$\min_{\forall \{i,j, j \neq l_i\}, T_{l_i,i} - T_{j,i} \geq 1} \sum_{i=1}^{n} \|T_{:,i} - V_{:,i}\|^2 \tag{15}$$

According to [15], the optimal solution for T can be obtained column by column.

(2) Fix T, S and update W: The partial derivative of $\mathcal{L}$ w.r.t. W is

$$\frac{\partial \mathcal{L}}{\partial W} = (X_s X_s^T W - X_s T^T + 2\alpha X L_s X^T W + \gamma G W + W) \qquad (16)$$

Let $\frac{\partial \mathcal{L}}{\partial W} = 0$, W can be updated by the following equation:

$$W = (X_s X_s^T + 2\alpha X L_s X^T + \gamma G + I)^{-1}(X_s T^T) \qquad (17)$$

(3) Fix T, W and update S: The problem about S can be formulated as

$$\min_{S} 2Tr(W^T X L_s X^T W) + 2\beta \sum_{i=1}^{n} \sum_{j=1}^{n} (s_{ij} \log s_{ij})$$

$$\text{s.t. } W \geq 0, W^T W = I, \sum_{j=1}^{n} s_{ij} = 1, s_{ij} > 0 \qquad (18)$$

For convenience, by defining $V = X^T W$, we have the following Lagrangian function of S:

$$L(S) = \sum_{i=1}^{n} \sum_{j=1}^{n} \|v^i - v^j\|_2^2 s_{ij} + 2\beta \sum_{i=1}^{n} \sum_{j=1}^{n} (s_{ij} \log s_{ij}) -$$

$$\sum_{i=1}^{n} \varphi_i (\sum_{i=1}^{n} s_{ij} - 1) - \sum_{i=1}^{n} \sum_{j=1}^{n} \phi_{ij} s_{ij} \qquad (19)$$

where φ and ϕ are the Lagrangian operators. By the KKT condition, we can derive the update rule for variable S as follows:

$$s_{i,j} = \frac{exp\left(-\frac{\|v_i - v_j\|_2^2}{2\beta}\right)}{\sum_{j=1}^{n} exp\left(-\frac{\|v_i - v_j\|_2^2}{2\beta}\right)} \qquad (20)$$

The above three steps are repeated until the objective converges or the maximum times of iteration reaches.

3 Experiments

3.1 Experimental Settings

To demonstrate the efficacy of DGTR, four emotional datasets are used in our experiments, including Berlin, CVE, IEMOCAP, and TESS [16]. In addition, four common emotions, i.e., anger (AN), happiness (HA), neutral (NE), and sadness (SA), are chosen. We compare DGTR with the following methods, i.e., traditional linear discriminant analysis (LDA), TCA [4], JDA [5], TJM [6], BDA [7], transfer linear discriminant analysis (TLDA) [17], joint transfer subspace learning and regression (JTSLR) [8], and transferable discriminant linear regression (TDLR) [9]. Moreover, the deep domain adaptation methods are also used, including dynamic adversarial adaptation network (DAAN) [18], multi-representation adaptation network (MRAN) [19], deep subdomain adaptation network (DSAN) [20], and batch nuclear-norm maximization (BNM) [21].

In our experiments, one dataset is served as the source domain and the other dataset is served as the target domain, resulting in 12 cross-domain SER tasks, i.e., C→B, I→B, T→B, B→C, I→C, T→C, B→I, C→I, T→I, B→T, C→T, and I→T. Each dataset is divided into 10 parts, among which seven parts are used for training and three parts are used for testing.

We pre-reduced the feature dimension for each group using PCA to retain 98% of energy. The values of the three trade-off parameters, i.e., dynamic graph regularization parameter α, maximum entropy parameter β, and sparse regularization parameter γ, are searched in the range of $\{10^{-3}, 10^{-2}, 10^{-1}, 1, 10, 10^2, 10^3\}$.

Table 1. Recognition accuracy (%) of different algorithms using low-level features.

Settings	Compared methods								DGTR
	LDA	TCA	JDA	TJM	BDA	TLDA	JTSLR	TDLR	
C→B	60.22	65.98	60.82	67.01	57.27	59.79	66.72	69.83	**71.13**
I→B	50.14	50.52	53.61	53.61	**59.21**	56.41	52.73	52.58	56.70
T→B	54.67	55.43	51.97	57.66	56.41	54.21	55.77	**58.59**	56.89
B→C	58.62	53.21	48.51	48.08	50.41	55.56	50.76	57.69	**67.87**
I→C	40.79	40.38	51.28	41.03	49.32	**54.49**	46.17	49.63	48.08
T→C	52.65	54.37	55.46	52.45	53.21	56.72	58.13	56.46	**62.18**
B→I	42.28	43.73	37.42	43.21	48.52	32.44	44.21	41.45	**50.85**
C→I	40.71	46.77	46.77	47.29	44.10	50.19	48.13	50.59	**50.97**
T→I	38.66	44.23	40.92	46.89	47.53	44.23	47.55	42.67	**49.56**
B→T	52.85	55.52	56.33	53.59	**63.78**	54.87	55.78	53.22	56.50
C→T	55.41	54.56	55.95	56.66	55.61	53.21	**58.73**	57.88	58.58
I→T	50.11	55.33	50.40	50.16	51.87	52.54	54.73	51.48	**59.38**
Average	49.76	51.67	50.79	51.47	53.10	52.06	53.28	53.51	**57.39**

3.2   Experimental Results and Analysis

Table 1 and Table 2 show the recognition results of different algorithms on the 12 cross-domain tasks using low-level and deep features, respectively. Compared with all baseline methods, it can be seen that whether using low-level features or deep features, our proposed DGTR method can achieve the best recognition results under 12 experimental settings. To be specific, in Table 1, the average accuracy of our method is 7.63% greater than that of the traditional LDA method. The reason is that LDA does not consider the difference between the

Table 2. Recognition accuracy (%) of different algorithms using deep features.

Settings	Compared methods							DGTR
	JDA	BDA	JTSLR	DAAN*	MRAN*	DSAN*	BNM*	
C→B	58.76	56.71	53.61	67.90	**70.68**	65.43	42.90	70.10
I→B	57.73	56.83	63.92	65.12	66.05	**67.59**	60.19	61.86
T→B	63.92	53.83	58.76	**66.05**	55.25	61.73	43.83	55.67
B→C	56.41	56.71	47.44	38.58	45.30	47.03	60.27	**71.79**
I→C	51.17	46.85	49.36	40.31	45.49	48.75	45.30	**51.28**
T→C	57.69	51.78	49.36	43.57	44.34	59.88	41.65	**62.26**
B→I	47.36	32.58	48.85	48.29	48.24	**48.98**	45.55	46.40
C→I	**43.88**	40.44	43.65	38.78	40.62	40.20	30.00	43.21
T→I	45.81	**45.98**	41.79	41.07	39.55	38.91	36.26	45.88
B→T	51.67	46.83	69.71	57.16	53.35	**70.11**	46.65	54.38
C→T	51.25	57.10	**62.71**	52.10	58.47	57.79	42.40	57.08
I→T	**56.25**	47.81	53.75	43.90	45.78	55.10	47.28	51.88
Average	53.49	49.45	53.58	50.23	51.09	55.12	45.19	**55.82**

source and target domain feature distributions. Besides, the regression-based transfer learning methods, like TDLR, JTSLR, and our method, achieve superior results compared with other transfer learning methods, i.e., TCA, JDA, TJM, BDA, and TLDA. This might be attributed to that the regression methods can utilize the abundant label information in the source domain to describe the relationships between corresponding features. In Table 2, it can be seen that most transfer learning methods perform better than deep domain adaptation methods.

We further investigate the sensitivity of the parameters in our proposed method. The results are depicted in Fig. 1. From the figure, we can notice that our method is stable and recognition accuracies are high within a large parameter range.

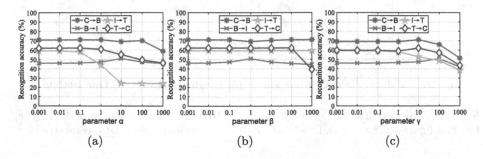

(a)   (b)   (c)

Fig. 1. Parameter sensitivity of the proposed DGTR w.r.t. (a) α, (b) β, and (c) γ.

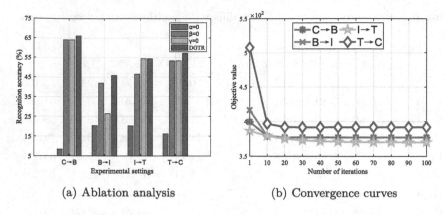

(a) Ablation analysis   (b) Convergence curves

Fig. 2. Ablation analysis and convergence curves of DGTR.

To verify the importance of each item in the proposed model, we conduct the ablation study. Our model includes three special cases. Setting $\alpha = 0$, which means the dynamic graph regularization is ignored; setting $\beta = 0$, which means the maximum entropy item is ignored; and setting $\gamma = 0$, which means the sparse regularization is ignored.

Figure 2 (a) shows the recognition accuracy of different cases. From the figure, we can see that the recognition accuracy decreases regardless of which parameter being 0. This proves that each term plays a positive role in our model.

We also give the convergence curves of DGTR, which are shown in Fig. 2(b). It can be seen that DGTR is stable within only a few ($T < 20$) iterations. which proves the convergence property of our method.

Moreover, we give the visualization analysis of our method using the t-SNE algorithm in Fig. 3. From the figure, we can find that the samples belonging to the same categories are close, and those from different categories are kept away from each other. This result demonstrates that DGTR can effectively reduce the feature distribution disparity across two domains.

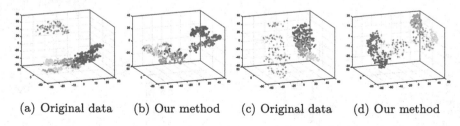

(a) Original data   (b) Our method   (c) Original data   (d) Our method

Fig. 3. t-SNE visualization on the tasks C→B (the first two figures) and B→C (the last two figures). The "$*$" and "$+$" indicate the source and target data, respectively.

4   Conclusion

In this paper, we propose an dynamic graph-guided transferable regression (DGTR) method for cross-domain SER. It utilizes a retargeted learning technique for discriminative linear regression in the source domain. Meanwhile, we introduce an adaptive maximum entropy graph as the distance metric across domains. Moreover, we impose an $\ell_{2,1}$-norm on the projection matrix to make the model robust. Experimental results show the superiority of DGTR over some state-of-the art methods.

Acknowledgment. This research was supported by the Natural Science Foundation of Shandong Province under Grants ZR2023MF063 and ZR2022MF314, and by the National Natural Science Foundation of China under Grant 61703360.

References

1. Akçay, M.B., Oğuz, K.: Speech emotion recognition: emotional models, databases, features, preprocessing methods, supporting modalities, and classifiers. Speech Commun. **116**, 56–76 (2020)
2. Song, P.: Transfer linear subspace learning for cross-corpus speech emotion recognition. IEEE Trans. Affect. Comput. **10**(02), 265–275 (2019)
3. Zhang, L., Gao, X.: Transfer adaptation learning: a decade survey. IEEE Trans. Neural Netw. Learn. Syst. (2022)
4. Pan, S.J., Tsang, I.W., Kwok, J.T., Yang, Q.: Domain adaptation via transfer component analysis. IEEE Trans. Neural Netw. **22**(2), 199–210 (2010)
5. Long, M., Wang, J., Ding, G., Sun, J., Yu, P.S.: Transfer feature learning with joint distribution adaptation. In: Proceedings of the IEEE International Conference on Computer Vision, pp. 2200–2207 (2013)
6. Long, M., Wang, J., Ding, G., Sun, J., Yu, P.S.: Transfer joint matching for unsupervised domain adaptation. In: Proceedings of the IEEE Conference on Computer Vision and Pattern Recognition, pp. 1410–1417 (2014)
7. Wang, J., Chen, Y., Hao, S., Feng, W., Shen, Z.: Balanced distribution adaptation for transfer learning. In: 2017 IEEE International Conference on Data Mining (ICDM), pp. 1129–1134. IEEE (2017)
8. Zhang, Y., Li, W., Tao, R., Peng, J., Du, Q., Cai, Z.: Cross-scene hyperspectral image classification with discriminative cooperative alignment. IEEE Trans. Geosci. Remote Sens. **59**(11), 9646–9660 (2021)
9. Li, S., Song, P., Zhao, K., Zhang, W., Zheng, W.: Coupled discriminant subspace alignment for cross-database speech emotion recognition. Proc. Interspeech **2022**, 4695–4699 (2022)
10. Zhang, X.Y., Wang, L., Xiang, S., Liu, C.L.: Retargeted least squares regression algorithm. IEEE Trans. Neural Netw. Learn. Syst. **26**(9), 2206–2213 (2014)
11. Mohar, B., Alavi, Y., Chartrand, G., Oellermann, O.: The Laplacian spectrum of graphs. Graph Theory Comb. Appl. **2**(871–898), 12 (1991)
12. Li, Z., Nie, F., Chang, X., Nie, L., Zhang, H., Yang, Y.: Rank-constrained spectral clustering with flexible embedding. IEEE Trans. Neural Netw. Learn. Syst. **29**(12), 6073–6082 (2018)
13. Fan, K.: On a theorem of Weyl concerning eigenvalues of linear transformations I. Proc. Natl. Acad. Sci. **35**(11), 652–655 (1949)

14. Li, X., Zhang, H., Zhang, R., Liu, Y., Nie, F.: Generalized uncorrelated regression with adaptive graph for unsupervised feature selection. IEEE Trans. Neural Netw. Learn. Syst. **30**(5), 1587–1595 (2018)
15. Wen, J., Zhong, Z., Zhang, Z., Fei, L., Lai, Z., Chen, R.: Adaptive locality preserving regression. IEEE Trans. Circuits Syst. Video Technol. **30**(1), 75–88 (2018)
16. Li, S., Song, P., Zheng, W.: Multi-source discriminant subspace alignment for cross-domain speech emotion recognition. IEEE/ACM Transactions on Audio, Speech, and Language Processing (2023)
17. Song, P., Zheng, W.: Feature selection based transfer subspace learning for speech emotion recognition. IEEE Trans. Affect. Comput. **11**(3), 373–382 (2018)
18. Yu, C., Wang, J., Chen, Y., Huang, M.: Transfer learning with dynamic adversarial adaptation network. In: 2019 IEEE International Conference on Data Mining (ICDM), pp. 778–786. IEEE (2019)
19. Zhu, Y., et al.: Multi-representation adaptation network for cross-domain image classification. Neural Netw. **119**, 214–221 (2019)
20. Zhu, Y., et al.: Deep subdomain adaptation network for image classification. IEEE Trans. Neural Netw. Learn. Syst. **32**(4), 1713–1722 (2020)
21. Cui, S., Wang, S., Zhuo, J., Li, L., Huang, Q., Tian, Q.: Towards discriminability and diversity: batch nuclear-norm maximization under label insufficient situations. In: Proceedings of the IEEE/CVF Conference on Computer Vision and Pattern Recognition, pp. 3941–3950 (2020)

AVMFAC: Acoustic Visual Multi-scale Feature Aggregation Conformer for Multimodal Sentiment Analysis

Qiuyan Zheng[✉]

Key Laboratory of Media Audio & Video, School of Information and Communication Engineering, Communication University of China, Beijing, China
zqy_213@cuc.edu.cn

Abstract. To gain a deeper understanding of user sentiments, multimodal sentiment analysis has gained significant attention. However, prior research has highlighted the dominance of the text modality, while audio and visual modalities have been less explored. To maximize the utilization of information from non-verbal modalities within multimodal data and to enhance the feature representation capabilities of audio and visual modalities, we introduce a multi-scale feature fusion framework based on the Conformer architecture. Initially, the Conformer module is employed to encode non-verbal modalities, yielding multi-scale hidden representations. We then incorporate attention mechanisms to consolidate sentiment orientation within each modality. Subsequently, an attention-based statistical pooling layer is utilized to fuse multimodal features for sentiment classification and regression tasks. Experimental results on the CH-SIMSv2s datasets demonstrate that our proposed framework achieves state-of-the-art performance.

Keywords: Multimodal sentiment analysis · Conformer · Multi-scale features · Attention mechanism

1 Introduction

With the rapid rise of short video platforms, more people are using social media to express themselves, creating diverse multimodal data rich in personal emotional content. Multimodal sentiment analysis deals with understanding emotions in videos, encompassing images, audio, and text.

Previous benchmarks often emphasized fusion techniques, relying on joint representation learning to create a unified multimodal view [6–8]. However, as [1] points out, extracting sentiment from text is comparatively easier due to pre-trained language models, while handling sparse non-verbal modalities poses greater challenges. Many studies tend to rely heavily on textual information, with significant classification accuracy drops when text is removed [1–3]. In real-world scenarios, text may suffer from imperfections due to speech recognition errors [4, 5], making effective use of non-verbal information a critical challenge in multimodal sentiment analysis.

To enhance acoustic and visual representations, we propose using the Conformer architecture for non-verbal modalities and BERT for text. We also introduce a multi-scale feature fusion framework that combines hierarchical visual and acoustic representations with textual ones. Finally, we employ attentive statistical pooling to create comprehensive sentiment representations. Our experiments utilize a Chinese dataset with videos from movies and TV shows, featuring diverse facial expressions and emotionally-rich vocalizations, making it a suitable testbed for non-verbal information exploration.

In summary, the main contributions of this work are as follows:

- We propose a multimodal sentiment analysis framework called AVMFA-Conformer (Acoustic Visual Multi-scale Feature Aggregation Conformer), which utilizes the Conformer architecture to enhance representation learning in acoustic and visual modalities. It effectively captures both local and global information from the visual modality by employing multi-head self-attention and convolutional neural networks.
- We introduce a straightforward multimodal fusion approach that emphasizes the expressive capabilities of acoustic and visual modalities. This method integrates features from the acoustic and visual modalities at various scales and employs self-attention mechanisms to consolidate emotional information within each modality.
- We conducted extensive experiments on the CH-SIMSv2s [13] dataset, and the results demonstrate that our proposed model surpasses previous state-of-the-art models in multimodal sentiment analysis tasks.

2 Related Work

Multimodal sentiment analysis has attracted significant attention in recent years, leading to the development of various models. LF-DNN [0] is a late fusion deep neural network that extracts modality-specific features and utilizes late fusion strat-egy for final prediction. On the other hand, EF-LSTM [9] is an early fusion model that combines input-level features and employs Long Short-Term Memory (LSTM) networks to learn multimodal representations. In contrast, TFN [7] employs tensor fusion to capture interactions among unimodal, bimodal, and trimodal data. LMF [10] improves upon TFN by using low-rank tensor fusion techniques to enhance model efficiency. MulT [6] is a multi-modal transformer that utilizes directional pairwise cross-modal attention to transform one modality to another. MISA [1] is a model that learns modality-invariant and modality-specific representations by combining similarity, reconstruction, and prediction losses. MTFN is a multi-task tensor fusion network that calculates a multi-dimensional tensor to capture interactions among unimodal, bimodal, and trimodal data.

In recent years, Transformer-based variants have emerged in different domains and achieved remarkable results. The Conformer [15] module, initially proposed for speech recognition tasks, incorporates CNN layers into the Transformer structure to simultaneously capture local and global features, leading to outstanding performance. It has since been applied to speech enhancement [23], speech separation [24] and speech verification [26] demonstrating excellent performance. In the visual domain, Conformer [25] adopts a hybrid network structure that combines CNN and Transformer in parallel, leveraging both convolutional operations and self-attention mechanisms to enhance feature representation learning. It has achieved promising results in object detection. However, in sentiment analysis tasks, no work has yet utilized the Conformer model, combining the ideas of CNN and Transformer to enhance feature expression capability.

3 Methods

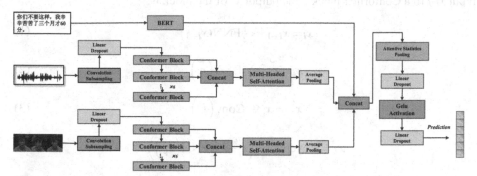

Fig. 1. The overall architecture of Acoustic Visual Multi-scale Feature Aggregation Con-former (AVMFA-Conformer)

An overview of our method is shown in Fig. 1. Each modality feature is first extracted using specific methods. Then they are fed into the model for further processing.

3.1 Feature Extraction

For fair comparisons, we utilize the standard low-level features that are provided by the respective benchmarks and utilized by the state-of-the-art methods.

Text Features. The pre-trained BERT [17] model was used to learn contextual word embeddings. This model consists of 12 stacked Transformer layers. The final text feature was obtained from the 768-dimensional hidden state representation.

Acoustic Features. The OpenSMILE [19] toolkit was used to extract low-level descriptor features from the eGeMAPS [18] feature set with a sampling rate of 16000 Hz. This feature set includes 25 dimensions such as MFCC1-4, F0, and Pitch.

Visual Features. The OpenFace [19] toolkit was employed to extract 177 dimensions facial features, including 68 facial landmarks, 17 facial action units, head pose, head direction, and gaze direction.

3.2 Conformer Block

The Conformer block consists of four stacked modules: the feed-forward module, self-attention module, convolution module, and the final second feed-forward module. The key components of the Conformer module are the multi-head self-attention (MHSA) and the convolution module. The MHSA in Conformer adopts the relative positional encoding scheme proposed in Transformer-XL [20]. The convolution module after MHSA consists of Pointwise convolution, 1D Depthwise convolution, and BatchNorm after the convolution layer, which helps in training deep models more easily. Each Conformer block includes two Macaron-like feed-forward modules (FNN), with 1/2 residual connections sandwiched between the MHSA and convolution modules (Conv). Mathematically, the input x_{i-1} to a Conformer block i, the output x_i of the block is:

$$\tilde{x}_i = x_{i-1} + \tfrac{1}{2}\text{FNN}(x_{i-1}) \tag{1}$$

$$x_i' = \tilde{x}_i + \text{MHSA}\left(\tilde{x}_i\right) \tag{2}$$

$$x_i'' = x_i' + \text{Conv}\left(x_i'\right) \tag{3}$$

$$x_i = \text{LayerNorm}\left(x_i'' + \tfrac{1}{2}\text{FNN}\left(x_i''\right)\right) \tag{4}$$

Note that $x_{i-1} \in R^{d \times T}$, and $x_i \in R^{d \times T}$, where d denotes the Conformer encoder dimension and T denotes the frame length.

3.3 MFA with Multi-headed Self-attention and Attentive Statistics Pooling

Previous studies [6] indicate that the low-level feature maps can also contribute towards the accurate classification for audio and image. Based on this experience, in our system, we concatenate the output feature maps from each Conformer block for each modality, and this aggregation leads to an obvious performance improvement. And then feed them into self-attention layer:

$$X' = \text{Concat}(x_1, x_2, \ldots, x_L). \tag{5}$$

where $X' \in R^{D \times T}$ and $X = [X_1, X_2, \ldots, X_T] \in R^{D \times T}$. L denotes the number of Conformer blocks and $D = d \times L$.

Furthermore, we perform a self-attention [21] followed by a concatenation of all the six transformed modality representations from Conformer blocks to capture unified emotional information within each modality.

The Transformer leverages an attention module that is defined as a scaled dot-product function:

$$\text{Attention}(Q, K, V) = \text{softmax}\left(\frac{QK^T}{\sqrt{d}}\right)V. \tag{6}$$

where, Q, K, and V are the query, key, and value matrices. The Transformer computes multiple such parallel attentions, where each attention output is called a head. The ith head is computed as:

$$head_i = \text{Attention}\left(QW_i^q, KW_i^k, VW_i^v\right). \tag{7}$$

$W_i^{q/k/v} \in R^{d \times d}$ are head-specific parameters to linearly project the matrices into local spaces.

Next, average pooling is applied to the hidden representations of the audio and visual modalities to align with the frame length of the text. Then, they are concatenated along the feature dimension. cc attentive statistics pooling [6, 22] to capture the importance of each frame. Specifically, for a frame-level feature X_t at time step t, we firstly calculate scalar score e_t and normalized score α_t as:

$$e_t = v^T f(WX_t + b) + k. \tag{8}$$

$$\alpha_t = \frac{\exp(e_t)}{\sum_{\tau=1}^{T} \exp(e_\tau)}. \tag{9}$$

where $W \in R^{D \times D}$, $b \in R^{D \times 1}$, $v \in R^{D \times 1}$ and k are the trainable parameters for attention. $f(\cdot)$ denotes the Tanh activation function. After that, the normalized score α_t is adopted as the weight to calculate the weighted mean vector $\widetilde{\mu}$ and weighted standard deviation $\widetilde{\sigma}$, which are formulated as:

$$\widetilde{\mu} = \sum_{t=1}^{T} \alpha_t X_t. \tag{10}$$

$$\widetilde{\sigma} = \sqrt{\sum_{t=1}^{T} \alpha_t X_t \odot X_t - \mu \odot \mu}. \tag{11}$$

where $\mu = \frac{1}{T} \sum_{\tau}^{T} X_\tau$ and $\odot$ denotes the Hadamard product. The output of the pooling layer is given by concatenating the weighted mean $\widetilde{\mu}$ and weighted standard deviation $\widetilde{\sigma}$. Finally, the sentiment embedding is extracted from a high dimension representation to a low dimension representation with Gelu using the fully-connected linear layer.

4 Experiments Setup

4.1 Dataset

In this study, we conducted experiments using the Chinese multimodal sentiment analysis dataset, CH-SIMSv2s which is the labeled part of CH-SIMSv2. It includes a larger number of instances with ambiguous and ironic text modalities, indicating a significant presence of instances with weak text modality dependence. Specifically, CH-SIMSv2s consists of 145 videos with a total of 4,402 video seg-ments. The classification labels are positive emotion (label: 1) and negative emotion (label: −1). The regression labels range from −1 to 1 and represent the intensity of emotion, with values {−1.0, −0.8, − 0.6, −0.4, −0.2, 0.0, 0.2, 0.4, 0.6, 0.8, 1.0} denoting the transition from negative to positive emotions.

4.2 Evaluation Criteria

The classification metrics include binary classification accuracy (Acc_2) and F1 score (F1_Score). In addition, Acc2_weak is used to further evaluate the performance of the model on weak emotion instances marked within the range [−0.4, 0.4]. The regression metrics consist of mean absolute error (MAE) and Pearson correlation (Corr) for fine-grained prediction assessment. Furthermore, R-square is used to compare the proportion of data explainability across different models.

4.3 Baselines

Previous Models. To validate the effectiveness of the proposed model, comparisons need to be made with existing models. Models that utilize unified multimodal annotations for supervision include the following: TFN uses a tensor fusion network to model single-modality, bimodal, and trimodal information in multimodal sentiment analysis. LMF improves upon TFN by using low-rank tensor fusion techniques to enhance model efficiency. MFN [8] and Graph-MFN [11] are memory fusion networks that model interactions within and across specific views, summarizing them through multi-view gated memory. By using cross-modal transformers, MulT transforms the information from the other two modalities to the target modality, extracting cross-modal features and modeling long-range temporal dependencies of modalities. MISA employs modality representation learning to decompose multimodal data into modality-specific representations and modality-invariant representations. MAG-BERT [12] applies multimodal adaptation gates at different layers of the BERT backbone. Self-MM [14] utilizes semi-supervised learning to guide single-modality representation learning and promote multimodal effects. Other methods that use single-modality annotations to guide single-modality representation learning and promote multimodal effects include: MTFN [27], MLF_DNN [27], MLMF [27].

State of the Art. The AV-MC [13] framework stands as the state-of-the-art (SOTA) model in CH-SIMSv2 dataset. The designed modality Mixup module can be regarded as an augmentation, which mixes the acoustic and visual modalities from different videos. Through drawing unobserved multimodal context along with the text, the model can learn to be aware of different non-verbal contexts for sentiment prediction.

5 Experiments Results

5.1 Quantitative Results

Experimental results for multimodal sentiment analysis are presented in Table 1, including the performance of several previously proposed models. All models underwent training and testing within the same experimental environment, utilizing five random seeds. The averaged results from these seed experiments were computed for each model to minimize result variability.

Most baseline models show subpar performance on datasets emphasizing acoustic and visual information. This is particularly evident in the Acc2_weak indicator, highlighting the current ineffectiveness of existing benchmark tests for fine-grained emotion intensity prediction. In contrast, the AVMFA-Conformer model outperforms the AV-MC model across all metrics. This suggests that the Conformer module, replacing the commonly used LSTM network in most benchmarks, is more effective in modeling both local and global features. The combination of multi-scale acoustic and visual features enriches sentiment polarity information, while the attention mechanism in the fusion stage enables the model to focus on pertinent information and reduce the weight of redundant data, ultimately achieving more precise sentiment classification.

Table 1. Comparison of performance of baseline models on the CH-SIMS v2s dataset. Models with (*) were trained on multitask learning, and the best results are highlighted in bold.

Model	Acc_2	F1_score	Acc2_weak	Corr	R_squre	MAE
LMF	72.28	71.98	69.32	49.26	38.15	40.14
MFN	78.28	78.24	69.42	67.21	37.11	31.78
Graph_MFN	71.95	70.98	68.98	45.89	19.07	41.36
MAG_BERT	75.01	75.11	70.9	61.13	40.66	35.89
TFN	79.24	79.29	70.72	69.66	39.57	33.77
EF_LSTM	79.52	79.6	71.82	67.16	42.71	32.28
Mult	79.68	79.39	72.6	68.32	47.15	32.71
MISA	77.37	77.4	71.16	66.66	47.54	34.32
Self_MM	79.57	78.21	71.5	65.21	30.73	33.1
AV-MC	80.66	80.72	72.54	73.33	52.59	**29.4**
MLF_DNN*	77.48	76.54	70.23	63.84	40.81	36.63
MTFN*	80.19	80.17	71.09	70.19	46.14	32.15
MLMF*	76.94	76.59	69.88	65.21	48.46	31.61
Ours	**83.44**	**83.43**	**76.52**	**73.95**	**53.77**	30.13

5.2 Ablation Study

In order to understand the contribution of each module in the model, ablation experiments were conducted as shown in Table 2.

Table 2. Ablation Study. Here, a﹨v means audio and visual, mfa means the multi-scale feature aggregation, conformer means the Conformer block, and (-) means removal of a particular component.

Model	Acc_2	F1_score	Acc2_weak	Corr	R_squre	MAE
a(-)mfa	82.5	82.52	75.11	73.37	52.43	30.61
v(-)mfa	82.18	82.23	74.2	72.59	51.45	31.06
a&v(-)mfa	81.84	81.86	73.58	72.59	51.15	31.18
a(-)conformer	82.68	82.62	75.28	73.43	52.99	30.42
v(-)conformer	79.92	79.91	71.84	70.59	48.06	31.65
a&v(-)conformer	79.06	79.03	71.13	70.49	48.01	31.65
a&v(-)self_attention	82.8	82.78	76.02	73.71	51.58	30.52
Ours	**83.44**	**83.43**	**76.52**	**73.95**	**53.77**	**30.13**

It can be observed that the performance of the model is least affected when only the acoustic modality is used without multi-scale feature aggregation or without using the Conformer encoder, indicating a weaker contribution of the acoustic modality. On the other hand, the performance of the model is more significantly affected when the visual modality loses low-level features or when the Conformer encoder is not used.

Specifically, without the Conformer encoder, the model's performance decreases by 2.88% in Acc_2, 4.18% in Acc2_weak, and 8.25% in R_square. This indicates that the Conformer encoder effectively captures the sentiment orientation in facial expressions, particularly evident in the CH-SIMSv2 dataset with rich facial expression information. Overall, the best performance is achieved when both modules are present, especially the visual Conformer module. In addition, experiments were conducted by removing the multi-scale features and using self-attention mechanism.

5.3 Impact of the Number of Conformer Blocks

The hidden representations output by the Conformer blocks serve as the input to the subsequent feature fusion module, which means that the number of Conformer blocks directly affects the quantity of feature representations received by the fusion module. Therefore, it is necessary to investigate the relationship between the number of Conformer blocks and the final performance. In this study, we simultaneously varied the number of Conformer blocks for both the audio and visual modalities. The specific results are shown in Table 3, and it can be observed that setting the number of blocks to 6 yields the best performance.

Table 3. The impact of the number of Conformer blocks on performance

Conformer blocks	Acc_2	F1_score	Acc2_weak	Corr	R_squre	MAE
2	82.19	82.19	74.74	72.81	51.81	30.93
3	82.73	82.79	75.32	72.97	52.78	30.59
4	82.61	82.58	75.44	72.86	50.73	31.07
5	82.22	82.22	74.95	73.36	52.33	30.56
6	**83.44**	**83.43**	**76.52**	**73.95**	**53.77**	**30.13**
8	81.78	81.79	74.33	72.44	50.84	30.84

6 Conclusion

We introduce the AVMFA-Conformer model, which leverages the Conformer framework alongside multiscale feature aggregation. The Conformer module efficiently extracts both local and global features from the acoustic and visual modalities, enriching the information for sentiment analysis. The incorporation of the MFA mechanism and attention pooling seamlessly integrates multiscale features from non-verbal data while diminishing the impact of redundant information within each modality. Our experiments on the publicly available CH-SIMSv2s dataset validate the efficacy of our model, particularly in enhancing the classification of weak sentiments. In our future research, we will explore the incorporation of multitask mechanisms and delve deeper into the role of cross-modal representations.

References

1. Hazarika, D., Zimmermann, R., Poria, S.: MISA: modality-invariant and -specific representations for multimodal sentiment analysis. CoRR abs/2005.03545 (2020). arXiv:2005.03545 https://arxiv.org/abs/2005.03545
2. Li, X., Chen, M.: Multimodal sentiment analysis with multi-perspective fusion network focusing on sense attentive language. In: Sun, M., Li, S., Zhang, Y., Liu, Y., He, S., Rao, G. (eds.) Chinese Computational Linguistics. CCL 2020. LNCS, vol. 12522, pp. 359–373. Springer, Cham. https://doi.org/10.1007/978-3-030-63031-7_26
3. Luo, H., Ji, L., Huang, Y., Wang, B., Ji, S., Li, T.: ScaleVLAD: improving multimodal sentiment analysis via multi-scale fusion of locally descriptors. arXiv preprint arXiv:2112.01368 (2021)
4. Shahin Amiriparian, S., et al.: On the impact of word error rate on acoustic-linguistic speech emotion recognition: an update for the deep learning era. arXiv preprint arXiv:2104.10121 (2021)
5. Wu, Y., et al.: Sentiment word aware multimodal refinement for multimodal sentiment analysis with ASR errors. arXiv preprint arXiv:2203.00257 (2022).
6. Tsai, Y.H.H., Bai, S., Liang, P.P., Kolter, J.Z., Morency, L.P., Salakhutdinov, R.: Multimodal transformer for unaligned multimodal language sequences. In: Proceedings of the 57th Annual Meeting of the Association for Computational Linguistics, vol. 2019, pp. 6558–6569 (2019)
7. Zadeh, A., Chen, M., Poria, S., Cambria, E., Morency, L.P.: Tensor fusion network for multimodal sentiment analysis. arXiv preprint arXiv:1707.07250 (2017)

8. Zadeh, A., Liang, P.P., Mazumder, N., Poria, S., Cambria, E., Morency, L.P.: Memory fusion network for multi-view sequential learning. arXiv preprint arXiv:1802.00927 (2018)
9. Williams, J., Kleinegesse, S., Comanescu, R., Radu, O.: Recognizing emotions in video using multimodal DNN feature fusion. In: Proceedings of Grand Challenge and Workshop on Human Multimodal Language (Challenge-HML). Association for Computational Linguistics, pp. 11–19 (2018)
10. Liu, Z., Shen, Y., Lakshminarasimhan, V.B., Liang, P.P., Zadeh, A., Morency, L.-P.: Efficient low-rank multimodal fusion with modality-specific factors. arXiv preprint arXiv:1806.00064 (2018)
11. Zadeh, A.B., Liang, P.P., Poria, S., Cambria, E., Morency, L.P.: Multimodal language analysis in the wild: CMU-MOSEI dataset and interpretable dynamic fusion graph. In: Proceedings of the 56th Annual Meeting of the Association for Computational Linguistics (vol. 1: Long Papers), pp. 2236–2246 (2018)
12. Rahman, W., et al.: Integrating multimodal information in large pretrained transformers. In: Proceedings of the 58th Annual Meeting of the Association for Computational Linguistics, pp. 2359–2369 (2020)
13. Liu, Y., Yuan, Z., Mao, H., et al.: Make acoustic and visual cues matter: CH-SIMS v2.0 dataset and AV-Mixup consistent module. In: Proceedings of the 2022 International Conference on Multimodal Interaction, pp. 247–258 (2022)
14. Yu, W., Xu, H., Yuan, Z., Wu, J.: Learning modality-specific representations with self-supervised multi-task learning for multimodal sentiment analysis. arXiv preprint arXiv:2102.04830 (2021)
15. Gulati, A., et al.: Conformer: convolution-augmented transformer for speech recognition. Proc. Interspeech **2020**, 5036–5040 (2020)
16. Mao, H., Yuan, Z., Xu, H., Yu, W., Liu, Y., Gao, K.: M-SENA: an integrated platform for multimodal sentiment analysis. In: Proceedings of the 60th Annual Meeting of the Association for Computational Linguistics (2022)
17. Devlin, J., Chang, M.W., Lee, K., Toutanova, K.: BERT: pre-training of deep bidirectional transformers for language understanding. arXiv preprint arXiv:1810.04805 (2018)
18. Eyben, F., et al.: The Geneva minimalistic acoustic parameter set (GeMAPS) for voice research and affective computing. IEEE Trans. Affect, Comput. **7**(2), 190–202 (2015)
19. Eyben, F., Wöllmer, M., Schuller, B.: OpenSMILE: the Munich versatile and fast open-source audio feature extractor. In: Proceedings of the 18th ACM International Conference on Multimedia, pp. 1459–1462 (2010)
20. Dai, Z., Yang, Z., Yang, Y., Carbonell, J., Le, Q.V., Salakhutdinov, R.: Transformer-XL: attentive language models beyond a fixed-length context. arXiv preprint arXiv:1901.02860 (2019)
21. Vaswani, A., et al.: Attention is all you need. In: Advances in Neural Information Processing Systems, pp. 5998–6008 (2017)
22. Okabe, K., Koshinaka, T., Shinoda, K.: Attentive statistics pooling for deep speaker embedding. arXiv preprint arXiv:1803.10963 (2018)
23. Koizumi, Y., et al.: DF-conformer: Integrated architecture of Conv-TasNet and conformer using linear complexity self-attention for speech enhancement. In: 2021 IEEE Workshop on Applications of Signal Processing to Audio and Acoustics (WASPAA), pp. 161–165. IEEE (2021)
24. Chen, S., et al.: Continuous speech separation with conformer. In: ICASSP 2021–2021 IEEE International Conference on Acoustics, Speech and Signal Processing (ICASSP), pp. 5749–5753. IEEE (2021)
25. Peng, Z., Huang, W., Gu, S., et al.: Conformer: Local features coupling global representations for visual recognition. In: Proceedings of the IEEE/CVF International Conference on Computer Vision, pp. 367–376 (2021)

26. Zhang, Y., Lv, Z., Wu, H., et al.: MFA-conformer: multi-scale feature aggregation conformer for automatic speaker verification. arXiv preprint arXiv:2203.15249 (2022)
27. Yu, W., Xu, H., Meng, F., et al.: CH-SIMS: a Chinese multimodal sentiment analysis dataset with fine-grained annotation of modality. In: Proceedings of the 58th Annual Meeting of the Association for Computational Linguistics, pp. 3718–3727 (2020)

Gait, Iris and Other Biometrics

Few-Shot Person Re-identification Based on Hybrid Pooling Fusion and Gaussian Relation Metric

Guizhen Chen, Guofeng Zou$^{(\boxtimes)}$, Jinjie Li, and Xiaofei Zhang

School of Electrical and Electronic Engineering, Shandong University of Technology, Zibo 255000, China
gfzou@sdut.edu.cn

Abstract. In practical scenarios, person re-identification tasks often face the problem of insufficient available pedestrian images. In response to this problem, a few-shot person re-identification method based on hybrid pooling fusion and Gaussian relation metric is proposed. Firstly, a hybrid pooling fusion method is proposed. In this method, max pooling and average pooling layers are introduced after each feature extraction layer, and the adaptive weight allocation mechanism is introduced in the fusion of post-pooling and non-pooling features, which realizes more representative pedestrian feature extraction. Secondly, a composite metric method of Gaussian relation metric is proposed in the metric module. This method realizes the comprehensive metric of pedestrian features in kernel space and relation level and improves the reliability of pedestrian similarity measurement. Finally, experiments on three small datasets, Market-Tiny, Duke-Tiny, and MSMT17-Tiny, demonstrate the effectiveness of the proposed method.

Keywords: Person re-identification · Hybrid pooling fusion · Gaussian relation metric · Few-shot

1 Introduction

Person re-identification [1] involves identifying specific pedestrians by analyzing pedestrian image information in surveillance video. Due to occlusion, illumination, perspective, and other reasons, obtaining many marked pedestrian image data is difficult. Therefore, only unlabeled and a small number of usable pedestrian images can be obtained in practice. This makes the deep person re-identification network [2] based on massive data-driven face severe challenges.

Few-shot learning [3] aims to efficiently adapt to new categories or tasks using a limited amount of labeled data. This method mainly solves the following problems: 1) Learning and recognition challenges involving missing or inaccurate class labels within extensive datasets. 2) Learning and recognition challenges arise from correct labeling but constrained dataset size. Notably, few-shot person re-identification also confronts challenges stemming from both of these categories.

W. Jia et al. (Eds.): CCBR 2023, LNCS 14463, pp. 249–258, 2023.
https://doi.org/10.1007/978-981-99-8565-4_24

In addressing the challenge of person re-identification in scenarios with limited annotations, Lv et al. [4] proposed a fusion model based on Bayesian inference, which uses the spatiotemporal information of the camera to improve the probability of generating correct positive sample pairs to improve the network performance. Ding et al. [5] proposed a clustering method based on dispersion, which comprehensively considers the gap between the classes within the cluster and effectively deals with the impact of unbalanced data distribution.

To solve the problem of insufficient sample size, scholars have proposed few-shot learning methods, mainly including generative model and meta-metric learning methods. Methods for generating model, Mehrotra et al. [6] proposed an adversarial residual pairwise network, which exploited the GAN framework's generative power to improve the model's recognition performance by learning residual pairs. Schwartz et al. [7] proposed a few-shot learning method of the Delta encoder, which used the Delta encoder to minimize the difference between synthetic and biological samples and improve the recognition ability. Such methods often have high network complexity and make it easy to introduce noise data, which reduces the model's generalization ability and recognition performance.

In contrast, the methods based on meta-metric learning have a simpler model structure and calculation process. It can learn the similarities and differences between tasks and quickly generalize them to new tasks. Vinyals et al. [8] proposed a matching network model, which uses the attention mechanism to realize the dynamic weighting of samples and dynamically adjust the attention to different categories to improve the model's recognition performance. Snell et al. [9] proposed a prototype network model, which learns a category prototype for each type of sample, and captures the feature distribution between categories through the learned prototype vector so that the model has good generalization performance. Sung et al. [10] proposed a relational network model in which the neural network was used to construct the correlation module, and the ReLU function was used to calculate the distance between samples to analyze the matching degree, thus improving the recognition performance of the model. Although such methods have shown good performance in the recognition tasks of birds and cars, they still have the following problems when dealing with the recognition tasks of complex images: (1) The feature extraction networks are relatively shallow, and it is difficult to capture enough rich and specific feature information when facing sample images with complex appearance and pose changes. (2) The metric methods are relatively simple, and it is easy to fall into the curse of dimensionality when facing high-dimensional sample features. Moreover, despite the plethora of studies addressing the challenge of few-shot learning with limited sample sizes, these studies have not been extensively employed in person re-identification, primarily because of various interfering factors.

To solve the above problems, this paper adopts the meta-metric learning method. We propose a few-shot person re-identification method based on hybrid pooling fusion and Gaussian relation metric. When dealing with pedestrian images with complex appearance and pose changes, the proposed algorithm can effectively alleviate the problems of insufficient extraction ability of feature extraction networks and unreliable similarity measurement. The main contributions of this work are summarized as follows:

- **Feature level:** Hybrid pooling fusion modules are introduced in different feature extraction layers. Firstly, the sample features obtained by each layer are processed by Max pooling and Average pooling operations simultaneously to obtain a feature representation with both local detail information and global statistical information. Then, the obtained feature representations are weighted and fused by the adaptive weighting mechanism according to their contribution to the person re-identification task to obtain more discriminative sample features.
- **Metric level:** A method combining Gaussian kernel and Relation metrics is introduced. On the one hand, the Gaussian kernel function's nonlinear mapping property better captures the complex relationship and similarity between features. On the other hand, the reliable relationship between pedestrians is established by the Relation metric. Combining the two measures fully uses the kernel similarity and relationship information between features to improve the recognition performance of the person re-identification.

2 Few-Shot Person Re-identification Method Based on Hybrid Pooling Fusion and Gaussian Relation Metric

The proposed network architecture consists of two fundamental components: a feature extraction module and a composite metric module. The feature extraction module incorporates various layers for feature extraction and hybrid pooling fusion modules. In parallel, the composite metric module includes the Gaussian kernel metric module and the Relation metric module. The comprehensive structure of this network is visually illustrated in Fig. 1.

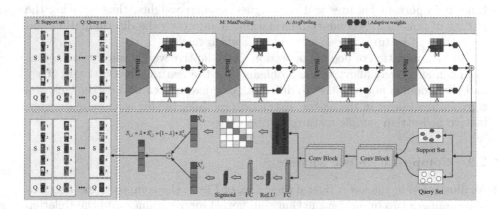

Fig. 1. Overall network architecture diagram

2.1 Hybrid Pooling Fusion Module

The white box between the Blocks layers in Fig. 1 shows that the hybrid pooling fusion module consists of Max pooling, Average pooling, and Adaptive weight assignment algorithms. Firstly, the Max pooling and Average pooling operations are introduced into the output of each feature extraction layer, and different sampling and statistical operations are performed on the features of each layer. Secondly, the Adaptive weight mechanism is used to assign weights to the output features after and without pooling according to their contribution to the person re-identification task. Finally, each layer's more representative and discriminative feature representation is obtained by the weighted fusion method and passed to the next layer for further processing.

Pooling Operations: We can obtain the statistical properties of different features by using Max pooling and average pooling. On the one hand, the Max pooling operation can extract the most significant feature of each layer feature map, the maximum value, to effectively capture the local details and edge features of pedestrian samples. On the other hand, the Average pooling operation provides global statistical features to obtain the overall distribution and smoothness of pedestrian samples by calculating the average of sample feature maps. Therefore, the Max pooling and Average pooling operations can obtain feature representations with both local detail information and global statistical information. This comprehensive feature representation can better describe the structure and characteristics of pedestrian images, improve features' diversity and expression ability, and thus improve recognition accuracy.

Adaptive Weight Mechanism: The non-trainable weight coefficients are converted into trainable parameter data types and bound to the model by introducing the nn.Parameter() function. This allows the model to adaptively assign weights according to the importance of corresponding features during training. Through this method, the essential features are weighted to highlight the critical features of pedestrians, such as body parts and texture information. At the same time, unimportant features will be assigned smaller weights, thus reducing the impact of noise and secondary information. It improves the discrimination and robustness of features in person re-identification tasks.

The combination of pooling operation and adaptive weight allocation mechanism can effectively alleviate the problems that the features contain more noise, and the model is not sensitive to different scale features caused by the lack of a convolutional layer in the feature extraction module. In this way, more discriminative pedestrian sample features can be extracted.

2.2 Composite Metric Module

As illustrated in the lower right dashed box of Fig. 1, the composite metric module comprises two branches: the Gaussian kernel metric branch and the Relation metric branch. Specifically, the sample features from the support set and query set, extracted via the feature extraction module, first pass through two Conv

Blocks. Then, the obtained features are input into the Gaussian kernel metric branch and Relation metric branch simultaneously to obtain the corresponding metric score.

The Gaussian kernel metric score formula is as follows:

$$S_{i,j}^G = K\left(f_{cm}f_\phi\left(x_i\right), f_{cm}f_\phi\left(x_j\right)\right) = e^{-\gamma\|f_{cm}f_\phi(x_i)-f_{cm}f_\phi(x_j)\|^2}. \tag{1}$$

where $S_{i,j}^G$ is the matching score of the Gaussian kernel metric module, $K()$ represents the Gaussian function formula, $K\left(x, y\right) = e^{-\gamma\|x-y\|^2}$, γ represents the hyperparameter of the Gaussian function, which is adaptively adjusted according to the similarity score, f_{cm} represents the two convolution blocks, f_ϕ represents the feature extraction module containing the hybrid pooling fusion module, x_i rdenotes the support set sample corresponding to the i-th category, and x_j represents the query set sample.

The Relation similarity score formula is as follows:

$$S_{i,j}^R = f_R\left(f_{cm}\left(\frac{1}{P}\sum_{p=1}^{P} f_\phi\left(x_{i,p}\right)\|f_\phi\left(x_j\right)\right)\right). \tag{2}$$

where $S_{i,j}^R$ represents the matching score generated by the relation metric module, f_R denotes the relation metric method, which comprises a fully connected layer, ReLU function, and Sigmoid function. Additionally, P signifies the total number of images within each pedestrian category, $x_{i,p}$ corresponds to the p-th sample belonging to the i-th category, and $\|$ signifies the feature concatenation operation.

The joint metric score formula for the dual metric module is as follows:

$$S_{i,j} = \lambda * S_{i,j}^G + (1 - \lambda) * S_{i,j}^R. \tag{3}$$

where λ signifies the weight coefficient assigned to the joint metric score.

The proposed method uses mean square error to calculate the loss value of the Gaussian kernel metric and relation metric and obtains the joint loss through the weighted fusion method. The specific formula is as follows:

$$loss = \frac{\varphi}{C \times Q}\sum_{i=0}^{C-1}\sum_{j=1}^{Q}\left(S_{i,j}^G\left(i\right) - 1(y_i = y_j)\right)^2 + \frac{1-\varphi}{C \times Q}\sum_{i=0}^{C-1}\sum_{j=1}^{Q}\left(S_{i,j}^R\left(i\right) - 1\left(y_i = y_j\right)\right)^2. \tag{4}$$

where φ represents the joint loss weight coefficient, C denotes the total number of distinct pedestrian categories within the support set, and Q signifies the number of samples within the query set. The variables y_i and y_j correspond to the labels of the support set and query set samples. When $y_i = y_j$, $1\left(y_i = y_j\right)$ is 1. Otherwise, it is 0.

The combination of the Gaussian kernel metric and relation metric can comprehensively consider the kernel similarity and complex relation information between pedestrian features. This method has more expressive power and discrimination in few-shot learning and can better solve the problem of person re-identification with scarce samples and significant intra-class differences.

Table 1. The Details of the Created Datasets. Tiny Datasets are composed of 200 randomly selected pedestrians from the Original Datasets.

	Dataset Name	Number of Pedestrians	Total Data Volume
Original Datasets	DukeMTMC-reID	1,812	36,411
	Market-1501	1,501	32,668
	MSMT17	4,101	126,441
Tiny Datasets	Duke-Tiny	200	10,775
	Market-Tiny	200	7228
	MSMT17-Tiny	200	13,199

3   Experiment and Analysis

3.1   Dataset Introduction

In this paper, we created three smaller datasets: Market-Tiny, Duke-Tiny, and MSMT17-Tiny, through random sampling from the original Market-1501, DukeMTMC reID, and MSMT17 datasets. The details are presented in Table 1.

3.2   Experimental Setup

In our experiments, we trained our model using three datasets: Market-Tiny, Duke-Tiny, and MSMT17-Tiny, under two distinct scenarios: 5-way 1-shot and 5-way 5-shot. The parameters λ and φ are set to 0.4 and 0.4, respectively, and the epoch is set to 200, with each epoch comprising 100 episodes, resulting in a total of 20,000 episodes during the entire training process. Each training episode sets the number of query samples per class to 12. In each episode, there were 65 sample images in the 1-shot scenario and 85 sample images in the 5-shot scenario.

After the end of each epoch, we perform 100 validation tasks to calculate the accuracy of the validation dataset while maintaining the limited number of query images in the training task. To evaluate the final recognition accuracy of the model, 600 episodes were evaluated.

3.3   Experiments of Various Combinations

To assess the impact of the proposed components on recognition results, we conducted multiple ablation experiments on three datasets: Market-Tiny, Duke-Tiny, and MSMT17-Tiny, using the relation network as the baseline. We verify the effectiveness of the hybrid pooling fusion module and Gaussian kernel metric. Among them, HP stands for hybrid pooling fusion module; GS stands for Gaussian kernel metric. The results are presented in Table 2.

Table 2. Tabular presentation of experimental analyses for different combinations in the 5-way scenario. (%)

Methods	Market-Tiny		Duke-Tiny		MSMT17-Tiny	
	1-shot	5-shot	1-shot	5-shot	1-shot	5-shot
Baseline	89.06	94.44	84.47	94.14	65.13	77.70
Baseline+HP	91.52	96.10	87.45	95.75	70.30	83.60
Baseline+GS	91.16	95.81	87.89	95.40	71.14	82.48
Baseline+HP+GS	**92.64**	**96.56**	**88.82**	**96.16**	**72.10**	**84.51**

Table 2 shows that based on the Relation network, after adding the hybrid pooling fusion module proposed in this paper, The average recognition accuracy of the network is improved in three datasets of Market-Tiny, Duke-Tiny and MSMT17-Tiny and two modes, by 2.46% and 1.66%, 2.98% and 1.61%, 5.17% and 5.90%, respectively. This demonstrates that this paper's hybrid pooling fusion module can extract more representative pedestrian features. Based on the relation network, after adding the Gaussian kernel metric, the average recognition accuracy of the network is improved by 3.42% and 1.26%, 2.10% and 1.37%, 6.01% and 4.78%, respectively, in the two modes of the three datasets. It shows that the composite metric method combining Gaussian kernel metric and relation metric can metric samples more reliably, thereby improving the recognition accuracy of the network. Finally, when the hybrid pooling fusion module and the Gaussian kernel metric method are added to the network at the same time, the average recognition accuracy of the network is greatly improved in the two modes of the three datasets, which is increased by 4.35% and 2.02%, 3.58% and 2.12%, 6.97% and 6.81%, respectively. This shows that using the two methods proposed in this paper simultaneously improves the robustness and effectiveness of the model and makes the model performance achieve the best effect.

3.4   Comparative Experiments with State-of-the-art Methods

To validate the efficacy of the suggested network, comparative experiments are carried out with 11 advanced few-shot learning methods on three datasets of Market-Tiny, Duke-Tiny, and MSMT17-Tiny. It includes the Matching network, Prototypical network, Relation network and MAML Network, CBG +Bsnet network, UARRnent network, FRN network, FRN+TDM network, BSNet network, DeepBDC network and SetFeat network. The experimental results are shown in Table 3.

The data in Table 3 shows that compared with existing few-shot learning methods, the proposed algorithm achieves the highest recognition accuracy in the context of two experimental scenarios conducted across three datasets. On the one hand, the feature embedding module of the above few-shot learning methods uses a single convolutional network. In contrast, the hybrid pooling fusion module proposed in this paper is introduced into the feature extraction layer, which

Table 3. Comparison with state-of-the-art techniques in the 5-way scenario. (%)

Method	Market-Tiny		Duke-Tiny		MSMT17-Tiny	
	1-shot	5-shot	1-shot	5-shot	1-shot	5-shot
Matching [8]	84.62	92.69	79.78	92.21	59.74	74.57
Prototype [9]	85.46	94.04	78.66	92.12	53.15	76.59
Relation [10]	89.06	94.44	84.47	94.14	65.13	77.70
MAML [11]	83.83	91.74	80.21	92.57	62.33	77.61
CBG+Bsnet [12]	88.97	94.85	85.07	93.10	68.51	80.11
UARenet [13]	89.59	95.09	84.22	94.17	68.57	82.19
FRN [14]	85.05	94.41	63.71	83.53	59.65	78.92
FRN+TDM [15]	89.72	94.79	75.95	90.48	67.85	82.14
BSNet [16]	88.84	94.15	85.77	92.78	68.67	81.22
DeepBDC [17]	89.53	95.86	82.65	93.61	70.02	83.52
SetFeat [18]	89.85	95.06	84.16	93.71	67.70	82.26
Ours	**92.64**	**96.56**	**88.82**	**96.16**	**72.10**	**84.51**

adaptively fuses pedestrian features under different distributions according to the importance of features to obtain more representative sample features. On the other hand, the method of learning two similarity measures simultaneously in this paper can effectively improve the robustness of the model. Compared with BSNet and CBG+BSNet, which also use the dual-metric method, the proposed dual-metric method can better deal with the noise features existing in the pedestrian sample feature space, and make the model have stronger nonlinear modeling ability, better robustness, and generalization performance.

In summary, when compared to other few-shot learning methods, the hybrid pooling fusion and Gaussian relation metric approach proposed in this paper demonstrate greater competitiveness in addressing the challenge of person re-identification with limited sample sizes.

3.5   Comparison of Visualization Results

In order to visualize the effect of the proposed network, the Gard-Cam visualization method is used to generate heat maps, and the Matching network, Prototypical network, Relation network, MAML network, CBG+Bsnet network, UARenet network, FRN Network, FRN+TDM network, BSNet network, DeepBDC network, and SetFeat network for effect comparison. The heatmap shows the output features of the network feature embedding module, where the darker the color is, the more attention the network pays to the region. It can be seen by observing the heat maps of different methods in Fig. 2. On the given pedestrian sample images, our methods focus more on areas that are more discriminative towards pedestrians. Therefore, in response to the problem of insufficient sample size, it has been proven that this method can extract more robust pedestrian features. The effectiveness of this method has been verified.

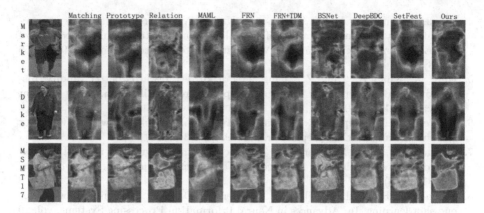

Fig. 2. Visualization of heat maps

4   Conclusion

This paper proposed a hybrid pooling fusion and Gaussian relation metric method for few-shot person re-identification to address the challenge of limited pedestrian data in the person re-identification task. The proposed hybrid pooling fusion mechanism was introduced into the feature embedding module to alleviate the insensitivity of the model to features of different scales caused by the lack of convolution layers, and more discriminative feature representations of pedestrian data could be extracted. In addition, the improved relation metric module comprehensively considered the kernel similarity and complex relationship information between pedestrian features to generate more reliable similarity measurement scores. For future endeavors, we intend to leverage the proposed algorithm as a foundational framework for conducting further research in cross-domain re-identification challenges, particularly within contexts characterized by limited pedestrian image data. We aim to address person re-identification issues within natural and uncontrolled open environments.

Acknowledgments. This work is supported by the Shandong Provincial Natural Science Foundation (No. ZR2022MF307), and the National Natural Science Foundation of China (No. 61801272).

References

1. Zou, G., Fu, G., Peng, X., Liu, Y., Gao, M., Liu, Z.: Person re-identification based on metric learning: a survey. Multimed. Tools Appl. **80**(17), 26855–26888 (2021)
2. Liu, Z., Feng, C., Chen, S., Hu, J.: Knowledge-preserving continual person re-identification using graph attention network. Neural Netw. **161**, 105–115 (2023)
3. Song, Y., Wang, T., Cai, P., Mondal, S.K., Sahoo, J.P.: A comprehensive survey of few-shot learning: Evolution, applications, challenges, and opportunities. ACM Comput. Surv. (2023)

4. Lv, J., Chen, W., Li, Q., Yang, C.: Unsupervised cross-dataset person re-identification by transfer learning of spatial-temporal patterns. In: Proceedings of the IEEE Conference on Computer Vision and Pattern Recognition, pp. 7948–7956 (2018)
5. Ding, G., Khan, S., Tang, Z., Zhang, J., Porikli, F.: Towards better validity: dispersion based clustering for unsupervised person re-identification. arXiv preprint arXiv:1906.01308 (2019)
6. Mehrotra, A., Dukkipati, A.: Generative adversarial residual pairwise networks for one shot learning. arXiv preprint arXiv:1703.08033 (2017)
7. Schwartz, E., et al.: Delta-encoder: an effective sample synthesis method for few-shot object recognition. In: Advances in Neural Information Processing Systems, vol. 31 (2018)
8. Vinyals, O., Blundell, C., Lillicrap, T., Wierstra, D., et al.: Matching networks for one shot learning. In: Advances in Neural Information Processing Systems, vol. 29 (2016)
9. Snell, J., Swersky, K., Zemel, R.: Prototypical networks for few-shot learning. In: Advances in Neural Information Processing Systems, vol. 30 (2017)
10. F., Yang, Y., Zhang, L., Xiang, T., Torr, P.H., Hospedales, T.M.: Learning to compare: Relation network for few-shot learning. In: Proceedings of the IEEE Conference on Computer Vision and Pattern Recognition, pp. 1199–1208 (2018)
11. Finn, C., Abbeel, P., Levine, S.: Model-agnostic meta-learning for fast adaptation of deep networks. In: International Conference on Machine Learning, pp. 1126–1135. PMLR (2017)
12. Lu, Y., Wang, Y., Wang, W.: Transformer-based few-shot and fine-grained image classification method. Comput. Eng. Appl. 1–11 (2022)
13. Meng, H., Tian, Y., Sun, Y., Li, T.: Few shot ship recognition based on universal attention relationnet. Chin. J. Sci. Instrum. 42(12), 220–227 (2021)
14. Wertheimer, D., Tang, L., Hariharan, B.: Few-shot classification with feature map reconstruction networks. In: Proceedings of the IEEE/CVF Conference on Computer Vision and Pattern Recognition, pp. 8012–8021 (2021)
15. Lee, S., Moon, W., Heo, J.-P.: Task discrepancy maximization for fine-grained few-shot classification. In: Proceedings of the IEEE/CVF Conference on Computer Vision and Pattern Recognition, pp. 5331–5340 (2022)
16. Li, X., Wu, J., Sun, Z., Ma, Z., Cao, J., Xue, J.-H.: BSNet: bi-similarity network for few-shot fine-grained image classification. IEEE Trans. Image Process. 30, 1318–1331 (2020)
17. Xie, J., Long, F., Lv, J., Wang, Q., Li, P.: Joint distribution matters: deep Brownian distance covariance for few-shot classification. In: Proceedings of the IEEE/CVF Conference on Computer Vision and Pattern Recognition, pp. 7972–7981 (2022)
18. Afrasiyabi, A., Larochelle, H., Lalonde, J.-F., Gagné, C.: Matching feature sets for few-shot image classification. In: Proceedings of the IEEE/CVF Conference on Computer Vision and Pattern Recognition, pp. 9014–9024 (2022)

Prompt-Based Transformer for Generalizable Person Re-identification with Image Masking

Jialu Liu and Meng Yang[✉]

School of Computer Science and Engineering, Sun Yat-sen University,
Guangzhou, China
liujlu6@mail2.sysu.edu.cn, yangm6@mail.sysu.edu.cn

Abstract. Domain generalizable (DG) person re-identification (ReID)
aims to perform well on the unseen target domains by training on multiple source domains with different distribution, which is a realistic but
challenging problem. Existing DG person ReID methods have not well
explored the domain-specific knowledge based on the Transformer. In
this paper, we propose a Prompt-based transformer framework which
embeds domain-specific knowledge into different domain prompts, which
are optionally optimized by different source domains. Furthermore, we
exploit a pretext task of masking and predicting for DG ReID to broaden
the understanding of model about data by learning from the signals of the
corresponding matching image, which enables interaction between image
pairs and improves the ability of generalization. Extensive experiments
demonstrate that our method achieves state-of-the-art performances on
the popular benchmarks.

Keywords: Domain generalizable person re-identification · Prompt
learning · Pretext task

1 Introduction

Person Re-Identification (ReID) aims to recognize the identity of a person via
retrieving a given pedestrian probe across non-overlapping camera views. It can
be seen as a general biometric recognition problem because the learned person
representation for ReID includes both biometric features (e.g., hair, skin, and
body pattern) and external appearance (e.g., clothes and accessories). Conventional supervised ReID technology has been extensively studied in [1–4]. However, directly applying the model pretrained to the unseen domain suffers from
significant performance degradation due to the domain shift. Moreover, the labeling work is expensive and time-consuming. To deal with these issues, some unsupervised domain adaptation (UDA) methods [5,6] are proposed. But it still need
to collect enough target domain training data for finetuning. Therefore, domain
generalization (DG) based methods [7,8] has recently emerged to address this

W. Jia et al. (Eds.): CCBR 2023, LNCS 14463, pp. 259–268, 2023.
https://doi.org/10.1007/978-981-99-8565-4_25

problem, which resorts to learning a model in available source domains and directly testing in the unseen domain, that is more practical and challenging.

Existing generalizable person Re-ID approaches can be divided into two categories: the meta-learning based methods and the Mixture of Experts (MoE) based methods. The method based on meta-learning [9,10] is aiming to mimic real train-test domain shift situations and modeling the domain-invariant representations. However, these methods do not consider the complementary information of domain-specific characteristics enough, which limits the generalization capability on the unseen target domain. Mixture of Experts (MoE) based mechanisms [8] have shown promising results in improving the generalization ability on target domains of Re-ID models, since it captures and utilizes domain-specific information well. However, these methods only choose some parameters, e.g. Batch Normalization, or some layers of the network, to model the domain-specific characteristics, which limits the interaction with the whole network to fully incorporate the domain knowledge.

To solve this issue, we propose a prompt-based transformer pipeline for domain generalizable Person ReID via modeling stronger domain experts. The transformer-based methods [13] have achieved striking performance in visual representation tasks thanks to the self-attention module for preserving more detailed relationship between different image patches. Furthermore, prompt learning approaches [14] has widely used in downstream tasks, integrating with task-specific information for model training. Inspired by the success of Transformer and prompt learning that are not explored in domain generalizable Person ReID, we design different domain prompt to carry different source domain knowledge, which is achieved by conditionally inputting the image combined with the corresponding domain prompt token. In this way, we can get robust domain experts for domain-specific leaning.

Moreover, self-supervised learning is proved to be effective to improve DG [11,12] because solving pretext tasks allows a model to learn generic features regardless of the target task, and hence less over-fitting to domain-specific biases. Therefore, we explore the usage of pretext tasks specifically for DG Re-ID. We argue that person re-identification is essentially an image matching task. It needs to pay more attention to the interaction between image pairs, which benefits to learn more stable representations for improving the generalization ability of model under various scenario conditions, instead of only the classification in semantic space and data transformation. Specifically, we extend the Masked Autoencoders (MAE) [31] to learn the relationship of matching image pairs via randomly masking a certainty portion of one image's patches, while keeping the other intact. They are encoded by a shared encoder and in decoder, the masked image will predict the missing patches and get complementary information from the matching full image via the cross-attention layers.

Our main contributions can be summarized as follows:

- We develop a prompt learning based transformer pipeline for domain generalization Re-ID to better capture domain-specific knowledge.

- We propose a pretext task focusing on image matching for DG ReID methods and prove its effectiveness.
- Extensive experiments demonstrate the effectiveness of our framework under various testing protocols.

2   Related Work

Generalizable Person Re-identification. Generalizable Re-ID aims to improve the generalization performance on unseen domains, which supposes the target data is invisible during training.

Style Normalization and Restitution (SNR) [26] encourage the separation of identity-relevant features and identity-irrelevant features for better discrimination. Memory-based Multi-Source Meta-Learning (M^3L) [28] network randomly splits the source domains into meta-train and meta-test to simulate the train-test process of domain generalization with a non-parametric classifier for stable identification. Meta Batch-Instance Normalization (MetaBIN) [10] proposes a learnable balancing parameter between Batch Normalization (BN) and Instance Normalization (IN) to learn generalizable and discriminative features. The Relevance-aware Mixture of Experts (RaMoE) [8] adds an expert branch for each source domain and designs a voting network for integrating multiple experts. However, it suffers from a large model size with the increase of the number of source domains, which limits the ability of application and the interaction with the whole network to fully incorporate the domain knowledge.

Pretext Tasks with Self-supervised Learning. Self-supervised learning methods are widely used in unsupervised feature representation learning and achieve excellent results in many tasks. It is often referred to as teaching the model with free labels generated from data itself such as the shuffling order of patch-shuffled images [11] or rotation degrees [29]. It is also widely used in person re-identification to model the similarity or dissimilarity between samples, e.g. ICE [30] mines hardest samples for the hard instance contrast, which reduces intra-class variance. However, these approaches often depend on careful selection of data augmentations to learn useful invariances.

3   The Proposed Method

In this paper we solve the domain generalizable Person ReID by designing domain prompts for the Transformer-based ReID model and introducing a mask-predict pretext task for domain generalization. Let $\{D_k\}_{k=1}^K$ denotes the K source domain datasets. Each domain $D_k = \{(x_i^k, y_i^k)\}_{i=1}^{N_k}$ has its own label space, where N_k is the total number of samples in the source domain D_k and y_i^k represents the groundtruth of sample x_i^k. During the inference time, we directly test on unseen target domains without additional model updating.

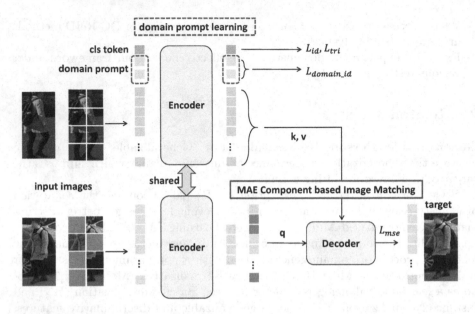

Fig. 1. The framework of the proposed Prompt-based transformer framework for DG person Re-ID with image matching. The inputs are a pair of positive samples w or w/o random mask with a certain proportion. In the domain prompt learning strategy, the images in D_k is conditionally input combined with the corresponding domain token $prompt_k$ to gather domain-specific information specifically. Furthermore, the pretext task for image pairs allows the decoder with cross-attention layers pay more attention to the interaction between images and hence less over-fitting to domain-specific biases.

The proposed Prompt-based transformer pipeline with image matching is shown in Fig. 1. We randomly sample a pair of positive samples as inputs and randomly mask one of the image with a certain proportion at the patch level. In the domain prompt learning strategy, the images in D_k is conditionally input combined with corresponding domain token $prompt_k$. In this case, the domain prompts can learn more discriminative domain feature in each source domain. In addition, we extend the MAE decoder with image matching pairs as the pretext task to allows the model to pay more attention to the generic features regardless of the target task, and hence less over-fitting to domain-specific biases.

3.1 Baseline

ViT is used as the backbone of our model, with the class token as the feature embedding. Then, we apply the classification loss and the triplet loss to optimize the network, with the features encoded in the same label space, formulated as:

$$\mathcal{L}_{base} = \mathcal{L}_{id} + \mathcal{L}_{tri}, \tag{1}$$

where

$$\mathcal{L}_{id} = -\frac{1}{N} \sum_{i=1}^{N} log p(y_i|x_i),$$ (2)

$$\mathcal{L}_{tri} = \max(0, d(x_i, x_i^+) - d(x_i, x_i^-) + \alpha).$$ (3)

where $d(x_i, x_i^+)$ represents the distance between the anchor and positive samples, $d(x_i, x_i^-)$ represents the distance between the anchor and negative samples, and α is a margin that controls the separation between positive and negative samples.

3.2 Domain Prompt Learning Strategy

The domain prompt learning strategy is aiming to generate domain prompts carrying with the domain-specific knowledge. The designed domain prompts are similar to the class token. They can pass all the self-attention layers and MLP layers. Different from the class token, the optimization of domain prompt is conducted in individual domain space, which is formulated as:

$$\mathcal{L}_{dom} = -\frac{1}{K} \sum_{k=1}^{K} \sum_{i=1}^{N_k} \frac{1}{N_k} log \hat{p}(y_i^k|x_i^k),$$ (4)

where $\hat{p}(y_i^k|x_i^k) = \theta(\phi(prompt_k))$. In this case, the whole model can take advantage of the domain information instead of some specific layers to give a more accurate prediction.

3.3 The MAE Component Based Image Matching

Masked autoencoders (MAE) are a type of denoising autoencoders that learn representations by reconstructing the original input from corrupted (i.e., masked) inputs. We argue that pedestrian re-identification is fundamentally an image matching task, which requires a focus on the interaction between image pairs, beyond the semantic space classification and data augmentation through self-transformation. Learning from matching image pairs allows the model to capture more robust representations ultimately and improve generalization.

We randomly mask a high percentage of image patches for image matching learning. Both masked and unmasked images are encoded by a parameter shared encoder. We extend the decoder blocks cross-attention layers, where the tokens from unmasked image guide the recovery of masked patches, i.e. the encoded unmasked tokens concatenated with recoverable parameters act as the query $\mathcal{Q} = [t_1, t_2, ..., t_v, mask_1, mask_2, ..., mask_m]$, where v and m is number of visible patches and masked patches respectively, and the corresponding encoded tokens of matching image acts as key and value $\mathcal{K}, \mathcal{V} = [t_1, t_2, ..., t_n]$ where n is the numbers of total image tokens and $n = v + m$. The task of reconstruction is training with Mean Squared Error (MSE) loss.

Finally, the overall training objective of the proposed method can be formulated as:

$$\mathcal{L}_{all} = \mathcal{L}_{base} + \mathcal{L}_{dom} + \mathcal{L}_{mse}.$$ (5)

Table 1. Comparison with state-of-the-art methods under protocol-2 and only the training sets in the source domains are used for training. The words in bold indicate the best performance.

Method	Reference	D+C+Ms→M		M+C+Ms→D	
		mAP	R-1	mAP	R-1
QAConv [24]	ECCV 2020	39.5	68.6	43.4	64.9
CBN [25]	ECCV 2020	47.3	74.7	50.1	70.0
SNR [26]	CVPR 2020	48.5	75.2	48.3	66.7
DAML [27]	CVPR 2021	49.3	75.5	47.6	66.5
M^3L [28]	CVPR 2021	51.1	76.5	48.2	67.1
Ours	**this paper**	**52.4**	75.8	**56.1**	**71.2**
Method	Reference	M+D+C→Ms		Ms+D+M→C	
		mAP	R-1	mAP	R-1
QAConv [24]	ECCV 2020	10.0	29.9	19.2	22.9
CBN [25]	ECCV 2020	15.4	37.0	25.7	25.2
SNR [26]	CVPR 2020	13.8	35.1	29.0	29.1
DAML [27]	CVPR 2021	11.7	31.1	28.6	29.3
M^3L [28]	CVPR 2021	13.1	32.0	30.9	31.9
MetaBIN [10]	CVPR 2021	14.8	36.1	29.3	29.4
Ours	**this paper**	**21.3**	**45.6**	**35.0**	**34.8**

4 Experiments

4.1 Datasets

We evaluate our approach on several person re-identification datasets: Market1501 [16], DukeMTMC-reID [17], MSMT17 [15], CUHK03 [18], CUHK-SYSU [19], PRID [20], GRID [21], VIPeR [22], and iLIDs [23]. For simplicity, we denote Market1501, DukeMTMC-reID, MSMT17, CUHK03, CUHK-SYSU as M, D, MS, C3, and CS in the following. For protocol-1, we use the training data in M+C3+CS+MS datasets and then tested on four small datasets (i.e., PRID, GRID, VIPeR, and iLIDs), respectively. For protocol-2, we choose one domain from M+MS+D+C3 for testing and the remaining three domains for training.

4.2 Implementation Details

All images are resized to 256 × 128. ViT pretrained on ImageNet is used as backbone. We set batch size to 64, including 16 identities and 4 images per identity. We optimize the model using the SGD optimizer employed with a momentum of 0.9 and the weight decay of 1e-4. The learning rate is initialized as 0.008 with cosine learning rate decay. In the pretext task of patch masking, we use a masking rate of 50%.

Table 2. Ablation study on the effectiveness of promp learning and the design of MAE based on matching image pairs. The experiment is conducted under protocol-1. The final results are highlighted in bold.

Method	→PRID		→GRID		→VIPeR		→iLIDs	
	mAP	R-1	mAP	R-1	mAP	R-1	mAP	R-1
Baseline	70.7	63.3	55.0	44.8	67.9	58.9	81.9	73.3
Baseline+prompt learning	70.5	62.0	56.0	47.0	68.5	58.9	83.2	75.0
Baseline+prompt learning+MAE	70.6	61.0	55.9	46.4	70.3	60.8	81.5	73.3
Baseline+prompt learning+Matching MAE	**72.2**	**64.0**	**56.9**	**47.2**	**71.5**	**62.7**	**84.0**	**76.7**

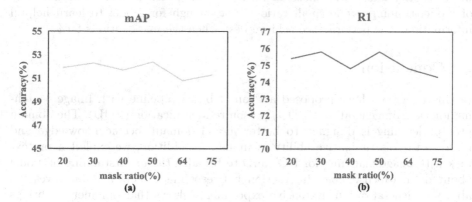

Fig. 2. The analysis of the mask ratio of the input images under the setting of D+C+MS→M in protocol-2.

4.3 Comparison with State-of-the-arts

To demonstrate the superiority of our method, we compare it with some state-of-the-art methods on four widely used benchmark datasets under protocol-2. The results are shown in Table 1. In our experiment, only the training sets in the source domains are used for training time. The results show that our methods could outperform previous methods by a large margin on all the benchmarks. Specifically, the results surpasses other methods by at least 5.0% and 4.0% in average mAP and Rank-1 respectively.

4.4 Ablation Studies

We study ablation studies on the effectiveness of each component under protocol-1, as shown in the Table 2. As seen, when adding the "prompt learning" into the baseline, the baseline can be gained in multiple different tasks, which validates that the prompt learning based method can help integrate the domain-specific information and distinguish between different source domains.

The second and forth rows denotes when we apply the pretext task base image matching, the performance can be further improved in different benchmark. In this way, the interaction between image pairs is well exploited for improving generalization. We also compare the method MAE which only explores the intrinsic information from the image itself as the third and forth rows, and the great performance drop also shows the superiority of our methods.

4.5 Parameter Analysis

We analyze the impact of the mask ratio of the input images at the setting of D+C+MS→M in protocol-2. As illustrated in Fig. 2, large mask ratio means more identity information need to be recovered, which increases the difficulty of model training, while small ratio is not enough for model to learn helpful information. The performance achieve best when the mask ratio is 50%.

5 Conclusion

In this paper, we have proposed a Prompt-based pipeline with Image Matching for Domain generalizable (DG) person re-identification (ReID). The domain prompt learning is designed to better model domain-specific knowledge and improve the discriminative ability of model. In addition, we exploit a pretext task with image matching for DG ReID to broaden the understanding of model about data, which enables interaction between image pairs and improves the ability of generalization. Extensive experiments shows that our method brings general improvements and achieves state-of-the-art performances on the popular benchmarks.

Acknowledgments. This work is partially supported by National Natural Science Foundation of China (Grants no. 62176271), and Science and Technology Program of Guangzhou (Grant no. 202201011681).

References

1. Zhong, Z., Zheng, L., Cao, D., Li, S.: Re-ranking person re-identification with k-reciprocal encoding. In: Proceedings of the IEEE Conference on Computer Vision and Pattern Recognition, pp. 1318–1327 (2017)
2. Sun, Y., Zheng, L., Yang, Y., Tian, Q., Wang, S.: Beyond part models: person retrieval with refined part pooling (and a strong convolutional baseline). In: Proceedings of the European Conference on Computer Vision, ECCV 2018, pp. 480–496 (2018)
3. Miao, J., Wu, Y., Liu, P., Ding, Y., Yang, Y.: Pose-guided feature alignment for occluded person re-identification. In: Proceedings of the IEEE/CVF International Conference on Computer Vision, pp. 542–551 (2019)
4. Hou, R., Ma, B., Chang, H., Gu, X., Shan, S., Chen, X.: IAUnet: global context-aware feature learning for person reidentification. IEEE Trans. Neural Netw. Learn. Syst. **32**(10), 4460–4474 (2020)
5. Zhong, Z., Zheng, L., Luo, Z., Li, S., Yang, Y.: Invariance matters: exemplar memory for domain adaptive person re-identification. In Proceedings of the IEEE/CVF Conference on Computer Vision and Pattern Recognition, pp. 598–607 (2019)

6. Dai, Y., Liu, J., Sun, Y., Tong, Z., Zhang, C., Duan, L. Y.: IDM: an intermediate domain module for domain adaptive person re-ID. In: Proceedings of the
IEEE/CVF International Conference on Computer Vision, pp. 11864–11874 (2021)
7. Jin, X., Lan, C., Zeng, W., Chen, Z., Zhang, L.: Style normalization and restitution for generalizable person re-identification. In: Proceedings of the IEEE/CVF
Conference on Computer Vision and Pattern Recognition, pp. 3143–3152 (2020)
8. Dai, Y., Li, X., Liu, J., Tong, Z., Duan, L. Y.: Generalizable person re-identification
with relevance-aware mixture of experts. In: Proceedings of the IEEE/CVF Conference on Computer Vision and Pattern Recognition, pp. 16145–16154 (2021)
9. Bai, Y., et al.: Person30K: a dual-meta generalization network for person re-
identification. In: Proceedings of the IEEE/CVF Conference on Computer Vision
and Pattern Recognition, pp. 2123–2132 (2021)
10. Choi, S., Kim, T., Jeong, M., Park, H., Kim, C.: Meta batch-instance normalization for generalizable person re-identification. In: Proceedings of the IEEE/CVF
conference on Computer Vision and Pattern Recognition, pp. 3425–3435 (2021)
11. Carlucci, F.M., D'Innocente, A., Bucci, S., Caputo, B., Tommasi, T.: Domain generalization by solving jigsaw puzzles. In Proceedings of the IEEE/CVF Conference
on Computer Vision and Pattern Recognition, pp. 2229–2238 (2019)
12. Maniyar, U., Deshmukh, A. A., Dogan, U., Balasubramanian, V.N.: Zero shot
domain generalization. arXiv preprint arXiv:2008.07443 (2020)
13. Dosovitskiy, A., et al.: An image is worth 16×16 words: transformers for image
recognition at scale. arXiv preprint arXiv:2010.11929 (2020)
14. Zhou, K., Yang, J., Loy, C.C., Liu, Z.: Learning to prompt for vision-language
models. Int. J. Comput. Vision **130**(9), 2337–2348 (2022)
15. Wei, L., Zhang, S., Gao, W., Tian, Q.: Person transfer GAN to bridge domain gap
for person re-identification. In: Proceedings of the IEEE Conference on Computer
Vision and Pattern Recognition, pp. 79–88 (2018)
16. Zheng, L., Shen, L., Tian, L., Wang, S., Wang, J., Tian, Q.: Scalable person re-
identification: a benchmark. In: Proceedings of the IEEE International Conference
on Computer Vision, pp. 1116–1124 (2015)
17. Li, W., Wang, X.: Locally aligned feature transforms across views. In: Proceedings
of the IEEE Conference on Computer Vision and Pattern Recognition, pp. 3594–
3601 (2013)
18. Li, W., Zhao, R., Xiao, T., Wang, X.: DeepReid: deep filter pairing neural network
for person re-identification. In: Proceedings of the IEEE Conference on Computer
Vision and Pattern Recognition, pp. 152–159 (2014)
19. Xiao, T., Li, S., Wang, B., Lin, L., Wang, X.: End-to-end deep learning for person
search. arXiv preprint arXiv:1604.01850, 2(2), 4 (2016)
20. Hirzer, M., Beleznai, C., Roth, P.M., Bischof, H.: Person re-identification by
descriptive and discriminative classification. In: Heyden, A., Kahl, F. (eds.) SCIA
2011. LNCS, vol. 6688, pp. 91–102. Springer, Heidelberg (2011). https://doi.org/
10.1007/978-3-642-21227-7_9
21. Loy, C.C., Xiang, T., Gong, S.: Time-delayed correlation analysis for multi-camera
activity understanding. Int. J. Comput. Vision **90**(1), 106–129 (2010)
22. Gray, D., Tao, H.: Viewpoint invariant pedestrian recognition with an ensemble
of localized features. In: Forsyth, D., Torr, P., Zisserman, A. (eds.) ECCV 2008.
LNCS, vol. 5302, pp. 262–275. Springer, Heidelberg (2008). https://doi.org/10.
1007/978-3-540-88682-2_21
23. Zheng, W.S., Gong, S., Xiang, T.: Associating groups of people. In: BMVC, pp.
1–11 (2009)

24. Liao, S., Shao, L.: Interpretable and generalizable person re-identification with query-adaptive convolution and temporal lifting. In: Vedaldi, A., Bischof, H., Brox, T., Frahm, J.-M. (eds.) ECCV 2020, Part XI. LNCS, vol. 12356, pp. 456–474. Springer, Cham (2020). https://doi.org/10.1007/978-3-030-58621-8_27

25. Zhuang, Z., et al.: Rethinking the distribution gap of person re-identification with camera-based batch normalization. In: Vedaldi, A., Bischof, H., Brox, T., Frahm, J.-M. (eds.) ECCV 2020, Part XII. LNCS, vol. 12357, pp. 140–157. Springer, Cham (2020). https://doi.org/10.1007/978-3-030-58610-2_9

26. Jin, X., Lan, C., Zeng, W., Chen, Z., Zhang, L.: Style normalization and restitution for generalizable person re-identification. In: Proceedings of the IEEE/CVF Conference on Computer Vision and Pattern Recognition, pp. 3143–3152 (2020)

27. Shu, Y., Cao, Z., Wang, C., Wang, J., Long, M.: Open domain generalization with domain-augmented meta-learning. In: Proceedings of the IEEE/CVF Conference on Computer Vision and Pattern Recognition, pp. 9624–9633 (2021)

28. Zhao, Y., Zhong, Z., Yang, F., Luo, Z., Lin, Y., Li, S., Sebe, N.: Learning to generalize unseen domains via memory-based multi-source meta-learning for person re-identification. In: Proceedings of the IEEE/CVF Conference on Computer Vision and Pattern Recognition, pp. 6277–6286) (2021)

29. Gidaris, S., Singh, P., Komodakis, N.: Unsupervised representation learning by predicting image rotations. arXiv preprint arXiv:1803.07728 (2018)

30. Chen, H., Lagadec, B., Bremond, F.: Ice: Inter-instance contrastive encoding for unsupervised person re-identification. In: Proceedings of the IEEE/CVF International Conference on Computer Vision, pp. 14960–14969 (2021)

31. He, K., Chen, X., Xie, S., Li, Y., Dollár, P., Girshick, R.: Masked autoencoders are scalable vision learners. In: Proceedings of the IEEE/CVF Conference on Computer Vision and Pattern Recognition, pp. 16000–16009 (2022)

Multiple Temporal Aggregation Embedding for Gait Recognition in the Wild

Shilei Zhu, Shaoxiong Zhang, Annan Li[✉], and Yunhong Wang

State Key Laboratory of Virtual Reality Technology and Systems, School of
Computer Science and Engineering, Beihang University, Beijing 100191, China
{zhushilei,zhangsx,liannan,yhwang}@buaa.edu.cn

Abstract. Gait recognition in the wild is a cutting-edge topic in biometrics and computer vision. Since people is less cooperative in the wild scenario, view angles, walking direction and pace cannot be controlled. It leads to high variance of effective sequence length and bad spatial alignment of adjacent frames, which degrades current temporal modeling method in gait recognition. To address the aforementioned issue, we propose a multi-level and multi-time span aggregation (MTA) approach for comprehensive spatio-temporal gait feature learning. With embedded MTA modules, a novel gait recognition architecture is proposed. Results of extensive experiments on three large public gait datasets suggest that our method achieves an excellent improvement on gait recognition performance, especially on the task of gait recognition in the wild.

Keywords: Gait Recognition in the Wild · Temporal Aggregation

1 Introduction

Gait recognition identifies pedestrians by their body shapes and walking patterns. Compared with other biometrics, e.g., iris, face, and fingerprint, gait is difficult to be imitated but easy to be captured at a relative long distance. Therefore, it has enormous potential in criminal investigations and security certification.

Conventional gait recognition is often set to constrained scenarios, which means the camera angle or walk direction is fixed and the pedestrian is highly cooperative. However, for gait recognition in the wild, such prerequisites are no longer available, which leads to a dramatic performance decline of current methods [2,4,5].

The challenge of gait recognition in the wild is relevant to many factors. In this paper we focus on a specific issue, i.e. the temporal feature fusion in deep ConvNets. The original convolutional neural networks are designed for general static image recognition. Gait is considered a pattern of both shape appearance and motion. The ConvNets are good at representing the former, to tackle with the latter temporal processing module is required. To facilitate the gait image sequence, existing methods either treat the sequence as a set [6] or tackle the temporal modeling as one dimensional or three dimensional convolution [7,8].

Lin et al. [8] use the local temporal aggregation (LTA) module to aggregate temporal features from consecutive frames. However, the LTA module is only used at the beginning of their framework. Fan et al. [7] use a module named MCM to do the aggregation at the end of their model. The success of these methods implies the potential of short-term temporal features for gait recognition. However, the aggregation operation only plays a role of pre-processing or post processing. Considering the bottom-up process of training a convolutional neural network, the temporal aggregation is actually either pure-holistic or pure-local. We argue that the temporal aggregation should be performed at multiple stages or levels of convolution for a comprehensive representation.

We also observe that the effective length, i.e. consecutive frames of good quality, of a gait silhouette sequence exhibits a high variance in the wild scenario. It is caused by the undersample issue introduced by short appearing period of people. To cover a wider range of time span or scale in temporal dimension, multiple temporal sampling is also necessary.

Based on the aforementioned observations, we propose a novel method for gait recognition in the wild by introducing the Multi-span and multi-level Temporal Aggregation (MTA). The proposed MTA can be embedded into many existing gait recognition framework. In this paper, we adopt the GaitBase [5] for its effectiveness and simplicity. Experimental results on both wild and conventional benchmarks show that the propose MTA is very effective.

In summary, we make the following several contributions.

- We propose a novel multi-level and multi-span aggregation method for temporal modeling of silhouette sequence for gait recognition in the wild.
- We conduct experiments on several public gait datasets, which demonstrate that multiple temporal features aggregation improves the performance on gait recognition task, especially on the gait recognition in the wild.

2   Related Works

Since deep learning has achieved a great progress, this paper only focus on deep gait recognition methods. A recent survey can be found in [9]. We investigate relevant studies from three aspects: the new challenge of gait recognition in the wild, notable works of deep gait recognition and the temporal modeling in deep gait recognition respectively.

2.1   Gait Recognition in the Wild

In the past decade, gait recognition in a controlled environment has made excellent progress [9]. Public gait datasets are typically collected with strict constraints. More specifically, subjects are asked to walk along a straight way in front of a green screen background [10] or simple background [11,12]. However, such requirements are not feasible in a real scenario. Partial and temporal occlusions, view variations introduced by arbitrary walk directions, diverse carrying articles and background clutters are inevitable [13]. These challenging factors make *Gait Recognition in the Wild* a different problem from conventional studies using constrained data. Recent reports [2,4,5] that the performance of approaches for conventional gait recognition drop dramatically in the wild benchmarks. Most current methods suffer an over 40% accuracy degradation.

This research topic is advanced by recent progress in public gait datasets. GREW dataset by Zhu et al. [2] first introduces the concept of *Gait Recognition in the Wild*. A similar dataset sample from supermarket surveillance video named Gait3D is also proposed [3]. New datasets enable the new study. Zheng et al. [4] propose a novel method for wild recognition by introducing channel-wise temporal switch. Since the topic is new the number of relevant study is small. However, the new topic is more challenging and of more important application potential.

2.2 Temporal Modeling in Deep Gait Recognition

Following the categorization by Zheng et al. [4], there are four kinds of temporal modeling methods in deep gait recognition, i.e. set-based, LSTM-based, 1D CNN-based, and 3D CNN-based respectively. GaitSet by Chao et al. [6] regard the gait sequence as an image set, and aggregate frame feature to set feature by pooling operation. It should be pointed out that such pooling operation is not equivalent to temporal pooling since the order is random. As a common sequence modeling tool, long short-term memory (LSTM) are adopted to gait recognition [20]. Besides pooling spatio-temporal convolution i.e. 3D convolution is another widely used temporal modeling method in ConvNets, MT3D and GaitGL by Lin et al. [8,21] employ 3D convolution to integrate spatial and temporal information. Although reasonable, 3D convolution suffers from efficiency issues. A compromised or balanced way of temporal modeling is use one dimensional convolution instead of 3D ones. GaitPart [7] and CSTL [22] are typical work of this category. Different from the aforementioned four approaches, Zheng et al. [4] propose to switch channels between frames to integrate temporal cues.

Since the sequence is well sampled and normalized in the constrained scenario gait recognition, simple temporal modeling method is sufficient. However, when facing the new challenge of gait recognition in the wild, such normalization is no longer available. In the wild scenario, the gait sequence is usually undersampled, which leads to big variations in effective sequence length. Besides that big individual variations also make the spatial registration of adjacent frames not well established. Thus, subtle motion is not naturally included in the convolution process. In general simple temporal modeling method in prior arts cannot meets the demand of recognition-in-the-wild. To this end, we propose a comprehensive temporal modeling method.

3   Proposed Method

We propose a novel framework to extract multi-level and multi-timespan features from gait silhouette sequence, which is referred as MTA (Multiple Temporal Aggregation). It consists of four components: 1) a backbone network to extract gait features from gait sequence; 2) a temporal pooling module to aggregate feature along temporal dimension; 3) a horizontal pyramid pooling module to obtain abundant multi-scale spatial feature; 4) separate fully-connected networks and BNNeck [14] layers for classification. The proposed framework is illustrated in Fig. 1. Since GaitBase [5] is a good baseline for gait recognition, the proposed model is based on GaitBase, where the key difference is a different backbone network.

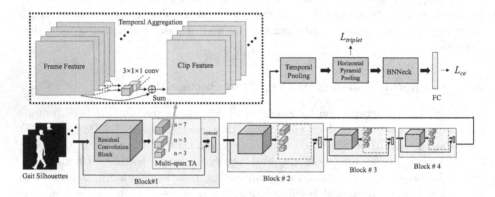

Fig. 1. Framework of the proposed gait recognition method. The *temporal aggregation* (*TA*) is performed at a multiple time spans (with scale $n = 3$, 5, and 7). Besides that the *TA* module is embedded into multiple convolutional blocks at different levels or stages. To establish a complete recognition pipeline, the stacked convolution-temporal aggregation blocks are followed by a temporal pooling module and a horizontal pyramid pooling module, a BNNeck module [14] and a fully-connected (*FC*) layer.

3.1   Backbone Network

The backbone network is used for extracting gait features from input silhouettes. In gait recognition, most methods take a relatively shallow network with several convolution layers as backbones. These models work well for gait datasets captured in a controlled environment with high-quality silhouettes [5]. However, for gait recognition in the wild, we find that such shallow architectures are insufficient because of the low-quality silhouettes introduced by occlusion and illumination variations. Since the ResNet provides a good deep architecture, we adopt a ResNet-like backbone based on GaitBase [5].

The original backbone of GaitBase [5] can only extract frame-level gait feature. It ignores the temporal features, which we consider very useful. To extract multi-level and multi-time span features, we introduce three temporal aggregation modules in different time span at the end of each block. Details of the temporal aggregation module will be introduced in the following section.

To further improve the fitting ability of backbone, we increase the depth of layers compared with the original GaitBase [5]. Specifically, our backbone has four blocks. The block structure is similar to GaitBase except for the layer numbers. The channel number of the four blocks are 32, 64, 128 and 256 respectively. To achieve a comprehensive multi-level feature representation, We use concatenating operation to combine temporal features extracted from previous levels:

$$Input_{x+1} = concat(O_x, O_{TA1}, ...O_{TAx-1}), \tag{1}$$

where $Input_{x+1}$ means the input of block $x+1$, $concat$ denotes for concatenating operation, O_x is the output of block x, and O_{TAn} means the output of temporal aggregation modules of block n.

3.2   Temporal Aggregation Module

The temporal aggregation module is designed to aggregate short-term temporal features. Specifically, we use a 3D convolution with a kernel size of $n \times 1 \times 1$ to aggregate adjacent n frame features by the convolution operation. As the convolution kernel sliding along the temporal dimension, it aggregates feature of adjacent frames. We consider that the temporal aggregation module can not only extract short-term features, which are considered to be discriminative for periodic gait [7], but also reduce the impact of noise on one frame by aggregating consecutive frames.

The inputs of temporal aggregation module are frame-level features extracted by convolutional layers. We use a residual structure. Specifically, the total feature can be formulated as:

$$F_{total} = ReLU(F_{frame} + F_{TA}), \tag{2}$$

where F_{frame} is the frame-level feature, F_{TA} means the temporal aggregation of this frame.

In addition, we consider that the pace and stride of a pedestrians can change frequently, so we use aggregation modules in three different time spans, i.e. $(3 \times 1 \times 1)$, $(5 \times 1 \times 1)$, and $(7 \times 1 \times 1)$ respectively. The temporal aggregation features can be formulated as

$$F_{TA} = Relu(F_{TA3} + F_{TA5} + F_{TA7}), \tag{3}$$

where $F_{TA3}+F_{TA5}+F_{TA7}$ indicates temporal aggregation features from $(3 \times 1 \times 1)$ and $(5 \times 1 \times 1)$ temporal aggregation modules. To extract multi-level clip features, we add the three temporal aggregation modules at the end of each block.

4   Experiments

4.1   Datasets

Existing public gait datasets can be roughly divided into two categories: constrained and less constrained. The constrained gait datasets are usually captured with stringent requirements for pedestrians. For example, in OU-MVLP [10], subjects are asked to walk in a straight-line path. Meanwhile, the background is simple or even a green screen. So that the silhouette of people can be easily obtained by background subtraction. On the contrary, less constrained gait datasets are directly sampled from captured real-world surveillance video. For example, some gait datasets are constructed from videos captured by cameras established in public places [2,3]. Pedestrians can walk freely but are not restricted on a certain route. To consider the performance of our method on both constrained and less constrained gait recognition tasks, we evaluate our method on the following three widely-used gait datasets: OU-MVLP [10], GREW [2] and Gait3D [3].

   GREW [2] is a large public gait dataset, which contains 26,345 subjects. GREW is sampled from real surveillance videos with manual annotations and thus it can be used for the so-called *Gait Recognition in the Wild*. We use the same protocol used in [5] including 20,000 subjects for training and 6,000 subjects for test.

   Gait3D [3] is another public wild gait dataset, which contains 4,000 subjects and over 25,000 sequences captured by 39 cameras of arbitrary 3D viewpoints in a supermarket. We also adopt the same protocol used in the OpenGait challenge [5], in which 3,000 subjects are used for training and 1,000 subjects for test.

   OU-MVLP [10] is one of the largest multi-view gait datasets. It contains 10,307 subjects, and each subject contains two sequences with 14 views ranging $0° - 90°$, $180° - 270°$. We use the same protocol as reference [6], i.e. 5,153 subjects for training and 5,154 subjects for test respectively.

4.2   Implementation Details

The hyper parameters of our model are set as the same on the three gait datasets except for batch size. Batch size is set to (32×4) for GREW and Gait3D, but (32×8) for OU-MVLP. SGD is selected as an optimizer in the training phase. We set the initial learning rate as 0.1 and the weight decay as 0.0005. The margin of triplet loss is set to 0.2. The length of each silhouette sequence is fixed and set to 30 in training phases, while the whole silhouettes are used in test phases. The number of training iterations is 180,000 for GREW and Gait3D and 110,000 for OU-MVLP. We choose Euclidean distance to calculate the similarity of gait embeddings generated from gait recognition models. The data augmentation strategy is also applied, including horizontal flipping, rotation, and random perspective on GREW and Gait3D for better performance. In the test phase, rank-n accuracy is used to evaluate the performance of our method.

Table 1. Average rank-n accuracies (%) on GREW dataset. Accuracies of GaitSet, GaitPart, and GaitGL are cited from [2].

Method	Rank-1	Rank-5	Rank-10	Rank-20
GaitSet [6]	46.28	63.58	70.26	76.82
GaitPart [7]	44.01	60.68	67.25	73.47
GaitGL [8]	47.28	63.56	69.32	74.18
MTSGait [4]	55.32	71.28	76.85	81.55
GaitBase [5]	60.1	–	–	–
MTA (Ours)	**72.85**	**84.15**	**87.75**	**90.48**

Table 2. Performance on Gait3D dataset. Performances of GaitSet, GaitPart, and GaitGL are cited from [3]

Method	Rank-1(%)	Rank-5(%)	mAP(%)	mINP
GaitSet [6]	42.60	63.10	33.69	19.69
GaitPart [7]	29.90	50.60	23.34	13.15
GaitGL [8]	23.50	38.50	16.40	9.20
MTSGait [4]	48.70	67.10	37.63	21.92
GaitBase [5]	64.6	–	–	–
MTA (Ours)	**71.10**	**84.79**	**63.29**	**37.10**

4.3 Comparison and Discussion

We conduct experiments on three gait datasets and compare performance with several state-of-the-art methods, i.e., GaitSet [6], GaitPart [7], GaitGL [8] and GaitBase [5].

The comparison on GREW and Gait3D datasets are displayed in Table 1 and Table 2. Our method achieves 72.85% rank-1 accuracy on the GREW dataset, which clearly outperforms the state-of-the-arts. Similar results can also be observed on the Gait3D dataset. The effectiveness and robustness of our method is well demonstrated on the gait recognition in the wild task, which implies that the proposed temporal aggregation can reduce the influence of challenging factors in the wild scenario.

There are considerable low-quality gait silhouette sequences in GREW and Gait3D datasets. One obvious reason is that there are many noises like background clutter, occlusion. The other challenge is the inaccurate silhouettes. Different from conventional gait sequence captured in front of green screen, the body boundary of pedestrian is automatically detected by model-based method like mask R-CNN [2]. Due to the aforementioned difficulties and the performance limit, quite a number of the silhouettes are incomplete. It is much more challenging than the pixel-level noise in the Gaussian Mixture Model background subtraction. We observe that such incompleteness does not necessarily appear con-

Table 3. Average rank-1 accuracies (%) on OU-MVLP dataset for 0°~90° views.

Method	Probe View							Average (0°~90°)
	0°	15°	30°	45°	60°	75°	90°	
GaitSet [6]	79.33	87.59	89.96	90.09	87.96	88.74	87.69	87.34
GaitPart [7]	82.57	88.93	90.84	91.00	89.75	89.91	89.50	88.93
SRN [24]	83.76	89.70	90.94	91.19	89.88	90.25	89.61	89.33
GaitGL [8]	84.9	90.2	91.1	91.5	91.1	90.8	90.3	89.99
3DLocal [25]	86.1	91.2	92.6	92.9	92.2	91.3	91.1	91.06
GQAN [26]	84.99	90.34	91.26	91.40	90.63	90.57	90.14	89.90
MTA (Ours)	84.3	89.4	90.9	91.3	89.8	90.4	89.4	89.36

Table 4. Average rank-1 accuracies (%) on OU-MVLP dataset for 180°~270° views.

Method	Probe View							Average	
	180°	195°	210°	225°	240°	255°	270°	180°~270°	All
GaitSet [6]	81.82	86.46	88.95	89.17	87.16	87.6	86.15	86.76	87.05
GaitPart [7]	85.19	88.09	90.02	90.15	89.03	89.10	88.24	88.55	88.74
SRN [24]	85.76	88.79	90.11	90.41	89.03	89.36	88.47	88.85	89.09
GaitGL [8]	88.5	88.6	90.3	90.4	89.6	89.5	88.8	89.39	89.7
3DLocal [25]	86.9	90.8	92.2	92.3	91.3	91.1	90.2	90.69	90.9
GQAN [26]	87.09	89.37	90.46	90.64	90.02	89.81	89.10	89.50	89.70
MTA (Ours)	87.3	88.4	89.7	89.9	87.9	88.8	87.8	88.54	89.0

tinuously. The proposed temporal aggregation of consecutive frames can reduce the negative effects to some extents. Other factor like temporal partial occlusions can also be tackled by this aggregation method.

The comparisons on OU-MVLP datasets are shown in Table 3 and 4. Our method achieves 89.0% average rank-1 accuracy. Compared with other state-of-the-art methods, our model shows competitive performance on this dataset. It should be pointed out that our method is not designed for tackling conventional gait recognition task. There is a sacrifice of accuracy for the robustness in the wild. Even though our method is still comparable to the leading methods on OU-MVLP. It shows that our method is not only an *Ad-hoc* method for the wild scenario but also a robust method for general gait recognition.

4.4   Ablation Study

In the proposed method, the key component is the multiple temporal aggregation module. We design three frameworks to analyze the contribution of this module. The first framework is without any temporal aggregation modules, and the remaining part is the same as the original framework. The second framework is

Table 5. Ablation experiments on GREW dataset.

Method	single-span	multi-spans	rank-1
MTA (ours)	x	x	62.31
	✓	x	70.28
	x	✓	72.85

with a multi-level temporal aggregation module with a single time span. In other words, we add a single temporal aggregation module at end of each backbone blocks. And the time span is $3 \times 1 \times 1$. The third framework is with the complete multiple temporal aggregation module, and the spans we set are $3 \times 1 \times 1$, $5 \times 1 \times 1$, and $7 \times 1 \times 1$ respectively. The only difference between single-span and multi-span is that the former performs aggregation in a single period, while the latter are carried out in three periods. Other parts of these frameworks and the experimental conditions are the same. We trained this framework on GREW [2] with 180k epochs. By comparing the performance of the three frameworks, we can find out the impact of both multi-level aggregation and multi-span aggregation.

The results are shown in Table 5. As can be seen, compared with the framework without any temporal aggregation module, the aggregation with multi-level but single-span achieves an excellent improvement (+7.97% rank-1 accuracy rate) on GREW [2]. It indicates that the multi-level temporal aggregation embedding works well on gait recognition tasks in the wild, even just with a single time span.

Compared with the single-span framework, the result shows that multi-span aggregation can further improves the results (+2.57% rank-1 accuracy rate on GREW). It implies that the gait cycle length and pace variations do have an impact on the performance of gait recognition in the wild and the multi-span strategy can reduce the negative influence.

It should be pointed out that due to limits in computing power we only investigate three time-spans and four levels. Although the model is larger than some exiting gait recognition model, the size is still normal. Some recent studies suggest that exploring big model can boost the performance. It can be expected that the performance of proposed method can be further improved by expanding the aggregation range and nesting larger backbones.

5   Conclusion

In this paper, we discussed the impact of short-term temporal features in the task of gait recognition in the wild. We consider that these features are discriminative for periodic gait and more robust in the wild scenario. We propose a novel aggregation method for gait recognition named MTA to extract multi-span and multi-level temporal features. The proposed MTA module can be embedded into many existing gait recognition architectures. Extensive experiments were conducted on three public gait datasets including OU-MVLP, GREW, and Gait3D.

The result shows that our method achieves excellent performance improvements on two gait datasets in the wild (GREW and Gait3d), and shows competitive performance on conventional constrained gait dataset (OU-MVLP). The result of ablation study also shows that multi-level and multi-span temporal aggregation module works well on gait datasets in the wild.

Acknowledgement. This work was supported by the Key Program of National Natural Science Foundation of China (Grant No. U20B2069).

References

1. Wu, Z., Huang, Y., Wang, L., Wang, X., Tan, T.: A comprehensive study on cross-view gait based human identification with deep CNNs. TPAMI **39**, 209–226 (2017)
2. Zhu, Z., et al.: Gait recognition in the wild: a benchmark. In: ICCV (2021)
3. Zheng, J., Liu, X., Liu, W., He, L., Yan, C., Mei, T.: Gait recognition in the wild with dense 3D representations and a benchmark. In: CVPR (2022)
4. Zheng, J., et al.: Gait recognition in the wild with multi-hop temporal switch. In: ACM Multimedia (2022)
5. Fan, C., Liang, J., Shen, C., Hou, S., Huang, Y., Yu, S.: OpenGait: revisiting gait recognition toward better practicality. In: CVPR (2023)
6. Chao, H., He, Y., Zhang, J., Feng, J.: GaitSet: regarding gait as a set for cross-view gait recognition. In: AAAI (2019)
7. Fan, C., et al.: Gaitpart: temporal part-based model for gait recognition. In: CVPR (2020)
8. Lin, B., Zhang, S., Yu, X.: Gait recognition via effective global-local feature representation and local temporal aggregation. In: ICCV (2021)
9. Sepas-Moghaddam, A., Etemad, A.: Deep gait recognition: a survey. TPAMI **45**, 264–284 (2023)
10. Takemura, N., Makihara, Y., Muramatsu, D., Echigo, T., Yagi, Y.: Multi-view large population gait dataset and its performance evaluation for cross-view gait recognition. CVA **10**, 1–14 (2018)
11. Yu, S., Tan, D., Tan, T.: A framework for evaluating the effect of view angle, clothing and carrying condition on gait recognition. In: ICPR (2006)
12. Song, C., Huang, Y., Wang, W., Wang, L.: CASIA-E: a large comprehensive dataset for gait recognition. TPAMI **45**, 2801–2815 (2023)
13. Fan, D.-P., Ji, G.-P., Xu, P., Cheng, M.-M., Sakaridis, C., Gool, L.C.: Advances in deep concealed scene understanding. Visual Intell. **1**, 16 (2023)
14. Luo, H., Gu, Y., Liao, X., Lai, S., Jiang, W.: Bag of tricks and a strong baseline for deep person re-identification. In: CVPR Workshops (2019)
15. Han, J., Bhanu, B.: Individual recognition using gait energy image. TPAMI **28**, 316–322 (2006)
16. Xing, W., Li, Y., Zhang, S.: View-invariant gait recognition method by three-dimensional convolutional neural network. JEI **27**, 013010 (2018)
17. Liang, J., Fan, C., Hou, S., Shen, C., Huang, Y., Yu, S.: GaitEdge: beyond plain end-to-end gait recognition for better practicality. In: Avidan, S., Brostow, G., Cissé, M., Farinella, G.M., Hassner, T. (eds.) ECCV 2022. Lecture Notes in Computer Science, vol. 13665, pp. 375–390. Springer, Cham (2022). https://doi.org/10.1007/978-3-031-20065-6_22

18. Xu, C., Makihara, Y., Li, X., Yagi, Y.: Occlusion-aware human mesh model-based gait recognition. TIFS **18**, 1309–1321 (2023)
19. Huang, X., Wang, X., He, B., He, S., Liu, W., Feng, B.: STAR: spatio-temporal augmented relation network for gait recognition. TBIOM **5**, 115–125 (2023)
20. Zhang, Y., Huang, Y., Yu, S., Wang, L.: Cross-view gait recognition by discriminative feature learning. TIP **29**, 1001–1015 (2020)
21. Lin, B., Zhang, S., Bao, F.: Gait recognition with multiple-temporal-scale 3D convolutional neural network. In: ACM Multimedia (2020)
22. Huang, X., et al.: Context-sensitive temporal feature learning for gait recognition. In: CVPR (2021)
23. Fu, Y., et al.: Horizontal pyramid matching for person re-identification. In: AAAI (2019)
24. Hou, S., Liu, X., Cao, C., Huang, Y.: Set residual network for silhouette-based gait recognition. TBIOM **3**, 384–393 (2021)
25. Huang, Z., et al.: 3D local convolutional neural networks for gait recognition. In: ICCV (2021)
26. Hou, S., Liu, X., Cao, C., Huang, Y.: Gait quality aware network: toward the interpretability of silhouette-based gait recognition. TNNLS (2022)

Frame Correlation Knowledge Distillation for Gait Recognition in the Wild

Guozhen Peng, Shaoxiong Zhang, Yuwei Zhao, Annan Li[✉],
and Yunhong Wang

State Key Laboratory of Virtual Reality Technology and Systems, School of
Computer Science and Engineering, Beihang University, Beijing 100191, China
{guozhen_peng,zhangsx,yuweizhao,liannan,yhwang}@buaa.edu.cn

Abstract. Recently, large deep models have achieved significant progress on gait recognition in the wild. However, such models come with a high cost of runtime and computational resource consumption. In this paper, we investigate knowledge distillation (KD) for gait recognition, which trains compact student networks by using a cumbersome teacher network. We propose a novel scheme, named Frame Correlation KD (FCKD), to transfer the frame correlation map (FCM) from the teacher network to the student network. Since the teacher network usually learns more frame correlations, transferring such FCM from teacher to student makes the student more informative and mimic the teacher better, thus improving the recognition accuracy. Extensive experiments demonstrate the effectiveness of our approach in improving the performance of compact networks.

Keywords: Gait recognition · Knowledge distillation · Frame correlation map

1 Introduction

Gait recognition is a task to identify pedestrians utilizing walking patterns without explicit cooperation. Compared with other biometrics characteristics such as fingerprints and face, gait is hard to disguise and does not require a close distance to capture, thus benefiting the application in criminal investigation, identity verification, and suspect tracking [1].

Gait recognition has achieved impressive progress [2–6] in the past decade. However, many researches [7–10] indicate that existing methods perform poorly in the wild. Different from in-the-lab datasets [11,12] performing well with relatively small and shallow neural networks, in-the-wild datasets [9,10] collected outdoors are more complex. To alleviate this problem, GaitBase [7] and DeepGaitV2 [8] have been proposed. They employ larger and deeper network architectures and have achieved state-of-the-art performance on outdoor datasets [9,10]. But large networks come with a high cost of runtime and computational resource consumption, which limits the application of gait recognition systems in widespread surveillance systems.

In order to obtain efficient and compact models, we study the knowledge distillation (KD) method, popularized by Hinton et al. [13], which represents a way of transferring the soft probabilities of a cumbersome teacher network to a compact student network for improved performance. KD has achieved significant success in various vision tasks. However, it is less studied in gait recognition. The reason is that gait networks trained with simple indoor datasets are small and shallow. It is challenging to use KD without a complex and large teacher network. With the recent GaitBase [7] and DeepGaitV2 [8] method, we are able to explore the effect of KD in gait recognition.

Gait has many modalities as input, such as skeleton, point clouds, silhouette sequence, and so on. Most methods recently consider a gait silhouette sequence as input in gait recognition. Compared with full-color images containing rich appearance clues, the gait silhouette sequence pays more attention to the motion, which derives from the frame-by-frame difference and correlations. To learn more temporal information, we propose a new KD scheme named Frame Correlation KD (FCKD), which focuses on transferring the frame correlation map (FCM) from the teacher network to the student network.

FCM contains the correlation between each pair of frames in a silhouette sequence. As a continuous process, gait exhibits small differences between adjacent frames but significant differences between further apart frames in a gait cycle. If a network accurately predicts the FCM, we can consider that it has the ability to determine whether two frames are adjacent. Furthermore, we can infer that such a network has learned the temporal information in a gait cycle. By mimicking such FCM of the teacher network, the improvement of the student is evident. As illustrated in Fig. 1, with our proposed method, DG2D(16)[1] [8] achieves a similar level of accuracy as GaitBase [7] with only 0.72 MegaBytes parameters[2].

To conclude, our main contributions are threefold:

1) We propose a new KD architecture for training accurate compact gait recognition networks.
2) We present a novel KD scheme (FCKD), which focuses on transferring the FCM of the teacher network to the student network and assists the student in learning more temporal information.
3) Extensive experiments demonstrate the effectiveness of our approach to improve the state-of-the-art compact networks on outdoor datasets [9,10].

2   Related Work

Gait Recognition. Deep neural networks have been the dominant solution to gait recognition in the past decade. Various methods were proposed to improve

---

[1] DG2D represents DeepGaitV2-2D and DG3D represents DeepGaitV2-3D. (16) represents that the number of first-stage channels is 16.
[2] We only consider the backbone for all experiments.

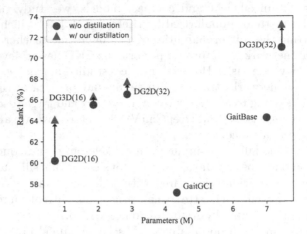

Fig. 1. Performance comparison on Gait3D [9]. Red triangles represent the results of FCKD and the others represent the results without KD. (32) and (16) represent the number of first-stage channels. We can get a higher Rank-1 result with FCKD, with no extra parameters increased.

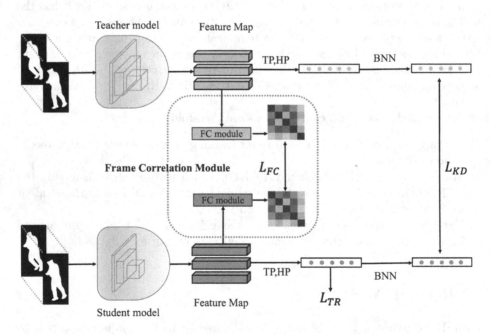

Fig. 2. Pipeline of the proposed Frame Correlation KD (FCKD). We introduce a FC module to obtain the frame correlation map (FCM). Knowledge transfer is then employed to the FCMs of the teacher network and student network. The vanilla KD loss is used in our approach.

the capability of networks and accordingly enhanced the effectiveness of gait recognition. For instance, GaitSet [2] deemed each sequence as an unordered set and utilized a maximum function to compress the sequence of frame-level spatial features. GaitPart [3] carefully explored the local information of input silhouette sequences and integrated temporal dependencies using the Micro-motion Capture Module. LagrangeGait [6] designed a second-order motion extraction module to capture second-order information in the temporal dimension and a lightweight view-embedding module taking the view itself into consideration. Although these methods have achieved successful performance on indoor datasets such as CASIA-B [11] and OU-MVLP [12], they performed not very well on the challenging outdoor dataset [9,10]. To solve these problems, Open-Gait [7] rethought deep gait networks' design principles for applications and proposed a simple and strong architecture named GaitBase. It took a ResNet-like [14] network as the backbone and demonstrated good performance on outdoor datasets. Under the encouragement of GaitBase, DeepGaitV2 [8] has been proposed recently, which achieved better results by employing a larger network.

Knowledge Distillation. Knowledge distillation (KD) has been widely developed in recent years. The concept, popularized by Hinton et al. [13], represents the process of training a compact student network with the objective of matching the soft probabilities of a cumbersome teacher network. It has been applied to various vision tasks such as image classification [13,15], semantic segmentation [16], video person re-identification [17,18].

However, KD has little application in gait recognition. Only GaitPVD [19] was proposed to solve cross-view gait recognition with the same structure of teacher and student, which limited its application in cross-architectures. Recently DeepGaitV2 [8] has gotten state-of-the-art performance with a large network. This encouraged us to propose an effective and cross-architectural architecture named FCKD to learn a well-performed compact network. Different from previous works using person pair distances [17] or triplet distances [18] in video person re-identification, we rely on a different aspect, which focuses on transferring the FCM of teacher network to student network.

3 Proposed Method

3.1 Overview

Gait recognition can be viewed as a task of predicting a label for each silhouette sequence from C categories. We employ the KD strategy to transfer the knowledge of a cumbersome network T to a compact network S for better training. Apart from a vanilla scheme, logits distillation, we present a Frame Correlation KD (FCKD) scheme, to transfer frame correlation knowledge from the cumbersome network to the compact network. The pipeline is illustrated in Fig. 2, where TP is Temporal Pooling operation, HP is Horizontal Pooling operation [20], and BNN is BNNeck [21]. In Sect. 3.2, we introduce vanilla KD. We then detail the FCKD in Sect. 3.3.

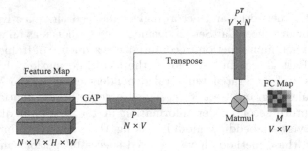

Fig. 3. Proposed FC module for computing the Frame Correlation Map (FCM) of a network. Here N is feature channels, V is the number of frames, H and W is the height and width of image respectively. GAP is the global average pooling. We compute the cosine similarity of each pair of features and obtain the final FCM.

3.2 Vanilla KD

In addition to the compact student network S, KD uses the cumbersome pre-trained teacher network T to help the student network. The results of them can be represented as $\mathbf{z}^s \in \mathbb{R}^C$ and $\mathbf{z}^t \in \mathbb{R}^C$, where C is the number of classes.

We directly use class probabilities produced from the teacher network as soft targets for training the student network. The loss function is given as

$$\mathbf{q}^t = softmax(\frac{\mathbf{z}^t}{\tau}), \quad \mathbf{q}^s = softmax(\frac{\mathbf{z}^s}{\tau}), \tag{1}$$

$$\mathcal{L}_{KD} = KL(\mathbf{q}^t \| \mathbf{q}^s), \tag{2}$$

where $\mathbf{q}^s$ represents the class probabilities from the student network, $\mathbf{q}^t$ represents the class probabilities from the teacher network, τ is a hyper-parameter to adjust two probabilistic distributions, and $KL(\cdot)$ is the Kullback-Leibler divergence between two probabilistic distributions.

3.3 Frame Correlation KD

As shown in Fig. 3, we propose a FC module to get a frame correlation map (FCM), which represents the gait frame correlation of a silhouette sequence. We first utilize global average pooling to compute the intermediate feature map $P \in \mathbb{R}^{N \times V}$. Then we compute the cosine similarity of each feature pair and obtain the final frame correlation map M. Formally, M is computed by

$$M = sim(P^T, P), \tag{3}$$

where T is transpose and $sim(\cdot)$ is a similarity function. Specifically, we use the cosine similarity for all experiments.

To transfer frame correlation knowledge from the teacher network to the student network, a straightforward approach is to minimize the distance between the FCMs of the teacher network and the student network. Specifically, we adopt the mean squared error (squared ℓ_2 norm) loss as below:

$$\mathcal{L}_{FC} = \sum_{i=1}^{v} \sum_{j=1}^{v} (M_{ij}^t - M_{ij}^s)^2, \tag{4}$$

where v is the number of frames, M^t and M^s represent the FCMs of teacher network and student network.

Student optimization. The FCKD objective is composed of two distillation loss items ($\mathcal{L}_{KD}$ and $\mathcal{L}_{FC}$) and a conventional triplet loss item ($\mathcal{L}_{TR}$). The whole student optimization process is

$$\mathcal{L} = \mathcal{L}_{TR} + \alpha \mathcal{L}_{KD} + \beta \mathcal{L}_{FC}, \tag{5}$$

where α and β are hyper-parameters to balance the contributions of the total loss $\mathcal{L}$. We do not use the conventional cross-entropy loss ($\mathcal{L}_{CE}$). The reason is that with the conventional cross-entropy loss ($\mathcal{L}_{CE}$) and KD loss, the result of the student is relatively weak.

Fig. 4. A silhouette sequence in Gait3D [9]. Adjacent frames are similar but further apart frames are dissimilar.

4   Experiments

In this section, we validate the effectiveness of our FCKD on outdoor datasets: Gait3D [9] and GREW [10].

4.1   Datasets and Evaluation Metrics

Gait3D [9] is one of the latest gait datasets in the wild. It contains 4,000 subjects and 25,309 sequences extracted from 39 cameras. 3D Skinned Multi-Person Linear and 2D silhouettes are provided. In our experiments, only 2D silhouette information is employed, as shown in Fig. 4. Following Gaitbase [7], 3,000 subjects are collected as the training set and the rest 1,000 subjects consist of the test set.

GREW [10] is one of the largest gait datasets in the wild, containing 26345 subjects and 128671 sequences collected from 882 cameras. It is divided into two parts with 20000 and 6000 subjects as the training set and the test set respectively.

Our experiments follow the official protocols strictly. Rank-1 accuracy is used as the primary evaluation metric. Rank-5 accuracy, Rank-10 accuracy, and mean average precision (mAP) are also used as evaluation metrics.

Table 1. Results for KD recognition on Gait3D. (128), (64), and (32) represent the number of first-stage channels.

Teacher	Params (M)	Rank-1 (%)	Student	Params (M)	Rank-1 (%)
DG3D (128)	118.32	75.6 (75.8[†])	DG3D (64)	29.72	74.6→74.7 (+0.1)
DG3D (64)	29.72	74.6 (72.8[†])	DG3D (32)	7.44	71.0→73.2 (+2.2)
DG3D (32)	7.44	71.0 (69.4[†])	DG3D (16)	1.86	65.5→66.3 (+0.8)
DG2D (64)	11.43	69.1 (68.2[†])	DG2D (32)	2.87	66.5→67.7 (+1.2)
DG2D (32)	2.87	66.5 (62.9[†])	DG2D (16)	0.72	60.2→64.1 (+3.9)

†Reported in the original paper [8].

4.2   Implementation Details

Network Architectures. As shown in Table 1, we set KD experiments for 3D and 2D respectively. In the 3D experiment, DG3D (128), DG3D (64), DG3D (32) serve as the teacher network for teaching DG3D (64), DG3D (32), DG3D (16) respectively. In the 2D experiment, DG2D (64), DG2D (32) serve as the teacher network for teaching DG2D (32), DG2D (16) respectively. We use 22-layer and [1, 4, 4, 1]-stage DeepGaitV2 for all experiments. Our code is on the codebase by Chao et al. [7] and all the networks are retrained.

Training Details. For hyper-parameters in Equation (5) and Eq. (1), we set $\alpha = 1$, $\beta = 0.04$ and $\tau = 1$ for all experiments. Since our code is on the codebase by Chao et al. [7], we used most of the default settings from it.

Table 2. Results on Gait3D dataset.

Method	Source	Params (M)	Rank-1 (%)	Rank-5 (%)	mAP (%)
Current state of art results					
GaitGL [5]	ICCV 2021	2.49	29.7	48.5	22.3
SMPLGait [9]	CVPR 2022	–	46.3	64.5	37.2
DANet [22]	CVPR 2023	–	48.0	69.7	–
GaitGCI [23]	CVPR 2023	–	50.3	68.5	39.5
GaitBase [7]	CVPR 2023	7.00	64.3 (64.6[†])	79.6	55.5
Results w/ and w/o distillation schemes					
DG2D (16) [8]	–	0.72	60.2	79.3	51.2
DG2D (ours)	–	0.72	64.1 (+3.9)	81.1	54.7
DG3D (32) [8]	–	7.44	71.0 (69.4[‡])	85.0	62.3
DG3D (VKD [17])	ECCV 2020	7.44	71.3 (+0.3)	84.9	63.3
DG3D (TCL [18])	ICASSP 2022	7.44	71.3 (+0.3)	85.8	63.3
DG3D (ours)	–	7.44	73.2 (+2.2)	85.5	64.1

†Reported in the original paper [7].
‡Reported in the original paper [8].

Table 3. Results on GREW dataset.

Method	Source	Params (M)	Rank-1 (%)	Rank-5 (%)	Rank-10 (%)
Current state of art results					
GaitGL [5]	ICCV 2021	2.49	47.3	63.6	69.3
GaitGCI [23]	CVPR 2023	–	68.5	80.8	84.9
GaitBase [7]	CVPR 2023	7.00	60.1	–	–
Results w/ and w/o distillation schemes					
DG2D (16) [8]	-	0.72	53.8	69.7	75.7
DG2D (ours)	–	0.72	59.0 (+5.2)	74.5	79.7
DG3D (32) [8]	-	7.44	71.2 (73.1[†])	83.3	87.3
DG3D (ours)	–	7.44	74.9 (+3.7)	86.1	89.6

†Reported in the original paper [8].

4.3 Results

KD Results. As can be seen from Table 1, our FCKD method helps the student network train significantly. Specifically, the improvements for DG3D (32) and DG2D (16) are 2.1% and 3.9%. However, the improvements for DG3D (64) and DG3D (16) are limited, with only 0.1% and 0.8% increase. For DG3D (16), it is too small to get a significant improvement. Different from DG2D (16), DG3D (16) needs to study both the spatial information of one silhouette image and the temporal dimension information of the input sequence. It is challenging for DG3D (16) with only 1.86 MegaBytes parameters. And for DG3D (64), as the difference in result accuracy compared to DG3D (128) is marginal, it has difficulties in learning more useful information.

Gait3D. We compare our proposed FCKD with other methods on Gait3D [9] dataset. The results are reported in Table 2. Compared with VKD [17] using person pair distances and TCL [18] using triplet distances, FCKD obtains better results. This demonstrates that learning frame correlation maps from the teacher network can effectively assist the student network in training. Finally, we obtain two networks with 64.1% and 73.2% accuracy, while their sizes are only 0.72 and 7.44 MegaBytes, respectively.

GREW. We then evaluate the proposed FCKD on GREW [10] dataset. As shown in Table 3, the improvements for DG3D (32) and DG2D (16) are 3.7% and 5.2%, which further confirms the effectiveness of our approach in improving the performance of compact networks.

4.4 Ablation Study

We investigate the effectiveness of different components in our FCKD architecture. Specifically, we employ DG3D (64) as the teacher network and DG3D (32) as the student network. As shown in Table 4, with our distillation term ($\mathcal{L}_{FC}$), the improvement for DG3D (32) is 2.2%. It indicates the effectiveness of FCKD. However, with the conventional cross-entropy loss ($\mathcal{L}_{CE}$) and KD loss,

Table 4. Ablation study on Gait3D.

Network	$\mathcal{L}_{TR}$	$\mathcal{L}_{CE}$	$\mathcal{L}_{KD}$	$\mathcal{L}_{FC}$	Rank-1 (%)
DG3D (64) (teacher)	✓	✓	×	×	74.6
DG3D (32) (student)	✓	✓	×	×	71.0
	✓	✓	✓	×	69.4
	✓	×	✓	×	71.0
	✓	×	✓	✓	73.2

the result of the student is relatively weak. The possible explanation is that the test of gait recognition is applied by comparing the similarity between the intermediate features and the features in the gallery. The soft label of the teacher network contains relational information between different classes, which is beneficial for the student network to learn the intermediate features of the teacher. Adding ground truth label information may affect the student to learn the soft labels. Consequently, it affects the student to learn the intermediate features of the teacher.

5 Conclusion

In this paper, we propose a novel Frame Correlation Knowledge Distillation (FCKD) for gait recognition in the wild. Different from previous works using person pair distances or triplet distances, we focus on transferring the FCM of the teacher network to the student network. Extensive experiments have been conducted on Gait3D and GREW. The results demonstrate that learning frame correlation maps from the teacher network can effectively assist the student network in training compared with other state-of-the-art gait recognition methods and KD methods.

Acknowledgement. This work was supported by the Key Program of National Natural Science Foundation of China (Grant No. U20B2069).

References

1. Nixon, M.S., Carter, J.N.: Automatic recognition by gait. Proc. IEEE **94**(11), 2013–2024 (2006)
2. Chao, H., He, Y., Zhang, J., Feng, J.: GaitSet: regarding gait as a set for cross-view gait recognition. In: AAAI Conference on Artificial Intelligence, vol. 33, pp. 8126–8133 (2019)
3. Fan, C., et al.: GaitPart: temporal Part-based Model for Gait Recognition. In: IEEE/CVF Conference on Computer Vision and Pattern Recognition, pp. 14225–14233 (2020)

4. Huang, X., et al.: Context-sensitive temporal feature learning for gait recognition. In: IEEE/CVF International Conference on Computer Vision, pp. 12909–12918 (2021)
5. Lin, B., Zhang, S., Yu, X.: Gait recognition via effective global-local feature representation and local temporal aggregation. In: IEEE/CVF International Conference on Computer Vision, pp. 14648–14656 (2021)
6. Chai, T., Li, A., Zhang, S., Li, Z., Wang, Y.: Lagrange motion analysis and view embeddings for improved gait recognition. In: IEEE/CVF Conference on Computer Vision and Pattern Recognition. pp. 20249–20258 (2022)
7. Fan, C., Liang, J., Shen, C., Hou, S., Huang, Y., Yu, S.: OpenGait: revisiting gait recognition towards better practicality. In: IEEE/CVF Conference on Computer Vision and Pattern Recognition, pp. 9707–9716 (2023)
8. Fan, C., Hou, S., Huang, Y., Yu, S.: Exploring deep models for practical gait recognition. arXiv preprint arXiv:2303.03301 (2023)
9. Zheng, J., Liu, X., Liu, W., He, L., Yan, C., Mei, T.: Gait recognition in the wild with dense 3d representations and a benchmark. In: IEEE/CVF Conference on Computer Vision and Pattern Recognition, pp. 20228–20237 (2022)
10. Zhu, Z., et al.: Gait recognition in the wild: a benchmark. In: IEEE/CVF International Conference on Computer Vision, pp. 14789–14799 (2021)
11. Yu, S., Tan, D., Tan, T.: A framework for evaluating the effect of view angle, clothing and carrying condition on gait recognition. In: International Conference on Pattern Recognition, vol. 4, pp. 441–444. IEEE (2006)
12. Takemura, N., Makihara, Y., Muramatsu, D., Echigo, T., Yagi, Y.: Multi-view large population gait dataset and its performance evaluation for cross-view gait recognition. IPSJ Trans. Comput. Vis. Appl. **10**, 1–14 (2018)
13. Hinton, G., Vinyals, O., Dean, J.: Distilling the knowledge in a neural network. arXiv preprint arXiv:1503.02531 (2015)
14. He, K., Zhang, X., Ren, S., Sun, J.: Deep residual learning for image recognition. In: IEEE/CVF Conference on Computer Vision and Pattern Recognition, pp. 770–778 (2016)
15. Guo, G., Han, L., Wang, L., Zhang, D., Han, J.: Semantic-aware knowledge distillation with parameter-free feature uniformization. Visual Intell. **1**, 6 (2023)
16. Shu, C., Liu, Y., Gao, J., Yan, Z., Shen, C.: Channel-wise knowledge distillation for dense prediction. In: IEEE/CVF International Conference on Computer Vision, pp. 5311–5320 (2021)
17. Porrello, A., Bergamini, L., Calderara, S.: Robust re-identification by multiple views knowledge distillation. In: Vedaldi, A., Bischof, H., Brox, T., Frahm, J.-M. (eds.) ECCV 2020. LNCS, vol. 12355, pp. 93–110. Springer, Cham (2020). https://doi.org/10.1007/978-3-030-58607-2_6
18. Wang, P., Wang, F., Li, H.: Image-to-video re-identification via mutual discriminative knowledge transfer. In: IEEE International Conference on Acoustics, Speech and Signal Processing, pp. 2125–2129. IEEE (2022)
19. Shang, L., Yin, D., Hu, B.: GaitPVD: part-based view distillation network for cross-view gait recognition. In: International Conference on Computer Science and Application Engineering, pp. 1–6 (2021)
20. Fu, Y., et al.: Horizontal pyramid matching for person re-identification. In: AAAI Conference on Artificial Intelligence, vol. 33, pp. 8295–8302 (2019)
21. Luo, H., Gu, Y., Liao, X., Lai, S., Jiang, W.: Bag of tricks and a strong baseline for deep person re-identification. In: IEEE/CVF Conference on Computer Vision and Pattern Recognition Workshops (2019)

22. Ma, K., Fu, Y., Zheng, D., Cao, C., Hu, X., Huang, Y.: Dynamic aggregated network for gait recognition. In: IEEE/CVF Conference on Computer Vision and Pattern Recognition, pp. 22076–22085 (2023)
23. Dou, H., Zhang, P., Su, W., Yu, Y., Lin, Y., Li, X.: GaitGCI: generative counter-factual intervention for gait recognition. In: IEEE/CVF Conference on Computer Vision and Pattern Recognition, pp. 5578–5588 (2023)

Alignment-Free Iris Cancellable Template Protection Scheme Based on Code-Blocks Encoding

Muhammad Jahangir[1], Ming Jie Lee[1(✉)], Ban-Hoe Kwan[1], Yenlung Lai[2], Zhe Jin[2], and Tong Yuen Chai[3]

[1] Lee Kong Chian Faculty of Engineering and Science, Universiti Tunku Abdul Rahman, 43000 Kajang, Malaysia
jahangir@1utar.my, {leemj,kwanbh}@utar.edu.my
[2] Anhui Provincial Key Laboratory of Secure Artificial Intelligence, Anhui Provincial International Joint Research Center for Advanced Technology in Medical Imaging, School of Artificial Intelligence, Anhui University, Hefei 230093, China
{yenlung,jinzhe}@ahu.edu.cn
[3] Taylor's University, 47500 Subang Jaya, Malaysia
tongyuen.chai@taylors.edu.my

Abstract. This paper introduces a novel irisCode template protection scheme, integrating the Indexing First One (IFO) hashing and Bloom filter methodologies. The scheme eliminates pre-alignment needs, while a proposed bit-binding strategy extends the IFO hashed code's utility for biometric cryptosystems without explicit error correction code construction. This strategy ensures authentication accuracy by preserving the Jaccard distance between input irisCodes. Testing on the CASIA v3-interval database confirms the superior performance of our approach over existing iris recognition methods.

Keywords: Iris Recognition · Biometric Template Protection

1 Introduction

Conventional recognition system relies on the personal ownership of secret data, i.e., "what we have" such as passwords, PINs, and access cards, for system access. The authentication methods rely on passwords, access cards, etc., and possess insufficiency because they can be easily lost, stolen, guessed, forgotten, or shared [1]. Moreover, there is a trade-off between password memorability and strength since complex password offer higher security but are difficult to be remembered by users.

Contrary to conventional recognition system, biometric recognition offers a more advanced approach by leveraging unique traits like fingerprint patterns, facial features, iris structures, hand geometry, voice patterns, palm-prints, signatures, and gaits.This approach eliminates the need for complex passwords or additional access cards, offering dependable and convenient authentication around the world [1,2].

W. Jia et al. (Eds.): CCBR 2023, LNCS 14463, pp. 291–300, 2023.
https://doi.org/10.1007/978-981-99-8565-4_28

In biometric authentication, Iris patterns offer a reliable method for identification due to their unique and stable nature. Iris recognition systems have improved with Daugman's irisCode, a binary array capturing iris details. During enrollment, an eye image generates an enrollment irisCode (I_e), which is stored for future authentication. For authentication, a user's iris image generates a query irisCode (I_q). If the Hamming distance (d) between I_e and I_q is below a threshold (t), the user is authenticated; otherwise, access is denied [2].

Security and Privacy Concerns in Iris Recognition: IrisCode stored in the database contains discriminative information about individual users that possess several security and privacy threats such as brute-force and reconstruction attacks, etc., which could reveal sensitive information about individual users [3]. Since the human iris is permanently associated with each individual, a compromised irisCode implies a permanent loss of identity.

Researchers have been actively working on irisCode protection in databases. One approach is using cryptographic techniques like one-way hash functions. However, achieving consistent and reliable hashes with biometric data variation is challenging due to the inherent variability in biometric acquisition. On the other hand, encrypting the irisCode requires a pre-shared secret, which introduces key management issues. Motivated by the aforementioned challenges, Biometric template protection (BTP) has emerged as an appropriate solution to safeguard biometric data stored in databases [4]. Biometric template protection is mainly divided into two categories:

1. Biometric Cryptosystem (BCS)
2. Cancellable Biometric (CB)

BCS and CB are designed to solve the current security and privacy threats [3]. The core idea of BCS is to 'bind' a cryptographic key with biometric data through key binding or to extract a key from biometric data directly for personal authentication. Over time, researchers have proposed various heuristic functions in the field of biometric authentication, as highlighted in the works of Barman et al. [5]. The majority of the proposed methods are based on two primary cryptographic constructions: the "fuzzy vault" introduced by Juels and Sudan [6], and the "fuzzy commitment" proposed by Juels and Wattenberg [4].

These cryptographic constructions aim to generate secure helper data, which is stored in the database as a replacement for the original probe biometric data. The helper data contains sufficient information for the genuine user to reconstruct a secret that was bound to it during the enrollment phase, enabling secure authentication.However, deploying such schemes reliably in practice poses challenges. One of the main obstacles is the inherent noise and randomness present in biometric data. In order to allow genuine users to regenerate a stable secret key from the helper data, error correction strategies are necessary. This introduces the problem of selecting an appropriate error correction code that offers sufficient error tolerance capability for genuine users while simultaneously preventing imposters from exploiting the error correction mechanism [7].

Cancellable biometrics is an important approach for generating secure and privacy-preserving biometric templates. This concept was originally introduced by Ratha et al. in their work [8]. It aims to transform the original biometric data in non-invertibly manner, creating a new representation suitable for authentication in transformed domain. By storing the transformed templates enhances the system's security, and in case of a compromise, new templates can be generated to prevent unauthorized access.

2 Literature Review

In recent years, significant advancements have been made in protecting irisCode stored in databases by employing a cancellable approach. The pioneering work by Chong et al. [11] introduced the irisCode-encoding scheme, which is based on the concept of random projection to project individual biometric features to a lower-dimensional subspace using a user-specific randomly generated orthogonal matrix (known as a token).Other cancellable schemes that utilized the random projection concept are also proposed by Zuo et al. [9] and Pillai et al. [10]. Both of their works require randomly generated matrices to project or distort (using a random permutation matrix) the original iris data to generate its protected instances. Ouda et al. [11] proposed to encode the irisCode to generate its protected instance, namely Bio-code, using a random key.

Starting in 2013, Rathgeb et al. [12] proposed an alignment-free cancellable biometrics based on adaptive Bloom Filter. This approach efficiently compared biometric templates like irisCode without alignment at pre-matching stages. The Bloom filter transformation involved partitioning irisCode into sub-matrices and converting them to Bloom filter vectors. It achieved non-invertibility by mapping biometric features to a Bloom filter using a many-to-one approach and an application-specific secret key for template renewal and irreversibility.The Bloom filter exhibited comparable accuracy to the original counterparts. However, the restoration of biometric templates was found to be successful with low complexity [13]. Additionally, using smaller key spaces for accuracy preservation posed unlinkability attack risks. Moreover Gomez et al. [14] enhanced the Bloom filter-based template protection proposed in [12] by introducing a Structure-Preserving Feature Re-Arrangement, significantly improving unlinkability and countering cross-matching attacks.

In 2017, Lai et al. [15] introduced a novel iris-cancellable biometrics scheme, Indexing-First-One (IFO) hashing to generate cancellable IFO hashed code. For IFO hashcode generation, the irisCode first undergoes random permutation, followed by a p-ordered Hadamard product. It follows that the positions of the first '1' in each row of the product code are recorded (Min-hashing), then modulo thresholding is applied for enhanced security, i.e., improve non-invertibility. A unique aspect of IFO hashing is that the normalized Hamming distance between enrollment ifo_e and query IFO codes ifo_q remains equivalent to the Jaccard distance between corresponding irisCodes, even post-IFO hashing, that is:

$$d_H(ifo_e, ifo_q) = d_{Jaccard}(I_q, I_e) + \varepsilon, \tag{1}$$

where, $d_H(,)$ is the normalized Hamming distance measure, $d_{Jaccard}(.,.)$ is the Jaccard distance measure, and ε is the error of approximation, converging to zero with increasing hashed code length. In IFO hashing, a pre-alignment step is necessary to ensure proper alignment for consistent and reliable hashing results.

Sadya et al. [16] proposed Locality Sampled Code (LSC) for cancellable irisCode generation. This approach utilizes the principles of Hamming hash-based Locality Sensitive Hashing (LSH) to extract random bit strings from irisCode. In order to achieve non-invertibility, LSC incorporates a modulo thresholding technique, similar to that used in IFO hashing. However, LSC necessitates a pre-processing step for irisCode to tackle alignment-related issues. The LSC process generates 33 shifted instances of the probe iris feature, which are subsequently transformed into LSC templates for comparative analysis.

Lee et al. [17] proposed a cancellable biometrics scheme called Random Augmented Histogram of Gradients (RHoG) for enhancing the security and privacy of iris templates. The RHoG method consists of two main processes. Firstly, the unaligned iris code is augmented using random augmentation seeds. This is followed by a gradient orientation grouping process to transform the resulting iris template into an alignment-robust cancellable template. As a result, the generated cancellable iris template exhibits alignment robustness, allowing direct comparison during the matching stages without the need for pre-alignment techniques.

3   Motivation and Contributions

Upon conducting an in-depth literature review, we discovered that existing solutions exhibit a complementary relationship through their heuristic designs. For instance, Bloom filters are invertible, but IFO medthod effectively address this issue, although it requires pre-alignment. This complementarity extends to combination of cancellable schemes and biometric cryptosystems. While cancellable schemes avoid error correction codes in template matching, they struggle with noise during stable key regeneration. This paper aims to explore the mutual complementarity between IFO and Bloom filter approaches, as well as between cancellable schemes and biometric cryptosystems. Our main contribution is an innovative irisCode template protection scheme that uniquely integrates IFO hashing and Bloom filters, providing high cancelability without alignment requirements. Additionally, we have introduced a bit-binding strategy to extend its applicability for biometric cryptosystems, eliminating the need for explicit error correction code construction. Experimental results show that our approach outperforms existing biometric template protection schemes, achieving the lowest Equal Error Rate (EER) on the CASIA-Irisv3-interval database, demonstrating its promising potential for secure iris recognition systems.

4   Overview Idea

We have adopted the alignment-free IFO methodology, integrated with the Bloom filter, to generate an IFO vector that boasts both alignment freedom and strong non-invertibility [18]. The principal contribution of our work is a novel template protection method, namely **Code-Block Encoding (CBE)** scheme, that fuses the biometric cryptosystem and the cancellable approach, thereby enhancing the robustness and security of the iris recognition system.

Bit Binding: Our method binds a single bit of information (0 or 1) to a pair of uniformly and randomly generated codewords (c_0, c_1). This process is conducted over a finite field $\mathbb{F}_q^n$, where n is the vector dimension and q is the field size. If the bit value is 0, a helper string h is formed by adding the enrollment IFO vector to c_0 (i.e., $h = ifo_e + c_0$). If the bit value is 1, c_1 is used for the same operation, resulting in $h = ifo_e + c_1$.

Bit Recovery: For the recovery of the information about b, given $\{c_0, c_1\}$, stored together with h as a whole helper data; one can compute the distance solution by subtracting a query IFO vector from the helper string and $\{c_0, c_1\}$ respectively, follows:

$$h - ifo_q - c_0 = d_H(ifo_e, ifo_q) + c_b - c_0, \text{and}$$
$$h - ifo_q - c_1 = d_H(ifo_e, ifo_q) + c_b - c_1,$$

which yields a resultant set of distance solutions

$$\mathcal{S} = \{d_H(ifo_e, ifo_q), d_H(ifo_e, ifo_q) + \delta\}$$
$$= \{d_{Jaccard}(I_q, I_e) + \varepsilon, d_{Jaccard}(I_q, I_e) + \varepsilon + \delta\}$$
$$\approx \{\underbrace{d_{Jaccard}(I_q, I_e)}_{\text{error-free term}}, \underbrace{d_{Jaccard}(I_q, I_e) + \delta}_{\text{error term}}\}$$

with $\delta = c_b - c_{(b+1) \mod (2)}$ denotes the error that leads to possibly larger Jaccard distance between the enroll irisCode and query irisCode due to the differences between the introduced codewords $\{c_0, c_1\}$. It's important to note that $\delta = 0$ only when the same codeword is used in both the binding b and recovery b processes. The second line above utilizes the inherent Jaccard distance preserving property of the IFO, following Eq. 1. The validity of the third line is based on the premise that the length of the IFO vector is sufficiently large leading to negligible ε.

Given the preceding discussion, it becomes apparent that for sufficiently large IFO vector lengths, we can derive an 'almost' error-free distance solution by simply selecting the minimum solution from the set $\mathcal{S}$. This corresponds to the Jaccard distance between the enrolled and query irisCodes. As a result, the bind bit value b, which should ideally correspond to the minimum distance solution, can be retrieved in the following manner:

$$b^* = \arg \min_{b \in \{0,1\}}(h - ifo_q - c_b). \tag{2}$$

Given that b^* corresponds to the solution with the minimum Jaccard distance $d_{Jaccard}(I_q, I_e)$, a tolerance threshold t can be imposed to ensure that the system releases b^* if and only if $d_{Jaccard}(I_q, I_e) \leq t$. This demonstrates the ability to retrieve bits based on the irisCode Jaccard distance, even after the application of IFO hashing.

5   Main Construction

The central construction of the code-blocks encoding process, which includes bit binding and retrieval, is visually represented in Fig. 1. This process consists of repeating the binding of bit information n times, resulting in sequences of helper strings $(h_1, \ldots, h_n)$ and a corresponding set of codewords $\{c_0, c_1\}_1, \ldots, \{c_0, c_1\}_n$. These helper strings and codewords sets are collectively stored as helper data in the database to assist in future bit retrieval processes. The retrieved bit information can then be employed for verification or authentication purposes.

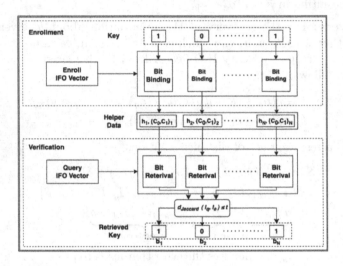

Fig. 1. Overview of the design for the proposed code-blocks encoding scheme.

5.1   Bit Binding

Initially, the enrollment irisCode with dimensions $I_e \in \{0,1\}^{20 \times 512}$ is processed using the Bloom Filter technique. The output from this step is then subjected to IFO transformation to generate an IFO vector $ifo_e \in \mathbb{F}_q^n$.

1. *Random Codewords Pair $\{c_0, c_1\}$ Generation*: Two irisCodes $r_0, r_1 \in \{0,1\}^{20 \times 520}$ are sampled uniformly at random. These are then processed through the Bloom filter and subsequently through the IFO hashing procedure to generate two random codewords $\{c_0, c_1\}$. The codewords are same size with the IFO vector.
2. *Random bit (b) generation*: A single bit of information $b \in \{0,1\}$ is sample uniformly at random.
3. *Helper Data generation*: Based on the value of b (either 0 or 1), perform an addition operation between the selected codeword (i.e., c_0 if $b = 1$, otherwise) and the IFO vector to generate the Helper-string $h = ifo_e + c_b$ to be stored together with $\{c_0, c_1\}$ in database.

5.2   Bit Retrieval

Given query irisCode with dimensions $I_e \in \{0,1\}^{20 \times 512}$ is processed using the Bloom Filter technique. The output from this step is then subjected to IFO transformation to generate an IFO vector $ifo_q \in \mathbb{F}_q^n$.

1. *Bit Recovery:* Perform subtraction in between the helper data h and query IFO vector ifo_q to yield an intermediate output of $ifo_q - h$. With the knowledge in the codewords pair $\{c_0, c_1\}$, return the recovered bit information as b^* based on the minimum value calculated by subtracting c_0 and c_1 from the intermediate output, which can be mathematically described as $b^* = \arg \min_{b \in \{0,1\}} (ifo_q - h - c_b)$. It follows that a tolerance threshold t can be imposed to ensure that the system releases b^* if and only if $d_{Jaccard}(I_q, I_e) \leq t$.

6   Experiments and Discussion

This section delivers an in-depth overview of our experimental setup, the database employed, and a thorough discussion and comparison of the results against state-of-the-art works.

Experiment Set-Up: For the iris-image preprocessing and irisCode extraction, we utilized tools from [19], specifically the Iris-Toolkit v3 from Wavelab USIT (University of Salzburg). Our proposed scheme was implemented in MATLAB (Version R2022b) on a personal computer equipped with a 500 GB HDD, an Intel Core i5 4th-Gen CPU operating at 4.80 Hz, and 16 GB DDR4 memory. To conduct the experiments, we employed the CASIA-IrisV3-Internal dataset, focusing on the left eye of subjects, each having 7 iris images. This resulted in a total of 868 irisCodes for evaluation.

Experiment Parameters: Several parameters need consideration in the original IFO hashing scheme, including the hashed code length (n), K-window (K), P-Hadamard multiplication (P), and the modulo threshold (τ). As our focus is on bit-binding and bit-retrieval performance, we've chosen not to emphasize the parameters (K, P, τ) related to IFO's cancelability. In line with the claims of [15], asserting that a smaller τ results in stronger non-invertibility of the IFO hashed code, we've set $K = n$, $P = 1$ and $\tau = 78$. Consequently, the parameters to be evaluated in our code-blocks encoding scheme are reduced to two: the IFO hashed code length n and the key length N. All the while, we have set $t = 0.8580$ for the tolerant threshold.

Experiment Protocol, Results, and Comparison: We executed both intra-class (genuine) and inter-class (imposter) matches, resulting in 4406 genuine and 19936 imposter comparisons over the retrieved bit string (key). It is important to note that the correct release of the retrieved bit is conditional on $d_{Jaccard}(I_q, I_e) \leq t$. Thus, our proposed scheme can operate under a fuzzy setting where the bit string does not necessarily need to be exactly equal.

We conducted two experiments: one requiring an exact match of the retrieved bit string, and another allowing for a certain Hamming distance. Our scheme achieved an EER of only 0.52% when a certain Hamming distance is allowed, outperforming existing state-of-the-art works (Table 1 and Table 2). When an exact match is required, our scheme showed promising performance with a low false acceptance rate (FAR) of less than 0.05%, while maintaining an acceptable false rejection rate of approximately 1.5% (Table 1). Figure 2 illustrates the intra-class and inter-class matching score distributions from our experiments using different $n = 100$ and $n = 20000$. As the hashed code length (n) increases, it can be clearly observed that the computed minimum distance solution (as per Eq. 2) for both inter-class and intra-class matching significantly overlaps with the actual Jaccard distance between the enrolled and queried irisCodes. This demonstrates the Jaccard distance-preserving property of our proposed code-based encoding scheme.

Table 1. FAR/FRR & EER's % under different parameter settings of key length (N) and IFO hashed code length (n) in CASIA-IrisV3-Internal.

Keylength N (column)	IFO Hashed Codelength n (row)							
	100		1000		10000		20000	
	FAR/FRR	EER	FAR/FRR	EER	FAR/FRR	EER	FAR/FRR	EER
8	13.7/0.5	1.79	0.9/0.7	0.8	0.5/1.3	0.6	0.3/1.5	0.6
16	13.6/0.8	1.48	0.9/0.4	0.62	0.06/1.2	0.57	0.03/1.4	0.54
32	9.2/0.9	1.50	1.4/0.4	0.69	0.07/1.1	0.55	0.03/1.3	0.55
64	2.1/2.3	1.32	1.8/0.4	0.55	0.09/1.1	0.62	0.04/1.1	0.53
128	1.9/0.5	1.06	2.8/0.3	0.56	0.1/1.0	0.54	0.03/1.2	0.52

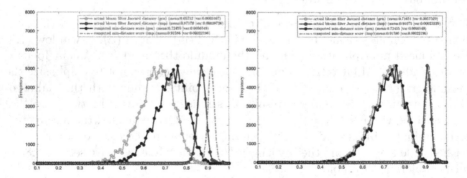

Fig. 2. The graph illustrates the inter-class (blue) and intra-class (red) score distributions and the computed minimum Jaccard distance during the bit retrieval in the proposed Code Block Encoding (CBE) scheme (black for intra-class and magenta for inter-class) for $n = 100$ (left) and $n = 20,000$ (right). (Color figure online)

Table 2. Comparison of EER's % between the proposed CBE and the state-of-the-art Iris template protection scheme for the CAISA-IrisV3-Interval dataset.

Author's	Year	Alignment Required	Iris Images	Protected EER (%)
Lai et al. [18]	2017	No	868 (Left)	0.69
Lai et al. [15]	2017	Yes	868 (Left)	0.54
Sadhya et al. [16]	2019	Yes	395 (Class)	0.105
Chai et al. [20]	2019	No	868 (Left)	0.62
Lee et al. [17]	2022	No	868 (Left)	0.62
Proposed CBE	2023	No	**868 (Left)**	**0.52**

6.1 Conclusions

This paper presents a Code-Block Encoding (CBE) scheme, an approach that synthesizes the benefits of biometric cryptosystems and cancellable template generation, traditionally used in irisCode template protection. The CBE method adeptly addresses the individual limitations of each strategy, providing the key binding ability of biometric cryptosystems without necessitating explicit error correction code construction, and ensuring accurate matching outcomes inherent to cancellable template generation. Experimental evidence showcases the CBE's ability to effectively handle exact matches and scenarios with allowable variations in retrieval bit information, suggesting its high potential for secure and high-performance Iris template protection.

Acknowledgment. This research study was funded by the National Natural Science Foundation of China (Nos. 62376003 & 62306003), Anhui Provincial Natural Science Foundation (Nos. 2308085MF200), and the UTAR research fund from Universiti Tunku Abdul Rahman (UTAR) (IPSR/RMC/UTARRF/2021-C2/2L01). Additionally, it received support from the Center for Cyber Security (CCS) at UTAR (Vote Account: 6552/0041).

References

1. Yan, J., Blackwell, A., Anderson, R., Grant, A.: Password memorability and security: empirical results. IEEE Secur. Priv. **2**(5), 25–31 (2004)
2. Daugman, J.: How iris recognition works. In: The Essential Guide to Image Processing, pp. 715–739. Elsevier (2009)
3. Rathgeb, C., Uhl, A.: A survey on biometric cryptosystems and cancelable biometrics. EURASIP J. Inf. Secur. **2011**(1), 1–25 (2011)
4. Juels, A., Wattenberg, M.: A fuzzy commitment scheme. In: Proceedings of the 6th ACM Conference on Computer and Communications Security, pp. 28–36 (1999)
5. Barman, S., Shum, H.P., Chattopadhyay, S., Samanta, D.: A secure authentication protocol for multi-server-based e-healthcare using a fuzzy commitment scheme. IEEE Access **7**, 12 557–12 574 (2019)
6. Juels, A., Sudan, M.: A fuzzy vault scheme. Des. Codes Crypt. **38**, 237–257 (2006)

7. Lai, Y., Dong, X., Jin, Z., Tistarelli, M., Yap, W.-S., Goi, B.-M.: Breaking free from entropy's shackles: cosine distance-sensitive error correction for reliable biometric cryptography. IEEE Trans. Inf. Forensics Secur. **18**, 3101–3115 (2023)
8. Ratha, N.K., Chikkerur, S., Connell, J.H., Bolle, R.M.: Generating cancelable fingerprint templates. IEEE Trans. Pattern Anal. Mach. Intell. **29**(4), 561–572 (2007)
9. Zuo, J., Ratha, N.K., Connell, J.H.: Cancelable iris biometric. In: 2008 19th International conference on pattern recognition, pp. 1–4. IEEE (2008)
10. Pillai, J.K., Patel, V.M., Chellappa, R., Ratha, N.K.: Secure and robust iris recognition using random projections and sparse representations. IEEE Trans. Pattern Anal. Mach. Intell. **33**(9), 1877–1893 (2011)
11. Ouda, O., Tsumura, N., Nakaguchi, T.: Tokenless cancelable biometrics scheme for protecting iris codes. In: 2010 20th International Conference on Pattern Recognition, pp. 882–885. IEEE (2010)
12. Rathgeb, C., Breitinger, F., Busch, C.: Alignment-free cancelable iris biometric templates based on adaptive bloom filters. In: 2013 International Conference on Biometrics (ICB), pp. 1–8. IEEE (2013)
13. Hermans, J., Mennink, B., Peeters, R.: When a bloom filter is a doom filter: security assessment of a novel iris biometric template protection system. In: 2014 International Conference of the Biometrics Special Interest Group (BIOSIG), pp. 1–6. IEEE (2014)
14. Gomez-Barrero, M., Rathgeb, C., Galbally, J., Busch, C., Fierrez, J.: Unlinkable and irreversible biometric template protection based on bloom filters. Inf. Sci. **370**, 18–32 (2016)
15. Lai, Y.-L., et al.: Cancellable iris template generation based on indexing-first-one hashing. Pattern Recogn. **64**, 105–117 (2017)
16. Sadhya, D., Raman, B.: Generation of cancelable iris templates via randomized bit sampling. IEEE Trans. Inf. Forensics Secur. **14**(11), 2972–2986 (2019)
17. Lee, M.J., Jin, Z., Liang, S.-N., Tistarelli, M.: Alignment-robust cancelable biometric scheme for iris verification. IEEE Trans. Inf. Forensics Secur. **17**, 3449–3464 (2022)
18. Lai, Y.-L., Goi, B.-M., Chai, T.-Y.: Alignment-free indexing-first-one hashing with bloom filter integration. In: 2017 IEEE International Conference on Intelligence and Security Informatics (ISI), pp. 78–82. IEEE (2017)
19. Rathgeb, C., Uhl, A., Wild, P., Hofbauer, H.: Design decisions for an iris recognition SDK. In: Bowyer, K.W., Burge, M.J. (eds.) Handbook of Iris Recognition. ACVPR, pp. 359–396. Springer, London (2016). https://doi.org/10.1007/978-1-4471-6784-6_16
20. Chai, T.-Y., Goi, B.-M., Tay, Y.-H., Jin, Z.: A new design for alignment-free chaffed cancelable iris key binding scheme. Symmetry **11**(2), 164 (2019)

BFNet: A Lightweight Barefootprint Recognition Network

Yi Yang[1], Yunqi Tang[1(✉)], Junjian Cui[2], and Xiaorui Zhao[2]

[1] School of Criminal Investigation, People's Public Security University of China,
Beijing 10038, China
20052263@ppsuc.edu.cn
[2] Dalian Everspry Sci&Tech Co., Ltd., Dalian 116085, China

Abstract. In recent years, barefootprint-based biometrics has emerged as a novel research area. Compared with other biometrics, barefootprints are more covert and secure. However, due to the absence of large-scale datasets and the limited training data, it is difficult to achieve high accuracy for barefootprint recognition. In this paper, a barefootprint dataset named BFD is first proposed containing 54118 images from 3000 individuals of different genders, ages and weights. A novel barefootprint recognition network named BFNet is secondly proposed, which is enhanced by adding SENet, adjusting the width and depth of the network, and using an improved triplet loss function. Experiments show that BFNet achieves an accuracy of 94.0% and 98.3% respectively in Top-1 and Top-10 for the barefootprint identification task. BFNet achieves 98.9% of Area Under Curve (AUC) for the barefootprint verification task, with the False Acceptance Rate (FAR) of 0.00106 and the Equal Error Rate (EER) of 0.054.

Keywords: Barefootprint Recognition · Attention Mechanism · Triplet Loss · Deep Learning

1 Introduction

Compared with other biometric traits such as fingerprints [1], faces [2], voiceprints [3], irises [4], signatures [5] and DNA [6], on which traditional biometric recognition is based, barefootprint is not only stable and unique, but also more covert and non-intrusive. With the increasing concern for personal privacy and security of biometric systems, barefootprint recognition has become a more secure, effective and reliable method in the field of biometric identification.

The barefootprint can be used as a biometric trait for biometrics because it possesses both uniqueness and stability. There are significant individual differences in human gait, foot bones and posture maintenance ability, and the variability in center of pressure (COP) between individuals increases with age [7]. However, consistent features such as size, shape and orientation can be reproduced over time [8], highlighting its homogeneity and stability [9]. Furthermore, given the rarity of walking barefootprint in public, barefootprint is a private and secure biometric feature.

W. Jia et al. (Eds.): CCBR 2023, LNCS 14463, pp. 301–311, 2023.
https://doi.org/10.1007/978-981-99-8565-4_29

Current barefootprint recognition methods are still limited by three urgent problems. First, most of the barefootprint datasets used in the current studies are self-built with a small size, which pose a challenge for training larger and deeper neural networks. Second, current methods require manual annotation of barefootprint images, which not only introduces subjectivity but also demands substantial manpower and resources. Third, the features embedded in barefootprints are mainly shape contour features, and the similarity between contours of different barefootprints is relatively high, which poses a greater challenge to the study of barefootprint recognition network [10], and there is no automatic barefootprint recognition network with high accuracy under the validation of large-scale datasets at present.

Compared with previous studies, a larger-scale barefootprint dataset was used to train a deep learning-based automatic barefootprint recognition network. Our network requires no manual labeling of barefootprint images and achieves higher accuracy on larger-scale datasets. The contributions of this article are as follows:

– The largest barefootprint dataset (BFD) to date, containing 54,118 images of bare-footprints from 3,000 individuals. Of these, 26,127 are of left feet and 27,991 are of right feet.
– The barefootprint recognition network (BFNet). The framework consists of a pre-processing module, a feature extraction module and a task module, and achieves an accuracy of up to 98.4% in the large-scale dataset without manual labeling at all.

2   Related Work

Barefootprints Recognition Methods Based on Collection Scenario. Depending on the volunteer's movement during collection, barefootprint identification can be divided into static and dynamic identification methods. Nakajima et al. identify individuals by the orientation and position between paired standing barefootprints [11]. Performance parameters such as error acceptance rate and accuracy were analysed by Rohit et al. through static barefootprints [12]. Dynamic barefootprint sequences were used for identification by Todd et al. [13].

Barefootprints Recognition Methods Based on Sample Type. Barefootprint samples include plantar photographs, ink stamped barefootprints, optical imaging barefootprints and foot pressure images. The first two mainly show the shape, contour, texture and detail features, while the latter two, in addition, provide a better representation of foot pressure features. Researchers have extracted barefootprint features from different types of samples [14] and performed barefootprint analysis [15] and identification [16].

Barefootprints Recognition Methods Based on Identification Approach. With advances in computer technology, barefootprint recognition methods have evolved from mathematical metrics to deep learning. In the early days, researchers manually extracted barefootprint features and calculated their Euclidean distances [17]. With the development of machine learning techniques, algorithms such as principal component analysis [18], Bayesian decision making [19] and support vector machines [20] were introduced for barefootprint recognition. Recently, deep learning has made breakthroughs in bare-footprint recognition, such as feature extraction using neural networks such as Alexnet

[21], VGG [22], Resnet [23] and Inception [24]. In addition, the combination of convolutional neural networks and deep hashing has proven effective in the field of podiatry image retrieval [25].

Compared with other methods, optical imaging barefootprint allows for better extraction of features such as texture, shape and pressure. Dynamic barefootprints can reflect features such as walking habits and posture. Therefore, a deep learning-based barefooprint recognition framework was proposed to automate the extraction of barefootprint features and greatly improve recognition efficiency and reliability.

3 Method

In our work, a framework for barefootprint recognition was proposed, as shown in Fig. 1, including a self-built barefootprint dataset (BFD), a data pre-processing module, a feature extraction module, and two task modules, including the barefootprint recognition task and the barefootprint verification task. In the feature extraction module, a barefootprint network (BFNet) was proposed for feature extraction, as shown in Fig. 2.

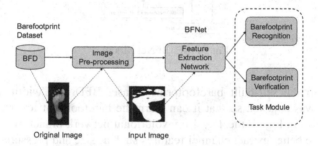

Fig. 1. The Framework of Our Method

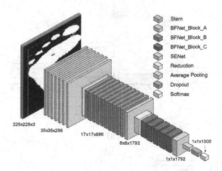

Fig. 2. The Structure of BFNet

3.1 Feature Extraction Network

Since the skip connect of the Inception_Resnet network structure can avoid the problem of gradient vanishing and output the features as compact 128-dimensional feature vectors

for feature recognition and further analysis, this network structure can extract the barefootprint features well in the field of barefootprint recognition. Therefore, a model named
BFNet was proposed for barefootprint recognition by enhancing Inception_Resnet_V1
network in three ways.

The SENet attention mechanism was added between the three BFNet_Block and
Reduction modules, as shown in Fig. 3, to allow the model to better focus on the barefootprint features. SENet, through Squeeze and Excitation operations, can adaptively
learn the importance of each channel and adjust the weight of important channel features according to the needs of barefootprint recognition tasks, thereby enhancing the
performance of the model [26].

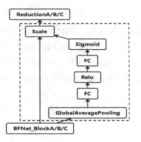

Fig. 3. SE_BFNet Module

To adapt to the self-built barefootprint dataset BFD, the width and depth of
BFNet_Block was adjusted so that it can learn the barefootprint features at different
scales. As shown in Fig. 4, the 1×1 convolutional network branch was added to the
BFNet_Block to better extract channel features such as size and pressure. The conventional convolutional network was replaced with a depth-separable convolutional network

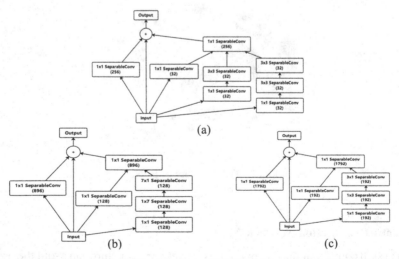

Fig. 4. BFNet_Block. (a) BFNet_Block_A; (b) BFNet_Block_B; (c) BFNet_Block_C.

in BFNet_Block [27]. By decomposing the convolution operation into Depthwise Convolution and Pointwise Convolution, it allows the model to make more flexible trade-offs between channel features and spatial features, reducing the number of parameters and computational effort, making the BFNet model smaller, more flexible and easier to train, and thus better adapted to the barefootprint dataset and the barefootprint recognition task.

3.2 Loss Function

In the field of deep learning, Triplet Loss is a commonly used loss function. Therefore, in this paper, an optimised version of Triplet Loss is employed to measure the similarity between barefoot samples. In the field of barefootprint recognition, Anchor and Positive are barefootprint images from the same individual, whereas Anchor and Negative are barefootprint images from different individuals. The minimum distance between the Positive and Negative is controlled by introducing a threshold α, and the purpose of the loss function is to make the loss as small as possible [28], where the loss is defined in Eq. (1).

The optimised triplet loss function replaces the squared Euclidean distance with the non-squared Euclidean distance [29], as defined in Eq. (2). When the barefootprint samples are close together, the non-square Euclidean distance has a larger value, which improves the learning efficiency of the model. When the barefootprint samples are far away, the gradient of the non-square Euclidean distance is smaller, effectively avoiding the problem of gradient explosion. In addition, this improvement also makes the threshold α directly for the physical distance of the Euclidean space, making the loss function more stable, efficient and readable. As shown in Eq. (3), the T is the combination of all possible triples in the dataset, and the x_i^a, x_i^p, x_i^n are Anchor, Positive and Negative, respectively.

$$Loss = \sum_i^N \left[\|f(x_i^\alpha) - f(x_i^p)\|_2^2 - \|f(x_i^a) - f(x_i^n)\|_2^2 + \alpha \right] \tag{1}$$

$$Loss = \sum_i^N \left[\|f(x_i^\alpha) - f(x_i^p)\|_2 - \|f(x_i^a) - f(x_i^n)\|_2 + \alpha \right] \tag{2}$$

$$\forall \left(f(x_i^\alpha), f(x_i^p), f(x_i^n) \right) \in T \tag{3}$$

4 Experiments and Evaluation

4.1 Image Acquisition and Image Pre-processing

For biometric recognition, having a large-scale barefootprint dataset becomes a key factor for the model to achieve high accuracy. There is no publicly available large-scale barefootprint dataset. Based on this, Dalian Everspry Barefootprint Sequence Collection and Analysis Comparison System V2.0 was used to collect 54,118 barefootprint images from 3,000 individuals to build the largest Barefootprint Dataset (BFD) at present. Of these, 26,127 are of left feet and 27,991 are of right feet.

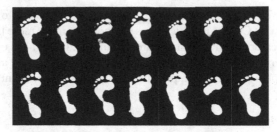

Fig. 5. Barefootprint samples from BFD.

The volunteer population was diverse in terms of gender, age, height and weight. They include both males and females, covering ages from 17 to 69, heights from 1.51 to 1.95 m, and weights from 40 to 109 kg. The barefootprint samples are shown in Fig. 5.

Pre-processing operations were performed on barefootprint images, where Fig. 6 shows the barefootprint optical image pre-processing process, including normalization operations, binarization, detection and annotation, rotation and alignment, cropping and scaling to better train the model.

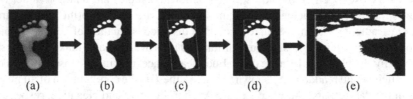

| (a) | (b) | (c) | (d) | (e) |

Fig. 6. Pre-processing Operations. (a) Original Image; (b) Binarization; (c) Detection and Annotation; (d) Rotation and Alignment; (e) Cropping and Scaling.

4.2 Experimental Settings

Data Preparation. The dataset was divided into a training set and a test set according to 8:2, with the training set using the ten-fold cross-validation method. For the barefootprint validation task, matching and mismatching image pairs were generated as the test set, generating a total of 115,020 image pairs.

Environment Setup. Our experiments were done on a GPU A100, Windows 10 environment, using the tensorflow 1.12 framework with python 3.6.

Parameters Setup. During training, each epoch comprised 20 batches. Each batch processed barefootprints from 45 individuals, with at least 2 images per person. The input size of the barefootprint images is 160 × 160 and the feature vector is 128 dimensions. According to the experimental results, the loss function works best when the distance threshold α is set to 0.2. The initial value of the learning rate was 0.1 and was optimised using Adaptive Gradient (AdaGrad).

4.3 Results and Analysis

Intergration Strategy. In order to verify where the attention mechanism is best placed in the BFNet, intergration strategy experiments were conducted. The experimental results show that the third approach obtained the highest top1 accuracy of 94% for the barefootprint recognition task on the dataset DBF, as shown in Table 1, which is 1.5% and 1.3% better than the other two approaches respectively. Therefore, method d was chosen to add an attention mechanism into BFNet (Fig. 7).

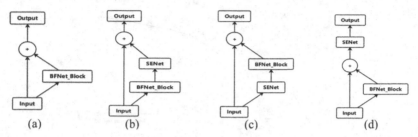

Fig. 7. Intergration Strategy. (a) BFNet_Block; (b) Standard SE_Block; (c) Pre_SE_Block; (d) Post_SE_Block.

Table 1. The Performance of Different Intergration Strategy.

Model	Top-1 Accuracy	Top-10 Accuracy
BFNet_Block	88.7%	97.5%
Standard SE_Block	92.5% (+3.8%)	98.1% (+0.6%)
Pre_SE_Block	92.7% (+4.0%)	98.2% (+0.7%)
Post_SE_Block	**94.0% (+5.3%)**	**98.3% (+0.8%)**

Barefootprint Recognition. Two tasks were used to show the performance of our approach in the field of barefootprint recognition. Task one is barefootprint recognition, where given a barefootprint image, the model predicts in a dataset which person this barefootprint belongs to. Our model BFNet performs a retrieval in the test set based on the feature vector and uses the classifier's prediction score as the basis for retrieval ranking. Experimental results show that our method achieves an accuracy of 94.0% in top1 and can reach a maximum accuracy of 98.4%. The Top1 to Top 20 accuracy of the model is shown in Table 2.

To test the effectiveness of our model, we also compared the model before and after the improvements. It can be seen from the Fig. 8 that the improved model is able to obtain higher recognition results in the Top-k accuracy for the barefootprint recogniton task.

Barefootprint Verification. Task two is barefootprint verification, where two barefootprint images were determined whether they belong to the same person. As this is a

Table 2. The Accuracy of Top-k ($1 \leq k \leq 20$).

Top-k	Top-1	Top-2	Top-3	Top-4	Top-5
Accuracy	94.0%	96.9%	97.2%	97.8%	97.9%
Top-k	Top-6	Top-7	Top-8	Top-10	Top-20
Accuracy	98.1%	98.2%	98.2%	98.3%	98.4%

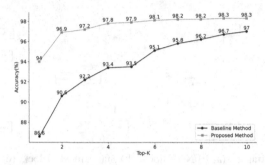

Fig. 8. The Comparison of Baseline Method and Proposed Method.

binary classification problem, a threshold was introduced for the determination. When the Euclidean distance between the feature vectors of two barefootprint images is greater than the threshold, these images were considered to belong to different individuals, and vice versa. The thresholds were randomly set in steps of 0.01 between 0 and 4 and the best threshold was determined based on the accuracy. The Receiver Operating Characteristic (ROC) Curve was plotted based on the True Positive Rate (TPR) and False Positive Rate (FPR) at different thresholds, as shown in Fig. 9. The experiments show that the model accuracy reaches 94.7% with the best threshold value and the Area Under Curve (AUC) is 0.989.

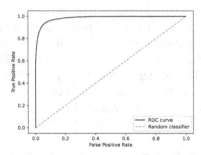

Fig. 9. ROC Curve.

To verify the security of the BFNet, the False Acceptance Rate (FAR) was introduced. This is the probability that the model misidentifies the barefootprints of different people as the same person, which is a more serious error in biometric systems. Therefore, more attention was focused on this evaluation metric. Experiments show that our model has a FAR of 0.00106, which is highly secure. The Equal Error Rate (EER) of our model is only 0.054, which means that the model has a low probability of false recognition. The results of all evaluation metrics are shown in Table 3.

Table 3. The Performance of Our Method

Model	AUC	ACC	FAR	EER
BFNet	0.989	0.947	0.00106	0.054

Comparison Experiments. To verify the effectiveness of the proposed method, we compare it with other models for barefootprint recognition task. The Table 4 shows that both Top-1 and Top-10 accuracy of BFNet are higher than other models, reflecting that the recognition performance of the proposed method is significantly better than other models.

Table 4. The comparison of BFNet and other models

Model	Top-1	Top-10
Inception_Resnet [30]	86.6%	97.0%
Inception [31]	86.1%	96.7%
Transformer [32]	79.9%	88.5%
Resnet50 [33]	92.6%	97.9%
VGG-16 [34]	85.7%	96.5%
BFNet	**94.0%**	**98.3%**

5   Conclusion and Future Work

In this paper, a large-scale barefootprint dataset (BFD) consisting of 54118 images from 3000 individuals is proposed, which is the largest publicly available dataset that can be used to evaluate barefootprint recognition algorithms. In addition, a barefootprint recognition network named BFNet is secondly proposed. By integrating attention mechanisms, depthwise separable convolutional networks, and an improved triplet loss function, as well as optimizing the network structure, the model can extract distinctive barefootprint features, including spatial features and channel features. Experimental results show that our model is able to achieve good results in both barefootprint recognition and barefootprint verification tasks.

In future work, we plan to further investigate how to handle the substantial differences in barefootprints from the same individual due to deformations, as well as how to perform feature extraction and barefootprint recognition for incomplete barefootprints.

Acknowledgments. This work is supported by Double First-Class Innovation Research Project for People's Public Security University of China (No. 2023SYL06).

References

1. Kumar, A., Zhou, Y.: Human identification using finger images. IEEE Trans. Image Process. **21**, 2228–2244 (2012)
2. Turk, M.A., Pentland, A.P.: Face recognition using eigenfaces. In: Proceedings of the 1991 IEEE Computer Society Conference on Computer Vision and Pattern Recognition, pp. 586–591 (1991)
3. Kubanek, M.: Method of speech recognition and speaker identification using audio-visual of polish speech and hidden Markov models. In: Saeed, K., Pejaś, J., Mosdorf, R. (eds.) Biometrics, Computer Security Systems and Artificial Intelligence Applications, pp. 45–55. Springer, Boston (2006). https://doi.org/10.1007/978-0-387-36503-9_5
4. Boles, W.W., Boashash, B.: A human identification technique using images of the iris and wavelet transform. IEEE Trans. Signal Process. **46**, 1185–1188 (1998)
5. Wei, P., Li, H., Hu, P.: Inverse discriminative networks for handwritten signature verification. In: 2019 IEEE/CVF Conference on Computer Vision and Pattern Recognition (CVPR), pp. 5757–5765 (2019)
6. Van Oorschot, R.A.H., Ballantyne, K.N., Mitchell, R.J.: Forensic trace DNA: a review. Invest. Genet. **1**, 14 (2010)
7. Ye, H., Kobashi, S., Hata, Y., Taniguchi, K., Asari, K.: Biometric system by foot pressure change based on neural network. In: 2009 39th International Symposium on Multiple-Valued Logic, pp. 18–23 (2009)
8. Han, D., Yunqi, T., Wei, G.: Research on the stability of plantar pressure under normal walking condition. In: Tan, T., Li, X., Chen, X., Zhou, J., Yang, J., Cheng, H. (eds.) CCPR 2016. CCIS, vol. 662, pp. 234–242. Springer, Singapore (2016). https://doi.org/10.1007/978-981-10-3002-4_20
9. Tong, L., Li, L., Ping, X.: Shape analysis for planar barefoot impression. In: Huang, D.-S., Li, K., Irwin, G.W. (eds.) ICIC 2006. Lecture Notes in Control and Information Sciences, vol. 345, pp. 1075–1080. Springer, Heidelberg (2006). https://doi.org/10.1007/978-3-540-37258-5_139
10. Nguyen, D.-P., Phan, C.-B., Koo, S.: Predicting body movements for person identification under different walking conditions. Forensic Sci. Int. **290**, 303–309 (2018)
11. Kazuki, N., Yoshiki, M., Tanaka, K., Toshiyo, T.: A new biometrics using footprint. IEEJ Trans. Ind. Appl. **121**, 770–776 (2001)
12. Khokher, R., Singh, R.C.: Footprint-based personal recognition using dactyloscopy technique. In: Manchanda, P., Lozi, R., Siddiqi, A. (eds.) Industrial Mathematics and Complex Systems. Industrial and Applied Mathematics, pp. 207–219. Springer, Singapore (2017). https://doi.org/10.1007/978-981-10-3758-0_14
13. Pataky, T.C., Mu, T., Bosch, K., Rosenbaum, D., Goulermas, J.Y.: Gait recognition: highly unique dynamic plantar pressure patterns among 104 individuals. J. R. Soc. Interface **9**, 790–800 (2012)
14. Wang, X., Wang, H., Cheng, Q., Nankabirwa, N.L., Zhang, T.: Single 2D pressure footprint based person identification. In: 2017 IEEE International Joint Conference on Biometrics (IJCB), pp. 413–419 (2017)
15. Nagwanshi, K.K., Dubey, S.: Statistical feature analysis of human footprint for personal identification using BigML and IBM Watson analytics. Arab. J. Sci. Eng. **43**, 2703–2712 (2017)

16. Zhengwen, F., Nian, W., Jinjian, J., Wenxia, B.: Clustering algorithm for static gait recognition based on low-dimensional plantar pressure features. Appl. Res. Comput. **32**, 2176–2178+2183 (2015)
17. Nakajima, K., Mizukami, Y., Tanaka, K., Tamura, T.: Footprint-based personal recognition. IEEE Trans. Biomed. Eng. **47**, 1534–1537 (2000)
18. Khokher, R., Singh, R.C., Kumar, R.: Footprint recognition with principal component analysis and independent component analysis. Macromol. Symp. **347**, 16–26 (2015)
19. Hang, L., Li, T., Xijian, P.: Feature analysis & identity recognition of planar barefoot impression. J. Comput.-Aided Design Comput. Graph. 659–664 (2008)
20. Kushwaha, R., Nain, N.: PUG-FB: Person-verification using geometric and Haralick features of footprint biometric. Multimed. Tools Appl. **79**, 2671–2701 (2019)
21. Abuqadumah, M.M.A., Ali, M.A.M., Al-Nima, R.R.O.: Personal authentication application using deep learning neural network. In: 2020 16th IEEE International Colloquium on Signal Processing & Its Applications (CSPA), pp. 186–190 (2020)
22. Keatsamarn, T., Pintavirooj, C.: Footprint identification using deep learning. In: 2018 11th Biomedical Engineering International Conference (BMEiCON), pp. 1–4 (2018)
23. Jinjie, Q.: Research on recognition algorithm of pressure barefootprint based on convolutional neural network. Anhui University (2021)
24. Ming, Z., Chang, J., Xiaoyong, Y., Kehua, Y., Jun, T., Nian, W.: A footprint image retrieval algorithm based on deep metric learning. forensic science and technology, pp. 1–9 (2022)
25. Wenxia, B., Wei, H., Dong, L., Nian, W., Fuxiang, H.: Deep supervised binary hash codes for footprint image retrieval. In: 2020 International Conference on Intelligent Computing and Human-Computer Interaction (ICHCI), pp. 138–141 (2020)
26. Hu, J., Shen, L., Sun, G.: Squeeze-and-excitation networks. In: 2018 IEEE/CVF Conference on Computer Vision and Pattern Recognition, pp. 7132–7141 (2018)
27. Chollet, F.: Xception: deep learning with depthwise separable convolutions. In: 2017 IEEE Conference on Computer Vision and Pattern Recognition (CVPR), pp. 1800–1807 (2017)
28. Schroff, F., Kalenichenko, D., Philbin, J.: FaceNet: a unified embedding for face recognition and clustering. In: 2015 IEEE Conference on Computer Vision and Pattern Recognition (CVPR), pp. 815–823 (2015)
29. Hermans, A., Beyer, L., Leibe, B.: In defense of the triplet loss for person re-identification (2017)
30. Szegedy, C., Ioffe, S., Vanhoucke, V., Alemi, A.: Inception-v4, inception-ResNet and the impact of residual connections on learning. In: Proceedings of the AAAI Conference on Artificial Intelligence, pp. 4278–4284. AAAI (2017)
31. Szegedy, C., et al.: Going deeper with convolutions. In: 2015 IEEE Conference on Computer Vision and Pattern Recognition (CVPR), pp. 1–9 (2015)
32. Vaswani, A., et al.: Attention is all you need. In: Advances in Neural Information Processing Systems (NIPS 2017), vol. 30 (2017)
33. He, K., Zhang, X., Ren, S., Sun, J.: Deep residual learning for image recognition. In: 2016 IEEE Conference on Computer Vision and Pattern Recognition (CVPR), pp. 770–778 (2016)
34. Liu, S., Deng, W.: Very deep convolutional neural network based image classification using small training sample size. In: 2015 3rd IAPR Asian Conference on Pattern Recognition (ACPR), pp. 730–734. IEEE, Kuala Lumpur (2015). https://doi.org/10.1109/ACPR.2015.748 6599

Gait Recognition by Jointing Transformer and CNN

Mingyu Cai, Ming Wang, and Shunli Zhang[✉]

Beijing Jiaotong University, Beijing, China
{23126412,slzhang}@bjtu.edu.cn

Abstract. Gait recognition is a biometric technology based on the human walking state. Unlike other biometric technologies, gait recognition can be used for remote recognition and the human walking pattern cannot be imitated. Gait recognition has wide applications in the field of criminal investigation, security and other fields. Most of the current mainstream algorithms use Convolutional Neural Network (CNN) to extract gait features. However, CNN only captures the local image features in most cases which may not inherently capture global context or long-range dependencies. In order to solve the above problems and to extract more comprehensive and precise feature representations, we propose a novel Gait recognition algorithm jointing Transformer and CNN by introducing the attention mechanism, called GaitTC. The framework consists of three modules, including the Transformer module, CNN module and feature aggregation module. In this paper, we conduct the experiments on CASIA-B dataset. The results of the experiments show that the proposed gait recognition method achieves relatively good performance.

Keywords: Gait recognition · Deep Learning · Transformer · CNN

1 Introduction

At present, with the continuous development of the computer vision, researchers have proposed many gait recognition methods. Most of the existing methods are bulit based on the CNN and can be roughly divided into two categories. One category is the template-based gait recognition framework. It mainly uses some statistical functions, including Max, Mean, etc., to calculate the gait statistics whithin a gait sequence cycle. These methods first extract the temporal features of the gait sequence, and then extract the spatial features through the CNN. The CNN has primarily been designed for local feature extraction, which may not effectively capture global information. As a result, there can be limitations or potential inaccuracies in recognition results when relying solely on CNN-based approaches. The other category mainly extracts the temporal and spatial features of the gait sequence with fixed input length. These methods may greatly limit the length of the input gait sequence and reduce the robustness of the model. Therefore, this paper proposes a novel gait recognition model by jointing Transformer and CNN, GaitTC, which has the following advantages:

W. Jia et al. (Eds.): CCBR 2023, LNCS 14463, pp. 312–321, 2023.
https://doi.org/10.1007/978-981-99-8565-4_30

(1) The Transformer can reduce the number of operations on sequence by using parallel computing, which greatly improves the efficiency.

(2) The Transformer restores positional dependence among image blocks by encoding the positions of segmented image blocks. This allows the model to better capture the spatial features.

In view of the existing problems of the existing gait recognition methods and the advantages of Transformer itself, this paper develops a new Transformer-CNN-based gait recognition framework to better extract the spatio-temporal features of gait sequences and to achieve higher performance. The main work and contributions of this paper are as follows:

(1) This paper proposes a new gait recognition framework based on Transformer and CNN, which can effectively extract the global feature of gait sequence by introducing Transformer. Compared with traditional Recurrent Neural Network(RNN) and CNN based methods, the proposed method with Transformer can improve the efficiency and better extract the global features.

(2) After the Transformer module, CNN is used to further extract the gait features of each frame. Then, the frame-level features are aggregated into sequence-level features to improve the representation ability of the gait features and the accuracy of the recognition.

(3) The proposed method is experimented on CASIA-B dataset, and compared with other gait recognition methods such as ViDP [1], CMCC [2], CNN-LB [3], GaitSet [4] in different wearing conditions and perspectives. The experimental results show that the the proposed method achieves good performance in most conditions.

2 Related Work

In this section, we provide a brief overview of the two important types of gait recognition methods: appearance-based methods and model-based methods.

2.1 Model-Based Methods

The model-based gait recognition methods mainly build the human model for gait recognition. These methods usually require a structure model to capture the static characteristics of human, and a motion model to capture the dynamic characteristics [5]. The structure model describes the structure of a person's body, including the stride, height, trunk and other body parts. The motion model is used to simulate the motion trend and trajectory of different body parts of a person during walking. The existing model-based gait recognition methods can be divided into two categories. One is to capture the evolution of these parameters over time by fitting a model. In these body parameter estimation methods, the angle of the body skeleton joints during walking is mainly obtained, such as the angular movement of knees and legs at different stages; the other is to estimate the parameters of the body (length, width, step frequency, etc.) directly from the original video. Gait recognition based on three-dimensional human body modeling belongs to this type. By analyzing video, image and other data, the motion parameters of the human body are obtained, and a complete gait sequence is constructed. Then the sequence is converted into the corresponding coordinate information to realize the extraction of human motion features, so as to reconstruct the 3D model of the human body. Zhao et al. [6] constructed a human skeleton model with 10 joints and 24 degrees of freedom by using multiple cameras to capture the movement process of the human body. In order to obtain better performance, several features extracted from different directions are combined into a complete set of features for recognition, which can improve the stability of this method. At the same time, a gait recognition method based on geometric description [7] has also been proposed. This method mainly learns the deep features of the gait sequence by locating the skeletal joint coordinates.

Although the above methods can provide more complex gait feature information and can effectively perform gait recognition in complex environments, in actual scenes such as shopping malls and banks, due to the inability to deploy a large number of cameras, it is not possible to shoot gait sequences from multiple angles of the camera at the same time; at the same time, realizing the 3D human body model requires a lot of computing resources and a lot of computer computing power, which is not conducive to the training and development of the model. How to meet the low-cost sequence extraction without consuming a lot of computer resources is one of the main problems.

2.2 Appearance-Based Methods

With the development and maturity of deep learning algorithms, many gait recognition methods based on deep learning have emerged. At present, most of the networks used in gait recognition are CNN and RNN.

Since CNNs have excellent image classification capabilities, gait recognition based on CNNs has also occured. Shiraga et al. [8] proposed the GEINet network structure. This network consists of three modules. The first two modules include a convolutional layer, a pooling layer, and a normalization layer, respectively. The last module is composed of two fully connected layers. At the same time, the input of the network is a gait energy map. The gait feature reflects the accumulation of gait energy during a person's walking process. Compared with other methods, GEINet focuses on subtle inter-subject differences in the same action sequence. Liao et al. [9] proposed a posture-based spatio-temporal network through the GEI, which has better effect on gait recognition in complex states. In addition, Huang et al. [10] proposed to extract the local features of human gait sequence according to the parts of the body. The human body composition is defined as six local paths, i.e. the head, left arm, right arm, trunk, left leg and right leg, and features are extracted from each path. At the same time, a 3D local CNN network is introduced into the backbone. The backbone contains three network blocks, and each block is composed of two CNN layers. Finally, the ReLU function is used as the activation function to output the obtained features. Wolf et al. [11] proposed a gait recognition method based on 3D CNN. This method captures the spatiotemporal information of the gait in multiple sequence frames. This method can well summarize the gait characteristics in a variety of perspective changes.

3   Method

In this section, we will introduce the implementation of the proposed method in detail. Firstly, we overview the proposed Transformer and CNN based gait recognition framework. Secondly, we explain the Transformer model in detail. Finally, we describe the CNN Module and Feature Aggregation Module.

3.1   GaitTC

We propose a Transformer-CNN-based gait recognition method built upon the traditional Transformer model. The overview structure of the proposed method is shown in Fig. 1 which is designed to generate more robust gait feature representations. To address the issue of limited effectiveness of the traditional Transformer model on small-scale datasets, we incorporate the CNN module after the Transformer model. Firstly, the Transformer module is used to extract the global features, and the corresponding attention weights of each image block are obtained. Then, CNN is used for local feature extraction. At the same time, CNN also makes up for the defect that the Transformer model has poor effect on the feature extraction in small-scale datasets.

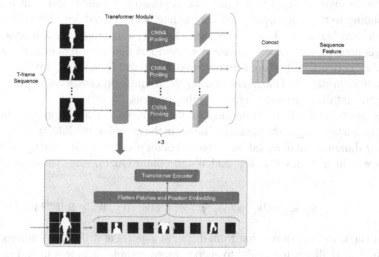

Fig. 1. The proposed gait recognition framework with Transformer and CNN

3.2   Network Structure

This section will mainly introduce the model of GaitTC. The model is mainly divided into three modules, namely Transformer module, CNN module and feature aggregation module. The Transformer module is mainly used to extract the most useful global information from the input gait sequence. Then, the output of the Transformer module is put into the CNN module to extract more comprehensive gait features. Finally, we use the feature aggregation module to fuse the features.

3.2.1 Transformer Module

This module uses the Transformer to operate the input gait silhouette. Firstly, the gait silhouette map is divided into image blocks and linearly projected, and then input into the Transformer module for processing. In the linear projection process, each input image block is mapped to a d-dimensional vector, and each vector needs to be multiplied by a linear matrix E. At this time, the image block is a vector with a dimension of d after smoothing. Next, in order to enable the model to encode the position of the image block vector, before entering the model, we embed the position information of each image block into the vector of the corresponding image block, and then embedded vector is connected with a learnable class marker. The internal value of the vector can be learned and adjusted during the model training process to obtain a feature representation with attention weight.

In the Transformer, the encoder module has two important sub-modules, which are Multi-Head Self-attention (MSA) and Multi-Layer Perceptron (MLP) modules. The encoder will receive the image block of the gait sequence as input, and the input image block will first pass through the normalization layer. In the normalization layer, the input values of all neurons are normalized in the feature dimension, which greatly reduces the training time and improves the training performance. Subsequently, the output of the normalization layer is input to the multi-head attention module, and then the output corresponding to the multi-head attention module is connected with the original input through the residual network. The output after the normalization layer will be sent to the multi-layer perceptron layer to simulate more complex nonlinear function relationships. The residual network will be used for two modules in the Transformer encoder to retain the gradient information of the module during the training process, avoiding the problem that the gradient disappears during the training process.

In the multi-head self-attention module, the multiple self-attention operations will be performed according to the number of heads in the attention module. In each attention head, the d-dimensional flattened image block vector p will be multiplied by the multiple attention weight matrices W_q, W_k, and W_v to obtain Query, Key, Value, as shown in Eq. (1):

$$[q, k, v] = [p \cdot W_q, p \cdot W_k, p \cdot W_v], (W_q, W_k, W_v \in \mathrm{R}^{d \times d_H}) \tag{1}$$

MSA captures the information from different aspects at different positions of each head, which also allows the model to encode more complex features in gait sequences in parallel. At the same time, due to the use of parallel computing mechanism, the time cost of multi-head attention calculation is similar to that of single-head attention mechanism, which improves the performance of the model to a certain extent and reduces the consumption of computing resources.

The multi-layer perceptron module contains two fully connected layers and a GeLU function. Finally, the Transformer module utilizes a residual structure to connect the output of the multi-layer perceptron with the original vector output through the multi-head attention mechanism, output the attention value between each image block and other image blocks, and then pass it to the next module for further feature extraction.

3.2.2 CNN Module and Feature Aggregation Module

The CNN module extracts features by extracting feature blocks with attention weights output of the Transformer. The module mainly includes three convolution pooling layers, and the kernel size, and step size of the convolution kernels in each layer are equal. In order to extract more detailed information, the convolution with the kennel size of 3 * 3 * 3 is used to extract the features of each frame. The feature contains the spatial information of each frame and the time information of the gait sequence, so that the feature representation is more complete. The higher-level features extracted by the convolution operation will be put into the feature aggregation module.

In the feature aggregation module, the model aggregates the features extracted from each subject under a fixed number of frames, that is, the features of each frame in the gait sequence are aggregated into a sequence set. The module will first calculate the maximum value, average value and median value of each element of the feature of each frame, respectively, and splice the obtained feature. In order to better represent the set-level features of each sequence, the spliced feature will be finally performed. Global average pooling and global maximum pooling are used to aggregate frame-level features, and the sum of the two is used as the feature representation of the final gait sequence.

4   Experimental Results

4.1   CASIA-B Dataset

The experiments in this paper were conducted on the current popular gait dataset CASIA-B, which contains 124 subjects. In order to make the experimental results more rigorous and reliable, we conduct the experiment in different sample scale conditions. According to the different proportions of sample division between the training set and the test set, the experiment is divided into three parts, which include small sample training (ST), medium sample training (MT) and large sample training (LT). The training set of small-scale samples contains 24 subjects, the medium-scale sample training set contains 62 subjects and the large-scale sample training set contains 74 subjects. The rest subjects will taken as the test set. Through different division of LT, MT and ST, the performance of the model under different conditions can be tested, which can better reflect the robustness of the model.

4.2   Results and Analysis

In this section, the experimental results of this model are compared with some excellent gait recognition algorithms, including CNN-LB, GaitSet, MGAN [12], AE [13], ViDP, CMCC and so on.

Small-scale sample data is closer to practical applications for gait recognition tasks, because for recognition tasks, the number of samples to be identified in practical applications(i.e., test data) is much larger than the number of samples during training (i.e., training data), so the accuracy of small-scale samples can better reflect the performance of the proposed method. According to the experimental results conducted in small-scale sample data (as shown in Table 1), it can be seen that the accuracy varies in different cross-views. Under normal conditions, the experients maintain better accuracy under cross-views such as 36°, 126°, and 144°, which is 13% higher than the 0° under the same condition. In the complex state, it is 10% higher than the 0°. Besides, according to the results, it can be observed that the accuracy of the proposed method is higher than the existing excellent methods in some cases. The results show that the proposed method achieves appealing performance at difficult angles such as 0°, 90° and 180°. However, the accuracy is slightly lower than GaitSet under the 36° view angle.

Table 1. The accuracy of the proposed GaitTC on the CASIA-B under the ST condition.

Gallery NM#1–4			0°–180°										
Probe			0	18	36	54	72	90	108	126	144	162	180	Mean
ST	NM	ViDP	–	–	–	59.1	–	50.2	–	57.5	–	–	–	–
		CMCC	46.3	–	–	52.4	–	48.3	–	56.9	–	–	–	–
		CNN-LB	54.8	–	–	77.8	–	64.9	–	76.1	–	–	–	–
		GaitSet	64.6	83.3	90.4	86.5	80.2	75.5	80.3	86.0	87.1	81.4	59.6	79.5
		GaitTC	**75.8**	**85.9**	**88.9**	**87.4**	**81.9**	**77.9**	**83.4**	**88.5**	**88.4**	**83.6**	**68.9**	**82.8**
	BG	GaitSet	55.8	70.5	**76.9**	**75.5**	**69.7**	63.4	68.0	75.8	**76.2**	70.7	52.5	68.6
		GaitTC	**64.6**	**73.8**	76.7	74.3	67.4	**64.1**	**69.0**	**77.0**	75.4	**70.8**	**58.3**	**70.1**
	CL	GaitSet	29.4	43.1	49.5	48.7	42.3	40.3	44.9	47.4	43.0	35.7	25.6	40.9
		GaitTC	**40.8**	**47.9**	**50.0**	45.8	**46.9**	**44.5**	**47.8**	**49.7**	**44.8**	**37.1**	**29.9**	**44.1**

Under the medium sample condition, the experimental results are shown in Table 2. The accuracy is improved compared with the small samples in some cases, but the accuracy maintains small margin compared to the GaitSet under normal conditon(NM) and walking with bag condition(BG). In the case of wearing coat or jacket (CL), the accuracy improvement is significant. Compared with the GaitSet, the accuracy of the proposed is higher by 5% to 10% in the case of wearing a jacket.

We can observe that as the number of training samples increases, the accuracy improves. However, in the practical application the number of training samples is often less than the number of the test, which requires the model to maintain good recognition ability in small-scale training. By comparing the results with other methods, the average accuracy reached 82.8% under NM conditions, 70.1% under BG conditions, and 44.1% under CL conditions, which are better than the GaitSet. Therefore, the proposed method has better performance and stronger robustness.

Secondly, in the same sample division, the model can work well under the NM condition. In the three divisions, the average accuracy of the NM is higher than BG and CL condition. At the same time, it can be observed from the results that the people in BG condition is easier to be identified than the CL condition. The accuracy in NM condition is 10% to 20% higher than that in complex condition (BG and CL). Furthermore, the gait recognition framework proposed in this paper achieves better gait recognition

Table 2. The accuracy of the proposed method GaitTC on the CASIA-B under the MT condition

Gallery NM#1–4			0°–180°										
Probe			0	18	36	54	72	90	108	126	144	162	180	Mean
MT	NM	AE	49.3	61.5	64.4	63.6	63.7	58.1	59.9	66.5	64.8	56.9	44.0	59.3
		MGAN	54.9	65.9	72.1	74.8	71.1	65.7	70.0	75.6	76.2	68.6	53.8	68.1
		GaitSet	86.8	95.2	98.0	94.5	91.5	89.1	91.1	**95.0**	**97.4**	93.7	80.2	92.0
		GaitTC	**87.2**	**95.4**	**97.5**	94.7	91.1	**88.4**	**91.9**	94.9	96.5	**93.9**	**83.9**	**92.3**
	BG	AE	29.8	37.7	39.2	40.5	43.8	37.5	43.0	42.7	36.3	30.6	28.5	37.2
		MGAN	48.5	58.5	59.7	58.0	53.7	49.8	54.0	51.3	59.5	55.9	43.1	54.7
		GaitSet	79.9	**89.8**	**91.2**	**86.7**	**81.6**	76.7	81.0	**88.2**	90.3	88.5	73.0	84.3
		GaitTC	**80.3**	88.3	90.8	86.3	81.3	77.3	**82.0**	87.4	**91.6**	**89.3**	**76.0**	**84.6**
	CL	AE	18.7	21.0	25.0	25.1	25.0	26.3	28.7	30.0	23.6	23.4	19.0	24.2
		MGAN	23.1	34.5	36.3	33.3	32.9	32.7	34.2	37.6	33.7	26.7	21.0	31.5
		GaitSet	52.0	66.0	72.8	69.3	63.1	61.2	63.5	66.5	67.5	60.0	45.9	62.5
		GaitTC	**64.9**	**77.1**	**76.1**	**74.4**	**71.4**	**68.0**	**69.9**	**73.1**	**71.4**	**68.4**	**55.1**	**70.0**

performance than other methods, and the accuracy in different partition is higher than other models. There are two main reasons: First, the Transformer module preferentially extracts the attention value of each image block, and retain the gradient of the original data through the residual network, which will be more convenient for the subsequent CNN pooling module to extract gait features. On the other hand, the Transformer module with global receptive field not only extracts the global feature representations in advance, but also further mines the local feature representations after introducing the CNN pooling module, thus improving the performance of the model (Table 3).

Table 3. The accuracy of the proposed method GaitTC on the CASIA-B under LT condition.

Gallery NM#1–4			0°–180°											
Probe			0	18	36	54	72	90	108	126	144	162	180	Mean
LT	NM	CNN-3D	87.1	93.2	97.0	94.6	90.2	88.3	91.1	93.8	96.5	96.0	85.7	92.1
		GaitSet	90.8	97.9	**99.4**	96.9	93.6	91.7	95.0	**97.8**	**98.9**	96.8	85.8	95.0
		GaitTC	**93.9**	**98.0**	98.9	**97.9**	**95.0**	**93.4**	**95.1**	97.2	97.6	**98.0**	**92.0**	**96.1**
	BG	CNN-LB	64.2	80.6	82.7	76.9	64.8	63.1	68.0	76.9	82.2	75.4	61.3	72.4
		GaitSet	83.8	91.2	91.8	88.8	83.3	81.0	84.1	90.0	92.2	94.4	79.0	87.2
		GaitTC	**89.4**	**94.0**	**97.9**	**95.7**	**94.7**	**91.2**	**92.3**	**95.5**	**95.4**	**93.7**	**88.5**	**93.5**
	CL	CNN-LB	37.7	57.2	66.6	61.1	55.2	54.6	55.2	59.1	58.9	48.8	39.4	54.0
		GaitSet	61.4	75.4	80.7	77.3	72.1	70.1	71.5	73.5	73.5	68.4	50.0	70.4
		GaitTC	**79.8**	**90.4**	**88.8**	**85.8**	**85.2**	**81.6**	**81.9**	**87.7**	**87.4**	**85.2**	**70.2**	**84.0**

5 Conclusion

In this work, we propose a novel Transformer-based gait recognition framework, GaitTC. It includes the Transformer model, CNN pooling module and feature aggregation module. The proposed model not only capture global context to extract the global feature representations, but also can obtain the local feature representation using the CNN pooling module. The multi-head self-attention mechanism in this model has good robustness to image noise and incompleteness. At the same time, the residual structure and the layer normalization structure further improve the performance of the algorithm. In the comparative experiments with other models, the accuracy of the model in this paper is higher than other models in most perspectives. The experimental results show that the model also shows excellent performance under three different sample scales.

References

1. Hu, M., Wang, Y., Zhang, Z., Little, J., et al.: View-invariant discriminative projection for multi-view gait-based human identification, pp. 2034–2045 (2013)
2. Kusakunniran, W., Wu, Q., Zhang, J., et al.: Recognizing gaits across views through correlated motion co-clustering. IEEE Trans. Image Process. **23**(2), 696–709 (2014)
3. Wu, Z., Huang, Y., Wang, L., et al.: A comprehensive study on cross-view gait based human identification with deep CNNs. IEEE Trans. Pattern Anal. Mach. Intell. **39**, 209–226 (2016)
4. Chao, H., Wang, K., He, Y., et al.: GaitSet: cross-view gait recognition through utilizing gait as a deep set. Cornell University – arXiv:2102.03247v1 (2021)
5. Rida, I., Almaadeed, N., Almaadeed, S.: Robust gait recognition: a comprehensive survey. IET Biomet. **8**, 14–28 (2018)
6. Zhao, G., Liu, G., Li, H., et al.: 3D gait recognition using multiple cameras, pp. 529–534 (2006)
7. Zheng, X., Li, X., Xu, K., et al.: Gait identification under surveillance environment based on human skeleton. arXiv preprint arXiv:2111.11720 (2021)

8. Shiraga, K., Makihara, Y., Muramatsu, D., et al.: GEINet: view-invariant gait recognition using a convolutional neural network. In: 2016 International Conference on Biometrics (ICB), Halmstad, Sweden, pp. 1–8 (2016)

9. Liao, R., Cao, C., Garcia, E.B., Yu, S., Huang, Y.: Pose-based temporal-spatial network (PTSN) for gait recognition with carrying and clothing variations. In: Zhou, J., et al. (eds.) CCBR 2017. LNCS, vol. 10568, pp. 474–483. Springer, Cham (2017). https://doi.org/10.1007/978-3-319-69923-3_51

10. Huang, Z., Xue, D., Shen, X., et al.: 3D local convolutional neural networks for gait recognition. In: 2021 IEEE/CVF International Conference on Computer Vision (ICCV), Montreal, QC, Canada (2022)

11. Wolf, T., Babaee, M., Rigoll, G.: Multi-view gait recognition using 3D convolutional neural networks. In: 2016 IEEE International Conference on Image Processing (ICIP), Phoenix, AZ, USA, pp. 14920–14929 (2016)

12. He, Y., Zhang, J., Shan, H., et al.: Multi-task GANs for view-specific feature learning in gait recognition. IEEE Trans. Inf. Forensics Secur. 102–113 (2018)

13. Yu S, Wang, Q., Shen, L., et al.: View invariant gait recognition using only one uniform model. In: 2016 23rd International Conference on Pattern Recognition (ICPR), Cancun, vol. 239, pp. 81–93 (2017)

Trustyworth, Privacy and Persondal Data Security

Random Undersampling and Local-Global Matching Mechanism for Cancellable Biometrics Against Authentication Attack

Ying Zhou[1], Ming Jie Lee[2], Hui Zhang[3], Xingbo Dong[1], and Zhe Jin[1(✉)]

[1] Anhui Provincial Key Laboratory of Secure Artificial Intelligence,
Anhui Provincial International Joint Research Center for Advanced Technology
in Medical Imaging, School of Artificial Intelligence, Anhui University,
Hefei 230093, China
wa22301072@stu.ahu.edu.cn, jinzhe@ahu.edu.cn
[2] Department of Internet Engineering and Computer Science, Lee Kong Chian
Faculty of Engineering and Science, Universiti Tunku Abdul Rahman,
43000 Kajang, Malaysia
[3] Anhui Provincial International Joint Research Center for Advanced Technology
in Medical Imaging, School of Computer Science and Technology,
Anhui University, Hefei 230093, China

Abstract. The trade-off between security and verification performance is inevitable towards biometric template protection. The system developer has to sacrifice some genuine acceptance rate and tune the matching threshold to tolerating more false acceptance. To alleviate this problem, we introduce a new method of feature transformation and matching, which consists of a random undersampling and local-global matching mechanism for the hashing-based cancellable biometrics. This method manages to enlarge the gap between the mean of genuine/ impostor score distributions. As such, the decision environment is improved and the biometric system could provide more resistance to authentication attacks. Comprehensive experiments are conducted on the fingerprint FVC2002 and FVC2004 datasets, and the results demonstrate that the proposed method improves the decision environment in terms of decidability and verification performance.

Keywords: Authentication Attack · Biometric Template Protection · Cancellable Biometrics · Decision Environment

1 Introduction

Cancellable biometrics (CB) [1,2] is an approach that utilizes a feature transformation-based technique by employing an auxiliary data-guided transformation function to convert the original biometric feature into an irreversible template, also known as a cancellable template. Let $f(\cdot)$ represent the cancellable transformation function, x and x' denote biometric features belonging to the same individual, and r represent the auxiliary data. In a cancellable biometric scheme, the cancellable template $f(x,r) \to c$ is generated, which preserves the relative similarity between x and x', even in the presence of minor differences. This ensures that $f(x,r) \sim f(x',r)$, allowing the authentication process to be conducted in the transformed domain without disclosing the original biometric information. Cancellable biometrics has gained widespread acceptance within the community due to its simplicity and satisfactory verification rates [3–5].

Numerous cancellable biometric schemes have been proposed, including Index-of-Max (IoM) hashing [6], which provides privacy protection for biometric features. However, IoM-based cancellable biometric systems still rely on decision schemes based on matching thresholds, which introduce security threats and fail to ensure the privacy of biometric features. Specifically, in a matching threshold-based decision environment, attackers can repeatedly guess biometric templates until they exceed the matching threshold and gain unauthorized access to the system [7]. From a statistical perspective, as the overlap region between the distributions of genuine and impostor matching scores increases, the performance of the system decreases [8–10].

In view of the above discussion, a straightforward method to improve the security of the system is to increase the matching threshold τ [9]. However, this leads to an increment in the false rejection rate (FRR) of the system, which refers to a case of trade-off between security and performance [11]. This problem is further exacerbated in classical cancellable biometrics due to the performance degradation issue [12,13].

In this paper, we deduce the performance degradation issue as the weak decision environment problem of biometric template protection. The concept of a weak decision environment is inspired by Daugman's work [14], where the decision environment refers to the performance indicator that is based on the separation between the genuine/impostor score distributions. In our context, the weak decision environment refers to the case where the means of genuine/impostor score distributions are close to each other, limiting the selection of a high matching threshold.

To improve the decision environment of the existing cancellable biometric schemes, we propose an enhanced matching mechanism that aims to maximize the intra/inter-class variances. In short, the proposed matching mechanism is a partial matching-based score quantization scheme that produces highly confident matching scores, where the mean of the genuine matching score distribution approaches 1, while the mean of the impostor matching score distribution approaches 0. This allows for a higher matching threshold while reducing the sacrifice of the verification performance of the system.

The contributions of this paper are highlighted as follows:

- We propose a random undersampling and local-global matching mechanism to enhance the verification performance and decidability (d') of existing cancellable biometric schemes. This mechanism increases the separation between the means of genuine and impostor score distributions, enabling the selection of a higher matching threshold and reducing the Equal Error Rate (EER).

– We conduct comprehensive experiments on benchmark datasets, including FVC2002 [15] and FVC2004 [16], to validate the improvement in verification performance for IoM hashing. The experimental results demonstrate that the proposed mechanism effectively enhances IoM hashing by achieving lower EER and higher d' compared to the unenhanced counterpart.

2   Related Work

Type-4 attacks in biometric systems exploit information from the system, such as matching scores, to estimate a biometric preimage. These attacks pose a serious threat, resembling feature reconstruction attacks when the stored biometric sample is not adequately protected. However, there is limited research on enhancing the tolerance of existing cancellable biometric schemes against this type of attack. To understand other attacks in biometric systems, refer to [17].

One straightforward approach to estimating a guessed biometric template is a brute-force attack, as formalized by Ratha et al. [2] for minutia point-based fingerprint systems. The attack complexity is determined by the probability of matching each guessed minutia to one in the enrolled fingerprint template. However, the exhaustive search required by this attack makes it inefficient for large template sizes.

Uludag and Jain [18] proposed a hill climbing-based attack model for unprotected minutiae-based fingerprint systems. This attack involves initializing guessed minutiae templates, iteratively injecting them into the system, selecting the best matching template based on intercepted scores, and performing operations like perturbation, insertion, replacement, and deletion on the guessed template. This attack reduces the number of guessed minutiae points using grid formulation and orientation quantization, improving efficiency compared to the brute-force approach.

Marta et al. [19,20] employed the Nelder-Mead algorithm to exploit the privacy aspect of online signature and face verification systems. They aimed to maximize the similarity score between the enrolled template and the guessed instance, using the Downhill Simplex algorithm inversely. This iterative attack process involved establishing multiple randomly guessed instances, computing centroids, identifying vertices with the highest and lowest matching scores, and updating the guessed templates with the Nelder-Mead algorithm. Successful attacks implied the reconstruction of the original biometric feature, highlighting the importance of biometric template protection (BTP).

Pashalidis [21] introduced the simulated annealing attack to demonstrate the possibility of type-4 attacks in BTP-enabled systems. This iterative modification process aims to improve the guessed biometric template until a desirable authentication outcome is achieved. By replacing a vicinity in the initially guessed fingerprint template with a randomly generated one, the attack gradually refines the template. Occasionally, the attack accepts replacements with lower matching scores to reduce the local optimal problem.

Galbally et al. [22] used genetic algorithms to reconstruct iris images without prior knowledge of the binary irisCode stored in the system. Rozsa et al.

[8] employed genetic algorithms to test the security and privacy aspects of a PMCC-protected fingerprint system. The attacks aimed to compromise security by guessing inputs for the PMCC scheme and achieve a sufficient matching score, while privacy referred to guessing the original fingerprint template. The privacy aspect was protected since the guessed template was not identical to the original.

Lai et al. [23] demonstrated the vulnerability of a face-based distance-preserving transformation scheme to type-4 attacks. They estimated a protected template highly similar to the pre-stored protected template using a known biometric sample. The attack involved obtaining a sample input and establishing a noise distribution based on it. Multiple noise samples were generated by perturbing the sample, and the attack stopped when the similarity score surpassed the matching threshold. This attack was particularly effective when the original face template was transformed into a smaller sub-space.

In summary, type-4 attacks exploit information from biometric systems to estimate a biometric preimage. Brute-force attacks, hill climbing-based attacks, and iterative algorithms like simulated annealing and genetic algorithms have been proposed to perform such attacks. Protecting the privacy and security of biometric templates through techniques like biometric template protection is crucial in mitigating the impact of these attacks.

3   Proposed Method

3.1   Overview

The proposed method enhances a biometric system's decision environment by separating the mean of genuine and impostor score distributions. It involves a two-phase matching mechanism: transformation and matching. In the transformation phase, the input biometric template is randomized and converted into multiple local cancellable templates. In the matching phase, the query template set is compared to the pre-stored template set, producing local similarity scores. These scores are quantized based on a local threshold, resulting in a final matching score calculated by averaging the quantized scores. This approach effectively separates the mean of genuine and impostor score distributions, with higher similarity yielding higher matching scores.

3.2   Transformation Phase (enrollment)

During the transformation (or enrollment) phase, the proposed scheme aims to convert the input biometric template into multiple instances of cancellable templates (see Fig. 1 and Fig. 2). Let $x \in \mathbb{R}^a$ represent the original biometric feature, where a is the feature dimension. Additionally, let $f(\cdot)$ denote the cancellable transformation function, $R \in \mathbb{R}^{q \times e}$ denote the auxiliary data, and $p = \{p_i \mid p_i \in [1, a]^k\}$ denote the permutation seed, where k controls the under-sampling size. The proposed scheme follows the following steps to generate a set of local cancellable templates $c = \{c_i\}$ (Algorithm 1):

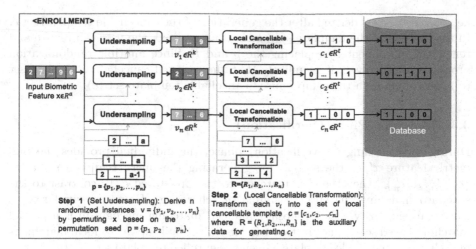

Fig. 1. Illustration of the proposed enhanced matching mechanism to transform the input biometric feature $x \in \mathbb{R}^a$ to the local cancellable template set $c = \{c_1, c_2, \ldots, c_n\}$.

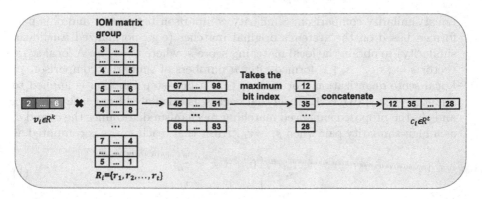

Fig. 2. Step 2 of the registration stage is shown in detail, using IOM as an example of the conversion method.

1. Random undersampling: Random undersampling is applied to x to obtain n permuted biometric features v_i. Using the random undersampling function $\text{perm}(\cdot)$, we compute $v_i = \text{perm}(x, p_i)$ for $i = 1, \ldots, n$. Here, each p_i is randomly chosen from $[1, a]^k$. The resulting v_i are independent of each other due to the random undersampling process.

2. Local cancellable template generation: Each v_i is transformed into a local cancellable template c_i by applying the cancellable transformation function with the auxiliary data R_i. Thus, we compute $c_i = f(v_i, R_i)$ for $i = 1, \ldots, n$. To enhance the randomness of the local cancellable templates, different auxiliary data R_i are employed for each c_i, forming a set of auxiliary data $R = \{R_i\}$.

At the end of enrollment, the cancellable template set $c = c_1, \ldots, c_n$ are stored in storage for authentication purposes. It is noted that the intermediate product, i.e., $v = v_1, ..., v_n$ is deleted after the generation of the cancellable template set c. In the event that the template storage is compromised, the user can revoke and renew the enrollment by replacing the p and R. Since multiple randomization processes are involved, it is unlikely that the renewed cancellable template set (c') can collide with the compromised cancellable template set (c).

3.3   Matching Phase (Verification)

During the matching (or verification) phase, the individual provides the biometric feature x' to the system for generating the query template set $c' = \{c_1', c_2', ..., c_n'\}$, then the c' is matched to the pre-stored c. In contrast to the standard matching that uses a simple matcher (e.g., Hamming similarity or Euclidean similarity), the proposal enhanced matching mechanism is a partial matching-based score quantization scheme that is built upon the local matchings of each local cancellable template. Given the enrolled template set $c = \{c_1, ..., c_n\}$ and the query template set $c' = \{c_1', c_2', ..., c_n'\}$, the procedures (algorithm 2) to obtain the global similarity score s_G are:

1) Local similarity comparison: Similarity comparison between c_i and c_i' is performed based on the system's original matcher (e.g., normalized Euclidean similarity) to obtain the local matching score s_i where $i = 1...n$. A local score vector $s = \{s_1, ..., s_n\}$ is formed after n numbers of similarity comparison.
2) Local score quantization: For each $s_i \in s$, a unit-step function is applied to quantize each s_i to 0 or 1. Given that each s_i is calculated from each pair of c_i and c_i' , the proposed enhanced matching mechanism determines the c_i and c_i' as a high-similarity pair when $s_i \geq \tau_L$. After that, each $s_i \in s$ is computed as

$$s_i = \begin{cases} 0, & \text{if } s_i < \tau_L \\ 1, & \text{if } s_i \geq \tau_L \end{cases} \tag{1}$$

where τ_L is the parameter to control the quantization process.
3) Global score calculation: Compute the global similarity score $s_G = \frac{1}{n} \sum_{i=1}^{n} s_i$ where each $s_i \in s$.
   The s_G is passed to the decision module to determine the identity of the individual based on the system matching threshold τ_G, where the individual is recognized as genuine user when $s_G \geq \tau_G$. If $s_G < \tau_G$, the individual is recognized as impostor. On the whole, the value of the s_G is amplified by the local matchings. Given the similar input x and x', the proposed enhanced matching mechanism produces the $c = \{c_1, ..., c_n\}$ and $c' = \{c_1', ..., c_n'\}$. Since the c_i and c' are highly similar, the enhanced matching mechanism could produce an s_G that is close to 1.

Algorithm 1: Enhanced matching mechanism - Transformation	**Algorithm 2:** Enhanced matching mechanism - Matching
Input(From User): Biometric feature x, Cancellable transformation $f(.)$, Permutation seeds $p = \{p_1, \ldots, p_n\}$, Transformation auxiliary data $R = \{R_1, \ldots, R_n\}$	**Input (From User):** Query template set $c' = \{c'_1, \ldots, c'_n\}$ **Input (From System):** Enrolled template set $c = \{c_1, \ldots, c_n\}$, Local quantization threshold τ_L

Algorithm 1

Parameters: number of local n
Output: A set of cancellable templates $c = \{c_1, c_2, \ldots, c_n\}$
for $i \leftarrow 1$ to n do
  // **Step 1: Set random undersampling**
  Random undersampling x based on p_i to produce v_i
  // **Step 2: Local cancellable transformation**
  Compute $c_i = f(v_i, R_i)$
return $c = \{c_1, \ldots, c_n\}$

Algorithm 2

Output: Global similarity score s_G
// **Step 1 and 2: Local similarity comparison + score quantization**
Initialize score vector $s = [0]_n$
for $i \leftarrow 1$ to n do
  $s_i = similarity(c_i, c'_i)$
  if $s_i \geq \tau_L$ then
    $s_i = 1$
  else
    $s_i = 0$
// **Step 3: Global score calculation**
Compute $s_G = \frac{1}{n} \sum_{i=1}^{n} s_i$
return s_G

4 Experiments and Discussions

This section presents the experiment results and discussions on the proposed enhanced matching mechanism. The experiments are conducted on a machine with Solid-State Drive (NVMe)@1024 GB, Intel Core i7-12700K CPU@3.61 GHz and Memory DDR4@64 GB. Realization of the schemes are written using MATLAB R2022b.

4.1   Dataset and Feature Extraction

This subsection shows the employed datasets and feature extraction methods in the experiments. For the fingerprint modality, six benchmarking datasets, i.e., $FVC2002(DB1, DB2, DB3)$ [15] and $FVC2004(DB1, DB2, DB3)$ [16] are employed. Each fingerprint subset consists of 100 subjects and 8 fingerprint images per subject. Fingerprint vector extraction technique [24] is adopted to extract the fingerprint vector $x \in \mathbb{R}^{256}$ from the fingerprint image. Given a fingerprint image, the fingerprint vector extraction processes are: (i) Extract the minutiae point set from the image and transform it to Minutia Cylinder Code (MCC) descriptor [25] and (ii) KPCA-based learning to convert the MCC descriptor to the fixed-length fingerprint vector $x \in \mathbb{R}^{256}$. Since the adopted technique is a learning-based method, the first 3 fingerprint images from each subject are employed for learning phase, while the remaining 5 fingerprint images are used to generate the fingerprint vector. A total of 500 (100 × 5) fingerprint vectors $x \in \mathbb{R}^{256}$ are extracted.

4.2   Matching Protocol and Evaluation Metric

We evaluated the verification performance using the FVC full matching protocol [26]. In our experiments, we generated these score distributions as follows:

For genuine matching attempts, we crossmatched all cancellable templates from the same subject, resulting in $n(C_m^2)$ genuine matching scores. For impostor matching attempts, we crossmatched cancellable templates generated from the first biometric feature of different subjects, resulting in C_n^2 impostor matching scores in each experiment. Each experiment produced 1000 genuine and 4950 impostor matching scores.

Each experiment was conducted five times with different sets of auxiliary information. This was done to obtain more precise readings of the EER and d' [14]. d' is an important metric to quantify the decision-making capability of the system using the formula:

$$d' = \frac{|\mu_{\text{gen}} - \mu_{\text{imp}}|}{\sqrt{0.5(\sigma_{\text{gen}}^2 + \sigma_{\text{imp}}^2)}} \tag{2}$$

A higher value of d' indicates a greater separation between the score distributions, indicating a higher decision-making power for the biometric system.

The experiments were conducted under the worst-case assumption where the auxiliary information (e.g., transformation key R for cancellable transformation and permutation seed P for the proposed enhanced matching mechanism) was accessible to the adversary (stolen-token scenario). The same auxiliary information was shared among the subjects in each experiment. In our experiments, we tested the proposed method based on the existing fingerprint-based cancellable biometric scheme, Index-of-Max (IoM) Hashing [6].

In the experiment, we have these parameters: downsampling times n, i.e., the number of p; downsampling size k, i.e., dimension of p; length of the iom matrix group l_{iom}; the number of matrices in the iom matrix group s; and local threshold τ_L. Where, we set k to 100, l_{iom} to 16, and the s to 100, and discuss the size of n and τ_L in the next section.

4.3 Parameter Estimation

Effect of Parameter τ_L: In the matching phase, a local matching is performed between pre-stored cancellable templates and query templates. This produces a local similarity score vector, denoted as s, where each element s_i ranges from 0 to 1. To enhance the matching mechanism, the scores in s are quantized to either 0 or 1 using a parameter called τ_L. However, setting τ_L inappropriately can lead to unfavorable scenarios.

When τ_L is set to a high value (Scenario-1), it becomes difficult for the genuine comparison scores (s_i) to meet the requirement of $s_i \geq \tau_L$. Consequently, a majority of the scores in s are quantized to 0, resulting in a very low final matching score (s_G) for genuine comparisons. This leads to a high FRR and low d' in the system.

When τ_L is set to a low value (Scenario-2), the impostor comparison scores (s_i) easily exceed τ_L and are quantized to 1. As a result, the calculated s_G value becomes high. This causes the impostor score distribution to overlap with the genuine score distribution, leading to a high false acceptance rate (FAR) and low d'.

To evaluate the effect of τ_L, experiments were conducted with different values of τ_L (with an interval of $\pm$ 0.1) while keeping the number of comparisons (n) fixed at 100 (see Table 1). The experiments focused on examining the impact of τ_L on FAR, FRR, and d'.

The experimental results, presented in tabulated form, confirmed the expected outcomes. When τ_L was set to a low value, the FAR was high and d' was low, as the impostor scores dominated and overlapped with genuine scores. Increasing τ_L significantly reduced FAR while slightly increasing FRR. However,

Table 1. Effect of different τ_L in IoM Hashing-based fingerprint system (FVC2002 [27] and FVC2004 [16]). The result is the average of five experiments.

Subset	τ_L	FAR	FRR	d'	Subset	τ_L	FAR	FRR	d'
	0.61	52.36	0.30	1.13		0.61	54.31	0.88	1.07
FVC2002 DB1	0.71	0.22	0.18	7.68	FVC2004 DB1	0.71	1.37	1.32	3.89
	0.81	0	23.24	1.06		0.81	0	44.96	0.84
	0.61	52.42	0.46	1.12		0.61	54.20	2.80	1.04
FVC2002 DB2	0.71	0.31	0.48	6.31	FVC2004 DB2	0.71	5.40	4.90	2.96
	0.81	0	18.94	1.24		0.81	0	52.26	0.71
	0.61	53.86	2.10	1.04		0.61	55.53	2.74	1.00
FVC2002 DB3	0.71	3.96	3.66	3.25	FVC2004 DB3	0.71	4.21	4.38	3.19
	0.81	0	51.88	0.74		0.81	0.02	38.52	0.93

the slight increase in FRR was deemed acceptable compared to the substantial decrease in FAR. For example, in the tested IoM-based fingerprint system in FVC2002 DB1, the performance changed from FAR = 52.36%, FRR = 0.30%, d'=1.13 to FAR = 0.22%, FRR = 0.18%, d'=7.68 when τ_L increased from 0.61 to 0.71. Further increments in τ_L led to continued improvement in d', but when τ_L was set too high, FRR began to increase due to genuine scores not surpassing τ_L, causing the final matching scores to resemble impostor scores.

The results demonstrated that an inappropriate setting of τ_L could lead to Scenario-1 and Scenario-2. However, it was observed that $\tau_L = 0.71$ yielded the best improvement in EER and d' for the tested schemes.

Effect of Parameter n: The final matching score is calculated by averaging the quantized local scores. In the proposed matching mechanism, the parameter n is employed to control the number of cancellable templates generated and the quantity of local similarity scores produced during the matching phase.

Several experiments are conducted by setting the n from 1 until 100 while the parameter τ_L is fixed to 0.71 (see Table 2). It is noted there is only 1 local similarity score when $n = 1$; and hence, the recognition performance of the system is easily affected by the outlier in the genuine and impostor matchings, which is not favorable. The experimental results for the targeted systems under different n are tabulated in the tables below. In addition, Fig. 3 visualizes the genuine and impostor score distributions for the IOM hashing-based finger system under the cases of (a) The cancellable biometric scheme is operated in its original construction, (b) The cancellable biometric scheme is enhanced by the proposed enhanced matching mechanism with parameter $n = 30$ and (c) The cancellable biometric scheme is enhanced by the proposed enhanced matching mechanism with parameter $n = 100$.

From Fig. 3, it is observed that the mean of genuine/impostor score distributions are close to each other when the IOM hashing is not enhanced. After applying the proposed enhanced matching mechanism, the mean of genuine/impostor score distributions is highly separated. In this sense, the proposed enhanced matching mechanism achieves the effect of improving d'.

From the Table 2, it is observed that the EERs are starting at the highest point when $n = 1$. This is as expected where the final matching score s_G is directly calculated by quantizing one local matching score s_i where $i = 1$. In this case, the outlier(s) in the genuine and impostor comparisons could easily affect the verification performance of the system. It is observed that the increment of n leads to the higher separation between the genuine/impostor score distributions (higher d') and better verification performance (lower EER) in the systems. This implies the parameter n is taking effect in enhancing the decision environment of the system in terms of EER and d'. The performance of the system has improved significantly when n increased from 1 to 30. After that, the improvement of the decision environment is at a slower pace when $n > 30$ and the trend of EER and d' slows down when $n > 100$. Considering the storage pressure, we decide to choose n = 100.

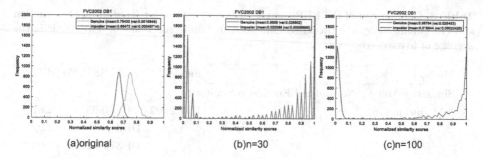

(a)original   (b)n=30   (c)n=100

Fig. 3. The genuine and impostor score distributions for the finger system are compared between the original and enhanced systems with n = 30 and n = 100, using threshold = 0.71.

Table 2. Effect of different n in IoM Hashing-based fingerprint system (FVC2002 and FVC2004 dataset). The result is the average of five experiments.

n	Equal Error Rate (EER)(%)	d'	n	Equal Error Rate (EER)(%)	d'	n	Equal Error Rate (EER)(%)	d'
	FVC2002 DB1			FVC2002 DB2			FVC2002 DB3	
1	6.93	2.87	1	6.96	2.92	1	14.28	2.06
5	1.37	6.16	5	2.11	5.54	5	8.30	2.97
10	1.42	6.46	10	1.82	5.69	10	5.68	3.05
15	0.56	6.90	15	1.45	5.89	15	5.04	3.12
30	0.42	7.27	30	0.69	6.03	30	4.12	3.15
50	0.28	7.62	50	0.52	6.25	50	4.17	3.24
100	0.20	7.68	100	0.40	6.31	100	3.81	3.25
150	0.16	7.63	150	0.38	6.24	150	3.52	3.26
200	0.19	7.71	200	0.41	6.31	200	3.08	3.27
250	0.13	7.71	250	0.38	6.29	250	3.21	3.25
	FVC2004 DB1			FVC2004 DB2			FVC2004 DB3	
1	11.83	2.30	1	11.83	2.30	1	15.25	2.04
5	7.01	3.46	5	10.02	2.67	5	9.35	2.93
10	3.76	3.57	10	10.54	2.80	10	9.35	2.93
15	3.48	3.72	15	6.54	2.85	15	6.21	3.09
30	2.07	3.77	30	7.38	2.87	30	5.00	3.11
50	1.95	3.86	50	6.15	2.93	50	5.03	3.14
100	1.34	3.89	100	5.35	2.96	100	4.18	3.19
150	1.11	3.89	150	4.49	2.95	150	4.03	3.17
200	0.96	3.90	200	4.14	2.95	200	3.96	3.19
250	0.90	3.90	250	3.93	2.95	250	3.60	3.19

In short, it is observed that $n = 100$ serves the best effect. Therefore, $n = 100$ is concluded to be the best-tuned setting in the experiment.

Summary of Parameter Estimation: It is concluded that the n should be set higher to improve the verification performance and d', while the τ_L is varied based on the tested system. The best-tuned setting of the proposed enhanced matching mechanism for the IoM hashing is $n = 100$, $\tau_L = 0.71$.

Table 3. Comparison of the EERs and d' in the system under (i) original construction and (ii) enhanced by the proposed enhanced matching mechanism. The result is the average of five experiments.

Method	Subset		EER(%)	d'
Similarity Metric: Normalized Euclidean Similarity				
IoM Hashing [6]	FVC2002	DB1	6.93	2.87
		DB2	6.96	2.92
		DB3	14.28	2.06
	FVC2004	DB1	11.83	2.30
		DB2	16.01	1.97
		DB3	15.25	2.04
IoM Hashing (enhanced) ($n =100$, $\tau_L = 0.71$)	FVC2002	DB1	0.20	7.68
		DB2	0.40	6.31
		DB3	3.81	3.25
	FVC2004	DB1	1.34	3.89
		DB2	5.35	2.96
		DB3	4.18	3.19

4.4   Performance and Security Analysis

Performance Analysis. This subsection presents the verification performance and decidability of the proposed enhanced matching mechanism. A comparison of the system performance in terms of EER and d' to the original counterparts (cancellable biometric schemes) is conducted for validating the improvement of EER and d'. The proposed enhanced matching mechanism is operated using the best-tuned parameters. From the Table 3, it is observed that the EERs of the system after applying the proposed enhanced matching mechanism is averagely lower compared to the unenhanced system. Besides that, it is observed that the d' of the cancellable biometric schemes is largely increased after applying the proposed matching mechanism. This is attributed to the local quantization mechanism in the proposed scheme that could maximize the intra/inter-class variances and enable the high separation between the mean of genuine/impostor matching score distributions.

Security Analysis. This section analyzes the feasibility of the attacker to recover the original biometric input x from the leaked information, thus showing that the proposed scheme can achieve biometric security and privacy protection. The proposed enhanced matching mechanism takes a single biometric template x as input and generates a cancellable template set $c = \{c_1, ..., c_n\}$. The transformation phase involves random undersampling of p into permuted biometric features $v = \{v_1, ..., v_n\}$, with $p = \{p_1, ..., p_n\}$ representing permutation seeds. The v_i are independent due to randomization. Each v_i undergoes a cancellable transformation to yield local cancellable templates c_i, where R_i represents auxiliary data for the cancellable biometric scheme. In summary, $v = \{v_1, ..., v_n\}$ and $R = \{R_1, ..., R_n\}$ are transformed into $c = \{c_1, ..., c_n\}$. Random undersampling ensures that each v_i contains partial information of X, resulting in uncorrelated c_i. The intermediate product v is deleted and not stored after the enrollment phase. Furthermore, we evaluate the resistance to similarity-based attack (SA) [28] for proposed method. By carrying out an SA, the experimental results demonstrate that the attack success rate is 0. Therefore, it would be challenging for attacker to reconstruct the original biometric feature. The proposed scheme can ensure the security and privacy of biometric features.

5   Conclusion and Future Work

In this paper, we propose an enhanced matching mechanism to improve the decision environment for the IoM hashing in terms of verification performance and d'. With the genericity, the enhanced matching mechanism could be propagated to any cancellable biometric scheme that accepts vectorized biometric features as input. Comprehensive experiments are conducted to examine the proposed enhanced matching mechanism on the benchmarking fingerprint FVC datasets. The effectiveness of the proposed enhanced matching mechanism varies due to several reasons: (i) employed cancellable biometric scheme, (ii) performance of original biometric feature (iii) transformation parameters (e.g., n and τ_L) and (iv) type of biometric system. As for future work, we aim to further improve the robustness of the matching process and allow higher τ_L to be employed.

Acknowledgments. This work was supported by the National Natural Science Foundation of China (Nos. 62376003, 62306003) and Anhui Provincial Natural Science Foundation (No. 2308085MF200).

References

1. Patel, V.M., Ratha, N.K., Chellappa, R.: Cancelable biometrics: a review. IEEE Signal Process. Mag. **32**(5), 54–65 (2015)
2. Ratha, N.K., Connell, J.H., Bolle, R.M.: Enhancing security and privacy in biometrics-based authentication systems. IBM Syst. J. **40**(3), 614–634 (2001)
3. Riaz, S.A., Khan, A.: Biometric template security: an overview. Sens. Rev. **38**(1), 120–127 (2018)
4. Noviana, E., Indrayanto, G., Rohman, A.: Advances in fingerprint analysis for standardization and quality control of herbal medicines. Front. Pharmacol. **13**, 853023 (2022)
5. Engelsma, J.J., Grosz, S., Jain, A.K.: PrintsGAN: synthetic fingerprint generator. IEEE Trans. Pattern Anal. Mach. Intell. **45**(5), 6111–6124 (2022)
6. Jin, Z., Hwang, J.Y., Lai, Y.-L., Kim, S., Teoh, A.B.J.: Ranking-based locality sensitive hashing-enabled cancelable biometrics: index-of-max hashing. IEEE Trans. Inf. Forensics Secur. **13**(2), 393–407 (2017)
7. Yang, W., Wang, S., Kang, J.J., Johnstone, M.N., Bedari, A.: A linear convolution-based cancelable fingerprint biometric authentication system. Comput. Secur. **114**, 102583 (2022)

8. Sun, Y., Li, H., Li, N.: A novel cancelable fingerprint scheme based on random security sampling mechanism and relocation bloom filter. Comput. Secur. **125**, 103021 (2023)

9. Siddhad, G., Khanna, P.: Max-min threshold-based cancelable biometric templates for low-end devices. J. Electron. Imaging **31**(3), 033025 (2022)

10. Manisha, Kumar, N.: CBRC: a novel approach for cancelable biometric template generation using random permutation and Chinese remainder theorem. Multimedia Tools Appl. **81**(16), 22027–22064 (2022)

11. Nandakumar, K., Jain, A.K.: Biometric template protection: bridging the performance gap between theory and practice. IEEE Signal Process. Mag. **32**(5), 88–100 (2015)

12. Lee, M.J., Jin, Z., Liang, S.-N., Tistarelli, M.: Alignment-robust cancelable biometric scheme for iris verification. IEEE Trans. Inf. Forensics Secur. **17**, 3449–3464 (2022)

13. Li, Y., Pang, L., Zhao, H., Cao, Z., Liu, E., Tian, J.: Indexing-min-max hashing: relaxing the security-performance tradeoff for cancelable fingerprint templates. IEEE Trans. Syst. Man Cybern. Syst. **52**(10), 6314–6325 (2022)

14. Daugman, J.: Biometric decision landscapes. University of Cambridge, Computer Laboratory, Technical report (2000)

15. Li, C., Hu, J.: Attacks via record multiplicity on cancelable biometrics templates. Concurrency Comput. Pract. Experience **26**(8), 1593–1605 (2014)

16. Maio, D., Maltoni, D., Cappelli, R., Wayman, J.L., Jain, A.K.: FVC2004: third fingerprint verification competition. In: Zhang, D., Jain, A.K. (eds.) ICBA 2004. LNCS, vol. 3072, pp. 1–7. Springer, Heidelberg (2004). https://doi.org/10.1007/978-3-540-25948-0_1

17. Gomez-Barrero, M., Galbally, J.: Reversing the irreversible: a survey on inverse biometrics. Comput. Secur. **90**, 101700 (2020)

18. Uludag, U., Jain, A.K.: Attacks on biometric systems: a case study in fingerprints. In: Security, Steganography, and Watermarking of Multimedia Contents VI, vol. 5306, pp. 622–633. SPIE (2004)

19. Gomez-Barrero, M., Galbally, J., Fierrez, J., Ortega-Garcia, J.: Hill-climbing attack based on the uphill simplex algorithm and its application to signature verification. In: Vielhauer, C., Dittmann, J., Drygajlo, A., Juul, N.C., Fairhurst, M.C. (eds.) BioID 2011. LNCS, vol. 6583, pp. 83–94. Springer, Heidelberg (2011). https://doi.org/10.1007/978-3-642-19530-3_8

20. Gomez-Barrero, M., Galbally, J., Fierrez, J., Ortega-Garcia, J.: Face verification put to test: a hill-climbing attack based on the uphill-simplex algorithm. In: 2012 5th IAPR International Conference on Biometrics (ICB), pp. 40–45. IEEE (2012)

21. Pashalidis, A.: Simulated annealing attack on certain fingerprint authentication systems. In: International Conference of the BIOSIG Special Interest Group (BIOSIG), pp. 1–11. IEEE (2013)

22. Galbally, J., Ross, A., Gomez-Barrero, M., Fierrez, J., Ortega-Garcia, J.: Iris image reconstruction from binary templates: an efficient probabilistic approach based on genetic algorithms. Comput. Vis. Image Underst. **117**(10), 1512–1525 (2013)

23. Learned-Miller, E., Huang, G.B., RoyChowdhury, A., Li, H., Hua, G.: Labeled faces in the wild: a survey. In: Kawulok, M., Celebi, M.E., Smolka, B. (eds.) Advances in Face Detection and Facial Image Analysis, pp. 189–248. Springer, Cham (2016). https://doi.org/10.1007/978-3-319-25958-1_8

24. Kho, J.B., Kim, J., Kim, I.-J., Teoh, A.B.: Cancelable fingerprint template design with randomized non-negative least squares. Pattern Recogn. **91**, 245–260 (2019)

25. Cappelli, R., Ferrara, M., Maltoni, D.: Minutia cylinder-code: a new representation and matching technique for fingerprint recognition. IEEE Trans. Pattern Anal. Mach. Intell. **32**(12), 2128 (2010)
26. Cappelli, R., Maio, D., Maltoni, D., Wayman, J.L., Jain, A.K.: Performance evaluation of fingerprint verification systems. IEEE Trans. Pattern Anal. Mach. Intell. **28**(1), 3–18 (2005)
27. Maio, D., Maltoni, D., Cappelli, R., Wayman, J.L., Jain, A.K.: FVC2002: second fingerprint verification competition. In: International Conference on Pattern Recognition, vol. 3, pp. 811–814. IEEE (2002)
28. Dong, X., Jin, Z., Jin, A.T.B.: A genetic algorithm enabled similarity-based attack on cancellable biometrics. In: 2019 IEEE 10th International Conference on Biometrics Theory, Applications and Systems (BTAS), pp. 1–8. IEEE (2019)

R-IoM: Enhance Biometric Security with Redundancy-Reduced Hashcode Reliability

ZhengHui Goh[1], Shiuan-Ni Liang[1], Zhe Jin[2], YenLung Lai[2(✉)], Ming-Jie Lee[3],
and Xin Wang[1]

[1] Monash University Malaysia, Subang Jaya, Malaysia
[2] Anhui Provincial Key Laboratory of Secure Artificial Intelligence, Anhui Provincial
International Joint Research Center for Advanced Technology in Medical Imaging,
School of AI, Anhui University, Hefei 230093, China
yenlung@ahu.edu.cn
[3] Lee Kong Chian Faculty of Engineering and Science, Universiti Tunku Abdul
Rahman, 43000 Kajang, Malaysia

Abstract. This research focuses on analyzing vulnerabilities in the
IoM hashing technique concerning its susceptibility to preimage attacks,
which poses a significant security concern in biometric template protection (BTP) systems. To address these vulnerabilities and achieve
a balanced trade-off between performance and security, we propose a
novel approach called R-IoM hashing. This method introduces innovative mitigation strategies to minimize information leakage and enhance
the resistance to preimage attacks. By employing a dimensionality reduction technique during the IoM hashing process, R-IoM hashing effectively eliminates extraneous data, ensuring improved security without
compromising computational efficiency. Through comprehensive experiments, we demonstrate the effectiveness of R-IoM hashing. Notably, this
approach maintains remarkably low error rates while showcasing robust
resilience against preimage attacks compared to conventional IoM hashing. This substantial improvement in security positions R-IoM hashing
as a promising solution for real-world BTP applications. Our research
underscores the importance of accurate distance measurement in feature comparison, identifies vulnerabilities in IoM hashing, and introduces a practical and efficient solution through R-IoM hashing to enhance
the reliability and security of biometric-based systems. This paper contributes valuable insights into biometric template protection and offers
a potential avenue for future research and implementation in security-
critical environments.

1 Introduction

Traditional authentication systems [1] predominantly rely on the personal pos-
session of confidential information, commonly referred to as "what we have",
including but not limited to passwords, Personal Identification Numbers (PINs),
and access cards. However, these methods are not infallible, as such credentials

W. Jia et al. (Eds.): CCBR 2023, LNCS 14463, pp. 340–349, 2023.
https://doi.org/10.1007/978-981-99-8565-4_32

can be easily lost, stolen, guessed, forgotten, or shared, presenting a significant vulnerability [2]. Furthermore, a notable trade-off exists between the memorability of passwords and their security strength; intricate passwords offer superior security but present challenges in recall for users.

In contrast, biometric recognition [3,4] presents a more sophisticated and secure alternative, utilizing distinct biometric characteristics as a form of authentication. Such characteristics span a wide array of individual anatomical and behavioral traits, encompassing fingerprint patterns, facial structures, iris configurations, hand dimensions, vocal characteristics, palm-prints, handwritten signatures, and even an individual's unique walk, or gait. This technique obviates the necessity for users to memorize complicated passwords or to carry supplementary access cards. Owing to their superior reliability, user-friendliness, and ubiquity, biometric recognition systems have been extensively adopted for personal authentication on a global scale.

Facial recognition [5,6], a widely adopted biometric authentication method, capitalizes on the unique features of an individual's face to verify identity. During enrollment, an individual's facial features are captured and converted into digital templates, which are saved in a database for future reference. However, this storage methodology exposes a significant vulnerability. If the database storing these facial templates is compromised, these templates could be stolen and potentially misused for unauthorized access or identity fraud. Unlike passwords or access tokens, which can be changed or reissued if compromised, facial templates are inherently linked to the user and cannot be altered or replaced. Therefore, securing the database and the facial templates it houses is a crucial task in ensuring the integrity and dependability of facial recognition systems.

Biometric template protection (BTP) methods [7–9] have been introduced to tackle the security concerns related to the storage of fingerprint templates. The primary goal of these methods is to fortify the stored templates against potential security breaches and more importantly, enable template revocation in the event of a compromise. A predominant category of BTP is Cancelable Biometrics (CB) [10], which involves the transformation of the biometric template into a new, protected form using a non-invertible function. This transformed template can then be stored in the database, with the original biometric data remaining secure. In the event of a database breach, these transformed templates cannot be reverted back to the original biometric data, preserving the privacy of the users. Furthermore, a new transformation function can be generated and a new template created if the original is compromised, effectively revoking the old template. Specifically, for a CB scheme to be effective and reliably implemented, they must satisfy certain essential criteria which are noninvertibility, revocability, unlinkability, and performance preservation [8].

1.1 IoM Hashing

The IoM hashing [11] is one of the state of the art cancellable biometric sheme that make use of the notion of Locality Sensitive Hashing (LSH) [12] to perform hashing on the input biometric feature and transform into a hashed template that can be securely stored in the database to replace the original counterpart. It is widely being studied due to its simplicity and high efficienty in generating cancellablel template.

Step 1. Given an input feature vector $w \in \mathbb{R}^\ell$, generate m random matrices $(H_1, \ldots, H_m)$, where each matrix $H_i \in (H_1, \ldots, H_m)$ is of dimension $\mathbb{R}^{n \times \ell}$ consists of entries that are independent and identically distributed according to a Gaussian distribution with mean 0 and variance 1, denoted as $\mathcal{N}(0, 1)$.

Step 2. (for $i = 1, \ldots, m$) Let $H_i w = z_i$, where $z_i = (z_{i1}, z_{i2}, \ldots, z_{in})$ is the output vector of n dimensions. Then, define

$$y_i = \underset{j \in \{1, 2 \ldots, n\}}{\arg \max}\ z_{ij} \in \mathbb{Z},$$

where $\arg \max$ operation returns the maximum index (position) value in the vector z_i corresponds to the maximum value among the relevant entries for $j = 1, \ldots, n$. The resultant output vector is denoted as $(y_1, \ldots, y_m) \in \mathbb{Z}^m$.

Below depicts a toy example of IoM hashing with $m = 2$, $n > 2$:

Input : Random matrices $\{H_1, H_2\}$, Feature vector $w \in \mathbb{R}^\ell$

$$H_1 \times w = \begin{bmatrix} a_{11} & a_{12} & \cdots & a_{1\ell} \\ a_{21} & a_{22} & \cdots & a_{2\ell} \\ \vdots & \vdots & \ddots & \vdots \\ a_{n1} & a_{n2} & \cdots & a_{n\ell} \end{bmatrix} \times \begin{bmatrix} w_1 \\ w_2 \\ \vdots \\ w_\ell \end{bmatrix} = \begin{bmatrix} 0.34 \\ -1.44 \\ \vdots \\ 0.29 \end{bmatrix} \Rightarrow y_1 = 0$$

$$H_2 \times w = \begin{bmatrix} b_{11} & b_{12} & \cdots & b_{1\ell} \\ b_{21} & b_{22} & \cdots & b_{2\ell} \\ \vdots & \vdots & \ddots & \vdots \\ b_{n1} & b_{n2} & \cdots & b_{n\ell} \end{bmatrix} \times \begin{bmatrix} w_1 \\ w_2 \\ \vdots \\ w_\ell \end{bmatrix} = \begin{bmatrix} -0.44 \\ 3.34 \\ \vdots \\ 0.19 \end{bmatrix} \Rightarrow y_2 = 1$$

Output : $\{H_1, H_2\}$, $(y_1, y_2) = (0, 1)$

IoM can be employed for two-factor authentication, where the projection matrices $\{H_1, \ldots, H_m\}$ are not stored along with the hashed code y in a database, rather used as auxiliary tokens associated with an individual. These tokens are then presented along with the corresponding biometric data w for authentication purposes.

Nonetheless, it is instructive to analyze the system under a *stolen token scenario* [13], where these projection matrices become publicly available. Under such circumstances, we assume for the purposes of this study that any auxiliary information such as the projection matrices, aside from y, is publicly accessible. This assumption forms the basis for our analysis in the rest of the paper.

2   Motivation

In many applications involving feature comparison, distance measurement plays a critical role [14]. Two of the most common distance metrics used for measuring the distance between features are the cosine distance and the Euclidean distance. The cosine distance is defined as $1 - \frac{A \cdot B}{\|A\|\|B\|}$, where A and B represent two feature vectors, and $\cdot$ denotes the dot product. In contrast, the Euclidean distance is given by $\|A - B\|_2 = \sqrt{\sum_{i=1}^{n}(a_i - b_i)^2}$, where a_i and b_i are the components of vectors A and B, respectively.

These distance metrics fundamentally consider the magnitude of the feature vectors in computation, i.e., the *absolute value* of $\|A\|$, $\|B\|$ or $\|A - B\|$. Therefore, when designing distance-sensitive hashing schemes such as LSH, it is essential to include or preserve such magnitude information. By doing so, we not only ensure the hashing process reflects the original data structure, but also potentially improve the performance of the subsequent machine learning or data mining tasks.

On the other hand, previous research has highlighted potential vulnerabilities of IoM hashing in BTP to preimage attacks [15–18]. These studies, such as Genetic algorithm enabled similarity based attack (GASA) [18] and Constrained-Optimized Similarity-based Attack (CSA) [16], have uncovered a specific relationship between the increase in IoM hashed codelength and its resemblance to a supervised learning problem that is prone to overfitting when the hashed code length is small. It has been observed that increasing the length of the hashed code can alleviate the overfitting issue, but it also exposes IoM hashing to a higher vulnerability to preimage attacks. This scenario illustrates the inherent trade-off between performance and security within systems that employ IoM hashing.

Motivated from above, this paper is primarily aimed at addressing the inherent trade-off issue by mitigating the storage of 'unwanted' data that could potentially ease pre-image attacks on a database. It is important to clarify that our goal is not to entirely prevent pre-image attacks on IoM hashing. Instead, we aim to curtail the dimensionality of IoM hashing without compromising its performance. By discarding 'unwanted' or extraneous information, we aim to limit information leakage, which in turn could dampen the efficacy of existing pre-image attacks on IoM hashing.

3   Methodology

We herein present the our proposed improvement over traditional IoM hashing. This methodology, termed as the Reduced-IoM (R-IoM) hashing scheme, aims to minimize the redundancy and dimensionality of the hashed code length. This optimization yields substantial benefits in terms of system storage and computational time, particularly within the context of authentication procedures. The R-IoM hashing can be summarized into two major steps:

Step 1. Given an input feature vector $w \in \mathbb{R}^{\ell}$, generate m random matrices $(H_1, \ldots, H_m)$, where each matrix $H_i \in (H_1, \ldots, H_m)$ is of dimension $\mathbb{R}^{n \times \ell}$ consists of entries that are independent and identically distributed according to a Gaussian distribution with mean 0 and variance 1, denoted as $\mathcal{N}(0, 1)$.

Step 2. (for $i = 1, \ldots, m$) Let $H_i w = z_i$, where $z_i = (z_{i1}, z_{i2}, \ldots, z_{in})$ is an output vector of n dimensions. Define

$$y_i = \text{sign}(\max_{j=1,2\ldots,n} (|z_{ij}|)) \in \{-1, 1\}. \tag{1}$$

In this context, the max operation retrieves the maximum value in the vector z_i, i.e., value that largest compared to zero, and the function $\text{sign}(.)$ discretizes this maximum value into the binary set $\{-1, 1\}$, based on its sign. Let h_i be the row of H_i that corresponds to this maximum value, such that $h_i w = y_i$. The resultant output vector is denoted as $(y_1, \ldots, y_m) \in \{-1, 1\}^m$ and the corresponding transform matrix formed as $\hat{H} = (h_1, \ldots, h_m) \in \mathbb{R}^{m \times \ell}$.

Below depicts a toy example of R-IoM hashing with $m = 2$, $n = 2$:

$Input$: Random matrices $\{H_1, H_2\}$, Feature vector $w \in \mathbb{R}^{\ell}$

$$H_1 \times w = \begin{bmatrix} a_{11} & a_{12} & \cdots & a_{1\ell} \\ a_{21} & a_{22} & \cdots & a_{2\ell} \\ \vdots & \vdots & \ddots & \vdots \\ a_{n1} & a_{n2} & \cdots & a_{n\ell} \end{bmatrix} \times \begin{bmatrix} w_1 \\ w_2 \\ \vdots \\ w_\ell \end{bmatrix} = \begin{bmatrix} 3.34 \\ -1.44 \\ \vdots \\ 0.99 \end{bmatrix}$$

$$\Rightarrow y_1 = 1, \ h_1 = [a_{11} \ a_{12} \ldots \ a_{1\ell}]$$

$$H_2 \times w = \begin{bmatrix} a_{11} & a_{12} & \cdots & a_{1\ell} \\ b_{21} & b_{22} & \cdots & b_{2\ell} \\ \vdots & \vdots & \ddots & \vdots \\ b_{n1} & b_{n2} & \cdots & b_{n\ell} \end{bmatrix} \times \begin{bmatrix} w_1 \\ w_2 \\ \vdots \\ w_\ell \end{bmatrix} = \begin{bmatrix} 1.34 \\ -2.44 \\ \vdots \\ 0.99 \end{bmatrix}$$

$$\Rightarrow y_2 = -1, \ h_2 = [b_{21} \ b_{22} \ldots \ b_{2\ell}]$$

$$Output : \hat{H} = (h_1, h_2) = \begin{bmatrix} a_{11} & a_{12} & \cdots & a_{1\ell} \\ b_{21} & b_{22} & \cdots & b_{2\ell} \end{bmatrix}, \ y = (y_1, y_2) = (1, -1)$$

To summarize, the proposed R-IoM comes with numerous notable features that different from the traditional IoM hashing:

1. Instead of merely tracking the index of the maximum value, R-IoM records the absolute maximum value, i.e., the value that holds the greatest distance

from zero. This methodology allows for the retention of crucial information within the vector, which becomes particularly significant when computing distances between hashed codes. This is underpinned by the fact that the magnitude of a vector substantially influences the distance computation, i.e., Cosine, Euclidean distances.

2. As more 'useful' information being retain as only the absolute maximum value after matrix multiplication ($H_i w$), it means that only the corresponding row h_i should take effect during hashing. This allow us to remove redundancy by only storing h_i rather than the whole matrix H_i involved during IoM hashing.

4 Experiment and Discussion

For input biometric samples, we employ MagFace [19], a pre-trained CNN model, to generate universal face feature embeddings of dimensionality $\ell = 512$ as input feature vector hashed code generation. In our evaluation, we utilize the Labelled Faces in the Wild (LFW) dataset [20], which consists of 7,701 images of 4,281 subjects.

Following the protocol described in Huang et al. [20], we divide 6,000 face pairs from the LFW dataset into two disjoint subsets for cross-validation. Each subset contains 3,000 genuine pairs (matching faces) and 3,000 impostor pairs (non-matching faces). We compute the pair-wise Hamming distance between the two hashed codes to evaluate the similarity between face pairs. This process yields 3,000 genuine and 3,000 impostor test scores, enabling us to assess the performance of the MagFace model on the LFW dataset for face recognition tasks.

Performance over Small Hashed Code Length (m): Figure 1 presents the Equal Error Rate (EER) results for both IoM hashing and the proposed R-IoM hashing methods from the experiments conducted. These experiments were carried out with a constant parameter of $n = 1000$ and a progressively increasing hashed code length of $m = 5, 10, 15, \ldots, 99$. The results clearly illustrate that the proposed R-IoM hashing method outperforms conventional IoM hashing overall. It's noteworthy that R-IoM hashing can attain an EER less than 1.5% at a hashed code length of 10, whereas IoM hashing only manages to achieve an EER greater than 10% under the same conditions.

Performance over Large Parameter n: It is worth recall that R-IoM produce output that is corresponds to maximum amplitude among n entries follows Eq. 1. The quantization process, through sign(.) is applied only to the largest entries in the projected data (after matrix multiplication). This selectiveness is vital, as these maximum values are typically distanced from the decision boundary of the sign(.) function, contributing to the stability of their sign.

As n enlarges, the entries chosen for quantization embody greater magnitudes and showcase more stable signs. These features support the sign(.) function in assigning either -1 or 1 depending on the initial sign of the data value, thereby yielding a substantially more robust and reliable hashed code representation.

Figure 2 vividly illustrates the distributions of genuine and imposter test scores as the parameter n progressively escalates from 2 to 100, with m held constant at 512. The genuine test scores-which are anticipated to display minimal variances between their hashed codes-provide a compelling testament to the robustness of our scheme. As n increases, the Hamming distance, a measure of error between the R-IoM hashed codes, tends towards zero, implying an exact match amongst authentic users. This convergence to zero not only demonstrates the efficacy of the proposed R-IoM methodology but also underlines its robustness in encoding accurate representations. In effect, the scheme offers high resistance to noise and minor input data fluctuations, resulting in reliable and consistent hash code representations. The resilience of this method underscores the potential for its application in security-sensitive domains that necessitate the utmost reliability and precision.

Efficacy over Pre-image Resistance: Table 1 displays the results of an attack study, conducted by [16], which includes the performance of two pre-image attacks on traditional IoM hashing using the LFW dataset. For assessing the effectiveness of these attacks, two new metrics were proposed: the Successful Attack Rate (SAR) and the False Acceptance Increment (FAI). SAR is determined by recording the acceptance rate of the generated preimage during the attack. FAI, on the other hand, is calculated by subtracting the False Match Rate (FMR) from the SAR (i.e., FAI = SAR − FMR). This calculation provides a more accurate depiction of the true attack performance, excluding false positives. Consequently, a higher FAI score suggests a more effective attack performance. Notably, R-IoM capability of preserving low EER even for hashed codelength smaller than 32 suggests stronger resistance over the studied pre-image attacks that demostrating less than 5% of SAR and 2.5% of FAI.

Table 1. Pre-image attack results recorded by [16], observably the efficacy of GASA and CSA drop as the hashcode length decreases.

Hashcode length (m)	GASA [18]		CSA [16]	
	SAR (%)	FAI (%)	SAR (%)	FAI (%)
8	10.94	1.16	11.06	1.28
16	12.41	2.97	11.14	1.70
32	3.96	1.27	4.83	2.14
64	5.40	3.16	12.03	9.79
128	7.54	6.44	42.13	41.03
256	24.11	23.39	92.08	91.36
512	64.12	63.51	99.19	98.58

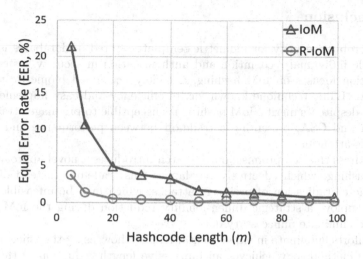

Fig. 1. EER vs hashedcode length m for both IoM hashing and R-IoM hashing.

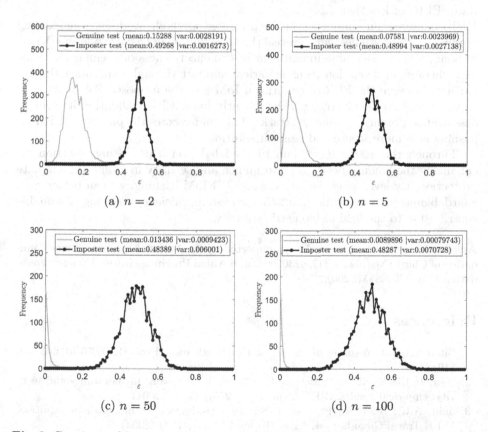

Fig. 2. Genuine and imposter test scores distributions with increasing n and constant $m = 512$.

5   Conclusion

Ensuring robust security for biometric templates stored in databases is critical for reliable individual recognition and authentication in security systems. Our investigation focuses on IoM hashing, a widely acclaimed biometric template protection (BTP) technique known for its efficiency and easy implementation. However, despite its merits, IoM hashing is susceptible to preimage attacks such as GASA and CSA, presenting a trade-off between performance and security that needs attention.

To address this compromise, our research introduces a novel approach called R-IoM hashing, which effectively rebalances this trade-off. Instead of aiming for complete eradication of preimage attacks, which may be infeasible, R-IoM hashing employs a strategic dimensionality reduction during the IoM hashing process to eliminate unnecessary data.

Our efforts culminate in experimental results showcasing the efficiency of R-IoM. The methodology achieves an impressive length reduction of the hashed code down to only $m = 10$, while maintaining a remarkably low Equal Error Rate (EER) of less than 1.5.

To reinforce our confidence in the proposed method, we draw from existing pre-image attack studies, which reveal that a reduction in hashed code length corresponds to a considerable impairment in the effectiveness of preimage attacks. This theoretical deduction gains empirical support through experimental comparisons between the EER of traditional IoM and the proposed R-IoM hashing methods. R-IoM demonstrates a significantly lower EER, validating its robustness against potential preimage attacks. This underscores the potential of R-IoM hashing as a more secure and resilient solution.

Through this research, we aim to shed light on a promising direction for enhancing the balance between performance and security in biometric template protection. By leveraging the advantages of R-IoM hashing, we can better safeguard biometric data while maintaining system efficiency, offering a valuable contribution to the field of biometric security.

Acknowledgement. This work was supported by the National Natural Science Foundation of China (Nos. 62376003, 62306003) and Anhui Provincial Natural Science Foundation (No. 2308085MF200).

References

1. Simmons, G.J.: A survey of information authentication. Proc. IEEE **76**(5), 603–620 (1988)
2. Yan, J., Blackwell, A., Anderson, R., Grant, A.: Password memorability and security: empirical results. IEEE Secur. Priv. **2**(5), 25–31 (2004)
3. Jain, A.K., Ross, A., Prabhakar, S.: An introduction to biometric recognition. IEEE Trans. Circuits Syst. Video Technol. **14**(1), 4–20 (2004)
4. Unar, J., Seng, W.C., Abbasi, A.: A review of biometric technology along with trends and prospects. Pattern Recogn. **47**(8), 2673–2688 (2014)

5. Zhao, W., Chellappa, R., Phillips, P.J., Rosenfeld, A.: Face recognition: a literature survey. ACM Comput. Surv. (CSUR) **35**(4), 399–458 (2003)
6. Hu, G., et al.: When face recognition meets with deep learning: an evaluation of convolutional neural networks for face recognition. In: Proceedings of the IEEE International Conference on Computer Vision Workshops, pp. 142–150 (2015)
7. Jain, A.K., Nandakumar, K., Nagar, A.: Biometric template security. EURASIP J. Adv. Signal Process. **2008**, 1–17 (2008)
8. Rathgeb, C., Busch, C.: Multi-biometric template protection: issues and challenges. In: New Trends and Developments in Biometrics, pp. 173–190 (2012)
9. Nandakumar, K., Jain, A.K.: Biometric template protection: bridging the performance gap between theory and practice. IEEE Signal Process. Mag. **32**(5), 88–100 (2015)
10. Ratha, N.K., Chikkerur, S., Connell, J.H., Bolle, R.M.: Generating cancelable fingerprint templates. IEEE Trans. Pattern Anal. Mach. Intell. **29**(4), 561–572 (2007)
11. Jin, Z., Hwang, J.Y., Lai, Y.-L., Kim, S., Teoh, A.B.J.: Ranking-based locality sensitive hashing-enabled cancelable biometrics: index-of-max hashing. IEEE Trans. Inf. Forensics Secur. **13**(2), 393–407 (2017)
12. Jafari, O., Maurya, P., Nagarkar, P., Islam, K.M., Crushev, C.: A survey on locality sensitive hashing algorithms and their applications. arXiv preprint arXiv:2102.08942 (2021)
13. Kong, A., Cheung, K.-H., Zhang, D., Kamel, M., You, J.: An analysis of biohashing and its variants. Pattern Recogn. **39**(7), 1359–1368 (2006)
14. Seifert, C.: Data mining: an overview. In: National Security Issues, pp. 201–217 (2004)
15. Dong, X., Jin, Z., Teoh, A., Tistarelli, M., Wong, K.: On the security risk of cancelable biometrics. arXiv preprint arXiv:1910.07770 (2019)
16. Wang, H., Dong, X., Jin, Z., Teoh, A.B.J., Tistarelli, M.: Interpretable security analysis of cancellable biometrics using constrained-optimized similarity-based attack. In: Proceedings of the IEEE/CVF Winter Conference on Applications of Computer Vision, pp. 70–77 (2021)
17. Lai, Y., Jin, Z., Wong, K., Tistarelli, M.: Efficient known-sample attack for distance-preserving hashing biometric template protection schemes. IEEE Trans. Inf. Forensics Secur. **16**, 3170–3185 (2021)
18. Dong, X., Jin, Z., Jin, A.T.B.: A genetic algorithm enabled similarity-based attack on cancellable biometrics. In: 2019 IEEE 10th International Conference on Biometrics Theory, Applications and Systems (BTAS), pp. 1–8. IEEE (2019)
19. Meng, Q., Zhao, S., Huang, Z., Zhou, F.: MagFace: a universal representation for face recognition and quality assessment. In: Proceedings of the IEEE/CVF Conference on Computer Vision and Pattern Recognition, pp. 14 225–14 234 (2021)
20. Huang, G.B., Mattar, M., Berg, T., Learned-Miller, E.: Labeled faces in the wild: a database forstudying face recognition in unconstrained environments. In: Workshop on Faces in 'Real-Life' Images: Detection, Alignment, and Recognition (2008)

SP²IN: Leveraging Fuzzy Commitment and LDPC Sum-Product Decoder for Key Generation from Face

Yafei Liu[1], Ying Zhou[1], Weiyu Zhou[1], Hui Zhang[2], Yufang Dong[3],
Xingbo Dong[1], and Zhe Jin[1(✉)]

[1] Anhui Provincial Key Laboratory of Secure Artificial Intelligence, Anhui Provincial
International Joint Research Center for Advanced Technology in Medical Imaging,
School of Artificial Intelligence, Anhui University, Hefei 230093, China
wa22301072@stu.ahu.edu.cn, jinzhe@ahu.edu.cn
[2] Anhui Provincial International Joint Research Center for Advanced Technology in
Medical Imaging, School of Computer Science and Technology, Anhui University,
Hefei 230093, China
[3] School of Medicine, Nankai University, Tianjin 300071, China

Abstract. Biometric authentication, with its unique and convenient
features, is gaining popularity as a secure access control method for
diverse systems and services. However, the inherent ambiguity of biometric data poses challenges when integrating it with cryptographic systems
that require 100% accuracy, such as personal information number generation. To address this, we propose SP^2IN, a face bio-cryptosystem that
utilizes a Low-Density Parity-Check Sum-Product decoder and fuzzy
commitment. In our innovative face biometric cryptosystem, we employ
fuzzy commitment for secure key extraction from biometric input, ensuring the protection of sensitive facial information without compromising the privacy of the raw data. To tackle facial biometric noise, we
use a Low-Density Parity-Check Sum-Product decoder for error correction against variations. Our system was rigorously tested on public face
datasets (LFW, AgeDB, CALFW), showcasing outstanding recognition
rates: 99.43% (LFW), 90.43% (CALFW), 92.63% (AgeDB30).

Keywords: Biometric cryptosystem · Face bio-cryptosystem · Fuzzy
Commitment · Key Generation · Secure Access Control

1 Introduction

As the demand for convenient authentication with high information security
continues to grow, conventional identification technologies relying on passwords
and credentials no longer suffice [1,2].

Biometrics, especially face recognition, has emerged as a dependable method
for individual identification owing to its inherent uniqueness and convenience.

Y. Liu and Y. Zhou—These authors contributed equally to this work.

W. Jia et al. (Eds.): CCBR 2023, LNCS 14463, pp. 350–362, 2023.
https://doi.org/10.1007/978-981-99-8565-4_33

However, due to the irrevocable nature of biometric features, once lost, it become permanently ineffective [3]. Furthermore, as the application of recognition systems expands, concerns about the security and privacy of the biometric features themselves have also drawn increasing attention [4]. Safeguarding the security of the feature templates used in recognition systems has become an ongoing research focus in the field of biometric recognition. To address these challenges, various biometric cryptosystem (BC) schemes have been proposed [3,5–7] for generating cryptographic keys from biometric data.

Among various BC schemes, the fuzzy commitment scheme [8] is a representative BC with two steps: commitment and de-commitment. Given a binary biometric vector $\mathbf{b}$, the commitment step selects a codeword $\mathbf{c} \in C$, where C is a set of n-bit codewords generated from certain Error Correction Codes (ECCs), with the same length as $\mathbf{b}$. The difference between the biometric and the codeword is denoted as $\delta = \mathbf{b}$ XOR $\mathbf{c}$. The commitment is represented as $\{hash(\mathbf{c}), \delta\}$, where $hash(\cdot)$ is a cryptographic hashing algorithm like SHA256. As $hash(\cdot)$ is a one-way hashing function, the commitment $\{hash(\mathbf{c}), \delta\}$ ensures no disclosure of any information about the biometric data. In the de-commitment step, given an input biometric data denoted by $\mathbf{b}'$, a codeword $\mathbf{c}'$ is calculated from the commitment: $\mathbf{c}' = \mathbf{b}'$ XOR δ. The codeword $\mathbf{c}'$ can be restored as the original $\mathbf{c}$ by the ECC if the distance between $\mathbf{b}'$ and $\mathbf{b}$ is smaller than a certain threshold. Fuzzy commitment has been applied to various biometric modalities, including iris [9], face [10], fingerprints [11], and others.

However, several challenges remain for the practical implementation of fuzzy commitment for face recognition systems. Ideally, face features should be the same for the same user and distinguishable for different users, but achieving this is unrealistic. ECCs may be one of the best options to achieve this task, but achieving 100% error correction for the same user and 0% for different users is highly unlikely in practice. Secondly, most existing fuzzy commitment schemes are evaluated with controlled biometric datasets, assuming cooperative scenarios [12], which is not usually practical in reality.

Motivated by the aforementioned challenges, we propose a new fuzzy commitment scheme based on the LDPC error correction coding approach integrated with the Sum-Product (SP) decoder for unconstrained face recognition. Specifically, state-of-the-art face recognition models are employed to generate discriminative features, followed by a feature transformation pipeline, which converts real-valued features into binary features suitable for error correction coding. Considering that the error rates of binary features from the same user tend to be relatively high due to intra-class variation, they often exceed the error-correcting capability of LDPC, we introduce a random masking technique, bitwise AND the binary features to decrease the bit error rate to a level that aligns with the error correction capability of LDPC.

The main contributions of this paper are as follows: 1) We introduce an SP decoder based fuzzy commitment BC, namely SP^2IN, which is modality-agnostic and applicable to any fixed-length biometric feature vector; 2) A comprehensive evaluation has been carried out on three public unconstrained face datasets, including LFW, CALFW, and AgeDB30. Our system demonstrates outstanding key recovery performance with genuine match rates of 99.43% on LFW, 90.43% on CALFW, and 92.63% on AgeDB30.

2   Related Work

The fuzzy commitment scheme, tailored for binary biometrics, draws inspiration from cryptographic bit commitment [8]. It allows for a certain degree of error in the submitted value by utilizing ECCs that fall within the error correction range of the code. Hao et al. [9] demonstrated an early application of the fuzzy commitment scheme to iris biometrics, employing a combination of two ECCs, namely Hadamard and Reed-Solomon. They utilized a (64, 7) Hadamard ECC capable of correcting at least 15 random bit errors and generating a 7-bit word. The 2048-bit iris template was partitioned into 32 blocks, each containing 64 bits. Additionally, a Reed-Solomon code (32, 20) was used to handle errors at the block level (burst) and correct up to 6 incorrect 7-bit words. The process resulted in a 140-bit key obtained by employing 32 input words to decode 20 output words. Despite these efforts, the key recovery rate showed a significant decline when tested on a challenging dataset. Bringer et al. [13] introduced an iterative soft decoding ECC, a combination of two Reed-Muller ECCs, which greatly improved the accuracy of the fuzzy commitment scheme.

Chen et al. [14] developed a fuzzy commitment system for ordered feature vectors utilizing BCH codes. In a similar vein, Li et al. (2012) proposed a binary fixed-length feature generation approach based on minute triplets to enable fingerprint fuzzy commitment, employing BCH codes. Additionally, Yang et al. [15] implemented a fuzzy commitment scheme based on BCH codes to establish associations between finger-vein templates and secret keys, storing the resulting helper data on a smart card.

In [16], a fuzzy commitment scheme based on the Euclidean distance is proposed. Unlike traditional security schemes that utilize binary feature vectors, this novel approach can accommodate real-valued feature vectors used in recent deep learning-based biometric systems. In [17], LDPC coding is employed to extract a stable cryptographic key from finger templates, integrated into a bio-cryptosystem scheme. In [18], an iris-based cryptographic key generation scheme is introduced, utilizing information analysis and following the principles of the fuzzy commitment scheme. This scheme employs high-entropy biometric templates, resulting in 400-bit cryptographic keys with 0% FAR and an FRR of 3.75%. In [19], the authors developed a face template protection method using multi-label learning and LDPC codes. Initially, random binary sequences are hashed to create a protected template, and during training, they are encoded with an LDPC encoder to generate diverse binary codes. Subsequently, deep multi-label learning is applied to map each user's facial features to distinct binary codes. Finally, the LDPC decoder removes the noise caused by intra-variations from the output of the CNN, achieving a high Genuine Accept Rate (GAR) with a 1% False Accept Rate (FAR) on PIE and the extended Yale B datasets.

The fuzzy commitment scheme has been proven to provide secure and privacy-preserving biometric authentication. However, certain areas have received relatively less attention in research. One such area is the optimization of error-correcting codes used in existing fuzzy commitment schemes for face recognition. Further investigation in this domain could lead to improved performance of ECCs in these schemes. Additionally, it is worth noting that commonly used datasets such as FRGC [20], FERET [21], PIE [22], and Extended Yale B [23] have been extensively employed in works like [19,24]. As a result, fuzzy commitment schemes for unconstrained face recognition scenarios have not been well explored, despite the fact that such unconstrained settings pose greater challenges and necessitate more robust solutions.

3   Proposed Method

3.1   Overview

During the registration phase, a given input image $\mathbf{x} \in R^{H*W*3}$ is used to extract discriminative features $\mathbf{v} \in R^{512}$ using state-of-the-art face recognition models by $\mathbf{v} = f(\mathbf{x})$, where $f(\cdot)$ represents the feature extractor. Then the binary instances $\mathbf{b}'_x \in \{0,1\}^n$, can be obtained by $\mathbf{b}'_x = g(\mathbf{v})$, where $g(\cdot)$ is the feature transformation function composed of feature quantization and binarization.

Next, a randomly generated key $\mathbf{k}$ is used to generate a set of n-bit codewords C using the LDPC encoder. The commitment is saved as $\{hash(\mathbf{c}), \delta\}$, where $\delta = \mathbf{b}'_x$ XOR $\mathbf{c}$. Here, $\mathbf{c}$ is a codeword $\mathbf{c} \in C$, and $hash(\cdot)$ donates a one-way hashing function, such as SHA256.

During the authentication and key retrieval phase, given a query image $\mathbf{y} \in R^{H*W*3}$ from the same person, a binary instance $\mathbf{b}'_y$ can be extracted in the same way, such as $\mathbf{b}'_y = g(f(\mathbf{y}))$. Then, the codeword $\mathbf{c}'$ can be recovered by $\mathbf{c}' = \mathbf{b}'_y$ XOR δ, where the stored δ can be de-committed. If the distance between $\mathbf{b}'_x$ and $\mathbf{b}'_y$ is within the ECC's error correction capability, the codeword $\mathbf{c}'$ can be restored to its original form $\mathbf{c}$ by the ECC system.

In this work, based on Arcface [25], we address the problem using a well-designed feature transformation function and SP decoder. The feature transformation function uses feature quantization and binarization techniques to convert deep features into binary instances. To ensure security, a key is generated by a pseudorandom number generator (PRNG) and encoded into a codeword by an LDPC encoder [26]. We adopt the lifting factor $z = 10$, therefore the code length is $N = 52*10$. The message length is $K = 10*10$. In the end, XOR is applied to codeword and binary templates to generate the commitment. During the authentication phase, the de-committed codeword is obtained using the SP decoder. In the subsequent subsections, a detailed discussion of the feature transformation and XOR masking is presented.

3.2   Binarization Transformation

The feature transformation has several objectives: 1) state-of-the-art face models generate fixed-length and real-valued vectors as features, so it is necessary to convert them into binary strings suitable for ECC; 2) Maintain recognition ability and accuracy in the binary domain; 3) Given a specific LDPC code scheme, bridge the gap between bit error rates observed from binary features of the same user and the error correction capabilities provided by the LDPC code.

We adopt the best feature quantization and binarization approaches presented in [24,27], namely the quantization based on equally probable intervals and the linearly separable subcode binarization (LSSC) [28]. In order to convert the vector $\mathbf{v}$ into an integer vector $\mathbf{z}$, the following equation is utilized:

$$\mathbf{z} = QLuT(\mathbf{v}) \in \{1, q\}^{512}, \tag{1}$$

here, the function $QLuT$ uses quantization schemes based on equal probability intervals, as suggested by Rathgeb et al. [1] and Drozdowski et al. [2]. The first step is to calculate the probability density of each feature element. Then, the feature space for each element is divided into q integer-labeled equally-probable intervals, according to the obtained probability density. Thus, each element of the feature vector is distributed an integer in corresponds to the interval it belongs to. The resulting quantized feature vector $\mathbf{z}$ is then used to map to a binary feature vector $\mathbf{b} \in \{0, 1\}^{512*m}$ using a second lookup table:

$$\mathbf{b} = BLuT_\varphi(\mathbf{z}) \in \{0, 1\}^{512*m}. \tag{2}$$

In Equation (2), $BLuT$ represents the index-permuted LSSC, while φ refers to the permutation seed. Note that $m = q - 1$, represents the bit length of the binary entries in $BLuT$. Note that the L1 norm of the distance between two binary values generated by LSSC is equal to the distance between the two quantized values.

3.3   Error Gap Optimization

To minimize the intra-class Hamming distance, we raise a random masking strategy. This strategy is used to bridge the gap between the bit error rate obtained from the intra-class binary features and the system's error correction capabilities. In this approach, a binary vector $\mathbf{r}$ is generated as a random bit string, with κ percent of the bits being set to 0. Each binary vector is then bitwise AND with the mask $\mathbf{r}$ to produce the new binary vector:

$$\mathbf{b}' = \mathbf{b} \text{ AND } \mathbf{r}, \tag{3}$$

where $\mathbf{r} = \text{sgn}(\mathbf{u} - \kappa)$, and $\mathbf{u} \in \mathcal{U}(0, 1)^{512*m}$. The distance between any two samples after masking can be computed as follows:

$$\begin{aligned} \mathbf{D} &= ||(\mathbf{b}' \text{ AND } \mathbf{r}) \text{ XOR } (\mathbf{b} \text{ AND } \mathbf{r})||_1 \\ &= ||\mathbf{b}' \text{ XOR } \mathbf{b}||_1 - 0.5 * ||\mathbf{r}||_1, \end{aligned} \tag{4}$$

The intra-class and inter-class Hamming distances can be mediated by different masks $\mathbf{r}$. A proper mask $\mathbf{r}$ should result in a smaller intra-class distance within the error correction capability, while a larger inter-class distance beyond the error correction capability. We iteratively find the best κ that can lead to 95% of the inter-class distance after masking to be larger than a given threshold τ. In other word,

$$P(||\mathbf{b_i} \text{ XOR } \mathbf{b_j}||_1 - 0.5 \times ||\mathbf{r}||_1 > \tau) = 0.95, \tag{5}$$

where $\mathbf{b_i}$ and $\mathbf{b_j}$ are from different users.

Note that $\mathbf{r}$ is set for application-specific and can be exposed to the public. In effect, $\mathbf{r}$ can also be user-specific, and using a user-specific $\mathbf{r}$ would improve the performance but also needs extra security measures to protect the $\mathbf{r}$. On the other hand, raising the τ parameter can result in a zero FMR, but this leads to the consequence of a lower genuine match rate (GMR) or utility.

4 Experiments and Results

4.1 Feature Extractors and Datasets

In our experiment, we used the advanced pre-trained model Arcface [29] (resnet100 [30] trained on the ms1mv3 [31] dataset). The experiment focused on recognition performance on three mainstream benchmarks: LFW [32], CALFW [33], and AgeDB-30 [34]. LFW contains 13,233 face images from 5,749 different identities and was also used to build the CALFW dataset, which focuses on challenges related to face recognition, particularly adversarial robustness, and similar-looking faces. AgeDB comprises 16,488 images of 568 celebrities with a challenging subset called AgeDB-30, featuring identities with a 30-year age difference. Both LFW and AgeDB-30 datasets contain 3,000 genuine and 3,000 impostor comparisons for evaluating face recognition performance.

4.2 Ablation Studies

This section evaluates the recognition performance of binary features generated at various LSSC intervals q. By estimating the cosine distance of deep facial features, the comparison scores between deep facial feature pairs are obtained. The accuracy of the identification performance is evaluated based on standard protocols. Decidability (d') [35] is also used to indicate the divisibility of paired and unpaired[1] comparison scores. The d' is defined as

$$d' = \frac{|\mu_m - \mu_{nm}|}{\sqrt{\frac{1}{2}(\sigma_m^2 + \sigma_{nm}^2)}}, \tag{6}$$

where μ_m and μ_{nm} are the means of the paired and the unpaired comparison trials score distributions, and σ_m and σ_{nm} are their standard deviations, respectively. The greater the decidability values, the better the ability to distinguish between paired and unpaired comparison trial scores.

---

[1] Paired corresponds to intra-user, unpaired corresponds to inter-user, these terms are used interchangeably.

As shown in Table 1, consistent with [24,27], the LSSC can achieve comparable performance to the deep features in terms of accuracy. Dividing the feature space into larger intervals generally leads to better performance. The performance reaches a plateau quickly using more than eight intervals.

Table 1. Ablation study of feature transformation (LFW, Arcface).

	accuracy	d'	paired	unpaired
Deep features	99.82 ± 0.27	7.97	14.71 ± 5.11	49.88 ± 3.58
LSSC-2 (sign)	99.68 ± 0.34	6.40	24.65 ± 4.80	49.94 ± 2.86
LSSC-4	99.75 ± 0.30	6.64	21.18 ± 3.90	41.64 ± 1.95
LSSC-8	99.82 ± 0.27	6.70	19.28 ± 3.48	37.49 ± 1.64
LSSC-16	99.83 ± 0.24	6.71	18.22 ± 3.26	35.24 ± 1.50

The parameter τ in (5) is used to control the generation of the masking bits, and we test the accuracy of the $\mathbf{b}'$ after masking with $\tau = [0.05, 0.5]$. As shown in Fig. 1, the accuracy of CALFW improves according to the increase in τ. It can also be seen that the performance is largely preserved compared to deep features. For example, the bit masking operation on features from Arcface can achieve an accuracy similar to their deep features counterparts.

Next, we must decide which τ is the best for the SP decoder. Features of CALFW extracted from Arcface are adopted as the testing dataset, and the key retrieval performance in GMR and FMR is evaluated. The result is shown in Fig. 2. It can be seen that FMR decreases as τ increases, but the GMR will also drop. The τ that drives FMR only above 0.1% is selected to keep a balance between FMR and GMR. It can be seen that SP can earn a 0.13% FMR at $\tau = 0.24$. This τ is adopted for the best parameters for the SP decoder for all datasets and feature extractors subsequently.

Moreover, Fig. 3 shows the distributions, at each phase, of the paired and unpaired Hamming distances. It can be seen that the feature transformation using LSSC and random masking preserves the separation of paired and unpaired distributions. On the other hand, we can find that the random masking (+ LSSC-4 + mask) can decrease the Hamming distance to comply with the requirements of the LDPC. Consequently, the paired distances can be decreased to 15.64% on CALFW, which is within the error correction capability and suitable for the adopted LDPC. Meanwhile, the unpaired distance is decreased to 26.02% on CALFW, which is still beyond the error correction capability.

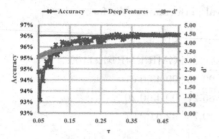

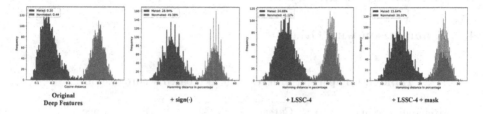

Fig. 1. Ablation study on τ concerning accuracy on transformed binary features (CALFW).

Fig. 2. Ablation study on τ concerning key retrieval accuracy (CALFW, 100 iterations).

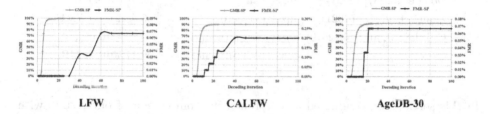

Fig. 3. Distribution of distances across different stages (CALFW).

Fig. 4. Key retrieval performance in GMR and FMR vs. decoding iterations.

4.3   Key Retrieval Performance of the Proposed Method

This section evaluates the performance under decoding iterations ranging from 1 to 100. The performance of different decoding strategies is shown in Fig. 4. We can observe that both GMR and FMR increase with decoding iterations. So, choosing the appropriate number of decoding iterations is crucial for system accuracy. Fewer iterations can lead to fewer FMR, while more iterations can lead to more GMR without overly compromising FMR. On the other hand, we observed that SP achieves favorable performance on LFW. Specifically, SP achieves a GMR of 99.33% (in Table 2) on Arcface in terms of GMR@0FMR.

In Table 2, we present the GMR and FMR values at 100 iterations (GMR|FMR@iter100 column). Under this setting, the GMR of CALFW and AgedDB30 can be improved significantly, while only slightly comprising on FMR. In comparison (SP-GMR@FMR0 vs. SP-GMR|FMR@iter100), Arcface

Table 2. Accuracy of key retrieval performance (Arcface).

Dataset	Deep Feat. GMR@FMR0	LSSC-4	SP	SP GMR|FMR@iter100
LFW	99.67	99.63	99.33	99.43|0.07
CALFW	91.53	91.13	85.27	90.43|0.20
AgedDB30	96.13	95.27	89.73	92.63|0.07
Average	95.78	95.34	91.44	–

can achieve 90.43% (85.27%) at FMR = 0.20% (0FMR), and 92.63% (89.73%) at FMR = 0.07% (0FMR).

4.4   Comparison with Others

Table 3. Comparison with relevant face-based secure systems.

Reference (year)	Category	Performance
Boddeti et al. [36] (2018)	homomorphic encryption	96.74%@0.1%FMR
Dong et al. [37] (2021)	fuzzy vault	Rank1 = 99.9%
Zhang et al. [38] (2021)	fuzzy extractor	30%@2.1e−7FMR
Gilkalaye et al. [16] (2019)	fuzzy commitment	36.94%@0.05%
Ours	fuzzy commitment	99.17%@0%FMR

In this section, we conducted a comprehensive comparison of our results with state-of-the-art secure face templates evaluated on LFW. Table 3 presents the performance of the proposed fuzzy commitment scheme with existing works on LFW. Compared to existing key generation schemes, our proposed approach outperforms them. The results demonstrate the effectiveness and superiority of our fuzzy commitment scheme in performance.

We would like to emphasize that the homomorphic encryption approach proposed in [36] is specifically designed for performing matching in the encryption domain. In contrast, the CNN approaches presented in [39] and [19] assign a unique binary code to each user during the enrollment phase, which is exclusively used for training the deep CNN. This means that re-training is required whenever a new user is added to the system, making these approaches impractical for real-world deployment.

5   Security Analysis

In our system, we ensure unlinkability and cancellability by generating a random key for each user during the enrollment process. This guarantees that once the

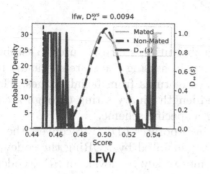
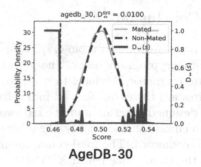

LFW   AgeDB-30

Fig. 5. Unlinkability evaluation.

stored commitment is compromised, a new commitment can be generated using a different random key, preserving the unlinkability property. Moreover, using different keys for different enrollments prevents information leakage from cross-matching attacks, where an adversary attempts to infer information by matching commitments from different applications.

In this section, we focus on evaluating the unlinkability property following a protocol outlined by [40]. The experiments were conducted using the SP parameters with Arcface on the LFW and AgeDB-30 datasets. A cross-matching attack is performed by comparing the binary commitments generated from the same person in different applications (with different $\mathbf{k}$). The adversary exploits the matching score distributions to determine whether the commitments belong to the same person. The matching distance of the same subject in different applications is referred to as the paired distance. In contrast, the matching distance of other subjects in various applications is referred to as the unpaired distance.

In [40], two distinct measures for linkability are defined: a local measure $D_{\leftrightarrow}(s) \in [0,1]$ and a global measure $D_{\leftrightarrow}^{sys}$. The local measure $D \leftrightarrow (s)$ evaluates the specific linkage scores s on a score-wise level. On the other hand, the global measure $D_{\leftrightarrow}^{sys} \in [0,1]$ assesses the unlinkability of the entire system and provides a standard for various systems, regardless of the score. A value of $D_{\leftrightarrow}^{sys} = 1$ indicates that the system is fully linkable for all scores of the paired subjects, meaning there is a high level of linkability among the commitments. Conversely, a value of $D_{\leftrightarrow}^{sys} = 0$ suggests that the system is fully unlinkable for all scores, indicating a high level of unlinkability among the commitments. The global measure $D_{\leftrightarrow}^{sys} = 0$, provides an overall evaluation of the system's unlinkability performance.

In evaluating our scheme, we compute the mated and Non-mated scores on the selected dataset among the commitments. The distributions of these scores are illustrated in Fig. 5. The results demonstrate that our scheme achieves good unlinkability, as indicated by the global measure $D_{\leftrightarrow}^{sys}$, which consistently reaches a value of 0.01 for all datasets. This signifies a high level of unlinkability among the commitments in our system.

6   Conclusion

This paper introduces a bio-cryptosystem that utilizes face features to establish a secure cryptographic key. The process involves using the state-of-the-art face feature extractor, Arcface, to generate face features from facial images. These features are then transformed into a fixed-length binary string through a carefully designed function and masked using a specific scheme.

To encode the secret key, the scheme incorporates LDPC to convert the key into a codeword. The final commitment is generated by XORing the codeword with the binary face features. When it comes to key retrieval, an SP decoder is used to decode the committed codeword and reconstruct the user's secret key.

The proposed bio-cryptosystem can be effectively applied in various key management scenarios, such as generating private keys for blockchain wallets and providing enhanced security for users. As a future direction, the authors suggest extending the proposed scheme to other biometric modalities and optimizing the execution efficiency, accuracy, and overall security even further.

Acknowledgments. This work was supported by the National Natural Science Foundation of China (Nos. 62376003, 62306003) and the Anhui Provincial Natural Science Foundation (No. 2308085MF200).

References

1. Yan, J., Blackwell, A., Anderson, R., Grant, A.: Password memorability and security: empirical results. IEEE Secur. Priv. **2**(5), 25–31 (2004)
2. Spafford, E.H.: OPUS: preventing weak password choices. Comput. Secur. **11**(3), 273–278 (1992)
3. Sandhya, M., Prasad, M.V.N.K.: Biometric template protection: a systematic literature review of approaches and modalities. In: Jiang, R., Al-maadeed, S., Bouridane, A., Crookes, D., Beghdadi, A. (eds.) Biometric Security and Privacy. SPST, pp. 323–370. Springer, Cham (2017). https://doi.org/10.1007/978-3-319-47301-7_14
4. EuropeanParliament, General Data Protection Regulation (GDPR). https://gdpr-info.eu/
5. Lei, J., Pei, Q., Wang, Y., Sun, W., Liu, X.: PRIVFACE: fast privacy-preserving face authentication with revocable and reusable biometric credentials. IEEE Trans. Dependable Secur. Comput. **19**, 3101–3112 (2021)
6. Walia, G.S., Aggarwal, K., Singh, K., Singh, K.: Design and analysis of adaptive graph based cancelable multi-biometrics approach. IEEE Trans. Dependable Secur. Comput. **19**, 54–66 (2020)
7. Xi, K., Hu, J.: Bio-cryptography. In: Stavroulakis, P., Stamp, M. (eds.) Handbook of Information and Communication Security, pp. 129–157. Springer, Heidelberg (2010). https://doi.org/10.1007/978-3-642-04117-4_7
8. Juels, A., Wattenberg, M.: A fuzzy commitment scheme. In: Proceedings of the 6th ACM Conference on Computer and Communications Security, ser. CCS 1999, ACM. New York, NY, USA, pp. 28–36. ACM (1999)
9. Hao, F., Anderson, R., Daugman, J.: Combining crypto with biometrics effectively. IEEE Trans. Comput. **55**(9), 1081–1088 (2006)

10. Kelkboom, E.J.C., Gökberk, B., Kevenaar, T.A.M., Akkermans, A.H.M., van der Veen, M.: "3D face": biometric template protection for 3D face recognition. In: Lee, S.-W., Li, S.Z. (eds.) ICB 2007. LNCS, vol. 4642, pp. 566–573. Springer, Heidelberg (2007). https://doi.org/10.1007/978-3-540-74549-5_60

11. Li, P., Yang, X., Qiao, H., Cao, K., Liu, E., Tian, J.: An effective biometric cryptosystem combining fingerprints with error correction codes. Expert Syst. Appl. **39**(7), 6562–6574 (2012)

12. Rathgeb, C., Uhl, A.: A survey on biometric cryptosystems and cancelable biometrics. EURASIP J. Inf. Secur. **2011**(1), 3 (2011)

13. Bringer, J., Chabanne, H., Cohen, G., Kindarji, B., Zémor, G.: Optimal iris fuzzy sketches. In: 2007 First IEEE International Conference on Biometrics: Theory, Applications, and Systems, pp. 1–6. IEEE (2007)

14. Chen, B., Chandran, V.: Biometric based cryptographic key generation from faces. In: 9th Biennial Conference of the Australian Pattern Recognition Society on Digital Image Computing Techniques and Applications, pp. 394–401. IEEE (2007)

15. Yang, W., et al.: Securing mobile healthcare data: a smart card based cancelable finger-vein bio-cryptosystem. IEEE Access **6**, 36939–36947 (2018)

16. Gilkalaye, B.P., Rattani, A., Derakhshani, R.: Euclidean-distance based fuzzy commitment scheme for biometric template security. In: 2019 7th International Workshop on Biometrics and Forensics (IWBF), pp. 1–6 (2019)

17. Dong, X., Jin, Z., Zhao, L., Guo, Z.: Bio can crypto: an LDPC coded biocryptosystem on fingerprint cancellable template. In: 2021 IEEE International Joint Conference on Biometrics, pp. 1–8. IEEE (2021)

18. Adamovic, S., Milosavljevic, M., Veinovic, M., Sarac, M., Jevremovic, A.: Fuzzy commitment scheme for generation of cryptographic keys based on iris biometrics. IET Biometrics **6**(2), 89–96 (2017)

19. Chen, L., Zhao, G., Zhou, J., Ho, A.T., Cheng, L.-M.: Face template protection using deep LDPC codes learning. IET Biometrics **8**(3), 190–197 (2019)

20. Phillips, P.J., et al.: Overview of the face recognition grand challenge. In: IEEE Computer Society Conference on Computer Vision and Pattern Recognition (CVPR 2005), vol. 1. pp, 947–954. IEEE (2005)

21. Phillips, P.J., Moon, H., Rizvi, S.A., Rauss, P.J.: The FERET evaluation methodology for face-recognition algorithms. IEEE Trans. Pattern Anal. Mach. Intell. **22**(10), 1090–1104 (2000)

22. Sim, T., Baker, S., Bsat, M.: The CMU pose, illumination, and expression (PIE) database. In: Proceedings of fifth IEEE International Conference on Automatic Face Gesture Recognition, pp. 53–58. IEEE (2002)

23. Georghiades, A.S., Belhumeur, P.N., Kriegman, D.J.: From few to many: illumination cone models for face recognition under variable lighting and pose. IEEE Trans. Pattern Anal. Mach. Intell. **23**(6), 643–660 (2001)

24. Rathgeb, C., Merkle, J., Scholz, J., Tams, B., Nesterowicz, V.: Deep face fuzzy vault: implementation and performance. Comput. Secur. **113**, 102539 (2022)

25. Deng, J., Guo, J., Xue, N., Zafeiriou, S.: ArcFace: additive angular margin loss for deep face recognition. In: Proceedings of the IEEE/CVF Conference on Computer Vision and Pattern Recognition, pp. 4690–4699 (2019)

26. Multiplexing and Channel Coding, Release 16. 3GPP Standard TS 38.212, V16.0.0 (2019)

27. Drozdowski, P., Struck, F., Rathgeb, C., Busch, C.: Benchmarking binarisation schemes for deep face templates. In:2018 25th IEEE International Conference on Image Processing, pp. 191–195. IEEE (2018)

28. Lim, M.-H., Teoh, A.B.J.: A novel encoding scheme for effective biometric discretization: linearly separable subcode. IEEE Trans. Pattern Anal. Mach. Intell. **35**(2), 300–313 (2012)

29. Dang, T.K., Truong, Q.C., Le, T.T.B., Truong, H.: Cancellable fuzzy vault with periodic transformation for biometric template protection. IET Biometrics **5**(3), 229–235 (2016)

30. He, K., Zhang, X., Ren, S., Sun, J.: Deep residual learning for image recognition. In: Proceedings of the IEEE Conference on Computer Vision and Pattern Recognition, pp. 770–778 (2016)

31. Deng, J., Guo, J., Zhang, D., Deng, Y., Lu, X., Shi, S.: Lightweight face recognition challenge. In: Proceedings of the IEEE/CVF International Conference on Computer Vision Workshops (2019)

32. Huang, G.B., Mattar, M., Berg, T., Learned-Miller, E.: Labeled faces in the wild: a database for studying face recognition in unconstrained environments. In: Workshop on Faces in Real-Life Images: Detection, Alignment, and Recognition (2008)

33. Zheng, T., Deng, W., Hu, J.: Cross-age LFW: a database for studying cross-age face recognition in unconstrained environments. arXiv preprint arXiv:1708.08197 (2017)

34. Moschoglou, S., Papaioannou, A., Sagonas, C., Deng, J., Kotsia, I., Zafeiriou, S.: AgeDB: the first manually collected, in-the-wild age database. In: Proceedings of the IEEE Conference on Computer Vision and Pattern Recognition Workshops, pp. 51–59 (2017)

35. Daugman, J.: Biometric decision landscapes. University of Cambridge, Computer Laboratory, Technical report (2000)

36. Boddeti, V.N.: Secure face matching using fully homomorphic encryption. In: 2018 IEEE 9th International Conference on Biometrics Theory, Applications and Systems (BTAS), pp. 1–10. IEEE (2018)

37. Dong, X., Kim, S., Jin, Z., Hwang, J.Y., Cho, S., Teoh, A.B.J.: A secure chaffless fuzzy vault for face identification system. ACM Trans. Multimedia Comput. Commun. Appl. **17**, 1–22 (2021)

38. Zhang, K., Cui, H., Yu, Y.: Facial template protection via lattice-based fuzzy extractors. Cryptology ePrint Archive (2021)

39. Kumar Jindal, A., Chalamala, S., Kumar Jami, S.: Face template protection using deep convolutional neural network. In: Proceedings of the IEEE Conference on Computer Vision and Pattern Recognition Workshops, pp. 462–470 (2018)

40. Gomez-Barrero, M., Galbally, J., Rathgeb, C., Busch, C.: General framework to evaluate unlinkability in biometric template protection systems. IEEE Trans. Inf. Forensics Secur. **13**(6), 1406–1420 (2017)

Homomorphic Encryption-Based Privacy Protection for Palmprint Recognition

Qiang Guo[1], Huikai Shao[1]([✉]), Chengcheng Liu[1], Jing Wan[1], and Dexing Zhong[1,2,3]

[1] School of Automation Science and Engineering, Xi'an Jiaotong University, Xi'an 710049, Shaanxi, China
shaohuikai@xjtu.edu.cn
[2] Pazhou Lab, Guangzhou 510335, China
[3] Research Institute of Xi'an Jiaotong University, Hangzhou 311215, Zhejiang, China

Abstract. Palmprint recognition is a promising biometric technology. Currently, the research on palmprint recognition focuses on the topic of feature extraction and matching. However, due to the characteristic that biometric traits cannot be modified at will, how to secure and protect the privacy of palmprint recognition is a neglected and valuable topic. In this paper, we propose a privacy-preserving framework for palmprint recognition based on homomorphic encryption. Specially, for any given eligible palmprint recognition network, it is encrypted layer by layer to obtain both image key and network key. Particularly, the introduced homomorphic encryption strategy does not cause any loss of recognition accuracy, which ensures the wide applicability of the proposed method. In addition, it greatly reduces the risk of exposing plaintext images and model parameters, thus circumventing potential attacks against data and models. Adequate experiments on constrained and unconstrained palmprint databases verify the effectiveness of our method.

Keyword: Palmprint recognition · Homomorphic encryption · Image key

1 Introduction

In recent years, biometric technologies have developed rapidly. Face recognition [1] and fingerprint recognition [2] are widely used in various industries. Due to its rich texture information, contactless capture and high privacy, palmprint recognition has also gained widespread attention [3]. Currently, privacy and security issue is one of the key problems that need to be solved in palmprint recognition from theory to application. Image theft and attacks against recognition models are the main attack methods, both of which can cause biometric systems to work incorrectly. Biometric data is often associated to personal information, and mistaken recognition results will pose a significant threat to property of user. Therefore, protecting palmprint image and model is an important topic for privacy protection.

In the past few years, many algorithms for biometric image encryption have been proposed. Conventional image encryption schemes cannot work without first decrypting them [4]. So the current approaches on biometric privacy security mostly focus around homomorphic encryption [5] and federated learning [6]. However, these methods still have the following problems: (1) biometric images are stored in plaintext in servers; (2) encrypted biometric systems aim to strike the balance between security and accuracy. To address these issues, we propose a palmprint image encryption and recognition framework based on homomorphic encryption.

The contributions can be briefly summarized as follows:

(1) An effective privacy-preserving framework is proposed for palmprint recognition. Homomorphic encryption is incorporated with palmprint recognition. The private information in the palmprint image is encrypted and invisible, which avoids attacks against the images.
(2) The specific key network can perform sophisticated inference on the encrypted palmprint images, and there is no degradation in recognition accuracy compared with the plaintext system.
(3) Experiments are conducted on several palmprint databases with constrained and unconstrained benchmarks, which show the effectiveness of the method.

2   Related Work

2.1   Palmprint Recognition

Palmprint recognition has gained the attention of researchers as a secure and friendly biometric identification technique. Before the deep learning theory was proposed, palmprint recognition methods were mainly classified as texture-based, code-based, and subspace-based methods [7]. Wu et al. [8] extracted a stable line feature consisting of main lines and wrinkles to describe the palmprint image. Zhong et al. [9] applied Deep Hash Network (DHN) to convert palmprint images into distinguished binary codes for recognition. As research progresses, many attacks against deep learning models are emerging. To solve the potential threats, we propose a convolutional network encryption method to improve the system security.

2.2   Homomorphic Encryption

The most widely used homomorphic encryption concept developed so far is the fully homomorphic encryption. Xiang et al. [10] proposed a privacy-preserving online face authentication system based on a fully homomorphic encryption scheme. Sun et al. [11] designed a face feature ciphertext recognition method by combining automorphism mapping and Hamming distance. However, these feature-level homomorphic encryption algorithms are difficult to prevent replay attacks. Byrne et al. [12] designed a KeyNet method for privacy protection of images in modern cameras. Inspired by this idea, this paper proposes an image-level homomorphic encryption algorithm to protect image privacy in palmprint recognition.

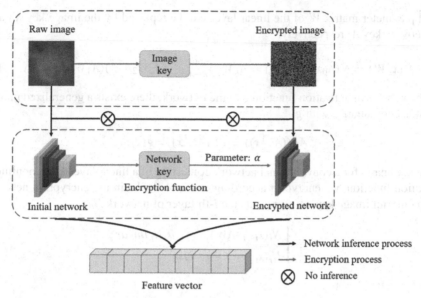

Fig. 1. Palmprint recognition framework based on image-level homomorphic encryption.

3   Method

As shown in Fig. 1, we propose a privacy-preserving framework for palmprint recognition based on image-level homomorphic encryption. The initial network is first passed through the encryption function to obtain the encrypted network. In the process of network encryption, the image key is gained, and the raw palmprint images can be converted to the encrypted images. Besides, the encryption function contains the privacy parameter α. A larger α means deeper encryption.

3.1   Image-Level Homomorphic Encryption

A secure encryption framework should assume the following public and private information: (1) the image key is secret and controlled by the administrator [12]; (2) the source convolutional network N is secret and the encrypted network is public; (3) the encrypted palmprint images are public, and the original images can only be recovered by a private image key.

Based on the above idea, we choose generalized doubly stochastic matrix as the basis of the encryption function.

For a network $N(x)$ with all linear layers, it can be simplified to the form of a product of weight matrices for each layer:

$$N(x; W) = \prod_k W_k x, \tag{1}$$

where k represents the number of network layers, W_k represents the network weight matrix of the k-th layer, and x is the input. Given a doubly stochastic matrix A, the input

x and parameter matrix W of the linear layer can be replaced by the image key A_0 and the network key A_i respectively:

$$\hat{N}(x; W) = N(A_0 x; AWA^{-1}) = A_k W_k A_{k-1}^{-1} \cdots (A_2 W_2 A_1^{-1})(A_1 W_1 A_0^{-1}) A_0 x. \quad (2)$$

For the non-linear activation function g in the network, there exists a generalized matrix A that is commutative with g:

$$Ag((A^{-1}x)) = g(AA^{-1}x) = g(x). \quad (3)$$

In summary, for a convolutional network consisting of a linear layer and a nonlinear excitation function, we encrypt it according to Eq. 4 to obtain the encryption network and palmprint image key. N_i represents the i-th layer of network $N(x)$:

$$N_i = \begin{cases} N_i(x_{i-1}, AWA_{i-1}^{-1}) & \text{if } N_i \ linear \\ N_i(x_{i-1}) & else \end{cases}. \quad (4)$$

3.2 Metric Learning-Based Palmprint Recognition

Deep metric learning determines identity by calculating the distance between palmprint images. So the direction of model optimization is to reduce the distance of intra-class samples and increase the distance of inter-class samples. In this paper, triplet loss [13] and arcface loss [14] are applied as the loss functions.

The inputs of triplet loss are anchor sample x_a, positive sample x_p and negative sample x_n. The optimization strategy is to constrain the distance between the anchor and negative samples to be larger than that between the anchor and positive samples by a threshold m:

$$L_{triplet} = max(D(x_a, x_p) - D(x_a, x_n) + m, 0), \quad (5)$$

where $D(\cdot)$ is the distance calculation function. In this paper, m is empirically set to 0.8.

Arcface loss is a loss function based on an improvement of softmax loss:

$$L_{arcface} = -\frac{1}{N} \sum_{i=1}^{N} \log \frac{e^{s(cos(\theta_{yi}+m))}}{e^{s(cos(\theta_{yi}+m))} + \sum_{j=1,j\neq y_i}^{n} e^{scos\theta_j}}, \quad (6)$$

where n and N represent the number of classes and batch size, and y_i represents the label of the i-th palmprint image. θ_j is the angle between the weight W_j and feature x_i of the i-th sample. θ_{yi} is the target optimization angle, and m is the optimization margin. In this paper, s and m are set to 0.5 and 30 based on experience.

4 Experiments and Results

4.1 Dataset

XJTU-UP palmprint database adopts an unconstrained collection method to acquire palmprint images. The organizers used five smartphones to capture the hand images of 100 volunteers under two lighting conditions. The brands of the mobile phones include Samsung (denoted as S), LG (denoted as L), Xiaomi (denoted as M), Huawei (denoted as H), and iPhone (denoted as I). The two lighting conditions include natural light (denoted as N) and lighting environment (denoted as F). Therefore, the whole database can be divided into ten sub-databases, *i.e.*, SN, SF, LN, LF, MN, MF, HN, HF, IN, and IF. Some typical ROI images are shown in Fig. 2.

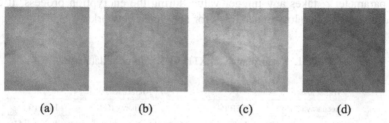

(a)   (b)   (c)   (d)

Fig. 2. Typical ROI samples in the XJTU-UP database. (a) is in HF, (b) is in HN, (c) is in IF, and (d) is in IN.

PolyU Multispectral Palmprint database is captured in four spectrum conditions (Blue, Green, Red, and Near-Infrared). The whole database can be divided into four sub-databases: Blue, Green, Red, and NIR. There are 6,000 palmprint images in each sub-database. Some typical ROI images are shown in Fig. 3.

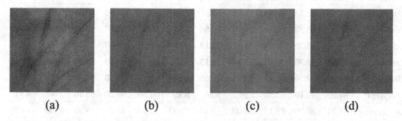

(a)   (b)   (c)   (d)

Fig. 3. ROI samples of PolyU Multispectral Palmprint database. (a) is in Blue, (b) is in Green, (c) is in NIR, and (d) is in Red. (Color figure online)

4.2 Implementation Details

In experiments, to illustrate the generality of our method, three network structures are adopted: LeNet-5 [15], the self-designed 11-layer network (ConvNet), and AlexNet [16]. For each database, the palmprint images are divided into two parts according to a 3:1

ratio: the training set and the test set. In this paper, accuracy and Equal Error Rate (EER) are utilized as evaluation indicators of performance.

The experiments are implemented using the Pytorch framework on NVIDIA GPU RTX 2080 SUPER and CPU i7-3.0 GHz processors. The initial learning rate is set to 0.0001 for training with epoch 40, batch size 32, and Adam optimizer.

4.3 Experimental Results

4.3.1 Performance of Encrypted Network

The performance of three networks before and after encryption in XJTU-UP database and PolyU Multispectral Palmprint database are shown in Tables 1 and 2. The abbreviations of "Alex" and "Conv" stand for AlexNet and ConvNet, respectively. * indicates that the privacy parameter α takes any integer value during the encryption process. It can be observed that there is no loss in accuracy for encrypted networks.

Table 1. Performance on XJTU-UP palmprint database

Database		Triplet loss						Arcface loss					
		Accuaray (%)			EER (%)			Accuaray (%)			EER (%)		
		LeNet	Alex	Conv	LeNet	Alex	Conv	LeNet	Alex	Conv	LeNet	Alex	Conv
HF	Unencrypted	80.50	90.80	93.70	18.98	9.64	6.27	90.10	92.10	92.00	9.82	8.13	8.44
	Encrypted*	80.50	90.80	93.70	18.98	9.64	6.27	90.10	92.10	92.00	9.82	8.13	8.44
HN	Unencrypted	74.40	80.30	91.20	26.62	18.80	8.84	82.70	90.20	88.30	18.18	10.27	12.53
	Encrypted*	74.40	80.30	91.20	26.62	18.80	8.84	82.70	90.20	88.30	18.18	10.27	12.53
IF	Unencrypted	88.20	93.10	94.40	11.47	7.16	6.04	94.00	94.10	92.90	6.09	6.31	7.33
	Encrypted*	88.20	93.10	94.40	11.47	7.16	6.04	94.00	94.10	92.90	6.09	6.31	7.33
IN	Unencrypted	71.20	87.10	94.70	29.38	13.29	5.60	80.70	88.10	85.10	18.84	12.44	16.04
	Encrypted*	71.20	87.10	94.70	29.38	13.29	5.60	80.70	88.10	85.10	18.84	12.44	16.04
LF	Unencrypted	84.90	93.20	92.80	14.98	6.36	7.38	91.10	95.50	89.00	8.53	4.76	11.91
	Encrypted*	84.90	93.20	92.80	14.98	6.36	7.38	91.10	95.50	89.00	8.53	4.76	11.91
LN	Unencrypted	75.30	85.70	90.10	25.47	14.13	10.31	86.50	90.00	88.90	13.20	10.36	11.64
	Encrypted*	75.30	85.70	90.10	25.47	14.13	10.31	86.50	90.00	88.90	13.20	10.36	11.64
MF	Unencrypted	87.20	92.10	93.50	12.62	8.36	6.89	92.50	95.50	94.20	7.96	4.71	6.27
	Encrypted*	87.20	92.10	93.50	12.62	8.36	6.89	92.50	95.50	94.20	7.96	4.71	6.27
MN	Unencrypted	75.70	86.50	89.10	24.00	13.47	11.33	87.60	88.60	85.90	13.11	11.29	15.16
	Encrypted*	75.70	86.50	89.10	24.00	13.47	11.33	87.60	88.60	85.90	13.11	11.29	15.16
SF	Unencrypted	88.40	92.50	94.00	11.29	7.20	6.40	90.40	95.80	92.20	9.24	4.53	8.22
	Encrypted*	88.40	92.50	94.00	11.29	7.20	6.40	90.40	95.80	92.20	9.24	4.53	8.22
SN	Unencrypted	74.70	82.70	89.60	24.80	17.64	10.13	84.60	87.80	88.90	16.44	11.91	11.64
	Encrypted*	74.70	82.70	89.60	24.80	17.64	10.13	84.60	87.80	88.90	16.44	11.91	11.64

Table 2. Performance on PolyU Multispectral Palmprint database

Database		Triplet loss						Arcface loss					
		Accuaray (%)			EER (%)			Accuaray (%)			EER (%)		
		LeNet	Alex	Conv	LeNet	Alex	Conv	LeNet	Alex	Conv	LeNet	Alex	Conv
Blue	Unencrypted	92.60	94.60	95.90	7.47	5.70	3.92	97.10	98.60	97.00	3.13	1.28	3.19
	Encrypted*	92.60	94.60	95.90	7.47	5.70	3.92	97.10	98.60	97.00	3.13	1.28	3.19
Green	Unencrypted	91.40	93.10	95.10	9.01	6.85	5.18	96.20	98.80	97.10	4.25	1.27	3.01
	Encrypted*	91.40	93.10	95.10	9.01	6.85	5.18	96.20	98.80	97.10	4.25	1.27	3.01
NIR	Unencrypted	90.60	95.10	97.00	9.79	4.79	2.84	97.30	99.20	96.70	2.63	0.98	2.92
	Encrypted*	90.60	95.10	97.00	9.79	4.79	2.84	97.30	99.20	96.70	2.63	0.98	2.92
Red	Unencrypted	90.40	95.10	96.00	10.04	4.86	4.06	97.30	98.60	97.10	2.61	1.47	2.93
	Encrypted*	90.40	95.10	96.00	10.04	4.86	4.06	97.30	98.60	97.10	2.61	1.47	2.93

4.3.2 Performance of Encrypted Image

Typical examples of encrypted images are shown in Fig. 4. The encryption method can accomplish personalized encryption for both RGB and grayscale spaces, and the encrypted images cannot be interpreted by other image keys.

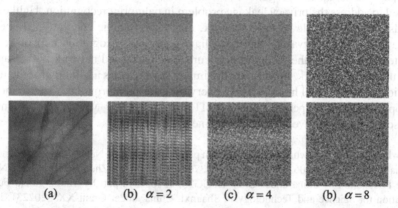

| (a) | (b) $\alpha = 2$ | (c) $\alpha = 4$ | (b) $\alpha = 8$ |

Fig. 4. Examples of encrypted images. (a) is the original image, (b) (c) (d) are the encrypted images of (a) under different privacy parameter α.

4.3.3 Hyperparameter Tuning

We use LeNet-5 network and Arcface loss on PolyU Multispectral Palmprint database to explore the effect of privacy parameter α on the performance of cryptographic network, and the results are as shown in Table 3. In the cases of mismatch between the network key and image key, when α is relatively small (such as 2 and 4), the decrease in recognition accuracy of cryptographic network is not yet significant, from 97.01% to 84.92%. But when it is taken as 8, the recognition accuracy decreases to 67.54%. It can be seen that with the increase of α, the privacy and security of palmprint image and system are also increasing, while the network parameters will also increase. Therefore, in the actual palmprint recognition system, appropriate privacy parameters should be chosen.

Table 3. The impact of privacy parameter α on network performance

Network State	α	Network parameters(M)	Keys	Accuarcy(%)
Unencrypted	–	54.79	–	97.01
Encrypted	2	54.81	No paired	95.23
Encrypted	4	54.89	No paired	84.92
Encrypted	8	59.84	No paired	67.54
Encrypted	8	59.84	Paired	97.01

5 Conclusion

In this paper, a palmprint recognition framework based on homomorphic encryption is proposed to address the privacy leakage problem in palmprint recognition. Unlike other mehtods towards a single specific network, our homomorphic encryption framework is more flexible and pervasive: any compliant palmprint recognition network can be encrypted. Meanwhile, the recognition accuracy of encrypted network is the same as that of the source network. In addition, the image key provides a solution for the implementation of image-level homomorphic encryption for palmprint data. The framework we proposed is fully experimented on XJTU-UP and PolyU Multispectral Palmprint databases, and competitive results are obtained.

Acknowledgments. This work was supported in part by the National Natural Science Foundation of China under Grant 62206218 and Grant 62376211, in part by Zhejiang Provincial Natural Science Foundation of China under Grant LTGG23F030006, in part by Young Talent Fund of Association for Science and Technology in Shaanxi, China, under Grant XXJS202231, in part by the Xi'an Science and Technology Project under Grant 23ZCKCGZH0001, and in part by Fundamental Research Funds for the Central Universities under Grant xzy012023061.

References

1. Liu, W., Kou, K.I., Miao, J., Cai, Z.: Quaternion scalar and vector norm decomposition: quaternion PCA for color face recognition. IEEE Trans. Image Process. **32**, 446–457 (2023)
2. Zhu, Y., Yin, X., Hu, J.: FingerGAN: a constrained fingerprint generation scheme for latent fingerprint enhancement. IEEE Trans. Pattern Anal. Mach. Intell. **45**(7), 8358–8371 (2023)
3. Shao, H., Zhong, D.: Multi-target cross-dataset palmprint recognition via distilling from multi-teacher. IEEE Trans. Instrum. Meas. **72**, 1–14 (2023)

4. Iezzi, M.: Practical privacy-preserving data science with homomorphic encryption: an overview. In: 8th IEEE International Conference on Big Data, pp. 3979–3988. IEEE, Atlanta (2020)
5. Kim, D., Guyot, C.: Optimized privacy-preserving CNN inference with fully homomorphic encryption. IEEE Trans. Inf. Forensics Secur. 18, 2175–2187 (2023)
6. Bugshan, N., Khalil, I., Rahman, M.S., Atiquzzaman, M., Yi, X., Badsha, S.: Toward trustworthy and privacy-preserving federated deep learning service framework for industrial internet of things. IEEE Trans. Ind. Inform. 19(2), 1535–1547 (2023)
7. Zhong, D., Du, X., Zhong, K.: Decade progress of palmprint recognition: a brief survey. Neurocomputing 328, 16–28 (2019)
8. Wu, X., Zhang, D., Wang, K.: Palm line extraction and matching for personal authentication. IEEE Trans. Syst. Man Cybern. Part A 36(5), 978–987 (2006)
9. Zhong, D., Shao, H., Du, X.: A hand-based multi-biometrics via deep hashing network and biometric graph matching. IEEE Trans. Inf. Forensics Secur. 14(12), 3140–3150 (2019)
10. Xiang, C., Tang, C., Cai, Y., Xu, Q.: Privacy-preserving face recognition with outsourced computation. Soft. Comput. 20(9), 3735–3744 (2016)
11. Sun, D., et al.: Face security authentication system based on deep learning and homomorphic encryption. Secur. Commun. Netw. 2022, 1–8 (2022)
12. Byrne, J., DeCann, B., Bloom, S.: Key-nets: optical transformation convolutional networks for privacy preserving vision sensors. In: 31st British Machine Vision Conference, pp. 1–26. Springer, UK (2020). https://doi.org/10.48550/arXiv.2008.04469
13. Hoffer, E., Ailon, N.: Deep metric learning using triplet network. In: Feragen, A., Pelillo, M., Loog, M. (eds.) SIMBAD 2015. LNCS, vol. 9370, pp. 84–92. Springer, Cham (2015). https://doi.org/10.1007/978-3-319-24261-3_7
14. Deng, J., Guo, J., Yang, J., Xue, N., Kotsia, I., Zafeiriou, S.: ArcFace: additive angular margin loss for deep face recognition. IEEE Trans. Pattern Anal. Mach. Intell. 44(10), 5962–5979 (2022)
15. LeCun, Y., Bottou, L., Bengio, Y., Haffner, P.: Gradient-based learning applied to document recognition. Proc. IEEE 86(11), 2278–2324 (1998)
16. Krizhevsky, A., Sutskever, I., Hinton, G.E.: ImageNet classification with deep convolutional neural networks. Commun. ACM 60(6), 84–90 (2017)

Medical and Other Applications

Generative AI Enables the Detection of Autism Using EEG Signals

Yisheng Li[1,2], Iman Yi Liao[3], Ning Zhong[4], Furukawa Toshihiro[4], Yishan Wang[1], and Shuqiang Wang[1(✉)]

[1] Shenzhen Institutes of Advanced Technology, Chinese Academy of Sciences, Beijing, China
sq.wang@siat.ac.cn
[2] Southern University of Science and Technology, Shenzhen, China
[3] University of Nottingham Malaysia Campus, Semenyih, Malaysia
[4] Maebashi Institute of Technology, Maebashi, Japan

Abstract. In disease detection, generative models for data augmentation offer a potential solution to the challenges posed by limited high-quality electroencephalogram (EEG) data. The study proposes a temporal-spatial feature-aware denoising diffusion probabilistic model (DDPM), termed TF-DDPM, as an EEG time-series augmentation framework for autism research. The module for predicting noise is CCA-UNet based on the channel correlation-based attention (CCA) mechanism, which considers the spatial and temporal correlation between channels, and uses depthwise separable convolution instead of traditional convolution, thereby suppressing the interference from irrelevant channels. Visualization and binary classification results on synthetic signals indicate that proposed method generates higher quality synthetic data compared to Generative Adversarial Networks (GAN) and DDPM.

Keywords: electroencephalogram (EEG) · Denoising Diffusion Probability Model (DDPM) · synthetic data

1 Introduction

Medical images have notably benefited from the advancements in deep learning techniques, leading to transformative applications in areas such as radiology, psychiatric diagnostics, and neuropathology [3,16,20]. EEG, which captures the electrical activity of the cerebral cortex by placing electrodes on the scalp, provides medical data with a high temporal resolution. Distinct EEG patterns are observed in individuals with neurodevelopmental disorders, like Autism Spectrum Disorder (ASD), when compared to neurotypical individuals. Such differences underscore the potential of EEG as a valuable diagnostic instrument for neural disorders [4–6].

However, the scarcity of high-quality medical data has become a limiting factor for the performance of deep learning models. These challenges manifest in various ways: an inability to achieve both high temporal and spatial resolutions, incomplete data information, and insufficient training data, etc. An

W. Jia et al. (Eds.): CCBR 2023, LNCS 14463, pp. 375–384, 2023.
https://doi.org/10.1007/978-981-99-8565-4_35

increasing number of data augmentation studies are being proposed to address these issues, with GAN being one of the most widely applied and technologically advanced methods [7–11]. GAN and its variants have been widely adopted in medical images augmentation, such as Magnetic Resonance Imaging (MRI) and Positron Emission Tomography (PET) Image, as well as in the fusion of multi-modal images [12–15,28,29]. Their potential is further realized in the domain of EEG data augmentation, particularly for artifact removal, imputation of missing sequences, and data expansion [1,2,17–20,33–35]. Nevertheless, the stability of GAN training and the issue of mode collapse remain research challenges [21].

A novel generative model, the Diffusion Model, offers more stable training and diversified data generation. It has been proven effective in image generation [22], and its potential application for EEG data augmentation is garnering increasing interest [23,24]. A noteworthy approach involves utilizing the EEGWave sub-model to predict noise, thereby eliminating artifacts in the synthetic data [25,31]. Currently, the majority of augmentation studies tend more towards converting EEG time series into spectral images, while the potential of frameworks that directly utilize time series as input has not been fully explored [30,32,35].

In this context, building upon DDPM, we introduce a novel model, TF-DDPM, designed to generate synthetic EEG data for autism research. The model employs EEG time series as input and utilizes a submodule, CCA-UNet, which integrates the CCA mechanism, to predict noise. The CCA mechanism, an enhancement of the self-attention mechanism, is considered a point-wise convolution method and, when combined with channel-wise convolution techniques, replaces the conventional inter-channel convolution. By considering the temporal and spatial correlations between various EEG channels, proposed method amplifies contributions from correlated channels while mitigating interference from uncorrelated ones. In comparison to WGAN-GP and DDPM, the synthetic signals generated by proposed model exhibits closer resemblance to real signals, both temporally and spatially. We validate this through visual interpretations and binary classification results between ASD and Typical Development (TD) cases.

2   Method

2.1   TF-DDPM

The TF-DDPM [22] is depicted in Fig. 1. At each time step t, a Gaussian-distributed noise ϵ_t with scale β_t is added to the original time series:

$$\mathbf{x}_t = \sqrt{\alpha_t}\mathbf{x}_{t-1} + \sqrt{\beta_t}\epsilon_t, \quad where \quad \alpha_t = 1 - \beta_t \tag{1}$$

After T steps, the original data $\mathbf{x}_0$ is transformed into noise data $\mathbf{x}_T$ that follows the standard Gaussian distribution. The process progressively transforms the distribution $q(\mathbf{x}_0)$ into $q(\mathbf{x}_T)$:

$$q(\mathbf{x}_T) = q(\mathbf{x}_0) \prod_{t=1}^{T} q(\mathbf{x}_t|\mathbf{x}_{t-1}), \quad where \quad q(\mathbf{x}_t|\mathbf{x}_{t-1}) = \mathcal{N}(\mathbf{x}_t; \sqrt{\alpha_t}\mathbf{x}_{t-1}, \beta_t\mathbf{I}) \tag{2}$$

A new $\mathbf{x}_T$ is initially sampled from $\mathcal{N}(\mathbf{0}, \mathbf{I})$. Then, the intractable posterior distribution $q(\mathbf{x}_{t-1}|\mathbf{x}_t)$ is approximated by $p_\theta(\mathbf{x}_{t-1}|\mathbf{x}_t)$, allowing the derivation of $p_\theta(\mathbf{x}_0)$, which in turn generates new data $\mathbf{x}_0$ that follows the same distribution as the original input. The optimization objective of maximizing the likelihood distribution $p_\theta(\mathbf{x}_0)$ can be rewritten in the following form via variational lower bound inference:

$$\max p_\theta(\mathbf{x}_0) = \min \mathbb{E}_q \left[\sum_{t=2}^{T} D_{KL}(q(\mathbf{x}_{t-1}|\mathbf{x}_t, \mathbf{x}_0) \parallel p_\theta(\mathbf{x}_{t-1}|\mathbf{x}_t)) \right] \tag{3}$$

Both $q(\mathbf{x}_{t-1}|\mathbf{x}_t, \mathbf{x}_0)$ and $p_\theta(\mathbf{x}_{t-1}|\mathbf{x}_t)$ are assumed to follow a Gaussian distribution:

$$q(\mathbf{x}_{t-1}|\mathbf{x}_t, \mathbf{x}_0) = \mathcal{N}(\mathbf{x}_{t-1}; \tilde{\mu}(\mathbf{x}_t, \mathbf{x}_0), \tilde{\beta}_t \mathbf{I}) \tag{4}$$

$$p_\theta(\mathbf{x}_{t-1}|\mathbf{x}_t) = \mathcal{N}(\mathbf{x}_{t-1}; \tilde{\mu}_\theta(\mathbf{x}_t, \mathbf{x}_0), \tilde{\beta}_t \mathbf{I}) \tag{5}$$

$$where \quad \tilde{\mu}(\mathbf{x}_t, \mathbf{x}_0) = \frac{1}{\sqrt{\alpha_t}}(\mathbf{x}_t - \frac{1-\alpha_t}{\sqrt{1-\bar{\alpha}_t}} \epsilon_t)$$

$$\tilde{\mu}_\theta(\mathbf{x}_t, \mathbf{x}_0) = \frac{1}{\sqrt{\alpha_t}}(\mathbf{x}_t - \frac{1-\alpha_t}{\sqrt{1-\bar{\alpha}_t}} \epsilon_\theta(\mathbf{x}_t, t, \mathbf{p}))$$

$$\tilde{\beta}_t = \frac{\beta_t(1-\bar{\alpha}_{t-1})}{1-\bar{\alpha}_t}$$

$$\bar{\alpha}_t = \alpha_1 \alpha_2 \cdots \alpha_t$$

where $\epsilon_\theta(\mathbf{x}_t, t, \mathbf{p})$ represents the predicted value of the noise ϵ_t, and $\mathbf{p}$ is the Pearson correlation coefficient tensor $PCMs$ introduced in Fig. 2. Consequently, the optimization objective is equivalent to minimizing the discrepancy between the two noises, as

$$D_{KL}(q(\mathbf{x}_{t-1}|\mathbf{x}_t, \mathbf{x}_0) \parallel p_\theta(\mathbf{x}_{t-1}|\mathbf{x}_t)) \propto \|\epsilon_t - \epsilon_\theta(\mathbf{x}_t, t, \mathbf{p})\|^2 \tag{6}$$

Therefore, the formula for the reverse process is given by:

$$\mathbf{x}_{t-1} = \frac{1}{\sqrt{\alpha_t}}(\mathbf{x}_t - \frac{1-\alpha_t}{\sqrt{1-\bar{\alpha}_t}} \epsilon_\theta(\mathbf{x}_t, t, \mathbf{p})) + \frac{\beta_t(1-\bar{\alpha}_{t-1})}{1-\bar{\alpha}_t}\mathbf{z}$$

$$where \quad \mathbf{z} \sim \mathcal{N}(\mathbf{0}, \mathbf{I}) \tag{7}$$

2.2   CCA-Unet

The CCA-UNet is employed for the prediction of noise, denoted as $\epsilon_\theta(\mathbf{x}_t, t, \mathbf{p})$. This framework is an enhancement of the UNet architecture used in the DDPM as presented in reference [22], as illustrated in Fig. 2. The primary components of the entire structure encompass three Down modules for the downsampling process and three Up modules for the upsampling process. Each Down module is

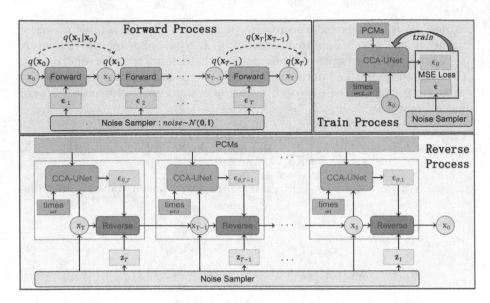

Fig. 1. The architecture of TF-DDPM. Three sections show the forward process, train process, and reverse process, respectively.

composed of two time embedding (Embed) blocks, one channel correlation-based attention (CCA) block, and a common convolution (Conv) block. In contrast, each Up module consists of two Embed blocks, one CCA block, one upsampling (Samp) block, and a Conv block. The Embed block also utilizes the CCA, which is treated as a point-wise convolution.

The UNet architecture integrates a multi-head attention mechanism. The self-attention query Q and key-value pairs (K, V) are directly derived by applying a linear transformation to the input X. In the CCA variant, the scalp electrode distribution with 129 electrodes is initially transformed into a 17×17 matrix. Only the elements representing the electrodes of C (either 125 or 126) channels are retained, with their values being their channel indices. All other elements are set to zero, for instance, the element denoting the reference electrode Cz.

Subsequently, the Pearson correlation coefficients between the C channels of N samples are computed, yielding the Pearson Correlation Matrix tensor, denoted as $PCMs \in \mathbb{R}^{N \times C \times 17 \times 17}$. This tensor is treated as an image and serves as an additional input within the CCA block. Within the CCA, the query $Q \in \mathbb{R}^{N \times C_{in} \times C}$ and the key $K \in \mathbb{R}^{N \times C_{out} \times C}$ are obtained by executing a two-dimensional convolution on $PCMs$, thereby transforming the 17×17 electrode distribution into a vector of length C, where C_{in} and C_{out} represent the input and output channel numbers, respectively. The $PCMs$ inherently depict the inter-channel correlations. Given that the convolution process modifies the channel number, we convert the C channels into a two-dimensional matrix based on the electrode distribution, ensuring the preservation of spatial correlations between channels. Consequently, the entire CCA module essentially acts as a point-wise convolution guided by channel correlation.

Therefore, within the Embed block, we enhance the standard convolution to a depthwise separable convolution. This involves initially employing the CCA for point-wise convolution, followed by channel-wise convolution. Such a modification effectively circumvents arbitrary inter-channel fusion and facilitates easier network training.

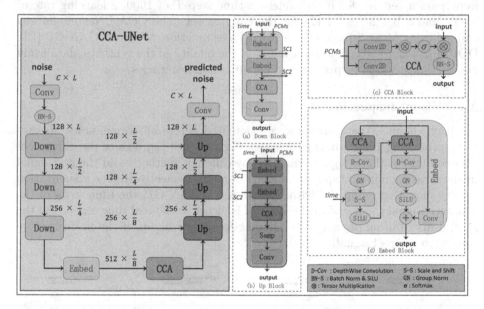

Fig. 2. The architecture of CCA-UNet with its sub-modules: (a) Down block, (b) Up block, (c) CCA block, (d) Embed block, and some abbreviations in the model diagram.

3 Experiments

3.1 Dataset

The experimental data for this study is sourced from the National Database for Autism Research under the project titled "Multimodal Developmental Neurogenetics of Females with ASD" [26]. The study engaged 143 participants diagnosed with ASD and 137 TD participants.

EEG recordings were acquired using a 128-channel HydroCel geodesic sensor net system, sampled at a frequency of 500 Hz. Sequentially, a 1 Hz high-pass filter, a 60 Hz notch filter, and a 100 Hz low-pass filter were employed to suppress noise. After excluding channels with an impedance exceeding 200 Kohm and unused channels, 125 channels were retained for the ASD dataset, and 126 channels for the TD dataset. Each channel consists of 512 data points. Our focus was solely on the resting-state data. Each epoch from every participant was treated as an individual sample. All epochs across all ASD/TD participants were considered as training sets for their respective categories.

3.2   Experimental Details

Separate models were trained for both ASD and TD class data, with identical hyperparameters set for both models: a time step T of 1000, a learning rate of 0.001, and a batch size of 128 for the training set. The CCA-UNet model was trained using Mean Squared Error (MSE) loss function. We set WGAN-GP [19], DDPM [22] as the baseline and evaluated the quality of the synthetic data using two methods: visual inspection and classification accuracies.

3.3   Visual Inspection

For each channel, the averages were calculated across all segments for all subjects, producing 125-channel time series. Figure 3 and Fig. 4 show the differences between the synthetic signal generated by different methods and the real signal in the time domain and space-frequency domain, respectively. The visualization results show that compared with DDPM and WGAN-GP, the time series of the synthetic signal generated by TF-DDPM is closer to the real time series, and the spatial distribution of energy in different frequency bands of the brain is more similar to the real signal.

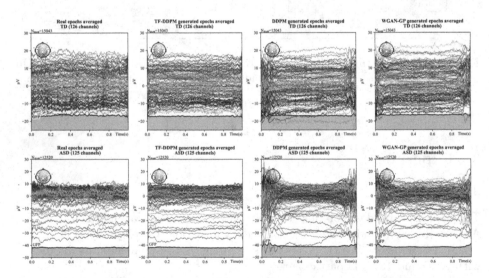

Fig. 3. Comparison of averaged real and generated data by different models. The first row shows TD images and the second row shows ASD images. Columns 1 to 4 show images from real data, TF-DDPM, DDPM, and WGAN-GP, respectively.

3.4 Classification Accuracies

Classification accuracies serves as a quantitative measure of the generation effect. We utilized a 1D-ResNet network as our classifier. Our evaluation method followed the approach proposed by [27]. We test the accuracy acc_1 of classifiers trained with synthetic data on real data to evaluate the substitutability of synthetic data. Similarly, we test the accuracy acc_2 of classifiers trained on real data with synthetic data to evaluate the authenticity of synthetic data. The test accuracy acc_3 obtained after training the classifier through the mixed set of synthetic data and real data is an auxiliary indicator, which can directly reflect the effect of data synthesis.

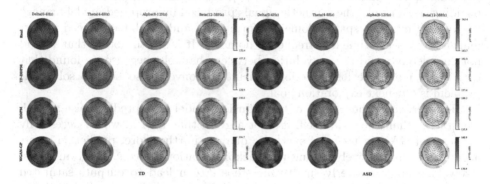

Fig. 4. Real and generated signal PSD top plots. The first four columns show TD images and the last four show ASD images. Rows 1 to 4 show images from real data, TF-DDPM, DDPM, and WGAN-GP respectively.

The classification results are summarized in Table 1. The three classification accuracies of the synthetic data generated by the proposed model are all higher than those of the other two models, indicating that our synthetic data has stronger substitutability and authenticity.

Table 1. The three classification accuracy rates tested by 1D-XResNet on the synthetic data generated by WGAN-GP, DDPM and TF-DDPM respectively.

Accuracy (%)	acc_1	acc_2	acc_3
WGAN-GP [19]	75.6	78.3	87.8
DDPM [22]	75.4	84.1	89.2
TF-DDPM	**84.3**	**88.2**	**93.7**

4   Conclusion

Although there are observable discrepancies between the synthetic data generated by TF-DDPM and actual data, such as smaller peaks and troughs in time series across channels and a generally lower energy in the alpha frequency band, the gap has been notably narrowed in comparison with DDPM and WGAN-GP. This improvement can be attributed to the deep separable convolution based on the channel attention mechanism. By placing heightened emphasis on the voltage values of more pertinent channels and sidelining those from irrelevant channels, the deep convolution effectively learns an underlying relationship between channels, a relationship that is guided by the Pearson correlation coefficient tensor. Subsequent channel-wise convolution prevents indiscriminate inter-channel blending. As a result, the synthetic signals produced by proposed model manage to preserve inherent spatial domain information, and exhibit enhanced performance in both the time and frequency domains. It is worth noting that we did not completely avoid the convolution between channels, because we found that this would make the loss function difficult to converge, so how to solve this problem is our next exploration goal.

However, since the essence of the diffusion model is to predict noise at each step rather than the data itself, it's not a given that DDPM would necessarily outperform GAN in terms of synthetic quality. Furthermore, prediction errors accumulate progressively during the backpropagation process. Both an excessively large and an overly small time steps T can lead to outputs saturated with noise. The diffusion parameter β_t also influences the output since it determines the scale of the noise being eradicated. In summary, it might be suggested that exploring the optimal T and diffusion parameters could be of considerable interest.

Acknowledgements. This work was supported by the National Natural Science Foundations of China under Grant 62172403, the Distinguished Young Scholars Fund of Guangdong under Grant 2021B1515020019, the Excellent Young Scholars of Shenzhen under Grant RCYX20200714114641211.

References

1. Luo, Y., Lu, B.: EEG data augmentation for emotion recognition using a conditional Wasserstein GAN. In: 2018 40th Annual International Conference of the IEEE Engineering in Medicine and Biology Society (EMBC), pp. 2535–2538 (2018)
2. Lee, W., Lee, J., Kim, Y.: Contextual imputation with missing sequence of EEG signals using generative adversarial networks. IEEE Access **9**, 151753–151765 (2021)
3. Yu, W., et al.: Morphological feature visualization of Alzheimer's disease via multi-directional perception GAN. IEEE Trans. Neural Netw. Learn. Syst. **34**(8), 4401–4415 (2023)
4. Jamal, W., et al.: Using brain connectivity measure of EEG synchrostates for discriminating typical and Autism Spectrum Disorder. In: Proceedings of the 2013 6th

International IEEE/EMBS Conference on Neural Engineering (NER), pp. 1402–1405 (2013)

5. Jamal, W., Das, S., Oprescu, I.A., Maharatna, K., Apicella, F., Sicca, F.: Classification of autism spectrum disorder using supervised learning of brain connectivity measures extracted from synchrostates. J. Neural Eng. **11**(4), 046019 (2014)

6. Truong, D., Makeig, S., Delorme, A.: Assessing learned features of Deep Learning applied to EEG. In: Proceedings of the 2021 IEEE International Conference on Bioinformatics and Biomedicine (BIBM), pp. 3667–3674 (2021)

7. Chlap, P., Min, H., Vandenberg, N., Dowling, J., Holloway, L., Haworth, A.: A review of medical image data augmentation techniques for deep learning applications. J. Med. Imaging Radiat. Oncol. **65**(5), 545–563 (2021)

8. Kebaili, A., Lapuyade-Lahorgue, J., Ruan, S.: Deep learning approaches for data augmentation in medical imaging: a review. J. Imaging **9**(4), 81 (2023)

9. Garcea, F., Serra, A., Lamberti, F., Morra, L.: Data augmentation for medical imaging: a systematic literature review. Comput. Biol. Med. **152**, 106391 (2023)

10. Hu, B., Zhan, C., Tang, B., Wang, B., Lei, B., Wang, S.: 3D brain reconstruction by hierarchical shape-perception network from a single incomplete image. IEEE Trans. Neural Netw. Learn. Syst. 1–13 (2023)

11. Goodfellow, I., et al.: Generative adversarial nets. In: Ghahramani, Z., Welling, M., Cortes, C., Lawrence, N., Weinberger, K.Q. (eds.) Advances in Neural Information Processing Systems 27, vol. 27. Curran Associates, Inc. (2014)

12. You, S., et al.: Fine perceptive GANs for brain MR image super-resolution in wavelet domain. IEEE Tran. Neural Netw. Learn. Syst. 1–13 (2022)

13. Hu, S., Lei, B., Wang, S., Wang, Y., Feng, Z., Shen, Y.: Bidirectional mapping generative adversarial networks for brain MR to PET synthesis. IEEE Trans. Med. Imaging **41**(1), 145–157 (2022)

14. Hu, S., Yu, W., Chen, Z., Wang, S.: Medical image reconstruction using generative adversarial network for Alzheimer disease assessment with class-imbalance problem. In: 2020 IEEE 6th International Conference on Computer and Communications (ICCC), pp. 1323–1327 (2020)

15. Hu, S., Shen, Y., Wang, S., Lei, B.: Brain MR to PET synthesis via bidirectional generative adversarial network. In: Martel, A.L., et al. (eds.) MICCAI 2020. LNCS, vol. 12262, pp. 698–707. Springer, Cham (2020). https://doi.org/10.1007/978-3-030-59713-9_67

16. Wang, S., Shen, Y., Zeng, D., Hu, Y.: Bone age assessment using convolutional neural networks. In: 2018 International Conference on Artificial Intelligence and Big Data (ICAIBD), pp. 175–178 (2018)

17. Panwar, S., Rad, P., Quarles, J., Huang, Y.: Generating EEG signals of an RSVP experiment by a class conditioned Wasserstein generative adversarial network. In: Proceedings of the 2019 IEEE International Conference on Systems, Man and Cybernetics (SMC), Bari (2019)

18. Zhang, K., et al.: Data augmentation for motor imagery signal classification based on a hybrid neural network. Sensors **20**(16), 4485 (2020)

19. Panwar, S., Rad, P., Jung, T.-P., Huang, Y.: Modeling EEG data distribution with a Wasserstein generative adversarial network to predict RSVP events. IEEE Trans. Neural Syst. Rehabil. Eng. **28**(8), 1720–1730 (2020)

20. Wang, S., et al.: An ensemble-based densely-connected deep learning system for assessment of skeletal maturity. IEEE Trans. Syst. Man Cybern. Syst. **52**(1), 426–437 (2022)

21. Arjovsky, M., Chintala, S., Bottou, L.: Wasserstein generative adversarial networks. In: Precup, D., Teh, Y.W. (eds.) Proceedings of the 34th International Conference on Machine Learning, vol. 70, pp. 214–223. JMLR (2017)

22. Ho, J., Chen, X., Srinivas, A., Duan, Y., Abbeel, P.: Denoising diffusion probabilistic models. arXiv:2006.11239 (2020)

23. Shu, K., Zhao, Y., Wu, L., Liu, A., Qian, R., Chen, X.: Data augmentation for seizure prediction with generative diffusion model. arXiv:2306.08256 (2023)

24. Tosato, G., Dalbagno, C.M., Fumagalli, F.: EEG synthetic data generation using probabilistic diffusion models. arXiv:2303.06068 (2023)

25. Author(s): Brain Signal Generation and Data Augmentation with a Single-Step Diffusion Probabilistic Model. Paper under double-blind review, presented at ICLR (2023)

26. Pelphrey, K.: Multimodal Developmental Neurogenetics of Females with ASD. NIMH Data Archive. (2012). https://nda.nih.gov/experiment.html?id=196& collectionId=2021

27. Alcaraz, J.M.L., Strodthoff, N.: Diffusion-based conditional ECG generation with structured state space models. arXiv preprint arXiv:2301.08227 (2023)

28. Wang, S., Chen, Z., You, S., Lei, B.: Brain stroke lesion segmentation using consistent perception generative adversarial network. Neural Comput. Appl. **34**, 8657–8669 (2022)

29. Gong, C., et al.: Generative AI for brain image computing and brain network computing: a review. Front. Neurosci. **17** (2023)

30. Miao, Z., Zhao, M.: Time-space-frequency feature Fusion for 3-channel motor imagery classification. arXiv preprint arXiv:2304.01461 (2023)

31. Torma, S., Szegletes, L.: EEGWave: a Denoising Diffusion Probabilistic Approach for EEG Signal Generation. EasyChair (2023)

32. Yan, Y., et al.: Topological EEG nonlinear dynamics analysis for emotion recognition. IEEE Trans. Cogn. Dev. Syst. **15**(2), 625–638 (2023)

33. Li, Y., Zhang, X.R., Zhang, B., Lei, M.Y., Cui, W.G., Guo, Y.Z.: A channel-projection mixed-scale convolutional neural network for motor imagery EEG decoding. IEEE Trans. Neural Syst. Rehabil. Eng. **27**, 1170–1180 (2019)

34. Zhang, C., Kim, Y.K., Eskandarian, A.: EEG-inception: an accurate and robust end-to-end neural network for EEG-based motor imagery classification. J. Neural Eng. **18**, 046014 (2021)

35. Shovon, T.H., Nazi, Z.A., Dash, S., Hossain, F.: Classification of motor imagery EEG signals with multi-input convolutional neural network by augmenting STFT. In: Proceedings of the 5th International Conference on Advances in Electrical Engineering (ICAEE), Dhaka (2019)

Boosting Medical Image Segmentation with Partial Class Supervision

Minxia Xu[1,2], Han Yang[3,4], Bo Song[3], Jinshui Miao[1,2], Weida Hu[1,2],
and Erkang Cheng[3(✉)]

[1] Hangzhou Institute for Advanced Study, University of Chinese Academy of
Sciences, Hangzhou, China
{xuminxia22,miaojinshui,wdhu}@ucas.ac.cn
[2] University of Chinese Academy of Sciences, Beijing, China
[3] Institute of Intelligent Machines, HFIPS, Chinese Academy of Sciences, Hefei,
China
matrix_yh@ustc.edu.cn, songbo@iim.ac.cn, twokang.cheng@gmail.com
[4] University of Science and Technology of China, Hefei, China

Abstract. Medical image data are often limited due to expensive acquisition and annotation processes. Directly using such limited annotated
samples can easily lead to the deep learning models overfitting on
the training dataset. An alternative way is to leverage the unlabeled
dataset which is free to obtain in most cases. Semi-supervised methods using a small set of labeled data and large amounts of unlabeled
data have received much attention. In this paper, we propose a novel
semi-supervised method for medical image segmentation that uses partial class supervision. Specifically, for a given multi-class label, we extend
it to generate several labeled images with partial classes annotated while
others remain unannotated. The unlabeled part in the partially annotated label is supervised by a pseudo-labels approach. In addition, we
project the labeled pixel values into pseudo-labels to achieve rectified
pixel-level pseudo-labels. In this way, our method can effectively increase
the number of training samples. The experimental results on two public medical datasets of heart and prostate anatomy demonstrate that
our method outperforms the state-of-the-art semi-supervised methods.
Additional experiments also show that the proposed method gives better results compared to fully supervised segmentation methods.

Keywords: Medical image segmentation · Data augmentation · Label
combination

1 Introduction

Accurate and reliable medical image segmentation is essential for computer-
aided diagnosis and surgical navigation systems and is required for many clin-
ical applications [1,2]. Medical image segmentation based on deep learning has
shown excellent results with state-of-the-art segmentation performance [3,4].

© The Author(s), under exclusive license to Springer Nature Singapore Pte Ltd. 2023
W. Jia et al. (Eds.): CCBR 2023, LNCS 14463, pp. 385–394, 2023.
https://doi.org/10.1007/978-981-99-8565-4_36

Deep-supervised models usually require a large number of training samples to achieve great segmentation performance. However, it is challenging to acquire accurate pixel-wise annotation for medical image segmentation tasks [5,6]. The annotation process relies on experienced physicians and is extremely expensive and time-consuming, especially for 3D image data. Therefore, for a collected medical image dataset, there are only a small number of images are labeled by experts and a large portion of the images are unannotated.

Recently, semi-supervised methods [7,8,24–26] aim to utilize a large amount of unlabeled data to achieve better segmentation performance. One line of research to alleviate the scarcity of medical image data challenge is to apply data augmentation. The goal of data augmentation is to generate large annotated training images with minimum effort. Recent data augmentation approaches can be roughly divided into single-sample and multi-sample augmentation. For example, single-sample data augmentation applies geometric transformations (e.g., translation, flipping, and color transformations) on a single image. These single-sample data augmentation methods perform small transformations on images and have limited ability to simulate diverse and realistic examples. Also, these methods are highly sensitive to the choice of parameters. The multi-sample augmentation is to combine several images together to generate training images and corresponding labels. For example, mixup [9–13] is the main approach to achieve multi-sample data augmentation. However, these methods are proposed for image classification tasks, and they may change the boundary of the target object, leading to unrealistic segmentation results. In particular, the shape and morphology of different objects (such as organs or tumors) in medical images are unique, and directing using multi-sample augmentation may lead to worse and unstable segmentation performance.

In semi-supervised segmentation methods, another line of research is to generate pseudo labels for those unannotated images. A segmentation network first produces segmentation probability results and some pseudo-label generation strategies simply use pre-defined thresholds to generate the groundtruth [14,15]. These methods can produce a large number of labels with high confidence while having some unreliable noise labels. To summarize, these pseudo-label generation approaches have the following drawbacks. First, with extremely imbalanced class distributions, high-confident pseudo labels are always biased toward the classes with major distributions [16]. Second, the discrepancy between easy and hard samples also makes it difficult to find the best thresholds for selecting high-confident pseudo labels. In order to solve these problems, Cross-Pseudo-Supervision (CPS) [17] employs network perturbations to train two different segmentation networks in parallel and constrain the pseudo-labels with consistency regularization.

Although these semi-supervised methods greatly improve the segmentation results by leveraging a large number of unlabeled images, these methods still require accurate and precise pixel-level annotations of all the categories. It remains difficult for experts to label every category in each image. This motivates us to use partially labeled images for medical image segmentation tasks. In

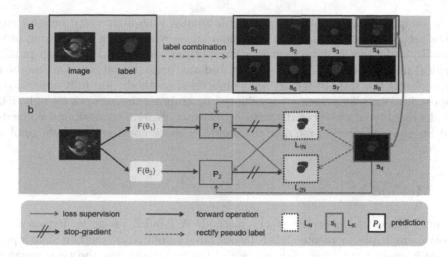

Fig. 1. Overview of the proposed label combination for medical image segmentation. After labeling arrangement, a single image can be expanded into multiple images consisting of different categories, as shown in Fig. a. During the training process, the labeled part of each image is supervised by the real label L_K, and the unlabeled part is supervised by the pseudo-label L_N, and the real label performs pixel-level correction on the pseudo-label, as shown in Fig. b. The two networks have the same structure and their weights, i.e., θ_1 and θ_2, are initialized differently.

this paper, we propose a novel data augmentation method to generate additional training samples. Our method aims to generate partially labeled images and use augmented partial supervision in the network design. Our method extends the pseudo-label generation approach in CPS to create partial pseudo-labels which can incorporate more supervision information into the training process.

Specifically, for an image with N distinct categories annotated, a label combination step is to select a set of labels from these N classes. We denote that K category is selected for supervision, and the remaining $N - K$ labels are unannotated. The labeled part in the image is supervised by the original annotation and the remaining pixels from $N - K$ classes are supervised by pseudo-label methods. Similar to CPS, we also perturb the two branch networks with different initialization parameters, constraining the reliability of pseudo-labels by the consistency principle. In addition, considering the characteristics of the label combination method, that is, each image contains accurately labeled categories, we map the selected K category annotation back to the pseudo-label mask and generate corrected pseudo supervision. Therefore, the pseudo supervision mask generated by our method contains augmented labels for the remaining $N - K$ category and partial real labels, which in turn improve the reliability of the label augmentation step.

To this end, our data augmentation method of label combination does not change the morphological information of medical objects. Our method effectively expands the amount of data and alleviates the problem of the insufficient sample size of medical images. Additionally, each augmented image combines pseudo-supervised labels and manual labels which eases the learning process. To evaluate our data augmentation method, we verified it on two public medical image datasets, ACDC dataset and the prostate dataset. Our method outperforms the state-of-the-art semi-supervised methods and fully-supervised approaches. Excellent accuracy is achieved by training the network for only 400 epochs roughly on these two datasets. In contrast, general semi-supervised medical image segmentation requires thousands or more epochs to provide similar results.

2   Method

Figure 1 shows the overview of our method. A labeled image is first used to generate multiple augmented labels by our label combination method. The input image is processed by two networks with identical structures and their weights are initialized differently. Following CPS, one network can generate pseudo labels for the other. In our method, for one label combination selection, a rectified pseudo label is created. Totally, we have two supervision losses on two different labels, L_K for the selected manual label and L_N is defined as our rectified pseudo label.

2.1   Network Architecture

Our segmentation network consists of two parallel branch networks F (shown in Fig. 1). These two networks are with the same structure and use different initialization weights θ_1 and θ_2. Therefore, these two networks perturb the same input image to produce two different segmentation confidence maps P_1 and P_2. The network and its outputs are defined as follows:

$$P_1 = F(x; \theta_1), Y_1^* = Max(P_1) \tag{1}$$

$$P_2 = F(x; \theta_2), Y_2^* = Max(P_2) \tag{2}$$

where P_1 and P_2 are the segmentation confidence maps with softmax normalization. Y_1^* and Y_2^* are the predicted one-hot maps calculated by P_1 and P_2.

2.2   Label Combination

Conventional semi-supervised segmentation methods aim to learn the segmentation network by simultaneously exploring labeled and unlabeled images. For example, CPS proposes a data augmentation method to generate pseudo labels for these unlabeled images. Different from it, our method can produce multiple augmented training samples by generating partially labeled annotation while the remaining pixels are recognized as unlabeled. The introduced data augmented method is achieved by the label combination step.

Mathematically, for an image x and its corresponding labels y in the original dataset D with N distinct categories. These categories denoted by $C = \{c_0, c_1, c_2, c_3, ...c_{N-1}\}$. During label combination, we select K classes as labeled, and the remaining $N-K$ categories are recognized as unannotated. In the experiments, we select $1,2,... N-2$ categories, and a maximum of $N-2$ categories is to avoid generate fully labeled foreground. Totally, for a given image, we can produce n augmented images, where $n = C_N^1 + C_N^2 + ... + C_N^{N-2}$. C_N^K denotes that number of choices that we select K categories from N classes. Compared to CPS which only expands training images for unlabeled images, our data augmentation can generate n times training samples for the labeled images. Our network design is to augment multiple partially labeled images from one fully-labeled image.

During the training, for each label combination, we can create two types of supervision. The first one is simply labeled by the selected K categories. We denote the partially labeled mask as:

$$L_K = \begin{cases} c_i, & \text{if } c_i \in K \\ 0, & \text{if } c_i \in N - K \end{cases} \qquad (3)$$

The other loss supervision is computed from pseudo labels. And a pseudo-label mask Y^* is first calculated. Then we add partial labels of selected K categories into the Y_i^* to generate the rectified pseudo label L_N as:

$$L_N = \begin{cases} L_K, & \text{if } c_i \in K \\ Y^*, & \text{if } c_i \in N - K \end{cases} \qquad (4)$$

These two types of labels are used as supervision in the loss part of the network.

2.3 Loss Function

The training objective consists of two losses: supervised loss L_s and pseudo-supervised loss L_{ps}. The supervision loss L_s is formulated to use the standard pixel-wise loss on the labeled images over the two parallel segmentation networks:

$$\mathcal{L}_s = \frac{1}{D^a} \sum_{x_i' \in D^a} \frac{1}{W \times H} \sum_{i=0}^{W \times H} (\mathcal{L}(P_{1i}, L_K) + \mathcal{L}(P_{2i}, L_K)), \qquad (5)$$

where W and H are the width and height of the input image.

The pixel-wise pseudo-supervised loss L_{ps} for the rectified pseudo mask L_N is:

$$\mathcal{L}_{ps} = \frac{1}{D^a} \sum_{x_i' \in D^a} \frac{1}{W \times H} \sum_{i=0}^{W \times H} (\mathcal{L}(P_{1i}, L_{2N}) + \mathcal{L}(P_{2i}, L_{1N})). \qquad (6)$$

For loss function $\mathcal{L}$, we use the weight cross entropy loss function and the Dice loss function. Considering the problem of category imbalance in medical image segmentation, we use weighted cross entropy $w = [w_0, w_1, w_2, ..., w_{N-1}]$ to impose more weight on categories with fewer annotations. Finally, the total training loss is $L = L_s + L_{ps}$.

3   Experiments

3.1   Dataset and Evaluation

Dataset: We evaluated the proposed approach on two public MRI datasets.

ACDC Dataset. ACDC dataset consists of 2-dimensional cineMRI images from 150 patients. The cine-MRI images were obtained using two MRI scanners of various magnetic strengths and different resolutions. For each patient, manual annotations of the right ventricle (RV), left ventricle (LV) and myocardium (MYO) are provided. It was hosted as part of the MICCAI ACDC challenge 2017.

Prostate Dataset. Prostate dataset contains 48 T2-weighted MRI 3D volumes of prostate. Expert annotations are provided for two structures of the prostate: the peripheral zone and the central gland. The 48 subjects in the Prostate dataset are randomly divided into 2 sets of 33 (training), and 15 (testing) subjects in the experiments. It was hosted in the medical decathlon challenge in MICCAI 2019.

Evaluation Metrics. We adopt the Dice coefficient to evaluate the performance of each method, which computes the similarity of two segmentation masks.

3.2   Implementation Details

Our approach is implemented using the pytorch framework, where the backbone of both branch networks is resnet50 and appended with dilated convolution. In addition, we initialize the weights of the two parallel networks with weights pre-trained on ImageNet. We train our model using the SGD approach with momentum fixed at 0.9 and weight decay set to 0.0001. We use the learning rate warmup approach, and the learning rate is decayed with the initial learning rate (0.001) multiplied by $(1 - \frac{iter}{max\_iter}) \times 0.9$. We train ACDC for 350 epochs, and Prostate for 400 epochs.

3.3   Experimental Results

Comparison with Semi-supervised Methods. As shown in Table 1, we compare our method with several previously reported semi-supervised methods on ACDC dataset and Prostate dataset. These semi-supervised method use the size of unlabeled (X_U) and test sets (X_t): (a) $|X_U| = 63$, $|X_t| = 30$ for ACDC dataset, (b) $|X_U| = 22$, $|X_t| = 15$ and val sets $|X_{val}| = 2$ for Prostate dataset. Due to the limited annotation images, small labeled sets $(|X_L| = 8$, or $|X_L| = 7)$ are used individually for Prostate or ACDC datasets. For label combination, we set $K = 1$ and $K = 2$ for the ACDC dataset and use $K = 1$ for Prostate dataset. We follow the experimental settings of other semi-supervised methods which divide the ACDC dataset into 70 images for training, and 30 images for testing. We also divide the ACDC dataset to 100 images for training, and 50 images for testing. The experimental results are denoted by $Ours'$ and $Ours^*$, respectively. We use the same dataset division for Prostate dataset.

Our methods with different varieties outperform these previously reported semi-supervised segmentation methods. The experimental results show that our data augmentation provides additional partial supervision and our segmentation model can boost the medical image segmentation performance. Our method with weight cross-entropy (WCE) loss supervision yields slightly better results than using DICE as the loss function. Network with both WCE and DICE as loss function gives the best performance.

Table 1. Comparison of the proposed method with other semi-supervised learning and data augmentation methods. *Ours'* means dividing the ACDC dataset as other semi-supervised methods (70(training), 30(tests); *Ours** means dividing the ACDC dataset to 100(training), 50(testing). Prostate dataset follows the same setting as ACDC dataset.

Method	Prostate	Method	ACDC
self -training [19]	0.598	URPC [27]	0.831
Mixup [12]	0.593	CPS [17]	0.788
Data Augment [20]	0.597	MC-Net [28]	0.865
DTC [21]	0.587	SS-Net [29]	0.868
CPS [17]	0.567	ACTION [30]	0.872
ICT [22]	0.567	MONA [31]	0.877
Pseudo-labels joint [23]	0.696	ARCO-SG [32]	0.894
Ours'(WCE+Dice)	**0.744**	*Ours'*(WCE+Dice)	**0.909**
*Ours** (Dice)	0.708	*Ours**(Dice)	0.890
*Ours** (WCE)	0.703	*Ours**(WCE)	0.899
*Ours** (WCE+Dice)	0.744	*Ours** (WCE+Dice)	0.900

Comparison with Fully-Supervised Methods. As shown in Table 2, we also conduct an experiment to compare our method with fully-supervised methods. The experimental results of fully-supervised methods on Prostate dataset are reported in [18]. Results of our method with label combination parameter $K = 1, 2, 3$ are listed in Table 2. Our method employs partial class supervision outperforms several fully-supervised approaches. Also, experimental settings with large K give better results. The main reason is that label combination with large K provides more augmented training images into the supervision of the training process.

Table 2. Comparison of the proposed method with other fully-supervised learning and data augmentation methods. The experimental results are reported [18]. The backbone of fully-supervised methods is nnUNet. NoDA: No augmentation; moreDA: sequential augmentation; Spatial SS: designed search space; TrivialAugment: natural image SOTA method; DDAug: MCTS + search space.

Method	Prostate($N = 3$)		
NoDA	0.7236		
moreDA	0.7123		
TrivialAugment	0.7258		
Spatial SS	0.7290		
DDAug	0.7320		
	$K = 1$	$K = 2$	$K = 3$
Ours	0.744	0.746	**0.753**

4   Conclusion

In this paper, we propose a new low-cost data augmentation method for semi-supervised medical image segmentation, which expands the sample size of the dataset and enhances the data diversity of the dataset through label combination. Different from most semi-supervised methods that only utilize unlabeled images in the data augmentation step, our label combination strategy provides a novel way to use labeled images in the data augmentation. A fully labeled image is expanded to a set of partially labeled images. To this end, our method can effectively alleviate the challenge of data insufficiency in the medical image analysis domain. Experimental results on ACDC and Prostate datasets demonstrate the effectiveness of this method, even superior to the fully supervised segmentation method.

References

1. Wang, G., et al.: DeepIGeoS: a deep interactive geodesic framework for medical image segmentation. IEEE Trans. Pattern Anal. Mach. Intell. **41**(7), 1559–1572 (2018)
2. Luo, X., et al.: MIDeepSeg: minimally interactive segmentation of unseen objects from medical images using deep learning. Med. Image Anal. **72**, 102102 (2021)
3. Shi, Z., et al.: A clinically applicable deep-learning model for detecting intracranial aneurysm in computed tomography angiography images. Nat. Commun. **11**(1), 6090 (2020)
4. Chen, J., et al.: TransUNet: transformers make strong encoders for medical image segmentation. arXiv preprint arXiv:2102.04306 (2021)
5. Yu, L., Wang, S., Li, X., Fu, C.-W., Heng, P.-A.: Uncertainty-aware self-ensembling model for semi-supervised 3D left atrium segmentation. In: Shen, D., et al. (eds.) MICCAI 2019. LNCS, vol. 11765, pp. 605–613. Springer, Cham (2019). https://doi.org/10.1007/978-3-030-32245-8_67

6. Jiao, R., Zhang, Y., Ding, L., Cai, R., Zhang, J.: Learning with limited annotations: a survey on deep semi-supervised learning for medical image segmentation. arXiv preprint arXiv:2207.14191 (2022)
7. Ouali, Y., Hudelot, C., Tami, M.: Semi-supervised semantic segmentation with cross-consistency training. In: Proceedings of the IEEE/CVF Conference on Computer Vision and Pattern Recognition, pp. 12 674–12 684 (2020)
8. Xia, Y., et al.: Uncertainty-aware multi-view co-training for semi-supervised medical image segmentation and domain adaptation. Med. Image Anal. **65**, 101766 (2020)
9. Kim, J.-H., Choo, W., Jeong, H., Song, H.O.: Co-mixup: saliency guided joint mixup with supermodular diversity. arXiv preprint arXiv:2102.03065 (2021)
10. Kim, J.-H., Choo, W., Song, H.O.: Puzzle mix: exploiting saliency and local statistics for optimal mixup. In: International Conference on Machine Learning, pp. 5275–5285. PMLR (2020)
11. Yun, S., Han, D., Oh, S.J., Chun, S., Choe, J., Yoo, Y.: Cutmix: regularization strategy to train strong classifiers with localizable features. In: Proceedings of the IEEE/CVF International Conference on Computer Vision, pp. 6023–6032 (2019)
12. Zhang, H., Cisse, M., Dauphin, Y.N., Lopez-Paz, D.: Mixup: beyond empirical risk minimization. arXiv preprint arXiv:1710.09412 (2017)
13. Zhang, K., Zhuang, X.: Cyclemix: a holistic strategy for medical image segmentation from scribble supervision. In: Proceedings of the IEEE/CVF Conference on Computer Vision and Pattern Recognition, pp. 11 656–11 665 (2022)
14. Wu, L., Fang, L., He, X., He, M., Ma, J., Zhong, Z.: Querying labeled for unlabeled: Cross-image semantic consistency guided semi-supervised semantic segmentation. IEEE Trans. Pattern Anal. Mach. Intell. (2023)
15. Feng, Z., et al.: DMT: dynamic mutual training for semi-supervised learning. Pattern Recogn. **130**, 108777 (2022)
16. Wang, Y., et al.: Balancing logit variation for long-tailed semantic segmentation. In: Proceedings of the IEEE/CVF Conference on Computer Vision and Pattern Recognition, pp. 19 561–19 573 (2023)
17. Chen, X., Yuan, Y., Zeng, G., Wang, J.: Semi-supervised semantic segmentation with cross pseudo supervision. In: Proceedings of the IEEE/CVF Conference on Computer Vision and Pattern Recognition, pp. 2613–2622 (2021)
18. Xu, X., Hsi, Y., Wang, H., Li, X.: Dynamic data augmentation via MCTS for prostate MRI segmentation. arXiv preprint arXiv:2305.15777 (2023)
19. Bai, W., et al.: Semi-supervised learning for network-based cardiac MR image segmentation. In: Descoteaux, M., Maier-Hein, L., Franz, A., Jannin, P., Collins, D.L., Duchesne, S. (eds.) MICCAI 2017. LNCS, vol. 10434, pp. 253–260. Springer, Cham (2017). https://doi.org/10.1007/978-3-319-66185-8_29
20. Chaitanya, K., Karani, N., Baumgartner, C.F., Becker, A., Donati, O., Konukoglu, E.: Semi-supervised and task-driven data augmentation. In: Chung, A.C.S., Gee, J.C., Yushkevich, P.A., Bao, S. (eds.) IPMI 2019. LNCS, vol. 11492, pp. 29–41. Springer, Cham (2019). https://doi.org/10.1007/978-3-030-20351-1_3
21. Luo, X., Chen, J., Song, T., Wang, G.: Semi-supervised medical image segmentation through dual-task consistency. In: Proceedings of the AAAI Conference on Artificial Intelligence, vol. 35, no. 10, pp. 8801–8809 (2021)
22. Verma, V., Kawaguchi, K., Lamb, A., Kannala, J., Solin, A., Bengio, Y., Lopez-Paz, D.: Interpolation consistency training for semi-supervised learning. Neural Netw. **145**, 90–106 (2022)

23. Chaitanya, K., Erdil, E., Karani, N., Konukoglu, E.: Local contrastive loss with pseudo-label based self-training for semi-supervised medical image segmentation. Med. Image Anal. **87**, 102792 (2023)
24. Bui, P.N., Le, D.T., Bum, J., Kim, S., Song, S.J., Choo, H.: Semi-supervised learning with fact-forcing for medical image segmentation. IEEE Access **11**, 99413–99425 (2023). https://doi.org/10.1109/ACCESS.2023.3313646
25. Wu, F., Zhuang, X.: Minimizing estimated risks on unlabeled data: a new formulation for semi-supervised medical image segmentation. IEEE Trans. Pattern Anal. Mach. Intell. **45**(5), 6021–6036 (2023). https://doi.org/10.1109/TPAMI.2022.3215186
26. Lee, M., Lee, S., Lee, J., Shim, H.: Saliency as pseudo-pixel supervision for weakly and semi-supervised semantic segmentation. IEEE Trans. Pattern Anal. Mach. Intell. **45**(10), 12341–12357 (2023). https://doi.org/10.1109/TPAMI.2023.3273592
27. Luo, X., et al.: Efficient semi-supervised gross target volume of nasopharyngeal carcinoma segmentation via uncertainty rectified pyramid consistency. In: de Bruijne, M., et al. (eds.) MICCAI 2021. LNCS, vol. 12902, pp. 318–329. Springer, Cham (2021). https://doi.org/10.1007/978-3-030-87196-3_30
28. Wu, Y., Xu, M., Ge, Z., Cai, J., Zhang, L.: Semi-supervised left atrium segmentation with mutual consistency training. In: de Bruijne, M., et al. (eds.) MICCAI 2021. LNCS, vol. 12902, pp. 297–306. Springer, Cham (2021). https://doi.org/10.1007/978-3-030-87196-3_28
29. Wu, Y., Wu, Z., Wu, Q., Ge, Z., Cai, J.: Exploring smoothness and class-separation for semi-supervised medical image segmentation. In: Wang, L., Dou, Q., Fletcher, P.T., Speidel, S., Li, S. (eds.) MICCAI 2022. LNCS, vol. 13435, pp. 34–43. Springer, Cham (2022). https://doi.org/10.1007/978-3-031-16443-9_4
30. You, C., Dai, W., Min, Y., Staib, L., Duncan, J.S.: Bootstrapping semi-supervised medical image segmentation with anatomical-aware contrastive distillation. In: Frangi, A., de Bruijne, M., Wassermann, D., Navab, N. (eds.) IPMI 2023. LNCS, vol. 13939, pp. 641–653. Springer, Cham (2023). https://doi.org/10.1007/978-3-031-34048-2_49
31. You, C., et al.: Mine your own anatomy: revisiting medical image segmentation with extremely limited labels. arXiv preprint arXiv:2209.13476 (2022)
32. You, C., et al.: Rethinking semi-supervised medical image segmentation: a variance-reduction perspective. arXiv preprint arXiv:2302.01735 (2023)

FV-REID: A Benchmark for Federated Vehicle Re-identification

Linhan Huang[1], Qianqian Zhao[2], Liangtai Zhou[1], Jianqing Zhu[1(✉)],
and Huanqiang Zeng[1]

[1] College of Engineering, Huaqiao University,
Quanzhou 362021, People's Republic of China
jqzhu@hqu.edu.cn
[2] College of Information Science and Engineering, Huaqiao University,
Xiamen 361021, People's Republic of China

Abstract. Vehicle re-identification is a crucial research direction in computer vision for constructing intelligent transportation systems and smart cities. However, privacy concerns pose significant challenges, such as personal information leakage and potential risks of data sharing. To address these challenges, we propose a federated vehicle re-identification (FV-REID) benchmark that protects vehicle privacy while exploring re-identification performance. The benchmark includes a multi-domain dataset and a federated evaluation protocol that allows clients to upload model parameters to the server without sharing data. We also design a baseline federated vehicle re-identification method called FVVR, which employs federated-averaging to facilitate model interaction. Our experiments on the FV-REID benchmark reveal that (1) the re-identification performance of the FVVR model is typically weaker than that of non-federated learning models and is prone to significant fluctuations and (2) the difference in re-identification performance between the FVVR model and the non-federated learning model would be more pronounced on a small-scale client dataset compared to a large-scale client dataset.

Keywords: Vehicle re-identification · Federated learning · Benchmark

1 Introduction

Vehicle re-identification [1–3] is an important research, which can be used to identify and track vehicles, enabling various applications such as traffic management [4], video surveillance [5], and criminal investigation [6]. However, as surveillance cameras are frequently dispersed across various locations and organizations, with data being centralized in their respective data centers, traditional vehicle re-identification methods based on centralized learning encounter a list of problems such as data privacy, data security, and data centralization.

In 2017, Google's research team proposed the concept of federated learning with the goal of enabling edge devices, such as smartphones, to participate in model training without sharing raw data. This federated learning approach effectively reduces the risk of privacy breaches by only exchanging model parameters

W. Jia et al. (Eds.): CCBR 2023, LNCS 14463, pp. 395–406, 2023.
https://doi.org/10.1007/978-981-99-8565-4_37

Fig. 1. An overview of privacy protection in federated vehicle-re-identification.

between clients and servers. Since its inception, many researchers [7–9] have been developing different methods to improve efficiency, accuracy, and privacy protection during model training. Consequently, federated learning has potential in real-world applications, such as healthcare [10–12], finance [13], and telecommunications [14]. We notice that researchers [15–17] have already applied federated learning to person re-identification and achieved certain progress. However, compared to person re-identification, vehicle re-identification faces a more complex spatio-temporal scope. Generally speaking, vehicles might travel a greater distance in a short time compared to persons, possibly leading to vehicle re-identification being conducted over a broader geographical range. Regarding the number of cameras, the most complex client dataset used federated person re-identification [15] only has 15 cameras, but in our constructed federated vehicle re-identification benchmark, the number of cameras in one client dataset reaches 326. Hence, federated vehicle re-identification would encounter great challenge.

In this paper, we propose a federated vehicle re-identification (FV-REID) benchmark to explore re-identification performance as well as protect vehicle privacy. The FV-REID benchmark includes four aspects. First, we gather five publicly available well-annotated vehicle image datasets (i.e., VeRi [18], VehicleID [19], VRID [20], Boxcars116k [21], and Cityflow [22]) as client datasets to create a multi-domain dataset for federated scenarios. Second, we design a federated evaluation protocol in which each client is allowed to upload model parameters to the server without sharing their data, thus ensuring privacy protection, as shown in Fig. 1. Third, we design a baseline federated vehicle re-identification method, called FVVR. It employs the most common aggregation strategy, namely, federated-averaging (FedAvg), to facilitate model interactions between the server and clients. We utilize ResNet50 as the backbone for both the server and client models and use the cross-entropy loss function for model training. Due to variations in the number of identities among clients, our FVVR method only aggregates parameters of the same backbone between the server and clients. We conduct extensive experiments on the FV-REID benchmark to establish the baseline performance for future studies.

2 Related Work

2.1 Vehicle Re-identification

In recent years, there has been extensive research of vehicle re-identification technology. Researchers have proposed various methods for feature extraction [2,3] and metric learning [23,24]. Shen et al. [2] designed a graph interactive transformer method, which combines graphs and transformers to enable cooperation between local and global features. Wang et al. [3] developed a multiscale attention network to exploit distinct features of vehicle images in the unknown domain. Chu et al. [23] introduced a viewpoint-aware metric learning method to enhance ReID accuracy. Yu et al. [24] proposed an unsupervised vehicle ReID approach using self-supervised metric learning based on a feature dictionary. These methods aim to improve the accuracy of vehicle re-identification. However, the issue of vehicle privacy protection and data security has not been adequately addressed. It is important to note that these methods have the potential to violate the personal privacy of vehicle owners if visual features, such as color, shape and identification information, are misused or leaked.

2.2 Federated Learning

Federated learning is receiving a lot of attention from both academic and industrial fields due to its great potential to protect data privacy. Recently, federated learning has been applied to person re-identification. For exmaple, Zhuang et al. [15] proposed a federated person re-identification benchmark and improved algorithms to optimize its performance. Sun et al. [16] focused on improving the normalization layer and improving the performance of federated learning in image classification tasks. Zhang et al. [17] proposed a federated spatial-temporal incremental learning approach to continuously optimize the models deployed in many distributed edge clients. Although vehicle re-identification is similar to person re-identification, the activity range of vehicles usually involves a larger space-time area, which increases the heterogeneity among different client datasets, making federated vehicle re-identification a significantly difficult task.

3 Federated Vehicle Re-identification Benchmark

3.1 Multi-domain Dataset

We use five different vehicle datasets VeRi [18], VehicleID [19], VRID [20], Boxcars116k [21] and Cityflow [22], which vary in number of images and cameras, camera angles, and camera environments to bulid a multi-domain dataset. Datasets statistics are shown in Table 1. The vehicle images in these datasets cover a broad distribution. VeRi comprises images from 20 cameras, VRID from 326 cameras, Boxcars116k from 137 cameras, and Cityflow from 40 cameras.

Table 1. Statistics of 5 client datasets of FV-REID benchmark.

Datasets		Cameras	Train		Test		
			IDs	Images	Query		Gallery
					IDs	Images	Images
VeRi		20	575	37743	200	1678	11579
VehicleID	Small	–	13164	113346	800	5693	800
	Medium				1600	11777	1600
	Large				2400	17377	2400
VRID		326	1000	5000	1000	2000	3000
Boxcars116k		137	11653	51691	11125	12734	26415
Cityflow		40	238	30410	95	1669	4856

3.2 Federated Evaluation Protocol

Each dataset is associated with a specific client, and in total, there are five clients and one server. To ensure that each client's data privacy is protected, there is no sharing of data between clients or between the clients and the server. This approach effectively safeguards the confidentiality of each client's data. In evaluating the accuracy of vehicle re-identification, we utilize two metrics: the rank-1 accuracy [25] and the mean average precision (mAP) [26]. While rank-1 is a useful indicator, mAP is a more comprehensive measure of performance, particularly when multiple gallery images are matched to a query. The server model is applied to report baseline performance. Furthermore, because VRID, Boxcars116k, and Cityflow have no standard re-identification data division, we design data divisions as follows. For VRID and Boxcars116k, the test set is divided into a query set, which contains 25% images of all identities in the test set, and a gallery set, which includes the remaining images in the test set. Due to Cityflow not releasing an annotated test set, we split the test set from the original training set. In particular, images of identity 1 to identity 95 are used for the test set, and the rest seems to be the training set. Overall, our approach prioritizes data privacy and accuracy in vehicle re-identification, ensuring that each client's data is kept secure while still achieving high levels of performance.

3.3 FVVR Baseline Method

As shown in Fig. 2, both the server and client models use the same backbone, namely ResNet50 [27], and the cross-entropy (CE) loss function. At the beginning of model training, the sever first initializes the global model, denoted as w_0, then the FVVR method is implemented as follows.

Step-1: The server sends a global model to clients. At the start of the t-th training round, it sends the global model ω^t to clients to participate in training.

Step-2: Clients implement local training. Each client connects the global model ω^t to its identity classifier ϑ^{t-1} to form a new model $(\omega^t, \vartheta^{t-1})$. Then, clients are updated as follows.

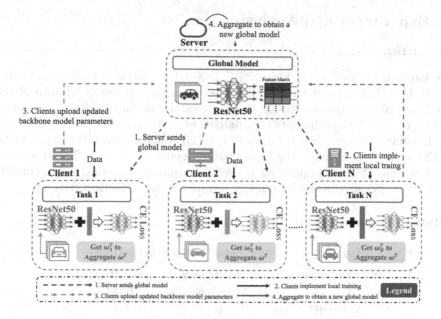

Fig. 2. Illustration of the FVVR baseline method.

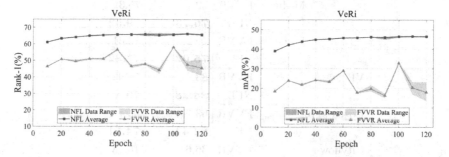

Fig. 3. Performance on VeRi.

$$(\omega_k^t, \vartheta_k^t) \leftarrow \begin{cases} (\omega^t, \mathrm{Init}(\vartheta_k)), t = 0 \\ (\omega^t, \vartheta_k^{t-1}), \text{otherwise} \end{cases}, \qquad (1)$$

where k is a client number; $\leftarrow$ represents gradient updating; ω_k^t, ϑ_k^t represent the backbone model and identity classifier of client k after training, respectively.

Step-3: Clients upload updated backbone model parameters ω^t.

Step-4: Sever aggregates client model parameters ω^t to obtain a new global model ω^{t+1} via federated-average [28], as follows.

$$\omega^{t+1} = \sum_{k \in C} \frac{n_k}{n} \omega_k^t, \qquad (2)$$

where C represents the set of clients, n represents the total image number of all client datasets; n_k is image number of the k-th client dataset. Steps 1 to 4 are continuous executed T times to obtain the final server model ω^T.

4 Experiment and Analysis

4.1 Setup

The hardware device is a GeForce RTX 4090 GPU. Software tools are Pytorch 1.10.0, CUDA 11.3, and Python 3.8. The operating system is Ubuntu 20.04. The ImageNet pre-trained ResNet50 is applied as the backbone for server and client models. The learning rate is initialized at 0.01, and as training progresses, the learning rate decreases 0.1 times every 20 rounds. The total round is set to 120, and in each round, the local training epoch is set to 1. The stochastic gradient descent (SGD) optimizer is used for training, and each batch consists of 32 256 × 256 sized images randomly sampled from each client dataset.

Table 2. Performance of the FVVR and non-federated learning (NFL) models.

Datasets		Model	Rank-1(%)	mAP(%)
VeRi		FVVR	58.05	32.91
		NFL	**66.25**	**46.51**
VehicleID	Small	FVVR	74.47	77.41
		NFL	**79.67**	**82.45**
	Medium	FVVR	72.77	75.32
		NFL	**76.73**	**79.52**
	Large	FVVR	70.22	72.81
		NFL	**75.02**	**77.82**
VRID		FVVR	83.27	70.92
		NFL	**88.28**	**79.21**
Boxcars116k		FVVR	63.04	55.11
		NFL	**82.44**	**74.51**
Cityflow		FVVR	36.61	15.93
		NFL	**42.98**	**22.68**

4.2 Federated Performance and Analysis

Table 2 shows the experimental results of FVVR on five datasets. For the VeRi dataset, the FVVR model's Rank-1 and mAP are 58.05% and 32.91%, respectively, while the non-federated learning (NFL) model's Rank-1 and mAP are 66.25% and 46.51%, respectively. It can be seen that Rank-1 and mAP of the FVVR model are 8.2% and 13.6% lower than those of the NFL model, respectively. For the VehicleID dataset, the test set is divided into three subsets [19]: small, medium, and large. For the large test subset, the FVVR model's Rank-1 and mAP are 70.22% and 72.81%, respectively, while the NFL model's Rank-1 and mAP are 75.02% and 77.82%, respectively. From the comparison results on FVVR model and NFL model, it can be observed that the performance of the

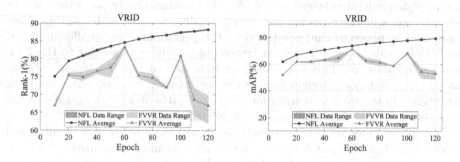

Fig. 4. Performance on VRID.

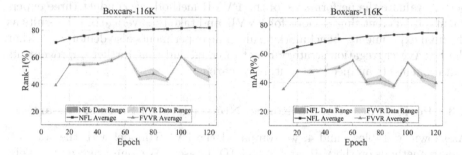

Fig. 5. Performance on Boxcars116k.

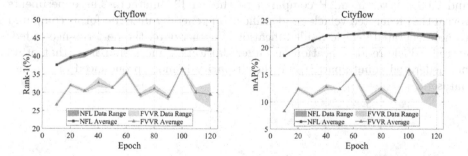

Fig. 6. Performance on Cityflow.

FVVR model is generally lower than that of the NFL model, which indicates that applying federated learning to vehicle re-identification impacts the model's performance, and there remain significant challenges to be addressed. Besides, it can also be observed that compared to the performance on smaller datasets, the FVVR model's performance on larger datasets is more similar to the NFL model's performance. This is because, as indicated in Eq. (2), larger datasets have a more significant weight during the aggregation process, reflecting their importance in the overall distribution of data. Furthermore, a larger dataset is more stable for learning, resulting in better performance.

To gain a more intuitive understanding of the experimental results and trends, Figs. 3, 4, 5, 6, and 7 show the Rank-1 accuracy and mAP of FVVR training for 120 epochs in the five datasets. We perform a test every ten epochs of communication and observe that the FVVR fluctuates continuously during the training process. For example, on the Citylflow dataset, Rank-1 is 36.61% at epoch 100, which is 7.73% higher than that at epoch 90.

Due to the heterogeneity of the client data, the convergence fluctuations using the FVVR method in the training process are relatively significant. Therefore, to better evaluate the performance of the FVVR method, we conduct three experiments in different time periods for FVVR and take the average of the results as the final experimental benchmark result. The experiments also demonstrate that the FedAvg aggregation strategy is not optimal and that further improvements and refinements are needed in future research.

4.3   Performance Comparison to Non-Federated State-of-the-art

As shown in Tables 3 and 4, we compared the FVVR model with the state-of-the-art methods on the VeRi and VehicleID datasets. We found that on the VeRi dataset, the FVVR's performance is 39.25% lower in Rank-1 and 55.09% lower in mAP compared to the RPTM method. Additionally, the server performance on the VeRi dataset has a significant gap compared to other advanced methods, while on the VehicleID dataset, the difference is marginal. For example, in the large subset of VehicleID, the FVVR performance is 22.68% lower in rank-1 and 7.69% lower in mAP compared to the RPTM method. The experiments reveal that federated vehicle re-identification generally underperforms compared to non-federated vehicle re-identification. Furthermore, the performance of federated vehicle re-identification on larger datasets is more similar to that of its non-federated counterpart, while the disparity is more pronounced on smaller datasets.

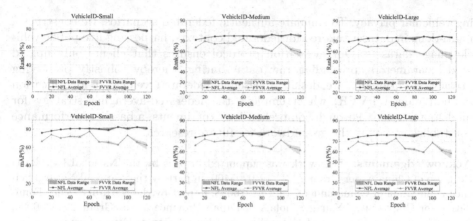

Fig. 7. Performance on small, medium, large subsets of VehicleID.

Table 3. Comparison of FVVR and state-of-the-art on VeRi.

Method	Rank-1	mAP	Reference
RPTM [29]	97.30	88.00	WACV 2023
VehicleNet [30]	96.78	83.41	IEEE TMM 2020
TransReID [31]	97.1	82.3	ICCV 2021
ANet [32]	96.8	81.2	Neurocomputing 2021
MSINet [33]	96.8	78.8	CVPR 2023
CAL [34]	95.4	74.3	ICCV 2021
Git [2]	96.86	80.34	IEEE TIP 2023
FVVR	58.05	32.91	Ours

Table 4. Comparison of FVVR and state-of-the-art on VehicleID.

Method	Small		Medium		Large		Reference
	Rank-1	mAP	Rank-1	mAP	Rank-1	mAP	
PNP LOSS [35]	95.5	–	94.2	–	93.2	–	AAAI 2022
RPTM [29]	95.5	84.8	93.3	81.2	92.9	80.5	WACV 2023
VehicleNet [30]	83.64	–	83.15	–	79.46	–	IEEE TMM 2020
ANet [30]	87.9	–	82.8	–	80.5	–	Neurocomputing 2021
CAL [34]	82.50	87.80	78.20	83.80	75.10	80.90	ICCV 2021
GiT [2]	84.65	90.12	80.52	86.77	77.94	84.26	IEEE TIP 2023
FVVR	74.47	77.41	72.77	75.32	70.22	72.81	Ours

5   Conclusion

This paper presents a federated vehicle re-identification (FV-REID) benchmark, aiming to delve deeper into vehicle re-identification performance while safeguarding vehicular privacy. To simulate authentic federated scenarios, we construct a multi-domain dataset tailored for federated contexts, harnessing five public vehicle image datasets. Our evaluation protocol ensures that clients only upload model parameters, precluding raw data sharing, thereby robustly preserving privacy. Additionally, we design a baseline federated vehicle re-identification method named FVVR, which employs the federated-averaging strategy for model interaction. Through comprehensive experiments, a baseline performance is established, laying the groundwork for future research.

Acknowledgements. This work was supported in part by the National Key R&D Program of China under Grant 2021YFE0205400, in part by the National Natural Science Foundation of China under Grant 61976098, in part by the Natural Science Foundation for Outstanding Young Scholars of Fujian Province under Grant 2022J06023, in part by the Key Program of Natural Science Foundation of Fujian Province under Grant 2023J02022, in part by the High-level Talent Innovation and Entrepreneurship Project of Quanzhou City under Grant 2023C013R.

References

1. Khan, S., Ullah, H.: A survey of advances in vision-based vehicle re-identification. Comput. Vis. Image Underst. **182**, 50–63 (2019)
2. Shen, F., Xie, Y., Zhu, J., Zhu, X., Zeng, H.: Git: graph interactive transformer for vehicle re-identification. IEEE Trans. Image Processing **32**, 1039–1051 (2023)
3. Wang, Y., Peng, J., Wang, H., Wang, M.: Progressive learning with multi-scale attention network for cross-domain vehicle re-identification. Sci. China Inf. Sci. **65**(6), 160103 (2022)
4. Humayun, M., Ashfaq, F., Jhanjhi, N., Alsadun, M.: Traffic management: multi-scale vehicle detection in varying weather conditions using yolov4 and spatial pyramid pooling network. Electronics **11**(17), 2748 (2022)
5. Berroukham, A., Housni, K., Lahraichi, M., Boulfrifi, I.: Deep learning-based methods for anomaly detection in video surveillance: a review. Bull. Electr. Eng. Inf. **12**(1), 314–327 (2023)
6. Win, K., Li, K., Chen, J., Viger, P., Li, K.: Fingerprint classification and identification algorithms for criminal investigation: a survey. Futur. Gener. Comput. Syst. **110**, 758–771 (2020)
7. Wu, X., Huang, F., Hu, Z., Huang, H.: Faster adaptive federated learning. In: AAAI, vol. 37, pp. 10379–10387 (2023)
8. Song, J., Wang, W., Gadekallu, T., Cao, J., Liu, Y.: EPPDA: an efficient privacy-preserving data aggregation federated learning scheme. IEEE Trans. Netw. Sci. Eng. **10**, 3047–3057 (2022)
9. Chen, S., Yu, D., Zou, Y., Yu, J., Cheng, X.: Decentralized wireless federated learning with differential privacy. IEEE Trans. Ind. Inf. **18**(9), 6273–6282 (2022)
10. Jiang, M., Wang, Z., Dou, Q.: Harmofl: harmonizing local and global drifts in federated learning on heterogeneous medical images. In: AAAI, vol. 36, pp. 1087–1095 (2022)
11. Khan, A., et al.: CD-FL: cataract images based disease detection using federated learning. Comput. Syst. Sci. Eng. **47**(2), 1733–1750 (2023)
12. Almadhor, A., et al.: Chest radiographs based pneumothorax detection using federated learning. Comput. Syst. Sci. Eng. **47**(2), 1775–1791 (2023)

13. Zheng, Z., Zhou, Y., Sun, Y., Wang, Z., Liu, B., Li, K.: Applications of federated learning in smart cities: recent advances, taxonomy, and open challenges. Connect. Sci. **34**(1), 1–28 (2022)
14. Wijethilaka, S., Liyanage, M.: A federated learning approach for improving security in network slicing. In: GLOBECOM 2022–2022 IEEE Global Communications Conference, pp. 915–920 (2022)
15. Zhuang, W., Gan X., Wen, Y., Zhang, S.: Optimizing performance of federated person re-identification: Benchmarking and analysis. ACM Trans. Multimedia Comput. Commun. Appl. **19**(1s), 1–18 (2023)
16. Sun, S., Wu, G., Gong S.: Decentralised person re-identification with selective knowledge aggregation. arXiv preprint arXiv:2110.11384 (2021)
17. Zhang, L., Gao, G., Zhang, H.: Spatial-temporal federated learning for lifelong person re-identification on distributed edges. IEEE Trans. Circ. Syst. Video Technol. (2023)
18. Liu, X., Liu, W., Mei, T., Ma, H.: A deep learning-based approach to progressive vehicle re-identification for urban surveillance. In: Leibe, B., Matas, J., Sebe, N., Welling, M. (eds.) ECCV 2016. LNCS, vol. 9906, pp. 869–884. Springer, Cham (2016). https://doi.org/10.1007/978-3-319-46475-6_53
19. Liu, H., Tian, Y., Yang, Y., Pang, L., Huang, T.: Deep relative distance learning: tell the difference between similar vehicles. In: CVPR, pp. 2167–2175 (2016)
20. Li, X., Yuan, M., Jiang, Q., Li, G.: Vrid-1: a basic vehicle re-identification dataset for similar vehicles. In International Conference on Intelligent Transportation Systems, pp. 1–8 (2017)
21. Sochor, J., Špaňhel, J., Herout, A.: Boxcars: improving fine-grained recognition of vehicles using 3-d bounding boxes in traffic surveillance. IEEE Trans. Intell. Transport. Syst. **20**(1), 97–108 (2018)
22. Tang, Z., et al.: Cityflow: a city-scale benchmark for multi-target multi-camera vehicle tracking and re-identification. In: CVPR, pp. 8797–8806 (2019)
23. Chu, R., Sun, Y., Li, Y., Liu, Z., Zhang, C., Wei, Y.: Vehicle re-identification with viewpoint-aware metric learning. In: ICCV, pp. 8282–8291 (2019)
24. Yu, J. Oh, H.: Unsupervised vehicle re-identification via self-supervised metric learning using feature dictionary. In: Conference on Intelligent Robots and Systems, pp. 3806–3813 (2021)
25. Luo, H.: A strong baseline and batch normalization neck for deep person re-identification. IEEE Trans. Multimedia **22**(10), 2597–2609 (2019)
26. Zheng, L., Shen, L., Tian, L., Wang, S., Wang J., Tian, Q.: Scalable person re-identification: a benchmark. In: ICCV, pp. 1116–1124 (2015)
27. He, K., Zhang, X., Ren, S., Sun, J.: Deep residual learning for image recognition. In: CVPR, pp. 770–778 (2016)
28. McMahan, B., Moore, E., Ramage, D., Hampson, S., y Arcas, B.: Communication-efficient learning of deep networks from decentralized data. Artif. Intell. Stat. 1273–1282 (2017)
29. Ghosh, A., Shanmugalingam, K., Lin, W.: Relation preserving triplet mining for stabilising the triplet loss in re-identification systems. In: WACV, pp. 4840–4849 (2023)
30. Zheng, Z., Ruan, T., Wei, Y., Yang, Y., Mei, T.: Vehiclenet: learning robust visual representation for vehicle re-identification. IEEE Trans. Multimedia **23**, 2683–2693 (2020)
31. He, S., Luo, H., Wang, P., Wang, F., Li, H., Jiang, W.: Transreid: transformer-based object re-identification. In: ICCV, pp. 15013–15022 (2021)

32. Quispe, R., Lan, C., Zeng, W., Pedrini, H.: Attributenet: attribute enhanced vehicle re-identification. Neurocomputing **465**, 84–92 (2021)
33. Gu, J., et al.: Msinet: twins contrastive search of multi-scale interaction for object reid. In: CVPR, pp. 19243–19253 (2023)
34. Rao, Y., Chen, G., Lu, J., Zhou, J.: Counterfactual attention learning for fine-grained visual categorization and re-identification. In: ICCV, pp. 1025–1034 (2021)
35. Li, Z., et al.: Rethinking the optimization of average precision: only penalizing negative instances before positive ones is enough. In: AAAI, vol. 36, pp. 1518–1526 (2022)

Alpha Local Difference Loss Function for Deep Image Matting

Jiehong Li[1], Peijie Huang[1(✉)], Wensheng Li[2], and Yihui Liang[2]

[1] College of Mathematics and Informatics, South China Agricultural University, Guangzhou, China
pjhuang@scau.edu.cn
[2] School of Computer, University of Electronic Science and Technology of China, Zhongshan Institute, Zhongshan, China

Abstract. In recent years, deep learning-based matting methods have received increasing attention due to their superior performance. The design of the loss function plays a important role in the performance of matting models. Existing loss functions train the network by supervising it to learn specific value, gradient, and detailed information of the ground-truth alpha matte. However, these loss functions only supervise network learning based on the value of alpha matte, and the matting network may not fully understand the uniqueness of the matting task. We introduce a loss function which supervises image features. On one hand, it effectively extracts useful information from the ground-truth alpha. On the other hand, this loss function combines the mathematical model of matting, which constrains the image features to satisfy local differences. Multiple experiments have shown that our loss function enhances the generalization ability of matting networks.

Keywords: Natural Image Matting · Loss Function · Deep Learning

1 Introduction

Image matting is a challenging tasks in computer vision that aims to separate the foreground from a natural image by predicting the transparency of each pixel. It has been applied in the field of biometric recognition, such as finger-vein [1], gait recognition [2,3], and face verification [4], as it can finely delineate the target contours, thus facilitating biometric recognition tasks.

The image $\mathbf{I}$ can be represented as a convex combination of the foreground $\mathbf{F}$ and the background $\mathbf{B}$.

$$\mathbf{I}_i = \alpha_i \mathbf{F}_i + (1 - \alpha_i)\mathbf{B}_i \qquad \alpha_i \in [0,1] \tag{1}$$

where α_i, $\mathbf{F}_i$, and $\mathbf{B}_i$ respectively represent the transparency, foreground color, and background color at position i in the image. This problem is a highly underdetermined mathematical problem. There are three unknowns and only one known in the equation. The trimap is introduced to provide additional constrains. It consists of three parts: the known foreground region where the alpha value is known to be 1, the known background region where the alpha value is 0, and an unknown region where the alpha value needs to be determined. Existing deep learning-based matting methods have greatly surpassed traditional methods in terms of the quality of alpha mattes, attracting a rapid increase in attention to deep learning-based matting methods.

The loss function is a fundamental component of deep learning, as it measures the difference between the predicted output of a model and the true labels. It provides guidance for model training and optimization objectives, allowing the model to gradually improve its prediction accuracy. The alpha prediction loss is computed as the average absolute difference between the predicted alpha matte and the ground-truth alpha matte. The composition loss, introduced by [5], utilizes the ground-truth foreground and background colors to supervise the network at the pixel level. Gradient loss [6] has been proposed to improve the sharpness of the predicted alpha matte and reduce excessive smoothness. The Laplacian Pyramid loss [7], a multi-scale technique, is employed to measure the disparities between the predicted alpha matte and the ground-truth alpha matte in local and global regions. Indeed, the loss functions used for image matting encompass supervision at the pixel level as well as supervision of the gradient and detail changes in the alpha channel, which improves the accuracy and quality of the matting results. But these loss functions only focus on the differences between the alpha matte predicted by the network and the ground-truth alpha matte. Consequently, the network may not effectively learn valuable information inherent in the ground-truth across different feature layers. In general, increasing the depth of a neural network can improve its representation ability to some extent. To better train the network, it is common to add auxiliary supervision to certain layers of the neural network. Some methods [8,9] supervise the multi-scale features obtained by the decoder at different scales. However, directly supervising neural networks with ground-truth alpha mattes causes the decoder at a small scale to strictly approximate the ground-truth alpha mattes, which may result in overfitting. Figure 1 provides an example. When the image matting method is applied to scenarios different from the training images, the prediction of the decoder at a small scale may not be accurate. Any prediction error of the decoder would degrade the quality of alpha mattes.

We introduce a loss function called Alpha Local Difference Loss(ALDL), which leverages the local differences within the ground-truth to supervise features at various resolution scales. Unlike gradient loss, ALDL captures the differences between the pixel and its surrounding pixels in the ground-truth, and utilizes these differences as constraints to supervise the features of the image. Gradient loss only describes the gradient of the central pixel in the x and y directions, without explicitly capturing the specific variations between the central pixel and local surrounding pixels. Furthermore, instead of applying strict supervision on early decoders [8,9], ALDL is a loose supervision that leads the matting network to learn the relationships between features, rather than strictly adhering to specific numerical values.

This work's main contributions can be summarized as follows:

(a) Input Image   (b) Trimap   (c) Ground-truth   (d) Matteformer   (e) Ours

Fig. 1. From left to right, the images are the input, trimap, ground-truth, the predicted results by the MatteFormer and ours. We can see that there are serious errors in the prediction of the intermediate details of alpha. These errors are the result of inaccurate alpha prediction caused by low-resolution feature estimation.

1. We propose a loss function called Alpha Local Difference Loss specifically designed for matting networks, which utilizes the supervision of local feature relationships. This loss function can be easily integrated into existing networks with hardly any need to add extra parameters.
2. Through experiments conducted on multiple networks and datasets, our Alpha Local Difference Loss demonstrates the ability to improve the generalization capability of matting networks, resulting in enhanced object details in the matting process.

2 Methodology

In this section, we illustrate how to define the difference between each point and its local neighboring points based on the local information of the ground-truth alpha. The local difference is embedded into the image features, and the Alpha Local Difference Loss is proposed to constrain the network in learning this difference. Furthermore, an analysis is conducted to determine which features in the neural network should be supervised.

2.1 Local Similarity of Alpha Labels and Features

Consistent with the assumption of closed-form matting [10], we assume that pixels within a local region have the same foreground color F and background color B. According to Eq. (1), we can obtain the pixel value difference ΔI between two points $\mathbf{x}$ and $\mathbf{y}$ within a local region. Similarly, by using the ground-truth alpha, we can also obtain the alpha value difference $\Delta \alpha$ between point $\mathbf{x}$ and $\mathbf{y}$.

$$I_x - I_y = \alpha_x F + (1 - \alpha_x) - \alpha_y F - (1 - \alpha_y)B = (\alpha_x - \alpha_y)(F - B) \quad (2)$$

$$\Delta I = \Delta \alpha (F - B) \quad (3)$$

$$\Delta f = \Delta \alpha (f_F - f_B) \quad (4)$$

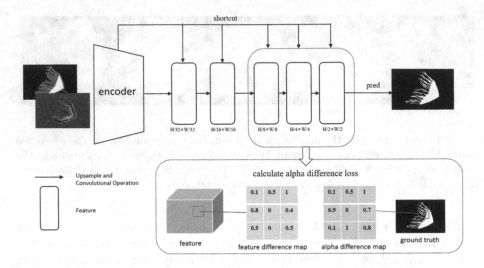

Fig. 2. The process of calculating ALDL

It can be observed that there is a linear relationship between the color value difference ΔI and the $F - B$ within a local region on the image. Because F and B are invariant within the local region, $F - B$ is a fixed vector. By analogy, we can consider feature difference Δf as a linear combination of features f_F and f_B. In spatial terms, for two features f_F and f_B within a local region, Eq. (4) is obtained. The features should also be constrained to satisfy this relationship as much as possible. This relationship embodies the intrinsic meaning of matting, and it is believed that it will help the network learn to synthesize Eq. (1).

2.2   The Design of Loss Function

For a position i, let $\partial \{i\}$ denote the set of points within the M1 $\times$ M2 region R, where M1 and M2 respectively denote the height and width of the R, and pixel i is located at the center position of the R. The set of values for the ground-truth alpha at position i is: $\partial \{\alpha_i\} = \{\alpha_{i1}, \alpha_{i2}, \alpha_{i3}, ..., \alpha_{iM1 \times M2}\}$. It is worth noting that α_{ij} is a scalar. We can compute the differences between α_i and each element in its set $\partial \{\alpha_i\}$.

$$dif\left(\alpha_i, \alpha_{ij}\right) = \alpha_i - \alpha_{ij} \tag{5}$$

$$sim_\alpha\left(\alpha_i, \alpha_{ij}\right) = 1 - \left|dif\left(\alpha_i, \alpha_{ij}\right)\right| \tag{6}$$

$$sim_f\left(f_i, f_{ij}\right) = \varphi(\cos(norm(f_i), norm(f_{ij}))) \tag{7}$$

$$loss = \sum_i \sum_j sim_\alpha\left(\alpha_i, \alpha_{ij}\right) - sim_f\left(f_i, f_{ij}\right) \tag{8}$$

$dif\left(\alpha_i, \alpha_{ij}\right)$ represents the difference between the alpha value of the central pixel i and the alpha values of other positions within the region R. To facilitate computation, we normalize the values between 0 and 1 using the sim_α function. The smaller the difference between α_i and α_{ij}, the closer the value of sim_α tends to approach 1. Given the feature $X \in R^{H/r \times W/r \times C}$, for any point at the location i in X, $\partial\left\{f_i\right\} = \left\{f_{i1}, f_{i2}, f_{i3}, ..., f_{iM1 \times M2}\right\}$, where $f_{iM1 \times M2} \in R^{1 \times 1 \times C}$, r is the downsampling factor. In order to align the resolution of alpha with the feature, the ground-truth alpha is downsampled to obtain $\partial\left\{\alpha_i^r\right\}$. Each element in the set $\partial\left\{\alpha_i^r\right\}$ and $\partial\left\{f_i\right\}$ corresponds to each other based on their spatial positions. It is worth noting that our goal is to correspond the vector Δf with the scalar $\Delta\alpha$, so the similarity between the two features is calculated to convert the vector into a scalar. The definitions of distance between features is (7), $norm(f_i)$ denotes the calculation of the norm of vector f_i, φ represents a mapping function, cos refers to the calculation of the cosine similarity. The aim is to maintain consistency in terms of both the differneces of alpha values and the differneces of features between each point and its neighboring adjacent points. Hence, the definition of Alpha Local Difference Loss is Eq. (8).

2.3   The Supervisory Position of ALDL

[11] indicates that different layers in a convolutional neural network tend to learn features at different levels. Shallow layers learn low-level features such as color and edges and the last few layers learn task-relevant semantic features. If the features at shallow layers are supervised to capture task-related knowledge, the original feature extraction process in the neural network would be overlooked. Therefore, we only supervise the features outputted by the decoder. Additionally, our supervision relationship is derived from the ground-truth alpha in local regions, which can be considered as extracting features at a lower-level semantic level. Alpha Local Difference Loss should not be used for supervising features representing higher-level semantic features with very low resolution. As shown in the Fig. 2, taking MatteFormer [9] as an example, its decoder outputs features with resolutions of 1/32, 1/16, 1/8, 1/4, and 1/2. Supervision is only applied to the features with resolutions of 1/8, 1/4, and 1/2 in the decoder, while the feature with a resolution of 1 is not supervised in order to reduce computational cost.

3   Experiments

To validate the effectiveness of the suggested Alpha Local Difference Loss function, we extensively perform experiments on various matting baselines using multiple benchmark datasets. The performance is assessed in real-world scenarios to verify its generalization capability.

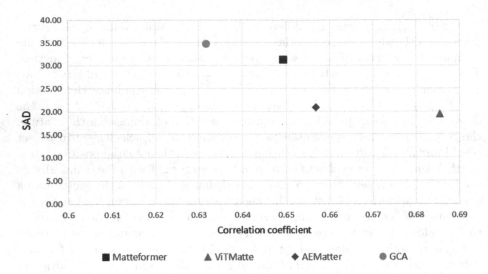

Fig. 3. Y-axis: the SAD error on AIM-500. X-axis: the correlation coefficient between the difference of alpha and the difference of feature.

Table 1. The effectiveness of implementing ALDL

	AIM-500				AM-2K				P3M			
	MSE	SAD	Grad	Conn	MSE	SAD	Grad	Conn	MSE	SAD	Grad	Conn
GCA	40.00	**35.25**	27.86	35.89	**14.49**	**9.23**	8.92	**8.17**	17.49	8.50	13.41	7.90
GCA+ALDL	**38.33**	35.65	**27.82**	**36.13**	15.28	9.45	**8.75**	8.50	**16.98**	**8.27**	**12.92**	**7.74**
MatteFormer	34.32	31.25	23.53	31.25	17.00	9.93	9.81	9.16	22.62	10.07	**14.39**	9.63
MatteFormer+ALDL	**31.11**	**28.23**	**21.79**	**28.21**	**15.68**	**9.68**	9.73	**8.93**	**21.42**	9.93	14.48	**9.51**
VitMatte	15.69	19.35	12.99	18.74	7.65	6.50	6.07	5.46	11.34	6.40	10.33	6.79
VitMatte+ALDL	**15.45**	**17.76**	**12.85**	**17.09**	**7.87**	**6.44**	**5.83**	**5.41**	**10.84**	**6.16**	**9.82**	**5.56**

- MSE values are scaled by 10^{-3}
- The best results are in bold

3.1 Datasets and Implementation Details

We train models on the Adobe Image Matting [5] dataset and report performance on the real-world AIM-500 [8], AM-2K [12], P3M [13]. AIM-500 contains 100 portrait images, 200 animal images, 34 images with transparent objects, 75 plant images, 45 furniture images, 36 toy images, and 10 fruit images. The AM-2k test set comprises 200 images of animals, classified into 20 distinct categories. P3M-500-NP contains 500 diverse portrait images that showcase diversity in foreground, hair, body contour, posture, and other aspects. These datasets comprise a plethora of human portrait outlines and exhibit numerous similarities to datasets employed for tasks like gait recognition and other biometric recognition tasks. Our implementation is based on PyTorch. No architectural changes are required. We only modify the loss function. The height M1 and width M2 of the local region R are both set to 3, and the center position of R belongs to an unknown region in the trimap. Various matting models utilize distinct loss functions. In order to effectively illustrate the efficacy of ALDL, we directly incorporate ALDL into the existing loss function. In line with the approach outlined in [14], four widely adopted metrics are employed to assess the quality of the predicted alpha matte. These metrics include the sum of absolute differences (SAD), mean squared errors (MSE), gradient errors (Grad), and connectivity errors (Conn). Four matting baselines, namely: GCA Matting [15], MatteFormer [9], VitMatte [16], AEMatter [17] are evaluated. GCA implements a guided contextual attention module to propagate opacity information based on low-level features. MatteFormer introduces prior-token for the propagation of global information. VitMatte proposes a robust matting method based on Vit [18].

3.2 Proof of the Local Similarity Hypothesis Between Alpha and Feature

In order to validate the effectiveness of the local similarity hypothesis in improving image matting, during the inference stage, we extracted the feature outputs from the intermediate layer. Based on (6) and (7), the correlation coefficient of sim_α and sim_f for each point in the unknown region of the trimap have been calculated. It can be observed that the higher the correlation coefficient, the better the matting performance of the method from Fig. 3. This indicates that if the features satisfy the local differences defined by ground-truth alpha, it can improve the quality of the matting.

3.3 Generalization

ALDL was applied to three different baselines and compared with their counterparts without ALDL, as shown in the Table 1. It can be observed that for MatteFormer and VitMatte, ALDL improves their generalization ability on three datasets. This suggests that constraining the relationships between local features can help the network better understand the matting task. The combination of GCA with ALDL demonstrates its generalization ability, particularly on the P3M dataset. GCA incorporates a shallow guidance module to learn feature relationships, but evaluating the quality of these relationships poses a challenge. In contrast, ALDL explicitly constrains local feature relationships using ground-truth alpha, aligning with the objective of GCA's shallow guidance module. Consequently, the addition of ALDL to GCA results in moderate performance improvements on the AIM-500 and AM-2K datasets. GCA consistently performs well according to the Grad metric, indicating that ALDL excels at capturing intricate details, accurately defining contours, and proves advantageous for downstream tasks involving matting.

Table 2. Ablation experiment of ALDL

MatteFormer	R1	R2	AIM-500				AM-2K				P3M			
			MSE	SAD	Grad	Conn	MSE	SAD	Grad	Conn	MSE	SAD	Grad	Conn
			34.32	31.25	23.53	31.25	17.00	9.93	9.81	9.16	22.62	10.07	14.39	9.63
	✓		**26.99**	**23.95**	**20.59**	**23.41**	**15.42**	**9.10**	**9.14**	**8.23**	**18.11**	**8.69**	**13.32**	**8.16**
		✓	33.16	29.10	23.23	28.92	15.63	9.39	9.94	8.52	22.18	9.74	14.65	9.28
GCA			40.00	**35.25**	27.86	35.89	**14.49**	**9.23**	8.92	**8.17**	17.49	8.50	13.41	7.90
	✓		**38.33**	35.65	**27.82**	**36.13**	15.28	9.45	**8.75**	8.50	**16.98**	**8.27**	**12.92**	**7.74**
		✓	39.04	35.23	28.34	35.82	15.39	9.81	8.96	8.80	17.31	8.53	13.26	7.80

- MSE values are scaled by 10^{-3}
- R1: ALDL supervises features with resolutions of 1/2, 1/4, 1/8. R2: ALDL supervises features with all resolutions of decoder output.

3.4 Ablation Study of Deep Supervision

An ablation experiment was conducted using MatteFormer, as its decoder's output features are supervised with ground-truth. The difference is that ALDL supervises the local differential relationships between features, while Matte-Former directly supervises the alpha values at the feature level. As shown in the Table 2, MatteFormer marked with R1 or R2 denotes removing the structure that originally outputs alpha values from the decoder and instead directly supervising the feature level with ALDL. GCA marked with R1 or R2 represents the application of the ALDL to the intermediate layer features of the decoder. Experimental results demonstrate that applying ALDL to features, which is a relatively weak constraint, yields better performance than directly supervising with alpha values. Additionally, since ALDL explores local information from ground-truth, which essentially belongs to low-level features, it is more suitable for shallow features rather than deep features.

4   Conclusion

This study focuses on the loss function of deep image matting methods. We analyzed the shortcomings in the loss functions of existing matting models, and proposed the alpha local difference loss function, which takes the ground-truth alpha matte and the composition formula of image matting as the starting point, to supervise the image features. Extensive experiments are performed on several test datasets using state-of-the-art deep image matting methods. Experimental results verify the effectiveness of the proposed ALDL and demonstrate that ALDL can improve the generalization ability of deep image matting methods.

Acknowledgements. This work was supported in part by National Natural Science Foundation of China (62002053,62276103), Guangdong Basic and Applied Basic Research Foundation (2020A1515110504), Natural Science Foundation of Guangdong Province (2021A1515011866, 2020A1515010696, 2022A1515011491), and of Sichuan Province (2022YFG0314), the Guangdong University Key Platforms and Research

Projects (2018KZDXM066), Key Research and Development Program of Zhongshan (2019A4018), the Major Science and Technology Foundation of Zhongshan City (2019B2009, 2019A40027, 2021A1003), and Zhongshan Science and Technology Research Project of Social welfare (210714094038458, 2020B2017), Natural Science Foundation of Guangdong Province (2021A1515011864).

References

1. Yang, J., Shi, Y.: Finger-vein network enhancement and segmentation. Pattern Anal. Appl. **17**, 783–797 (2014)
2. Hofmann, M., Schmidt, S.M., Rajagopalan, A.N., Rigoll, G.: Combined face and gait recognition using alpha matte preprocessing. In: 2012 5th IAPR International Conference on Biometrics (ICB), pp. 390–395. IEEE (2012)
3. Han, Y., Wang, Z., Han, X., Fan, X.: Gaitpretreatment: robust pretreatment strategy for gait recognition. In: 2022 International Conference on Communications, Computing, Cybersecurity, and Informatics (CCCI), pp. 1–6. IEEE (2022)
4. Wasi, A., Gupta, M.: Dfvnet: real-time disguised face verification. In: 2022 IEEE India Council International Subsections Conference (INDISCON), pp. 1–5. IEEE (2022)
5. Xu, N., Price, B., Cohen, S., Huang, T.: Deep image matting. In: Proceedings of the IEEE Conference on Computer Vision and Pattern Recognition, pp. 2970–2979 (2017)
6. Tang, J., Aksoy, Y., Oztireli, C., Gross, M., Aydin, T.O.: Learning-based sampling for natural image matting. In: Proceedings of the IEEE/CVF Conference on Computer Vision and Pattern Recognition, pp. 3055–3063 (2019)
7. Hou, Q., Liu, F.: Context-aware image matting for simultaneous foreground and alpha estimation. In: Proceedings of the IEEE/CVF International Conference on Computer Vision, pp. 4130–4139 (2019)
8. Yu, Q., et al.: Mask guided matting via progressive refinement network. In: Proceedings of the IEEE/CVF Conference on Computer Vision and Pattern Recognition, PP. 1154–1163 (2021)
9. Park, G., Son, S., Yoo, J., Kim, S., Kwak, N.: Matteformer: transformer-based image matting via prior-tokens. In: Proceedings of the IEEE/CVF Conference on Computer Vision and Pattern Recognition, pp. 11696–11706 (2022)
10. Levin, A., Lischinski, D., Weiss, Y.: A closed-form solution to natural image matting. IEEE Trans. Pattern Anal. Mach. Intell. **30**(2), 228–242 (2007)
11. Zhang, L., Chen, X., Zhang, J., Dong, R., Ma, K.: Contrastive deep supervision. In: Avidan, S., Brostow, G., Cisse, M., Farinella, G.M., Hassner, T. (eds.) ECCV 2022. LNCS, vol. 13866, pp. 1–19. Springer, Heidelberg (2022). https://doi.org/10.1007/978-3-031-19809-0_1
12. Li, J., Zhang, J., Maybank, S.J., Tao, D.: Bridging composite and real: towards end-to-end deep image matting. Int. J. Comput. Vision **130**(2), 246–266 (2022)
13. Li, J., Ma, S., Zhang, J., Tao, D.: Privacy-preserving portrait matting. In: Proceedings of the 29th ACM International Conference on Multimedia, pp. 3501–3509 (2021)
14. Rhemann, C., Rother, C., Wang, J., Gelautz, M., Kohli, P., Rott, P.: A perceptually motivated online benchmark for image matting. In: 2009 IEEE Conference on Computer Vision and Pattern Recognition, pp. 1826–1833. IEEE (2009)

15. Li, Y., Lu, H.: Natural image matting via guided contextual attention. In: Proceedings of the AAAI Conference on Artificial Intelligence, vol. 34, pp. 11450–11457 (2020)
16. Yao, J., Wang, X., Yang, S., Wang, B.: Vitmatte: boosting image matting with pretrained plain vision transformers. arXiv preprint arXiv:2305.15272 (2023)
17. Liu, Q., Zhang, S., Meng, Q., Li, R., Zhong, B., Nie, L.: Rethinking context aggregation in natural image matting. arXiv preprint arXiv:2304.01171 (2023)
18. Dosovitskiy, A., et al.: An image is worth 16×16 words: transformers for image recognition at scale. arXiv preprint arXiv:2010.11929 (2020)

Enhanced Memory Adversarial Network for Anomaly Detection

Yangfan Liu, Yanan Guo[✉], Kangning Du, and Lin Cao

Key Laboratory of Information and Communication Systems,
Ministry of Information Industry, Beijing Information Science
and Technology University, Beijing 100101, China
yananguo@bistu.edu.cn

Abstract. Video anomaly detection (VAD) aims to detect abnormal behaviors or events during video monitoring. Recent VAD methods use a proxy task that reconstructs the input video frames, quantifying the degree of anomaly by computing the reconstruction error. However, these methods do not consider the diversity of normal patterns and neglect the scale differences of the abnormal foreground image between different video frames. To address these issues, we propose an unsupervised video anomaly detection method termed enhanced memory adversarial network, which integrates a dilated convolution feature extraction encoder and a feature matching memory module. The dilated convolution feature extraction encoder extracts features at different scales by increasing the receptive field. The feature matching memory module stores multiple prototype features of normal video frames, ensuring that the query features are closer to the prototypes while maintaining a distinct separation between different prototypes. Our approach not only improves the prediction performance but also considers the diversity of normal patterns. At the same time, it reduces the representational capacity of the predictive networks while enhancing the model's sensitivity to anomalies. Experiments on the UCSD Ped2 and CUHK Avenue dataset, comparing our method with existing unsupervised video anomaly detection methods, show that our proposed method is superior in the AUC metric, achieving an AUC of 96.3% on the UCSD Ped2 dataset, and an AUC of 86.5% on the CUHK Avenue dataset.

Keywords: Anomaly detection · Dilated convolution · Feature matching

1 Introduction

With the widespread application of video surveillance technology, video anomaly detection has emerged as an essential component in areas such as security protection [1], autonomous driving [2], industrial intelligence [3], medical assistance [4]. Video anomaly detection is the process of detecting abnormal behaviors or events during video monitoring.

W. Jia et al. (Eds.): CCBR 2023, LNCS 14463, pp. 417–426, 2023.
https://doi.org/10.1007/978-981-99-8565-4_39

Video anomaly detection is typically implemented using a proxy task [5] that reconstructs the input video frames or predicts the future frames, quantifying the degree of anomaly by computing the reconstruction or prediction error. Existing proxy task can be classified into two categories: reconstruction discrimination and future frame prediction method. Representative reconstruction discrimination algorithms include convolution autoencoder [5], U-Net [6], and generative adversarial networks [7]. In cases where the abnormality features subtle and gradual changes, these reconstruction-based methods struggle to capture the presence of anomalies, does not explicitly consider the diversity of normal patterns. The future frame prediction approach assumes that normal events occur in an orderly manner, while abnormal events are sudden and unpredictable. In order to suppress the generalization ability of the Auto-encoder, Gong et al. [8] proposed a Memory-augmented Auto-encoder (MemAE) for anomaly detection. MemAE receives information from the encoder and then uses it as a query to retrieve some similar memory slots which are then combined to yield new encoding features for the decoder to reconstruct. The MemAE is trained on normal data, thus encouraged to store normal patterns in the memory. Park et al. [9] proposed an unsupervised learning approach to anomaly detection that explicitly considers the diversity of normal patterns, while reducing the representation capacity of CNNs. They utilize a memory module with a novel update scheme, in which the items within the memory capture prototypical patterns of normal data. However, these methods do not guarantee sufficient similarity between different memory contents and different query features, thus limiting the enhancement of query features. Additionally, the types of anomalous behaviors are diverse, and the sizes and scales of anomalous regions in video frames vary. When quantifying the degree of anomaly through reconstruction error, for certain abnormal video frames with relatively small anomalous regions, the reconstruction error is minor, leading to potential misclassification as normal frames.

To address above problem, we propose an enhanced memory adversarial network anomaly detection framework that contains a dilated convolution feature extraction encoder and a feature matching memory module, which is used for efficient video anomaly detection tasks. The proposed network aims to increase the prediction error of abnormal frames, reduce the prediction error of normal frames, thereby improving the accuracy of our anomaly detection, and enhancing the network's sensitivity to anomalies. Due to the remarkable capability of dilated convolutions to capture significant information across larger areas, we propose a dilated convolution feature extraction encoder that facilitates the extraction of features at various scales. To constrain the generalization ability of the prediction network, we added a feature matching memory module between the encoder and decoder of the generator. This module can learn and store multiple prototypes feature exist in the feature space of normal video frames. By using these prototypes feature, we match and enhance the features of video frames. Additionally, we propose to use the infoNCE loss [10] in the feature matching memory module to ensure that the query features are closer to the memory items while maintaining a distinct separation between different memory items.

2   Method

The overall architecture is shown in Fig. 1. Our model consists of a generator network, a discriminator network and an optical flow network. We first input consecutive frames $I_{se} = \{I_1, I_2, ..., I_n\}$ into the dilated convolution feature extraction encoder. It utilizes dilated convolutions with varying dilation rates to extract features of different scales from these input frames. Then these features are fed into feature matching memory module and connect them to the nearest memory item to enhance the features. Next, the enhanced features are input into the decoder to generate the future frames $\hat{I}_t$. The ground truth is I_t. When abnormal frames are input, a large error between the predicted frame and the ground truth indicates that anomalous events have occurred. Additionally, we introduce LiteFlownet [11] optical flow network to enhance the motion feature correlation between adjacent frames, which makes $\hat{I}_t$ closer to I_t. Finally, we employ a patch GAN discriminator [12] to discern the predicted frames during adversarial training. Each of the components are discussed next.

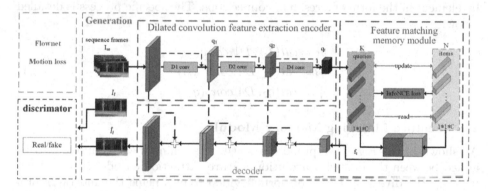

Fig. 1. The overall architecture of our proposed method.

2.1   Dilated Convolution Feature Extraction Encoder

From a given sequence of n frames I_{se}, the high level features can be extracted by encoder. However, different input frames may contain features of varying sizes and scales. In order to extract features of different scales, we employ dilated convolutions to increase the receptive field. In regular convolution, the size and shape of each convolution kernel define its receptive field, which determines the range of the input image it can "see". Dilated convolution, on the other hand, enlarges the span of the convolution kernel by inserting zero values, thus expanding the range of the receptive field. Figure 2 illustrates that a dilated convolution with a 3×3 kernel and a dilation rate of 2 is equivalent regular convolution with a 5×5 kernel. Hence, we employ dilated convolutions with different dilated rates to extract features of different scales.

Fig. 2. (a) is the dilated convolution receptive field with an dilated rate of 2, (b) is the regular convolution receptive field.

Firstly, we utilize dilated convolution $D1\ conv$ with a dilation rate of 1 to extract small-scale features from the input I_{se}. Then, we employ dilated convolution $D2\ conv$ with a dilation rate of 2 to extract medium-scale features. Finally, dilated convolution $D4\ conv$ with a dilation rate of 4 are used to extract large-scale features. Additionally, the multi-scale features are summed element by element in the form of a residual connections. The specific process is detailed below:

$$q_1 = cat(I_{se}, D1\ conv(I_{se}))$$
$$q_2 = cat(q_1, D2\ conv(q_1)) \tag{1}$$
$$q_t = cat(q_2, D4\ conv(q_2))$$

2.2 Feature Matching Memory Module

As shown in the Fig. 1, we propose a feature matching memory module to be added between the dilated convolution feature extraction encoder and decoder, it study the diverse patterns of normal video frames helps the generator produce high-quality predictions for normal frames and low-quality predictions for abnormal frames, thereby limiting the excessive expressive power of the prediction network. Inspired by [9], feature matching memory module contains M items, which prototypical patterns of normal data on the items in the memory. It read and update the M items to store the diverse patterns of normal video, an InfoNCE [10] loss is introduced to encourage the query features to be close to the nearest memory item and the memory items are far enough apart.

Read. In order to enhance the features $q_t \in \mathbb{R}^{H \times W \times C}$ from dilated convolution feature extraction encoder, we need to read the items. The features q_t are inputed into feature matching memory module and divided into $H \times W$ query features $q_t^k \in \mathbb{R}^{1 \times 1 \times C}(k = 1, 2, ..., K; K = H \times W)$ along the channel dimension. For each query q_t^k, the SoftMax function is applied to calculate the cosine similarity $w_t^{k,n}(n = 1, ..., N)$ between it and each memory items p_n to obtain matching probabilities, as follows:

$$w_t^{k,n} = \frac{exp((p_n)^T q_t^k)}{\sum_{n'=1}^{N} exp((p_n)^T q_t^k)} \tag{2}$$

For each query feature q_t^k, we calculate a weighted average of the matching probability weight $w_t^{k,m}$ and memory item p_n, resulting in the processed feature $\hat{p}_t^k \in \mathbb{R}^{1 \times 1 \times C}$ as follows:

$$\hat{p}_t^k = \sum_{n=1}^{N} w_t^{k,n} p_n \tag{3}$$

Once the corresponding $\hat{p}_t^k$ is found for each q_t^k query, $\hat{p}_t^k$ will form a feature tensor of the same size as q_t, denoted as $\hat{p}_t \in \mathbb{R}^{H \times W \times C}$. The q_t and p_t are then concatenated along the feature channel dimension to obtain a feature tensor f_t as the input to the decoder, as follows:

$$f_t = cat(q_t; \hat{p}_t) \in \mathbb{R}^{H \times W \times 2C} \tag{4}$$

Update. For each memory item p_n, we find all the query features q_t^k corresponding to p_n, and update it using these query features q_t^k based on the weights $w_t^{k,n}$, as follows:

$$p_n \longleftarrow f(p_n + \sum_k \frac{w_t^{k,n}}{z} q_t^k) \quad \text{where} \quad z = max_{k \in \varphi_n}(w_t^{k,n}) \tag{5}$$

The function $f(.)$ represents the $L2$ norm, which is employed to maintain the $L2$ norm of the updated memory item $||p_n||_2$ as 1. Additionally, the variable Z denotes the maximum similarity among the set of matching probabilities, ensuring that the normalized weighting coefficient remains within the range of 0 to 1. Furthermore, the set φ_n comprises indices k that correspond to the query feature q_t^k matched with p_n.

In order to encourage the query features to be close to the nearest memory item in feature matching memory module, reduce intraclass differences, and ensure that the memory items in the module are far enough apart to consider diverse patterns of normal video frames, we introduce the infoNCE loss as follows:

$$l_{nce} = \sum_t^T -log\frac{exp(p_{n+}q_t^k/\tau)}{\sum_n^N exp(p_n q_t^k/\tau)} \quad \text{where} \quad n^+ = \underset{n \in N}{\operatorname{argmax}} w_t^{k,n} \tag{6}$$

Where n^+ is an index of the nearest memory item for the query q_t^k, and τ is a temperature hyper-parameter per. The set p_n contains one memory item that is closest to the query feature and $N - 1$ memory items that are far from the query feature.

Intuitively, this loss is the log loss of a N-way softmax-based classifier that tries to classify q_t as p_n. It helps each query feature find the memory item with the highest matching degree, while ensuring that different memory items are sufficiently far apart to avoid confusion. Therefore, it can effectively assist the feature matching memory module in classifying different memory items p_n, so as to learn diverse patterns of normal video frames, provide better prediction for normal frames and worse prediction for abnormal frames, and alleviate the problem of over-generalization of prediction networks.

3   Experiments

3.1   Implementation Details

We resize each video frame uniformly to the size of 256×256 and use the first 4 frames to predict the 5th frame. For the feature matching memory module, we set H and W of the query feature map to 32, the C to 512, and the M to 10. The generator was optimized using the Adam optimizer, with a learning rate of $2e^{-4}$, while the discriminator was optimized using the Adam optimizer, with a learning rate of $2e^{-5}$. All models are trained end-to-end using PyTorch, with an Nvidia GTX TITAN Xp. The frame-level area under the curve (AUC) was used in evaluating the performance of our proposed network.

3.2   Comparison with Existing Methods

Table 1 presents a performance comparison between our proposed method and other existing approaches on two widely-used anomaly datasets. These methods are classified into three categories: reconstruction discrimination methods, future frame prediction methods, and other methods. Our method demonstrates strong performance on both the UCSD Ped2 and CUHK Avenue dataset, achieving AUC scores of 96.3% and 86.5%, respectively.

Compared to the other methods, the result of our method is more accurate on the Avenue dataset, our method also performs best on all the two datasets. Particularly, the performance of our method is respectively 0.4% and 2.3% better than method presented by Hu et al. [18] on the UCSD Ped2 dataset and the Avenue dataset in reconstruction discrimination methods. Moreover, in contrast to future frame prediction methods, our approach exhibits 0.5% better performance on the Avenue. Notably, our method's frame-level AUC exceeds that of the future frame prediction methods presented by Liu et al. [1] as an anomaly detection baseline. This result highlights the superior performance of our network compared to recent anomaly detection methods in terms of AUC.

3.3   Ablation Study

Given that our network contains two major processing units such as feature matching memory module and dilated convolution feature extraction encoder, an ablation study was carried out in order to evaluate their effectiveness in terms of performance. Table 2 shows result for the combinations of two components: 1) Not using any modules. 2) when the feature matching memory module are excluded, the network has the dilated convolution feature extraction encoder. 3) the effectiveness of the feature matching memory module, excluding the dilated convolution feature extraction encoder, is demonstrated in the third row. 4) The overall performance of the entire network is presented in the bottom row.

Table 1. Comparison with existing methods for video anomaly detection in terms of AUC (%) on two benchmark datasets.

Type	Methods	Ped2	Avenue
Other	Tang et al. [13]	96.3	85.1
	Morais et al. [14]	-	86.3
Reconstruction	Fan et al. [15]	92.2	83.4
	Wu et al. [16]	92.8	85.5
	Zhou et al. [17]	94.9	86.1
	Hu et al. [18]	95.9	84.2
Predict	Liu et al. [1]	95.4	85.1
	Yang et al. [19]	95.9	85.9
	Zhou et al. [20]	96.0	86.0
	Ours	96.3	86.5

Table 2. Comparison between different processing units in the proposed network in terms of AUC. Note: DCFE_encoder represents dilated convolution feature extraction encoder, and FMM_module represents feature matching memory module.

DCFE_encoder	FMM_module	Avenue	Ped2
		85.1	95.4
✓		85.6	95.7
	✓	86.1	95.9
✓	✓	86.5	96.3

The AUC performance of the proposed network with different combinations of components on the Ped2 and Avenue dataset is shown in Table 2. The performance of the baseline, which enhanced by incorporating additional components such as the feature matching memory module and dilated convolution feature extraction encoder. The network utilizing all two modules achieved the highest performance, reaching 96.3% for the Ped2 dataset and 86.5% for the CUHK Avenue dataset. These results validate the effectiveness of the dilated convolution feature extraction encoder in extracting features of different scales. Furthermore, the feature matching memory module significantly contributed to accurately restoring various patterns of normal frames.

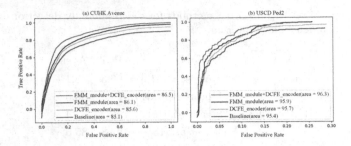

Fig. 3. Four ROC curves are plotted corresponding to four combinations in Table 2. Note: DCFE_encoder represents dilated convolution feature extraction encoder, and FMM_module represents feature matching memory module.

In particular, Fig. 3 shows the frame-level ROC curves using different modules for Avenue and Ped2 dataset, respectively. Wherein the black curve represents the feature matching memory module, the green curve represents the dilated convolution feature extraction encoder, and the blue curve represents the baseline. The red curve represents the combination of dilated convolution feature extraction encoder and feature matching memory module, reaching 86.5% for Avenue dataset.

3.4 Visual Analysis

In order to visually and clearly validate the effectiveness of the method proposed in this paper, we conducted a visual validation on the Avenue dataset, and the detection results and visualization results of some test videos are shown in Fig. 4. Figure 4 (1) shows the PSNR results of the test set, with the pink area indicating a sharp decrease in PSNR, corresponding to the abnormal parts in the video clips. Figure 4 (2) displays the visualization results of the pink abnormal area, showing the predicted frame, target frame, and the difference map of the abnormal parts. The red box in the difference map outlines the contour of the corresponding abnormality.

In the test video segments, there were three significant decreases in PSNR scores, indicating a large prediction error between the predicted frames and the ground truth frames, which implies the occurrence of abnormal events. In parts (a), (b), and (c), a significant decrease in the PSNR score occurs, and the visual interface shows some abnormal events, and the difference heatmap also displayed the outline of the abnormal objects. All three segments exhibited anomalous screens, lacking correlation between the preceding and following video frames. The visualization results further confirmed the model's effectiveness in detecting diverse anomalies.

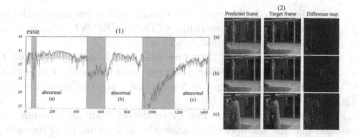

Fig. 4. The figure (1) represents the PSNR score of the test video in the CUHK Avenue dataset. Three pink areas represent abnormal events. The figure (2) shows the predicted frame and target frame and difference map corresponding to the abnormal events in the upper figure. The red boxed area indicates the abnormal region. (Color figure online)

4 Conclusions

This study presents an enhanced memory adversarial network which integrates the dilated convolution feature extraction encoder and feature matching memory module to address the challenges encountered in video anomaly detection. These challenges include the excessive expressive power of neural networks, lack of explicit consideration for the diversity of normal patterns, and insufficient sensitivity to abnormal events. Experiments on two anomaly benchmark datasets show that our network outperforms the existing methods. The ablation study shows that both the dilated convolution feature extraction encoder and the feature matching memory module have been very effective in improving system performance. Moreover, the stability and accuracy of the video anomaly detection model are further improved.

References

1. Liu, W., Luo, W., Lian, D., Gao, S.: Future frame prediction for anomaly detection - a new baseline. In: Proceedings of the IEEE Conference on Computer Vision and Pattern Recognition, pp. 6536–6545 (2018)
2. Di Biase, G., Blum, H., Siegwart, R., Cadena, C.: Pixel-wise anomaly detection in complex driving scenes. In: Proceedings of the IEEE/CVF Conference on Computer Vision and Pattern Recognition, pp. 16918–16927 (2021)
3. Wang, Y., Peng, J., Zhang, J., Yi, R., Wang, Y., Wang, C.: Multimodal industrial anomaly detection via hybrid fusion. In: Proceedings of the IEEE/CVF Conference on Computer Vision and Pattern Recognition, pp. 8032–8041 (2023)
4. Xiang, T., et al.: SQUID: deep feature in-painting for unsupervised anomaly detection. In: Proceedings of the IEEE/CVF Conference on Computer Vision and Pattern Recognition, pp. 23890–23901 (2023)
5. Zhao, Y., Deng, B., Shen, C., Liu, Y., Lu, H., Hua, X.S.: Spatio-temporal autoencoder for video anomaly detection. In: Proceedings of the 25th ACM International Conference on Multimedia, pp. 1933–1941 (2017)

6. Nguyen, T.N., Meunier, J.: Anomaly detection in video sequence with appearance-motion correspondence. In: Proceedings of the IEEE/CVF International Conference on Computer Vision, pp. 1273–1283 (2019)
7. Zaheer, M.Z., Lee, J.H., Astrid, M., Lee, S.I.: Old is gold: redefining the adversarially learned one-class classifier training paradigm. In: Proceedings of the IEEE/CVF Conference on Computer Vision and Pattern Recognition, pp. 14183–14193 (2020)
8. Gong, D., et al.: Memorizing normality to detect anomaly: memory-augmented deep autoencoder for unsupervised anomaly detection. In: Proceedings of the IEEE/CVF International Conference on Computer Vision, pp. 1705–1714 (2019)
9. Park, H., Noh, J., Ham, B.: Learning memory-guided normality for anomaly detection. In: Proceedings of the IEEE/CVF Conference on Computer Vision and Pattern Recognition, pp. 14372–14381 (2020)
10. He, K., Fan, H., Wu, Y., Xie, S., Girshick, R.: Momentum contrast for unsupervised visual representation learning. In: Proceedings of the IEEE/CVF Conference on Computer Vision and Pattern Recognition, pp. 9729–9738 (2020)
11. Hui, T.W., Tang, X., Loy, C.C.: LiteFlowNet: a lightweight convolutional neural network for optical flow estimation. In: Proceedings of the IEEE Conference on Computer Vision and Pattern Recognition, pp. 8981–8989 (2018)
12. Isola, P., Zhu, J.Y., Zhou, T., Efros, A.A.: Image-to-image translation with conditional adversarial networks. In: Proceedings of the IEEE Conference on Computer Vision and Pattern Recognition, pp. 1125–1134 (2017)
13. Tang, Y., Zhao, L., Zhang, S., Gong, C., Li, G., Yang, J.: Integrating prediction and reconstruction for anomaly detection. Pattern Recogn. Lett. **129**, 123–130 (2020)
14. Morais, R., Le, V., Tran, T., Saha, B., Mansour, M., Venkatesh, S.: Learning regularity in skeleton trajectories for anomaly detection in videos. In: Computer Vision and Pattern Recognition, pp. 11996–12004 (2019)
15. Fan, Y., Wen, G., Li, D., Qiu, S., Levine, M.D., Xiao, F.: Video anomaly detection and localization via Gaussian mixture fully convolutional variational autoencoder. Comput. Vis. Image Underst. **195**, 102920 (2020)
16. Wu, P., Liu, J., Li, M., Sun, Y., Shen, F.: Fast sparse coding networks for anomaly detection in videos. Pattern Recogn. **107**, 107515 (2020)
17. Zhou, J.T., Du, J., Zhu, H., Peng, X., Liu, Y., Goh, R.S.M.: Anomalynet: an anomaly detection network for video surveillance. IEEE Trans. Inf. Forensics Secur. **14**(10), 2537–2550 (2019)
18. Hu, J., Zhu, E., Wang, S., Liu, X., Guo, X., Yin, J.: An efficient and robust unsupervised anomaly detection method using ensemble random projection in surveillance videos. Sensors **19**(19), 4145 (2019)
19. Yang, Y., Zhan, D., Yang, F., Zhou, X.D., Yan, Y., Wang, Y.: Improving video anomaly detection performance with patch-level loss and segmentation map. In: 2020 IEEE 6th International Conference on Computer and Communications (ICCC), pp. 1832–1839 (2020)
20. Zhou, J.T., Zhang, L., Fang, Z., Du, J., Peng, X., Xiao, Y.: Attention-driven loss for anomaly detection in video surveillance. IEEE Trans. Circuits Syst. Video Technol. **30**(12), 4639–4647 (2019)

CrowdFusion: Refined Cross-Modal Fusion Network for RGB-T Crowd Counting

Jialu Cai, Qing Wang, and Shengqin Jiang[✉]

School of Computer Science, Nanjing University of Information Science
and Technology, Nanjing 210044, China
jiangshengmeng@126.com

Abstract. Crowd counting is a crucial task in computer vision, offering
numerous applications in smart security, remote sensing, agriculture and
forestry. While pure image-based models have made significant advancements, they tend to perform poorly under low-light and dark conditions.
Recent work has partially addressed these challenges by exploring the
interactions between cross-modal features, such as RGB and thermal, but
they often overlook redundant information present within these features.
To address this limitation, we introduce a refined cross-modal fusion
network for RGB-T crowd counting. The key design of our method lies
in the refined cross-modal feature fusion module. This module initially
processes the dual-modal information using a cross attention module,
enabling effective interaction between the two modalities. Subsequently,
it leverages adaptively calibrated weights to extract essential features
while mitigating the impact of redundant ones. By employing this strategy, our method effectively combines the strengths of dual-path features.
Building upon this fusion module, our network incorporates hierarchical
layers of fused features, which are perceived as targets of interest at various scales. This hierarchical perception allows us to capture crowd information from both global and local perspectives, enabling more accurate
crowd counting. Extensive experiments are conducted to demonstrate
the superiority of our proposed method.

Keywords: Crowding counting · Self-attention · RGB-T ·
Transformer

1 Introduction

Crowd counting involves the process of determining the number of people in
images with varying crowd densities [6, 8, 9]. It poses a significant challenge due
to obstacles like occlusions, scale variations, and complex backgrounds. Although
object detection-based methods also encounter these issues, crowd counting faces
even more demanding scenarios, including densely packed crowds and varying
shooting perspectives. These inherent characteristics of the task demonstrate
its applicability in various domains, such as traffic target detection, biometrics,

W. Jia et al. (Eds.): CCBR 2023, LNCS 14463, pp. 427–436, 2023.
https://doi.org/10.1007/978-981-99-8565-4_40

and agricultural and forestry yield prediction. Over the past few years, considerable efforts have been dedicated to this field in order to achieve more robust performance.

Currently, crowd counting methods predominantly utilize RGB or grayscale images as input to the network. Early approaches employed convolutional neural networks (CNNs) for directly regressing crowd numbers. However, this approach often led to large loss values, making the network susceptible to overfitting. To address this challenge, Zhang et al. [1] proposed the use of density maps instead of direct number regression. They also introduced a multi-column convolutional architecture to enable multi-scale target perception. Subsequent works in crowd counting have largely focused on the density regression task. While CNNs excel at capturing local features, they encounter difficulties in learning global long-distance dependencies. To tackle this issue, Vaswani et al. [3] introduced a self-attention mechanism capable of capturing global dependencies. Building upon this idea, TransCrowd [4] was the first to employ a pure Transformer model for crowd counting. Another notable work, MAN [5], integrated global attention and learnable local attention into their considered network. This combination improved the model's performance in capturing both local and global information.

These works have laid a solid foundation for in-depth exploration and application in this field. However, models relying solely on single RGB or grayscale inputs struggle to adapt effectively to low-light scenes. To overcome these limitations, researchers have started incorporating additional modalities to enhance performance across various scenarios. Under well-illuminated conditions, RGB images offer rich information, while thermal images struggle to differentiate individuals from the background. Conversely, in dark environments, thermal images provide clearer information, while RGB images become less informative. CFF [19] proposed the use of depth information as an auxiliary task to improve RGB crowd counting performance. IADM [12] introduced a cross-modal collaborative representation learning framework and released the RGBT-CC dataset, the first dataset for RGB-T crowd counting. MAFNet [11] designed a dual-branch RGB-T crowd counting network that utilized an attention mechanism to capture global long-range information from both RGB and thermal modalities. DEFNet [20] employed a combination of techniques, including multi-modal fusion, receptive field enhancement, and multi-layer fusion, to enhance crowd visibility while suppressing background noise. These studies primarily focus on fusing two modalities, leading to significant performance improvements. However, they overlook the potential redundancy between the two types of information, which limits the overall performance improvement of the network.

To overcome the aforementioned challenges, we propose a refined cross-modal fusion network for RGB-T crowd counting. By leveraging information from both RGB and thermal modalities in parallel, CrowdFusion addresses the limitations imposed by relying on a single modality. Our method introduces a refined cross-modal feature fusion module that facilitates effective feature interaction. The primary objective is to combine the information from both modalities while mitigating the impact of feature redundancy. To achieve this, the module incorporates a cross-attention mechanism that combines complementary modal information. Moreover, adaptive calibration weights are employed to alleviate feature redundancy. This ensures that the fused features capture the most relevant and informative aspects of the crowd counting task. Furthermore, our model aggregates features at different levels to facilitate the perception of targets at various scales. This multi-level feature aggregation enhances the model's ability to handle crowd counting in diverse scenarios. Through extensive experiments conducted on the RGBT-CC dataset, we demonstrate the superiority of our proposed method, highlighting its performance compared to some existing methods.

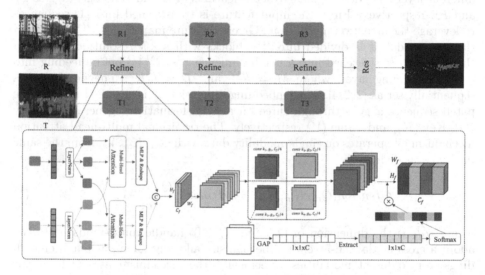

Fig. 1. The overall framework of the proposed method.

2   Proposed Method

The overall framework of the proposed CrowdFusion is schematically shown in Fig. 1. Given image pairs of RGB-T, we first send them to a shared backbone to generate multi-scale feature maps for the crowd counting task. The pairs of features from different stages are fed into the refined cross-modal feature fusion module. Then, the fusion features are aggregated before final density regression layers.

2.1   Backbone

Without loss of generality, we adopt the initial 10 layers from the pre-trained VGG-16 [17] as our backbone. We divide the backbone into three stages. In addition to the first maxpooling layer, we use the output after the next two maxpooling layers as the first two stages and the final output as the last stage. The

RGB input R and thermal input T are fed to the shared backbone, respectively, for modality-specific representation learning. The features from each stage are extracted through the backbones and then fed to the refined cross-modal feature fusion module for feature interaction.

2.2 Refined Cross-Modal Feature Fusion Module

The refined cross-modal feature module consists of feature interaction and adaptive calibration. It can be used for aggregation and refinement of features at different levels. We denote the extracted features of R and T at ith stage as F_t^i and F_r^i, respectively. First, the input feature is transformed into 1D sequences to leverage the attention mechanism. Given a feature map $F_m \in \mathbb{R}^{H \times W \times C}$ from the mth modal, it is divided into $\frac{HW}{k^2}$ blocks with $k \times k$ resolution, and then these blocks are stretched into a patch sequence $x \in R^{M \times D}$ before feeding into patch embedding layer, where $M = \frac{HW}{K^2}$ and $D = CK^2$. The patch size is sequentially set as $[2, 2, 4]$. The embedding dimension D is specified as 512. The patch sequence x goes through three linear transformations, generating Query (Q), Key (K), and Value (V) respectively. The traditional multi-head attention mechanism [3] operates on single-modality data with Q_m, K_m, V_m from the same modality, as defined by

$$Attention(Q_m, K_m, V_m) = softmax\left(\frac{Q_m K_m^T}{\sqrt{d_k}} V_m\right), \qquad (1)$$

where $\sqrt{d_k}$ is the dimension of Q_m and K_m. To handle multi-modal data, we adopt a cross-modal self-attention mechanism, allowing for input patch embeddings from different modalities. Specifically, the mechanism uses Q from one modality (e.g., thermal) and K, V from another (e.g., RGB):

$$CrossAttention\,(Q_t, K_r, V_r) = softmax\left(\frac{Q_t K_r^T}{\sqrt{d_k}} V_r\right), \qquad (2)$$

$$CrossAttention\,(Q_r, K_t, V_t) = softmax\left(\frac{Q_r K_t^T}{\sqrt{d_k}} V_t\right), \qquad (3)$$

where Q_r, K_r, V_r and Q_t, K_t, V_t represent RGB and thermal features, respectively. The multi-head attention outputs $\hat{F}_t$ and $\hat{F}_r$ are concatenated for further refinement.

Previous works [10,11] also interact features through complex attention mechanisms, but they ignore the redundancy of information between the two. To solve this problem, we utilize a feature refining method [7,18] to purify the cross-modal features. First, we divide the concatenated features $f \in \mathbb{R}^{H_f \times W_f \times C_f}$ into four parts. The feature maps from each part are denoted as $f_r \in \mathbb{R}^{H_f \times W_f \times C'}$ where $C' = \frac{C_f}{4}$ and $r \in \{1, 2, .., 4\}$. In each part, the multi-scale spatial information is learned independently, and a local cross-channel interaction is established. To decrease the computational cost, group convolution is utilized. We set the multi-scale kernel size $k \in [3, 5, 7, 9]$ with the corresponding group size

$g \in [1, 4, 8, 16]$. Here, g and k satisfy the following condition: $g = 2^{\frac{k-1}{2}}$. The method for multi-scale feature f_r extraction is as follows:

$$f_r = Conv\left(f, g_r, k_r \times k_r\right), r \in \{1, 2, .., 4\}. \tag{4}$$

The processed feature maps are then concatenated. After extracting multi-scale feature maps, we perform channel-wise attention weight extraction on different scales of feature maps. The specific calculation is as follows:

$$d_r = \sigma(W_2 \delta(W_1\left[Avg(f_r)\right])), d_r \in \mathbb{R}^{C' \times 1 \times 1} \tag{5}$$

where Avg represents global average pooling operator, W_1 and W_2 represent the fully-connected layers, δ is $ReLU$ operation and σ refers to $Sigmoid$ function. The entire multi-scale channel attention weight vector is then computed as:

$$d = Cat(d_1, d_2...d_r). \tag{6}$$

A soft attention mechanism is employed to dynamically select different spatial scales across channels, guided by the compact feature descriptor d_r. A soft weight $soft_r$ is assigned by $Softmax$ function. Afterwards, we perform a multiplication between the calibrated weights of the multi-scale channel attention $soft_r$ and the feature maps of the corresponding scale f_j^r as follows:

$$Z_r = f_r \odot soft_r, \tag{7}$$

where $\odot$ represents the channel-wise multiplication. Finally, the refined outputs are expressed as follows:

$$M = Cat(Z_1, Z_2, ..., Z_r), r \in \{1, 2, .., 4\}. \tag{8}$$

For each stage, we obtain refined feature maps M_i, and then aggregate these feature maps together before sending them to the final regression layer. We upsample the final feature to $1/8$ of the input resolution. Then we use a simple regression head which consists of one 3×3 convolution layers and one 1×1 convolution layer. Instead of using [22], we use a Bayesian loss [21] to measure the difference between the network output and groundtruth.

3   Experiment Analysis

In this section, we will first briefly introduce the dataset and evaluation metrics and then give some detailed information about the experiment. Then, our method is compared with some state-of-the-art (SOTA) methods. Finally, the effectiveness of our method is verified by ablation studies.

3.1 Dataset and Metrics

We utilize the RGBT-CC [12] dataset, with 1030 training, 200 validation, and 800 testing RGB-T image pairs, each of 640×480 resolution. We evaluate performance using Root Mean Square Error (RMSE) and Grid Average Mean Absolute Error (GAME):

$$RMSE = \sqrt{\frac{1}{N} \sum_{i=1}^{N} (P_i - \hat{P}_i)^2}, \tag{9}$$

and

$$GAME(l) = \frac{1}{N} \sum_{i=1}^{N} \sum_{j=1}^{4^l} |\hat{P}_i^j - P_i^j|, \tag{10}$$

where N is the total test image pairs, and P_i and $\hat{P}_i$ are the ground truth and estimated counts, respectively. Note that $GAME(0)$ equates to Mean Absolute Error (MAE).

3.2 Implementation Details

All the experiments of our method are implemented on the platform of PyTorch with a GeForce RTX 3090 GPU. The initial learning rate and weight decay are set to be 1e−5 and 1e−4, respectively. We choose Adam as the optimizer with batch size 1.

3.3 Comparison with SOTA Methods

In order to conduct quantitative comparisons, our method is compared to recent prominent approaches including, HDFNet [13], SANet [2], BBSNet [14], MVMS [15], IADM [12], BL [21], CSCA [10] and CmCaF [16] on RGBT-CC [12]. As depicted in Table 1, our proposed method demonstrates exceptional performance. Compared to CSRNet+IADM [12], our method surpasses it by achieving improvements of 21.52%, 17.49%, 17.69%, and 13.38% for GAME(0)–(3), respectively, and a 23.00% improvement in RMSE. In comparison to the recent method CSRNet+CSCA [10], our approach achieves notable improvements of 17.27%, 24.08%, 27.89%, 24.80%, 23.45% for GAME(0)–(3), and RMSE, respectively. When compared to CmCaF [16], our method exhibits significant advantages in GAME(0)–(2) and RMSE, while showing similar performance in GAME(3). Furthermore, we present qualitative results of our network output under different crowd densities in the dataset, as depicted in Fig. 2. The prediction results highlight the effectiveness of our method, although we acknowledge a certain gap in the predicted values, particularly in the third column of image pairs. This discrepancy can be attributed to significant scale changes, complex lighting environments, and severe occlusion. In summary, the above results validate the superiority of our proposed method.

Table 1. Comparison of some SOTA methods with ours on RGBT-CC.

Method	GAME(0)	GAME(1)	GAME(2)	GAME(3)	RMSE
HDFNet [13]	22.36	27.79	33.68	42.48	33.93
SANet [2]	21.99	24.76	28.52	34.25	41.6
BBSNet [14]	19.56	25.07	31.25	39.24	32.48
MVMS [15]	19.97	25.10	31.02	38.91	33.97
MCNN+IADM [12]	19.77	23.80	28.58	35.11	30.34
BL [21]	18.70	22.55	26.83	34.62	32.67
CSRNet+IADM [12]	17.94	21.44	26.17	33.33	30.91
CSRNet+CSCA [10]	17.02	23.30	29.87	38.39	31.09
BL+IADM [12]	15.61	19.95	24.69	32.89	28.18
CmCaF [16]	15.87	19.92	24.65	**28.01**	29.31
Ours	**14.08**	**17.69**	**21.54**	28.87	**23.80**

3.4   Ablation Study on Refined Cross-Modal Feature Fusion Module

We first establish a baseline to show the improvement of our proposed module. This baseline is to gather the features of the cross-modal inputs through a shared backbone, and then directly feed them into the density regression layer to obtain the predicted output. The experimental results are presented in Table 2. As shown, our method achieves 8.63%, 7.24%, 6.79%, 3.67% improvement in GAME(0)–(3), and 13.17% improvement in MSE. This indicates the effectiveness of the proposed module.

Table 2. Ablation study on the refined cross-modal feature fusion module on RGBT-CC.

Method	GAME(0)	GAME(1)	GAME(2)	GAME(3)	RMSE
Baseline	15.41	19.07	23.11	29.97	27.41
Baseline + MAF [11]	16.33	19.14	22.53	28.78	27.83
Baseline + CSCA [10]	15.22	18.37	21.91	28.44	27.04
CrowdFusion	14.08	17.69	21.54	28.87	23.80

We further compare our method with other cross-modal fusion methods, namely MAF [11] and CSCA [10]. For a fair comparison, we place them in the same baseline and then aggregate their features to obtain the output of the network. As shown in Table 2, our method has achieved significant performance improvements on GAME(0)–(2) and RMSE. This indicates that our proposed module can effectively refine the cross-modal features extracted from the shared backbone. GAME(3) achieves similar performance to MAF and CSCA. It can be seen that as the number of regional blocks increases, the prediction performance of the network decreases. This indicates that the network pays too much attention to the global counting effect, while the prediction in local areas is not good.

Fig. 2. Qualitative results. The first, second, and third rows correspond to RGB image, thermal image, and density map predicted by our network, respectively.

3.5   Ablation Study on Loss Function

The network used in this work uses a density map-free loss, i.e., Bayesian loss [21]. To this end, we further explore the impact of DM loss [22] on network performance. It built a new OT loss to improve the network's predictive ability in low-density regions. The comparison results are presented in Table 3. It can be seen that Bayesian loss is superior to DM loss. Although it exhibits excellent performance in high-density scenarios, its performance is limited to relatively sparse datasets. Therefore, we select Bayesian loss as the optimization objective.

Table 3. Ablation study on different loss functions on RGBT-CC.

Method	GAME(0)	GAME(1)	GAME(2)	GAME(3)	RMSE
Ours+DM loss [22]	18.81	21.12	24.47	30.06	40.79
Ours+Bayesian loss [21]	14.08	17.69	21.54	28.87	23.80

4   Conclusion

In this paper, we introduce a refined cross-modal fusion network for RGB-T crowd counting. Our method focuses on enhancing the cross modal feature fusion module to effectively process dual-modal information. We introduce a cross-attention module that facilitates interaction between the two modalities, enabling improved feature representation. Moreover, we incorporate adaptive calibration techniques to extract informative features while reducing the impact of redundant ones. To further enhance the feature fusion process, our network employs hierarchical layers of fused features, which capture targets of interest at different scales. This hierarchical perception allows for a comprehensive understanding of crowd information from both global and local perspectives, leading to more accurate crowd counting. We evaluate our proposed method on the RGBT-CC dataset and demonstrate its superior performance compared to several existing methods.

Acknowledgment. This work is supported by the National Natural Science Foundation of China (No. 62001237), the Joint Funds of the National Natural Science Foundation of China (No. U21B2044), the Jiangsu Planned Projects for Postdoctoral Research Funds (No. 2021K052A), the China Postdoctoral Science Foundation Funded Project (No. 2021M701756), the Startup Foundation for Introducing Talent of NUIST (No. 2020r084).

References

1. Zhang, Y., Zhou, D., Chen, S., Gao, S., Ma, Y.: Single-image crowd counting via multi-column convolutional neural network. In: Proceedings of the IEEE Conference on Computer Vision and Pattern Recognition, pp. 589–597 (2016)
2. Cao, X., Wang, Z., Zhao, Y., Su, F.: Scale aggregation network for accurate and efficient crowd counting. In: Ferrari, V., Hebert, M., Sminchisescu, C., Weiss, Y. (eds.) ECCV 2018. LNCS, vol. 11209, pp. 757–773. Springer, Cham (2018). https://doi.org/10.1007/978-3-030-01228-1_45
3. Vaswani, A., et al.: Attention is all you need. In: Advances in Neural Information Processing Systems 30 (2017)
4. Liang, D., Chen, X., Xu, W., Zhou, Y., Bai, X.: TransCrowd: weakly-supervised crowd counting with transformers. SCIENCE CHINA Inf. Sci. **65**(6), 1–14 (2022)
5. Lin, H., Ma, Z., Ji, R., Wang, Y., Hong, X.: Boosting crowd counting via multifaceted attention. In: Proceedings of the IEEE/CVF Conference on Computer Vision and Pattern Recognition, pp. 19628–19637 (2022)
6. Tian, Y., Chu, X., Wang, H.: CCTrans: simplifying and improving crowd counting with transformer. arXiv preprint arXiv:2109.14483 (2021)
7. Hu, J., Shen, L., Sun, G.: Squeeze-and-excitation networks. In: Proceedings of the IEEE Conference on Computer Vision and Pattern Recognition, pp. 7132–7141 (2018)
8. Idrees, H., Saleemi, I., Seibert, C., Shah, M.: Multi-source multi-scale counting in extremely dense crowd images. In: Proceedings of the IEEE Conference on Computer Vision and Pattern Recognition, pp. 2547–2554 (2013)
9. Guo, D., Li, K., Zha, Z.J., Wang, M.: DADNet: dilated-attention-deformable ConvNet for crowd counting. In: Proceedings of the ACM International Conference on Multimedia, pp. 1823–1832 (2019)
10. Zhang, Y., Choi, S., Hong, S.: Spatio-channel attention blocks for cross-modal crowd counting. In: Wang, L., Gall, J., Chin, T.J., Sato, I., Chellappa, R. (eds.) ACCV 2022. LNCS, vol. 13842, pp. 90–107. Springer, Cham (2022). https://doi.org/10.1007/978-3-031-26284-5_2

11. Chen, P., Gao, J., Yuan, Y., Wang, Q.: MAFNet: a multi-attention fusion network for RGB-T crowd counting. arXiv preprint arXiv:2208.06761 (2022)
12. Liu, L., Chen, J., Wu, H., Li, G., Li, C., Lin, L.: Cross-modal collaborative representation learning and a large-scale RGBT benchmark for crowd counting. In: Proceedings of the IEEE/CVF Conference on Computer Vision and Pattern Recognition, pp. 4823–4833 (2021)
13. Pang, Y., Zhang, L., Zhao, X., Lu, H.: Hierarchical dynamic filtering network for RGB-D salient object detection. In: Vedaldi, A., Bischof, H., Brox, T., Frahm, J.-M. (eds.) ECCV 2020. LNCS, vol. 12370, pp. 235–252. Springer, Cham (2020). https://doi.org/10.1007/978-3-030-58595-2_15
14. Fan, D.-P., Zhai, Y., Borji, A., Yang, J., Shao, L.: BBS-Net: RGB-D salient object detection with a bifurcated backbone strategy network. In: Vedaldi, A., Bischof, H., Brox, T., Frahm, J.-M. (eds.) ECCV 2020. LNCS, vol. 12357, pp. 275–292. Springer, Cham (2020). https://doi.org/10.1007/978-3-030-58610-2_17
15. Zhang, Q., Chan, A.B.: Wide-area crowd counting via ground-plane density maps and multi-view fusion CNNs. In: Proceedings of the IEEE/CVF Conference on Computer Vision and Pattern Recognition, pp. 8297–8306 (2019)
16. Li, H., Zhang, S., Kong, W.: RGB-D crowd counting with cross-modal cycle-attention fusion and fine-coarse supervision. IEEE Trans. Industr. Inf. 19(1), 306–316 (2022)
17. Simonyan, K., Zisserman, A.: Very deep convolutional networks for large-scale image recognition. arXiv preprint arXiv:1409.1556 (2014)
18. Zhang, H., Zu, K., Lu, J., Zou, Y., Meng, D.: EPSANet: an efficient pyramid squeeze attention block on convolutional neural network. In: Wang, L., Gall, J., Chin, T.J., Sato, I., Chellappa, R. (eds.) ACCV 2022. LNCS, vol. 13843, pp. 1161–1177. Springer, Cham (2022). https://doi.org/10.1007/978-3-031-26313-2_33
19. Shi, Z., Mettes, P., Snoek, C.G.: Counting with focus for free. In: Proceedings of the IEEE/CVF International Conference on Computer Vision, pp. 4200–4209 (2019)
20. Zhou, W., Pan, Y., Lei, J., Ye, L., Yu, L.: DEFNet: dual-branch enhanced feature fusion network for RGB-T crowd counting. IEEE Trans. Intell. Transp. Syst. 23(12), 24540–24549 (2022)
21. Ma, Z., Wei, X., Hong, X., Gong, Y.: Bayesian loss for crowd count estimation with point supervision. In: Proceedings of the IEEE International Conference on Computer Vision, pp. 6142–6151 (2019)
22. Wang, B., Liu, H., Samaras, D., Nguyen, M.H.: Distribution matching for crowd counting. In: Advances in Neural Information Processing Systems 33, pp. 1595–1607 (2020)

Cross-Modal Attention Mechanism for Weakly Supervised Video Anomaly Detection

Wenwen Sun, Lin Cao[✉], Yanan Guo, and Kangning Du

Key Laboratory of Information and Communication Systems, Ministry of Information Industry, Beijing Information Science and Technology University, Beijing 100101, China
CharLin@bistu.edu.cn

Abstract. Weakly supervised video anomaly detection aims to detect anomalous events with only video-level labels. Nevertheless, most existing methods ignore motion anomalies and the features extracted from pre-trained I3D or C3D contain unavoidable redundancy, which leads to inadequate detection performance. To address these challenges, we propose a cross-modal attention mechanism by introducing optical flow sequence. Firstly, RGB and optical flow sequences are input into pre-trained I3D to extract appearance and motion features. Then, we introduce a cross-modal attention module to reduce the task-irrelevant redundancy in these appearance and motion features. After that, optimized appearance and motion features are fused to calculate the clip-level anomaly scores. Finally, we employ the MIL ranking loss to enable better separation between the anomaly scores of anomalous and normal clips to achieve accurate detection of anomalous events. We conduct extensive experiments on the ShanghaiTech and UCF-Crime datasets to verify the efficacy of our method. The experimental results demonstrate that our method performs comparably to or even better than existing unsupervised and weakly supervised methods in terms of AUC, obtaining AUC of 91.49% on the ShanghaiTech dataset and 85.49% on the UCF-Crime dataset, respectively.

Keywords: Video anomaly detection · Weakly supervised · Cross-modal attention mechanism

1 Introduction

With the gradual increase in security awareness, increasingly more surveillance cameras are being deployed in public places (e.g., shopping malls, banks, intersections, etc.). The primary function of video surveillance is to detect abnormal events such as road accidents, criminal activities, etc. Currently, anomalous events are commonly defined as events that deviate from the norm. Video anomaly detection aims to discover anomalous events, and locate their start and

W. Jia et al. (Eds.): CCBR 2023, LNCS 14463, pp. 437–446, 2023.
https://doi.org/10.1007/978-981-99-8565-4_41

end timestamps in the video [1]. Previous algorithms for video anomaly detection mainly focus on unsupervised anomaly detection [2–5]. However, these methods are prone to false detection for new, unlearned normal events. Furthermore, these methods, focusing solely on learning the feature representation of normal events, fail to optimize the false detection of abnormal events. Consequently, the accuracy of abnormal event detection is low.

To address the above problems, researchers have proposed weakly supervised video anomaly detection methods [6–10]. These methods utilize normal and abnormal videos with video-level labels to train the models which can learn more distinguishing features between normal and abnormal events. Moreover, models trained with anomalous events can learn the feature representation of abnormal events, which can lower the false detection rate of abnormal events and further enhance the detection performance of abnormal events. Sultani et al. [6] proposed a MIL ranking model to detect abnormal events. Tian et al. [10] proposed a weakly supervised anomaly detection method based on feature magnitude learning. Zhong et al. [7] proposed a graph convolutional network to tackle the noise labels and applied a supervised action classifier to weakly supervised anomaly detection. Zhang et al. [8] proposed a Temporal Convolutional Network (TCN) to encode preceding adjacent snippets to solve real-time anomaly detection tasks. Wan et al. [9] proposed dynamic multiple-instance learning loss and center loss for video anomaly detection. They use the former to expand the inter-class distance between normal and anomalous instances, while the latter is utilized to narrow the intra-class distance of normal instances. However, these methods have two main limitations. The first one is ignoring motion information. There are two main types of anomalies in videos namely appearance and motion anomalies [11]. Appearance anomalies can be considered as unusual object appearance in a scene, such as a bicycle or truck appearing on a pedestrian walkway. Motion anomalies can be considered as unusual object motion in a scene, such as road accidents or fighting. Therefore, the information for appearance and motion modality are both crucial for anomaly detection [12]. However, the aforementioned works use only RGB sequences which can represent appearance information effectively yet not represent motion information, resulting in low detection rate of anomalous events. The second one is that features extracted from pre-trained I3D or C3D contain redundant information. The aforementioned works directly use features extracted from pre-trained I3D [13] or C3D [14] to detect abnormal events. However, these features are trained for the video action classification yet not specific for the video anomaly detection, resulting in unavoidable redundancy.

To address the above limitations, we propose a cross-modal attention mechanism by introducing optical flow sequences. Firstly, RGB and optical flow sequences are input into pre-trained I3D network to extract appearance and motion features. However, the features extracted from pre-trained I3D have task-irrelevant redundancy. Therefore, we introduce the Cross-modal Attention Module (CAM) to reduce the redundancy. Specifically, both appearance and motion features are input into the CAM. One of them acts as the primary modality, while the other serves as the secondary modality. We utilize the global information from the primary modality and the cross-modal local information from the secondary modality to filter out the task-irrelevant redundancy. Then, optimized appearance and motion features are fused to calculate the clip-level anomaly scores. Finally, we employ the highest scored instances in the anomalous and normal videos to calculate the MIL ranking loss which enables better separation between the anomaly scores of abnormal normal instances. The MIL ranking loss is utilized to train the network to obtain an anomaly detection model which can accurately identify anomalous events in the video.

2   Method

The overall architecture of our method is shown in Fig. 1. A given pair of videos, namely an abnormal video B_a (i.e., positive bag) and a normal video B_n (i.e., negative bag), is divided into N RGB snippets $\{v_i^{RGB}\}_{i=1}^{N}$ and optical flow snippets $\{v_i^{Flow}\}_{i=1}^{N}$ (i.e. instances). Then we employ pre-trained I3D network to extract appearance features $F_{appearance} = \{f_i^{apperance}\}_{i=1}^{N}$ and motion features $F_{motion} = \{f_i^{motion}\}_{i=1}^{N}$ for RGB snippets $\{v_i^{RGB}\}_{i=1}^{N}$ and optical flow snippets $\{v_i^{Flow}\}_{i=1}^{N}$. After that, we propose the Cross-modal Attention Module (CAM) to reduce the task-irrelevant redundancy in these appearance$F_{appearnace}$ and motion features F_{motion}. The optimized appearance features $\bar{F}_{appearnace} = \{\bar{f}_i^{apperance}\}_{i=1}^{N}$ and motion features $\bar{F}_{motion} = \{\bar{f}_i^{motion}\}_{i=1}^{N}$ are fused, and then fed into three fully connected layers to calculate the anomaly scores (i.e. $\{s_i^a\}_{i=1}^{N}$, $\{s_i^b\}_{i=1}^{N}$) for each instance in the positive and negative bags. Finally, we train the network with the MIL ranking loss to enable better separation between the anomaly scores of anomalous clips and that of normal clips.

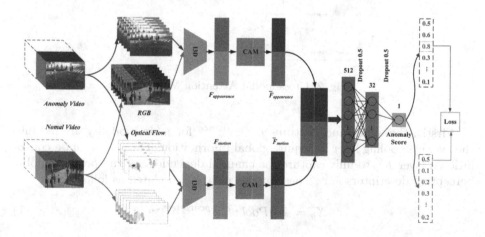

Fig. 1. Overview of our proposed method.

2.1   Cross-Modal Attention Module

To obtain the features for appearance and motion modality, the RGB snippets $\left\{v_i^{RGB}\right\}_{i=1}^N$ and the optical flow snippets $\left\{v_i^{Flow}\right\}_{i=1}^N$ are input into pre-trained I3D network, respectively. However, the I3D network is pre-trained on the Kinetics dataset which is for video action classification tasks yet not for video anomaly detection tasks. Thus, the appearance and motion features extracted from pre-trained I3D contain inevitable redundancy.

Inspired by literature [15], we introduce the Cross-modal Attention Module (CAM) to address the above challenge. The features for appearance and motion modality are fed into CAM. One of them acts as the primary modality, while the other serves as the secondary modality. The primary modality provides the modality-specific global information context, whereas the secondary modality provides the cross-modal local information. Then, global and local information are aggregated to filter out task-independent redundancy in the primary modality. The CAM is shown in Fig. 2. For the convenience of expression, we take the example that the appearance modality is the primary modality and the motion modality is the secondary modality. When the roles of the two modalities are switched, the same operations are performed.

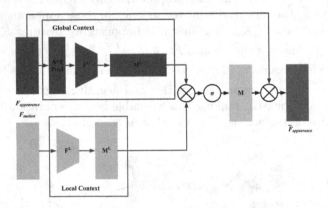

Fig. 2. Cross-modal Attention Module

Firstly, the appearance features $F^{appearance}$ for main modality are fed into the average pooling layer to acquire global information. Then, we adopt a convolutional layer F^G to fully capture the channel dependencies and produce global perceptual descriptors M^G. These processes are formulated as follows.

$$X_g = AvgPool\left(F^{appearance}\right) \tag{1}$$

$$M^G = F^G\left(X_g\right) \tag{2}$$

Since multiple modalities provide information from different perspectives, we obtain cross-modal local information from the motion features F^{motion} for auxiliary modality to detect task-independent redundancy in main modality. We introduce the convolutional layer F^L to produce a cross-modal local perception descriptor M^L as follows.

$$M^L = F^L \left(F^{motion} \right) \tag{3}$$

We obtain the channel descriptor M for feature optimization by multiplying the modality-specific global-aware descriptor M^G with the cross-modal local-focused descriptor M^L. We adopt the Sigmoid function to produce channel-level optimization weights that optimize the features $F^{appearance}$ for primary modality. Therefore, the information redundancy is filtered out through the cross-modal attention mechanism. These processes are formulated as follows.

$$M = M^G \otimes M^L \tag{4}$$

$$\bar{F}^{appearance} = \sigma(M) \otimes F^{appearance} \tag{5}$$

Where $\sigma \left(\cdot \right)$ is the Sigmoid function, $\otimes$ denotes the multiplication operator.

Then the optimized appearance features $\bar{F}^{appearance}$ and motion features $\bar{F}^{motion}$ are fused as follows.

$$v = cat(\bar{F}^{appearance}, \bar{F}^{motion}) \tag{6}$$

2.2 Ranking Loss

Inspired by literature [6], we combine the ranking loss function and hinge loss function to form the loss function that enables better separation between the anomaly scores of abnormal and normal instances. The loss function is formulated below.

$$l\left(B_a, B_n \right) = \max \left(0, 1 - \max_{i \in B_a} f\left(v_a^i \right) + \max_{i \in B_n} f\left(v_n^i \right) \right) \tag{7}$$

Where v_a is the fused features of the positive bag, v_n is the fused features of the negative bag, $f\left(v_a \right)$ and $f\left(v_n \right)$ denote the scores of instances in the positive and negative bags respectively, $\max_{i \in B_a} f\left(v_a^i \right)$ and $\max_{i \in B_n} f\left(v_n^i \right)$ represent the highest scores of instances in the positive and negative bags respectively.

Since videos consist of a sequence of segments, the anomaly score should vary smoothly between video segments. Moreover, since abnormal behaviors rarely occur and last for short time in real-world scenarios, the abnormal scores of the instances in the positive bags should be very sparse. Therefore, we introduce smoothness item and sparsity item b as follows.

$$a = \sum_{i}^{n-1} \left(f\left(v_a^i \right) - f\left(v_a^{i+1} \right) \right)^2 \tag{8}$$

$$b = \sum_{i}^{n} f\left(v_a^i\right) s.t. f\left(v_a^i\right) \neq \max\left(f\left(v_a^i\right)\right) \tag{9}$$

To prevent overfitting during network training, we also introduce regularization term $\|W\|_F$. The final ranking loss function is formulated below.

$$L\left(W\right) = l\left(B_a, B_n\right) + \lambda_1 a + \lambda_2 b + \|W\|_F \tag{10}$$

Where λ_1 and λ_2 are the weights of smoothness item and sparsity item respectively.

3 Experiments

3.1 Dataset

ShanghaiTech is a medium-sized dataset from fixed-angle street video surveillance. It has 13 different background scenes and 437 videos including 307 normal videos and 130 abnormal videos.

UCF-Crime is a large-scale anomaly detection dataset. The dataset covers 13 types of anomalies. The training set consists of 800 normal videos and 810 abnormal videos with video-level labels. The test set consisted of 150 normal videos and 140 abnormal videos with frame-level labels.

3.2 Comparison with State-of-the-Art Methods

To verify the effectiveness of our proposed method, we compare it with existing methods on the ShanghaiTech and UCF-Crime datasets, respectively. The detection results on the ShanghaiTech and UCF-Crime datasets are shown in Table 1, respectively.

It can be seen from Table 1 that the AUC score of our method has obvious advantages over unsupervised methods on the two datasets. These methods, including Frame-Pred [3], Mem-AE [2], MNAD [4], GCL [16] and GODS [20], are prone to false detection for new, unlearned normal events. Furthermore, these methods, focusing solely on learning the feature representation of normal events, fail to optimize the false detection of abnormal events. Consequently, the accuracy of anomaly detection is low. Some studies, including GCN [7], Zhang et al. [8], Sultani et al. [6], Peng et al. [21], AR-Net [9] and CLAWS [17], employ weak supervision for anomaly detection, enabling the learning of more distinguishing features between normal and abnormal events. These approaches further enhance the detection performance of abnormal events compared to unsupervised anomaly detection methods. However, the above methods have several challenges. These challenges include ignore motion anomalies and redundancy in extracted RGB and optical flow features. Our proposed method utilizes motion features and appearance features from optical flow sequences and RGB sequences respectively to improve the detection rate of abnormal events, and then introduces a cross-modal attention mechanism to filter out the task-irrelevant redundancy. Therefore, our proposed method achieves promising performance.

Table 1. The detection results on the ShanghaiTech dataset

Supervision	Method	AUC (%) ShanghaiTech	AUC (%) UCF
Unsupervised	Lu et al. [19]	-	65.51
	Frame-Pred [3]	73.40	-
	Mem-AE [2]	71.20	-
	MNAD [4]	70.50	-
	GODS [20]	-	70.46
	GCL [16]	78.93	71.04
Weakly Supervised	GCN [7]	84.44	82.12
	Zhang et al. [8]	82.50	78.66
	Sultani et al. [6]	85.33	77.92
	AR-Net [9]	91.24	-
	CLAWS [17]	89.67	83.03
	Peng et al. [21]	-	84.89
	Ours	91.49	85.02

3.3 Ablation Studies

To verify the effectiveness of each part of our proposed method, we conduct ablation studies on the ShanghaiTech and UCF-Crime datasets. We design the following 4 sets of experiments. (1) We use the method of Sultani et al. [6] as baseline. Such method uses the I3D network to extract features from RGB sequence and then inputs these features into the network model consisting of 3 fully connected layers. (2) We replace the RGB sequence used by baseline with optical flow sequence. (3) We add optical flow sequence. (4) We add both optical flow sequence and CAM module. The performance of the 4 sets of experiments on the ShanghaiTech dataset and the UCF-Crime dataset are shown in Table 2.

Table 2. Ablation studies on ShanghaiTech and UCF-Crime dataset

Number	Baseline	RGB	Optical	CAM	AUC (%) ShanghaiTech	AUC (%) UCF
1	✓	✓	-	-	85.33	77.92
2	✓	-	✓	-	88.10	81.1
3	✓	✓	✓	-	89.60	83.56
4	✓	✓	✓	✓	91.49	85.02

It can be seen from Table 2 that the baseline achieves only 85.33% AUC and 77.92% AUC on the ShanghaiTech and UCF-Crime datasets, respectively. When we replace the RGB sequence used by baseline with optical flow sequence, the AUC increases to 88.10% and 81.1% on the ShanghaiTech and UCF-Crime datasets, respectively. When we add optical flow sequence, the AUC is boosted to 89.60% and 83.56% on the ShanghaiTech and UCF-Crime datasets, respectively. The above results indicate that optical flow sequence contributes to the overall performance. When both optical flow sequence and CAM module are added, the AUC increases to 91.49% and 85.02% on the ShanghaiTech and UCF-Crime datasets, respectively. This experiment verifies the effectiveness of the proposed CAM module. The above results show that our proposed method achieves the best performance.

3.4 Visual Analysis

To verify the effectiveness of our proposed method more intuitively, we visualize the detection performance of our proposed method on some test videos from the UCF-Crime dataset, and show the visualization results in Fig. 3.

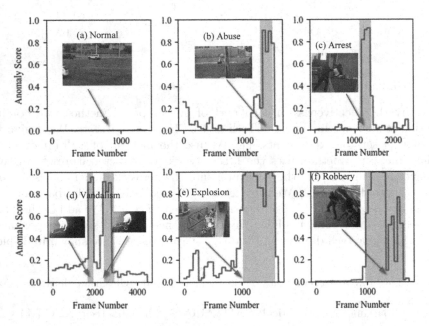

Fig. 3. The visualization results on some test videos from the UCF-Crime dataset

Specifically, Fig. 3(a) represents the visualization results for normal videos. It can be seen from Fig. 3(a) that the abnormal score generated by normal video is low, and almost close to 0. Figure 3(b)–(e) respectively represent the visualization results of abnormal videos including abuse, arrest, vandalism, and explosion, where pink shadowed areas indicate the time period in which the abnormal event occurred. It can be seen from Fig. 3(b)–(e) that the abnormal score increases rapidly when the abnormal event occurs, but the abnormal score is low in normal state. Figure 3(f) shows the visualization results of the abnormal robbery video. It can be seen from Fig. 3(f) that the score of some abnormal frames is low due to the perspective distortion problem caused by the object being far away from the camera and the occlusion problem. Therefore, overall performance of our proposed method is excellent.

4 Conclusion

In this article, we propose a weakly supervised video anomaly detection method based on a cross-modal attention mechanism. Firstly, RGB and optical flow sequences are input into pre-trained I3D to extract appearance and motion features. Then, a cross-modal attention mechanism optimization is introduced to reduce redundant information in these appearance features and motion features. After that, optimized appearance and motion features are fused to calculate the clip-level anomaly scores. Finally, the MIL ranking loss is utilized to train the network to obtain an anomaly detection model which can accurately identify anomalous events in the video. Extensive experiments on the ShanghaiTech and UCF-Crime datasets show that our method outperforms the current state-of-the-art methods. In the future, we consider how to use optical flow sequence to more effectively assist RGB sequence to obtain better video anomaly detection performance.

References

1. Lv, H., Zhou, C., Cui, Z., Xu, C., Li, Y., Yang, J.: Localizing anomalies from weakly-labeled videos. IEEE Trans. Image Process. **30**, 4505–4515 (2021)
2. Gong, D., Liu, L., Le, V., Saha, B., Mansour, M. R., Venkatesh, S., Hengel, A.V.D.: Memorizing normality to detect anomaly: memory-augmented deep autoencoder for unsupervised anomaly detection. In: Proceedings of the IEEE/CVF International Conference on Computer Vision, pp. 1705–1714 (2019)
3. Liu, W., Luo, W., Lian, D., Gao, S.: Future frame prediction for anomaly detection - a new baseline. In: Proceedings of the IEEE Conference on Computer Vision and Pattern Recognition, pp. 6536–6545 (2018)
4. Park, H., Noh, J., Ham, B.: Learning memory-guided normality for anomaly detection. In: Proceedings of the IEEE/CVF Conference on Computer Vision and Pattern Recognition, pp. 372–381 (2020)
5. Yu, G., et al.: Cloze test helps: effective video anomaly detection via learning to complete video events. In: Proceedings of the 28th ACM International Conference on Multimedia, pp. 583–591 (2020)
6. Sultani, W., Chen, C., Shah, M.: Real-world anomaly detection in surveillance videos. In: Proceedings of the IEEE Conference on Computer Vision and Pattern Recognition, pp. 6479–6488 (2018)
7. Zhong, J.X., Li, N., Kong, W., Liu, S., Li, T.H., Li, G.: Graph convolutional label noise cleaner: train a plug-and-play action classifier for anomaly detection. In: Proceedings of the IEEE/CVF Conference on Computer Vision and Pattern Recognition, pp. 1237–1246 (2019)
8. Zhang, J., Qing, L., Miao, J.: Temporal convolutional network with complementary inner bag loss for weakly supervised anomaly detection. In: 2019 IEEE International Conference on Image Processing, pp. 4030–4034 (2019)

9. Wan, B., Fang, Y., Xia, X., Mei, J.: Weakly supervised video anomaly detection via center-guided discriminative learning. In: 2020 IEEE International Conference on Multimedia and Expo, pp. 1–6 (2020)

10. Tian, Y., Pang, G., Chen, Y., Singh, R., Verjans, J.W., Carneiro, G.: Weakly-supervised video anomaly detection with robust temporal feature magnitude learning. In: Proceedings of the IEEE/CVF International Conference on Computer Vision, pp. 4975–4986 (2021)

11. Ramachandra, B., Jones, M.J., Vatsavai, R.R.: A survey of single-scene video anomaly detection. IEEE Trans. Pattern Anal. Mach. Intell. **44**(5), 2293–2312 (2020)

12. Sánchez, F.L., Hupont, I., Tabik, S., Herrera, F.: Revisiting crowd behaviour analysis through deep learning: taxonomy, anomaly detection, crowd emotions, datasets, opportunities and prospects. Inf. Fusion **64**, 318–335 (2020)

13. Carreira, J., Zisserman, A.: Quo vadis, action recognition? A new model and the kinetics dataset. In: Proceedings of the IEEE Conference on Computer Vision and Pattern Recognition, pp. 6299–6308 (2017)

14. Tran, D., Bourdev, L., Fergus, R., Torresani, L., Paluri, M.: Learning spatiotemporal features with 3d convolutional networks. In: Proceedings of the IEEE International Conference on Computer Vision, pp. 4489–4497 (2015)

15. Hong, F.T., Feng, J.C., Xu, D., Shan, Y., Zheng, W.S.: Cross-modal consensus network for weakly supervised temporal action localization. In: Proceedings of the 29th ACM International Conference on Multimedia, pp. 1591–1599 (2021)

16. Zaheer, M.Z., Mahmood, A., Khan, M.H., Segu, M., Yu, F., Lee, S.I.: Generative cooperative learning for unsupervised video anomaly detection. In: Proceedings of the IEEE/CVF Conference on Computer Vision and Pattern Recognition, pp. 744–754 (2022)

17. Zaheer, M.Z., Mahmood, A., Astrid, M., Lee, S.-I.: CLAWS: clustering assisted weakly supervised learning with normalcy suppression for anomalous event detection. In: Vedaldi, A., Bischof, H., Brox, T., Frahm, J.-M. (eds.) ECCV 2020. LNCS, vol. 12367, pp. 358–376. Springer, Cham (2020). https://doi.org/10.1007/978-3-030-58542-6_22

18. Sohrab, F., Raitoharju, J., Gabbouj, M., Iosifidis, A.: Subspace support vector data description. In: 2018 24th International Conference on Pattern Recognition, pp. 722–727 (2018)

19. Lu, C., Shi, J., Jia, J.: Abnormal event detection at 150 FPS in MATLAB. In: Proceedings of the IEEE International Conference on Computer Vision, pp. 2720–2727 (2013)

20. Wang, J., Cherian, A.: GODS: generalized one-class discriminative subspaces for anomaly detection. In: Proceedings of the IEEE/CVF International Conference on Computer Vision, pp. 8201–8211 (2019)

21. Wu, P., Liu, J.: Learning causal temporal relation and feature discrimination for anomaly detection. IEEE Trans. Image Process. **30**, 3513–3527 (2021)

Author Index

Printed in the United States
by Baker & Taylor Publisher Services